*fourth edition*

# Problem Solving, Abstraction, and Design Using C++

*fourth edition*

# Problem Solving, Abstraction, and Design Using C++

FRANK L. FRIEDMAN    ELLIOT B. KOFFMAN

*Temple University*

**PEARSON**

Addison
Wesley

Boston  San Francisco  New York
London  Toronto  Sydney  Tokyo  Singapore  Madrid
Mexico City  Munich  Paris  Cape Town  Hong Kong  Montreal

| | |
|---|---|
| *Senior Acquisitions Editor* | Michael Hirsch |
| *Assistant Editor* | Elizabeth Paquin |
| *Production Supervisor* | Marilyn Lloyd |
| *Project Management* | Argosy Publishing |
| *Composition and Art* | Argosy Publishing |
| *Copyeditor* | Suzanne Goraj |
| *Proofreader* | Heather Moehn |
| *Indexer* | Ed Rush |
| *Marketing Manager* | Nathan Schultz |
| *Marketing Coordinator* | Lesly Hershman |
| *Text Design* | Sandra Rigney |
| *Cover Design* | Joyce Cosentino Wells |
| *Text Image* | © 2003 Mark Downey/Photodisc, Getty Images |
| *Cover Image* | © 2003 Gerald L. French/Panoramic Images, Chicago |
| *Prepress and Manufacturing* | Caroline Fell |

Access the latest information about Addison-Wesley titles from our World Wide Web site:
http://www.aw.com/cs

Many of the designations used by manufacturers and sellers to distinguish their products are claimed as trademarks. Where those designations appear in this book, and Addison-Wesley was aware of a trademark claim, the designations have been printed in initial caps or all caps.

The programs and applications presented in this book have been included for their instructional value. They have been tested with care, but are not guaranteed for any particular purpose. The publisher does not offer any warranties or representations, nor does it accept any liabilities with respect to the programs or applications.

**Library of Congress Cataloging-in-Publication Data**
Friedman, Frank L.
  Problem solving, abstraction & design using C++ / Frank L. Friedman, Elliot B. Koffman.
  —4th ed.
     p.cm.
  Includes index.
  ISBN: 0-321-19718-6
C++ (Computer program language) I. Title: Problem solving, abstraction and design using C++. II. Koffman, Elliot B. III. Title.

QZ76.73.C153F74 2003
005.13'3—dc21

ISBN 0-321-19718-6
1 2 3 4 5 6 7 8 9 10-DOC -06050403

To my wife, Martha, my children, Dara and Shelly
and my Mom, Sylvia
In loving memory of my father, George,
whose inspiration lives on.

*FLF*


To my wife, Caryn
my children, Richard, Deborah, and Robin
my daughter- and son-in-law Jacquie and Jeff
and my grandchildren Dustin and Jonathan
with much thanks for your love and support.

*EBK*

# Preface

This is a textbook for a one- or two-semester course in problem solving and program design. It is suitable for use by students with no programming background as well as those with a one-semester course, or the equivalent, in another programming language. Students' backgrounds will determine the time required to cover the earlier chapters of the text and the extent of coverage possible for later chapters.

The earlier editions of this book represented the culmination of an eight-year effort, partially sponsored by the National Science Foundation,[1] to define an introductory-level course that presented the rudimentary principles of software engineering and object-oriented programming along with an introduction to the C++ programming language. Our primary goal is to motivate and introduce sound principles of program design and abstraction in a first programming course. Early in the book we introduce topics such as program style, documentation, algorithm and data structuring, procedure- and data-oriented modularization, component reuse, and program verification. The focus throughout is on the problem solving/software design process, from problem analysis to program design and coding.

The textbook fits the objectives of the first course in programming following an imperative first approach as described in the ACM/IEEE Computing Curricula 2001 (courses CS101 or CS111). Because it also introduces object-oriented programming and the C++ Standard Template Library (STL) as well as recursion and dynamic data structures, it may also be used as the textbook for the second course in the 3-semester sequence, CS102. The textbook can also be used in an objects early approach to the first programming course as classes are introduced in Chapter 1 and used in Chapter 3. However, we recommend that you move Chapter 9, Class Definition and Use, forward in that case. It could be studied anytime after Chapter 6.

# Features of the Fourth Edition

The fourth edition is totally compatible with the ANSI standard for C++. It introduces data type bool in Chapter 2 and the string class in Chapter 3. Integrated in the text are new sections on containers, which describe several Standard Template Library classes. We cover the vector class and iterators in Chapter 11 and the list, stack, and queue classes in Chapter 13. We've added a new section on arrays of characters and C-style strings in Chapter 9.

We've improved the writing style in this new edition and simplified the presentation whenever possible. The new design and the use of color also help make the text more accessible to students. We introduced new lists of chapter objectives at the start of each chapter and updated the interviews by leading computer scientists.

# Balancing Object–Oriented and Procedural Approaches

Object-oriented concepts and classes are introduced early in the book, starting in Section 1.3. Sections 2.4 and 3.7 discuss the use of two system-defined classes, iostream and string, and we refer to the use of classes and objects throughout most of the text.

An issue of concern to faculty is the relative order of arrays, structs, and classes. As in the last edition, we introduce arrays and structs first (Chapter 9) and then introduce the definition and coding of classes (Chapter 10). Some faculty may prefer to reverse the order, and this is entirely possible. The chapter on classes uses arrays only in the implementation of class simpleString, which can be omitted or deferred until after arrays are covered.

We continue to emphasize the design of classes and data modeling in Chapter 11, which introduces template classes, an indexed-list class, the STL vector class, friend functions, and operator overloading. We also use template classes in Chapter 13, where we discuss dynamic data structures: lists, stacks, queues, and trees. We discuss the use of the STL container classes and iterators and also show students how to implement their own classes. An illustration of the C++ inheritance and virtual function mechanisms is provided in Appendix E. We've done our best to follow a balanced path between the strictly objects-first and totally procedure-focused programming metaphors. We agree with the objects-first concept, but not at the expense of the fundamentals of algorithm organization and design. Students in a first course can and should be taught the basic elements of procedural design. Our task is to do so within the context of an early focus on the importance of data modeling, reuse, and other fundamental principles of good software development.

## Software Engineering and Object–Oriented Concepts

Many fundamental software engineering and object-oriented concepts are illustrated in the text: user-defined types, modeling problem domain entities and their relationships, minimal interfaces, high-level cohesion, information hiding, separation of concerns, parameterized components, and inheritance. Abstraction is stressed from the start. Numerous complete case examples are provided throughout the text; these follow a standard software development method, from the specification and analysis of a problem to a first stage of design to the final coding.

Issues of program style are presented throughout in special displays. The concept of a program as a sequence of control structures is introduced in Chapter 3 and discussed in more detail in Chapters 4 (on selection structures) and 5 (repetition structures). Our decision to introduce software engineering concepts in a first-year course is apparent in these early chapters . We've introduced functions and classes as early as possible at the introductory level—functions in Chapters 3 and 6, and the use and definition of classes in Chapters 3 and 10, respectively. We also provide several sections that discuss testing, debugging, and program verification.

## Outline of Contents

Conceptually, the text may be partitioned into three sections. Chapters 1 through 6 provide introductory material on functions and top-down design, presenting detailed coverage of selection and repetition structures and program design strategies for using these structures. The connection between good problem-solving skills and effective software development is established early in the first three chapters. Included in the first two chapters are sections on problem solving and an introduction to a software development methodology based on a systematic approach to problem solving. The problem-solving approach outlined in these chapters is applied consistently to all other case studies in the text. Chapter 2 also contains an introduction to the basic elements of C++, including two sections in which we discuss abstraction, data modeling, and object-oriented programming. In Chapter 3, we continue the emphasis on basic problem-solving skills with a discussion of top-down design anddivide and conquer. The reuse of program components is discussed and additional detail is provided on the  string class and its member functions.

Top-down procedural decomposition is further illustrated in Chapters 4 through 6. Decision structures are introduced in Chapter 4, and repetition structures are presented in Chapter 5. In Chapter 6, we revisit the C++ function, introducing functions with output arguments and providing a complete case study illustrating much of what has been learned to this point. An optional section on recursion is also included at the end of Chapter 6.

Chapters 7 through 9 cover simple data types, input and output, structured data types (arrays and structs), and classes.  Chapter 7 contains a more detailed discussion of simple data types, including additional commentary on data abstraction as well as a description of the internal and external distinctions among the simple types. In Chapter 9, the structured types (arrays and structs) are first introduced. Simple searching and sorting algorithms are discussed and the use of structured types as function arguments is illustrated.

Chapter 8 provides an introduction to external file input/output. Although studying external files may seem premature at this point, we believe it is appropriate. Programs don't exist in a vacuum; they manipulate data that often come from external sources and they produce results that may subsequently be manipulated by other programs. It's therefore important for students to gain a relatively early exposure to some fundamental concepts related to file input and output, as long as this exposure does not disrupt the presentation of other essential ideas. Of course, by the time Chapter 8 is reached, students will have already been introduced to the basics of stream input and output, including a minimal use of formatting functions and input/output manipulators (Chapter 5).

For students with the equivalent of a one-semester programming course in another language, Chapters 1 through 9 can be covered fairly quickly, perhaps in as little as five or six weeks. For students with little or no background, this coverage may take ten to twelve weeks.

Chapters 10 and 11 cover intermediate-level concepts that would normally be covered at the end of CS1 or the beginning of CS2. Chapter 10 covers the definition and use of classes and objects. Chapter 11 focuses on data modeling. We begin with a discussion of multidimensional arrays and arrays of structs and classes, and then extend our modeling capability with illustrations of the use of class templates and the vector class.

Chapters 12 and 13 cover more advanced topics in some depth: recursion (Chapter 12), and linked lists, stacks, queues, and trees (Chapter 13). This material will be covered in the second semester of the first-year sequence.

## Coverage of Pointers

Pointers are introduced only where they really belong—in the discussion of dynamic data structures (Chapter 13). The pointer is one of the more dangerous, relatively unprotected aspects of the C++ language and need not be an essential part of an introductory text. Use of the new and delete operators and the allocation and deallocation of memory cells in the heap are discussed at the beginning of Chapter 13. We illustrate the manipulation of dynamic data structures such as simple linked lists, stacks and queues, and binary trees.

## Pedagogical Features

Several pedagogical features also enhance the usefulness of the text as an instructional tool. These include the following:

- Consistent use of analysis and design aids such as data requirements tables and program structure charts
- End-of-section self-check and programming exercises (answers to the odd number self-check exercises are provided in the text)
- End-of-chapter self-check exercises (answers are provided)
- End-of-chapter programming projects
- Numerous examples and case studies carried through from analysis and design to implementation
- Syntax displays containing the syntax and semantics of each new C++ feature introduced
- Program style and design guideline displays
- Detailed syntax and run-time error discussions at the end of each chapter
- Chapter reviews and review questions

## Appendices

Separate appendices are provided, summarizing information about character sets, C++ reserved words, C++ operators, and function libraries (with descriptions and specific page numbers). There is an appendix illustrating inheritance and virtual functions, an appendix on Visual C++, and an appendix on Borland C++ Builder.

## Supplemental Materials

The following supplements are available to all readers of this book at www.aw.com/cssupport:

*Source Code*

The following instructor supplements are only available to qualified instructors. Please contact your local Addison-Wesley Sales Representative, or send e-mail to aw.cse@aw.com, for information about how to access them:

*PowerPoint Slides to follow the organization of the text*

*Laboratory assignments keyed to the textbook*

*Instructor's Manual with Solutions including:*
- A statement of objectives for each chapter
- All programs, functions, and classes from the text
- Solutions to even-numbered self-check exercises
- Solutions to review questions
- Commentary on the analysis and design of selected programming projects
- The implementation of selected programming projects
- Sample exam questions

*Test Bank consisting of short answer, multiple choice, and true/false questions for each chapter*

## Acknowledgements

Many people helped with the development of this book. Primary contributors to the first edition included Paul LaFollette, Paul Wolfgang, and Rajiv Tewari of Temple University. Temple graduate students Donna Chrupcala, Bruce Weiner, and Judith Wilson also contributed significantly to the development of the first edition. Steve Vinoski provided detailed comments concerning the C++ material in many of the later chapters.

The principal reviewers and class testers were enormously helpful in suggesting improvements and finding errors. For the first edition, these included Allen Alexander (Delaware Technical and Community College), Ruth Barton and Richard Reid (Michigan State University), Larry Cottrell (University of Central Florida), H. E. Dunsmore and Russell Quong (Purdue University), Donna Krabbe (College of Mount St. Joseph), Sally Kyvernitis (Neumann College), Xiaoping Jia (DePaul University), Xiannong Meng and Rick Zaccone (Bucknell), Jeff Buckwalter and Kim Summerhays (University of San Francisco), and Jo Ellen Perry (University of North Carolina). Valuable proof-reading and editing assistance were provided by Sally Kyvernitis, Donna Skalski, and Frank Friedman's daughters Dara and Shelley.

We are also very grateful to the principal reviewers of the third edition for their hard work and timely responses. They include: William E. Bulley (Merit Network, Inc.), Greg Comeau (Comeau Computing), Bruce Gilland (University of Colorado at Boulder), William I. Grosky (Wayne State University), Bina Ramamurthy (SUNY at Buffalo), and W. Brent Seales (University of Kentucky). Our thanks, also, to Temple student Ayisha Mertens, who tested the programs appearing in this edition.

Frank Friedman is particularly indebted to several members of the staff at the Software Engineering Institute (Pittsburgh), particularly Mary Shaw, Norm Gibbs (now at Guilford College), and Gary Ford, for their support during the year in which the seeds that lead to this book were sown.

As always, it has been a pleasure working with the people of Addison-Wesley throughout this endeavor. Susan Hartman Sullivan, Executive Editor for the Computing Editorial Group and our editor and good friend for the past several years, initiated the revision. Michael Hirsch, previously the marketing manager for computer science and now a Senior Acquisitions Editor, was closely involved in all phases of the development of the manuscript. Patty Mahtani, Manager of Product Development, Computing supervised the development and production of the new edition. Elizabeth Paquin, Assistant Editor, provided timely assistance at a moment's notice. Sally Boylan of Argosy Publishing coordinated the conversion of the manuscript to a finished book. Suzanne Goraj thoroughly copyedited the manuscript and provided many suggestions for improvement.

*Cheltenham, PA*
*F. L. F.*
*E. B. K.*

# Contents

*chapter four*     Selection Structures: **if** and **switch** Statements     165

*chapter seven*    Simple Data Types   347

*chapter ten*    User-Defined Classes    489

*chapter eleven*        Data Abstraction and Object-Oriented Design    553

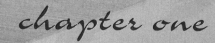

## chapter one

# Introduction to Computers, Problem Solving, and Programming

**Chapter Objectives**

- To learn the different categories of computers
- To understand the role of each component in a computer
- To understand the purpose of an operating system
- To learn the differences between machine language, assembly language, and higher level languages
- To understand what processes are required to run a C++ program
- To learn how to solve a programming problem in a careful, disciplined way
- To understand and appreciate ethical issues related to the use of computers and programming

SINCE THE 1940s—a period of little more than 50 years—the development of the computer has spurred the growth of technology into realms only dreamed of at the turn of the twentieth century. Computers have changed the way we live and how we do business. Many of us use computers to register for courses, to send and receive electronic mail (e-mail), to shop and bank from home, to retrieve information from the World Wide Web, to research and write term papers, and to do other homework assignments. Computers are a key component of automatic teller machines (ATMs), and computers are built into our cars and most household appliances. Computers can receive, store, process, and output information of all kinds: numbers, text, images, graphics, and sound, to name a few.

Although we're often led to believe otherwise, computers cannot "think." Basically, computers are devices for performing computations at incredible speeds (more than a billion instructions per second) and with great accuracy. But, to accomplish anything useful, a computer must be provided with a list of instructions, or a program. Programs are usually written in special computer programming languages—such as C++, the subject of this book and one of the most versatile programming languages available today.

In this chapter, we introduce the computer and its components and then present an overview of programming languages. Finally, we describe a method for developing software (programs), and we use it to write a basic C++ program.

## 1.1   Overview of Computers

Most of us deal with computers every day, and we probably use computers for word processing or for surfing the World Wide Web. And some of us may even have studied programming in high school. But it wasn't always this way. Not long ago, most people considered computers to be mysterious devices whose secrets were known only by a few computer wizards.

### Early Computers

If we take the literal definition for a computer as "a device for counting or computing," then we could consider the abacus to have been the first computer. The first electronic digital computer was designed in the late 1930s by Dr. John Atanasoff and graduate student Clifford Berry at Iowa State University. They designed their computer to help them perform mathematical computations in nuclear physics.

The first large-scale, general-purpose electronic digital computer, called the ENIAC, was completed in 1946 at the University of Pennsylvania with funding from the U.S. Army. The ENIAC weighed 30 tons and occupied a 30-by–50-foot space. It was used to compute ballistics tables, predict the weather, and make atomic energy calculations. Its designers were J. Presper Eckert and John Mauchley.

To program the ENIAC, engineers had to connect hundreds of wires and arrange thousands of switches in a certain way. In 1946, Dr. John von Neumann of Princeton University proposed the concept of a **stored-program** computer—a computer whose program was stored in computer memory. Von Neumann knew that the data stored in computer memory could easily be changed by a program. He reasoned that programs, too, could be stored in computer memory and changed far more easily than by

**stored-program computer (von Neumann architecture)** A computer design based on the concept of storing a computer program along with its data in computer memory.

connecting wires and setting switches. Von Neumann designed a computer based on this idea. His design was a success and greatly simplified computer programming. The **von Neumann architecture** is the basis of the digital computer as we know it today.

## Categories of Computers

Early computers used vacuum tubes as their basic electronic component. Technological advances in the design and manufacture of these components led to new generations of computers that were considerably smaller, faster, and less expensive than their predecessors.

In the 1970s, the Altair and Apple computer companies manufactured the first **microcomputers**. The computer processor in a microcomputer is an electronic component called a **microprocessor**, which is about the size of a postage stamp. Because they are so small and relatively inexpensive, microprocessors are found in watches, pocket calculators, cameras, home appliances, and automobiles, as well as in computers.

Most offices have one or more personal computers. Typical models cost less than $2000 and sit on a desk, yet have as much computational power as the giants of 20 years ago that cost more than $100,000 and filled a 9-by-12-foot room. Today's computers come in even smaller models that can fit inside a briefcase or a person's hand (see Figure 1.1).

Personal computers are used by one person at a time. Businesses and research labs use larger and faster computers called **minicomputers** and **mainframes**, which can be used by many people simultaneously. **Supercomputers**, the most powerful mainframe computers, can perform in seconds computations that might take hours or even days on other computers.

## Sharing Computer Resources

**Time sharing** is used on mainframes and minicomputers to allow simultaneous access to the computing resources. The problem with time sharing is that users have to wait their turn to access the resources. In the early days, these waits could take minutes. And if the computer stops working, all users are affected, as they must wait for the computer to be restarted.

Although microcomputers don't have the huge resources of minicomputers and mainframes, they provide their users with dedicated resources. Also if one microcomputer stops working, others are not affected. The major disadvantage of early personal or workstation computers was that they were isolated from the vast resources of the larger machines. In Section 1.2, we see how computer networks solve this problem.

**microcomputer**
A computer that uses a very small processor.
**microprocessor**
The processor found in a microcomputer.

**minicomputer**
A computer for businesses or research laboratories that can be used by many people simultaneously.
**mainframe**
A computer with more computational power than a minicomputer that is often used by major corporations.
**supercomputer**
The most powerful kind of mainframe computer, performing in seconds computations that might take hours or days on other computers.

**time sharing**
A process that allows simultaneous access to a single computer by a number of users.

**Figure 1.1**    Laptop computer and hand-held computer

## EXERCISES FOR SECTION 1.1

Self–Check

1. List the different kinds of computers from smallest to largest.

2. Why do you think each computer user in a time-shared environment is unaware that others are also using the computer?

3. Describe the contributions of Atanasoff and Berry, Eckert and Mauchley, and von Neumann.

## 1.2  Computer Hardware

**hardware**
The actual computer equipment.
**software**
The set of programs associated with a computer.
**program**
A list of instructions that a computer uses to manipulate data to perform a task.

A computer system consists of two major components: **hardware**—the actual equipment used to perform the computations—and **software**—that is, the programs. **Programs** let us communicate with a computer by giving it the instructions it needs to operate. We discuss hardware in this section and software in the next.

Despite their differences in cost, size, and capabilities, modern computers resemble each other in many basic ways. Essentially, most consist of the following hardware components:

- Main memory
- Secondary memory, including storage media such as hard disks, floppy disks, and CD-ROMs
- Central processing unit (CPU)

- Input devices, such as a keyboard and mouse
- Output devices, such as a monitor and printer
- Network connection, such as a modem or Ethernet interface

Figure 1.2 shows how these components interact in a computer when a program is executed; the arrows show the direction of information flow.

The program must be transferred from *secondary memory* to *main memory* before it can be executed. Data must be supplied from some source. The person using a program (the *program user*) may supply data through an *input device* such as a mouse or a keyboard, from a *data file* located in secondary storage, or from a remote machine via the network connection. The data are stored in the computer's *main memory* where they can be accessed and manipulated by the *central processing unit*. The results of this manipulation are stored back in *main memory*. Finally, the information (results) in main memory may be displayed through an *output device* such as a monitor or printer, stored in secondary storage, or sent to another computer via the network. In the remainder of this section, we describe these components in more detail.

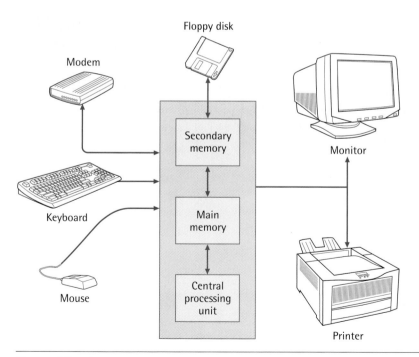

**Figure 1.2**   Computer components

## Memory

Memory is an essential component in any computer. Before discussing the types of memory—main and secondary—let's look at what it consists of and how the computer works with it.

### Anatomy of Memory

**memory cell**
An individual storage location in memory.

**address of a memory cell**
The relative position of a memory cell in the computer's main memory.

**contents of a memory cell**
The information stored in a memory cell, either a program instruction or data.

Imagine the memory of a computer as a sequence of storage locations called **memory cells**. To store and access information, the computer must have some way of identifying the individual memory cells, so each memory cell has a unique **address** that indicates its position in memory. Figure 1.3 shows a computer memory consisting of 1000 memory cells with addresses 0 through 999. Most computers have millions of individual memory cells, each with its own address.

The data stored in a memory cell are called the **contents** of the cell. In Figure 1.3, the contents of memory cell 3 is the number −26 and the contents of memory cell 4 is the letter H.

Memory cells can also contain program instructions. Cells 6 through 8 in Figure 1.3 store instructions to add two numbers (from cells 1 and 3) and store the result in memory cell 5. You'll recall that in a von Neumann computer, a program's instructions must be stored in main memory before they

| Address | Contents |
|---:|:---:|
| 0 | −27.2 |
| 1 | 354 |
| 2 | 0.005 |
| 3 | −26 |
| 4 | H |
| 5 | 400 |
| 6 | RTV 001 |
| 7 | ADD 003 |
| 8 | STO 005 |
| ⋮ | ⋮ |
| 998 | X |
| 999 | 75.62 |

**Figure 1.3**   A thousand memory cells in main memory

can be executed. Whenever we open a new program, we change the computer's operation by storing the new instructions in memory.

## Bytes and Bits

A memory cell is actually a grouping of smaller units called bytes. A **byte** is the amount of storage required to store a single character, such as the letter H in cell 4 of Figure 1.3. The number of bytes a memory cell can contain varies from computer to computer.

A byte is composed of even smaller units of storage called bits (see Figure 1.4). There are eight bits to a byte. "**Bit**" derives from the words *bi*nary digi*t* and is the smallest element a computer can deal with. Binary refers to a number system based on two numbers, 0 and 1; therefore, a bit is either a 0 or a 1.

**byte**
The amount of storage required to store a single character.

**bit (binary digit)**
A binary unit representing a 0 or a 1.

## Storing and Retrieving Information in Memory

A particular pattern of zeros and ones (that is, bits) represents each value in memory, whether it's a number, a letter, or an instruction such as ADD 003. A computer can either store or retrieve a value. When **storing** a value, the computer sends electronic signals to set each bit of a selected memory cell to either 0 or 1; storing a value destroys the previous contents of the cell. When **retrieving** a value from a memory cell, the computer copies the pattern of 0s and 1s stored in that cell to another storage area for processing; copying does *not* destroy the contents of the cell whose value is retrieved. This process is the same regardless of the kind of information—character, number, or program instruction—to be stored or retrieved.

**storing a value in memory**
Setting the individual bits of a memory cell to 0 or 1, destroying its previous contents.

**retrieving a value from memory**
Copying the contents of a particular memory cell to another storage area for processing.

## Main Memory

Main memory, made of electronic circuitry on small computer chips, stores programs, data, and results. Most computers have two types of main memory: **random access memory (RAM)** for temporary storage of programs, data, and results, and **read-only memory (ROM)**, which stores programs or data permanently.

RAM temporarily stores programs while they are being executed by the computer. It also temporarily stores information—e.g., numbers, names, or pictures—that is being processed by the computer. RAM is

**random access memory (RAM)**
The part of main memory that temporarily stores programs, data, and results.

**read-only memory (ROM)**
The part of main memory that permanently stores programs or data.

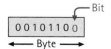

**Figure 1.4** Relationship between a byte and a bit

**volatile memory**
Memory whose contents disappear when you switch off the computer.

usually **volatile memory,** which means that when you switch off the computer, you will lose everything stored in RAM. To prevent this, you should store the contents of RAM in semipermanent secondary memory (discussed below) before switching off your computer.

In contrast, ROM stores information permanently. The computer can retrieve (or read) information but it can't store (or write) information in ROM—hence its name, read-only memory. Because they're not volatile, the instructions and data stored in ROM don't disappear when you switch off the computer. Most modern computers contain an internal ROM that stores the instructions needed to get the computer running when you first switch it on.

Usually a computer contains much more RAM than internal ROM. The amount of RAM can often be increased (up to a specified maximum), but the amount of internal ROM is usually fixed. When we refer to main memory in this text, we mean RAM because that is the part of main memory that is normally accessible to the programmer.

RAM is relatively fast memory, but is limited in size and is not permanent memory. These features are in contrast to secondary memory, which, although slower than RAM, is larger and more permanent.

## Secondary Memory

**disk**
A semipermanent storage medium whose contents can be changed.
**file**
A collection of related information stored on a disk.
**source file**
A file that contains a program.
**data file**
A file that contains data for a program.
**output file**
A file that contains results generated by running a program.
**hard disk**
A disk that is built into the computer and normally cannot be removed.
**floppy disk/Zip disk**
A personal, portable disk that can be used with different computers.

Secondary memory provides semipermanent data-storage capability through secondary storage devices. Such memory is considered semipermanent because its contents can be changed. Secondary memory is usually a magnetic medium such as tape or disk. Audiocassette tapes, for example, are a magnetic medium on which music is stored; computer tapes and disks provide storage for digital information (sequences of 0s and 1s). Magnetic media can easily be erased and recorded over.

The most common form of secondary memory is a **disk.** Information stored on a disk is organized into separate collections called **files.** One file may contain a program (a **source file**). Another file may contain the data to be processed by that program (a **data file**). A third file may contain the results generated by a program (an **output file**).

There are two common kinds of magnetic disks for personal computers: the **hard disk** (also called a *fixed disk*) and the **floppy disk.** Most personal computers contain one hard disk that can't be removed from its disk drive. A hard disk can store much more data than a single floppy disk can, and the CPU can access the data on a hard disk much more quickly. Normally the programs that are needed to operate the computer system are stored on its hard disk.

A floppy disk is a small mylar sheet coated with magnetizable material and housed in a hard plastic container. Floppy disks are mostly used to store programs and data for individual users and to move small amounts of information between personal computers. Floppy disks are being replaced by newer technologies (for example, Zip disks and flash memory cards). These disks store more data and access it more quickly but still have the portability of floppy disks.

Another common storage medium is the **CD-ROM**. A CD-ROM uses optical technology to store information on plastic disks that are similar to CDs used in a CD audio player. A computer CD stores data (numbers, characters, graphics, instructions) that can be transferred to the computer's main memory or secondary memory and are a convenient way to distribute commercial software. CD-ROM, also provide a flexible means of storing data that do not change—for example, images, sound, and large quantities of text such as encyclopedias. CD-ROMs are also less expensive and more reliable than magnetic media. Newer technologies enable the user to rewrite CDs.

> CD-ROM (Compact Disk–Read Only Memory)
> A plastic disk used to permanently store information that is read by optical technology.

You can further increase the size of secondary memory by purchasing additional storage devices. Secondary memory has much more storage capacity than main memory does. On most computers, you can add main memory by installing additional memory chips, but main memory is considerably more expensive per byte than is secondary memory. Data in main memory are volatile and disappear when you switch off the computer; data in secondary memory are semipermanent or permanent and are not lost when the computer is switched off. You should store all your programs as files in secondary memory and transfer a program file into main memory when you want it executed.

## Central Processing Unit

The **central processing unit (CPU)** has two roles: coordinating all computer operations and performing arithmetic and logical operations on data. The CPU follows instructions in computer programs to determine which operations to carry out and in what order. It then transmits control signals to the other computer components. For example, when instructed to read a data item, the CPU sends the necessary control signals to the input device.

> central processing unit (CPU)
> Coordinates all computer operations and performs arithmetic and logical operations on data.

To process a program stored in main memory, the CPU retrieves each instruction in sequence (called **fetching an instruction**), decodes the instruction, and then retrieves any data needed to carry out that instruction. Next, the CPU processes the data it retrieved and stores the results in main memory.

> fetching an instruction
> Retrieving an instruction from main memory.

The CPU can perform arithmetic operations such as addition, subtraction, multiplication, and division. It can also compare the contents of two memory cells—for example, deciding which contains the larger value or if the values are equal—and make decisions based on the results of that comparison.

**integrated circuit (IC)**
An electronic device containing a large number of circuits/components housed inside a silicon case.

**microprocessor**
A central processing unit packaged in an integrated circuit.

**register**
A high-speed memory location inside the CPU.

**keyboard**
A computer input device for typing sequences of letter or digit characters.

**cursor**
A moving place marker that indicates the position on the screen where the next character will be displayed.

**function keys**
A special keyboard key used to select a particular operation; the operation selected depends on the program being used.

**mouse**
A handheld input device that moves a cursor on the computer screen to select an operation.

**icon**
A picture representing a computer operation that is activated by clicking a mouse.

The circuitry of a modern CPU is housed in a single **integrated circuit** (IC) or chip—millions of miniature circuits manufactured on a sliver of silicon. An integrated circuit that is a full central processing unit is called a **microprocessor**. A CPU's current instruction and data values are stored temporarily inside the CPU in special high-speed memory locations called **registers**.

## Input/Output Devices

We use input/output (I/O) devices to communicate with the computer—to enter data for a computation and to observe the results of that computation. The most common input device is a keyboard and the most common output device is a monitor.

A computer **keyboard** resembles a typewriter keyboard (see Figure 1.5). When you press a letter or digit key, that character is sent to main memory and is displayed on the monitor at the position of the **cursor**, a moving place marker. A computer keyboard has extra keys for special purposes. For example, on the keyboard shown in Figure 1.5, the 12 keys in the top row labeled F1 through F12 are **function keys**. The functions of these keys depend on the program currently being executed; that is, pressing F4 in one program will usually not produce the same results as pressing F4 in another program. Other special keys let you delete characters, move the cursor, and "enter" a line of data you typed at the keyboard.

Another common input device is a **mouse**, a handheld pointing device. Moving the mouse on your desk causes the mouse cursor, a small arrow or symbol on the screen, to move in the same direction as the mouse. You can use the mouse to select an operation by pointing and clicking: moving the mouse cursor to a word or picture (called an **icon**) that represents the computer operation and then pressing a mouse button to start the operation selected.

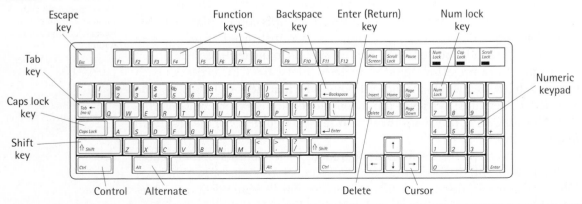

**Figure 1.5**    Computer keyboard

A **monitor** displays the output of currect computer operations. Once the image disappears from the monitor screen, it is lost. If you want a hard copy (a printed version) of some information, you must send that information to a different output device, a printer.

## Computer Networks

Network technology was invented to connect computers together and let them share resources. Unlike a mainframe, which is a single computer shared by many users, a **network** is made of many computers that share resources. Within an organization, a **local area network (LAN)** lets many personal computers access sharable resources from a larger computer called a **server**. A network that links individual computers and local area networks over a large geographic area is called a **wide area network (WAN)**. The best-known WAN is the **Internet**, which is composed of university, corporate, government, and public-access networks. The World Wide Web is accessed via the Internet.

Today, most computers are attached to the Internet and many are connected to a local area network as well. Computers can be networked either with hardware connections and cables that transmit digital signals directly or with a **modem** (**mo**dulator/**dem**odulator) and a telephone line. The modem for a personal computer converts digital signals to analog signals that can be sent over telephone lines. The modem at the destination computer converts the analog signals back to digital signals that can be understood by the destination computer. There are also modems that transmit digital signals at much faster speed over telephone lines (DSL modems) or cable TV lines (cable modems).

## The World Wide Web

The **World Wide Web (the Web)** was introduced in 1989; it is the newest and the most popular feature on the Internet. The Web was developed at CERN (the European Laboratory for Particle Physics) as an effective and uniform way of accessing all the information on the Internet. Today you can use the Web to send, view, retrieve, and search for information or to create a Web page. (There are no controls or checks for accuracy on the Web; you should keep this in mind when reading or using such information.)

To access and navigate the Web, you need a **Web browser**. A Web browser is a program with a **graphical user interface (GUI)** that displays the text and graphics in a Web document and activates the **hyperlinks** to other documents. Clicking on a link to a Web document causes that document to be transferred from the computer where it is stored to your own computer.

---

**monitor**
A computer output device for providing a temporary display of information.

**network**
An interconnected collection of computers that share resources.

**local area network (LAN)**
A network of computers in a single organization.

**server**
A computer that provides resources to other computers in a network.

**wide area network (WAN)**
A network such as the Internet that connects computers and LANs over a large geographic area.

**Internet**
An interconnected grouping of computer networks from all over the world; provides access to the World Wide Web.

**modem (modulator/demodulator)**
A device that converts digital signals to analog signals and analog signals back to digital signals.

**World Wide Web**
A collection of interconnected documents that may be accessed from virtually any computer in the world.

**Web browser**
A program that lets users display and view a Web document and activate links to other documents.

**graphical user interface (GUI)**
Displayed pictures and menus that allow users to select commands and data.

**hyperlink**
A connection in a Web document to other related documents that users can activate by pressing a mouse button.

## EXERCISES FOR SECTION 1.2

### Self-Check

1. What are the contents of memory cells 1 and 998 in Figure 1.3? What memory cells contain the letter H and the number 75.62?

2. Explain the purpose of main memory, secondary memory, CPU, and the disk. What input and output devices will be used with your computer? What is a computer network?

3. List the following in order of smallest to largest: byte, bit, ROM, RAM, hard disk, floppy disk, Zip disk.

4. What do you think each of the instructions in memory cells 6 though 8 in Figure 1.3 means?

5. Which came first, the Internet or the World Wide Web?

6. Indicate whether each of these devices usually provides temporary, semipermanent, or permanent storage: ROM, RAM, floppy disk, Zip disk, CD-ROM, hard disk.

7. Which device from the list in Exercise 6 does a word processor use to store a letter while it is being typed? To store the letter after you are finished? To store a software package you purchase? To store some very large files you no longer need?

8. Explain the use of a Web browser and hyperlinks in a Web document.

9. If a computer were instructed to sum the contents of memory cells 1 and 3 of Figure 1.3 and store the result in memory cell 5, what would be stored in memory cell 5?

10. One bit can have two values, 0 or 1. A combination of 2 bits can have values 00, 01, 10, 11. List the values you can have with 3 bits. Do the same for 4 bits. Write a formula that tells you how many values you can have with n bits.

# 1.3    Computer Software

In the previous section, we surveyed the components of a computer system, collectively called hardware. We also covered the basic operations by which a computer accomplishes tasks: repeated fetching and execution of instructions. In this section, we focus on these all-important lists of instructions, called computer programs or computer software. We will first consider the software that makes the hardware accessible to the user, then look at the various levels of computer languages in which software is written and at the process of creating and running a new program.

## Operating System

The computer programs that control the interaction of the user with the computer hardware compose the **operating system (OS)**. The operating system may be compared to the conductor of an orchestra, for it is responsible for directing all computer operations and managing all computer resources. Usually, part of the operating system is stored permanently in a read-only memory (ROM) chip so it will be available as soon as the computer is turned on. (A computer can look at the values in ROM but can't write new values to the chip.) This portion of the OS contains the instructions that will load into RAM the rest of the operating system code, which typically resides on disk. Loading the operating system into RAM is called **booting the computer**.

Among the operating system's many responsibilities are the following:

1. Communicating with the computer user: receiving commands and carrying them out or rejecting them with an error message.
2. Managing allocation of memory, processor time, and other resources for various tasks.
3. Collecting input from the keyboard, mouse, and other input devices, and providing this data to the currently running program.
4. Conveying program output to the screen, printer, or other output device.
5. Accessing data from secondary storage.
6. Writing data to secondary storage.

In addition, the OS of a computer with multiple users must verify each user's right to use the computer and ensure that each user can access only data for which he or she has authorization.

Table 1.1 lists some widely used operating systems. An OS with a command-line interface displays a brief message called a **prompt** that indicates readiness to receive input; the user can then type a command at the keyboard. Listing 1.1 shows the entry of a UNIX command (`ls  temp/misc`) requesting a list of the names of all the files (`Gridvar.cpp`, `Gridvar.exe`, `Gridok.dat`) in subdirectory `misc` of directory `temp`. Here, the prompt is `mycomputer:~>`. (In this and all subsequent listings showing program runs, input typed by the user is shown in color to distinguish it from computer-generated text.)

In contrast, operating systems with a GUI interface provide the user with a desktop (the user screen) that shows a collection of icons and menus.

**operating system (OS)**
Software that controls a user's interaction with the computer hardware and software and that manages the computer resources.

**booting the computer**
Starting the computer by loading part of the operating system from disk into memory (RAM) and executing it.

**prompt**
A message displayed by the computer indicating its readiness to receive data or a command from the user.

Table 1.1    Some Widely Used Operating Systems Characterized by Interface Type

| Command-Line Interface | Graphical User Interface |
|---|---|
| UNIX | Macintosh OS |
| MS-DOS | Windows XP |
| VMS | Windows NT |
| | OS/2 Warp |
| | UNIX + X Window System |
| | Linux |

Listing 1.1    Entering a UNIX command to display a directory

```
mycomputer:~> ls temp/misc
Gridvar.cpp      Gridvar.exe      Gridok.dat

mycomputer:~>
```

To issue commands, the user moves the mouse cursor to point to the appropriate icon or menu selection and clicks a button once or twice. Figure 1.6 shows the effect of double-clicking on the Recycle Bin icon at the top-left corner of a Windows XP desktop. The window titled Recycle Bin appears on the screen. It has a menu line showing the words File, Edit, View, and Help; clicking on one of these menu item drops down a list of choices for further action. There is a second menu line below the first, with icons that can be clicked on to perform specific tasks. The Recycle Bin window itself shows the documents and folders that are currently in the Recycle Bin. The shaded area on the left shows other tasks that you can perform (called Recycle Bin Tasks), and a list of "Other places" that you can navigate to.

## Application Software

**application programs**
Software used for a specific task such as word processing, accounting, or database management.

**Application programs** are designed to accomplish specific tasks. For example, a word-processing application such as Microsoft Word or WordPerfect creates a document, a spreadsheet application such as Excel automates tedious numerical calculations and generates charts that depict data, and a database management application such as Access enables data storage and quick keyword-based access to large collections of records.

**installing software**
Making an application available on a computer by copying it from floppy disks or a CD-ROM to a hard disk.

Computer users typically buy application software CD-ROMs and **install the software** by copying it to their hard disk. When buying software, verify that the program you are purchasing is compatible with both your operating system and your computer hardware. Programmers use

**Figure 1.6**   Clicking on the Recycle Bin Icon in Windows XP

programming languages, the subject of the next section, to write most commercial software.

## Programming Languages

Developing new software requires writing lists of instructions for a computer to execute. Software developers rarely write instructions in **machine language**, a language of binary numbers directly understood by a computer. A drawback of machine language is that it is not standardized: every type of CPU has a different machine language. This same drawback also applies to the somewhat more readable **assembly language**, a language in which computer operations are represented by mnemonic codes rather than binary numbers, and variables can be given names rather than binary memory addresses.

Table 1.2 shows a small machine language program fragment that adds two numbers and an equivalent fragment in assembly language. Notice that each assembly language instruction corresponds to exactly one machine language instruction. (The assembly language memory cells labeled A and B are space for data; they are not instructions.) The symbol ? indicates that we don't know the contents of the memory cells with addresses 00000100 and 00000101.

To write programs that are independent of the CPU on which they will be executed, software designers use **high-level languages**, which combine algebraic expressions and English words. For example, the machine/assembly

**machine language**
A list of binary instructions for a particular CPU.

**assembly language**
A language whose instructions are in the form of mnemonic codes and variable names.

**high-level language**
A machine programming language that combines algebraic expressions and English words.

**Table 1.2**    A Program in Machine and Assembly Language

| Memory Addresses | Machine Language Instructions | Assembly Language Instructions |
|---|---|---|
| 00000000 | 00010101 | RTV  A |
| 00000001 | 00010110 | ADD  B |
| 00000010 | 00110101 | STO  A |
| 00000011 | 01110111 | HLT |
| 00000100 | ? | A  ? |
| 00000101 | ? | B  ? |

language program fragment shown in Table 1.2 would be a single statement in a high-level language:

```
a = a + b;
```

This statement means "Add the data in memory cells a and b, and store the result in memory cell a (replacing its previous value)."

Many high-level languages are available. Table 1.3 lists some of the most widely used ones along with the application areas that first popularized them.

## Object-Oriented Programming

We will focus on C++, an object-oriented programming language derived from C. C++ was developed by Bjarne Stroustrup of AT&T's Bell Laboratories in the mid-1980s and was formally standardized in 1998. Object-oriented programming languages are popular because they make it easier to reuse and adapt previously written software. Another object-oriented language listed in Table 1.3 is Java, which is widely used on the Web.

**Table 1.3**    Common High-Level Languages

| High-Level Language | Original Purpose |
|---|---|
| BASIC | Teaching college students how to use the computer in their courses |
| C | Writing system software |
| C++ | Extension of C supporting object-oriented programming |
| COBOL | Performing business data processing |
| FORTRAN (**For**mula **tran**slation) | Performing engineering and scientific applications |
| Java | A highly portable object-oriented language used for programming on the Web |
| Lisp | Performing artificial intelligence applications that require manipulating abstract symbols |

An object is an entity that has particular properties. Some of these properties can be encoded into a computer program as data and some can be encoded as **methods** for operating on the data.

As an example of an object, consider a hypothetical automobile. You may visualize wheels, a steering wheel, a body shape, and a color. These are the attributes, or data, of the automobile. You can also imagine the actions associated with operating an automobile, such as starting the engine, driving forward or in reverse, and applying the brakes. These activities are analogous to methods. The attributes and methods we use to characterize an automobile are an **abstraction**, or model, of an automobile.

The description of an automobile thus provides a definition of a hypothetical automobile. As such, it describes a **class**—the class *automobile*. The class definition can be used as a template to construct actual **objects**, or instances of the class, such as your car and your parents' car. Both cars have all the attributes of an automobile, but they differ in detail—for example, one may be red and the other white.

The distinction between the terms *class* and *object* sometimes gets a bit blurry. A class definition, or class, describes the properties (attributes) of an abstract or hypothetical object. Actual objects are instances of the class. An object's data fields provide storage for information, and an object's methods process or manipulate this information. Some of the data stored in an object may be computed using a method. For example, fuel efficiency can be computed from the power of the engine and the weight of the car (along with some other factors). Table 1.4 shows some attributes of the class *automobile* and two objects of that class.

Classes can have other classes as components. For example, a car has an engine and wheels; both components can be defined as separate classes. Finally, classes can be organized into a hierarchy of **subclasses** and **superclasses**, where a subclass has all the properties of a superclass and some additional properties that are not part of the superclass. Figure 1.7 shows that the class *automobile* is a subclass of the class *vehicle* (an automobile is a vehicle that has passenger seats), and the class *vehicle* is a superclass of the class *automobile*. The class *truck* is also a subclass of the class *vehicle* (a truck

**method**
An operation that can be performed on an object's data.
**abstraction**
A representation or model of a physical object.
**class**
An entity that defines the properties of a hypothetical object.
**object**
A member, or instance, of a class that has all the properties described by the class definition.

**subclass**
A class that is derived from a superclass but with additional attributes.
**superclass**
A class that serves as a base class for other classes with additional attributes.

**Table 1.4**   The Relationship Between a Class and Objects of the Class

| Class **automobile** | Object **yourCar** | Object **parentsCar** |
| --- | --- | --- |
| Color | Red | White |
| Make | Toyota | Buick |
| Model | Coupe | Sedan |
| Year | 1999 | 2003 |

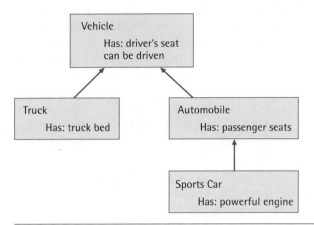

**Figure 1.7**    A class hierarchy

is a vehicle that has a truck bed), and the class *vehicle* is also a superclass of the class *truck*. The class *sports car* is a subclass of the class *automobile* (a sports car is an automobile with a powerful engine), so it is also a subclass of the class *vehicle* but not of the class *truck*. The classes *vehicle* and *automobile* are both superclasses of the class *sports car*.

Objects in a subclass inherit properties (both data and methods) from a superclass. For example, all three subclasses shown in Figure 1.7 have a driver's seat and can be driven (properties inherited from class *vehicle*).

These basic principles help programmers organize their solutions to problems. In particular, rather than starting each program from scratch, programmers use object-oriented programming because it encourages reuse of code (programs) that are already written. They can use existing classes as components of new classes, or they can create new classes that are subclasses of existing classes. Either way, methods that were programmed for the existing classes can be used with objects of the new classes. In this book, we will focus on using existing classes as components of new classes rather than creating subclasses of existing classes.

## EXERCISES FOR SECTION 1.3

### Self-Check

1. What do you think the four high-level language statements below mean?

    **a.** `profit = gross - net;`

    **b.** `fahren = 1.8 * celsius + 32;`

```
c.    fraction = percent / 100.0;
d.    sum = sum + x;
e.    newPrincipal = oldPrincipal * (1.0 + interest);
```

2. List two reasons why it would be preferable to write a program in C++ rather than machine language.

3. Explain the relationship between the data and methods of a class.

4. What are two ways that object-oriented programming facilitates code reuse by programmers?

5. What is an abstraction in programming?

6. Is an object an instance of a class or vice versa?

## 1.4 Processing a High-Level Language Program

Although programmers find it much easier to express problem solutions in high-level languages, computers do NOT understand these languages. Before a high-level language program can be executed, it must be translated into the target computer's machine language. The program that does this translation is called a **compiler**. Figure 1.8 illustrates the role of the compiler in the process of developing and testing a high-level language program. Both the input to and (when successful) the output from the compiler are programs.

The input to the compiler is a **source file** containing the text of a high-level language program. The software developer creates this file with a word processor or **editor**. The source file is in text format, which means that it is a collection of character codes. For example, you might type a program into a file called `myprog.cpp`. The compiler will scan this source file, checking to see if it follows the high-level language's rules of **syntax** (grammar). If the program is syntactically correct, the compiler saves, in an **object file**, the machine language instructions that carry out the program's purpose. For program `myprog.cpp`, the object file created might be named `myprog.obj`. This file's format is binary, which means that you should not send it to a printer, display it on your monitor, or try to work with it in a word processor because it will appear to be meaningless garbage. If the source program contains syntax errors, the compiler lists these errors but does not create an object file. The developer must return to the editor, correct the errors, and recompile the program.

Although an object file contains machine language instructions, not all of the instructions are complete. High-level languages provide the software developer with many named chunks of code for operations that he or she will likely need. Almost all high-level language programs use at least one

**compiler**
Software that translates a high-level language program into machine language.

**source file**
File containing a program written in a high-level language; the input for a compiler.

**editor**
Software used to create, edit (change), and store a source file on disk.

**syntax**
Grammar rules of a programming language.

**object file**
File of machine language instructions that is the output of a compiler.

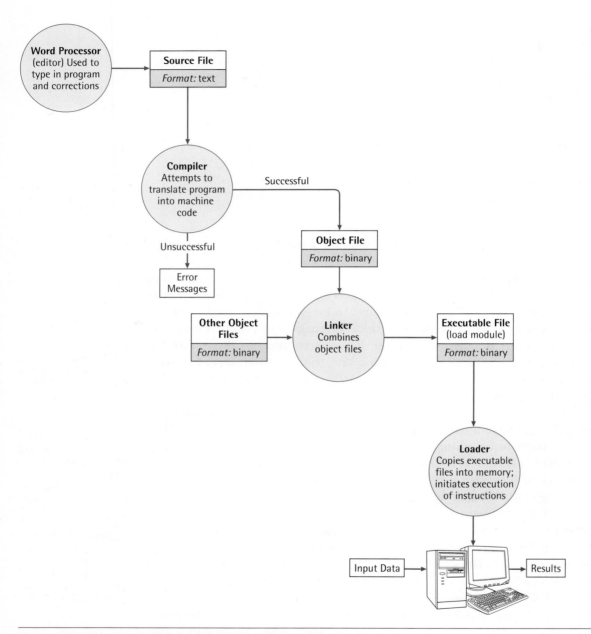

**Figure 1.8**   Preparing a high-level language program for execution

linker
Software that combines
object files to create an
executable machine lan-
guage program.

of these code chunks, which reside in other object files available to the system. The **linker program** combines code from other object files with the
new object file, creating a complete machine language program that is

ready to run. For your sample program, the linker might name the executable file it creates `myprog.exe`.

As long as `myprog.exe` is just stored on your disk, it does nothing. To run it, the **loader** must copy all its instructions into memory and direct the CPU to begin execution with the first instruction. As the program runs, it takes input data from one or more sources and sends results to output and/or secondary storage devices.

Some computer systems require the user to ask the OS to separately carry out each step illustrated in Figure 1.8. However, many high-level language compilers are now sold as part of an **integrated development environment (IDE)**, a package that combines a simple editor with a compiler, linker, and loader. IDEs give the developer menus from which to select steps, and if the developer tries a step that is out of sequence, the environment simply fills in the missing steps automatically.

One caution: the IDE might not automatically save to disk the source, object, and executable files created by the programmer; it may simply leave these programs in memory. This approach saves the time and disk space needed to make copies, and keeps the code available in memory for application of the next step in the translation/execution process. But the developer can risk losing the only copy of the source file if a serious program error causes termination of the IDE program. To prevent such a loss, users must explicitly save the source file to disk after every modification before attempting to run the program. Appendixes F and G describe two widely used IDEs.

## Executing a Program

To execute a program, the CPU must examine each program instruction in memory and send out the command signals required to carry out the instruction. Although normally the instructions are executed in sequence, as we will discuss later, it is possible to have the CPU skip over some instructions or execute some instructions more than once.

While a program runs, data can be entered into memory and manipulated in some specified way. Special program instructions are used for entering a program's data (called **input data**) into memory. After the input data have been processed, instructions for displaying or printing values in memory can be executed to display the program results. The lines displayed by a program are called the **program output**.

Let's look at the example shown in Figure 1.9—executing a water bill program stored in memory. Step 1 of the program enters into memory data that describe the amount of water used. In Step 2, the program manipulates the data and stores the results of the computations in memory. In the final step, the computed results are displayed as a water bill.

**loader**
Software that copies an executable machine language program into memory and starts its execution.

**integrated development environment (IDE)**
Software package combining an editor, a compiler, a linker, a loader, and tools for finding errors.

**input data**
The data values that are entered by a program.

**program output**
The lines displayed by a program.

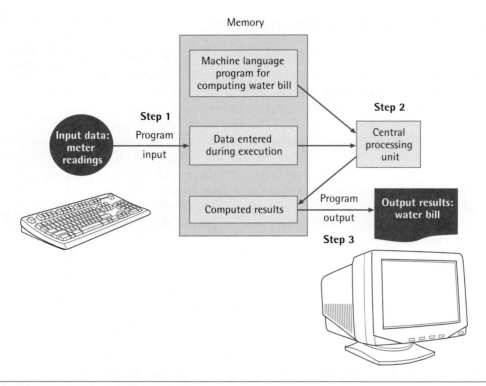

**Figure 1.9**   Execution of a water bill program

## EXERCISES FOR SECTION 1.4

Self-Check

1. Would a syntax error be found in a source program or an object program? What system program would find a syntax error if one existed? What system program would you use to correct it?

2. Explain the differences between a source program, an object program, and an executable program. Which do you create, and which does the compiler create? Which does the linker or loader create?

3. What is an IDE? What does the program developer need to be concerned about when using an IDE?

4. Explain how you could lose your source program if an error occurs while running a program using an IDE.

# 1.5   The Software Development Method

Programming is a problem-solving activity. If you are a good problem solver, you have the potential to become a good programmer, so one goal of this book is to help you improve your problem-solving ability. Problem-solving methods vary with subject area. Business students learn to solve problems with a *systems approach*, while engineering and science students use the *engineering and scientific method*. Programmers use the *software development method*.

We will focus on the first five steps listed below. The last step applies to commercial software, not student programs.

1. Specify the problem requirements.
2. Analyze the problem.
3. Design the algorithm to solve the problem.
4. Implement the algorithm.
5. Test and verify the completed program.
6. Maintain and update the program.

### PROBLEM

*Specifying the problem requirements* forces you to state the problem clearly and unambiguously to gain a precise understanding of what is required for its solution. Your objective is to eliminate unimportant aspects and zero in on the root problem. This goal may not be as easy to achieve as it sounds. You may, for instance, need more information from the person who posed the problem.

### ANALYSIS

*Analyzing the problem* involves identifying the problem *inputs* (the data you have to work with), *outputs* (the desired results), and any additional requirements for or constraints on the solution. At this stage, you should also determine the format in which the results should be displayed (for example, as a table with specific column headings) and develop a list of problem variables and their relationships. These relationships may be expressed as formulas.

If Steps 1 and 2 are not done properly, you will solve the wrong problem. Read the problem statement carefully (1) to obtain a clear idea of the problem and (2) to determine the inputs and outputs. It may be helpful to underline phrases in the problem statement that identify the inputs and outputs, as in the following example:

> Compute and display the *total cost of apples* given the number of *pounds of apples* purchased and the *cost per pound of apples*.

Next, summarize the information contained in the underlined phrases:

### Problem Inputs
quantity of apples purchased (in pounds)
cost per pound of apples (in dollars per pound)

### Problem Output
total cost of apples (in dollars)

Once you know the problem inputs and outputs, develop a list of formulas that specify relationships between them. The general formula

Total cost = Unit cost × Number of units

computes the total cost of any item purchased. Using the variables for our particular problem, we get the formula

Total cost of apples = Cost per pound × Pounds of apples

This process of modeling a problem to extract the essential variables and their relationships is called **abstraction**.

**abstraction**
The process of modeling a problem to extract the essential variables and their relationships.

## DESIGN

*Designing the algorithm to solve the problem* requires you to develop a list of steps (an **algorithm**) to solve the problem and then verify that the algorithm solves the problem as intended. Writing the algorithm is often the hardest part of the problem-solving process. Don't try to solve every detail of the problem at the beginning; instead, use top-down design. In **top-down design** (also called *divide and conquer*), you first list the major steps, or subproblems, that need to be solved, then solve the original problem by solving each of its subproblems. Most computer algorithms consist of at least the following subproblems.

**algorithm**
A list of steps for solving a problem.

**top-down design**
Breaking a problem into its major subproblems and then solving the subproblems.

ALGORITHM FOR A PROGRAMMING PROBLEM
1. Get the data.

2. Perform the computations.

3. Display the results.

Once you know the subproblems, you can attack each one individually. The perform-the-computations step, for example, may need to be broken down into a more detailed list of steps through a process called **algorithm refinement**.

**algorithm refinement**
Developing a detailed list of steps to solve a particular step in an algorithm.

You are using top-down design when creating an outline for a term paper. You first create an outline of the major topics, then refine it by filling in subtopics for each major topic. Once the outline is complete, you begin writing the text for each subtopic.

**Desk-checking** is an important, and often overlooked, part of algorithm design. To desk check an algorithm, you must carefully perform each algorithm step (or its refinements) just as a computer would and verify that the algorithm works as intended. You'll save time and effort if you locate algorithm errors early in the problem-solving process.

desk-checking
The step-by-step simulation of the computer execution of an algorithm.

## IMPLEMENTATION

*Implementing the algorithm* (Step 4 in the software development method) involves writing it as a program—converting each algorithm step into one or more statements in a programming language.

## TESTING

*Testing and verifying the program* requires testing the completed program to verify that it works as desired. Don't rely on just one test case; run the program several times using different sets of data, making sure that it works correctly for every situation provided for in the algorithm.

## MAINTENANCE

*Maintaining and updating the program* involves modifying a program to remove previously undetected errors and to keep it up-to-date as government regulations or company policies change. Many organizations maintain a program for five years or more, often after the programmers who originally coded it have left.

A disciplined approach is essential if you want to create programs that are easy to read, understand, and maintain. You must follow accepted program style guidelines (which will be stressed in this book) and avoid tricks and programming shortcuts.

## Caution: Failure Is Part of the Process

Although a step-by-step approach to problem solving is helpful, it does not guarantee that following these steps will result in a correct solution the first time, every time. The importance of verification highlights an essential truth of problem solving: The first (and also the second, third, or twentieth) attempt at a solution *may be wrong*. Probably the most important distinction between outstanding problem solvers and less proficient ones is that the former are not discouraged by initial failures. Instead, they see the faulty and near-correct early solutions as pointing toward a better understanding of the problem. One of the most inventive problem solvers of all time, Thomas Edison, is noted for his positive interpretation of the thousands of failed experiments that contributed to his incredible record of invention; he always saw those failures in terms of the helpful data they yielded about what did *not* work.

**EXERCISES FOR SECTION 1.5**

Self-Check

1. List the steps of the software development method.

2. Do you desk-check an algorithm before you refine it or after you refine it? Explain your answer.

# 1.6   Applying the Software Development Method

Throughout this book, we use the first five steps of the software development method to solve programming problems. These example problems, presented as *Case Studies*, begin with a statement of the *problem*. This is followed by an *analysis*, where we identify the data requirements for the problem: the problem inputs and the desired outputs. Next, we formulate the *design* of the initial algorithm and then we refine it. Finally, we *implement* the algorithm as a C++ program. We also provide a sample run of the program and discuss how to *test* the program.

Now let's walk through a sample case study. This example includes a running commentary on the process, which you can use as a model in solving other problems.

*case study*   **Converting Miles to Kilometers**

**PROBLEM**

Your summer surveying job requires you to study some maps that give distances in kilometers and some that use miles. You and your coworkers prefer to deal in metric measurements. Write a program that performs the necessary conversion.

**ANALYSIS**

The first step in solving this problem is to determine what you are asked to do. You must convert from one system of measurement to another, but are you supposed to convert from kilometers to miles, or vice versa? The problem states that you prefer to deal in metric measurements, so you must convert distance measurements in miles to kilometers. Therefore, the problem input is *distance in miles* and the problem output is *distance in kilometers*. To write the program, you need to know the relationship between miles and kilometers. Consulting a metric table shows that one mile equals 1.609 kilometers.

The data requirements and relevant formulas are listed below. The memory cell that will contain the problem input is identified by `miles`, and `kms` identifies the memory cell that will contain the program result, or the problem output.

## DATA REQUIREMENTS

*Problem Input*

`miles`         *the distance in miles*

*Problem Output*

`kms`         *the distance in kilometers*

*Relevant Formula*

1 mile = 1.609 kilometers

## DESIGN

The next step is to formulate the algorithm that solves the problem. Begin by listing the three major steps, or subproblems, of the algorithm.

ALGORITHM
1. Get the distance in miles.

2. Convert the distance to kilometers.

3. Display the distance in kilometers.

Now decide whether any steps of the algorithm need further refinement or whether they are perfectly clear as stated. Step 1 (getting the data) and Step 3 (displaying a value) are basic steps and require no further refinement. Step 2 is fairly straightforward, but some detail might help:

*Step 2 Refinement*

**2.1** The distance in kilometers is 1.609 times the distance in miles.

We list the complete algorithm with refinements below to show you how it all fits together. The refinement of Step 2 is numbered as Step 2.1 and is indented under Step 2.

ALGORITHM WITH REFINEMENTS
1. Get the distance in miles.

2. Convert the distance to kilometers.

    **2.1** The distance in kilometers is 1.609 times the distance in miles.

3. Display the distance in kilometers.

Let's desk check the algorithm before going further. If Step 1 gets a distance of 10.0 miles, Step 2.1 would convert it to 1.609 × 10.00 or 16.09 kilometers. This correct result would be displayed by Step 3.

## IMPLEMENTATION

To implement the solution, you must write the algorithm as a C++ program. You would first tell the C++ compiler about the problem data requirements—that is, what memory cell names you are using and what kind of data will be stored in each memory cell. Next, convert each algorithm step into one or more C++ statements. If an algorithm step has been refined, convert the refinements, not the original step, into C++ statements.

Listing 1.2 shows the C++ program along with a sample execution. The algorithm steps are in lines that begin with //; the program statements follow the algorithm steps. The sample execution is highlighted in the color screen. The input data typed in by the program user are in color. Don't worry about understanding the details of this program yet; we explain the program in the next chapter.

## TESTING

How do you know the sample run is correct? You should always examine program results carefully to make sure that they make sense. In this run, a distance of 10.0 miles is converted to 16.09 kilometers, as it should be. To verify that the program works properly, enter a few more test values of miles. You don't need to try more than a few test cases to verify that a simple program like this is correct.

**Listing 1.2**   Converting miles to kilometers

```
// miles.cpp
// Converts distance in miles to kilometers.

#include <iostream>
using namespace std;

int main()                              // start of main function
{
    const float KM_PER_MILE = 1.609;   // 1.609 km in a mile
    float miles,                        // input: distance in miles
          kms;                          // output: distance in kilometers

    // Get the distance in miles.
    cout << "Enter the distance in miles: ";
    cin >> miles;
```

(continued)

**Listing 1.2** Converting miles to kilometers (continued)

```
    // Convert the distance to kilometers.
    kms = KM_PER_MILE * miles;

    // Display the distance in kilometers.
    cout << "The distance in kilometers is " << kms << endl;

    return 0;                         //Exit the main function
}
```

```
Enter the distance in miles: 10.0
The distance in kilometers is 16.09
```

## EXERCISES FOR SECTION 1.6

Self-Check

1. Change the algorithm for the metric conversion program to convert distance in kilometers to miles.

2. List the data requirements, formulas, and algorithm for a program that converts a volume from quarts to liters.

# 1.7   Professional Ethics for Computer Programmers

We end this introductory chapter with a discussion of professional ethics for computer programmers. Like other professionals, computer programmers and software system designers (called software engineers) need to follow certain standards of professional conduct.

## Privacy and Misuse of Data

As part of their jobs, programmers may have access to large data banks or databases containing sensitive information on financial transactions or personnel, or information that is classified as "secret" or "top secret." Programmers should always behave in a socially responsible manner and not retrieve information that they are not entitled to see. They should not use information to which they are given access for their own personal gain, or do anything that would be considered illegal, unethical, or harmful to others. Just as doctors and lawyers must keep patient information confidential, programmers must respect an individual's rights to privacy.

A programmer who changes information in a database containing financial records for his or her own personal gain—for example, changes the amount of money in a bank account—is guilty of **computer theft** or **computer fraud**. This is a felony that can lead to fines and imprisonment.

## Computer Hacking

You may have heard about "computer hackers" who break into secure data banks by using their own computer to call the computer that controls access to the data bank. Classified or confidential information retrieved in this way has been sold to intelligence agencies of other countries. Other hackers have tried to break into computers to retrieve information for their own amusement or as a prank, or just to demonstrate that they can do it. Regardless of the intent, this activity is illegal, and the government will prosecute anyone who does it. Your university probably addresses this kind of activity in your student handbook. The punishment is likely similar to that for other criminal activity, because that is exactly what it is.

Another illegal activity sometimes practiced by hackers is attaching harmful code, called a **virus**, to another program so that the virus code copies itself throughout a computer's disk memory. A virus can cause sporadic activities to disrupt the operation of the host computer—for example, unusual messages may appear on the screen at certain times—or cause the host computer to erase portions of its own disk memory, destroying valuable information and programs. Viruses are spread from one computer to another in various ways—for example, if you copy a file that originated on another computer that has a virus, or if you open an e-mail message that is sent from an infected computer. Certainly, data theft and virus propagation should not be considered harmless pranks; they are illegal and carry serious penalties.

## Plagiarism and Software Piracy

Using someone else's programs without permission is also unprofessional behavior. Although it is certainly permissible to use modules from libraries that have been developed for reuse by their own company's programmers, you cannot use another programmer's personal programs or programs from another company without getting permission beforehand. Doing so could lead to a lawsuit, with you or your company having to pay damages.

Modifying another student's code and submitting it as your own is a fraudulent practice—specifically, plagiarism—and is no different than copying paragraphs of information from a book or journal article and calling it your own. Most universities have severe penalties for plagiarism that may include failing the course and/or being dismissed from the university. Be aware that even if you modify the code slightly or substitute your own comments or different variable names, you are still guilty of plagiarism if you are using another person's ideas and code. To avoid any question of plagiarism, find out beforehand your instructor's rules about working with others on a project. If group efforts are not allowed, make sure that you work independently and submit only your own code.

Many commercial software packages are protected by copyright laws against **software piracy**—the practice of illegally copying software for use on another computer. If you violate this law, your company or university can be fined heavily for allowing this activity to occur. Besides the fact that software piracy is against the law, using software copied from another computer increases the possibility that your computer will receive a virus. For all these reasons, you should read the copyright restrictions on each software package and adhere to them.

> **software piracy**
> Violating copyright agreements by illegally copying software for use in another computer.

## Misuse of a Computer Resource

Computer system access privileges or user account codes are private property. These privileges are usually granted for a specific purpose—for example, for work to be done in a particular course or for work to be done during the time you are a student at your university. The privilege should be protected; it should not be loaned to or shared with anyone else and should not be used for any purpose for which it was not intended. When you leave the institution, this privilege is normally terminated and any accounts associated with the privilege will be closed.

Computers, computer programs, data, and access (account) codes are like any other property. If they belong to someone else and you are not explicitly given permission to use them, then do not use them. If you are granted a use privilege for a specific purpose, do not abuse the privilege or it will be taken away.

Legal issues aside, it is important that we apply the same principles of right and wrong to computerized property and access rights as to all other property rights and privileges. If you are not sure about the propriety of something you want to do, ask first. As students and professionals in computing, we set an example for others. If we set a bad example, others are sure to follow.

## EXERCISES FOR SECTION 1.7

### Self-Check

1. Some computer users will not open an e-mail message unless they know the person who sent it. Why might someone adopt this policy?

2. Find out the penalty for plagiarism at your school.

# Chapter Review

1. The basic components of a computer are main and secondary memory, the CPU, and input and output devices.

2. Main memory is organized into individual storage locations called memory cells.

   - Each memory cell has a unique address.
   - A memory cell is a collection of bytes; a byte is a collection of eight bits.
   - A memory cell is never empty, but its initial contents may be meaningless to your program.
   - The current contents of a memory cell are destroyed whenever new information is stored in that cell.
   - Programs must be copied into the memory of the computer before they can be executed.
   - Data cannot be manipulated by the computer until they are first stored in memory.

3. Information in secondary memory is of two types: program files and data files. Secondary memory stores information in semipermanent form and is less expensive than main memory.

4. A computer cannot think for itself; a programming language is used to instruct it in a precise and unambiguous manner to perform a task.

5. The three categories of programming languages are machine language (meaningful to the computer), high-level language (meaningful to the programmer), and assembly language, which is similar to machine language except that it uses special mnemonic codes for operations and names for memory cells instead of numeric addresses.

6. Several system programs are used to prepare a high-level language program for execution. An *editor* enters a high-level language program into memory. A *compiler* translates a high-level language program (the source program) into machine language (the object program). The *linker* links this object program to other object files, creating an executable program, and the *loader* loads the executable program into memory. Sometimes these steps are combined into an Integrated Development Environment (IDE).

7. Programming a computer can be fun, if you're patient, organized, and careful. The software development method for solving problems using a computer can be of considerable help in your programming work. We emphasize five major steps in this problem-solving process:

   - Problem specification
   - Problem analysis

- Program design
- Program implementation
- Program testing

8. Through the operating system, you can issue commands to the computer and manage files.

9. Follow ethical standards of conduct in everything you do pertaining to computers. This means don't copy software that is copyright protected, don't hack into someone else's computer, don't send files that may be infected to others, and don't submit someone else's work as your own or lend your work to another student.

## Quick–Check Exercises

1. A _____ may translate statements in _____ language into several statements in _____ language while a statement in _____ language usually is translated into one statement in _____ language.

2. After a program has been executed, all program results are automatically displayed. True or false?

3. Specify the correct order for these operations: execution, translation, loading, linking.

4. A high-level language program is saved on disk as a(n) _____ file.

5. The _____ finds syntax errors in the _____ file.

6. Before linking, a machine-language program is saved on disk as a(n) _____ file.

7. After linking, a machine-language program is saved on disk as a(n) _____ file.

8. The _____ program is used to create and save the source file.

9. Computers are becoming (more/less) expensive and (bigger/smaller) in size.

10. List the five steps of the software development method that you should use to write your programs.

11. Determine whether each characteristic below applies to main memory or secondary memory.
    a. Faster to access
    b. Volatile
    c. May be extended almost without limit
    d. Less expensive

   **e.** Used to store files
   **f.** Central processor accesses it to obtain the next machine-language instruction for execution
   **g.** Provides semipermanent data storage

12. In object-oriented programming, explain the difference between the terms *class* and *object.*

13. The _____ of an object operate on the _____ of the object.

14. In a class hierarchy, a _____class inherits data and methods from its _____class.

## Answers to Quick–Check Exercises

1. Compiler, high-level, machine, assembler, machine

2. false

3. translation, linking, loading, execution

4. source

5. compiler, source

6. object

7. executable

8. editor

9. less, smaller

10. problem specification, problem analysis, program design, program implementation, program testing

11. main (a, b, f), secondary (c, d, e, g)

12. A class describes the properties of a category of objects whereas an object is a specific instance of a class.

13. methods, data or attributes

14. sub, super

## Review Questions

1. List at least three kinds of information stored in a computer.

2. List two functions of the CPU.

3. List two input devices, two output devices, and two secondary storage devices.

4. A computer can think. True or false?

5. What programs are combined in an IDE?

6. Describe two advantages of programming in a high-level language such as C++.

7. What processes are needed to transform a C++ program to a machine language program that is ready for execution?

8. Explain the relationship between memory cells, bytes, and bits.

9. What is the difference between a command-line interface and a GUI? Which are you using? Which kind is used on a PC?

10. Name three high-level languages and describe their main usage.

11. What are the differences between RAM and ROM? Which contains the instructions that execute when you first boot your computer? Which can be extended? Which contains information that does not disappear when you turn your computer off?

12. What is the major reason for programming in an object-oriented language?

13. In the following problem statement, identify the problem inputs, problem outputs, and some relevant formulas.

You are writing a program to help balance your checkbook. This program displays the new balance in your account after you enter the starting balance and a transaction. Each transaction has two data items: an indication of whether the transaction is a deposit or a withdrawal and the dollar amount of the transaction.

# Bjarne Stroustrup

*Bjarne Stroustrup is the designer of the C++ programming language. He is currently the College of Engineering Chair in Computer Science professor at Texas A&M University and a member of AT&T Labs' Systems and Information Research center. In 1993 Stroustrup won the ACM Grace Murray Hopper award for his early work on C++, and in 1990 he was named one of America's twelve top young scientists by* Fortune *magazine. Stroustrup has also authored several books, including* The C++ Programming Language *and* The Design and Evolution of C++, *which are the definitive C++ reference books.*

**What is your educational background? Why did you decide to study computer science?**

I have a master's in mathematics with computer science from the University of Århus in Denmark and a Ph.D. in computer science from Cambridge University in England. I liked math, but wanted something that had a practical application. Thinking about that led me to computers.

**What was your first job in the computer industry? What did it entail?**

I first had a series of programming jobs while I was studying in Århus, which helped me avoid serious study debts. I programmed ledger [billing] systems for small firms such as lumberyards, accounting systems, payroll systems, etc. Interestingly enough, this involved my collaborating with both computer salesmen and people running businesses. (They knew their businesses, but nothing about computers.)

In such collaboration, I designed a system and modified it for better usability. In addition, I did the complete detailed design and implementation. That taught me a lot—especially that a program is only a part of a larger system and that people directly depend on it.

My first full-time job was as a researcher at AT&T Bell Labs. I experimented with distributed systems and eventually with programming and programming languages as tools for building systems.

**What drove the development of C++? Which specific issues were you trying to address when you developed the language?**

I was working with some problems in distributed systems and networking. I needed a tool that would help me to structure my programs well and also allow me to write efficient code. I designed C++ to give me the design techniques of Simula and the low-level flexibility and efficiency of C. The further evolution of C++ has been dominated by the same aim of enabling code that is simultaneously elegant and efficient.

**Which person in the computer science field has inspired you?**

I have always had a deep respect for Kristen Nygaard. He is one of the designers of Simula [the first programming language to support object-oriented programming, designed in the mid-1960s], a gentleman, and a thoroughly enjoyable person to be with. Together with his friend and colleague, Ole-Johan Dahl, he received the 2002 Turing award.

### Do you have any advice for students learning C++?

Study systems and programming, not just programming languages. A language is a tool, so it should be studied in the context of problems that deserve to be solved. Studying a language in isolation is sterile.

Start C++ with an up-to-date ISO-standard-conforming implementation and use standard library facilities, such as strings, vectors, maps, and iostreams, right from the beginning. Do not fiddle with pointers, C-style strings, and other low-level facilities until you understand the basics of scope, functions, looks, variables, etc. and until you have a real need. Focus on concepts and techniques. Learn programming language features as needed to express ideas. Don't think that a single programming language is all you'll ever need to know.

### What advice do you have for students entering the computer science field?

Don't just study computers. Learn something that will give you an idea of what to use computers for. Consider making computer science a minor or the major with some other interesting field as a minor.

Study something just because it is hard and interesting at least once in your life; not everything has to be obviously useful or directly applicable to something specific.

### How do you see C++ evolving over the next few years?

The standards committee just issued a set of minor corrections and clarifications. That shows the dedication to stability and detail that is necessary for a mature language. However, no living language can remain unchanged for more than a few years, and a more significant revision of the standard is in progress. The emphasis will be on providing a larger and better standard library. The changes to the core language will be close to 100% compatible and focus on providing better support for library building. You can get an idea of some of the libraries considered for the next standard by looking at boost.org. These include smart pointers, regular expressions, and threads. The language extensions currently under consideration focus on better support for generic programming and on making the language rules more regular and easier to understand. Beyond that, I hope to see better support for distributed computing. The emphasis on performance and suitability for systems programming will be maintained.

## chapter two

# Overview of C++

## Chapter Objectives

- To become familiar with the general form of a C++ program and the basic elements in a program
- To learn how to include standard library files in a program
- To appreciate the importance of writing comments in a program
- To understand the use of data types and the differences between the numeric types for real numbers and integers
- To be able to declare variables with and without initial values
- To understand how to write assignment statements to change the values of variables
- To learn how C++ evaluates arithmetic expressions and how to write them
- To learn how to read data values into a program and to display results
- To learn how to use files for input/output
- To understand the differences between syntax errors, run-time errors, and logic errors, and how to avoid them and to correct them.

THIS CHAPTER INTRODUCES C++—a high-level programming language developed in the mid-1980s by Bjarne Stroustrup at AT&T's Bell Laboratories. C++ is widely used in industry because it supports object-oriented programming and incorporates all of the features of the popular C programming language. Throughout this book, we will follow the standard for the C++ language approved in 1998. Our focus in this chapter will be on the C++ statements for entering data, performing simple computations, and displaying results.

# 2.1   C++ Language Elements

One advantage of C++ is that it allows programmers to write programs that resemble everyday English. Even though you don't yet know how to write your own programs, you can probably read and understand parts of the program in Listing 1.2, which is repeated in Listing 2.1. In this section, we will describe the different language elements in this program and explain their syntax.

## Comments

The first two lines in the program shown in Listing 2.1

```
// miles.cpp
// Converts distances from miles to kilometers.
```

**comment**
Text in a program that makes the code more understandable to the human reader but is ignored—that is, not translated—by the compiler.

start with the symbol pair // that indicates that these lines are **comments**— text used to clarify the program to the person who is reading it but ignored by the C++ compiler, which does not attempt to translate comments into machine language. We show all comments in italics; your C++ system may not. The first comment line gives the name of the file containing this program (`miles.cpp`), and the second describes in English what the program does. (You can download all program files from the Web site for this book—see the Preface.) We discuss the use of comments in Section 2.5.

The C++ syntax for comments is described in the syntax display that follows. We use this stylistic form throughout the text to describe C++ language features.

Listing 2.1   Converting miles to kilometers

```
// miles.cpp
// Converts distance in miles to kilometers.

#include <iostream>
using namespace std;

int main()            // start of main function
{
       const float KM_PER_MILE = 1.609;  // 1.609 km in a mile
       float miles,                       // input: distance in miles
             kms;                         // output: distance in kilometers
```

(continued)

**Listing 2.1** Converting miles to kilometers (continued)

```
    // Get the distance in miles.
    cout << "Enter the distance in miles: ";
    cin >> miles;

    // Convert the distance to kilometers.

    kms = KM_PER_MILE * miles;

    // Display the distance in kilometers.

    cout << "The distance in kilometers is " << kms << endl;

    return 0;                        // Exit main function

}
```

---

**Comment**

**Form:**   `// comment`
        `/* comment */`

**Example:** `// This is a comment`
         `/* and so is this */`

**Interpretation:** A double slash indicates the start of a comment. Alternatively, the symbol pair `/*` may be used to mark the beginning of a comment that is terminated by the symbol pair `*/`. Comments are listed with the program but are otherwise ignored by the C++ compiler.

## Compiler Directive #include

The first line of Listing 2.1 after the comments—

```
#include <iostream>
```

is a **compiler directive**, a statement that is processed before the program is translated. This directive causes the statements from the header file for class `iostream` to be inserted at this spot in our program. A **header file** describes the data and operations in a class so that the compiler can check that the class is used correctly.

The left and right angle brackets < > indicate that class `iostream` is part of the C++ **standard library**, a component that contains a number of

**compiler directive**
A C++ program line beginning with # that is processed by the compiler before translation begins.

**header file**
A file that describes the data and operations in a class.

**standard library**
A collection of C++ predefined classes provided with a C++ system.

predefined classes such as `iostream` that provide important functionality for the C++ language. For example, class `iostream` has operators that enable a program to read input data typed at the keyboard and to display information on the screen. Libraries enable us to *reuse* C++ code modules that have already been written and tested, saving us from the burden of creating this code ourselves. There may be many `#include` statements, and possibly other compiler directives, in each program that you write.

---

**Compiler Directive `#include`**

**Form:**    `#include <filename>`

**Example:**  `#include <iostream>`

**Interpretation:**   Prior to translation, this line is replaced by the C++ standard library file header named inside the angle brackets. Usually compiler directives, such as `#include`, appear at the beginning of a program, but they will work as long as they appear before they are used.

**Note:**   A compiler directive should not end with a semicolon.

---

## Namespace `std`

The line

```
using namespace std;
```

indicates that we will be using objects that are named in a special region of the C++ compiler called `namespace std` (short for standard). Because the C++ standard library is defined in the standard namespace, this line will appear in all our programs. The `using` statement ends with a semicolon.

---

**`using namespace`**

**Form:**    `using namespace` *region*`;`

**Example:**  `using namespace std;`

**Interpretation:**   This line indicates that our program uses objects defined in the namespace specified by *region*. This line should follow the `#include` lines.

---

## Function `main`

The line

```
int main()        // start of function main
```

indicates the start of function `main`. A **function** is a collection of related statements that perform a specific operation. For example, the `main` function in Listing 2.1 is the program for converting from kilometers to miles. The word `int` indicates that the `main` function should return an integer value to the operating system. The empty parentheses after `main` indicate that no special information is passed to this function by the operating system. We added a comment (beginning with `//`) to the end of this line to clarify its meaning to you, the program reader. The body of function `main`, or any other function, is enclosed in curly braces `{ }` and it consists of the rest of the lines in Listing 2.1. Execution of a C++ program always begins with the first line in the body of function `main`.

**function**
A collection of related statements that perform a specific operation. These statements are executed as a unit.

---

**`main`  function definition**

**Form:**
```
int main()
{
      function body
}
```

**Example:**
```
int main()
{
      cout << "Enjoy C++" << endl;
      return 0;
}
```

**Interpretation:**  A program begins its execution with function **main**. The body of the function is enclosed in curly braces. The function body should end with the line

```
return 0;
```

which causes function **main** to return a value of 0 to the operating system when it finishes execution.

---

## Declaration Statements

A function body consists of two kinds of statements: *declaration statements* and *executable statements*. The declarations tell the compiler what data are needed in the function. For example, the declaration statements

```
const float KM_PER_MILE = 1.609;  // 1.609 km in a mile
float miles,         // input: distance in miles
      kms;           // output: distance in kilometers
```

tell the compiler that the function `main` needs three data items named `KM_PER_MILE`, `miles`, and `kms`. `KM_PER_MILE` is the conversion constant

1.609. To create this part of the function, the programmer uses the problem data requirements identified during problem analysis. We describe the syntax of declaration statements in Section 2.3.

## Executable Statements

The executable statements cause some action to take place when a program is executed. Executable statements that begin with cout (pronounced c–out) display output on the screen. The first such line

```
cout << "Enter the distance in miles: ";
```

displays the prompt (in black type) in the first line of the sample execution repeated below:

```
Enter the distance in miles: 10.0
```

cout (pronounced c-out) refers to the standard output device, the screen. The symbol pair << is the insertion operator, so named because it inserts characters into the text displayed on the screen. In this case, it inserts the characters shown in quotes, which ask the user to type in a distance in miles. The program user types in the number 10.0. The next statement in function main

```
cin >> miles;
```

reads the data value (10.0) into the variable miles. cin (pronounced c–in) refers to the standard input device, the keyboard. The symbol pair >> is the extraction operator, so named because it "extracts" characters typed at the keyboard and stores them in memory. The statement

```
kms = KM_PER_MILE * miles;
```

computes the equivalent distance in kilometers by multiplying miles by the number (1.609) stored in KM_PER_MILE; the result (16.09) is stored in memory cell kms.

Then, the statement

```
cout << "The distance in kilometers is " << kms << endl;
```

displays a *string* (the characters enclosed in double quotes) followed by the value contained in kms. The word endl stands for "endline" and ends the output line shown next:

```
The distance in kilometers is 16.09
```

Finally, the line

```
return 0;                      // Exit main function
```

causes the function exit. The function returns a value of 0 to the operating system which indicates that it exited normally. We describe these executable statements in Section 2.4.

## EXERCISES FOR SECTION 2.1

Self-Check

1. Explain what is wrong with the following declaration statement and correct it.

```
float miles,     /*  input: distance in miles
         kms;        output: distance in kilometers   */
```

2. Explain what is wrong with the comments below and correct them.

   a.  `/* This is a comment?  /*`

   b.  `/* How about this one /* it seems like a comment`

      `*/ doesn't it? */`

3. Indicate which of the following are translated into machine language: compiler directives, comments, `using namespace` statement, variable declarations, executable statements.

4. What is the purpose of the `#include`? Of the `using  namespace` statement? Which does not end with a semicolon?

Programming

1. Write the declarations for a program that converts a weight in pounds to a weight in kilograms.

2. Write the C++ statements to ask for and read the weight in pounds.

*[handwritten]* Cout << "ENTER WEIGHT IN POUNDS: ";
*[handwritten]* Cin >> POUNDS;   cr Cin >> float pounds;

## 2.2   Reserved Words and Identifiers

### Reserved Words

Each line of the program in Listing 2.1 contains a number of different syntactic elements, such as reserved words, identifiers, and special character

reserved word
(keyword)
A word that has a spe-
cific meaning in C++.

symbols (for example, //). The **reserved words** (or **keywords**) have a specific meaning in C++, and they cannot be used for other purposes. Table 2.1
lists the reserved words used in Listing 2.1. Appendix B contains a complete list of reserved words.

**Table 2.1**   Reserved Words in Listing 2.1

| Reserved Words | Meaning |
| --- | --- |
| const | Constant; indicates a data element whose value cannot change |
| float | Floating point; indicates that a data item is a real number |
| include | Preprocessor directive; used to insert a library file |
| int | Integer; indicates that the main function returns an integer value |
| namespace | Region where program elements are defined |
| return | Causes a return from a function to the unit that activates it |
| using | Indicates that a program is using elements from a particular namespace |

## Identifiers

Table 2.2 lists the identifiers from Listing 2.1. We use identifiers to name the
data elements and objects manipulated by a program. The identifiers cin,
cout, and std are predefined in C++, but the others were chosen by us. You
have quite a bit of freedom in selecting the identifiers that you use as long
as you follow these syntactic rules:

1. An identifier must always begin with a letter or underscore symbol
   (the latter is not recommended).

2. An identifier can consist only of letters, digits, and underscores.

3. You cannot use a C++ reserved word as an identifier.

**Table 2.2**   Identifiers in Listing 2.1

| Identifier | Use |
| --- | --- |
| cin | C++ name for standard input stream |
| cout | C++ name for standard output stream |
| km | Data element used for storing the distance in kilometers |
| KM_PER_MILE | Data element used for storing the conversion constant |
| miles | Data element used for storing the distance in miles |
| std | C++ name for the standard namespace |

The following are some valid identifiers.

```
letter1, Letter1, letter2, inches, cent, centPerInch,
cent_per_inch, hello
```

Table 2.3 shows some invalid identifiers.

## Uppercase and Lowercase Letters

The C++ programmer must use uppercase and lowercase letters with care, because the compiler considers such usage significant. The names `Rate`, `rate`, and `RATE` are viewed by the compiler as *different* identifiers. Adopting a consistent pattern in the way you use uppercase and lowercase letters will be helpful to the readers of your programs. All reserved words in C++ use only lowercase letters.

## PROGRAM STYLE    Choosing Identifier Names

We discuss program style throughout the text in displays like this one. A program that "looks good" is easier to read and understand than one that is sloppy. Most programs will be examined or studied by someone other than the original programmers. In industry, programmers spend considerably more time on program maintenance (that is, updating and modifying the program) than they do on its original design or coding. A program that is neatly stated and whose meaning is clear makes everyone's job simpler.

Pick a meaningful name for a user-defined identifier, so its use is immediately clear. For example, the identifier `salary` would be a good name for a memory cell used to store a person's salary, whereas the identifier `s` or `bagel` would be a bad choice.

If an identifier consists of two or more words, C programmers place the underscore character (_) between words to improve the readability of the

**Table 2.3**   Invalid Identifiers

| Invalid Identifier | Reason Invalid |
| --- | --- |
| `1Letter` | Begins with a number |
| `float` | Reserved word |
| `const` | Reserved word |
| `Two*Four` | Character * not allowed |
| `Joe's` | Character ' not allowed |
| `two-dimensional` | Underscore allowed but not hyphen |

name (`dollars_per_hour` rather than `dollarsperhour`). C programmers write constants in all uppercase letters (for example, `KM_PER_MILE`).

In this book, we will follow the C style for constants, but we will use a different naming convention for multiple-word variables called "Hungarian notation." Instead of using underscore characters, we will capitalize the first letter of each word—except for the first word. Therefore, we prefer the identifier `dollarsPerHour` to `dollars_per_hour`. Your instructor may recommend a different convention. Whichever convention you choose, make sure you use it consistently.

Choose identifiers long enough to convey your meaning, but avoid excessively long names because you are more likely to make a typing error in a longer name. For example, use the shorter identifier `lbsPerSqIn` instead of the longer identifier `poundsPerSquareInch`.

If you mistype an identifier, the compiler may detect this as a syntax error and display an *undefined identifier* error message during program translation. But if you mistype a name so that the identifier looks like another, the compiler may not detect your error. For this reason and to avoid confusion, do not choose names that are similar to each other. Especially avoid selecting two names that are different only in their use of uppercase and lowercase letters (such as `LARGE` and `large`), or in the presence or absence of an underscore (`xcoord` and `x_coord`).

## EXERCISES FOR SECTION 2.2

### Self-Check

1. Can reserved words be used as identifiers?

2. Why is it important to use consistent programming style?

3. Indicate which of the symbols below are C++ reserved words, or valid or invalid identifiers.

```
float        cout       Bill        "hello"   rate      start
var          xyz123     123xyz      'a'       include
return
x=y*z        Prog#2     thisIsLong
so_is_this   hyphen-ate under_score
```

4. Explain the difference between Hungarian notation and C-style notation.

Programming

1.  Write a multiline comment with your name, your instructor's name, and the course name. Use both methods for multiline comments.

2.  (Continuation of programming exercises 1 and 2 from Section 2.1) Write the C++ statement to multiply the weight in pounds by the conversion constant and store the resulting weight in kilograms. Write the C++ statement(s) to display the weight in kilograms.

## 2.3   Data Types and Declarations

### Data Types

A **data type** is a set of values and operations that can be performed on those values. (A value that appears in a C++ program line is called a **literal**. In C++, some data types are predefined in the language and some are defined in class libraries. In this section, we describe four predefined data types and one that is defined in the standard library.

data type
A set of values and operations that can be performed on those values.
literal
A value that appears in a C++ program line.

### Data Type `int`

In mathematics, integers are positive or negative whole numbers. Examples are 5, –52, and 343,222 (written in C++ as 343222). A number without a sign is assumed to be positive. C++ has three data types to represent integers— `short`, `int`, and `long`. Each data type is considered to be an abstraction (or model) for the integers because it represents a subset of all the integers. Each integer is represented as a binary number. The number of bytes allocated for storing an integer value limits the range of integers that can be represented. The difference between these three types is that some compilers use more bytes to represent `int` values than `short` values and more bytes to represent `long` values than `int` values. In these compilers, you can represent larger integers with type `int` than you can with type `short`, and larger integers with type `long` that you can with type `int`.

We will use the data type `int` throughout this text. The predefined constants `INT_MIN` and `INT_MAX` represent the smallest and largest values of type `int`, respectively. Use the line

```
cout << INT_MIN << " through " << INT_MAX << endl;
```

in a program to show the range of integer values for your computer.

In C++, you write integers (and all other numbers) without commas. Some valid integers are

```
-10500        435        15        -25
```

We can read and display integer values and can perform the common arithmetic operations (add, subtract, multiply, and divide) on type `int` values.

## Data Type `float`

A real number has an integral part and a fractional part that are separated by a decimal point. Examples are 2.5, 3.66666666, –.000034, and 5.0. C++ has three data types to represent real numbers—`float`, `double`, and `long double`. Just as it is for integers, the number of bytes used to represent each of these types is different, so the range and precision of real numbers that can be represented varies. We will use type `float` in this text.

We can use scientific notation to represent very large and very small values. In normal scientific notation, the real number $1.23 \times 10^5$ is equivalent to 123000.0, where the exponent 5 means "move the decimal point 5 places to the right." In C++ scientific notation, we write this number as `1.23e5` or `1.23e+5`. If the exponent has a minus sign, the decimal point is moved to the left (e.g., `0.34e-4` is equivalent to `0.000034`). Table 2.4 shows examples of both valid and invalid real numbers in C++.

C++ uses different formats (see Figure 2.1) to represent real numbers (floating-point format) and integers (fixed-point format). In **fixed-point format**, the binary number corresponding to an integer value is stored directly in memory. In **floating point-format**, a positive real number is represented as a **mantissa** (a binary fraction between 0.5 and 1.0) and an integer exponent (power of 2) analogous to scientific notation. Therefore, the

**fixed-point format**
The internal storage form for an integer.
**floating-point format**
The internal storage form for a real number.
**mantissa**
A binary fraction between 0.5 and 1.0 used in floating-point format.

**Table 2.4**  Valid and Invalid Real Numbers

| Valid | Invalid |
|---|---|
| `3.14159` | `-15e-0.3` (`0.3` invalid exponent) |
| `0.005` | `12.5e.3` (`.3` invalid exponent) |
| `.12345` | `.123E3` (needs lowercase *e*) |
| `12345.0` | `e32` (doesn't start with a digit) |
| `16` | `a34e03` (doesn't start with a digit) |
| `15.0e-04` (value is `0.0015`) | |
| `2.345e2` (value is `234.5`) | |
| `1.15e-3` (value is `0.00115`) | |
| `12e+5` (value is `1200000.0`) | |

**Figure 2.1** Internal formats for integers and real numbers

integer 10 and the real number 10.0 are stored differently in memory, so they can't be used interchangeably. As with integers, we can read and display real numbers and perform the common arithmetic operations (add, subtract, multiply, and divide).

## Data Type `bool`

The `bool` data type (named after mathematician George Boole who invented a two-valued algebra) has just two possible values: false and true. We can use this data type to represent conditional values so that a program can make decisions. For example, "if the first number is bigger than the second number, then switch their values." We discuss this data type in more detail in Chapter 4.

## Data Type `char`

Data type `char` represents an individual character value—a letter, digit, or special symbol that can be typed at the keyboard. Each character is unique. For example, the character for the digit one (`'1'`) is distinct from the character for the letter "el" (`'l'`), even though they might look identical on a computer screen. Each type `char` literal is enclosed in apostrophes (single quotes) as shown below.

```
'A'  'z'  '2'  '9'  '*'  ':'  '"'  ' '
```

The next-to-last literal above represents the character " (a quotation mark); the last literal represents the blank character, which is typed by pressing the apostrophe key, the space bar, and the apostrophe key.

Each type `char` value is stored in a byte of memory. The digit character `'1'` has a different storage representation than the integer 1.

Although a type `char` literal in a program requires apostrophes, you don't need them for a type `char` data value. When entering the letter z as a character data item to be read by a program, press just the z key.

Characters are used primarily in strings, a topic we will introduce shortly. A special set of symbols, called an **escape sequence**, allows you to do simple textual control. Each escape sequence is written as a type `char` literal consisting of a backslash \ followed by another character. Table 2.5

**escape sequence** A two-character sequence beginning with a backslash \ that represents a special character.

**Table 2.5** Escape Sequences

| Escape Sequence | Meaning |
|---|---|
| `'\n'` | linefeed |
| `'\b'` | backspace |
| `'\r'` | carriage return |
| `'\t'` | tab |
| `'\"'` | double quote |
| `'\'` | single quote |
| `'\f'` | formfeed |
| `'\\'` | backslash |

shows some common escape sequences. The first four escape sequences represent characters that control the appearance of text that is displayed. The last row shows that C++ uses two backslash characters to represent the backslash character.

## `string` Class

Besides these built-in data types, C++ provides definitions for a number of other data types in its standard library. The ability to extend C++ by using data types defined in libraries is one of the primary advantages of C++ and object-oriented languages in general. We will use two of these classes, `string` and `iostream`, in much of our programming. We discuss the `string` class next and some features of class `iostream` in Section 2.4.

**string literal**
A sequence of characters enclosed in quotation marks displayed as prompts or as labels for a program's results.

A **string literal** (or string) is a sequence of characters enclosed in quotation marks. String literals are often displayed as prompts or as labels for a program's results ("the value of x is"). The next line contains five string literals.

```
"A"    "1234"    "true"    "the value of x is "
"Enter speed in mph: "
```

Note that the string `"A"` is stored differently from the character `'A'`. Similarly, the string `"1234"` is not stored the same way as the integer `1234` and cannot be used in a numerical computation. The string `"true"` is also stored differently from the `bool` value `true`. A string can contain any number of characters, but all must be on the same line. Programmers often use string literals in lines that begin with `cout`. C++ displays the characters in the string literal exactly as they appear without the enclosing quotes.

In C++, strings can be read, stored, compared, joined together, and taken apart. A program that performs any of these operations on string data must contain the compiler directive

```
#include <string>
```

before the main function definition. This directive is not needed if you only use strings as literals in lines that begin with `cout`.

## Purpose of Data Types

Why have different data types? The reason is that they allow the compiler to know what operations are valid and how to represent a particular value in memory. For example, a whole number is stored differently in a type `float` variable than in a type `int` variable. Also, a type `float` value usually requires more memory space than an `int` value. A string will also take up more memory space than a `float` or `char` under most circumstances.

If you try to manipulate a value in memory in an incorrect way (for example, adding two `bool` values), the C++ compiler displays an error message telling you that this is an incorrect operation. Or if you try to store the wrong kind of value (such as a string in a data field that is type `int`), you get an error message. Detecting these errors keeps the computer from performing operations that don't make sense.

## Declarations

The memory cells used for storing a program's input data and its computational results are called **variables** because the values stored in variables can change (and usually do) as the program executes. The **variable declarations** in a C++ program communicate to the compiler the names of all variables used in a program. They also tell the compiler what kind of information will be stored in each variable and how that information will be represented in memory. You must declare each variable before its first use in a function.

A variable declaration begins with an identifier (for example, `float`) that tells the C++ compiler the type of data (for example, a real number) stored in a particular variable. The declaration statement

**variable**
A name associated with a memory cell whose contents can change during program execution.

**variable declarations**
Statements that communicate to the compiler the names of variables and the kind of information stored in each variable.

```
float miles,       // input: distance in miles
      kms;         // output: distance in kilometers
```

gives the names of two variables (`miles`, `kms`) used to store real numbers. Note that C++ ignores the comments on the right of each line describing the use of each variable. The two lines above make up a single C++ declaration statement.

The statement

```
string lastName;
```

declares an identifier, `lastName`, for storing a string. Since `string` is a class, it is more accurate to refer to `lastName` as an object (or class instance) instead of a variable.

---

### Variable and Object Declarations

**Form:**    *type identifier-list;*

**Examples:** `float x, y;`
`int me, you;`
`float week = 40.0;`
`string flower = "rose";`

**Interpretation:**    Storage is allocated for each identifier in the *identifier-list*. The *type* of data (`float`, `int`, etc.) to be stored in each variable or object is specified. Commas are used to separate the identifiers in the *identifier-list*. The last two lines show how to store an initial value (`40.0`, `"rose"`) in a variable or object. This value can be changed during program execution. A semicolon appears at the end of each declaration.

---

## Constant Declarations

**constant**
A memory cell whose contents cannot change.

**constant declaration**
A statement that communicates to the compiler the name of a constant and the value associated with it.

We often want to associate names with special program **constants**—memory cells whose values cannot change. This association may be done using a **constant declaration**. The constant declaration

```
const float KM_PER_MILE = 1.609;   // 1.609 km in a mile
```

specifies that the identifier `KM_PER_MILE` will be associated with the program constant 1.609. Because the identifier `KM_PER_MILE` is a constant, C++ will not allow you to change its value. You should consistently use `KM_PER_MILE` instead of the value 1.609 in the program. This makes it easier to read and understand the program. Make sure you only associate constant identifiers with data values that should never change (e.g., the num-

---

### Constant Declaration

**Form:**    `const` *type constant-identifier = value;*

**Example:**  `const float PI = 3.14159;`

**Interpretation:**    The specified *value* is associated with the *constant-identifier*. This *value* cannot be changed at any time by the program. A semicolon appears at the end of each declaration.

**Note:**    By convention, we place constant declarations before any variable or object declarations in a C++ function.

---

ber of kilometers in a mile is always 1.609). You should never declare an input data item or output result as a constant.

## EXAMPLE 2.1

Listing 2.2 contains a C++ program that reads character and string data and displays a personalized message to the program user.

The line starting with **char** declares two variables (**letter1**, **letter2**) used to store the first two initials of the name of the program user. The line beginning with **string** declares an object **lastName** used to store the last name of the user. The instruction

```
cin >> letter1 >> letter2 >> lastName;
```

reads the two letters, **E** and **B**, and the last name, **Koffman**, all typed by the program user, and stores them in the three variables listed (**E** in **letter1**, **B** in **letter2**, and **Koffman** in **lastName**). The next line

```
cout << "Hello " << letter1 << ". " << letter2 << ". "
     << lastName << "! ";
```

displays `Hello E. B. Koffman!`. The two string literals ". " cause a period and one blank space to be displayed after each initial. Finally, the last **cout** line displays the rest of the second line shown in the program output.

Listing 2.2    Printing a welcoming message

```cpp
// File: hello.cpp
// Displays a user's name

#include <iostream>
#include <string>
using namespace std;

int main()
{
   char letter1, letter2;   // input and output: first two initials
   string lastName;         // input and output: last name

   // Enter letters and print message.
   cout << "Enter 2 initials and a last name: ";
   cin >> letter1 >> letter2 >> lastName;
   cout << "Hello " << letter1 << ". " << letter2 << ". "
        << lastName << "! ";
   cout << "We hope you enjoy studying C++." << endl;

   return 0;
}
```

(continued)

Listing 2.2    Printing a welcoming message  (continued)

```
Enter 2 initials and a last name: EB Koffman
Hello E. B. Koffman! We hope you enjoy studying C++.
```

## EXERCISES FOR SECTION 2.3

Self-Check

1. What is the difference between a predefined type and a class type? Which has data stores that are variables and which has data stores that are objects? Is `string` a predefined type or a class type?

2. List the four types of predefined data.

3. **a.**  Write the following C++ scientific notation numbers in normal decimal notation:

    345E-4   3.456E+6   345.678E+3

   **b.**  Write the following numbers in C++ scientific notation with one digit before the decimal point:

    5678   567.89   0.00567

4. Indicate which of the following literal values are legal in C++ and which are not. Identify the data type of each valid literal value.

    15    'XYZ'    '*'    $    25.123    15.    -999    .123    'x'
    "X"    '9'    '-5'    True    'True'

5. What would be the best variable type for the area of a circle in square inches? How about the number of cars passing through an intersection in an hour? Your name? The first letter of your last name?

6. Distinguish between character and integer types.

7. What is the difference between:

```
char color = 'r';
string colorS = "r";
```

8. What is the difference between these three declarations?

```
string aPresident;
string pres = "Bush";
const string LAST_PRES = "Clinton";
```

**9.** What is the difference between these three declarations?

```
string name;
string pres = "Bush";
const string FIRST_PRES = "Washington";
```

Programming

1. Write the variable declarations and a constant declaration for a program that calculates the area and circumference of a circle given its radius.

2. Write declarations for variables to store the number of seconds it takes to run the 50-yard dash, the number of siblings a person has, a person's street address, a person's grade point average (G.P.A.), and a person's gender (M or F).

3. Write the declarations for a program with variables for `firstName`, `lastName`, and `middleInitial`.

## 2.4  Executable Statements

The **executable statements** follow the declarations in a function. They are the C++ statements used to write or code the algorithm and its refinements. The C++ compiler translates the executable statements into machine language; the computer executes the machine language version of these statements when we run the program.

**executable statement**
A C++ statement that is translated into machine language instructions that are executed.

### Programs in Memory

Before examining the executable statements in the miles-to-kilometers conversion program (Listing 2.1), let's see what computer memory looks like before and after that program executes. Figure 2.2(a) shows the program loaded into memory and the program memory area before the program executes. The question marks in memory cells `miles` and `kms` indicate that the values of these cells are undefined before program execution begins. During program execution, the data value 10.0 is copied from the input device into the variable `miles`. After the program executes, the variables are defined as shown in Figure 2.2(b). We will see why next.

### Assignment Statements

An **assignment statement** stores a value or a computed result in a variable, and is used to perform most arithmetic operations in a program. The assignment statement

**assignment statement**
A statement used to store a value or a computed result in a variable.

```
kms = KM_PER_MILE * miles;
```

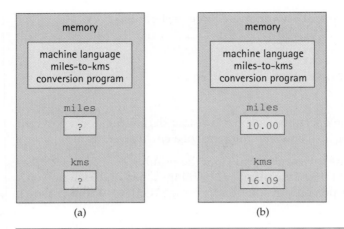

**Figure 2.2** Memory (a) before and (b) after execution of a program

assigns a value to the variable `kms`. The value assigned is the result of the multiplication (`*` means multiply) of the constant `KM_PER_MILE` (`1.609`) by the variable `miles`. The memory cell for `miles` must contain valid information (in this case, a real number) before the assignment statement is executed. Figure 2.3 shows the contents of memory before and after the assignment statement executes; only the value of `kms` is changed.

In C++ the symbol `=` is the assignment operator. Read it as "becomes," "gets," or "takes the value of" rather than "equals" because it is *not* equivalent to the "equal sign" of mathematics. In mathematics, this symbol states a relationship between two values, but in C++ it represents an action to be carried out by the computer.

Section 2.6 continues the discussion of type `int` and `float` expressions and operators.

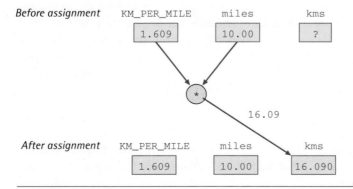

**Figure 2.3** Effect of `kms = KM_PER_MILE * miles;`

## EXAMPLE 2.2

In C++ you can write assignment statements of the form

```
sum = sum + item;
```

where the variable **sum** appears on both sides of the assignment operator. This is obviously not an algebraic equation, but it illustrates a common programming practice. This statement instructs the computer to add the current value of **sum** to the value of **item**; the result is then stored back into **sum**. The previous value of **sum** is destroyed in the process, as illustrated in Figure 2.4. The value of **item**, however, is unchanged.

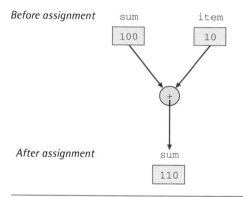

**Figure 2.4**   Effect of **sum = sum + item;**

## EXAMPLE 2.3

You can also write assignment statements that assign the value of a single variable or constant to a variable. If **x** and **newX** are type **float** variables, the statement

```
newX = x;
```

copies the value of variable **x** into variable **newX**. The statement

```
newX = -x;
```

instructs the computer to get the value of **x**, negate that value, and store the result in **newX**. For example, if **x** is **3.5**, **newX** is **-3.5**. Neither of the assignment statements above changes the value of **x**.

## Input/Output Operations

**input operation**
An instruction that reads data from an input device into memory.

Data can be stored in memory in two different ways: through assignment to a variable or by reading the data from an input device through an **input operation**. Use an input operation if you want the program to manipulate different data each time it executes.

As it executes, a program performs computations and assigns new values to variables and objects. These program results can be displayed on the screen through an **output operation**.

**output operation**
An instruction that displays information stored in memory.

Several C++ class libraries provide instructions for performing input and output. In this section, we will discuss how to use the input/output operations defined in the C++ class iostream.

**stream**
A sequence of characters associated with an input device, an output device, or a disk file.

In C++, a **stream** is a sequence of characters associated with an input device, an output device, or a disk file. Class iostream defines object cin as the stream associated with the standard input device (the keyboard). Class iostream defines object cout as the stream associated with the standard output device (the screen). Class iostream also defines the input operator >> and output operator <<. If you insert the compiler directive

```
#include <iostream>
```

before the main function, you can use cin and cout and the operators >> and << in your program.

## Input Statements

The statement

```
cin >> miles;
```

indicates that the input operator >> (also called the *extraction operator*) should read data into the variable miles. Where does the extraction operator get the data it stores in variable miles? It gets the data from cin, the standard input device. In most cases the standard input device is the keyboard; consequently, the computer will attempt to store in miles whatever data the program user types at the keyboard.

If miles is declared as type float, the input operation will proceed correctly only if the program user types in a number. Figure 2.5 shows the effect of this input statement.

When finished entering data, the program user should press the RETURN or ENTER key. Any space characters preceding the data item will be ignored during the input operation. This is true for the input of type int, float, char, bool, and string data.

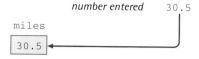

*number entered* 30.5

**Figure 2.5** Effect of `cin >> miles;`

---

**The Input (Extraction) Operator >>**

**Form:**     `cin >> data-store;`

**Example:** `cin >> age >> firstInitial;`

**Interpretation:** The extraction operator `>>` causes data typed at the keyboard to be read into the indicated *data-store* (variable or object) during program execution. The program extracts one data item for each data-store. The symbol pair `>>` precedes each data-store.

The order of the data you type in must correspond to the order of the data-stores in the input statement. You must insert one or more blank characters between numeric and string data items, and you may insert blanks between consecutive character data items and strings. The input operator `>>` skips any blanks that precede the data value to be read. This operator stops reading when a character (normally a space) that cannot legally be a part of the value being read in is encountered. Press the ENTER or RETURN key after entering all data items.

---

The program in Listing 2.2 reads a person's first two initials and last name. The input statement

```
cin >> letter1 >> letter2 >> lastName;
```

causes data to be extracted from the input stream object `cin` and stored in the variables `letter1` and `letter2` and object `lastName`. One character will be stored in `letter1` and one in `letter2` (type `char`). Figure 2.6 shows the effect of this statement when the characters `EBKoffman` are typed. Note that the result would be the same if one or more blanks appear before `E`, `B`, or `Koffman`.

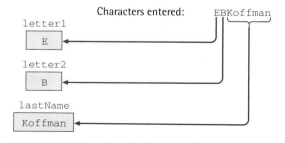

**Figure 2.6** Effect of `cin >> letter1 >> letter2 >> lastName;`

The number of characters extracted from `cin` depends on the type of the variable or object in which the data will be stored. The next nonblank character is stored for a type `char` variable. For a type `float`, `int`, or `string` variable, the program continues to extract characters until it reaches a character that cannot be part of the data item (usually the result of pressing the space bar or the RETURN or ENTER key).

How do we know when to enter the input data and what data to enter? Your program should display a prompt as a signal that informs the program user what data to enter and when. (Prompts are discussed in the next section.)

## Program Output

In order to see the results of a program execution, we must have some way of displaying data stored in variables. In Listing 2.1, the output statement

```
cout << "The distance in kilometers is "
     << kms << endl;
```

displays a line of program output containing two data elements: the string literal `"The distance  ...  is "` and the value of kms (type `float`). The characters inside the quotes are displayed, but the quotes are not. The output operator `<<` (also called the *insertion operator*) causes the data on the right of each occurrence of the operator to be inserted into the output stream object `cout`. Thus the previous output statement displays the line

```
The distance in kilometers is 16.09
```

In Listing 2.2, the line

```
cout << "Hello " << letter1 << ". " << letter2 << ". "
     << lastName << "! ";
```

displays

```
Hello E. B. Koffman!
```

In this case, the values of `letter1`, `letter2`, and `lastName` are displayed after the string `"Hello"`. The punctuation and space characters come from the other strings in the output statement.

Finally, the lines

```
cout << "Enter the distance in miles: ";
cout << "Enter 2 initials and a last name: ";
```

---

**The Output (Insertion) Operator <<**

**Form:**      cout << *data-element*;

**Example:**   cout << "My height in inches is " << height
          << endl;

**Interpretation:** The *data-element* can be a variable, object, constant, or literal (such as a **string** or **float** literal). Each data-element must be preceded by the output operator. The output operator causes the value of the data-element that follows it to be displayed. Each value is displayed in the order in which it appears. An **endl** at the end of the output statement advances the screen cursor to the next line. A string is displayed without the quotes.

      If no **endl** appears, the screen cursor will not advance to the next line. The next output statement will display characters on the same line as the previous one.

---

in Listings 2.1 and 2.2, respectively, display **prompts** or **prompting messages**. You should always display a prompt just before an input statement executes to inform the program user to enter data. The prompt should provide a description of the data to be entered—for example, distance in miles. If you don't display a prompt, the user will not know that the program is waiting for data or what data to enter.

The **screen cursor** is a moving place marker that indicates the position on the screen where the next character will be displayed. After executing an output statement, the cursor does not automatically advance to the next line of the screen. For this reason, the data you type in after a prompt will normally appear on the same line as the prompt. This is also the reason the two output statements in Listing 2.2

**prompt (prompting message)**
A message displayed by the computer indicating its readiness to receive data or a command from the user.

**screen cursor**
A moving place marker that indicates the position on the screen where the next character will be displayed.

```
cout << "Hello " << letter1 << ". " << letter2 << ". "
     << lastName << "! ";
cout << "We hope you enjoy studying C++." << endl;
```

display the single output line

```
Hello E. B. Koffman! We hope you enjoy studying C++.
```

But there are also many times when we would like to end one line and start a new one. We can do this by displaying the predefined constant endl (pronounced as *end-line*) when we wish to end a line.

To help you remember which operator follows cin and which follows cout, visualize the operator as an arrow indicating the direction of information flow. Data flows from cin to a variable (cin >>) and from a variable to cout (cout <<).

## EXAMPLE 2.4

### INSERTING BLANK LINES

The statements

```
cout << "The distance in kilometers is "
     << kms << endl << endl;
cout << "Conversion completed." << endl;
```

display the lines

```
The distance in kilometers is 16.09

Conversion completed.
```

A blank line occurs because we inserted `endl` twice in succession (`<< endl << endl`). Inserting `endl` always causes the display to be advanced to the next line. If there is nothing between the two `endl`s, a blank line appears in the program output. Most of the time, you will want to place `<< endl` at the end of an output statement.

## The **return** Statement

The last line in the `main` function (Listing 2.1)

```
return 0;
```

transfers control from your program to the operating system. The value 0 is considered the result of function `main`'s execution. By convention, returning 0 from function `main` indicates to the operating system that your program executed without error.

---

**Return Statement**

**Form:**    `return` *expression*`;`

**Example:**  `return 0;`

**Interpretation:**  The `return` statement transfers control from a function back to the activator of the function. For function **main**, control is transferred back to the operating system. The value of *expression* is returned as the result of function execution.

---

## EXERCISES FOR SECTION 2.4

Self-Check

1. Show the output displayed by the program lines below when the data entered are 3.0 and 5.0.

```
cout << "Enter two numbers: ";
cin >> a >> b;
a = a - 5.0;
b = a * b;
cout << "a = " << a << endl;
cout << "b = " << b << endl;
```

2. Show the contents of memory before and after the execution of the program lines shown in Self-Check Exercise 1.

3. Show the output displayed by the lines below.

```
cout << "My name is: ";
cout << "Doe, Jane" << endl;
cout << "I live in ";
cout << "Ann Arbor, MI ";
cout << "and my zip code is " << 48109 << endl;
```

4. How would you modify the code in Exercise 3 so that a blank line would be displayed between the two sentences?

Programming

1. Write the C++ instructions that first ask a user to type three integers and then read the three user responses into the variables `first`, `second`, and `third`. Do this in two different ways.

2. a. Write a C++ statement that displays the value of x as indicated in the line below.

```
The value of x is _____
```

   b. Assuming `radius` and `area` are type `float` variables, write a statement that displays this information in the following form:

```
The area of a circle with radius _____ is _____
```

3. Write a program that asks the user to enter the list price of an item and the discount as a percentage, and then computes and displays the sale

price and the savings to the buyer. For example, if the list price is $40 and the discount percentage is 25%, the sale price would be $30 and the savings to the buyer would be $10. Use the formulas

percentAsFraction = percent / 100.0

discount = listPrice * percentAsFraction

salePrice = listPrice – discount

# 2.5   General Form of a C++ Program

Now that we have discussed the individual statements that can appear in C++ programs, we'll review the rules for combining them into programs. We'll also discuss the use of punctuation, spacing, and comments in a program.

As shown in Listing 2.3, each program begins with compiler directives that provide information about classes to be included from libraries. Examples of such directives are `#include <iostream>` and `#include <string>`. Unlike the `using` statement and the statements of the `main` function body, the compiler directives do not end in semicolons.

A C++ program defines the `main` function after the `using` statement. An open curly brace `{` signals the beginning of the `main` function body. Within this body, we first see the declarations of all the variables and objects to be used by the `main` function. Next come the executable statements that are translated into machine language and eventually executed. The executable statements we have looked at so far perform computations or input/output operations. The end of the `main` function body is marked by a closing curly brace `}`.

Listing 2.3   General Form of a C++ Program

```
compiler directives
using namespace std;

int main()
{
   declaration statements
   executable statements
}
```

C++ treats most line breaks like spaces, so a C++ statement can extend over more than one line. (For example, the variable declaration in Listing 2.1 extends over two lines.) You should not split a statement that extends over more than one line in the middle of an identifier, a reserved word, or a numeric or string literal.

You can write more than one statement on a line. For example, the line

```
cout << "Enter the distance in miles: "; cin >> miles;
```

contains an output statement that displays a prompt and an input statement that gets the data requested. We recommend that you place only one statement on a line; that will improve readability and make it easier to maintain a program.

## Program Style    Spaces in Programs

The consistent and careful use of blank spaces can improve the style of a program. A blank space is required between consecutive words in a program line.

The compiler ignores extra blanks between words and symbols, but you may insert space to improve the readability and style of a program. You should always leave a blank space after a comma and before and after operators such as *, -, and =. You should indent the body of the main function and insert blank lines between sections of the main function.

Although stylistic issues have no effect whatever on the meaning of the program as far as the computer is concerned, they can make it easier for people to read and understand the program. But take care not to insert blank spaces where they do not belong. You can't place a space between special character pairs (for example, //, /*, */, >>, or <<), or write the identifier MAX_ITEMS as MAX ITEMS.

## Comments in Programs

Programmers can make a program easier to understand by using comments to describe the purpose of the program, the use of identifiers, and the purpose of each program step. Comments are part of the **program documentation** because they help others read and understand the program. The compiler, however, ignores comments and they are not translated into machine language.

A comment can appear by itself on a program line, at the end of a line following a statement, or embedded in a statement. In the following variable

**program documentation** Information (comments) that make it easier to read and understand a program.

declaration statement, the first comment is embedded in the declaration, while the second one follows the semicolon that terminates the declaration.

```
float miles,      // input - distance in miles
        kms;      // output - distance in kilometers
```

We document most variables in this way.

## Program Style    Using Comments

Each program should begin with a header section that consists of a series of comments specifying

- The programmer's name
- The date of the current version
- A brief description of what the program does

If you write the program for a class assignment, you should also list the class identification and your instructor's name:

```
/*
 * Programmer: William Bell Date completed: May 9, 2003
 * Instructor: Janet Smith Class: CIS61
 *
 * Calculates and displays the area and circumference of
 * a circle
 */
```

As shown above, programmers often use the symbol pairs /*, */ to surround multiline comments instead of placing the symbol pair // before each line.

Before you implement each step in the initial algorithm, you should write a comment that summarizes the purpose of the algorithm step. This comment should describe what the step does rather than simply restate the step in English. For example, the comment

```
// Convert the distance to kilometers.
kms = KM_PER_MILE * miles;
```

is more descriptive than (so preferable to)

```
// Multiply KM_PER_MILE by miles and store result in kms.
kms = KM_PER_MILE * miles;
```

## EXERCISES FOR SECTION 2.5

Self-Check

1. Change the following comments so they are syntactically correct.

```
/* This is a comment? *\
/* This one /* is a comment */ isn't it? */
```

2. Correct the syntax errors in the following program, and rewrite the program so that it follows our style conventions. What does each statement of your corrected program do? What output does it display?

```
/*
 * Calculate and display the product of two input values
 //
#include [iostream]
void main(float)
{int Y,    /* first input value */
        y,      /* second input value */
     sum; /* product of inputs */
cin << Y << sum;
Y * y = sum;
cout >> sum >> " = "   >> Y   " * " y;
return 0;}
```

Programming

1. Write a program that performs the implementation step for the case study presented in Section 1.5.

   Problem: Determine the total cost of apples given the number of pounds of apples purchased and the cost per pound of apples.

   Run this using several sets of input data. Try special values such as 0 and 1 for pounds of apples.

# 2.6   Arithmetic Expressions

To solve most programming problems, you will need to write arithmetic expressions that manipulate numeric data. This section describes the operators used in arithmetic expressions and rules for writing and evaluating the expressions.

**Table 2.6**    Arithmetic Operators

| Arithmetic Operator | Meaning | Examples |
|---|---|---|
| + | addition | 5 + 2 is 7 |
| | | 5.0 + 2.0 is 7.0 |
| − | subtraction | 5 - 2 is 3 |
| | | 5.0 - 2.0 is 3.0 |
| * | multiplication | 5 * 2 is 10 |
| | | 5.0 * 2.0 is 10.0 |
| / | division | 5.0 / 2.0 is 2.5 |
| | | 5 / 2 is 2 |
| % | remainder | 5 % 2 is 1 |

Table 2.6 shows all the arithmetic operators. Each operator manipulates two *operands,* which may be constants, variables, or other arithmetic expressions. The operators +, -, *, and / may be used with type int or float operands. As shown in the last column, the data type of the result is the same as the data type of its operands. An additional operator, the remainder operator (%), can be used with integer operands to find the remainder of longhand division. We will discuss the division and remainder operators next.

## Operators / and %

When applied to two positive integers, the division operator (/) computes the integral part of the result of dividing its first operand by its second. For example, the value of 7.0 / 2.0 is 3.5, but the value of 7 / 2 is the integral part of this result, or 3. Similarly, the value of 299.0 / 100.0 is 2.99, but the value of 299 / 100 is the integral part of this result, or 2. If the / operator is used with a negative and a positive integer, the result may vary from one C++ implementation to another. For this reason, you should avoid using division with negative integers. The / operation is undefined when the divisor (the second operand) is 0. Table 2.7 shows some examples of integer division.

**Table 2.7**    Results of Integer Division

| | |
|---|---|
| 3 / 15 = 0 | 18 / 3 = 6 |
| 15 / 3 = 5 | 16 / −3  system dependent |
| 16 / 3 = 5 | 0 / 4 = 0 |
| 17 / 3 = 5 | 4 / 0  is undefined |

The remainder operator (%) returns the *integer remainder* of the result of dividing its first operand by its second. For example, the value of 7 % 2 is 1 because the integer remainder is 1.

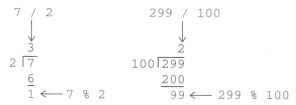

You can use longhand division to determine the result of a / or % operation with integers. The calculation on the left shows the effect of dividing 7 by 2 using longhand division: we get a quotient of 3 (7 / 2) and a remainder of 1 (7 % 2). The calculation on the right shows that 299 % 100 is 99 because we get a remainder of 99 when we divide 299 by 100.

The magnitude of $m$ % $n$ must always be less than the divisor $n$, so if $m$ is positive, the value of $m$ % 100 must be between 0 and 99. The % operation is undefined when $n$ is zero and varies from one implementation to another if $n$ is negative. Table 2.8 shows some examples of the % operator.

The formula

$m$ equals $(m / n) * n + (m$ % $n)$

defines the relationship between the operators / and % for an integer dividend of $m$ and an integer divisor of $n$. We can see that this formula holds for the two problems discussed earlier by plugging in values for $m$, $n$, $m / n$, and $m$ % $n$. In the first example that follows, $m$ is 7 and $n$ is 2; in the second, $m$ is 299 and $n$ is 100.

```
  7   equals  (7 / 2)     * 2 + (7 % 2)
      equals     3        * 2 + 1
299   equals  (299 / 100) * 100 + (299 % 100)
      equals      2        * 100 + 99
```

**Table 2.8**   Results of % Operation

| | |
|---|---|
| 3 % 5 = 3 | 5 % 3 = 2 |
| 4 % 5 = 4 | 5 % 4 = 1 |
| 5 % 5 = 0 | 15 % 5 = 0 |
| 6 % 5 = 1 | 15 % 6 = 3 |
| 7 % 5 = 2 | 15 % -7  system dependent |
| 8 % 5 = 3 | 15 % 0  is undefined |

## EXAMPLE 2.5

If you have **p** people and **b** identical boats, the expression

```
p / b
```

tells you how many people to put in each boat. For example, if **p** is **18** and **b** is **4**, then four people would go in each boat. The formula

```
p % b
```

tells you how many people would be left over (**18 % 4** is **2**).

## Data Type of a Mixed–Type Expression

The data type of each variable must be specified in its declaration, but how does C++ determine the type of an expression? The data type of an expression depends on the type of its operands. For example, the expression

```
m + n
```

mixed-type
expression
An expression involving
operands of type int
and type float.

is type int if both m and n are type int; otherwise, it is type float. A C++ expression is type int only if all its operands are type int, and a C++ expression is type float if any of its operands are type float. For example, 5 / 2 is type int, but 5 / 2.5 is type float. The latter expression, containing an integer and a floating-point operand, is called a **mixed-type expression**. The type of a mixed-type expression involving integer and floating-point data must be float.

In evaluating a mixed-type expression such as 5 / 2.5, C++ cannot perform the division directly because the internal representations of the numbers 5 and 2.5 are in different formats (fixed-point for 5, floating-point for 2.5). Consequently, C++ must first compute and store the floating-point equivalent of 5 in a new memory cell and then divide the contents of that cell (5.0) by the contents of the cell containing 2.5. C++ "converts" the type int value to type float instead of the other way around because there is no type int value that is equivalent to the real number 2.5.

## Mixed–Type Assignment Statement

When an assignment statement is executed, the expression is first evaluated and then the result is assigned to the variable listed to the left of the assignment operator (=). Either a type float or type int expression may be assigned to a type `float` variable. If the expression is type `int`, a real number with a fractional part of zero will be stored in a type `float` variable. For example, if a is type `float`, the statement

```
a = 10;
```

stores the floating-point value `10.0` in a. In a mixed-type assignment such as

```
a = 10 / 3;
```

the expression is type `int` and the variable a is type `float`. A common error is to assume that since a is type `float`, the expression should be evaluated as if its operands were type `float` as well. If you make this error, you will calculate the expression value incorrectly as `3.3333....` Remember, the expression is evaluated before the assignment is made, and the type of the variable being assigned has no effect on the expression value. The expression `10 / 3` evaluates to `3`, so `3.0` is stored in a.

In a similar vein, consider the assignment statement below when n is type `int`.

```
n = 10.5 + 3.7;
```

The expression is type `float`, and it is evaluated before the assignment. Its value is `14.2`, so the integral part of `14.2`, or `14`, is stored in n. Again, be careful not to evaluate the expression as if its operands were the same type as the variable being assigned. If you make this error, you might calculate the expression result incorrectly as `13` (`10 + 3`).

## Expressions with Multiple Operators

In our programs so far, most expressions have involved a single arithmetic operator; however, expressions with multiple operators are common in C++. Expressions can include both unary and binary operators. **Unary operators** take only one operand. In these expressions, we see the unary negation (–) and plus (+) operators.

unary operator
An operator that has one operand.
binary operator
An operator that has two operands.

```
x = -y;
p = +x * y;
```

**Binary operators** require two operands. When + and – are used to represent addition and subtraction, they are binary operators.

```
x = y + z;
z = y - x;
```

To understand and write expressions with multiple operators, we must know the C++ rules for evaluating expressions. For example, in the expression x + y / z, is + performed before / or is + performed after /? Is the expression x / y * z evaluated as (x / y) * z or as x / (y * z)? Verify for yourself that the order of evaluation does make a difference by substituting some simple values for x, y, and z. In both expressions, the / operator is evaluated first; the reasons are explained in the C++ rules for evaluation of arithmetic expressions that follow. These rules are based on familiar algebraic rules.

## Rules for Evaluating Expressions

1. *Parentheses rule:* All expressions in parentheses must be evaluated separately. Nested parenthesized expressions must be evaluated from the inside out, with the innermost expression evaluated first.

2. *Operator precedence rule:* Operators in the same expression are evaluated in the following order:

```
unary +, -     first
*, /, %        next
binary +, -    last
```

3. *Associativity rule:* Binary operators in the same subexpression and at the same precedence level (such as + and -) are evaluated left to right (*left associativity*). Unary operators in the same subexpression and at the same precedence level (such as + and -) are evaluated right to left (*right associativity*).

These rules will help you understand how C++ evaluates expressions. Use parentheses as needed to specify the order of evaluation. Often it is a good idea in complicated expressions to use extra parentheses to document clearly the order of operator evaluation. For example, the expression

```
x * y * z + a / b - c * d
```

can be written in a more readable form using parentheses:

```
(x * y * z ) + (a / b) - (c * d)
```

In Figure 2.8, we see a step-by-step evaluation of the same expression for a radius value of 2.0. You may want to use a similar notation when computing by hand the value of an expression with multiple operators.

## EXAMPLE 2.6

The formula for the area of a circle

    a = πr2

can be written in C++ as

    area = PI * radius * radius;

where the value of the constant **PI** is **3.14159**. Figure 2.7 shows the *evaluation tree* for this formula. In this tree, which you read from top to bottom, arrows connect each operand with its operator. The order of operator evaluation is shown by the number to the left of each operator; the letter to the right of the operator indicates which evaluation rule applies.

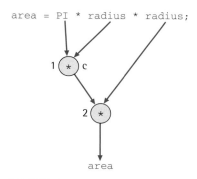

**Figure 2.7**   Evaluation tree for **area = PI * radius * radius;**

```
area    =    PI    *    radius    *    radius
            3.14159 *      2.0              2.0
               6.28318             *        2.0
                          12.56636
```

**Figure 2.8**   Step-by-step evaluation

## EXAMPLE 2.7

The formula for the average velocity, *v*, of a particle traveling on a line between points $p_1$ and $p_2$ in time $t_1$ to $t_2$ is

$$v = \frac{p_2 - p_1}{t_2 - t_1}$$

This formula can be written and evaluated in C++ as shown in Figure 2.9.

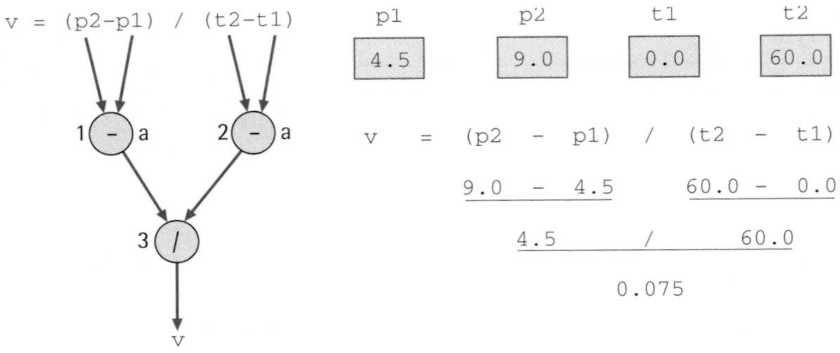

v = (p2-p1) / (t2-t1)

**Figure 2.9**   Evaluation for v = (p2 - p1) / (t2 - t1);

## EXAMPLE 2.8

Consider the expression

    z - (a + b / 2) + w * -y

containing type **int** variables only. The parenthesized expression

    (a + b / 2)

is evaluated first (rule 1) beginning with **b / 2** (rule 2). Once the value of **b / 2** is determined, it can be added to **a** to obtain the value of **(a + b / 2)**. Next, **y** is negated (rule 2). The multiplication operation can now be performed (rule 2) and the value for **w * -y** is determined. Then, the value of **(a + b / 2)** is subtracted from **z** (rule 3). Finally, this result is added to **w * -y**. The evaluation tree and step-by-step evaluation for this expression are shown in Figure 2.10.

## EXAMPLE 2.9

The evaluation of multiple operator expressions containing both type **int** and **float** values can be quite tricky to follow. Don't make the mistake of just converting all operands to type **float**, but evaluate each operator and its operands separately. Consider the statement

    m = x + k / 2;

shown in Figure 2.11, with **x = 5.5** (type **float**), **k = 5** (type **int**), and **m** (type **int**).

First, **k / 2** is evaluated (rule 2). Because both **k** and **2** are type **int**, the result is type **int** (**k / 2 = 2**). Next, **x + 2** is evaluated. Because **x** is type **float**, **2** is first converted to **2.0** so the expression **5.5 + 2.0** is evaluated. The result **7.5** is then truncated to **7** before it is assigned to the type **int** variable **m**.

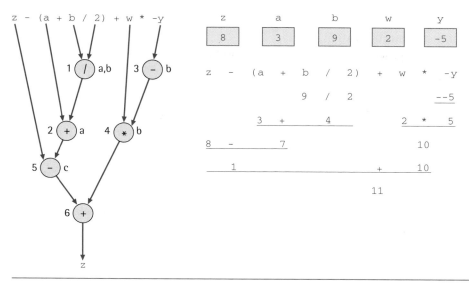

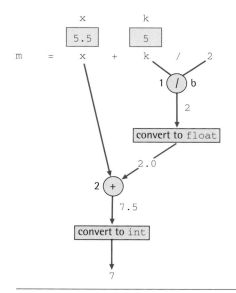

**Figure 2.10**   Evaluation for `z - (a + b / 2) + w * -y;`

**Figure 2.11**   Evaluation tree for `m = x + k / 2;`

## Writing Mathematical Formulas in C++

You may encounter two problems when writing mathematical formulas in C++: The first concerns multiplication, which is often implied in a mathematical formula by writing the two multiplicands next to each other—for example, $a = bc$. In C++, however, you must always use the $*$ operator to indicate multiplication, as in

```
a = b * c;
```

The other difficulty arises in formulas using division in which we normally write the numerator and denominator on separate lines:

$$m = \frac{y - b}{x - a}$$

In C++, however, all assignment statements must be written in a linear form. Consequently, parentheses are often needed to separate the numerator from the denominator and to clearly indicate the order of evaluation of the operators in the expression. The formula above would thus be written in C++ as

```
m = (y - b) / (x - a);
```

## EXAMPLE 2.10

This example illustrates how several mathematical formulas can be written in C++.

| Mathematical Formula | C++ Expression |
|---|---|
| 1. $b^2 - 4ac$ | b * b - 4 * a * c |
| 2. $a + b - c$ | a + b - c |
| 3. $\dfrac{a + b}{c + d}$ | (a + b) / (c + d) |
| 4. $\dfrac{1}{1 + y^2}$ | 1 / (1 + y * y) |
| 5. $a \times - (b + c)$ | a * -(b + c) |

The points illustrated are summarized as follows:

- Always specify multiplication explicitly by using the operator $*$ where needed (formulas 1 and 4).
- Use parentheses when required to control the order of operator evaluation (formulas 3 and 4).
- Two arithmetic operators can be written in succession if the second is a unary operator (formula 5).

## *case study* Finding the Value of a Coin Collection

This case study provides an example of manipulating type `int` data (using `/` and `%`).

### PROBLEM

Your niece has been saving nickels and pennies. She wants to exchange her coins at the bank, so she needs to know the value of her coins in dollars and cents.

### ANALYSIS

To solve this problem, you need a count of nickels and a count of pennies in the collection. From those counts, you determine the total value of coins in cents. Next, you can do an integer division using 100 as the divisor to get the dollar value; the remainder of this division will be the loose change that she should receive. In the data requirements table below, you list the total value in cents (`totalCents`) as a **program variable** because it is needed as part of the computation process but is not a required problem output.

**program variable**
A variable needed to store a computation in a program.

DATA REQUIREMENTS

**Problem Input**

| | |
|---|---|
| `string name` | *// your niece's first name* |
| `int nickels` | *// the count of nickels* |
| `int pennies` | *// the count of pennies* |

**Problem Output**

| | |
|---|---|
| `int dollars` | *// the number of dollars she should receive* |
| `int change` | *// the loose change she should receive* |

**Additional Program Variable**

| | |
|---|---|
| `int totalCents` | *// the total number of cents* |

FORMULAS
one dollar equals 100 pennies
one nickel equals 5 pennies

### DESIGN

The algorithm is straightforward and is presented next.

INITIAL ALGORITHM
1. Read in your niece's first name.

2. Read in the count of nickels and pennies.

3. Compute the total value in cents.

4. Find the value in dollars and loose change.

5. Display the value in dollars and loose change.

Steps 3 and 4 require further refinement.

**Step 3 Refinement**
**3.1.** `totalCents` is 5 times `nickels` plus `pennies`.

**Step 4 Refinement**
**4.1.** `dollars` is the integer quotient of `totalCents` and 100.

**4.2.** `change` is the integer remainder of `totalCents` and 100.

## IMPLEMENTATION

Listing 2.4 shows the program. The statement

```
totalCents = 5 * nickels + pennies;
```

implements algorithm Step 3.1. The statements

```
dollars = totalCents / 100;
change = totalCents % 100;
```

use the `/` and `%` operators to implement algorithm Steps 4.1 and 4.2, respectively.

## TESTING

To test this program, try running it with a combination of nickels and pennies that yields an exact dollar amount with no change left over. For example, 35 nickels and 25 pennies should yield a value of 2 dollars and no cents. Then increase and decrease the amount of pennies by 1 (26 and 24 pennies) to make sure that these cases are also handled properly.

**Listing 2.4**  Value of a coin collection

```cpp
// File: coins.cpp
// Determines the value of a coin collection

#include <iostream>
#include <string>
using namespace std;

int main()
{
    string name;        // input: niece's first name
    int pennies;        // input: count of pennies
    int nickels;        // input: count of nickels
    int dollars;        // output: value of coins in dollars
    int change;         // output: value of coins in cents
    int totalCents;     // total cents represented

    // Read in your niece's first name.
    cout << "Enter your first name: ";
    cin >> name;

    // Read in the count of nickels and pennies.
    cout << "Enter the number of nickels: ";
    cin >> nickels;
    cout << "Enter the number of pennies: ";
    cin >> pennies;

    // Compute the total value in cents.
    totalCents = 5 * nickels + pennies;

    // Find the value in dollars and change.
    dollars = totalCents / 100;
    change = totalCents % 100;

    // Display the value in dollars and change.
    cout << "Good work " << name << '!' << endl;
    cout << "Your collection is worth " << dollars << " dollars and "
        << change << " cents." << endl;

    return 0;
}
```

```
Enter your first name: Sally
Enter the number of nickels: 30
Enter the number of pennies: 77
Good work Sally!
Your collection is worth 2 dollars and 27 cents.
```

## EXERCISES FOR SECTION 2.6

### Self-Check

1. For the program fragment below, what values are printed?

```
int x, y, z;
float w;
x = 15;
w = x / 2;
y = 2 * x % 4;
z = 2 + x % 4;
cout << w << " " << x << " " << y << " " << z;
```

2. Evaluate the following expressions with 5 and 21 as operands:

   **a.**  21 / 5     5 / 21     21 % 5     5 % 21

   Repeat this exercise for the following pairs of integers:

   **b.**  5, 6    c. 3, 33    d. 20, 8

3. Show that the formula $m = (m / n) * n + (m \% n)$ holds when $m = 45$ and $n = 5$ (both of type int).

4. Show the step-by-step evaluation of the expressions below.

```
(y % z * (5 + w)) + x / y
(w + x / z) - x / (w - 5)
```

5. Given the declarations

```
const float PI = 3.14159;
const int MAX_I = 1000;
float x, y;
int a, b, i;
```

   indicate which C++ statements below are valid and find the value of each valid statement. Also, indicate which are invalid and why. Assume that a is 3, b is 4, and y is –1.0.

   **a.**  i = a % b;          **b.**  i = (MAX_I - 990) / a;
   **c.**  i = a % y;          **d.**  i = (990 - MAX_I) / a;
   **e.**  i = PI * a;         **f.**  x = PI * y;
   **g.**  x = PI / y;         **h.**  i = (MAX_I - 990) % a;
   **i.**  x = a % (a / b);    **j.**  i = a % 0;
   **k.**  i = b / 0;          **l.**  i = a % (MAX_I - 990);
   **m.**  x = a / y;          **n.**  i = a % (990 - MAX_I);
   **o.**  x = a / b;

6. What values are assigned by the legal statements in Exercise 5 above, assuming a is 5, b is 2, and y is 2.0?

7. Assume that you have the following variable declarations:

```
int color, lime, straw, yellow, red, orange;
float black, white, green, blue, purple, crayon;
```

Evaluate each of the statements below given the following values: color is 2, black is 2.5, crayon is −1.3, straw is 1, red is 3, and purple is 0.3e+1.

  a.  white = color * 2.5 / purple;
  b.  green = color / purple;
  c.  orange = color / red;
  d.  blue = (color + straw) / (crayon + 0.3);
  e.  lime = red / color + red % color;
  f.  purple = straw / red * color;

8. Let a, b, c, and x be the names of four type float variables, and let i, j, and k be the names of three type int variables. Each of the statements below contains a violation of the rules for forming arithmetic expressions. Rewrite each statement so that it is consistent with these rules.

  a.  x = 4.0 a * c;        b.  a = ac;
  c.  i = 5j3;             d.  k = 3(i + j);
  e.  x = 5a / bc;

## Programming

1. Write an assignment statement that might be used to implement the equation below in C++.

$$q = \frac{ka(t_1 - t_2)}{b}$$

2. Write a program that reads two int values into $m$, $n$ and displays their sum, their differences ($m - n$ and $n - m$), their product, their quotients ($m / n$ and $n / m$) and both $m \% n$ and $n \% m$. If the numbers are 4 and 5, the line that shows their sum should be displayed as:

```
5 + 4 = 9
```

Use this format for each output line.

3. Extend the program in Listing 2.4 to handle dimes and quarters as well as nickels and pennies.

# 2.7    Interactive Mode, Batch Mode, and Data Files

**interactive mode**
A mode of program execution in which the user interacts with a running program, entering data as requested.
**batch mode**
A noninteractive mode of program execution that requires all program data to be supplied before execution begins.

There are two basic modes of computer operation: interactive and batch. The programs we have written so far are intended to be run in **interactive mode**, a mode of program execution in which the user can interact with the program and enter data while the program is executing. In **batch mode**, all data must be supplied beforehand and the program user cannot interact with the program while it is executing. Batch mode is an option on most computers.

If you use batch mode, you must prepare a batch data file before executing your program. On a time-shared or personal computer, a batch data file is created and saved in the same way as a program or source file.

## Input Redirection

**input/output redirection**
Using operating system commands to associate the standard input device with an input file instead of the keyboard and/or the standard output device with an output file instead of the screen.

Listing 2.5 shows the miles to kilometers conversion program rewritten as a batch program. We assume that the input is associated with a data file instead of the keyboard. In most systems this can be done relatively easily through **input/output redirection** using operating system commands. For example, in the UNIX operating system, you can instruct your program to take its input from file `mydata` instead of the keyboard, by placing the symbols

```
< mydata
```

at the end of the command line that causes your compiled and linked program to execute. If you normally used the UNIX command line

```
metric
```

to execute this program, your new command line would be

```
metric < mydata
```

## Program Style    Echo Prints Versus Prompts

In Listing 2.5, the statement

```
cin >> miles;
```

reads the value of `miles` from the first (and only) line of the data file. Because the program input comes from a data file, there is no need to precede this statement with a prompt. Instead, we follow the input statement with the output statement

**Listing 2.5** Batch version of miles-to-kilometers conversion program

```cpp
// File: milesBatch.cpp
// Converts distance in miles to kilometers.

#include <iostream>
using namespace std;

int main()
{
    const float KM_PER_MILE = 1.609; // 1.609 km in a mile
    float miles,                      // input: distance in miles
          kms;                        // output: distance in kilometers

    // Get the distance in miles.
    cin >> miles;
    cout << "The distance in miles is " << miles << endl;

    // Convert the distance to kilometers.
    kms = KM_PER_MILE * miles;

    // Display the distance in kilometers.
    cout << "The distance in kilometers is " << kms << endl;

    return 0;
}
```

```
The distance in miles is 10
The distance in kilometers is 16.09
```

```cpp
cout << "The distance in miles is " << miles << endl;
```

which displays, or *echo prints*, the value just read into `miles`. This statement provides a record of the data to be manipulated by the program; without it, we would have no easy way of knowing what value was read. Whenever you convert an interactive program to a batch program, make sure you replace each prompt with an echo print that follows each input statement.

## Output Redirection

You can also redirect program output to a disk file instead of the screen. Then you could print the output file to obtain a hard-copy version of the program output. In UNIX, you would type

```
> myoutput
```

to redirect output from the screen to file `myoutput`. The command

```
metric > myoutput
```

executes the compiled and linked code for the metric conversion program, reading program input from the keyboard and writing program output to the file `myoutput`. However, it would be difficult to interact with the running program because all program output, including any prompts, are sent to the output file. It would be better to use the command

```
metric < mydata > myoutput
```

which reads program input from the data file `mydata` and sends program output to the output file `myoutput`.

## EXERCISES FOR SECTION 2.7

### Self-Check

1. Explain the difference in placement of `cout` statements used to display prompts and `cout` statements used to echo data. Which are used in interactive programs and which are used in batch programs? How are input data provided to an interactive program? How are input data provided to a batch program?

### Programming

1. Rewrite the program in Listing 2.4 as a batch program. Assume data are read from the file `mydata`.

2. Change the main function below to an interactive version.

```cpp
int main() {
    int m, n;        // input - 2 numbers
    int sum;         // output - their sum

    cin >> m >> n;
    cout << "m is " << m << ", n is " << n << endl;

    sum = m + n;
    cout << "Their sum is " << sum << endl;

    return 0;
}
```

3. Write a batch version of the solution to Programming Exercise 2 in Section 2.6 (repeated below). Your output should be sent to an output file.

Show the UNIX command that reads data from file `inData` and writes results to output file `outData`.

Write a program that reads two int values into *m*, *n* and displays their sum, their differences (*m* − *n* and *n* − *m*), their product, their quotients (*m* / *n* and *n* / *m*) and both *m* % *n* and *n* % *m*. If the numbers are 4 and 5, the line that shows their sum should be displayed as:

```
5 + 4 = 9
```

Use this format for each output line.

## 2.8   Common Programming Errors

As you begin to program, you will soon discover that a program rarely runs correctly on the first try. Murphy's law—"If something can go wrong, it will"—seems to have been written with the computer program in mind. In fact, errors are so common that they have their own special name— *bugs*—and the process of correcting them is called **debugging**. (According to computer folklore, computer pioneer Dr. Grace Murray Hopper diagnosed the first hardware error caused by a large insect found inside a computer component.) To alert you to potential problems, we will provide a section on common errors at the end of each chapter.

> debugging
> The process of removing errors from a program.

When the compiler detects an error, it displays an error message that indicates you made a mistake and what the likely cause of the error might be. Unfortunately, error messages are often difficult to interpret and are sometimes misleading. As you gain some experience, you will become more proficient at locating and correcting errors.

Three kinds of errors—syntax errors, run-time errors, and logic errors—can occur, as discussed in the following sections.

### Syntax Errors

A **syntax error** occurs when your code violates one or more of the grammar rules of C++ and is detected by the compiler as it attempts to translate your program. If a statement has a syntax error, it cannot be completely translated, and your program will not execute.

> syntax error
> A violation of a C++ grammar rule that prevents a program from being translated.

Listing 2.6 shows a version of the miles-to-kilometers conversion program with errors introduced.

One C++ system gives the following error messages:

```
[C++ Error] miles.cpp(12): E2141 Declaration syntax error.
```

```
[C++ Error] miles.cpp(15): E2380 Unterminated string or
          character constant.
[C++ Error] miles.cpp(16): E2379 Statement missing ;.
[C++ Error] miles.cpp(19): E2451 Undefined symbol 'kms'.
[C++ Warning] miles.cpp(25): W8080 'miles' is declared but
          never used.
[C++ Warning] miles.cpp(25): W8004 'KM_PER_MILE' is
          assigned a value that is never used.
```

On some systems, if you click on an error message, the statement containing the error will be highlighted. The missing comma after miles in the variable declaration statement causes error message E2141 above (Declaration syntax error). The missing quote at the end of the prompt string in the first executable statement causes error message E2380. Because of the missing quote, C++ considers the rest of the line to be part of the string including the ; at the end of the line. This causes error message E2379. If you click on this message, you will find that the line beginning with cin is highlighted; however, the missing ; is actually in the line just above. This kind of displacement of error messages is fairly common—you sometimes

**Listing 2.6**   Miles-to-kilometers conversion program with syntax errors

```cpp
// milesError.cpp
// Converts distances from miles to kilometers.

#include <iostream>
 using namespace std;

 int main()        // start of function main
 {
      const float KM_PER_MILE = 1.609;  // 1.609 km in a mile
      float miles                        // input: distance in miles
           kms;                          // output: distance in kilometers

      // Get the distance in miles.
      cout << "Enter the distance in miles:  ;
      cin >> miles;

      // Convert the distance to kilometers.
      kms = KM_PER_MILE * miles;

      // Display the distance in kilometers.
      cout << "The distance in kilometers is " << kms << endl;
      return 0;
 }
```

need to check one or more lines that precede the highlighted line to find an error. The incorrect variable declaration statement also causes error message E2451, which is associated with the assignment statement. If you fix the variable declaration, this error message will also go away. Finally, the last two error messages (W8080 and W8004) are considered warning messages. They will not stop the program from being executed, but they do indicate suspicious behavior in the program.

Your strategy for correcting syntax errors should take into account the fact that one error can lead to many error messages. It is often a good idea to concentrate on correcting the errors in the declaration statements first. Then recompile the program before you attempt to fix other errors. Many of the other error messages will disappear once the declarations are correct.

## Run–Time Errors

**Run-time errors** are detected and displayed by the computer during the execution of a program. A run-time error occurs when the program directs the computer to perform an illegal operation, such as dividing a number by zero. When a run-time error occurs, the computer will stop executing your program and will display a diagnostic message that indicates the line where the error was detected.

**run-time error**
An error detected by the computer during program execution.

The program in Listing 2.7 compiles successfully but cannot run to completion if the first integer entered is greater than the second. In this case, integer division causes the first assignment statement to store zero in temp. Using temp as a divisor in the next line causes a run-time error such as "Floating point division by zero".

## Undetected Errors

Some execution errors will not prevent a C++ program from running to completion, but they may lead to incorrect results. It is essential that you predict the results your program should produce and verify that the actual output is correct.

A very common source of incorrect results is the input of character and numeric data. Listing 2.8 shows only the data entry statements for the coin program from Listing 2.4 If your niece happens to type in her entire name instead of just her first name, a curious result will occur. You indicate the end of a string data item by pressing the space bar or the RETURN key, so her first name will be extracted correctly. But the characters that remain in the input stream (the space and last name) will mess up the data entry for variables nickels and pennies. Because the input stream is not empty, C++ attempts to extract these data from the current input stream instead of

Listing 2.7    Program with a potential run-time error

```cpp
// File: runtimeError.cpp
// Provides a possible "division by zero" run-time error.

#include <iostream>
using namespace std;

int main()
{

        int first, second;
        float temp, ans;

        cout << "Enter 2 integers: ";
        cin >> first >> second;

        temp = second / first;
        ans = first / temp;

        cout << "The result is " << ans << endl;

        return 0;

}
```

waiting for the user to type in these numbers. Since the next data character to be processed is a letter, C++ will simply leave the values of nickels and pennies unchanged, which will lead to unpredictable results.

Listing 2.8    Data entry statements for coins program

```cpp
// Read in your niece's first name.
cout << "Enter your first name: ";
cin >> name;

// Read in the count of nickels and pennies.
cout << "Enter the number of nickels: ";
cin >> nickels;
cout << "Enter the number of pennies: ";
cin >> pennies;
```

The output from one incorrect run of the program is shown below. Notice that the prompts for nickels and pennies appear on the second line and the user is unable to type in the numbers requested. The program runs to completion using whatever "garbage" values were originally in variables `nickels` and `pennies`.

```
Enter your first name: Sally Smith
Enter the number of nickels: Enter the number of pennies:
Good work Sally!
Your collection is worth 210060 dollars and 0 cents.
```

### Logic Errors

*Logic errors* occur when a program follows a faulty algorithm. Because such errors usually do not cause run-time errors and do not display error messages, they are very difficult to detect. You can detect logic errors by testing the program thoroughly, comparing its output to calculated results. You can prevent logic errors by carefully desk checking the algorithm and the program before you type it in.

Because debugging a program can be very time-consuming, plan your program solutions carefully and desk-check them to eliminate bugs early. If you are unsure of the syntax for a particular statement, look it up in the text.

## Chapter Review

1. You learned how to use C++ statements to perform some basic operations: to read information into memory, to perform computations, and to display the results of the computation. You can do all of this using symbols (variable names and operators, such as +, -, *, and /) that are familiar and easy to remember.

2. Use the compiler directive `#include` to reuse files containing classes and functions in previously defined libraries. Use the statement `using namespace std;` to indicate that you are referencing C++ elements defined in the standard namespace.

3. Comments make programs easier to read and understand. Use comments to document the use of variables and to introduce the major steps of the algorithm. A comment in a program line is preceded by the symbol pair `//` and it extends to the end of a line. You can also use the symbol pairs `/*`, `*/` to bracket multiline comments.

4. C++ statements contain reserved words (predefined in C++) and identifiers chosen by the programmer. Identifiers should begin with a letter and can consist of letters, digits, and the underscore character only. Use a standard naming convention for identifiers. We suggest using all uppercase for constants and using all lowercase for one-word names of variables and objects. For variables with multiword names, start

each word after the first with an uppercase letter (no underscores). Use underscore characters between words of a constant identifier.

5. A data type specifies a set of values and the operations that can be performed on those values. We will use the C++ predefined data types `float`, `int`, `char`, and `bool`. Types `float` and `int` are abstractions for the integers and real numbers. C++ uses floating-point representation for real numbers and fixed-point representation for integers. C++ uses the data type `char` to represent single characters that are enclosed in apostrophes in a program. The apostrophes are not considered part of the data element and are not stored in memory. Data type `bool` represents the two values `false` and `true`.

6. C++ uses the data type `string` (defined in the standard library) to represent sequences of characters that are enclosed in quotes in a program. The quotes are not considered part of the data element and are not stored in memory.

7. We can write arithmetic expressions using type `float` and `int` data. The rules of evaluation are similar to the rules of algebra, but we must be aware of the data type of an expression. If an operator has only type `int` data for its operands, the result will be type `int`; otherwise, it will be type `float`. Be careful when evaluating expressions with type `int` and type `float` data. If an operator has both kinds of data for its operands, C++ converts the type `int` value to a type `float` value before performing the operation.

8. C++ uses assignment statements to assign a computational result to a variable. Remember, the expression is evaluated first, following the rules summarized in point 7 above. Afterward, the result is assigned to the indicated variable. For a mixed-type assignment, C++ must perform a type conversion just before storing the expression result.

9. C++ uses the standard library class `iostream` for modeling input and output streams—sequences of characters associated with a file or device. C++ uses `cin` and `cout` to represent the keyboard and screen, respectively. C++ uses `<<` as the stream insertion operator, also called the output operator because it writes data to an output stream. C++ uses `>>` as the stream extraction operator, also called the input operator because it reads data into a variable.

10. The syntax rules of C++ are precise and allow no exceptions. The compiler will be unable to translate C++ instructions that violate these rules. Remember to declare every identifier used as a constant or variable and to terminate program statements with semicolons.

The table on the next page summarizes the new C++ constructs.

## Summary of New C++ Constructs

| Construct | Effect |
| --- | --- |
| **Compiler Directive**<br>`#include <iostream>` | A compiler directive that causes the class `iostream` to be placed in the program where the directive appears. |
| **Using Statement**<br>`using namespace std;` | Indicates that the program is using names defined in the region `namespace std` (standard). |
| **Constant Declaration**<br>`const float TAX = 25.00;`<br>`const char STAR = '*';` | Associates the constant identifier `TAX` with the floating-point constant `25.00` and the constant identifier `STAR` with the character constant `'*'`. |
| **Variable Declaration**<br>`float x, y, z;`<br>`int me, it;` | Allocates memory cells named `x`, `y`, and `z` for storage of floating-point numbers and cells named `me` and `it` for storage of integers. |
| **Assignment Statement**<br>`distance = speed * time;` | Assigns the product of `speed` and `time` as the value of `distance`. |
| **Input Statement**<br>`cin >> hours >> rate;` | Enters data into the variables `hours` and `rate`. |
| **Output Statement**<br>`cout << "Net = " << net << endl;` | Displays the string `"Net = "` followed by the value of `net`. `endl` advances the screen cursor to the next line after this information is displayed. |

## Quick-Check Exercises

1. What value is assigned to `x` (type `float`) by the following statement?

   ```
   x = 25 % 3 / 3.0;
   ```

2. What value is assigned to `x` by the statement below, assuming `x` is 10.0?

   ```
   x = x / 20;
   ```

3. Show the form of the output line displayed by the following `cout` lines when `total` is 152.55.

   ```
   cout << "The value of total is: " << endl;
   cout << "$" << total << endl;
   ```

4. Show the form of the output line displayed by the following `cout` line when `total` is 352.74.

```
cout << "The final total is $" << total << endl;
```

5. Indicate which type of data you use to represent the following items: number of cats in your house; each initial of your name; your full name; the average temperature during the last month.

6. In which step of the software development method are the problem input and output data identified? In which step do you develop and refine the algorithm?

7. In reading two integers using the statement

```
cin >> m >> n;
```

what character should be entered following the first value? What should be entered after the second number?

8. When reading two characters using the input operator >>, does it matter how many blanks (if any) appear

   a. before the first character?
   b. between the first and second characters?
   c. after the second character?

9. How does the compiler determine how many and what type of data values are to be entered when an `input` statement is executed?

10. What is the syntactic purpose of the semicolon in a C++ program?

11. Does the compiler listing show syntax or run-time errors?

Answers to Quick–Check Exercises

1. `0.333333`

2. `0.5`

3. The value of total is:

   `$152.55`

4. The final total is `$352.74`

5. `int, char, string, float`

6. problem analysis, design

7. a blank, RETURN key

8. For (a) and (b), the number of blanks is irrelevant; any number is allowed or there may be no blanks; the input operator will simply skip all leading blanks and stop reading after the first nonblank is read. For (c), there is no need for any blanks; press the RETURN key after entering the second character.

9. The number of values to be entered depends on the number of variables in the input list. The type of data is determined by the type of each variable.

10. It terminates a C++ statement.

11. syntax errors

## Review Questions

1. What type of information should be specified in the program header section comments?

2. Circle those identifiers below that are valid names for variables.

```
salary          two fold        amount*pct        myprogram
1stTime         R2D2            firstTime         program
CONST           income#1        main              MAIN
Jane's          int             variable          PI
```

3. What is illegal about the following declarations and assignment statement?

```
const float PI = 3.14159;
float c, r;
PI = c % (2 * r * r);
```

4. What do the following statements do? Which identifier cannot have its value changed?
   a. float x = 3.5;
   b. string flower = "rose";
   c. const int FEETINMILE = 5280;

5. List and define the rules of order of evaluation for arithmetic expressions.

6. Write the data requirements, necessary formulas, and algorithm for Programming Project 6 in the next section.

7. If the average size of a family is 2.8 and this value is stored in the variable familySize, provide the C++ statement to display this fact in a readable way (leave the display on the same line).

8. List three language-defined data types of C++.

9. Convert the program statements below to read and echo data in batch mode.

```
cout << "Enter three numbers separated by spaces: "
     << endl;
cin >> x >> y >> z;
cout << "Enter two characters: ";
cin >> ch1 >> ch2;
```

10. Write an algorithm that allows for the input of an integer value, triples it, adds your age to it (also an input), and displays the result.

11. Assuming a (10) and b (6) are type int variables, what are the values of the following expressions:

   a. a / b

   b. a % b

   c. a * b

   d. a + b

12. Assuming a and b are type int variables, which of the following expressions evaluate to the same value?

   a. a + b * c

   b. (a + b) * c

   c. a + (b * c)

13. Differentiate among syntax errors, run-time errors, and logic errors.

## Programming Projects

1. Write a program to convert a temperature in degrees Fahrenheit to degrees Celsius.

   DATA REQUIREMENTS
   
   **Problem Input**
   
   int fahrenheit    // *temperature in degrees Fahrenheit*

   **Problem Output**
   
   float celsius    // *temperature in degrees Celsius*

   **Formula**
   
   celsius = (5/9) * (fahrenheit − 32)

2. Write a program to read two data items and print their sum, difference, product, and quotient.

DATA REQUIREMENTS
**Problem Input**

```
int x, y            // two items
```

**Problem Output**

```
int sum             // sum of x and y
int difference      // difference of x and y
int product         // product of x and y
float quotient      // quotient of x divided by y
```

3. You have been watching the World's Strongest Man competition on television. The competitors perform amazing feats of strength such as pulling trucks along a course, flipping huge tires, lifting large objects onto raised platforms, etc. You can tell the items are quite heavy but the British announcer keeps referring to the weights in stones. Write a program that converts the weight in stones to the equivalent weight in pounds where 1 stone is 14 pounds.

4. Write a program that prints your first initial as a block letter. (Hint: Use a 6 × 6 grid for the letter and print six strings. Each string should consist of asterisks (*) interspersed with blanks.)

5. Write a program that reads in the length and width of a rectangular yard (in meters) and the length and width of a rectangular house (in meters) placed in the yard. Your program should compute the time (in minutes) required to cut the lawn around the house. Assume the mowing rate in square meters per minutes is entered as a data item.

6. Write a program that reads and stores the numerators and denominators of two fractions as integer values. For example, if the numbers 1 and 4 are entered for the first fraction, the fraction is $1/4$. The program should print the product of the two fractions as a fraction and as a decimal value. For example, $1/4 * 1/2 = 1/8$ or $0.125$.

7. Write a program that reads the number of years ago that a dinosaur lived and then computes the equivalent number of months, days, and seconds ago. Use 365.25 days per year. Test your program with a triceratops that lived 145 million years ago and a brontosaurus that lived 182 million years ago. (Hint: Use type `double` for all variables.)

8. Arnie likes to jog in the morning. As he jogs, he counts the number of strides he makes during the first minute and then again during the last minute of his jogging. Arnie then averages these two and calls this average the number of strides he makes in a minute when he jogs.

Write a program that accepts this average and the total time Arnie spends jogging in hours and minutes and then displays the distance Arnie has jogged in miles. Assume Arnie's stride is 2.5 feet (also a data item). There are 5280 feet in a mile (a constant).

9. Write a program that reads a number of seconds between 0 and 18,000 (5 hours) and displays the hours, minutes, and seconds equivalent.

10. Redo Programming Project 6—but this time compute the sum of the two fractions.

11. The Pythagorean theorem states that the sum of the squares of the sides of a right triangle is equal to the square of the hypotenuse. For example, if two sides of a right triangle have lengths 3 and 4, then the hypotenuse must have a length of 5. The integers 3, 4, and 5 together form a Pythagorean triple. There is an infinite number of such triples. Given two positive integers, $m$ and $n$, where $m > n$, a Pythagorean triple can be generated by the following formulas:

$$side1 = m^2 - n^2$$
$$side2 = 2mn$$
$$hypotenuse = \sqrt{side1^2 + side2^2}$$

Write a program that reads in values for $m$ and $n$ and prints the values of the Pythagorean triple generated by the formulas above.

12. Write a program to compute the rate of growth, expressed as a percentage, of an insect population. Take as input the initial size of the population and its size one week later. Then compute the rate of growth and predict the size of the population in yet another week, assuming that growth continues at the same rate.

13. Write a program that reads in an integer that is greater than 1,000 and less than 1,000,000. Recall that the number must be entered without a comma. Display the number with a comma inserted where it belongs. (Hint: use the % operator.)

14. Write a program that asks a user to enter the distance of a trip in miles, the miles per gallon estimate for the user's car, and the average cost of a gallon of gas. Your program should calculate and display the number of gallons of gas needed and the estimated cost of the trip.

15. Write a program that dispenses change. The program should read the amount of the purchase and the amount paid and then display the number of dollars, quarters, dimes, nickels, and pennies given in change. (Hint: Convert the purchase amount and the amount paid to pennies.) Calculate the difference (changeDue). Use the % operator to determine how many dollars to pay. Subtract that number of pennies

from changeDue and continue this process for quarters, dimes, etc. Your answer may be off by a penny. Do you have any idea why this might be the case? How could you correct this?

16. Your summer surveying job requires you to study some maps that give distances in kilometers and some that use miles. You and your co-workers prefer to deal in miles. Write a program that performs the necessary conversion.

# Josée Lajoie

*Josée Lajoie served as chair of the core language working group for the ANSI/ISO C++ Standard Committee and worked as a staff development analyst in the IBM Canada Laboratory C/C++ Compiler group. In addition, she is the co-author of* The C++ Primer *and a regular columnist on the evolution of the C++ language standard for the* C++ Report.

**What is your educational background?**
I have a bachelor's degree in electrical engineering from L'École Polytechnique at the University of Montreal, which I obtained in 1986, and I am currently pursuing a master's degree in computer graphics at the University of Waterloo. This master's degree includes both computer science and fine arts courses.

**What was your first job in the computer industry? What did it entail?**
I worked at IBM as a member of a team building a C compiler for IBM's mainframes. My work was to help develop the compiler front end—that is, the portion of the compiler that analyzes C programs for their syntactic and semantic validity. Over the course of a year and half, I developed with two other coworkers a C compiler front end to support the syntax and semantic requirements of the ANSI C standard.

**Which person in the computer science field has inspired you?**
Grace Hopper, for her pioneering spirit and her determination. Before computers were widely used, Grace Hopper believed that a much wider audience could use computers if tools existed that were both programmer-friendly and application-friendly. She worked on the development of early compilers to facilitate the use of computers in business and other nonscientific applications.

**Do you have any advice for students learning C++?**
I think people should learn by first using existing C++ libraries and code. They should start by writing small programs that use the features of an existing library. Then, when they become familiar with how to use the library, they should examine the library interface more closely, look at how the library features were designed and implemented, and if they can, read up on the design decisions behind the library implementation. The C++ Standard Library is a good example of a library that can be used in this way.

**Do you have any advice for students entering the computer science field?**
I would like to encourage students who are interested in studying computer science, but who do not see themselves as fitting the stereotypical description of a

computer scientist as portrayed in the media, to pursue their interests. The field needs people who are innovative, artistic, and good communicators just as much as it needs people who are good in math.

### What do you think the future of the C++ language is?

I think the language itself will remain the way it is for very many years to come. The C++ language tool set is quite extensive, and I think sufficient to implement a great variety of good libraries.

What I hope will happen is that the support offered by the C++ Standard Library will grow importantly over the next few iterations of the C++ standard. Five years after a standard has been published, individuals and companies can request changes to bring the standard closer to widely accepted industry practices. I hope that, as more C++ libraries become available, they will be added to the list of C++ Standard Libraries, and that users developing new products will be able to choose from a wide variety of domain-specific libraries available with every standard C++ implementation.

### You were a key member of the ANSI/ISO C++ Standard committee. Why was it important to standardize C++?

Standardization is important for users, especially for users writing applications that must be ported to a great variety of architectures. A standard gives these users the guarantee that the code they are writing on one platform will compile and run on another platform where standard C++ is supported, provided that their implementation follows the rules prescribed in the standard. Similarly with the library. The standard

guarantees that the standard libraries used by their implementation will be available on other platforms where the C++ standard library is supported, and that they won't have to rewrite their code to use another, sometimes quite different, system-specific library. Having a standard means that implementers can port their applications faster to other platforms.

### What were the main changes to the C++ definition?

The most important change to the original definition of C++ is the addition of the Standard Template Library, which is a good library not only because it provides important basic tools such as containers and algorithms that programmers use very often, but also because it is a very well-designed piece of software that shows better than anything else the power of C++ and how it can be used to write very good libraries.

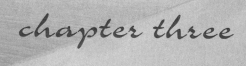

## chapter three

# Top-Down Design with Functions and Classes

### Chapter Objectives

- To learn about functions and how to use them to modularize programs
- To understand the capabilities of functions in the C++ math library
- To introduce structure charts as a system documentation tool
- To understand how control flows between functions
- To learn how to pass information to functions using arguments
- To learn how to return a value from a function
- To understand how to use class **string** and **string** objects and functions

PROGRAMMERS WHO SOLVE PROBLEMS using the software development method can use information collected during the analysis and design phases to help plan and complete the finished program. Also, programmers can use segments of earlier program solutions as components in their new programs. Therefore, they don't have to construct each new program from square one.

In the first section of this chapter, we demonstrate how you can tap existing information and code in the form of predefined functions to write programs. In addition to using existing information, you can use top-down design techniques to simplify the development of algorithms and the structure of the resulting programs. To apply top-down design, you start with the broadest statement of the problem solution and work down to more detailed subproblems.

We also introduce the structure chart, which documents the relationships among subproblems. We illustrate the use of procedural abstraction to develop modular programs that use separate functions to implement each subproblem's solution. Finally, we continue our discussion of data abstraction and provide further detail on class **string** and its member functions.

# 3.1   Building Programs from Existing Information

Programmers seldom start off with a blank slate (or empty screen) when they develop a program. Often some—or all—of the solution can be developed from information that already exists or from the solution to another problem, as we demonstrate next.

Carefully following the software development method generates important system documentation before you even begin coding. This documentation—a description of a problem's data requirements (developed during the analysis phase) and its solution algorithm (developed during the design phase)—summarizes your intentions and thought processes.

You can use this documentation as a starting point in coding your program. For example, you can begin by editing the problem data requirements to conform to the C++ syntax for constant and variable declarations, as shown in Listing 3.1 for the miles-to-kilometers conversion program. This approach is especially helpful if the documentation was created with a word processor and is in a file that you can edit.

**Listing 3.1**   Edited data requirements and algorithm for a conversion program

```cpp
// File: miles.cpp
// Converts distance in miles to kilometers.

#include <iostream>
using namespace std;

int main()                  // start of main function
{
    const float KM_PER_MILE = 1.609; // 1.609 km in a mile
    float miles,                      // input: distance in miles
          kms;                        // output: distance in kilometers

    // Get the distance in miles.

    // Convert the distance to kilometers.
       // Distance in kilometers is 1.609 * distance in miles.

    // Display the distance in kilometers.

    return 0;
}
```

To develop the executable statements in the `main` function, first use the initial algorithm and its refinements as program comments. The comments describe each algorithm step and provide program documentation that guides your C++ code. Listing 3.1 shows how the program will look at this point. After the comments are in place in the `main` function, you can begin to write the C++ statements. Place the C++ code for an unrefined step directly under that step. For a step that is refined, either edit the refinement to change it from English to C++ or replace it with C++ code. We illustrate this entire process in the next case study.

*case study*　　　　Finding the Area and Circumference of a Circle

### PROBLEM

Get the radius of a circle. Compute and display the circle's area and circumference.

### ANALYSIS

Clearly, the problem input is the circle radius. Two output values are requested: the circle's area and circumference. These variables should be type `float` because the inputs and outputs may contain fractional parts. The geometric relationship of a circle's radius to its area and circumference are listed below, along with the data requirements.

#### DATA REQUIREMENTS

**Problem Constant**

`PI = 3.14159`

**Problem Input**

`float radius`　　*// radius of a circle*

**Problem Output**

`float area`　　　*// area of a circle*
`float circum`　　*// circumference of a circle*

#### FORMULAS

*area of a circle* $= \pi \times radius^2$
*circumference of a circle* $= 2 \times radius$

### DESIGN

After identifying the problem inputs and outputs, list the steps necessary to solve the problem. Pay close attention to the order of the steps.

#### INITIAL ALGORITHM

1. Get the circle radius.
2. Compute the area of circle.

> **3.** Compute the circumference of circle.

ALGORITHM REFINEMENTS

Next, refine any steps that don't have an obvious solution (Steps 2 and 3).

**Step 2 Refinement**

2.1. Assign `PI * radius * radius` to area.

**Step 3 Refinement**

3.1. Assign `2 * PI * radius` to circum.

### IMPLEMENTATION

Listing 3.2 shows the C++ program so far. Function `main` consists of the initial algorithm with its refinements as comments. To write the final program, convert the refinements (Steps 2.1 and 3.1) to C++ and write C++ code for the unrefined steps (Steps 1 and 4). Listing 3.3 shows the final program.

### TESTING

The sample output in Listing 3.3 provides a good test of the solution because it is relatively easy to compute by hand the area and circumference for a radius value of 5.0. The radius squared is 25.0, so the value of the area is correct. The circumference should be ten times $\pi$, which is also an easy number to compute by hand.

---

**Listing 3.2**    Outline of area and circumference program

```
// Computes and displays the area and circumference of a circle

int main()
{
   const float PI = 3.14159;
   float radius;          // input: radius of circle
   float area;            // output: area of circle
   float circum;          // output: circumference of circle

   // Get the circle radius.

   // Compute area of circle.
      // Assign PI * radius * radius to area.

   // Compute circumference of circle.
      // Assign 2 * PI * radius to circum.

   // Display area and circumference.

   return 0;
}
```

**Listing 3.3**    Finding the area and circumference of a circle

```cpp
// File: circle.cpp
// Computes and displays the area and circumference of a circle

#include <iostream>
using namespace std;

int main()
{
    const float PI = 3.14159;
    float radius;           // input: radius of circle
    float area;             // output: area of circle
    float circum;           // output: circumference of circle

    // Get the circle radius.
    cout << "Enter the circle radius: ";
    cin >> radius;

    // Compute area of circle.
    area = PI * radius * radius;

    // Compute circumference of circle.
    circum = 2 * PI * radius;

    // Display area and circumference.
    cout << "The area of the circle is " << area << endl;
    cout << "The circumference of the circle is " << circum << endl;

    return 0;
}
```

```
Enter the circle radius: 5.0
The area of the circle is 78.539749
The circumference of the circle is 31.415901
```

## *case study*    Computing the Weight of a Batch of Flat Washers

Another way in which programmers use existing information is by *extending the solution for one problem to solve another.* For example, you can easily solve this new problem by building on the solution to the previous one.

### PROBLEM

You work for a hardware company that manufactures flat washers. To estimate shipping costs, your company needs a program that computes the weight of a specified quantity of flat washers.

## ANALYSIS

A flat washer resembles a small donut. To compute the weight of a single flat washer, you need to know its rim area, its thickness, and the density of the material used in its construction. The last two quantities are problem inputs. However, the rim area (see Figure 3.1) must be computed from two measurements that are provided as inputs: the washer's outer diameter and its inner diameter (diameter of the hole).

In the following data requirements, we list the washer's inner and outer radius (half the diameter) as program variables. We also list the rim area and weight of one washer (`unitWeight`) as program variables.

DATA REQUIREMENTS
**Problem Constant**
`PI = 3.14159`

**Problem Inputs**
`float holeDiameter`    *// diameter of hole*
`float edgeDiameter`    *// diameter of outer edge*
`float thickness`       *// thickness of washer*
`float density`         *// density of material used*
`float quantity`        *// number of washers made*

**Problem Outputs**
`float weight`          *// weight of batch of washers*

**Program Variables**
`float holeRadius`      *// radius of hole*
`float edgeRadius`      *// radius of outer edge*
`float rimArea`         *// area of rim*
`float unitWeight`      *// weight of 1 washer*

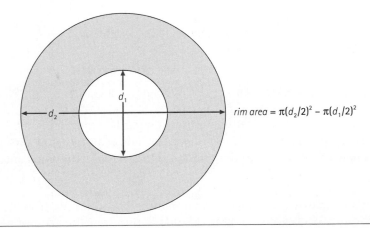

$$rim\ area = \pi(d_2/2)^2 - \pi(d_1/2)^2$$

**Figure 3.1**   The rim area of a washer

**Relevant Formulas**

*area of circle* $= \pi \times radius^2$
*radius of circle = diameter / 2*
*rim area = area of outer circle – area of hole*
*unit weight = rim area $\times$ thickness $\times$ density*

## DESIGN

We list the algorithm next, followed by the refinement of Steps 3 and 4.

INITIAL ALGORITHM

1. Get the washer's inner diameter, outer diameter, and thickness.
2. Get the material density and quantity of washers manufactured.
3. Compute the rim area.
4. Compute the weight of one flat washer.
5. Compute the weight of the batch of washers.
6. Display the weight of the batch of washers.

ALGORITHM REFINEMENTS

**Step 3 Refinement**

**3.1** Compute `holeRadius` and `edgeRadius`.

**3.2** `rimArea` is `PI * edgeRadius * edgeRadius -`
              `PI * holeRadius * holeRadius`

**Step 4 Refinement**

**4.1** `unitWeight` is `rimArea * thickness * density`

## IMPLEMENTATION

To write this program, edit the data requirements to write the variable declarations and use the initial algorithm with refinements as a starting point for the executable statements. Listing 3.4 shows the C++ program.

## TESTING

To test this program, run it with inner and outer diameters such as 2 centimeters and 4 centimeters that lead to easy calculations for rim area (3 * `PI` square centimeters). You can verify that the program is computing the correct unit weight by entering 1 for quantity, and then verify that the batch weight is correct by running it for larger quantities.

Listing 3.4    Washer program

```cpp
// File: washers.cpp
// Computes the weight of a batch of flat washers.

#include <iostream>
using namespace std;

int main()
{
      const float PI = 3.14159;
      float holeDiameter;    // input - diameter of hole
      float edgeDiameter;    // input - diameter of outer edge
      float thickness;       // input - thickness of washer
      float density;         // input - density of material used
      float quantity;        // input - number of washers made
      float weight;          // output - weight of washer batch
      float holeRadius;      // radius of hole
      float edgeRadius;      // radius of outer edge
      float rimArea;         // area of rim
      float unitWeight;      // weight of 1 washer

      // Get the inner diameter, outer diameter, and thickness.
      cout << "Inner diameter in centimeters: ";
      cin >> holeDiameter;
      cout << "Outer diameter in centimeters: ";
      cin >> edgeDiameter;
      cout << "Thickness in centimeters: ";
      cin >> thickness;

      // Get the material density and quantity manufactured.
      cout << "Material density in grams per cubic centimeter: ";
      cin >> density;
      cout << "Quantity in batch: ";
      cin >> quantity;

      // Compute the rim area.
      holeRadius = holeDiameter / 2.0;
      edgeRadius = edgeDiameter / 2.0;
      rimArea =  PI * edgeRadius * edgeRadius -
                 PI * holeRadius * holeRadius;

      // Compute the weight of a flat washer.
      unitWeight = rimArea * thickness * density;

      // Compute the weight of the batch of washers.
      weight = unitWeight * quantity;
```

(continued)

**Listing 3.4**  Washer program (continued)

```
                // Display the weight of the batch of washers.
                cout << "The expected weight of the batch is "
                     << weight << " grams." << endl;
                return 0;
        }
        Inner diameter in centimeters: 1.2
        Outer diameter in centimeters: 2.4
        Thickness in centimeters: 0.1
        Material density in grams per cubic centimeter: 7.87
        Quantity in batch: 1000
        The expected weight of the batch is 2670.23 grams.
```

## EXERCISES FOR SECTION 3.1

### Self-Check

1. Describe the data requirements and algorithm for a program that computes the number of miles you can drive a car given the estimated number of miles per gallon and the number of gallons of gas you purchased as input data. Also compute and display the cost of the gasoline based on the cost per gallon (a data item).

2. Write a program outline from the algorithm you developed in Exercise 1. Show the declaration part of the program and the program comments corresponding to the algorithm and its refinements.

3. Change the solution to Exercise 1 to calculate the estimated cost of a trip given the distance of the trip, the estimated number of miles per gallon, and the average cost of a gallon of gasoline.

### Programming

1. Add refinements to the program outline below and write the final C++ program.

```
// Computes the sum and average of two numbers

#include <iostream>
using namespace std;

int main()
{
    // Declare any constants and variables you need.
    // Read two numbers.
    // Compute the sum of the two numbers.
    // Compute the average of the two numbers.
    // Display sum and average.
```

```
        return 0;
    }
```

2. Write a complete C++ program for Self-Check Exercise 2.

3. Write a complete C++ program for Self-Check Exercise 3.

4. Assume that flat washers are manufactured by stamping them out from a rectangular piece of material of uniform thickness. Extend the washer program to compute (a) the number of square centimeters of material needed to manufacture a specified quantity of flat washers and (b) the weight of the leftover material.

## 3.2   Library Functions

A main goal of software engineering is to write error-free code. Code reuse—reusing program fragments that have already been written and tested whenever possible—is one efficient way to accomplish this goal. Stated more simply, why reinvent the wheel?

C++ promotes reuse by providing many predefined classes and functions in its standard library. The standard library `cmath` contains many functions that perform mathematical computations. For example, it defines a function named `sqrt` that performs the square root computation. The function call in the assignment statement

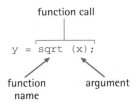

activates the code for function `sqrt`, passing the *argument* x to the function. You activate a function by writing a *function call*. After the function executes, the function result is substituted for the function call. If x is `16.0`, the assignment statement above is evaluated as follows:

1. x is `16.0`, so function `sqrt` computes $\sqrt{16.0}$, or `4.0`.
2. The function result `4.0` is assigned to y.

A function can be thought of as a "black box" that is passed one or more input values and automatically returns a single output value. Figure 3.2 illustrates this for the call to function `sqrt`. The value of x (`16.0`) is the function input, and the function result, or output, is $\sqrt{16.0}$ (result is `4.0`).

If w is 9.0, C++ evaluates the assignment statement

```
z = 5.7 + sqrt(w);
```

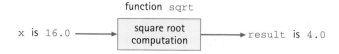

**Figure 3.2** Function `sqrt` as a "black box"

as follows:

1. `w` is `9.0`, so function `sqrt` computes $\sqrt{9.0}$ , or `3.0`.
2. The values `5.7` and `3.0` are added together.
3. The sum, `8.7`, is stored in `z`.

## EXAMPLE 3.1

The program in Listing 3.5 displays the square root of two numbers provided as input data (`first` and `second`) and the square root of their sum. To do so, we must call the function `sqrt` three times:

```
answer = sqrt(first);
answer = sqrt(second);
answer = sqrt(first + second);
```

For the first two calls, the function arguments are variables (`first` and `second`). The third call shows that a function argument can also be an expression (`first + second`). For all three calls, the result returned by function `sqrt` is assigned to variable `answer`. Because the definition of function `sqrt` is found in the standard library `cmath`, the program begins with

```
#include <cmath>                        // sqrt function
```

### Program Style      Use of Color to Highlight New Constructs

In Listing 3.5, program lines that illustrate new constructs are in color, so that you can find them easily. We will continue to use color for this purpose in listings.

### C++ Library Functions

Table 3.1 lists the names and descriptions of some of the most commonly used functions along with the name of the standard file to `#include` in order to have access to each function. A list of standard library functions appears in Appendix C.

**Listing 3.5**   Illustration of the use of the C++ `sqrt` function

```cpp
// File: squareRoot.cpp
// Performs three square root computations

#include <cmath>            // sqrt function
#include <iostream>         // i/o functions
using namespace std;

int main()
{
   float first;             // input: one of two data values
   float second;            // input: second of two data values
   float answer;            // output: a square root value

   // Get first number and display its square root.
   cout << "Enter the first number: ";
   cin >> first;
   answer = sqrt(first);
   cout << "The square root of the first number is "
        << answer << endl;

   // Get second number and display its square root.
   cout << "Enter the second number: ";
   cin >> second;
   answer = sqrt(second);
   cout << "The square root of the second number is "
        << answer << endl;

   // Display the square root of the sum of first and second.
   answer = sqrt(first + second);
   cout << "The square root of the sum of both numbers is "
        << answer << endl;
   return 0;
}
```

```
Enter the first number: 9
The square root of the first number is 3
Enter the second number: 25
The square root of the second number is 5
The square root of the sum of both numbers is 5.83095
```

If one of the functions in Table 3.1 is called with a numeric argument that is not of the argument type listed, the argument value is converted to the required type before it is used. Conversions of type `int` or type `float` to type double cause no problems, but a conversion of type `float` or type double to

**Table 3.1** Some Mathematical Library Functions

| Function | Standard Library | Purpose: Example | Argument(s) | Result |
|---|---|---|---|---|
| abs(x) | <cstdlib> | Returns the absolute value of its integer argument: if x is -5, abs(x) is 5 | int | int |
| ceil(x) | <cmath> | Returns the smallest integral value that is not less than x: if x is 45.23, ceil(x) is 46.0 | double | double |
| cos(x) | <cmath> | Returns the cosine of angle x: if x is 0.0, cos(x) is 1.0 | double (radians) | double |
| exp(x) | <cmath> | Returns $e^x$ where e = 2.71828...: if x is 1.0, exp(x) is 2.71828 | double | double |
| fabs(x) | <cmath> | Returns the absolute value of its type double argument: if x is -8.432, fabs(x) is 8.432 | double | double |
| floor(x) | <cmath> | Returns the largest integral value that is not greater than x: if x is 45.23, floor(x) is 45.0 | double | double |
| log(x) | <cmath> | Returns the natural logarithm of x for x > 0.0: if x is 2.71828, log(x) is 1.0 | double | double |
| log10(x) | <cmath> | Returns the base-10 logarithm of x for x > 0.0: if x is 100.0, log10(x) is 2.0 | double | double |
| pow(x, y) | <cmath> | Returns $x^y$. If x is negative, y must be integral: if x is 0.16 and y is 0.5, pow(x, y) is 0.4 | double, double | double |
| sin(x) | <cmath> | Returns the sine of angle x: if x is 1.5708, sin(x) is 1.0 | double (radians) | double |
| sqrt(x) | <cmath> | Returns the non-negative square root of x ($\sqrt{x}$) for x $\geq$ 0.0: if x is 2.25, sqrt(x) is 1.5 | double | double |
| tan(x) | <cmath> | Returns the tangent of angle x: if x is 0.0, tan(x) is 0.0 | double (radians) | double |

type int leads to the loss of any fractional part, just as in a mixed-type assignment. For example, if we call the abs function (in library cstdlib) with an argument value of -3.47, the argument is converted to -3 and the result returned is the type int value 3. For this reason, there is another absolute value function (fabs in library cmath) for floating-point arguments.

Most of the functions in Table 3.1 perform common mathematical computations. The arguments for log and log10 must be positive; the argument for sqrt cannot be negative. The arguments for sin, cos, and tan must be expressed in radians, not in degrees.

## EXAMPLE 3.2

We can use the C++ functions **sqrt** and **pow** to compute the roots of a quadratic equation in x of the form

$$ax^2 + bx + c = 0.$$

These two roots are defined as

$$root_1 = \frac{-b + \sqrt{b^2 - 4ac}}{2a} \qquad root_2 = \frac{-b - \sqrt{b^2 - 4ac}}{2a}$$

when the *discriminant* $(b^2 - 4ac)$ is greater than zero. If we assume that this is the case, we can use these assignment statements to assign values to **root1** and **root2**.

```
// Compute 2 roots, root1 & root2, for discriminant values > 0.
disc = pow(b, 2) - 4.0 * a * c;
root1 = (-b + sqrt(disc)) / (2.0 * a);
root2 = (-b - sqrt(disc)) / (2.0 * a);
```

## EXAMPLE 3.3

If we know the lengths of two sides (*b* and *c*) of a triangle and the angle between them in degrees (α) (see Figure 3.3), we can compute the length of the third side, *a*, by using the formula

$$a^2 = b^2 + c^2 - 2bc(\cos(\alpha))$$

To use the **cmath** library cosine function (**cos**), we must express its argument angle in radians instead of degrees. To convert an angle from degrees to radians, we multiply the angle by π/180. If we assume **PI** represents the constant π, the assignment statement that follows computes the length of the unknown side.

```
a = sqrt(pow(b,2) + pow(c,2)
    - 2 * b * c * cos(alpha * PI / 180.0));
```

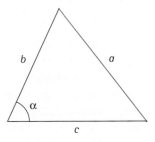

**Figure 3.3**   Triangle with unknown side *a*

## A Look Ahead

C++ allows us to write our own functions such as `findArea` and `findCircum`:

- Function `findArea(r)` returns the area of a circle with radius `r`.
- Function `findCircum(r)` returns the circumference of a circle with radius `r`.

We can reuse these functions in two programs shown earlier in this chapter (see Listings 3.3 and 3.4). The program in Listing 3.3 computes the area and the circumference of a circle. The statements

```
area = findArea(radius);
circum = findCircum(radius);
```

can be used to find these values. The expression part for each of the assignment statements is a function call with argument `radius` (the circle radius). The result returned by each function execution is assigned to the variable listed to the left of the = (assignment) operator.

For the flat washer program (Listing 3.4), we can use the statement

```
rimArea = findArea(edgeRadius) - findArea(holeRadius);
```

to compute the rim area for a washer. This statement is clearer than the one shown in the original program. We show how to write these functions in Section 3.5.

## EXERCISES FOR SECTION 3.2

### Self-Check

1. Rewrite the following mathematical expressions using C++ functions:

   **a.** $\sqrt{u} + v \times$          **c.** $\sqrt{(x - y}$

   **b.** $\log_e (x^y)$          **d.** $\left| a/c - wz \right|$

2. Evaluate the following:

   **a.**  `floor(16.2)`

   **b.**  `floor(16.7 + 0.5)`

   **c.**  `ceil(-9.2) * pow(4.0, 3)`

   **d.**  `sqrt(fabs(floor(-24.8)))`

   **e.**  `log10(10000.0)`

Programming

1. Write statements that compute and display the absolute difference of two type `double` variables, $x$ and $y$ ($|x - y|$).

2. Write a complete program that prompts the user for the Cartesian coordinates of two points $(x_1, y_1)$ and $(x_2, y_2)$ and displays the distance between them computed using the following formula:

$$distance = \sqrt{(x_1 - x_2)^2 + (y_1 - y_2)^2}$$

3. Write a program that prompts the user for the lengths of two sides of a triangle and the angle between them (in degrees) and calculates the length of the third side.

# 3.3   Top–Down Design and Structure Charts

**top-down design**
A problem-solving method in which the programmer breaks a problem up into its major subproblems and then solves the subproblems to derive the solution to the original problem.

**structure chart**
A documentation tool that shows the relationships among the subproblems of a problem.

Often the algorithm needed to solve a problem is more complex than those we have seen so far and the programmer has to break up the problem into subproblems to develop the program solution. In attempting to solve a subproblem at one level, we introduce new subproblems at lower levels. This process, called **top-down design**, proceeds from the original problem at the top level to the subproblems at each lower level. The splitting of a problem into its related subproblems is analogous to the process of refining an algorithm. The following case study introduces a documentation tool—the **structure chart**—that will help you to keep track of the relationships among subproblems.

*case study*    Drawing Simple Figures

PROBLEM

You want to draw some simple diagrams on your screen. Two examples are the house and female stick figure shown in Figure 3.4.

ANALYSIS

The house is formed by displaying a triangle without its base on top of a rectangle. The stick figure consists of a circular shape, a triangle, and a triangle without its base. We can draw both figures with four basic components:

**Figure 3.4**   House and stick figure

- a circle
- a base line
- parallel lines
- intersecting lines

## DESIGN

To create the stick figure, you can divide the problem into three subproblems.

> INITIAL ALGORITHM
> 1. Draw a circle.
> 2. Draw a triangle.
> 3. Draw intersecting lines.

> ALGORITHM REFINEMENTS

Because a triangle is not a basic component, you must refine Step 2:

**Step 2 Refinement**
**2.1.** Draw intersecting lines.
**2.2.** Draw a base line.

You can use a structure chart to show the relationship between the original problem and its subproblems (Figure 3.5). The original problem (Level 0) is in the darker color and its three subordinate subproblems are shown at Level 1. The subproblem "Draw a triangle" is also in color because it has its own subproblems (shown at Level 2).

The subproblems appear in both the algorithm and the structure chart. The algorithm, not the structure chart, shows the order in which you carry out each step to solve the problem. The structure chart simply illustrates the subordination of subproblems to each other and to the original problem.

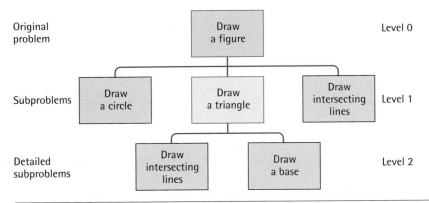

**Figure 3.5** Structure chart for drawing a stick figure

## EXERCISES FOR SECTION 3.3

Self–Check

1. Draw the structure chart for the subproblem of drawing a house (see Figure 3.4).

2. Draw the structure chart for the problem of drawing a rocket ship that consists of a triangle on top of a rectangle that is on top of a second rectangle. The bottom rectangle rests on a triangular base.

3. In which phase of the software development method do you apply top-down design to break the problem into subproblems?

# 3.4 Functions without Arguments

One way that programmers use top-down design in their programs is by designing their own functions. Often a programmer will write one function subprogram for each subproblem in the structure chart. In this section we show how to use and define your own functions, focusing on simple functions that have no arguments and return no value.

As an example of top-down design with functions, you could use the `main` function in Listing 3.6 to draw the stick figure. In that figure, the three algorithm steps are coded as calls to three C++ function subprograms. For example, the statement

```
// Draw a circle.
drawCircle();
```

**Listing 3.6** Function prototypes and `main` function for drawing a stick figure

```
// Draws a stick figure (main function only)

#include <iostream>
using namespace std;

// Functions used  . . .
void drawCircle();     // Draws a circle

void drawTriangle();   // Draws a triangle

void drawIntersect(); // Draws intersecting lines

void drawBase();       // Draws a horizontal line

int main()
{
    // Draw a circle.
    drawCircle();
    // Draw a triangle.
    drawTriangle();
    // Draw intersecting lines.
    drawIntersect();

    return 0;
}
```

in function `main` calls function `drawCircle` to implement the algorithm
step *Draw a Circle.* We call function `drawCircle` just like we call the functions in library `cmath`. The empty parentheses after the function name indicate that `drawCircle` requires no arguments.

---

**Function Call Statement (Function Without Arguments)**

**Form:**    *fname()*;

**Example:**  `drawCircle();`

**Interpretation:**   The function *fname* is activated. After *fname* finishes execution,
the program statement that follows the function call will be executed.

---

## Function Prototypes

Just like other identifiers in C++, a function must be declared before it can be referenced. One way to declare a function is to insert a function prototype before the `main` function. A function prototype tells the C++ compiler the data type of the function, the function name, and information about the arguments that the function expects. The data type of a function is determined by the type of value returned by the function. In Listing 3.6, the prototype for `drawCircle` is written as:

```
void drawCircle();
```

**void** function
A function that does not return a value.

The reserved word `void` indicates that `drawCircle` is a **void function**—that is, its type is `void`—because it doesn't return a value. The empty parentheses after the function name indicate that `drawCircle` has no arguments.

---

### Function Prototype (Function Without Arguments)

**Form:**    *ftype fname()*;

**Example:**  `void skipThree();`

**Interpretation:** The identifier *fname* is declared to be the name of a function. The identifier *ftype* specifies the data type of the function result.

**Note:** *ftype* is **void** if the function does not return a value. The argument list **( )** indicates that the function has no arguments. The function prototype must appear before the first call to the function. We recommend you place all prototypes before function **main**.

---

## Function Definitions

Although the prototype specifies the number of arguments a function takes and the type of its result, it doesn't specify the function operation. To do this, you need to provide a definition for each function subprogram similar to the definition of the `main` function. Listing 3.7 shows the definition for function `drawCircle`.

Listing 3.7    Function `drawCircle`

```
// Draws a circle
void drawCircle()
{
   cout << "    *  " << endl;
   cout << " *    *" << endl;
   cout << "  * *  " << endl;
}
```

The function heading is similar to the function prototype in Listing 3.6 except that it doesn't end with a semicolon. The function body, enclosed in braces, consists of three output statements that cause the computer to display a circular shape. We omit the `return` statement because `drawCircle` doesn't return a result.

The function call statement

```
drawCircle();
```

causes the three output statements to execute. Control returns to the `main` function after the circle shape is displayed.

---

**Function Definition (Function Without Arguments)**

**Syntax:**
```
ftype fname()
{
    local declarations
    executable statements
}
```

**Example:**
```
// Displays a block-letter H
void printH()
{
    cout << "**    **"    << endl;
    cout << "**    **"    << endl;
    cout << "******"      << endl;
    cout << "******"      << endl;
    cout << "**    **"    << endl;
    cout << "**    **"    << endl;
}
```

**Interpretation:** The function *fname* is defined. In the function heading, the identifier *ftype* specifies the data type of the function result. Notice that there are no semicolons after the function heading. The braces enclose the function body. Any identifiers that are declared in the optional *local declarations* are defined only during the execution of the function and can be referenced only within the function. The *executable statements* of the function body describe the data manipulation to be performed by the function.

**Note:** *ftype* is `void` if the function does not return a value. The argument list `( )` indicates that the function has no arguments.

---

Each function body may contain declarations for its own variables. These variables are considered *local* to the function; in other words, they can be referenced only within the function. There will be more on this topic later.

The structure chart in Figure 3.5 shows that the subproblem *Draw a triangle* (Level 1) depends on the solutions to its subordinate subproblems *Draw intersecting lines* and *Draw a base* (both Level 2). Listing 3.8 shows how you can use top-down design to code function `drawTriangle`. Instead of using output statements to display a triangular pattern, the body of function `drawTriangle` calls functions `drawIntersect` and `drawBase` to draw a triangle.

## Placement of Functions in a Program

Listing 3.9 shows the complete program with function subprograms. The subprogram prototypes precede the `main` function (after any `#include` directives) and the subprogram definitions follow the `main` function. The relative order of the function definitions doesn't affect their order of execution; that is determined by the order of execution of the function call statements.

## Program Style    Use of Comments in Function Declarations and Definitions

Listing 3.9 includes several comments. A comment precedes each function and describes its purpose. The same comment follows the prototype declaration. For clarity, the right brace at the end of each function may be followed by a comment, such as

```
// end fname
```

identifying that function.

## Order of Execution of Functions

The prototypes for the function subprograms appear before the `main` function, so the compiler processes the function prototypes before it translates the `main` function. The information in each prototype lets the compiler correctly translate a call to that function. The compiler translates a function call statement as a transfer of control to the function.

After compiling the `main` function, the compiler translates each function subprogram. During translation, when the compiler reaches the end of a function body, it inserts a machine language statement that causes a *transfer of control* back from the function to the calling statement.

**Listing 3.8**    Function `drawTriangle`
___

```
// Draws a triangle
void drawTriangle()
{
     drawIntersect();
     drawBase();
}
```
___

**Listing 3.9** Program to draw a stick figure

```cpp
// File: stickFigure.cpp
// Draws a stick figure

#include <iostream>
using namespace std;

// Functions used  . . .
void drawCircle();     // Draws a circle

void drawTriangle();   // Draws a triangle

void drawIntersect();  // Draws intersecting lines

void drawBase();       // Draws a horizontal line

int main()
{
   // Draw a circle.
   drawCircle();

   // Draw a triangle.
   drawTriangle();

   // Draw intersecting lines.
   drawIntersect();

   return 0;
}

// Draws a circle
void drawCircle()
{
   cout << "   *   " << endl;
   cout << " *   *" << endl;
   cout << " * * " << endl;
}  // end drawCircle

// Draws a triangle
void drawTriangle()
{
   drawIntersect();
   drawBase();
}  // end drawTriangle
```

(continued)

**Listing 3.9**    Program to draw a stick figure  (continued)

```
// Draws intersecting lines
void drawIntersect()
{
    cout << "    /\\   " << endl;
    cout << "   /  \\ " << endl;
    cout << "  /    \\" << endl;
}   // end drawIntersect

// Draws a horizontal line
void drawBase()
{
    cout << " _ _ _ _ _ _" << endl;
}   // end drawBase
```

Figure 3.6 shows the `main` function and function `drawCircle` of the stick figure program in separate areas of memory. Although the C++ statements are shown in Figure 3.6, it is actually the object code corresponding to each statement that is stored in memory.

When we run the program, the first statement in the `main` function is the first statement executed (the call to `drawCircle` in Figure 3.6). When the computer executes a function call statement, it transfers control to the function that is referenced (indicated by the top arrow in Figure 3.6). The computer allocates any memory that may be needed for variables declared in the function and then performs the statements in the function body. After the last statement in function `drawCircle` is executed, control returns to the `main` function (indicated by the bottom arrow in Figure 3.6), and the computer releases any memory that was allocated to the function. After the return to the `main` function, the next statement is executed (the call to `drawTriangle`).

## Advantages of Using Function Subprograms

There are many advantages to using function subprograms. Their availability changes the way an individual programmer organizes the solution to a

```
in main function

drawCircle();          void drawCircle()
                       {
drawTriangle();            cout <<...
                           cout <<...
drawIntersect();           cout <<...
                           return to calling function
                       }//end drawCircle
```

**Figure 3.6**    Flow of control between `main` function and subprogram

programming problem. For a team of programmers working together on a large program, subprograms make it easier to apportion programming tasks: Each programmer will be responsible for a particular set of functions. Finally, subprograms simplify programming tasks because existing functions can be reused as the building blocks for new programs.

## Procedural Abstraction

Function subprograms allow us to remove from the main function the code that provides the detailed solution to a subproblem. Because these details are provided in the function subprograms and not in the main function, we can write the main function as a sequence of function call statements as soon as we have specified the initial algorithm and before we refine any of the steps. We should delay writing the function for an algorithm step until we have finished refining that step. With this approach to program design, called **procedural abstraction**, we defer implementation details until we're ready to write an individual function subprogram. Focusing on one function at a time is much easier than trying to write the complete program all at once.

**procedural abstraction**
A programming technique in which the main function consists of a sequence of function calls and each function is implemented separately.

## Reuse of Function Subprograms

Another advantage of using function subprograms is that functions can be executed more than once in a program. For example, function drawInter-sect is called twice in Listing 3.9 (once by drawTriangle and once by the main function). Each time drawIntersect is called, the list of output statements in drawIntersect is executed and a pair of intersecting lines is drawn. Without functions, the output statements that draw the lines would

## EXAMPLE 3.4

Let's write a function (Listing 3.10) that displays instructions to a user of the program that computes the area and the circumference of a circle (see Listing 3.3). This simple function demonstrates one of the benefits of separating the statements that display user instructions from the **main** function body: Editing these instructions is simplified when they are separated from the code that performs the calculations.

If you place the prototype for function instruct

```
void instruct();
```

just before the **main** function, you can insert the function call statement

```
instruct();
```

as the first executable statement in the **main** function. The rest of the **main** function consists of the executable statements shown earlier. We show the output displayed by calling function **instruct** at the bottom of Listing 3.10.

Listing 3.10   Function `instruct`

```cpp
// Displays instructions to user of area/circumference
program

void instruct()
{
    cout << "This program computes the area and " << endl;
    cout << "circumference of a circle. " << endl << endl;
    cout << "To use this program, enter the radius of the "
         << endl;
    cout << "circle after the prompt" << endl << endl;
    cout << "Enter the circle radius: " << endl << endl;
    cout << "The circumference will be computed in the same
"
         << endl;
    cout << "units of measurement as the radius. The area "
         << endl;
    cout << "will be computed in the same units squared."
         << endl << endl;
}  // end instruct
```

```
This program computes the area and
circumference of a circle.

To use this program, enter the radius of
the circle after the prompt

Enter the circle radius:

The circumference will be computed in the same
units of measurement as the radius. The area
will be computed in the same units squared.
```

be listed twice in the `main` function, thereby increasing the `main` function's length and the chance of error.

Finally, once you have written and tested a function, you can use it in other programs or functions. The functions in the stick figure program, for example, could easily be reused in programs that draw other diagrams.

## Displaying User Instructions

The simple functions introduced in this section have limited capability. Without the ability to pass information into or out of a function, we can use functions only to display multiple lines of program output, such as instructions to a program user or a title page or a special message that precedes a program's results.

## EXERCISES FOR SECTION 3.4

### Self-Check

1. Assume that you have functions printH, printI, printM, and printO, each of which draws a large block letter (for example, printO draws a block letter O). What is the effect of executing the following main function?

```
int main()
{
    printO();
    cout << endl;
    printH();
    skipThree(); // see Programming Exercise 1

    printH();
    cout << endl;
    printI();
    cout << endl;
    printM();
}
```

2. Draw a structure chart for a program with three function subprograms that displays HI  HO in a vertical column of block letters.

3. If you write a program followed by a collection of functions, do the functions execute in the order in which they are listed before the main function (the function prototypes), the order in which they are listed after the main function (the function definitions), or neither? If your answer is neither, what determines the order in which the functions execute?

### Programming

1. Write a function that skips three lines when it is called.

2. Write a function drawParallel that draws parallel lines and a function drawRectangle that uses drawParallel and drawBase to draw a rectangle.

3. Write a complete program for the problem described in Self-Check Exercise 2.

4. Rewrite the miles-to-kilometers conversion program shown in Figure 2.1, so that it includes a function that displays instructions to its user.

5. Show the revised program that calls function instruct for the circle area and circumference problem.

6. Write a `main` method that solves Self-Check Exercise 2 for Section 3.3. Assume you have functions `drawRectangle` (see Programming Exercise 2), `drawTriangle`, and `drawIntersect`.

## 3.5   Functions with Input Arguments

Programmers use functions like building blocks to construct large programs. Functions are more like Lego blocks (Figure 3.7) than the smooth-sided wooden blocks you might have used as a young child to demonstrate your potential as a budding architect. Your first blocks were big and did not link together, so buildings over a certain size would topple over. Legos, in contrast, have one surface with little protrusions and one surface with little cups. By placing the protrusions into the cups, you could build rather elaborate structures.

What does this have to do with programming? Simple functions such as `drawCircle` and `instruct` are like wooden blocks. They can display information on the screen, but they are not particularly useful. To be able to construct more interesting programs, we must provide functions with "protrusions" and "cups" so they can be easily interconnected.

The arguments of a function are used to carry information into the function subprogram from the main function (or from another function subprogram) or to return multiple results computed by a function subprogram. Arguments that carry information into the function subprogram are called **input arguments**; arguments that return results are called **output arguments**. We can also return a single result from a function by executing a `return` statement in the function body. We study functions with input arguments in this section and functions with output arguments in Chapter 6.

**input arguments**
Arguments that pass information into a function.

**output arguments**
Arguments that return results from a function.

Figure 3.7   Lego blocks

The use of arguments is a very important concept in programming. Arguments make function subprograms more versatile because they enable a function to manipulate different data each time it is called. For example, in the statement

```
rimArea = findArea(edgeRadius) - findArea(holeRadius);
```

each call to function `findArea` calculates the area of a circle with a different radius.

## EXAMPLE 3.5

Function `drawCircleChar` (Listing 3.11) is an improved version of function `drawCircle` that enables the caller to specify the character drawn in the circle. When function `drawCircleChar` is called, the character that is its actual argument is passed into the function and is substituted for the formal parameter `symbol` (type `char`). The actual argument character is displayed wherever `symbol` appears in an output statement.

The function call

```
drawCircleChar('*');
```

draws the stick figure head shown earlier in Figure 3.4. Figure 3.8 shows the execution of this function call. You can use the function call

```
drawCircleChar('#');
```

to display the same circle shape, but with the character # displayed instead of *.

You must provide a prototype that declares `drawCircleChar` before function `main`. The prototype should indicate that `drawCircleChar` is type `void` (returns no result) and has an argument of type `char`. The prototype follows.

```
drawCircleChar(char);
```

You only need to specify the data type of the formal parameter, not its name, but you may specify the name if you like.

Listing 3.11   Function `drawCircleChar`

```cpp
// Draws a circle using the character specified by symbol
void drawCircleChar(char symbol)
{
   cout << "   " << symbol << endl;
   cout << " " << symbol << "   " << symbol << endl;
   cout << "   " << symbol << " " << symbol << endl;
}  // end drawCircle
```

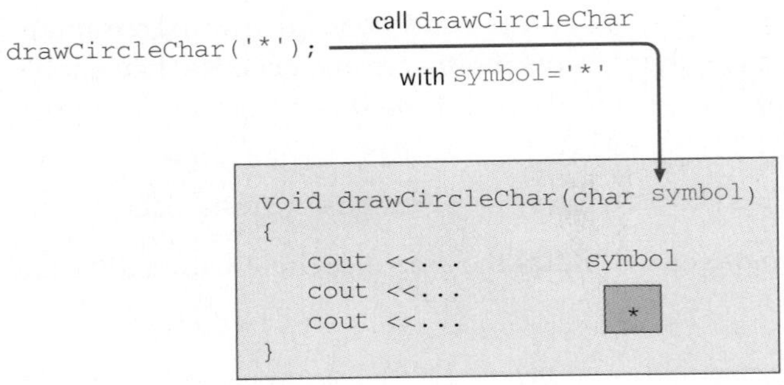

**Figure 3.8** Execution of `drawCircleChar('*')`

## void Functions with Input Arguments

In the last section, we used `void` functions such as `instruct` and `drawCircle` to display several lines of program output. Recall that a `void` function does not return a result. The next example shows a new function, `drawCircleChar`, that has an input argument.

## Functions with Input Arguments and a Single Result

Next we show how to write functions with input arguments that return a single result, as diagrammed in Figure 3.9. We can reference these functions in expressions just like the library functions described in Section 3.2.

Let's reconsider the problem of finding the area and circumference of a circle using functions with just one argument. Section 3.2 described functions `findCircum` and `findArea`, each of which has a single input argument (a circle radius) and returns a single result (the circumference or area). Listing 3.12 shows these functions.

Each function heading begins with the word `float`, indicating that the function result is a real number. Both function bodies consist of a single `return` statement. When either function executes, the expression in its `return` statement is evaluated and returned as the function result. If `PI` is the constant `3.14159`, calling function `findCircum` causes the expression `2.0 * 3.14159 * r` to be evaluated. To evaluate this expression, C++ substitutes the actual argument used in the function call for the formal parameter `r`.

For the function call below

```
radius = 10.0;
circum = findCircum(radius);
```

the actual argument, `radius`, has a value of `10.0`, so the function result is `62.8318` (`2.0 * 3.14159 * 10.0`). The function result is assigned to `circum`. Figure 3.10 shows the execution of this function call.

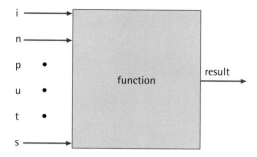

**Figure 3.9**  Function with input arguments and one result

**Listing 3.12**  Functions `findCircum` and `findArea`

```
// Computes the circumference of a circle with radius r.
// Pre: r is defined and is > 0.
//      PI is a constant.
//      Library cmath is included.
float findCircum(float r)
{
    return (2.0 * PI * r);
}


// Computes the area of a circle with radius r.
// Pre:  r is defined and is > 0.
//       PI is a constant.
//       Library cmath is included.
float findArea(float r)
{
    return (PI * pow(r, 2));
}
```

The function call to `findArea`

```
area = findArea(radius);
```

causes C++ to evaluate the expression `3.14159 * pow(r, 2)`, where pow is
a library function (part of cmath) that raises its first argument to the power
indicated by its second argument (`pow(r, 2)` computes r2). When `radius`
is `10.0`, pow returns `100.0` and `findArea` returns a result of `314.59`, which
is assigned to `area`. This example shows that a user-defined function can
call a C++ library function.

You must provide prototypes that declare these functions before function `main`. The prototypes should indicate that each function is type `float`

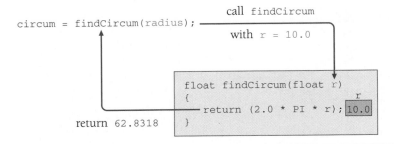

**Figure 3.10**   Execution of `circum = findCircum(radius);`

(returns a type `float` result) and has a formal parameter of type `float`. The prototypes follow.

```
float findArea(float);
float findCircum(float);
```

Like the function definition, the function prototype specifies the function type and its name. In the formal parameter list, you need to specify only the formal parameter types, not their names, but you can specify both. The function prototype, but not the heading, ends with a semicolon. Because function prototypes and function headings are so similar, we recommend that you write one of them first, and edit a copy of it (using your

---

**Function Definition (Input Arguments and One Result)**

**Syntax:**
```
// function interface comment
ftype fname( formal-parameter-declaration-list)
{
    local variable declarations
    executable statements
}
```

**Example:**
```
// Finds the cube of its argument.
// Pre: n is defined.
int cube(int n)
{
    return (n * n * n);
} // end cube
```

**Interpretation:** The function *fname* is defined. In the function heading, the identifier *ftype* specifies the data type of the function result. The *formal-parameter-declaration-list*, enclosed in parentheses, declares the type and name of each function parameter. Commas separate the parameters. Notice that there are no semicolons after the function heading. The braces enclose the function body. Any identifiers that are declared in the optional *local declarations* are defined only during the execution of the function and can be referenced only within the function. The *executable statements* of the function body describe the data manipulation to be performed by the function in order to compute the result value. Execution of a **return** statement causes the function to return control to the statement that called it. The function returns the value of the expression following **return** as its result.

**Note:** *ftype* is **void** if the function does not return a value. The argument list **( )** indicates that the function has no arguments.

---

**Function Prototype (With Parameters)**

**Form:**       *ftype fname(formal-parameter-type-list);*

**Example:**  `int cube(int);`

**Interpretation:** The identifier *fname* is declared as the name of a function whose type is *ftype*. This declaration provides all the information that the C++ compiler needs to know to translate correctly all references to the function. The function definition will be provided after the **main** function. The *formal-parameter-type-list* enclosed in parentheses shows the data type of each formal parameter. Commas separate the data types. A semicolon terminates the prototype.

**Note:** C++ permits the specification of formal parameter names in function prototypes, as in

`int cube(int n);`

In this case, the heading of the function definition and the prototype should be identical except that the prototype ends with a semicolon.

---

word-processor) to create the other. Make sure you perform whatever editing operations are required—that is, remove (or add) a semicolon and remove (or add) the formal parameter names.

## Program Style       Function Interface Comments

The comments that begin each function in Listing 3.12 contain all the information required in order to use the function. The function interface comments begin with a statement of what the function does. Then the line

    // Pre: r is defined.

describes the **precondition**—the condition that should be true before the function is called. You may also want to include a statement describing the **postcondition**—the condition that must be true after the function executes.

**precondition**
A condition assumed to be true before a function call.

**postcondition**
A condition assumed to be true after a function executes.

completes execution, if some details of this postcondition are not included in the initial statement of the function's purpose.

We recommend that you begin all function definitions in this way. The function interface comments provide valuable documentation to other programmers who might want to reuse your functions in a new program.

## Program Style        Problem Inputs versus Input Parameters

Make sure you understand the distinction between *problem inputs* and *input parameters*. *Problem inputs* are variables that receive their data from the program user through execution of an input statement. *Input parameters* receive their data through execution of a function call statement. Beginning programmers sometimes make the mistake of attempting to read a data value for a function's input parameter in the function body. The data passed to an input parameter must be defined *before* the function is called, not *after*.

## EXAMPLE 3.6

Function `scale` (Listing 3.13) multiplies its first argument (a real number) by 10 raised to the power indicated by its second argument (an integer). For example, the function call

```
scale(2.5, 2)
```

returns the value `250.0` ($2.5 \times 10^2$). The function call

```
scale(2.5, -2)
```

returns the value `0.025` ($2.5 \times 10^{-2}$).
In function `scale`, the statement

```
scaleFactor = pow(10, n);
```

calls function `pow` to raise `10` to the power specified by the second formal parameter n. Local variable `scaleFactor`, defined only during the execution of the function, stores this value. The `return` statement defines the function result as the product of the first formal parameter, `x`, and `scaleFactor`.

Listing 3.14 shows a very simple **main** function written to test function `scale`. The output statement calls function `scale` and displays the function result after it is returned. The arrows drawn in Listing 3.14 show the information flow between the two actual arguments and formal parameters. To clarify the information flow, we omitted the function interface comment. The argument list correspondence is shown below.

| Actual Argument | corresponds to | Formal Parameter |
|---|---|---|
| num1 | | x |
| num2 | | n |

## Functions with Multiple Arguments

Functions `findArea` and `findCircum` each have a single argument. We can also define functions with multiple arguments.

**Listing 3.13**   Function `scale`

```
// Multiplies its first argument by the power of 10
// specified by its second argument.
// Pre : x and n are defined and library cmath is
//       included.
float scale(float x, int n)
{
    float scaleFactor;      // local variable
    scaleFactor = pow(10, n);
    return (x * scaleFactor);
}
```

**Listing 3.14**   Testing function `scale`

```
// File testScale.cpp
// Tests function scale.

#include <iostream>
#include <cmath>
using namespace std;

// Function prototype
float scale(float, int);

int main()
{
    float num1;
    int num2;
    // Get values for num1 and num2
    cout << "Enter a real number: ";
    cin >> num1;
    cout << "Enter an integer: ";
    cin >> num2;

    // Call scale and display result.
    cout << "Result of call to function scale is "
         << scale(num1, num2)        // actual arguments
         << endl;
    return 0;                        // information flow
}
float scale(float x, int n)          // formal parameters
```

(continued)

**Listing 3.14** Testing function `scale` (continued)

```
{
        float scaleFactor;              // local variable
        scaleFactor = pow(10, n);
        return (x * scaleFactor);
}
```

```
Enter a real number: 2.5
Enter an integer: -2
Result of call to function scale is 0.025
```

## Argument/Parameter List Correspondence

When using multiple-argument functions, you must be sure to include the correct number of arguments in the function call. Also, the order of the actual arguments used in the function call must correspond to the order of the formal parameters listed in the function prototype or heading.

Finally, if the function is to return meaningful results, assignment of each actual argument to the corresponding formal parameter must not cause any loss of information. Usually, you should use an actual argument of the same data type as the corresponding formal parameter, although this is not always essential. For example, the <cmath> library description indicates that both parameters of the function pow are of type double. Function scale calls pow with two actual arguments of type int. This call doesn't cause a problem because there is no loss of information when an int is assigned to a type double variable. If you pass an actual argument of type float or double to a formal parameter of type int, loss of the fractional part of the actual argument would likely lead to an unexpected function result. Next, we summarize these constraints on the **number**, **order**, and **type** (**not**) of input arguments.

## Argument/Parameter List Correspondence

- The **number** of actual arguments used in a call to a function must be the same as the number of formal parameters listed in the function prototype.
- The **order** of arguments in the lists determines correspondence. The first actual argument corresponds to the first formal parameter, the second actual argument corresponds to the second formal parameter, and so on.
- Each actual argument must be of a data type that can be assigned to the corresponding formal parameter with no unexpected loss of information.

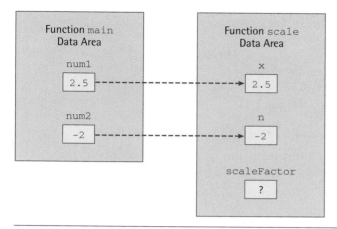

**Figure 3.11**   Data areas after call `scale(num1, num2);`

## The Function Data Area

Each time a function call is executed, an area of memory is allocated for storage of that function's data. Included in the function data area are storage cells for its formal parameters and any local variables that may be declared in the function. The function data area is always lost when the function terminates; it is re-created empty (all values undefined) when the function is called again.

Figure 3.11 shows the `main` function data area and the data area for function `scale` after the function call `scale(num1, num2)` executes. The values `2.5` and `-2` are passed into the formal parameters `x` and `n`, respectively. The local variable, `scaleFactor`, is initially undefined; the execution of the function body changes the value of this variable to `0.01`.

The local variable `scaleFactor` can be accessed only in function `scale`. Similarly, the variables `num1` and `num2` declared in function `main` can be accessed only in function `main`. If you want a function subprogram to use the value stored in `num1`, you must provide `num1` as an actual argument when you call the function.

## Testing Functions Using Drivers

A function is an independent program module, and as such it can be tested separately from the program that uses it. To run such a test, you should write a short **driver** function that defines the function arguments, calls the function, and displays the value returned. For example, the function `main` in Listing 3.14 acts as a driver to test function `scale`.

**driver**
A short function written to test another function by defining its arguments, calling it, and displaying its result.

## EXERCISES FOR SECTION 3.5

### Self-Check

1. Evaluate each of the following:
   a. `scale(2.55 + 5.23, 4 / 2)`
   b. `findCircum(3.0)`
   c. `findArea(2.0)`
   d. `scale(findArea(5.0), -1)`

2. Explain the effect of reversing the function arguments in the call to `scale` shown in Example 3.6—that is, `scale(num2, num1)`.

3. How does the use of function arguments make it possible to write larger, more useful programs?

4. Write the function prototypes for functions `drawCircleChar`, `findCircum`, and `findArea`.

### Programming

1. Revise the flat-washer program (Listing 3.4) to use function subprograms `findArea`, `findRimArea`, `findUnitWeight`, and `instruct`. Show the complete program.

2. Write a function that calculates the elapsed time in minutes between a start time and an end time expressed as integers on a 24-hour clock (8:30 P.M. = 2030). You need to deal only with end times occurring later on the same day as the start time. Also write a driver program to test your function.

3. Assume your friend has solved Programming Exercise 2. Write another function that uses your friend's function to calculate the speed (km/h) one must average to reach a certain destination by a designated time. Function inputs include same-day departure and arrival times as integers on a 24-hour clock and the distance to the destination in kilometers. Also write a driver program to test your function.

## 3.6   Scope of Names

**scope of a name**
The region in a program where a particular meaning of a name is visible or can be referenced.

The **scope of a name** refers to the region in a program where a particular meaning of a name is visible or can be referenced. For example, we stated earlier that variable num1 (declared in main in Listing 3.14) can be referenced only in function main, which means that that is its scope. Let's consider the names in the program outline shown in Listing 3.15. The identifiers MAX and LIMIT are defined as constants and their scope begins at their definition and continues to the end of the source file. This means that all three functions can access the constants MAX and LIMIT.

The scope of the function subprogram name funTwo begins with its prototype and continues to the end of the source file. This means that function funTwo can be called by functions one, main, and itself. The situation is different for function one because one is also used as a formal parameter name in function funTwo. Therefore, function one can be called by the main function and itself but not by function funTwo. This shows how you can use the same name for different purposes in different functions—generally not a good idea because it is confusing to human readers of the program, but C++ has no problem handling it.

All of the formal parameters and local variables in Listing 3.15 are visible only from their declaration to the closing brace of the function in which they are declared. For example, from the line that is marked with the comment // header 1 to the line marked // end one, the identifier anArg means an integer parameter in the data area of function one. From the line with the comment // header 2 through the line marked // end funTwo, this name refers to a character parameter in the data area of funTwo. In the rest of the file, the name anArg is not visible.

**Listing 3.15**  Outline of program for studying scope of names

```
void one(int anArg, double second);     // prototype 1

int funTwo(int one, char anArg);        // prototype 2

const int MAX = 950;
const int LIMIT = 200;

int main()
{
   int localVar;
   . . .
} // end main

void one(int anArg, double second)      // header 1
{
   int oneLocal;                        // local 1
   . . .
} // end one

int funTwo(int one, char anArg)         // header 2
{
   int localVar;                        // local 2
   . . .
} // end funTwo
```

Table 3.2 shows which identifiers are visible within each of the three functions.

**Table 3.2** Scope of Names in Listing 3.15

| Name | Visible in One | Visible in funTwo | Visible in main |
|---|---|---|---|
| MAX | yes | yes | yes |
| LIMIT | yes | yes | yes |
| main | yes | yes | yes |
| localVar (in main) | no | no | yes |
| one (the function) | yes | no | yes |
| anArg (int parameter) | yes | no | no |
| second | yes | no | no |
| oneLocal | yes | no | no |
| funTwo | yes | yes | yes |
| one (formal parameter) | no | yes | no |
| anArg (char parameter) | no | yes | no |
| localVar (in funTwo) | no | yes | no |

## EXERCISES FOR SECTION 3.6

Self-Check

1. Develop a table similar to Table 3.2 for the identifiers declared in Listing 3.14.

2. Develop a table similar to Table 3.2 for the program below.

```
#include <iostream>
using namespace std;

const float PI = 3.14159;

// function prototypes
float findCircum(float);
float findArea(float);

int main()
{
    float radius;
    float circumf, area;
```

```
    cout << "Enter radius: ";
    cin >> radius;

    circumf = findCircum(radius);
    area = findArea(radius);

    cout << "For a circle with radius " << radius
         << ", area is " << area
         << ", circumference is " << circumf << endl;

    return 0;
}

float findCircum(float r)
{
    return (2.0 * PI * r);
}

float findArea(float r)
{
    return (PI * pow(r, 2));
}
```

# 3.7 Extending C++ through Classes: Using Class `string`

You have seen the advantages of procedural abstraction and the use of functions as program building blocks. C++ also facilitates **data abstraction** through its class feature, which enables users to define new data types and their associated operations. In this section we study the `string` class, which is part of the C++ standard library. In Chapter 10, we show how to define your own classes.

**data abstraction** Modeling real-world data using the data types available in a programming language or additional class types.

## The `string` Class

In Section 2.3 we introduced the C++ `string` class, which defines a new data type `string` and many operators for `string` objects. Two attributes of a `string` object are the character sequence it stores and the length of that sequence. Some of the common operators you have seen so far (`<<`, `>>`, `=`, `+`) can be used with `string` objects. Listing 3.16 illustrates how we use these familiar operators and some new ones with `string` objects as operands.

**Listing 3.16** Illustrating `string` operations

```cpp
// File: stringOperations.cpp
// Illustrates string operations

#include <iostream>
#include <string>
using namespace std;

int main()
{
    string firstName, lastName;   // inputs - first and
                                  //          last names
    string wholeName;             // output - whole name
    string greeting = "Hello ";   // output - a greeting
                                  //          string

    // Read first and last names.
    cout << "Enter your first name: ";
    cin >> firstName;
    cout << "Enter your last name: ";
    cin >> lastName;

    // Join names in whole name
    wholeName = firstName + " " + lastName;

    // Display results
    cout << greeting << wholeName << '!' << endl;
    cout << "You have " << (wholeName.length() - 1)
        << " letters in your name." << endl;

    // Display initials
    cout << "Your initials are " << firstName.at(0)
        << lastName.at(0) << endl;

    return 0;
}
```

```
Enter your first name: Caryn
Enter your last name: Jackson
Hello Caryn Jackson!
You have 12 letters in your name.
Your initials are CJ
```

## Declaring **string** Objects

The declarations

```
string firstName, lastName;    // inputs - first and last
                               //          names
string wholeName;              // output - whole name
```

allocate storage for three `string` objects that initially contain empty strings (a string with zero characters). You can store new data in these strings through a string assignment or by reading a string value typed at the keyboard. You can also store data in a `string` object when you declare it. The statement

```
string greeting = "Hello ";  // output - a greeting string
```

stores the string `"Hello "` in the `string` object `greeting`.

## Reading and Displaying **string** Objects

In Section 2.4, we saw that the extraction operator can be used with `string` operands. The statement

```
cin >> firstName;
```

reads keyboard data into `firstName`. It stores in `firstName` all data characters up to (but not including) the first blank or return. You must not enclose these characters in quotes. The statement

```
cout << greeting << wholeName << '!' << endl;
```

displays `string` objects `greeting` and `wholeName` followed by the character value `'!'`.

What if you want to read a data string that contains a blank? For example, you may want to read the characters `Van Winkle` into `lastName`. You can do this using the `getline` function. For example, the statement

```
getline(cin, lastName, '\n');
```

reads into `string` object `lastName` all characters typed at the keyboard (stream `cin`) up to (but not including) the character `'\n'`. The escape sequence `'\n'` is a text control character (see Table 2.5) and it represents the *newline* character. You enter this character at the keyboard by pressing RETURN or ENTER. (On some systems, you may need to press ENTER twice.)

You can specify another terminator character by changing the third argument. For example, use `'*'` as the third argument to make the symbol `*` the terminator character. In this case, you can type your data string over multiple lines, and it will not terminate until you enter the symbol `*`. All data characters entered, including any newline characters (but not the `*`), will be stored in the `string` object used as the second argument.

## String Assignment and Concatenation

The assignment statement

```
wholeName = firstName + " " + lastName;
```

stores in `wholeName` the new string formed by joining the three strings that are operands of the operator +, which means to join, or *concatenate*, when its operands are strings. Notice that we insert a space between string objects `firstName` and `lastName` by joining the string value `" "`, not the character value `' '`. Remember to use quotes, not apostrophes, to enclose string values in C++ statements.

## Operator Overloading

**operator overloading**
The ability of an operator to perform different operations depending on the data type of its operands.

Until now, the operator + has always meant addition, but now we see that it means concatenation when its operands are `string` objects. We use the term **operator overloading** to indicate that an operator's function may vary depending on its operands. Operator overloading is a very powerful concept because it allows C++ to give multiple meanings to a single operator; C++ can determine the correct interpretation of the operator from the way we use it.

## Dot Notation: Calling Functions `length` and `at`

Listing 3.16 also uses member functions `length` and `at` from the `string` class. To call these functions (and most member functions), we use *dot notation*. Rather than passing an object as an argument to a member function, we write the name of the object, a dot (or period), and then the function to be applied to this object. The function reference

```
wholeName.length()
```

applies member function `length` (no arguments) to string object `whole-Name`. This call to function `length` returns a value of 13 (`wholeName` contains the 13-character string `"Caryn Jackson"`); however, we subtract one before printing the result because of the blank character between the first and last names:

```
cout << "You have " << (wholeName.length() - 1)
    << " letters in your name." << endl;
```

The expression

```
firstName.at(0)
```

retrieves the character in `firstName` that is at position 0, where we number the characters from the left, starting with 0 for the first character, 1 for the second, and so on. By this numbering system, the last character in `string` object `whole-Name` (the letter n) is at position `wholeName.length() - 1`, or position 12.

---

**Dot Notation**

**Syntax:** *object. function-call*

**Example:** `firstName.at(0)`

**Interpretation:** The member function specified in the *function-call* is applied to *object*.

**Note:** The member function may change the attributes of *object*.

---

## Member Functions for Word-Processing Operations

We would like to be able to perform on a `string` object all the operations that are available on most word processors. C++ provides member functions for searching for a string (`find`), inserting a string at a particular position (`insert`), deleting a portion of a string (`erase`), and replacing part of a string with another string (`replace`). We illustrate some simple examples of these functions next.

For the strings `firstName`, `lastName`, and `wholeName` in Listing 3.16, the expression

```
wholeName.find(firstName)
```

returns 0 (the position of the first character of "Caryn" in "Caryn Jackson") and the expression

```
wholeName.find(lastName)
```

returns 6 (the position of the first character of "Jackson" in "Caryn Jackson").

The first statement below inserts a string at the beginning of `string` object `wholeName` (at position 0) and the second statement inserts a string in the middle of `wholeName` (at new position 10).

```
wholeName.insert(0, "Ms. ");     // Change to
                                 // "Ms. Caryn Jackson"
wholeName.insert(10, "Heather "); // Change to
                                 // "Ms. Caryn Heather Jackson"
```

Notice that member function `insert` changes the string stored in object `wholeName`.

You can use the following statement to change the middle name from Heather to Amy:

```
wholeName.replace(10, 7, "Amy"); // Change to
                                 // "Ms. Caryn Amy Jackson"
```

This statement means: start at position 10 of `wholeName` (at the letter `H`) and replace the next seven characters (`Heather`) with the string `"Amy"`. Finally, you can delete the new middle name altogether by using the statement

```
wholeName.erase(10, 4);          // Change back to
                                 // "Ms. Caryn Jackson"
```

which means: start at position 10 and erase four characters (`Amy` and a space) from `string` object `wholeName`.

## Assigning a Substring to a **string** Object

You can also store a *substring* (portion of a string) in another `string` object using member function `assign`. For example, if `title` is a `string` object, the statement

```
title.assign(wholeName, 0, 3);   // Store "Ms." in title
```

stores in `title` the first three characters of `wholeName`. The content of `wholeName` is not changed.

Table 3.3 summarizes the member functions described in this section.

**Table 3.3**  Some Member Functions in the `string` Class

| Function | Purpose |
|---|---|
| `getline(cin, aString, '\n')` | Extracts data characters up to (but not including) the first newline character from stream `cin` and stores them in `aString`. The first newline character is extracted from `cin` but not stored in `aString`. |
| `aString.length()` | Returns the count of characters (an integer) in `aString`. |
| `aString.at(i)` | Returns the character in position i of `aString` where the leftmost character is at position 0 and the rightmost character is at position `aString.length() - 1`. |
| `aString.find(target)` | Returns the starting position (an integer) of string target in `aString`. If target is not in `aString`, returns a value that is outside the range of valid positions; that is, it returns a value $< 0$ or a value $\geq$ the length of `aString`. |
| `aString.insert(start, newString)` | Inserts `newString` at position `start` of `aString`. |
| `aString.replace(start, count, newString)` | Starting at position `start` of `aString`, replaces the next count characters with `newString`. |
| `aString.erase(start, count)` | Starting at position `start` of `aString`, removes the next count characters. |
| `aString.assign(oldString, start, count)` | Starting at position `start` of `oldString`, assigns to `aString` the next count characters. |

## EXERCISES FOR SECTION 3.7

**Self-Check**

1. Explain the effect of each of the following; assume a data line containing the characters `Jones***John Boy` is typed in.

```
String name;
cout << "name: ";
getline(cin, name, '\n');
int start = name.find("***");
name.erase(start, 3);
name.insert(start, ", ");
cout << name << endl;
```

2. Trace each of the following statements:

```
string author;
author = "John";
author = author + " Steinbeck";
cout << author.length() << endl;
cout << author.at(0) << author.at(4) << endl;
```

```
cout << author.at(author.length() - 1)
     << endl;
cout << author.find("n");
cout << author.find("nb");
author.insert(4, "ny");
author.replace(0, 6, "Jonathan");
author.erase(3, 5);
```

3. Write a statement that stores in `wholeName` the strings stored in `firstName` and `lastName` in the form *lastName, firstName*.

Programming

1. Write a program that reads three strings and displays the strings in all possible sequences, one sequence per output line. Display the symbol * between the strings on each line.

# 3.8   Common Programming Errors

Remember to use a `#include` compiler directive for every standard library that your program accesses. If you're including a user-defined library, enclose the header file name in quotes, not angle brackets.

If you're using function subprograms, place their prototypes in the source file before the `main` function. Place the actual function definitions after the `main` function.

Syntax or run-time errors may occur when you use functions. The acronym **not** summarizes the requirements for argument list correspondence. Provide the required **n**umber of arguments and make sure the **o**rder of arguments is correct. Make sure that each function argument is the correct **t**ype or that conversion to the correct type will lose no information. For user-defined functions, verify that each argument list is correct by comparing it to the formal parameter list in the function heading or prototype. Also be careful when using functions that are undefined on some range of values. For example, if the argument for function `sqrt`, `log`, or `log10` is negative, a run-time error will occur. The following are additional errors to look for.

- *Semicolons in a function heading and prototype:* A missing semicolon at the end of a function prototype may cause a `"Statement missing ;"` or `"Declaration terminated incorrectly"` diagnostic. (A prototype is a declaration and must be terminated with a semicolon.) However, make sure you don't insert a semicolon after the function heading.
- *Wrong number of arguments:* If the number of arguments in a function call is not the same as the number in the prototype, your compiler may generate an error message such as the following:

```
Incorrect number of arguments in call to intPower(int, int).
```

As shown above, in most cases the error message lists the function pro-totype—intPower(int, int) in this case—to help you determine the exact nature of the error.

- *Argument mismatches:* Verify that each actual argument in a function call is in the right position relative to its corresponding formal parameter. You do this by comparing each actual argument to the type and description of its corresponding formal parameter in the function pro-totype. Remember, the actual argument name is not what's important; it's the positional correspondence that's critical.

  C++ permits most type mismatches that you're likely to create and usu-ally won't generate even a warning message. Instead, the compiler will perform a *standard conversion* on the actual argument, converting it to the type specified by the formal parameter. These conversions may produce incorrect results, which in turn can cause other errors during the execu-tion of your program. If you pass a real number to a type char formal parameter, your compiler may generate a warning diagnostic such as

```
Float or double assigned to integer or character data type.
```

- *Function prototype and definition mismatches:* The compiler will not detect type mismatches between a function prototype and the function defini-tion, but they might be detected by the linker program for your C++ system.

```
undefined symbol intPower(int, int) in module square.
```

  This message may be caused by a missing function definition or by the use of a function prototype that doesn't match the function definition. If the parameters in a function prototype don't match those in the defi-nition, the linker assumes that the prototype refers to a different func-tion, one for which there is no definition.

- *Return statement errors:* All functions that you write, except for type void functions, should terminate execution with a return statement that includes an expression indicating the value to be returned. The data type of the value returned should match the type specified in the function heading. Make sure that you don't omit the expression (or even worse, the entire return statement). If you forget to specify a return value when one is expected, you'll see a message such as

```
Return value expected.
```

or

```
Function should return a value ...
```

If you specify a return value for a void function, you'll see a message such as

```
Function cannot return a value ...
```

- *Missing object name in call to a member function:* If you omit the object name and dot when attempting to apply a member function to an object, you'll get an error message such as

```
Call to undefined function
```

Because the object name is missing, the compiler can't determine the class library in which the function is defined and assumes the function definition is missing.

- *Missing #include line or incorrect library name in #include:* If you forget to include a library header file or write the wrong header (for example, <cmath> instead of <string>), you'll see multiple error messages because the compiler will not be able to access the symbols and functions defined in that library. The error messages will tell you that symbols and functions from that library are undefined. A similar error occurs if you omit the using namespace std; statement.

- *Argument mismatch in a call to a member function:* If you have argument type mismatches or an incorrect number of arguments in a call to a member function, you'll get an error message such as

```
Could not find a match for getline(string, char)
```

This message is displayed if you call function getline with a string and char argument instead of a stream, string, and char argument.

- *Logic errors in your program—testing a program and checking your results:* Many errors, such as the incorrect specification of computations (in writing mathematical formulas) may go undetected by the compiler, yet produce incorrect results. For example, if you're given the formula

$$y = 3k^2 - 9k + 7$$

to program, and you write the C++ code

```
y = 9 * pow(k, 2) 2 3 - k + 7
```

(accidentally reversing the coefficients 9 and 3), no error will be detected by the compiler. As far as the compiler is concerned, no mistake has been made—the expression is perfectly legal C++ code.

## Separately Testing Function Subprograms

There is usually just one way to find logic errors, and that's by testing your program using carefully chosen *test data samples* and verifying, for each sample, that your answer is correct. Such testing is a critical part of the programming process and cannot be omitted.

As we proceed through the text, we will have more to say about testing strategies. We discussed one testing strategy that involves breaking down a problem into subproblems, writing the solutions to the subproblems using separate functions, and then separately testing these functions with short driver functions. This strategy can help simplify the testing process and make it easier for you to perform a more thorough test of your entire program.

# Chapter Review

1. Develop your program solutions from existing information. Use the system documentation derived from applying the software development method as the initial framework for the program.

   - Edit the data requirements to obtain the `main` function declarations.
   - Use the refined algorithm as the starting point for the executable statements in the `main` function.

2. If a new problem is an extension of a previous one, modify the previous program rather than starting from scratch.

3. Use C++ library functions to simplify mathematical computations through the reuse of code that has already been written and tested. Write a function call (consisting of the function name and arguments) to activate a library function. After the function executes, the function result is substituted for the function call.

4. Use a structure chart to show subordinate relationships between subproblems.

5. Utilize modular programming by writing separate function subprograms to implement the different subproblems in a structure chart. Ideally, your `main` function will consist of a sequence of function call statements that activate the function subprograms.

6. You can write functions without arguments and results to display a list of instructions to a program user or to draw a diagram on the screen. Use a function call consisting of the function name followed by an empty pair of parentheses `( )` to activate such a function.

7. Write functions that have input arguments and that return a single result to perform computations similar to those performed by library

functions. When you call such a function, each actual argument value is assigned to its corresponding formal parameter.

8. Place prototypes (similar to function headings) for each function sub-program before the `main` function, and place the function definitions after the `main` function in a source file. Use `()` to indicate that a function has no parameters. List only the formal parameter types, not their names, in the prototype. Use a semicolon after the prototype but not after the function heading.

9. You can use the standard `string` class and its member functions to process textual data. Insert the compiler directive `#include <string>` and the statement `using namespace std;` in your program. You should use dot notation to apply a member function to an object (*object.function-call*).

## Summary of New C++ Constructs

| Construct | Effect |
|---|---|
| Function Prototype<br>`void display();` | Prototype for a function that has no arguments and returns no result. |
| `float average(float, float);` | Prototype for a function with two type `float` input arguments and a type `float` result. |
| Function Call<br>`display();` | Calls void function `display`, causing it to begin execution. When execution is complete, control returns to the statement in the calling function that immediately follows the call. |
| `x = average(2, 6.5) + 3.0;` | Calls function `average` with actual arguments 2 and `6.5`. When execution is complete, adds `3.0` to the function result and stores the sum in variable `x`. |
| Member Function Call Using Dot Notation<br>`cout << wholeName.at(0);` | Calls `string` member function at, applying it to object `wholeName`. Displays the first character in `wholeName`. |
| Function Definition<br>`// Displays a diamond of stars`<br>`void display()` | Definition of a function that has no arguments and returns no result. |

```
// Displays a diamond of stars
void display()
{
    cout << "    *    " << endl;
    cout << "   * *   " << endl;
    cout << "  *   *  " << endl;
    cout << " *     * " << endl;
    cout << "  *   *  " << endl;
    cout << "   * *   " << endl;
    cout << "    *    " << endl;
```

## Summary of New C++ Constructs (continued)

| Construct | Effect |
|---|---|
| ```} // end display``` | |
| ```// Computes average of two integers```<br>```float average(float, float)```<br>```{``` | Definition of a function with two type `float` input arguments and a type `float` result. |
| ```return (m1 + m2) / 2.0;```<br>```} // end average``` | Returns a type `float` result. |

### Quick-Check Exercises

1. Each function in a program executes exactly once. True or false?

2. State the order of declarations used in a program source file.

3. What is the difference between an actual argument and a formal parameter? How is correspondence between arguments and parameters determined?

4. Can you use an expression for a formal parameter or for an actual argument? If so, for which?

5. What is a structure chart? Explain how a structure chart differs from an algorithm.

6. What does the function below do?

   ```
   void nonsense(char c, char d)
   {
       cout << "*****" << endl;
       cout << c << "!!!" << d << endl;
       cout << "*****" << endl;
   } // end nonsense
   ```

7. Given the function nonsense from Exercise 6, describe the output that's produced when the following lines are executed.

   ```
   nonsense('a', 'a');
   nonsense('A', 'Z');
   nonsense('!', '!');
   ```

8. Explain what dot notation is and how you use it.

9. Trace the statements below:

   ```
   string flower = "rose";
   flower = flower + " of Sharon";
   cout << flower.at(0) << flower.at(8) << endl;
   cout << flower.find("s") << " " << flower.find("S")
   ```

```
<< endl;
flower.replace(5, 2, "from");
flower.erase(0, 4);
flower.insert(0, "thorn");
```

10. Explain the role of a function prototype and a function definition. Which comes first? Which must contain the formal parameter names? Which ends with a semicolon?

11. Write the following equation as a C++ statement using functions exp, log, and pow:

$$y = (e^n \ln b)^2$$

## Answers to Quick-Check Exercises

1. False; a function is only executed when it is called. It can execute more than once or not at all.

2. We declare function prototypes before function main. Next comes function main followed by any other function definitions. Within each function, we declare any local constants and variables that are defined only during the execution of that function.

3. An actual argument is listed in a function call; a formal parameter is used inside the function body to describe the function operation. When a function call executes, the value of each actual argument is passed into the corresponding formal parameter. Correspondence is determined by relative position in the lists of arguments and parameters (that is, the first actual argument corresponds to the first formal parameter, and so on).

4. An actual argument can be an expression but not a formal parameter.

5. A structure chart is a diagram used to show an algorithm's subproblems and their interdependence, so it shows the hierarchical relationship between subproblems. An algorithm lists the sequence in which subproblems are performed.

6. It would display a line of five stars, followed by a line showing the first argument, three exclamation points, and the second argument, followed by a line of five stars.

7. It displays the following:

```
*****
a!!!a
*****
*****
```

```
A!!!Z
*****
*****
!!!!!
*****
```

8. In dot notation, you write an object name, a dot, and a member function name. You use dot notation to apply the member function to the object that precedes the dot.

9. Allocate a `string` object `flower` and initialize it to `"rose"`.
   Change `flower` to `"rose of Sharon"`.
   Display `rs`.
   Display `2 8`.
   Change `flower` to `"rose from Sharon"`.
   Change `flower` to `" from Sharon"`.
   Change `flower` to `"thorn from Sharon"`.

10. A function prototype gives the C++ compiler enough information to translate each call to the function. The function definition provides a complete description of the function operation and is translated into machine language by the compiler. The prototype comes first; the definition must contain formal parameter names; the prototype ends with a semicolon.

11. `y = pow(exp(n * log(b)), 2);`

## Review Questions

1. Discuss the strategy of divide and conquer.

2. Provide guidelines for the use of function interface comments.

3. Briefly describe the steps you would take to derive an algorithm for a given problem.

4. The diagram that shows the algorithm steps and their interdependencies is called a _____.

5. What are three advantages of using functions?

6. A C++ program is a collection of one or more _____, one of which must be named _____.

7. When is a function executed? What is the difference between a function prototype and its definition? Which comes first?

8. Is the use of functions a more efficient use of the programmer's or the computer's time? Explain your answer.

9. Write a program that reads into a string object a name with three blanks between the first and last names. Then extract the first and last names and store them in separate string objects. Write a function subprogram that displays its string argument two times. Call this function to display the first name four times and then to display the last name six times.

10. Write a program that reads into a string object your name with the symbol * between first and last names. Then extract your first and last names and store them in separate string objects. Write a function subprogram that displays its string argument three times. Call this function to display your first name three times and then to display your last name three times.

## Programming Projects

1. Add one or more of your own unique functions to the stick figure program presented in Section 3.2. Create several more pictures combining the `drawCircle`, `drawIntersect`, `drawBase`, and `drawParallel` functions with your own. Make any modifications to these functions that you need in order to make the picture components fit nicely.

2. Write functions that display each of your initials in block letter form. Use these functions to display your initials.

3. Write three functions, one that displays a circle, one that displays a rectangle, and one that displays a triangle. Use these functions to write a complete C++ program from the following outline:

```cpp
int main()
{
    // Draw circle.
    // Draw triangle.
    // Draw rectangle.
    // Display 2 blank lines.
    // Draw triangle.
    // Draw circle.
    // Draw rectangle.

    return 0;
}
```

4. Write a computer program that computes the duration of a projectile's flight and its height above the ground when it reaches the target. As part of your solution, write and call a function that displays instructions to the program user.

### Problem Constant

```
G = 32.17        // gravitational constant
```

### Problem Inputs

```
float theta      // input - angle (radians) of elevation
float distance   // input - distance (ft) to target
float velocity   // input - projectile velocity (ft/sec)
```

### Problem Outputs

```
float time       // output - time (sec) of flight
float height     // output - height at impact
```

### Relevant Formulas

$$time = \frac{distance}{velocity \times cos\,(theta)}$$

$$height = velocity \times sin(theta) \times time - \frac{g \times time^2}{2}$$

Try your program on these data sets.

| Inputs | Data Set 1 | Data Set 2 |
|---|---|---|
| Angle of elevation | 0.3 radian | 0.71 radian |
| Velocity | 800 ft/sec | 1,600 ft/sec |
| Distance to target | 11,000 ft | 78,670 ft |

5. Write a program that takes a positive number with a fractional part and rounds it to two decimal places. For example, 32.4851 would round to 32.49, and 32.4431 would round to 32.44.

6. Four track stars entered the mile race at the Penn Relays. Write a program that will read the last name and the race time in minutes and seconds for one runner and compute and print the speed in feet per second and in meters per second after the runner's name. (*Hints:* There are 5280 feet in one mile, and one kilometer equals 3281 feet; one meter is equal to 3.281 feet.) Test your program on each of the times below.

| Name | Minutes | Seconds |
|---|---|---|
| Deavers | 3 | 52.83 |
| Jackson | 3 | 59.83 |
| Smith | 4 | 00.03 |
| Rivera | 4 | 16.22 |

Write and call a function that displays instructions to the program user. Write two other functions, one to compute the speed in meters per second and the other to compute the speed in feet per second.

7. A cyclist coasting on a level road slows from a speed of 10 miles/hr to 2.5 miles/hr in one minute. Write a computer program that calculates

the cyclist's constant rate of deceleration and determines how long it will take the cyclist to come to rest, given an initial speed of 10 miles/hr. (*Hint:* Use the equation

$$a = (v_f - v_i) \,/\, t,$$

where $a$ is acceleration, $t$ is time interval, $v_i$ is initial velocity, and $v_f$ is the final velocity.) Write and call a function that displays instructions to the program user and another function that computes and returns the deceleration given $v_f$, $v_i$, and $t$.

8. In shopping for a new house, you must consider several factors. In this problem the initial cost of the house, estimated annual fuel costs, and annual tax rate are available. Write a program that will determine the total cost after a five-year period for each set of house data below. You should be able to inspect your program output to determine the "best buy."

   | Initial House Cost | Annual Fuel Cost | Tax Rate |
   |---|---|---|
   | $175,000 | $2500 | 0.025 |
   | $200,000 | $2800 | 0.025 |
   | $210,000 | $2050 | 0.020 |

   To calculate the house cost, add the fuel cost for five years to the initial cost, then add the taxes for five years. Taxes for one year are computed by multiplying the tax rate by the initial cost. Write and call a function that displays instructions to the program user and another function that computes and returns the house cost given the initial cost, the annual fuel cost, and the tax rate.

9. Write a program that reads a string containing exactly four words (separated by * symbols) into a single string object. Next, extract each word from the original string and store each word in a string object. Then concatenate the words in reverse order to form another string. Display both the original and final strings. (*Hint:* To extract the words, you should use the `find` member function to find each symbol *, assign the characters up to the * to one of the four string objects, and then remove those characters from the original string.)

10. Write a program to take a depth (in kilometers) inside the earth as input data; compute and display the temperature at this depth in degrees Celsius and Fahrenheit. The relevant formulas are

    *Celsius* = 10 × (*depth*) + 20     (*Celsius temperature at depth in km*)
    *Fahrenheit* = 1.8 × (*Celsius*) + 32

    Include two functions in your program. Function `celsiusAtDepth` should compute and return the Celsius temperature at a depth measured in kilometers. Function `toFahrenheit` should convert a Celsius temperature to Fahrenheit.

11. The ratio between successive speeds of a six-speed gearbox (assuming that the gears are evenly spaced to allow for whole teeth) is

$$\sqrt[5]{M/m}$$

where $M$ is the maximum speed in revolutions per minute and $m$ is the minimum speed. Write a function `speedsRatio` that calculates this ratio for any maximum and minimum speeds. Write a `main` function that prompts for maximum and minimum speeds (rpm), calls `speedsRatio` to calculate the ratio, and displays the results.

12. Write a program that calculates and displays the volume of a box and the surface area of a box. The box dimensions are provided as input data. The volume is equal to the area of the base times the height of the box. Define and call a function `rectangleArea` to calculate the area of each rectangle in the box.

# Mark Hall

*Mark Hall is an expert on compilers. He works at Microsoft as the development manager for the Visual C++ compiler. Before that he was a computer scientist at Pyramid Technology. He received his B.S. in computer science from the College of William and Mary and his Ph.D. from the University of Colorado.*

**How did you decide to study computer science?**

I was sitting in my kitchen one night, filling out a college application that asked, "What do you think you'd like to do when you grow up?" and one of the choices on there was computer design. That interested me because as a kid I was always taking stuff apart to see how it worked. I'm sure I broke as much as I fixed, but it taught me a lot of great debugging skills.

Back then, computers were kind of a new thing. I can remember my brother saying, "Computers? Hah! There will never be any jobs in computers." I'm sure that bit of sibling rivalry was the deciding factor in choosing a career in computers.

The reason I got into the compiler area was because of an undergraduate course I took, in which we studied Frank DeRemer's landmark thesis in parser generators. That was very inspiring to me. I thought, "Wow, I can't believe that works." It really taught me what the phrase "elegant algorithm" meant. It's the combination of theory and down-to-the-metal coding that makes compiler work the choice for me.

**Describe your work at Microsoft.**

For the last seven years I've been the development manager for the C++ compiler, which is one of many tools that make up the Visual C++ product. Everyone on the team comes up with the ideas. It's my job to decide which ones we can do and who on the team will do each task. I allocate time between new features, supporting existing customers' needs, and improving compliance with the C++ standard. It's a delicate balancing act that I believe gives Visual C++ developers the best tool possible for targeting Microsoft platforms.

**What's a typical day like for you at work? What kinds of things might you be doing?**

Everyone who works for me is an excellent programmer, but few have formal compiler training. So I spend time each day explaining how to best implement something that involves the theoretical part of the compiler. I build all of the Windows NT source code every day to make sure bugs don't creep into the compiler. When a new one shows up, I isolate the cause and give it to the responsible developer. I fix a lot of bugs myself. Finally, of course, I attend a lot of meetings.

**What is the most challenging part of your job?**

I'd say the most difficult part of the job for me is making the hard trade-offs needed to ship the product. We have limited resources, competitive pressures, and changing markets, so we never get to implement all of the features or fix all the bugs we want to. Something always ends up getting delayed. This is frustrating, but at some point the customer needs the product and the access it provides to the new platform features. You have to make the hard call and ship the product.

**Do you have any advice about programming in C++?**

Many people are scared of C++ because there's a lot of stuff that looks complicated, but remember, you don't have to use all of the features; you can use C++ any way you want. If you're using C and think it's good, C++ can actually be used as a better C. You can get the same performance, but you get a lot better type checking, and therefore fewer bugs.

**How do you see Visual C++ evolving over the next few years?**

We'll certainly have more Intelli-Sense. IntelliSense makes writing code easier and more error-free. While you're typing a name of a class, for instance, then all the mem-ber functions or the data members that are legal at that point will pop up on your screen, and you get to pick one. It's called name comple-tion, and it's an extremely useful feature. We'll also have better con-formance and faster build times. Finally, we will aggressively support any new Microsoft platforms

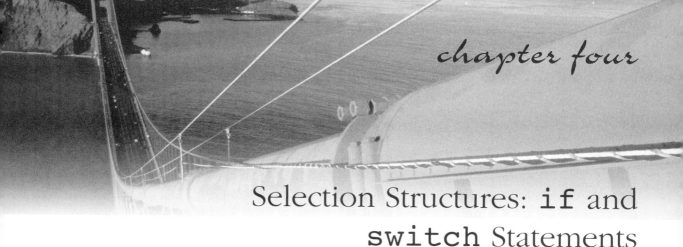

*chapter four*

# Selection Structures: `if` and `switch` Statements

## Chapter Objectives

- To become familiar with the 3 kinds of control structures: sequence, selection, repetition and to understand compound statements
- To learn how to compare numbers, characters, and strings
- To learn how to use the relational, equality, and logical operators to write expressions that are type bool (true or false)
- To learn how to write selection statements with one and two alternatives using the if statement
- To learn how to implement decisions in algorithms using the `if` statement
- To understand how to select among more than two alternatives by nesting `if` statements
- To learn how to use the switch statement as another technique for selecting among multiple alternatives

THIS BOOK TEACHES a disciplined approach that results in programs that are easy to read and less likely to contain errors. An important element of this technique is the use of top-down design to divide an algorithm into individual steps. We can use a small number of control structures to code the individual algorithm steps.

At this point, we've used just one of these control mechanisms, sequence. In this chapter and the next, we'll introduce two other important control structures: selection and repetition.

This chapter will also show how to use the C++ `if` and `switch` statements to select one group of statements for execution from several alternative groups. These control statements will allow a program to evaluate its data and to select a path of execution to follow based on the data. The chapter also discusses conditions and logical expressions, which the `if` statement relies on.

## 4.1    Control Structures

**control structure**
A combination of individual instructions into a single logical unit with one entry point and one exit point that regulates the flow of execution in a program.

**compound statement**
A group of statements bracketed by { and } that are executed sequentially.

**Control structures** regulate the flow of execution in a program or function, combining individual instructions into a single logical unit with one entry point and one exit point. There are three categories of control structures for controlling execution flow: (1) *sequence*, (2) *selection*, and (3) *repetition*. Until now, we've been using only sequential flow. A **compound statement**, written as a group of statements bracketed by { and }, is used to specify sequential control.

```
{
    statement₁;
    statement₂;
    .
    .
    .
    statementₙ;
}
```

Sequential flow means that each statement is executed in sequence, starting with $statement_1$, followed by $statement_2$, and so on through $statement_n$.

This chapter describes how to write algorithms and programs that use **selection control**, a control structure that enables the program to execute one of several alternative statements or groups of statements. With selection control, flow doesn't necessarily follow from one statement to the next as in sequential control, but may skip some statements and execute others based on selection criteria.

**selection control**
A control structure that chooses among alternative program statements.

## 4.2    Logical Expressions

In C++, the primary selection control structure is the `if` statement. We can use an `if` statement to select from several alternative executable statements. For example, the `if` statement

```
if (weight > 100.00)
   shipCost = 10.00;
else
   shipCost = 5.00;
```

selects one of the two assignment statements listed by testing the condition
weight > 100.00. If the condition is true (weight is greater than 100.00),
it selects the statement shipCost = 10.00;. If the condition is false
(weight is not greater than 100.00), it selects the statement shipCost =
5.00;. It is never possible for both assignment statements to execute after
testing a particular condition.

In order to write if statements, we must first understand how to write
the conditions that the if statement relies on to make a selection.

## Logical Expressions Using Relational and Equality Operators

A program selects among alternative statements by testing the value of key
variables. In C++, **logical expressions**, or **conditions**, are used to perform
such tests. Each logical expression has two possible values, true or false.
Such an expression is called a condition because it establishes a criterion for
either executing or skipping a group of statements.

**logical expression
(condition)**
An expression that is
either true or false.

Most conditions that we use to perform comparisons will have one of
these forms:

*variable    relational-operator    variable*
*variable    relational-operator    constant*
*variable    equality-operator    variable*
*variable    equality-operator    constant*

Table 4.1 lists the relational and equality operators. Be careful not to
confuse the assignment operator (single =) with the equality operator
(double ==).

**Table 4.1**    Relational and Equality Operators

| Operator | Meaning | Type |
|---|---|---|
| < | less than | relational |
| > | greater than | relational |
| <= | less than or equal to | relational |
| >= | greater than or equal to | relational |
| == | equal to | equality |
| != | not equal to | equality |

## EXAMPLE 4.1

Table 4.2 shows some sample conditions in C++. Each condition is evaluated assuming these variable and constant values:

| x | power | maxPower | y | item | minItem | momOrDad |
|---|-------|----------|---|------|---------|----------|
| -5 | 1024 | 1024 | 7 | 1.5 | -999.0 | 'm' |

**Table 4.2** Sample Conditions

| Operator | Condition | English Meaning | Value |
|----------|-----------|-----------------|-------|
| <= | x <= 0 | x less than or equal to 0 | true |
| < | power < maxPower | power less than maxPower | false |
| >= | x >= y | x greater than or equal to y | false |
| > | item > minItem | item greater than minItem | true |
| == | momOrDad == 'm' | momOrDad equal to 'm' | true |
| != | num != sentinel | num not equal to sentinel | false |

### Logical Expressions Using Logical Operators

With the three logical operators—`&&` (and), `||` (or), `!` (not)—we can form more complicated conditions or compound logical expressions. Examples of logical expressions formed with the `&&` (and) and `||` (or) operators are

```
(salary < minSalary) || (dependents > 5)
(temperature > 90.0) && (humidity > 0.90)
```

The first logical expression determines whether an employee is eligible for special scholarship funds. It evaluates to `true` if *either* the condition

```
(salary < minSalary)
```

or the condition

```
(dependents > 5)
```

is true. The second logical expression describes an unbearable summer day, with temperature and humidity both in the nineties. The expression evaluates to true only when *both* conditions are true.

The operands of `||` and `&&` are themselves logical expressions and each has a type `bool` value (`true` or `false`). The compound logical expression also has a type `bool` value. None of the parentheses used in these expressions are required; they are used here just for clarity.

The third logical operator, `!` (not), has a single type `bool` operand and yields the **logical complement**, or **negation**, of its operand (that is, if the variable `positive` is `true`, `!positive` is `false` and vice versa). The logical expression

```
winningRecord && (!probation)
```

logical complement (negation)
The logical complement of a condition has the value true when the condition's value is false; the logical complement of a condition has the value false when the condition's value is true.

manipulates two `bool` variables (`winningRecord`, `probation`). A college team for which this expression is true has a winning record and is not on probation, so it may be eligible for the postseason tournament. Note that the expression

```
(winningRecord == true) && (probation == false)
```

is logically equivalent to the one above; however, the first one is preferred because it's more concise and more readable.

Simple expressions such as

```
x == y
x < y
```

can be negated by applying the unary operator `!` to the entire expression.

```
!(x == y)
!(x < y)
```

However, using the logical complement of the relational operator often works just as well in these situations:

```
x != y
x >= y
```

The best time to use the `!` operator is when you want to reverse the value of a long or complicated logical expression that involves many operators. For example, expressions such as

```
(salary < minSalary) || (numberDependents > 5)
```

are most easily negated by enclosing the entire expression in parentheses and preceding it with the `!` operator.

```
!((salary < minSalary) || (numberDependents > 5))
```

Table 4.3 shows that the `&&` operator (and) yields a true result only when both its operands are true. Table 4.4 shows that the `||` operator (or) yields a false result only when both its operands are false. The `not` operator `!` has a single operand; Table 4.5 shows that the `not` operator yields the logical complement, or negation, of its operand (that is, if `flag` is `true`, `!flag` is `false` and vice versa). Remember to use logical operators only with logical expressions.

## Operator Precedence

The precedence of an operator determines its order of evaluation in an expression. Table 4.6 shows the precedence from highest to lowest of all C++ operators you've seen so far. The unary operators (including `!`) have the highest precedence followed by the arithmetic, relational, equality operators, and then the binary logical operators. To prevent errors and to clarify the meaning of expressions, use parentheses freely.

**Table 4.3**    `&&` Operator

| Operand$_1$ | Operand$_2$ | Operand$_1$ `&&` Operand$_2$ |
|---|---|---|
| true | true | true |
| true | false | false |
| false | true | false |
| false | false | false |

**Table 4.4**    `||` Operator

| Operand$_1$ | Operand$_2$ | Operand$_1$ `||` Operand$_2$ |
|---|---|---|
| true | true | true |
| true | false | true |
| false | true | true |
| false | false | false |

**Table 4.5**    `!` Operator

| Operand | `!`Operand |
|---|---|
| true | false |
| false | true |

**Table 4.6**   Operator Precedence

| Operator | Precedence | Description |
|---|---|---|
| `!, +, -` | Highest | Logical not, unary plus, unary minus |
| `*, /, %` | | Multiplication, division, modulus |
| `+, -` | | Addition, subtraction |
| `<, <=, >=, >` | | Relational inequality |
| `==, !=` | | Equal, not equal |
| `&&` | | Logical and |
| `||` | | Logical or |
| `=` | Lowest | Assignment |

The expression

```
x < min + max
```

involving the `float` variables `x`, `min`, and `max` is interpreted correctly in C++ as

```
x < (min + max)
```

because + has higher precedence than <. The expression

```
min <= x && x <= max
```

is also correct, but providing the extra parentheses

```
(min <= x) && (x <= max)
```

makes the expression clearer.

Because ! has higher precedence than ==, C++ incorrectly interprets the expression

```
!x == y
```

as

```
(!x) == y
```

To avoid this error, insert the parentheses where needed:

```
!(x == y)
```

## EXAMPLE 4.2

Expressions 1 to 4 below contain different operands and operators. Each expression's value is given in the corresponding comment, assuming x, y, and z are type `float`, `flag` is type `bool`, and the variables have the values:

| x | y | z | flag |
|---|---|---|---|
| 3.0 | 4.0 | 2.0 | false |

1. `!flag`                            `// !false is true`
2. `x + y / z <= 3.5`                 `// 5.0 <= 3.5 is false`
3. `!flag || (y + z >= x - z)`        `// true || true is true`
4. `!(flag || (y + z >= x - z))`      `// !(false || true) is false`

Figure 4.1 shows the evaluation tree and step-by-step evaluation for expression 3.

## Writing Conditions in C++

To solve programming problems, you must convert conditions expressed in English to C++. Many algorithm steps require testing to see if a variable's value is within a specified range of values. For example, if min represents the lower bound of a range of values and max represents the upper bound (min is less than max), the expression

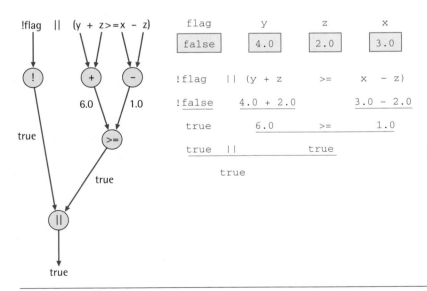

**Figure 4.1**   Evaluation tree and step-by-step evaluation of `!flag || (y + z >= x - z)`

```
(min <= x) && (x <= max)
```

tests whether x lies within the range min through max, inclusive. In Figure 4.2, this range is shaded. The expression is true if x lies within this range and false if x is outside the range.

**Figure 4.2** Range of true values for `(min <= x) && (x <= max)`

## EXAMPLE 4.3

Table 4.7 shows some English conditions and their corresponding C++ expressions. Each expression is evaluated assuming x is 3.0, y is 4.0, and z is 2.0.

The first logical expression shows the C++ code for the English condition "x and y are greater than z." You may be tempted to write this as

```
x && y > z        // invalid logical expression
```

However, if you apply the precedence rules to this expression, you quickly see that it doesn't have the intended meaning. Also, the type float variable x is an invalid operand for the logical operator &&.

The third logical expression shows the C++ code for the mathematical relationship $z \le x \le y$. The boundary values, 2.0 and 4.0, are included in the range of x values that yield a true result.

The last table entry shows a pair of logical expressions that are true when x is outside the range bounded by z and y. We get the first expression in the pair by complementing the expression just above it. The second expression states that x is outside the range if z is larger than x or x is larger than y. In

**Table 4.7** English Conditions as C++ Expressions

| English Condition | Logical Expression | Evaluation |
|---|---|---|
| x and y are greater than z | `(x > z) && (y > z)` | `true && true is true` |
| x is equal to 1.0 or 3.0 | `(x == 1.0) || (x == 3.0)` | `false || true is true` |
| x is in the range z to y, inclusive | `(z <= x) && (x <= y)` | `true && true is true` |
| x is outside the range z to y | `!(z <= x && x <= y)` | `!(true && true) is false` |
| | `(z > x) || (x > y)` | `false || false is false` |

Figure 4.3, the shaded areas represent the values of x that yield a true result. Both y and z are excluded from the set of values that yield a true result.

**Figure 4.3**   Range of true values for `(z > x) || (x > y)`

## Comparing Characters and Strings

In addition to comparing numbers, it's also possible to compare characters and strings of characters using the relational and equality operators. Several examples of such comparisons are shown in Table 4.8.

In writing such comparisons, you can assume that both the uppercase and lowercase letters appear in alphabetical order, and that the *digit characters* are ordered as expected: `'0' < '1' < '2' < ... < '9'`. For the relationships among other characters (such as `'+'`, `'<'`, `'!'`, etc.) or between two characters not in the same group (for example, `'a'` and `'A'`, or `'B'` and `'b'`, or `'c'` and `'A'`), see Appendix A.

If you include library `string`, you can compare `string` objects (see the last four examples in Table 4.8). C++ compares two strings by comparing corresponding pairs of characters in each string, starting with the leftmost pair. The result is based on the relationship between the first pair of different characters (for example, for `"acts"` and `"aces"`, the result depends on characters t and e). The last comparison involves a string (`"aces"`) that begins with a shorter *substring* (`"ace"`). The substring `"ace"` is considered less than the longer string `"aces"`. We'll say more about character comparisons in Chapter 7.

**Table 4.8**   Examples of Comparisons

| Expression | Value |
| --- | --- |
| `'a' < 'c'` | true |
| `'X' <= 'A'` | false |
| `'3' > '4'` | false |
| `('A' <= ch) && (ch <= 'Z')` | true if ch contains an uppercase letter; otherwise false |
| `"XYZ" <= "ABC"` | false (X <= A) |
| `"acts" > "aces"` | true ( t > e) |
| `"ace" != "aces"` | true (strings are different) |
| `"ace" < "aces"` | true (shorter string is smaller) |

## Boolean Assignment

Assignment statements can be written to assign a type `bool` value to a `bool` variable. If `same` is type `bool`, the statement

    same = true;

assigns the value `true` to `same`. Since assignment statements have the general form

    variable = expression;

you can use the statement

    same = (x == y);

to assign the value of the logical expression (`x == y`) to `same`. The value of `same` is `true` when x and y are equal; otherwise, `same` is `false`.

## EXAMPLE 4.4

The following assignment statements assign values to two type `bool` variables, `inRange` and `isLetter`. Variable `inRange` gets `true` if the value of n is between 210 and 10; variable `isLetter` gets `true` if ch is an uppercase or a lowercase letter.

    inRange =  (n > -10) && (n < 10);
    isLetter = (('A' <= ch) && (ch <= 'Z')) ||
               (('a' <= ch) && (ch <= 'z'));

The expression in the first assignment statement is `true` if n satisfies both conditions listed (n is greater than 210 and n is less than 10); otherwise, the expression is `false`. The expression in the second assignment statement uses the logical operators `&&`, `||`. The first subexpression (before `||`) is `true` if ch is an uppercase letter; the second subexpression (after `||`) is true if ch is a lowercase letter. Consequently, `isLetter` gets `true` if ch is either an uppercase or lowercase letter; otherwise, `isLetter` gets `false`.

## EXAMPLE 4.5

The statement below assigns the value `true` to `even` if n is an even number:

    even = (n % 2 == 0);

Because all even numbers are divisible by 2, the remainder of n divided by 2 (the C++ expression n % 2) is 0 when n is an even number. The expression in parentheses above compares the remainder to 0, so its value is `true` when the remainder is 0 and its value is `false` when the remainder is nonzero.

## Writing **bool** Values

Most logical expressions appear in control structures, where they determine the sequence in which C++ statements execute. You'll rarely have a need to read `bool` values as input data or display `bool` values as program results. If necessary, however, you can display the value of a `bool` variable using the output operator `<<`. If `flag` is `false`, the statement

```
cout << "The value of flag is " << flag;
```

displays the line

```
The value of flag is 0
```

If you need to read a data value into a type `bool` variable, you can represent the data as an integer; use 0 for `false` and 1 for `true`.

## Using Integers to Represent Logical Values

Earlier C++ compilers did not implement type `bool`. Instead they used the `int` data type to model type `bool` data. Internally C++ uses the integer value 0 to represent `false` and any nonzero integer value (usually 1) to represent `true`. A logical expression that evaluates to 0 is considered false; a logical expression that evaluates to nonzero is considered true.

## EXERCISES FOR SECTION 4.2

### Self-Check

1. Assuming `x` is 15 and `y` is 10, what are the values of the following conditions?

   a.  `x != y`   b. `x < y`   c. `x >= (y - x)`   d. `x == (y + x - y)`

2. Evaluate each expression below if `a` is 10, `b` is 12, `c` is 8, and `flag` is false.

   a.  `(c == (a * b)) || !flag`

   b.  `(a != 7) && flag || ((a + c) <= 20)`

   c.  `!(b <= 12) && (a % 2 == 0)`

   d.  `!((a < 5) || (c < (a + b)))`

3. Evaluate the following logical expressions. Assume `x` and `y` are type `float` and `p`, `q`, and `r` are type `bool`. The value of `q` is `false`. Why is it not necessary to know the value of `x`, `y`, `p`, `q`, or `r`?

   **a.**  `x < 5.1 || x >= 5.1 || y != 0`

   **b.**  `p && q || q && r`

**4.** Draw evaluation trees for the following:

   **a.**  `a == (b + a - c)`

   **b.**  `(c == (a + b)) || !flag`

   **c.**  `(a <> 7) && (c >=6) || flag`

Programming

**1.** Write a logical expression that is true for each of the following conditions.

   **a.**  `gender` is `'m'` or `'M'` and `age` is greater than or equal to 62 or `gender` is `'f'` or `'F'` and `age` is greater than or equal to 65.

   **b.**  `water` is greater than 0.1 and also less than 1.5.

   **c.**  `year` is divisible by 4 but not divisible by 100. (Hint: use %.)

   **d.**  `speed` is not greater than 55.

**2.** Write logical assignment statements for the following:

   **a.**  Assign a value of `true` to `between` if n is in the range -k and +k, inclusive; otherwise, assign a value of `false`.

   **b.**  Assign a value of `true` to `lowercase` if ch is a lowercase letter; otherwise, assign a value of `false`.

   **c.**  Assign a value of `true` to `isDigit` if `next` is a digit character ('0' through '9', inclusive).

   **d.**  Assign a value of `true` to `divisor` if m is a divisor of n; otherwise assign a value of `false`.

   **e.**  Assign the value of `true` to `isLeapYear` if year is divisible by 400 or if year is divisible by 4 but not by 100. For example, 2000 is a leap year, 2004 is a leap year, 2008 is a leap year . . . but 2100 is not a leap year. Every fourth century is a leap year (2000, 2400, 2800, and so on).

# 4.3    Introduction to the `if` Control Statement

You now know how to write a C++ expression that is the equivalent of a question such as "is x an even number?" Next, we need to investigate a way to use the value of the expression to select a course of action. In C++, the `if` statement is the primary selection control structure.

## `if` Statement with Two Alternatives

The `if` statement

```
if (gross > 100.00)
    net = gross - tax;
else
    net = gross;
```

selects one of the two assignment statements listed. It selects the statement immediately following the condition (`gross > 100.00`) if the condition is true (that is, `gross` is greater than `100.00`); it selects the statement following the reserved word `else` if the logical expression is false (i.e., `gross` is not greater than `100.00`). It is never possible for both statements to execute after testing a particular condition. You must always enclose the condition in parentheses, but must not place a semicolon after the condition.

Figure 4.4 provides a **flowchart**—a diagram that uses boxes and arrows to show the step-by-step execution of a control structure—for the `if` control statement above. A diamond-shaped box in a flowchart represents a decision. There's always one path into a decision and there are two paths out (labeled true and false).

The figure shows that the condition (`gross > 100.00`) enclosed in the diamond-shaped box is evaluated first. If the condition is true, program control follows the arrow labeled true, and the assignment statement in the rectangle on the right is executed. If the condition is false, program control

**flowchart**
A diagram that shows the step-by-step execution of a control structure.

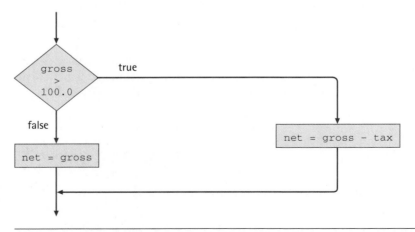

**Figure 4.4**    Flowchart of `if` statement with two alternatives

follows the arrow labeled false, and the assignment statement in the rectangle on the left is executed.

## **if** Statement with Dependent Statement

The if statement above has two alternatives, but only one will be executed for a given value of gross. Example 4.6 illustrates that an if statement can also have a single alternative that is executed only when the condition is true.

### EXAMPLE 4.6

The if statement below has one dependent statement that is executed only when x is not equal to zero. It causes product to be multiplied by x; the new value is saved in product, replacing the old value. If x is equal to zero, the multiplication is not performed. Figure 4.5 shows a flowchart for this if statement.

```
// Multiply product by a non zero x only.
if (x != 0)
    product = product * x;
```

## **if** Statement Conditions with Characters and Strings

The if statements in the next few examples evaluate conditions with character or string operands.

   In all our examples so far, the true and false alternatives of an if statement consist of a single C++ statement. In the next section, we'll see how to write true and false tasks consisting of more than one statement.

**Figure 4.5**   Flowchart of if statement with a dependent statement

## EXAMPLE 4.7

The `if` statement below has two alternatives. It displays either `"Hi Mom"` or `"Hi Dad"` depending on the character stored in variable `momOrDad` (type `char`).

```
if (momOrDad == 'm')
    cout << "Hi Mom" << endl;
else
    cout << "Hi Dad" << endl;
```

## EXAMPLE 4.8

The `if` statement below has one dependent statement; it displays the message `"Hi Mom"` only when `momOrDad` has the value `'m'`. Regardless of whether or not `"Hi Mom"` is displayed, the message `"Hi Dad"` is always displayed.

```
if (momOrDad == 'm')
    cout << "Hi Mom" << endl;
cout << "Hi Dad" << endl;
```

## EXAMPLE 4.9

The `if` statement below displays the result of a string search operation. If the search string is found, the position is printed; otherwise, a message is printed indicating that the search string was not found. The call to `string` member function `find` (see Table 3.3) returns to `posTarget` (type `int`) the starting position in `testString` (type `string`) of `target` (type `string`). If `target` is not found, `find` returns a value that is not in the allowable range (0 through $k-1$ where $k$ is the length of `testString`). The `if` statement tests whether the value returned to `posTarget` is in range before reporting the search result. If `testString` is `"This is a string"` and `target` is `"his"`, the `if` statement would display `his found at position 1`.

```
posTarget = testString.find(target);
if ((0 <= posTarget) && (posTarget < testString.length()))
    cout << target << " found at position " << posTarget
         << endl;
else
    cout << target << " not found!" << endl;
```

## EXAMPLE 4.10

The next `if` statement replaces one substring (`target`) with another (`newString`). If `target` is found in `testString`, function `find` returns the position of `target`. The condition will be true and the **true task** (following the condition) of the `if` statement replaces it with `newString`. Recall that the three arguments of `string` member function `replace` (see Table 3.3) are the starting position of the string to be replaced (`posTarget`), the number of characters to be removed (`target.length()`), and the replacement string (`newString`). If `testString` is `"This is a string"`, `target` is `"his"`, and `newString` is `"here"`, `testString` will become `"There is a string"`. If the condition is false, the **false task** (following the word `else`) displays a message.

> **true task**
> Statement(s) after the condition that execute when the condition is true.
> **false task**
> Statement(s) after `else` that execute when the condition is false.

```
posTarget = testString.find(target);
if ((0 <= posTarget) && (posTarget < testString.length()))
   testString.replace(posTarget, target.length(),
                      newString);
else
   cout << target << " not found - no replacement!" << endl;
```

## Format of the `if` Statement

In all the `if` statement examples, *statement*$_T$ and *statement*$_F$ are indented. If you use the word `else`, enter it on a separate line, aligned with the word `if`. The format of the `if` statement makes its meaning apparent. Again, this is done solely to improve program readability; the format used makes no difference to the compiler.

---

**if Statement with Dependent Statement**

**Form:**      `if ( condition )`
             *statement*$_T$

**Example:**   `if (x > 0.0)`
             `positiveProduct = positiveProduct * x;`

**Interpretation:**   If the *condition* evaluates to true, then *statement*$_T$ is executed; otherwise, it is skipped.

---

---

**if Statement with Two Alternatives**

**Form:**     `if (` *condition* `)`
          *statement$_T$*
          `else`
          *statement$_F$*

**Example:**  `if (x >= 0.0)`
          `cout << "Positive" << endl;`
          `else`
          `cout << "Negative" << endl;`

**Interpretation:**  If the *condition* evaluates to true, then *statement$_T$* is executed and *statement$_F$* is skipped; otherwise, *statement$_T$* is skipped and *statement$_F$* is executed.

---

## EXERCISES FOR SECTION 4.3

### Self-Check

1. What does the following fragment in part a display when **x** is 10? When **x** is 20? What does the fragment in part b display?

    a. ```
       if (x < 12)
           cout << "less" << endl;
       else
           cout << "done"  << endl;
       ```

    b. ```
       var1 = 15.0;
       var2 = 25.12;
       if (2 * var1 >= var2)
           cout << "O.K." << endl;
       else
           cout << "Not O.K." << endl;
       ```

2. What value is assigned to **x** for each segment below when **y** is 10.0?

    a. ```
       x = 20.0;
       if (y != (x - 10.0))
           x = x - 10.0;
       else
           x = x / 2.0;
       ```

    b. ```
       if (y < 5.0 && y >= 0.0)
           x = 5 + y;
       else
           x = 2 - y;
       ```

3. Trace the execution of the if statement in Example 4.10 for the values of target and newString below. For each part, assume testString is "Here is the string" before the if statement executes.
   a. target is "the", newString is "that"
   b. target is "Here", newString is "There"
   c. target is "Where", newString is "There"

Programming

1. Write C++ statements to carry out the steps below.
   a. Store the absolute difference of x and y in result, where the absolute difference is (x - y) or (y - x), whichever is positive. Don't use the abs or fabs function in your solution.
   b. If x is zero, add 1 to zeroCount. If x is negative, add x to minusSum. If x is greater than zero, add x to plusSum.

2. Write your own absolute value function that returns the absolute value of its input argument.

# 4.4  if Statements with Compound Alternatives

So far, we've seen if statements in which only one statement executes in either the true case or the false case. You may also write if statements that execute a series of steps by using compound statements, statements bracketed by { }. When the symbol { follows the condition or the keyword else, the C++ compiler either executes or skips all statements through the matching }. Assignment statements, function call statements, or even other if statements may appear in these alternatives.

## EXAMPLE 4.11

Suppose you're a biologist studying the growth rate of fruit flies. The if statement

```
if (popToday > popYesterday)
{
    growth = popToday - popYesterday;
    growthPct = 100.0 * growth / popYesterday;
    cout << "The growth percentage is " << growthPct;
}
```

computes the population growth from yesterday to today as a percentage of yesterday's population. The compound statement after the condition executes only when today's population is larger than yesterday's. The first assignment computes the increase in the fruit fly population, and the second assignment converts it to a percentage of the original population, which is displayed.

## EXAMPLE 4.12

As the manager of a clothing boutique, you want to keep records of your financial transactions, which can be either payments you make for goods received or deposits made to your checking account. Payments are designated by a `transactionType` value of `'c'`. The true task in the `if` statement below processes a payment; the false task processes a deposit. In both cases, an appropriate message is printed and the account balance is updated. Both the true and false statements are compound statements.

```
if (transactionType == 'c')
{   // process check
    cout << "Check for $" << transactionAmount << endl;
    balance = balance - transactionAmount;
}
else
{   // process deposit
    cout << "Deposit of $" << transactionAmount << endl;
    balance = balance + transactionAmount;
}
```

**Program Style**    Writing `if` Statements with Compound True or False Statements

Each `if` statement in this section contains at least one compound statement bracketed by { }. The placement of the braces is a stylistic preference. Your instructor may want the opening { at the end of the same line as the condition. The closing } of a compound `if` may also appear on the same line as the `else`:

```
} else {
```

Some programmers prefer to use braces even when the statement following `if` or `else` is a single statement. This way all `if` statements look the same, and there will be no danger of forgetting braces when needed. Whichever style you choose, be consistent in its use.

### Tracing an `if` Statement

A critical step in program design is to verify that an algorithm or C++ statement is correct before you spend extensive time coding or debugging it. Often a few extra minutes spent in verifying the correctness of an algorithm saves hours of coding and testing time.

hand trace (desk check)
The step-by-step simulation of an algorithm's execution.

A **hand trace**, or **desk check**, is a careful, step-by-step simulation on paper of how the computer executes the algorithm or statement. The results of this simulation should show the effect of each step's execution using data that are relatively easy to process by hand. We illustrate this next.

## EXAMPLE 4.13

In many programming problems you must order a pair of data values in memory so that the smaller value is stored in one variable (say, x) and the larger value in another (say, y). The next if statement rearranges any two values stored in x and y so that the smaller number is in x and the larger number is in y. If the two numbers are already in the proper order, the compound statement is not executed.

```
if (x > y)
{                   // exchange values in x and y
    temp = x;    // store original value of x in temp
    x = y;       // store original value of y in x
    y = temp;    // store original value of x in y
}
```

Although the values of x and y are being switched, an additional variable, temp, is needed to store a copy of one of these values. Variables x, y, and temp should all be the same data type.

Table 4.9 traces the execution of this if statement when x is 12.5 and y is 5.0. The table shows that temp is initially undefined (indicated by ?). Each line of the table shows the part of the if statement that is being executed, followed by its effect. If any variable gets a new value, its new value is shown on that line. If no new value is shown, the variable retains its previous value. The last value stored in x is 5.0, and the last value stored in y is 12.5.

The trace in Table 4.9 shows that 5.0 and 12.5 are correctly stored in x and y when the condition is true. To verify that the if statement is correct, you should select other data that cause the condition to evaluate to false. Also, you should verify that the statement is correct for special situations. For example, what would happen if x were equal to y? Would the statement still provide the correct result? To complete the hand trace, you would need to show that the algorithm handles this special situation properly.

**Table 4.9** Step-by-Step Hand Trace of if Statement

| Statement Part | x | y | temp | Effect |
|---|---|---|---|---|
| | 12.5 | 5.0 | ? | |
| if (x > y) | | | | 12.5 > 5.0 is true |
| { | | | | |
| temp = x; | | | 12.5 | Store x in temp |
| x = y; | 5.0 | | | Store original y in x |
| y = temp; | | 12.5 | | Store original x in y |
| } | | | | |

In tracing each case, you must be careful to execute the statement step-by-step exactly as the computer would execute it. Often programmers assume how a particular step will be executed and don't explicitly test each condition and trace each step. A trace performed in this way is of little value.

## EXERCISES FOR SECTION 4.4

### Self-Check

1. Insert braces where needed below to avoid syntax or logic errors. Indent as needed to improve readability. The last statement should execute regardless of the value of **x** or **y**.

```
if (x > y)

x = x + 10.0;
cout << "x bigger than y" << endl;

else
   y = y + 10.0;
cout << "x smaller than y" << endl;
cout << "x is " << x
        << "y is " << y << endl;
```

2. What would be the syntax error in Self-Check Exercise 1?

3. What would be the effect of placing braces around the last three statements in Self-Check Exercise 1?

4. Correct the following `if` statement:

```
if (num1 < 0)
{
    product = num1 * num2 * num3;
    cout << "Product is " << product << endl;
else
    sum = num1 + num2 + num3;
    cout << "Sum is " << sum << endl;
}
```

### Programming

1. Write an `if` statement that assigns to **ave** the average of a set of n numbers when n is greater than 0. If n is not greater than 0, assign 0 to **ave** and display an error message. The average should be computed by dividing `total` by n.

2. Write an interactive program that contains a compound `if` statement and may be used to compute the area of a square (area = side$^2$) or triangle (area = $1/2 \times$ base $\times$ height) after prompting the user to type the first character of the figure name (`t` or `s`).

## 4.5 Decision Steps in Algorithms

Algorithm steps that select from a choice of actions are called **decision steps**. The algorithm in the following case contains decision steps to compute an employee's gross and net pay after deductions. The decision steps are coded as `if` statements.

**decision step**
An algorithm step that selects one of several alternatives.

*case study* **Payroll Problem with Functions**

### STATEMENT

Your company pays its hourly workers once a week. An employee's pay is based upon the number of hours worked (to the nearest half hour) and the employee's hourly pay rate. Weekly hours exceeding 40 are paid at a rate of time and a half. Employees who earn over $100 a week must pay union dues of $15 per week. Write a payroll program that will determine the gross pay and net pay for an employee.

### ANALYSIS

The problem data include the input data for hours worked and hourly pay, and two required outputs: gross pay and net pay. There are also several constants: the union dues ($15), the minimum weekly earnings before dues must be paid ($100), the maximum hours before overtime must be paid (40), and the overtime rate (1.5 times the usual hourly rate). With this information, we can begin to write the data requirements for this problem. We can model all data using the `float` data types.

DATA REQUIREMENTS
**Problem Constants**

```
MAX_NO_DUES = 100.00      // maximum earnings (dollars) without
                          // paying union dues
DUES = 15.00              // union dues (dollars) to be paid
MAX_NO_OVERTIME = 40.0    // maximum hours without overtime pay
OVERTIME_RATE = 1.5       // time and a half for overtime
```

**Problem Input**

```
float hours      // hours worked
float rate       // hourly rate
```

### Problem Output

```
float gross      // gross pay
float net        // net pay
```

## PROGRAM DESIGN

The problem solution requires that the program read the hours worked and the hourly rate before performing any computations. After reading these data, we need to compute and then display the gross pay and net pay.

The structure chart for this problem (Figure 4.6) shows the decomposition of the original problem into five subproblems. We'll write three of the subproblems as functions. For these three subproblems, the corresponding function name appears under its box in the structure chart.

We added to the structure chart *data flow* information that shows the input and output of each program step. The structure chart shows that the step *enter data* provides values for `hours` and `rate` as its output (data flow arrow points up). Similarly, the step *compute gross pay* uses `hours` and `rate` as input to the function (data flow arrow points down) and provides `gross` as the function output.

We can now write the initial algorithm.

INITIAL ALGORITHM

1. Display user instructions (function `instructUser`).

2. Enter hours worked and hourly rate.

3. Compute gross pay (function `computeGross`).

4. Compute net pay (function `computeNet`).

5. Display gross pay and net pay.

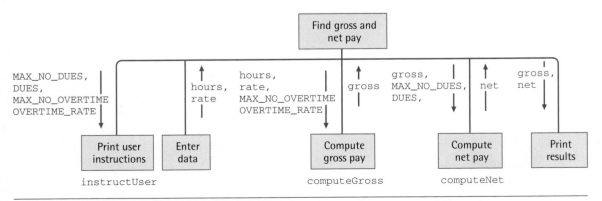

**Figure 4.6**   Structure chart for payroll problem

We now focus on the three lower-level functions listed in parentheses in the algorithm. We begin by defining the interfaces between these functions and the main function.

## ANALYSIS AND DESIGN FOR **INSTRUCTUSER** (ALGORITHM STEP 1)

In our analysis of the lower-level functions, we'll assume that the constant identifiers MAX_NO_DUES, DUES, MAX_NO_OVERTIME, and OVERTIME_RATE are declared before function main. This makes them **global constants**, which means that their values can be referenced in all functions without the need to pass them as arguments.

> global constant
> A constant declared before function main that can be referenced in all functions.

> INTERFACE FOR **instructUser**
>
> **Input Arguments**
>
> (none)
>
> **Function Return Value**
>
> (none—a void function)
> This function simply displays a short list of instructions and information about the program for the user. The information includes the values of the four program constants and other information to ensure that the user has an overview of what the program does and how the user should enter the input data.

## ANALYSIS AND DESIGN FOR **COMPUTEGROSS** (ALGORITHM STEP 3)

The function computeGross needs to know the hours worked and the hourly rate for the employee. It also needs the values of the constants (MAX_NO_OVERTIME and OVERTIME_RATE) involved in determining the employee's gross pay.

> INTERFACE FOR **computeGross**
>
> **Input Arguments**
>
> ```
> float hours          // number of hours worked
> float rate           // hourly pay rate (dollars)
> ```
>
> **Function Return Value**
>
> ```
> float gross
> ```
>
> FORMULA
> Gross pay = Hours worked × Hourly pay

To compute gross pay, we first need to determine whether any overtime pay is due. If there is, we should compute regular pay and overtime pay and return their sum. If not, we simply compute gross pay as the product of hours and rate. We list the local data needed and refine the algorithm step (Step 3) as a *decision step*.

**Local Data for `computeGross`**

```
float  gross        // gross pay (dollars)
float  regularPay   // pay for first 40 hours of work
float  overtimePay  // pay for hours in excess of 40 (dollars)
```

**Algorithm for `computeGross`**

**3.1.** If the hours worked exceeds 40.0 (max hours before overtime)

> **3.1.1.** Compute `regularPay`.
>
> **3.1.2.** Compute `overtimePay`.
>
> **3.1.3.** Add `regularPay` to `overtimePay` to get `gross`.

Else

> **3.1.4.** Compute `gross` as `hours * rate`.

pseudocode
A mixture of English and
C++ reserved words that
is used to describe an
algorithm step.

The decision step above is expressed in **pseudocode**—a mixture of English and C++ reserved words that is used to describe algorithm steps. In the pseudocode above, we use indentation and the reserved words `if` and `else` to show the flow of control.

## ANALYSIS AND DESIGN FOR COMPUTENET (STEP 4)

Once we have the gross pay (returned by `computeGross`), we can compute net pay. The constants representing the union dues cutoff value ($100) and the dues ($15) are required as well as the value of gross salary.

INTERFACE FOR computeNet
**Input Arguments**

```
float  gross        // gross pay (dollars)
```

**Function Return Value**

```
float  net          // net pay (dollars)
```

FORMULA
```
net pay = gross pay 2 deductions
```

Next, we list the local data needed for `computeNet` and refine the algorithm step (Step 4).

**Local Data for `computeNet`**

```
float  net          // net pay (dollars)
```

### Algorithm for `computeNet`

4.1. If the gross pay is larger than $100.00

    **4.1.1.**  Deduct the dues of $15 from gross pay.

Else

    **4.1.2.**  Deduct no dues.

## IMPLEMENTATION

We now write the main function along with the prototypes for the lower-level functions (see Listing 4.1).

## TESTING

To test this program, we need to be sure that all possible alternatives work properly. For example, to test function `computeNet`, we need three sets of data, one for the `if` (gross salary greater than $100), one for the `else` (gross salary less than $100), and one for the pivotal point (gross salary exactly $100). Listing 4.2 shows program output from a sample run.

**Listing 4.1**  Payroll problem with functions

```
// File: payrollFunctions.cpp
// Computes and displays gross pay and net pay given an hourly
//    rate and number of hours worked. Deducts union dues of $15
//    if gross salary exceeds $100; otherwise, deducts no dues.

#include <iostream>
using namespace std;

// Functions used  . . .
void instructUser();
float computeGross(float, float);
float computeNet(money);

const float MAX_NO_DUES = 100.00;    // max earnings before dues (dollars)
const float dues = 15.00;            // dues amount (dollars)
const float MAX_NO_OVERTIME = 40.0;  // max hours before overtime
const float OVERTIME_RATE = 1.5;     // overtime rate
```

(continued)

**Listing 4.1**    Payroll problem with functions (continued)

```cpp
int main ()
{
    float hours;            // input: hours worked
    float rate;             // input: hourly pay rate (dollars)
    float gross;            // output: gross pay (dollars)
    float net;              // output: net pay (dollars)

    // Display user instructions.
    instructUser();
    // Enter hours and rate.
    cout << "Hours worked: ";
    cin >> hours;
    cout << "Hourly rate: $";
    cin >> rate;

    // Compute gross salary.
    gross = computeGross(hours, rate);

    // Compute net salary.
    net = computeNet(gross);

    // Print gross and net.
    cout << "Gross salary is $" << gross << endl;
    cout << "Net salary is $" << net << endl;

    return 0;
}

// Displays user instructions
void instructUser()
{
    cout << "This program computes gross and net salary." << endl;
    cout << "A dues amount of " << DUES << " is deducted for" << endl;
    cout << "an employee who earns more than " << MAX_NO_DUES << endl
         << endl;
    cout << "Overtime is paid at the rate of " << OVERTIME_RATE << endl;
    cout << "times the regular rate for hours worked over "
         << MAX_NO_OVERTIME endl << endl;
    cout << "Enter hours worked and hourly rate" << endl;
    cout << "on separate lines after the prompts." << endl;
```

(continued)

**Listing 4.1**   Payroll problem with functions (continued)

```
      cout << "Press <return> after typing each number." << endl << endl;
   }  // end instructUser

// Find the gross pay
float computeGross
   (float hours,                 // IN: number of hours worked
    float rate)                  // IN: hourly pay rate (dollars)
{
   // Local data  . . .
   float gross;                  // RESULT: gross pay (dollars)
   float regularPay;             // pay for first 40 hours
   float overtimePay;            // pay for hours in excess of 40

   // Compute gross pay.
   if (hours > MAX_NO_OVERTIME)
   {
      regularPay = MAX_NO_OVERTIME * rate;
      overtimePay = (hours - MAX_NO_OVERTIME) * OVERTIME_RATE * rate;
      gross = regularPay + overtimePay;
   }
   else
      gross = hours * rate;

   return gross;
}  // end computeGross

// Find the net pay
float computeNet
   (float gross)                 // IN: gross salary (dollars)
{
   // Local data  . . .
   float net;                    // RESULT: net pay (dollars)

   // Compute net pay.
   if (gross > MAX_NO_DUES)
      net = gross - DUES;   // deduct dues amount
   else
      net = gross;          // no deductions

   return net;
}  // end computeNet
```

Listing 4.2    Sample run of payroll program with functions

```
This program computes gross and net salary.
A dues amount of $15.00 is deducted for
an employee who earns more than $100.00

Overtime is paid at the rate of 1.5
times the regular rate on hours worked over 40

Enter hours worked and hourly rate
on separate lines after the prompts.
Press <return> after typing each number.

Hours worked: 50
Hourly rate: $6
Gross salary is $330
Net salary is $315
```

## Program Style    Global Constants Enhance Readability and Maintenance

The four program constants used in this case are not essential. We could just as easily have placed the constant values (40.0, 1.5, 100.00, and 15.00) directly in the code. For example, we could have written the decision in computeNet as

```
if (gross > 100.00)
    net = gross - 15.00; // deduct amount dues
else
    net = gross;         // no deductions
```

However, the use of constant identifiers rather than constant values has two advantages. First, the original if statement is easier to understand because it uses descriptive names such as MAX_NO_DUES rather than numbers, which have no intrinsic meaning. Second, a program written with constant identifiers is much easier to maintain than one written with constant values. For example, if we want to use different constant values in the payroll program in Listing 4.1, we need to change only the constant declarations. However, if we had inserted constant values directly in the if statement, we'd have to change the if statement and any other statements that manipulate or display the constant values.

The constants have global scope, which means that any function can reference them. Although you must not give variables global scope, you can give constants global scope because the value of a constant, unlike a variable, cannot be changed in a lower-level function. If a constant is used by more than one function, you should declare it as a global constant. The alternatives would be to pass it as an argument to each function or to duplicate its definition in each function. Giving it global scope shortens argument lists and ensures that all functions have the same value for the constant.

## A Reminder About Identifier Scope

Notice that identifier `gross` is declared as a local variable in functions `main` and `computeGross`, and as a formal argument in function `computeNet`. The scope of each declaration is the function that declares it. To establish a connection between these independent declarations of the identifier `gross`, we use argument list correspondence or the function return mechanism. The variable `gross` in function `main` is passed as an actual argument (corresponding to formal argument `gross`) in the call to `computeNet`. Function `computeGross` returns as its result the value of its local variable `gross`; the statement in function `main` that calls `computeGross`

```
gross = computeGross(hours, rate );
```

assigns the function result to `main`'s local variable `gross`.

## Adding Data Flow Information to Structure Charts

In Figure 4.6, we added data flow information to the structure chart showing the input and output of each of the top-level problem solution steps. The data flow information is an important part of the program documentation. It shows what program variables are processed by each step and the manner in which these variables are processed. If a step gives a new value to a variable, then the variable is considered an *output of the step.* If a step displays a variable's value or uses it in a computation without changing its value, the variable is considered an *input of the step.* For example, the step "compute net pay" consists of a function that processes variables `gross` and `net`. This step uses the value of the variable `gross`, as well as the constants `MAX_NO_DUES` and `DUES` (its inputs) to compute `net` (its output).

Figure 4.6 also shows that a variable may have different roles in different subproblems of the structure chart. When considered in the context of the original problem statement, `hours` and `rate` are problem inputs (data supplied by the program user). However, when considered in the context of the subproblem "enter data," the subproblem's task is to deliver values for `hours` and `rate` to the main function, so they're considered outputs from this step.

When considered in the context of the subproblem "compute gross pay," the subproblem's task is to use `hours` and `rate` to compute a value of `gross`, so they're considered inputs to this step. In the same way, the role of the variables `gross` and `net` changes as we go from step to step in the structure chart.

## Commentary—The Software Development Method

The sequence of steps taken to solve the payroll problem with functions follows exactly the process outlined for the software development method presented in Chapter 1:

1. Analyze the problem statement to be sure that the problem specification is clear and complete.

2. Identify the relevant problem data including constants, input data, and output requirements as well as their data types.

3. Use top-down design to develop your solution. Break the main problem into simpler, smaller subproblems that can be solved with separate functions. Construct the structure chart, showing the data flow between modules and an algorithm that shows the sequence of steps required for the problem solution.

4. Refine your subproblems starting with an analysis similar to Step 1 above.

Once Steps 1 through 4 have been completed, you can write the main function and the prototypes for the lower-level functions. Next, design each of the subproblems following Steps 1 through 4, as was done for the main function. The layered approach to software design will enable you to focus first on the description of the data elements to be modeled and the data types that are most natural for modeling these elements.

This approach will also help you manage more complex problems by breaking them down into simpler, more easily solvable components. You'll see the benefits of this approach more clearly as problems become more complicated and you're able to build a complex system out of independent and reusable components that are relatively easy to understand and modify.

## EXERCISES FOR SECTION 4.5

### Self-Check

1. What are the benefits of using constant identifiers instead of literals in a program?

2. List three benefits of using the software design method applied in solving the payroll problem.

3. List all changes that would have to be made to the payroll program in Listing 4.1 if the union dues amount were changed from $15 to $25.

4. The input arguments to function `computeGross` included the employee's hourly rate, hours worked, overtime rate, and the maximum number of hours that could be worked without overtime. Should we have also included the union dues amount and the maximum earnings before union dues had to be paid? Why or why not?

Programming
1. Describe all modifications that would be required in the analysis, design, implementation, and testing of the payroll program if the problem statement were changed to include the requirement to deduct 18 percent in federal income tax if earnings exceeded $250.

2. Write function `readHours` that reads in hours worked and returns the value entered and function `readRate` that reads in hourly pay rate and returns the value entered.

3. Write function `printResults` that displays in a meaningful way the values of its two arguments that represent gross pay and net pay.

4. Modify the program in Listing 4.1 to use the functions in Programming Exercises 2 and 3.

# 4.6   Checking the Correctness of an Algorithm

As we said earlier, verifying the correctness of an algorithm is a critical step in algorithm design and can save hours of coding and testing time.

In Section 4.4, we simulated the execution of an `if` statement that switches the values of two variables. We now trace the execution of the refined algorithm for the payroll problem solved in the last section.

### Refined Algorithm
1. Display user instructions.

2. Enter hours worked and hourly rate.

3. Compute gross pay.

  3.1. If the hours worked exceed `40.0` (max hours before overtime)

    3.1.1. Compute `regularPay`.

    3.1.2. Compute `overtimePay`.

> **3.1.3.** Add `regularPay` to `overtimePay` to get gross.
>
> Else
>
> **3.1.4.** Compute gross as hours * rate.

4. Compute net pay.

   **4.1.** If `gross` is larger than $100.00

   > **4.1.1.** Deduct the dues of $15.00 from gross pay.
   >
   > Else
   >
   > **4.1.2.** Deduct no dues.

5. Display gross and net pay.

In Table 4.10, each step is listed at the left in the order of its execution. The last column shows the effect of each step. If a step changes the value of a variable, then the table shows the new value. If no new value is shown, the variable retains its previous value. For example, the table shows that step 2 stores the data values `30.0` and `10.00` in the variables `hours` and `rate`; `gross` and `net` are still undefined (indicated by `?` in the first table row).

The trace in Table 4.10 shows that `300.0` and `285.0` are stored in `gross` and `net` and then displayed. To verify that the algorithm is correct, you'd need to select other data that cause the two conditions to evaluate to different combinations of their values. Since there are two conditions and each has two possible values (`true` or `false`), there are two times two, or four, different combinations that should be tried. An exhaustive hand trace of the algorithm would show that it works for all combinations.

Besides the four cases discussed above, you should verify that the algorithm works correctly for unusual data. For example, what would happen if `hours` were `40.0` (value of `MAX_NO_OVERTIME`) or if `gross` were `100.0` (value of `MAX_NO_DUES`)? Would the algorithm still provide the correct

**Table 4.10** Trace of Algorithm for Payroll Problem

| Algorithm Step | hours | rate | gross | net | Effect |
|---|---|---|---|---|---|
|  | ? | ? | ? | ? |  |
| 2. Enter hours and rate | 30.0 | 10.00 |  |  | Reads the data |
| 3.1. If hours > 40.0 |  |  |  |  | hours > 40 is false |
| 3.1.4. gross gets hours * rate |  |  | 300.0 |  | Compute gross as hours * rate |
| 4.1. If gross > $100.00 |  |  |  |  | gross > 100.00 is true |
| 4.1.1. Deduct the dues of $15 |  |  |  | 285.0 | Deduct the dues of $15.00 |
| 5. Display gross and net |  |  |  |  | Displays 300.00 and 285.00 |

result? To complete the hand trace, you'd need to show that the algorithm handles these special situations properly.

In tracing each case, you must be careful to execute the algorithm exactly as the computer would execute it. Don't assume how a particular step will execute.

### EXERCISES FOR SECTION 4.6

Self-Check

1. Provide sample data that cause both conditions in the payroll problem to be true and trace the execution for these data.

2. If hours is greater than MAX_NO_OVERTIME and gross is less than MAX_NO_DUES, which assignment steps in the algorithm would be performed? Provide a trace.

## 4.7 Nested if Statements and Multiple-Alternative Decisions

Until now, we used if statements to implement decisions involving up to two alternatives. In this section, we use **nested if statements** (one if statement inside another) to code decisions with several alternatives.

**nested if statement**
An if statement with another if statement as its true task or its false task.

### EXAMPLE 4.14

The following nested if statement has three alternatives. It increases one of three variables (numPos, numNeg, or numZero) by one depending on whether x is greater than zero, less than zero, or equal to zero, respectively. The boxes show the logical structure of the nested if statement: the second if statement is the **false** task following the **else** of the first if statement.

```
if (x > 0)
      numPos = numPos + 1;
else
      if (x < 0)
            numNeg = numNeg + 1;
      else // x equals 0
            numZero = numZero + 1;
```

The execution of the nested `if` statement proceeds as follows: the first condition `(x > 0)` is tested; if it is true, `numPos` is incremented and the rest of the `if` statement is skipped. If the first condition is false, the second condition `(x < 0)` is tested; if it is true, `numNeg` is incremented; otherwise, `numzero` is incremented. It's important to realize that the second condition is tested only when the first condition is false.

Table 4.11 traces the execution of this statement when x is –7. Because `x > 0` is false, the second condition is tested.

---

**Table 4.11**    Trace of `if` Statement in Example 4.14 for x = –7

| Statement Part | Effect |
|---|---|
| `if (x > 0)` | –7 > 0 is false |
| `else` | |
|    `if (x < 0)` | –7 < 0 is true |
|      `numNeg = numNeg + 1;` | add 1 to numNeg |

---

## Comparison of Nested `if` Statements and a Sequence of `if` Statements

Beginning programmers sometimes prefer to use a sequence of `if` statements rather than a single nested `if` statement. For example, the previous `if` statement is rewritten as the following sequence of `if` statements.

```
// Less efficient sequence of if statements
if (x > 0)
   numPos = numPos + 1;
if (x < 0)
   numNeg = numNeg + 1;
if (x == 0)
   numZero = numZero + 1;
```

Although this sequence is logically equivalent to the original, it's neither as readable nor as efficient. Unlike the nested `if`, the sequence doesn't show clearly that exactly one of the three assignment statements is executed for a particular x. It's less efficient because all three of the conditions are always tested. In the nested `if` statement, only the first condition is tested when x is positive.

## Writing a Nested `if` as a Multiple-Alternative Decision

Nested `if` statements can become quite complex. If there are more than two alternatives and indentation is not consistent, it may be difficult to determine the logical structure of the `if` statement. For example, in the following nested `if` statement

```
if (condition₁)
   //  statement₁
      . . .
   if (condition₂)
   // statement₂
      . . .
else
   // statement₃
      . . .
```

does the else match up with the first if as shown by the identation or with the second if? The answer is the second if because an else is always associated with the closest if without an else. In the situation discussed in Example 4.14 in which each false task (except the last) is followed by an if and matching else, you can code the nested if as the *multiple-alternative decision* described next.

---

### Multiple-Alternative Decision Form

**Form:**
```
if (condition₁)
   statement₁;
else if (condition₂)
   statement₂;

   .
   .
   .

else if (conditionₙ)
   statementₙ;
else
   statementₑ;
```

**Example:**
```
// Increment numPos, numNeg, or numZero
// depending on x.
if (x > 0)
   numPos = numPos + 1;
else if (x < 0)
   numNeg = numNeg + 1;
else // x == 0
   numZero = numZero + 1;
```

**Interpretation:** The conditions in a multiple-alternative decision are evaluated in sequence until a true condition is reached. If a condition is true, the statement following it is executed and the rest of the multiple-alternative decision is skipped. If a condition is false, the statement following it is skipped and the next condition is tested. If all conditions are false, then *statementₑ* following the last **else** is executed.

## EXAMPLE 4.15

Suppose you want to match exam scores to letter grades for a large class of students. The following table describes the assignment of grades based on each exam score.

| Exam Score | Grade Assigned |
|---|---|
| 90 and above | A |
| 80 to 89 | B |
| 70 to 79 | C |
| 60 to 69 | D |
| Below 60 | F |

The multiple-alternative decision in function **displayGrade** (Listing 4.3) displays the letter grade assigned according to this table. If a student has an exam score of 85, the last three conditions would be true; however, a grade of B would be assigned because the first true condition is (**score >= 80**).

**Listing 4.3**   Function **displayGrade**

```
// Displays the letter grade corresponding to an exam
// score assuming a normal scale.
void displayGrade(int score)          // IN: exam score
{
   if (score >= 90)
      cout << "Grade is A" << endl;
   else if (score >= 80)
      cout << "Grade is B" << endl;
   else if (score >= 70)
      cout << "Grade is C" << endl;
   else if (score >= 60)
      cout << "Grade is D" << endl;
   else
      cout << "Grade is F" << endl;
}
```

## Order of Conditions

When more than one condition in a multiple-alternative decision is true, only the task following the first true condition is executed. Therefore, the order of the conditions can affect the outcome.

Writing the decision as follows would be incorrect. All passing scores (60 or above) would be incorrectly categorized as a grade of D because the first condition would be true and the rest would be skipped.

```
// incorrect grade assignment
if (score >= 60)
   cout << "Grade is D" << endl;
else if (score >= 70)
   cout << "Grade is C" << endl;
else if (score >= 80)
   cout << "Grade is B" << endl;
else if (score >= 90)
   cout << "Grade is A" << endl;
else
   cout << "Grade is F" << endl;
```

The order of conditions can also have an effect on program efficiency. If we know that low exam scores are much more likely than high scores, it would be more efficient to test first for scores below 60, next for scores below 70 , and so on (see Programming Exercise 3 at the end of this section).

## EXAMPLE 4.16

You could use a multiple-alternative `if` statement to implement a decision table that describes several alternatives. Let's assume that you're an accountant setting up a payroll system for a small firm having five different ranges for salaries up to $150,000, as shown in Table 4.12. Each table line shows the base tax amount (column 2) and tax percentage (column 3) for a particular salary range (column 1). Given a salary, you can calculate the tax by adding the base tax for that salary range to the product of the percentage of excess and the amount of salary over the minimum salary for that range.

For example, the second line of the table specifies that the tax due on a salary of $20,000.00 is $2,250.00 plus 16 percent of the excess salary over $15,000.00 (i.e., 16 percent of $5,000.00, or $800.00). Therefore, the total tax due is $2,250.00 plus $800.00, or $3,050.00.

The `if` statement in function `computeTax` (Listing 4.4) implements the tax table. If the value of **salary** is within the table range (0.00 to 150,000.00), exactly one of the statements assigning a value to **tax** will be executed. Table 4.13 shows a hand trace of the `if` statement when **salary** is $20,000.00. You can see that the value assigned to **tax**, $3050.00, is correct. Remember not to include symbols such as the dollar sign or commas in a `float` literal.

**Table 4.12**    Decision Table for Example 4.16

| Range | Salary | Base Tax | Percentage of Excess |
|---|---|---|---|
| 1 | 0.00 to 14,999.99 | 0.00 | 15 |
| 2 | 15,000.00 to 29,999.99 | 2250.00 | 16 |
| 3 | 30,000.00 to 49,999.99 | 4650.00 | 18 |
| 4 | 50,000.00 to 79,999.99 | 8250.00 | 20 |
| 5 | 80,000.00 to 150,000.00 | 14,250.00 | 25 |

**Listing 4.4**    Function `computeTax`

```
// Compute the tax due based on a tax table
float computeTax(float salary)    // IN: salary amount
{
   if (salary < 0.00)
      tax = -1;
   else if (salary < 15000.00)              // first range
      tax = 0.15 * salary;
   else if (salary < 30000.00)              // second range
      tax = (salary - 15000.00) * 0.16 + 2250.00;
   else if (salary < 50000.00)              // third range
      tax = (salary - 30000.00) * 0.18 + 4650.00;
   else if (salary < 80000.00)              // fourth range
      tax = (salary - 50000.00) * 0.20 + 8250.00;
   else if (salary <= 150000.00)            // fifth range
      tax = (salary - 80000.00) * 0.25 + 14250.00;
   else
      tax = -1;

   return tax;
}
```

**Table 4.13**    Trace of `if` Statement in Listing 4.4 for salary equals $20000.00

| Statement Part | salary | tax | Effect |
|---|---|---|---|
| | 20000.00 | ? | |
| `if (salary < 0.00)` | | | 20000.00 < 0.00 is false |
| `else if (salary < 15000.00)` | | | 20000.00 < 15000.00 is false |
| `else if (salary < 30000.00)` | | | 20000.00 < 30000.00 is true |
| `   tax = (salary - 15000.00)` | | | Evaluates to 5000.00 |
| `      * 0.16` | | | Evaluates to 800.00 |
| `      + 2250.00` | | 3050.00 | Evaluates to 3050.00 |

## Program Style    Validating the Value of Variables

If you validate the value of a variable before using it in computations, you can avoid processing invalid or meaningless data. Instead of computing an incorrect tax amount, function computeTax returns -1.0 (an impossible tax amount) if the value of salary is outside the range covered by the table (0.0 to 150,000.00). The first condition sets tax to -1.0 if salary is negative. All conditions evaluate to false if salary is greater than 150000.00, so the task following else sets tax to -1.0. The function calling computeTax should display an error message if the value returned to it is -1.0.

## Short-Circuit Evaluation of Logical Expressions

When evaluating logical expressions, C++ uses a technique called **short-circuit evaluation**. This means that evaluation of a logical expression stops as soon as its value can be determined. For example, if the value of (single == 'y') is false, then the logical expression

**short-circuit evaluation** Stopping evaluation of a logical expression as soon as its value can be determined.

```
(single == 'y') && (gender == 'm') && (age >= 18)
```

must be false regardless of the value of the other conditions (i.e., false && ( ...) must always be false). Consequently, there's no need to continue to evaluate the other conditions when (single == 'y') evaluates to false.

## EXAMPLE 4.17

If x is zero, the if condition

```
if ((x != 0.0) && (y / x > 5.0))
```

is false because (x != 0.0) is false, and false && ( ...) must always be false. Thus there's no need to evaluate the subexpression (y / x > 5.0) when x is zero. In this case, the first subexpression guards the second and prevents the second from being evaluated when x is equal to 0. However, if the subexpressions were reversed, the expression

```
if ((y / x > 5.0) && (x != 0.0))
```

would cause a "division by zero" run-time error when the divisor x is zero. Therefore, the order of the subexpressions in this condition is critical.

## EXERCISES FOR SECTION 4.7

Self-Check
1. Trace the execution of the nested `if` statements in Listing 4.4 for a salary of $135,000.

2. What would be the effect of reversing the order of the first two `if` statements in Listing 4.4?

3. Evaluate the expressions below, with and without short-circuit evaluation, if x equals 6 and y equals 7.

   a. `((x > 10) && (y / x <= 10))`
   b. `((x <= 10) || (x / (y - 7) > 3))`

4. Write pseudo code for the following: if the transaction is a deposit, add the transaction amount to the balance and display the new balance; else, if the transaction is a withdrawal and the transaction amount is less than or equal to the balance, deduct the transaction amount from the balance and display the new balance; else, if the transaction is a withdrawal but the amount is greater than the balance, deduct a PENALTY amount (a constant) from the balance and display a "withdrawal exceeds balance" warning message; else display an "illegal transaction" message.

Programming
1. Implement the decision table below using a nested `if` statement. Assume that the grade point average is within the range 0.0 through 4.0.

   | Grade Point Average | Transcript Message |
   | --- | --- |
   | 0.0 to 0.99 | Failed semester—registration suspended |
   | 1.0 to 1.99 | On probation for next semester |
   | 2.0 to 2.99 | (no message) |
   | 3.0 to 3.49 | Dean's list for semester |
   | 3.5 to 4.0 | Highest honors for semester |

2. Implement the solution to Self-Check Exercise 4 using a string to represent the transaction type.

3. Rewrite the `if` statement for Example 4.15 using only the relational operator < in all conditions.

4. The Air Force has asked you to write a program to label supersonic aircraft as military or civilian. Your program is to be given the plane's observed speed in kilometers per hour (km/h) and its estimated length in meters. For planes traveling in excess of 1100 km/h, you'll label those longer than 52 meters "`civilian`" and those shorter as "`mili-`"

`tary"`. For planes traveling at slower speeds, you'll issue an `"aircraft type unknown"` message.

# 4.8   The `switch` Control Statement

The `switch` control statement may also be used in C++ to select one of several alternatives. The `switch` statement is especially useful when the selection is based on the value of a single variable or a simple expression (called the `switch` *selector*). The value of this expression may be of type `int`, `char`, or `bool`, but not of type `float` or `string`.

## EXAMPLE 4.18

The `switch` statement

```
switch (momOrDad)
{
   case 'M': case 'm':
      cout << "Hello Mom - Happy Mother's Day" << endl;
      break;
   case 'D': case 'd':
      cout << "Hello Dad - Happy Father's Day" << endl;
      break;
}
```

behaves the same way as the `if` statement below when the character stored in `momOrDad` is one of the four letters listed (M, m, D, or d).

```
if ((momOrDad == 'M') || (momOrDad == 'm'))
   cout << "Hello Mom - Happy Mother's Day" << endl;
else if ((momOrDad == 'D') || (momOrDad == 'd'))
   cout << "Hello Dad - Happy Father's Day" << endl;
```

The message displayed depends on the value of the `switch` selector `momOrDad` (type `char`). If the `switch` selector value is `'M'` or `'m'`, the first message is displayed. If the `switch` selector value is `'D'` or `'d'`, the second message is displayed. The character constants `'M'`, `'m'` and `'D'`, `'d'` are called *case labels*.

Once a particular case label statement has been executed, the reserved word `break` causes control to be passed to the first statement following the `switch` control statement.

switch Statement

**Form:**
```
switch (selector)
{
  case label₁ : statements₁;
              break;
  case label₂ : statements₂;
              break;

            •
            •
            •

  case labelₙ : statementsₙ;
              break;
  default:    statement_d; // optional
}
```

**Example:**
```
// Display a musical note
switch (musicalNote)
{
  case 'c':
      cout << "do";
      break;
  case 'd':
      cout << "re";
      break;
  case 'e':
      cout << "mi";
      break;
  case 'f':
      cout << "fa";
      break;
  case 'g':
      cout << "sol";
      break;
  case 'a':
      cout << "la";
      break;
  case 'b':
      cout << "ti";
      break;
  default:
      cout << "An invalid note was read."
           << endl;
}
```

> **Interpretation:**  The *selector* expression is evaluated and compared to each of the **case** labels until a match is found. The selector expression should be an integral type (for example, **int**, **char**, **bool**, but not **float** or **string**). Each *label* is a single, constant value, and each one must have a different value from the others. When a match between the value of the *selector* expression and a **case** *label* is found, the statements following the case *label* are executed until a **break** statement is encountered. Then the rest of the **switch** statement is skipped.
>
>   If no case *label* matches the *selector*, the entire switch body is skipped unless it contains a **default** label. If there is a **default** label, the statements following the **default** are executed. The statements following a **case** *label* may be one or more C++ statements, which means that you don't need to make multiple statements into a single compound statement using braces.

## EXAMPLE 4.19

The **switch** statement in Listing 4.5 finds the average life expectancy of a standard lightbulb based on the bulb's wattage. Since the value of the variable **watts** controls the execution of the **switch** statement, **watts** must have a value before the statement executes. Case labels **40** and **60** have the same effect (also, case labels **75** and **100**).

**Listing 4.5**   switch statement to determine life expectancy of a lightbulb

```
// Determine average life expectancy of a standard
// lightbulb.
switch (watts)
{
   case 25:
      life = 2500;
      break;
   case 40:
   case 60:
      life = 1000;
      break;
   case 75:
   case 100:
      life = 750;
      break;
   default:
      life = 0;
}
```

## Proper Use of **break**

Don't forget to use the reserved word `break` at the end of a statement sequence in a `switch` statement. If the `break` is omitted, then execution will continue, or *fall through*, to the next statement sequence. This is usually an error in logic.

## Comparison of Nested **if** Statements and the **switch** Statement

You can use a nested `if` statement, which is more general than the `switch` statement, to implement any multiple-alternative decision. The `switch` statement is more readable in many contexts and should be used whenever practical. Case labels that contain type `float` values or strings are not permitted.

    You should use the `switch` statement when each label set contains a reasonable number of case labels (a maximum of ten). However, if the number of values is large, use a nested `if`. You should use a `default` label in a `switch` statement wherever possible. The discipline of trying to define a default will help you to consider what will happen if the value of your `switch` statement's selector expression falls outside the range of your set of case labels.

## Using a **switch** Statement to Select Alternative Functions

Instead of placing lengthy statement alternatives in the body of a switch, you should consider moving this code to a function. This leads to a very common use for the `switch` statement: selecting a particular function from a group of possible choices.

### EXAMPLE 4.20

Assume the type `char` variable `editOp` contains a data value (`D`, `I`, or `R`) that indicates the kind of text edit operation to be performed on `string` object `textString`. We use the `switch` statement in function `edit` (Listing 4.6) to call a function that performs the selected operation, passing `textString` as a function argument. Each function returns the modified string as its result. The modified string is assigned to `textString` and is returned by function `edit`.

    Using this structure, we place the code for each edit operation in a separate function. These functions might prompt the user for specific information, such as a substring to insert, replace, or delete, and perform all necessary operations on this data (by calling member functions from the `string` class).

**Listing 4.6**   String editing function edit

```
// Perform string editing function.
string edit(string textString,        // IN: string to edit
            char editOp)               // IN: edit operation
{
   switch (editOp)
   {
     case 'D': case 'd':               // Delete a substring
        textString = doDelete(textString);
        break;
     case 'I': case 'i':               // Insert a substring
        textString = doInsert(textString);
        break;
     case 'R': case 'r':               // Replace a substring
        textString = doReplace(textString);
        break;
     case 'Q': case 'q' :              // Quit editing
        cout << "All done!" << endl;
        break;
     default:
        cout << "An invalid edit code was entered." << endl;
   }
   return textString;

} //end edit
```

Program decomposition into separate components is the key here. The details of how our string is processed can be written without affecting the simple *control code* in the switch statement.

## EXERCISES FOR SECTION 4.8

Self-Check
1. What will be printed by the following carelessly constructed switch statement if the value of color is 'R'? Fix the error in this statement.

```
switch (color)
{
   case 'R': case 'r':
      cout << "red" << endl;
   case 'B': case 'b':
      cout << "blue" << endl;
      case 'Y': case 'y':
      cout << "yellow" << endl;
}
```

If `color` were type `string`, could you use `"Red"` and `"red"` as `case` labels for the first selection? Explain your answer.

2. Write an `if` statement that corresponds to the `switch` statement below.

```
switch (x > y)
{
   case 1 :
      cout << "x greater" << endl;
      break;
   case 0 :
      cout << "y greater or equal" << endl;
      break;
}
```

3. Why can't we rewrite our nested `if` statement examples from Section 4.7 using `switch` statements?

4. Why is it preferable to include a `default` label in a `switch` statement?

5. What would be the effect of omitting the first `break` statement in Listing 4.5? Would this be a syntax error, run-time error, or logic error?

Programming

1. Write a `switch` statement that prints a message indicating whether `nextCh` (type `char`) is an operator symbol (+, -, *, /, %), a punctuation symbol (comma, semicolon, parenthesis, brace, bracket), or a digit. Your statement should print the category selected. Include a `default` label.

2. Write a nested `if` statement equivalent to the `switch` statement described in Programming Exercise 1.

3. Implement the solution to Self-Check Exercise 4 of Section 4.7 using a type `char` variable for the transaction type. Assume `'d'` or `'D'` indicates a deposit and `'w'` or `'W'` indicates a withdrawal. Use a `switch` statement.

# 4.9   Common Programming Errors

Common errors using `if` statements involve writing the condition incorrectly and failure to enclose compound statements in braces. A common error for `switch` statements is omitting a `break` statement.

- *Parentheses:* For the most part, the defined precedence levels of C++ will prevent you from making a syntax error when writing conditions. But they will also allow you to do things you may not intend. The rule of thumb is, when in doubt, use parentheses.

- *Operators:* You can use the logical operators, `&&`, `||`, and `!`, only with logical expressions. Remember that the C++ operator for equality is the double symbol ==. Don't mistakenly use the assignment operator (single =) in its place. Your logical expression will probably compile, but the logic will be incorrect.

■ *Compound statements:* Don't forget to bracket a compound statement used as a true or false task in an `if` control statement with braces. If the { } bracket is missing, only the first statement will be considered part of the task. This could lead to a syntax error—or, worse, a logic error that could be very difficult to find. In the following example, the { } bracket around the true task is missing. The compiler assumes that only the statement

```
sum = sum + x;
```

is part of the true task of the `if` control statement. This creates a "misplaced else" syntax error. Of course, the correct thing to do is to enclose the compound statement in braces.

```
if (x > 0)                          // missing { }
    sum = sum + x;
    cout << "Greater than zero" << endl;
else
    cout << "Less than zero" << endl;
```

■ *Nested `if` statement:* When writing a nested `if` statement, try to select the conditions so that the multiple-alternative form shown in Section 4.7 can be used. If the conditions are not mutually exclusive (i.e., if more than one condition may be true), the most restrictive condition should come first.

■ `switch` *statements:* When using a `switch` statement, make sure the `switch` selector and `case` labels are of the same type (`int`, `char`, or `bool` but not `float`). If the selector evaluates to a value not listed in any of the `case` labels, the `switch` statement will fall through without any action being taken. For this reason, it's often wise to guard the `switch` with a `default` label. This way you can ensure that the `switch` executes properly in all situations. Be very careful in your placement of the `break` statements. Missing `break` statements will allow control to fall through to the next `case` label.

## Chapter Review

1. Control structures are used to control the flow of statement execution in a program. The compound statement is a control structure for sequential execution.

2. Selection control structures are used to represent decisions in an algorithm and pseudocode is used to write them in algorithms. Use the `if` statement or `switch` statement to code decision steps in C++.

3. Expressions whose values indicate whether certain conditions are true can be written

   - using the relational operators (<, <=, >, >=) and equality operators ( ==, !=) to compare variables and constants.
   - using the logical operators (&& (and), || (or), ! (not)) to form more complex conditions.

4. Data flow information in a structure chart indicates whether a variable processed by a subproblem is used as an input or an output, or as both. An input provides data that are manipulated by the subproblem, and an output returns a value copied from an input device or computed by the subproblem. The same variable may be an input to one subproblem and an output from another.

5. A hand trace of an algorithm verifies whether it is correct. You can discover errors in logic by carefully hand tracing an algorithm. Hand tracing an algorithm before coding it as a program will save you time in the long run.

6. Nested `if` statements are common in C++ and are used to represent decisions with multiple alternatives. Programmers use indentation and the multiple-alternative decision form when applicable to enhance readability of nested `if` statements.

7. The `switch` statement implements decisions with several alternatives, where the alternative selected depends on the value of a variable or expression (the *selector* expression). The *selector* expression can be type `int`, `bool`, or `char`, but not type `double` or `string`.

## Summary of New C++ Constructs

| Construct | Effect |
|---|---|
| **`if` Control Statement** | |
| *With Dependent Statement* | |
| `if (y != 0)`<br>`    result = x / y;` | Divides `x` by `y` only if `y` is nonzero. |
| *Two Alternatives* | |
| `if (x >= 0)`<br>`    cout << x << " is positive"`<br>`        << endl;`<br>`else`<br>`    cout << x << " is negative"`<br>`        << endl;` | If `x` is greater than or equal to 0, display the message "`is positive`"; otherwise, display the message "`is negative`". |

## Summary of New C++ Constructs (continued)

| Construct | Effect |
|---|---|

*Several Alternatives*

```
if (x < 0)
{
    cout << "Negative" << endl;
    absX = -x;
}
else if (x == 0)
{
    cout << "Zero" << endl;
    absX = 0;
}
else
{
    cout << "Positive" << endl;
    absX = x;
}
```

One of three messages is printed, depending on whether x is negative, positive, or zero. absX is set to represent the absolute value or magnitude of x.

Prints one of five messages based on the value of nextCh (type char). If nextDh is 'D', 'd' or 'F', 'f', the student is put on probation.

**switch Statement**

```
switch (nextCh)
{
    case 'A': case 'a':
        cout << "Excellent" << endl;
        break;
    case 'B': case 'b':
        cout << "Good" << endl;
        break;
    case 'C': case 'c':
        cout << "Fair" << endl;
        break;
    case 'D': case 'd':
    case 'F': case 'f'':
        cout << "Poor, student is"
             << " on probation"
             << endl;
        break;
    default :
        cout << "Invalid grade."
             << endl;
}
```

Prints one of five messages based on the value of nextCh (type char). If nextDh is 'D', 'd' or 'F', 'f', the student is put on probation.

## Quick-Check Exercises

1. An `if` statement implements a(n) _____ in an algorithm or program.

2. What is a compound statement?

3. A `switch` statement is often used instead of _____.

4. What values can a logical expression have?

5. Are the conditions (`x != y`) and `!(x == y)` logically equivalent or different? Explain your answer.

6. A hand trace is used to verify that a(n) _____ is correct.

7. Correct the syntax errors below.

```
if x > 25.0
    y = x
    cout << x << y << endl;
else
    y = z;
    cout << y << z << endl;
```

8. What value is assigned to `fee` by the `if` statement below (a) when speed is 50? (b) When speed is 51? (c) When speed is 15? (d) When speed is 130?

```
if (speed > 35)
    fee = 20;
else if (speed > 50)
    fee = 40;
else if (speed > 75)
    fee = 60;
```

9. Can you implement the `if` statement for question 8 as a `switch` statement? If yes, what are the advantages or disadvantage of doing it?

10. Answer Exercise 8 for the `if` statement below. Which `if` statement is correct?

```
if (speed > 75)
    fee = 60;
else if (speed > 50)
    fee = 40;
else if (speed > 35)
    fee = 20;
else
    fee = 0;
```

11. What output line(s) are displayed by the statements below (a) when grade is 'W'? (b) When grade is 'C'? (c) When grade is 'c'? (d) When grade is 'P'?

```
switch (grade)
{
    case 'A':
        points = 4;
        break;
    case 'B':
        points = 3;
        break;
    case 'C':
        points = 2;
        break;
    case 'D':
        points = 1;
        break;
    case 'F':
    case 'I':
    case 'W':
        points = 0;
        break;
}
if (('A' <= grade) && (grade <= 'D'))
    cout << "Passed, points earned = " << points << "."
         << endl;
else
    cout << "Failed, no points earned." << endl;
```

12. Explain the difference between the statements on the left and the statements on the right below. For each of them, what is the final value of x if the initial value of x is 0?

```
if (x >= 0)              if (x >= 0)
    x = x + 1;               x = x + 1;
else if (x >= 1)         if (x >= 1)
    x = x + 2;               x = x + 2;
```

13. **a.** Evaluate the expression below when x is 25:

```
true  &&  (x % 10 >= 0)  &&  (x / 10 <= 3)
```

   **b.** Is either pair of parentheses required? Is the constant `true` required?

   **c.** Write the complement of the expression.

## Answers to Quick-Check Exercises

1. decision

2. a block that combines one or more statements into a single statement

3. nested `if` statements or a multiple-alternative `if` statement

4. true or false

5. They are logically equivalent because they always have the same logical value.

6. algorithm

7. 
```
if (x > 25.0)
   {
      y = x;
      cout << x << y << endl;
   }
else
   {
      y = z;
      cout << y << z << endl;
   }
```

8. 20, 20, undefined, 20

9. You could use speed as a *selector* expression, but it would be impractical because the list of `case` labels would be very long.

10. 20, 40, 0, 60; this one

11. (a) when `grade` is `'W'`: `Failed, no points earned.`
    (b) when `grade` is `'C'`: `Passed, points earned = 2.`
    (c) when `grade` is `'c'`: `Failed, no points earned.`
    (d) when `grade` is `'P'`: `Failed, no points earned.`

12. A nested `if` statement is on the left; a sequence of `if` statements is on the right. x becomes 1 on the left; x becomes 3 on the right.

13. (a) true, remainder is 5 and quotient is 2.
    (b) no, no
    (c) Removing false and unnecessary parentheses: `!(x % 10 > 0  && x % 10 <= 3)`

## Review Questions

1. Making a decision between two alternatives is usually implemented with a(n) _____ statement in C++.

2. How does a relational operator differ from a logical operator?

3. What is short-circuit logical evaluation? What are its benefits?

4. Trace the following program fragment and indicate which function will be called if a data value of 35.5 is entered.

```
cout << "Enter a temperature: ";
cin >> temp;
if (temp > 32.0)
    notFreezing();
else
    iceForming();
```

5. Write a nested `if` statement to display a message indicating the educational level of a student based on his or her number of years of schooling (0, none; 1 through 6, elementary school; 7 through 8, middle school; 9 through 12, high school; 13 through 16, college; greater than 16, graduate school). Print a message to indicate bad data as well.

6. Write a `switch` statement to select an operation based on the value of `inventory`. Increment `totalPaper` by `paperOrder` if `inventory` is `'b'` or `'c'`; increment `totalRibbon` by 1 if `inventory` is `'e'`, `'f'`, or `'d'`; increment `totalLabel` by `labelOrder` if `inventory` is `'a'` or `'x'`. Do nothing if `inventory` is `'m'`. Display an error message if `inventory` is any other value.

7. Implement a decision structure for the following computation:

   ■ If your taxable income is less than or equal to $15,000, pay no taxes.

   ■ If your taxable income is greater than $15,000 but less than or equal to $44,000, pay taxes at a rate of 20 percent on the amount in excess of $15,000.

   ■ If your taxable income is greater than $44,000 but less than or equal to $68,150, pay taxes at the rate of 22 percent on the first $44,000 and 28 percent on the amount in excess of $44,000.

   ■ If your taxable income is greater than $68,150 but less than or equal to $121,300, pay taxes at the rate of 28 percent on the first $58,150 and 31 percent on the amount in excess of $58,150.

   ■ If your taxable income is greater than $121,300 but less than or equal to $263,750, pay taxes at the rate of 31 percent on the first $121,300 and 36 percent on the amount in excess of $121,300.

- If your taxable income is greater than $263,750, pay taxes at a rate of 36 percent on the first $263,750 and 39.6 percent on the amount in excess of $263,750.

8. Write a type `bool` function that returns `true` if its argument (a year) is a leap year. A leap year occurs every fourth year. Not every century is a leap year; every *fourth* century is a leap year. This means that 1900 is not a leap year, 2000 is a leap year, and 2100 is not a leap year.

## Programming Projects

1. Write functions to draw a circle, square, and triangle. Write a program that reads a letter c, s, or t and, depending on the letter chosen, draws either a circle, square, or triangle.

2. Write a program that reads in four words (as character strings) and displays them in increasing as well as in decreasing alphabetic sequence.

3. Write a program that reads in a room number, its capacity, and the size of the class enrolled so far and prints an output line showing the classroom number, capacity, number of seats filled, number of seats available, and a message indicating whether the class is filled. Call a function to display the following heading before the first output line:

```
Room    Capacity    Enrollment    Empty Seats    Filled/
                                                 Not Filled
```

Display each part of the output line under the appropriate heading. Test your program with the following classroom data:

| Room | Capacity | Enrollment |
|------|----------|------------|
| 426  | 25       | 25         |
| 327  | 18       | 14         |
| 420  | 20       | 15         |
| 317  | 100      | 90         |

4. Write a program that displays a "message" consisting of three block letters where each letter is an X or an O. The program user's data determines whether a particular letter will be an X or O. For example, if the user enters the three letters XOX, the block letters X, O, and X will be displayed.

5. Write a program to simulate a state police radar gun. The program should read an automobile speed and print the message `"speeding"` if the speed exceeds 55 mph.

6. While spending the summer as a surveyor's assistant, you decide to write a program that transforms compass headings in degrees (0 to 360) to compass bearings. A compass bearing consists of three items: the direction you face (north or south), an angle between 0 and 90 degrees, and the direction you turn before walking (east or west). For example, to get the bearing for a compass heading of `110.0` degrees, you would first face due south (180 degrees) and then turn `70.0` degrees east (`180.0` - `110.0`). Be sure to check the input for invalid compass headings.

7. Write a program that interacts with the user like this:

```
(1) Carbon monoxide
(2) Hydrocarbons
(3) Nitrogen oxides
(4) Nonmethane hydrocarbons
Enter pollutant number>> 2
Enter number of grams emitted per mile>> 0.35
Enter odometer reading>> 40112
Emissions exceed permitted level of 0.31 grams/mile.
```

Use the table of emissions limits below to determine the appropriate message.

|  | First Five Years or 50,000 Miles | Second Five Years or Second 50,000 Miles |
|---|---|---|
| carbon monoxide | 3.4 grams/mile | 4.2 grams/mile |
| hydrocarbons | 0.31 grams/mile | 0.39 grams/mile |
| nitrogen oxides | 0.4 grams/mile | 0.5 grams/mile |
| nonmethane hydrocarbons | 0.25 grams/mile | 0.31 grams/mile |

8. The New Telephone Company has the following rate structure for long-distance calls:

- The regular rate for a call is $0.10 per minute.
- Any call started at or after 6:00 P.M. (1800 hours) but before 8:00 A.M. (0800 hours) is discounted 50 percent.
- Any call longer than 60 minutes receives a 15 percent discount on its cost (after any other discount is subtracted).
- All calls are subject to a 4 percent federal tax on their final cost.

Write a program that reads the start time for a call based on a 24-hour clock and the length of the call. The gross cost (before any discounts or tax) should be printed, followed by the net cost (after discounts are deducted and tax is added). Use separate functions to print instructions to the program user and to compute the net cost.

9. Write a program that will calculate and print out bills for the city water company. The water rates vary, depending on whether the bill is for home use, commercial use, or industrial use. A code of h means home use, a code of c means commercial use, and a code of i means industrial use. Any other code should be treated as an error. The water rates are computed as follows:

- Code h: $5.00 plus $0.0005 per gallon used
- Code c: $1000.00 for the first 4 million gallons used and $0.00025 for each additional gallon
- Code i: $1000.00 if usage does not exceed 4 million gallons; $2000.00 if usage is more than 4 million gallons but does not exceed 10 million gallons; and $3000.00 if usage exceeds 10 million gallons

Your program should prompt the user to enter an account number (type int), the code (type char), and the gallons of water used (type float). Your program should echo the input data and print the amount due from the user.

10. Write a program to control a bread machine. Allow the user to input the type of bread as W for White and s for Sweet. Ask the user if the loaf size is double and if the baking is manual. The program should fail if the user inputs are invalid. The following table is a time chart for the machine used for each bread type. Print a statement for each step. If the loaf size is double, increase the baking time by 50 percent. If baking is manual, stop after the loaf-shaping cycle and instruct the user to remove the dough for manual baking. Use a function to print program instructions.

Time Chart for Making Bread

| Operation | White Bread | Sweet Bread |
|---|---|---|
| Primary kneading | 15 mins | 20 mins |
| Primary rising | 60 mins | 60 mins |
| Secondary kneading | 18 mins | 33 mins |
| Secondary rising | 20 mins | 30 mins |
| Loaf shaping | 2 seconds | 2 seconds |
| Final rising | 75 mins | 75 mins |
| Baking | 45 mins | 35 mins |
| Cooling | 30 mins | 30 mins |

11. Write a function that returns the digit value (an integer) corresponding to the letter passed to it as an argument based on the encoding on your telephone handset. For example, if the argument is the letter a, b, or c (uppercase or lowercase), your function should return the digit 2. If the argument is not one of the letters of the alphabet, return a value of

–1. Write a program that tests your function. Implement two versions of the function: one using a `switch` statement and one using a nested `if` statement. Write a program that tests your functions.

12. Write a function `dayNumber` that returns the day number (1 to 366) in a year for a date that is provided as input data. Your function should accept the month (1 through 12), day, and year as integers. As an example, January 1, 1994 is day 1. December 31, 1993 is day 365. December 31, 1996 is day 366 since 1996 is a leap year. A year is a leap year if it's divisible by four, except that any year divisible by 100 is a leap year only if it's also divisible by 400. Write and use a second function that returns true if its argument, a year, is a leap year.

13. Write a program that reads in two dates (using three integers for each) and displays a message showing the date that comes first. Use the following algorithm: `if` the first date's year is smaller, it comes first; `else if` the second date's year is smaller, it comes first; `else` check the month to determine which date comes first in a similar way. If the months are the same, check the day.

14. Write a function that uses Euclid's algorithm to calculate the greatest common divisor of its two integer arguments where both arguments are positive and the first argument should be greater than or equal to the second. For example, `euclid(10, 2)` is 2, `euclid(20, 12)` is 4. Euclid's algorithm (`int euclid(int m, int n)`) for finding the greatest common divisor of m and n follows:

```
if (m is less than n)    // the arguments are in the
                         //      wrong order
    return the result of euclid(n, m) // reverse the
                                      // arguments
else if (n divides m)    // n is a divisor of m
    return n
else
    return euclid(n, remainder of m divided by n)
```

The above algorithm is called a recursive algorithm because function `euclid` calls itself (a legal operation in C++). If the first condition is true, the arguments need to be reversed before the greatest common divisor can be found by recalling function `euclid`. If the second condition is true, the smaller argument, n, must be the divisor we're seeking. Otherwise, the result can be determined by recalling function `euclid` to find the greatest common divisor of n and the remainder of m divided by n. Verify that this algorithm works for the examples shown in the first paragraph. Then write this function and test it out.

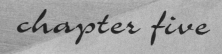

## chapter five

# Repetition and Loop Statements

## Chapter Objectives

- To understand why repetition is an important control structure in programming
- To learn about loop control variables and the three steps needed to control loop repetition
- To learn how to use the C++ `for`, `while`, and `do-while` statements for writing loops and when to use each statement type
- To learn how to accumulate a sum or a product within a loop body
- To learn common loop patterns such as counting loops, sentinel-controlled loops, flag-controlled loops, and menu-driven loops
- To understand nested loops and how the outer loop control variable and inner loop control variable are changed in a nested loop
- To learn how to debug programs using a debugger
- To learn how to debug programs by adding diagnostic output statements

IN THE PROGRAMS YOU'VE WRITTEN so far, the statements in the program body execute only once. But in most commercial software that you're likely to use, you can repeat a process many times. For example, when using an editor program or a word processor, you can move the cursor to a program line and perform as many edit operations as you need to.

Repetition, you'll recall, is the third type of program control structure (*sequence, selection, repetition*), and the repetition of steps in a program is called a **loop**. In this chapter we describe when to use loops in programs and common loop patterns in programming. We also describe three C++ loop control statements:

while, for, and do-while. In addition to explaining how to write loops using each statement, we describe the advantages of each and explain when it's best to use each one. Like if statements, loops can be nested, and this chapter demonstrates how to write and use nested loops in your programs.

## 5.1    Counting Loops and the `while` Statement

Just as the ability to make decisions is an important programming tool, so too is the ability to specify repetition of a group of operations. For example, a company that has seven employees will want to repeat the gross pay and net pay computations in its payroll program seven times, once for each employee. The **loop body** contains the statements to be repeated.

**loop**
A control structure that repeats a group of statements in a program.
**loop body**
The statements that are repeated in a loop.

Writing out a solution to a specific problem can help you create a general algorithm to solve similar problems. After solving the sample case, ask yourself some of the following questions to determine whether loops will be required in the general algorithm:

1. Were there any steps I repeated as I solved the problem? If so, which ones?

2. If the answer to question 1 is yes, did I know in advance how many times to repeat the steps?

3. If the answer to question 2 is no, how did I know how long to keep repeating the steps?

Your answer to the first question indicates whether your algorithm needs a loop and what steps to include in the loop body if it does need one. Your answers to the other questions will help you determine which loop structure to choose for your solution.

**counter-controlled loop (counting loop)**
A loop whose repetition is managed by a loop control variable whose value represents a count.
**loop control variable**
A variable that is used to regulate how many times a loop should be repeated.

The loop shown in pseudocode below is called a **counter-controlled loop** (or **counting loop**) because its repetition is managed by a **loop control variable** whose value represents a count. A counter-controlled loop follows the following general format:

**Counting Loop**
Set *loop control variable* to an initial value of 0.
while *loop control variable* < *final value*
     . . .
      Increase *loop control variable* by 1.

We use a counter-controlled loop when we can determine prior to loop execution exactly how many loop repetitions will be needed to solve the problem. This number should appear as the *final value* in the while condition.

## The while Statement

Listing 5.1 shows a program fragment that computes and displays the gross pay for seven employees. The loop body is the compound statement that starts on the third line. The loop body gets an employee's payroll data and computes and displays that employee's pay. After seven weekly pay amounts are displayed, the statement following the loop body executes and displays the message All employees processed.

The three colored lines in Listing 5.1 control the looping process. The first statement

```
countEmp = 0;                 // no employees processed yet
```

stores an initial value of 0 in the variable countEmp, which represents the count of employees processed so far. The next line evaluates the condition countEmp < 7. If the condition is true, the compound statement for the loop body executes, causing a new pair of data values to be read and a new pay to be computed and displayed. The last statement in the loop body,

```
countEmp = countEmp + 1; // increment count of employees
```

adds 1 to the current value of countEmp. After executing the last step in the loop body, control returns to the line beginning with while, and the condition is reevaluated for the next value of countEmp. The loop body executes once for each value of countEmp from 0 to 6. Eventually, countEmp becomes 7, and the condition evaluates to false. When this happens, the loop body is not executed and control passes to the display statement that follows the loop body.

**Listing 5.1**  Program fragment with a loop

```cpp
countEmp = 0;                 // no employees processed yet
while (countEmp < 7)          // test the count of employees
{
    cout << "Hours: ";
    cin >> hours;
    cout << "Rate : $";
    cin >> rate;
    pay = hours * rate;
    cout << "Weekly pay is " << pay << endl;
    countEmp = countEmp + 1;  // increment count of
                              //    employees
}
cout << "All employees processed" << endl;
```

**loop repetition condition**
The condition that is evaluated to determine whether to execute the loop body (condition is true) or to exit from the loop (condition is false).

The logical expression following the reserved word `while` is called the **loop repetition condition**. The loop is repeated when this condition is true. We say that the loop is *exited* when this condition is false.

The flowchart in Figure 5.1 summarizes what we've explained so far about `while` loops. In the flowchart, the expression in the diamond-shaped box is evaluated first. If that expression is true, the loop body is executed, and the process is repeated. The `while` loop is exited when the expression becomes false. If the loop repetition condition is false when it's first tested, then the loop body is not executed at all.

Make sure you understand the difference between the `while` statement in Listing 5.1 and the `if` statement:

```
if (countEmp < 7)
{
    . . .
}
```

In an `if` statement, the compound statement after the condition executes at most only once. In a `while` statement, the compound statement (loop body) may execute more than once.

### Syntax of the `while` Statement

In Listing 5.1, variable `countEmp` is the loop control variable because its value determines whether or not the loop body is repeated. The loop control variable `countEmp` must be (1) *initialized*, (2) *tested*, and (3) *updated* for the loop to execute properly. Each step is summarized as follows:

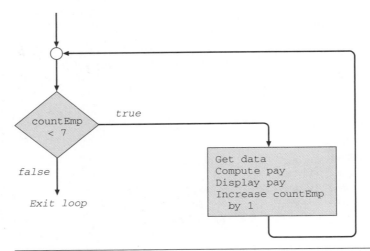

**Figure 5.1** Flowchart for a `while` loop

1. *Initialize:* `countEmp` is set to a starting value of 0 (initialized to 0) before the `while` statement is reached.

2. *Test:* `countEmp` is tested before the start of each loop repetition (called an *iteration* or a *pass*).

3. *Update:* `countEmp` is updated (its value increases by 1) during each iteration.

Similar steps must be performed for every `while` loop. Without the initialization, the initial test of `countEmp` is meaningless. The updating step ensures that the program progresses toward the final goal (`countEmp >= 7`) during each repetition of the loop. If the loop control variable is not updated, the loop will execute "forever." Such a loop is called an **infinite loop**.

**infinite loop**
A loop that executes forever.

---

**`while` Statement**

**Form:**        `while (loop repetition condition)`
                     `statement;`

**Example:** `// display n asterisks`
```
countStar = 0;
while (countStar < n)
{
    cout << "*";
    countStar = countStar + 1;
}
```

**Interpretation:** The *loop repetition condition* (a condition to control the loop process) is tested; if it's true, the *statement* (loop body) is executed and the *loop repetition condition* is retested. The *statement* is repeated as long as (while) the *loop repetition condition* is true. When this condition is tested and found to be false, the `while` loop is exited and the next program statement after the `while` statement is executed.

**Notes:** If the *loop repetition condition* evaluates to false the first time it's tested, *statement* is not executed.

---

## EXERCISES FOR SECTION 5.1

**Self-Check**

1. What will happen in the execution of the loop in Listing 5.1

   a. if the update statement

      `countEmp = countEmp + 1;`

      is omitted?

**b.** if the initialization statement

```
countEmp = 0;
```

is omitted?

2. Predict the output of this program fragment:

```
i = 0;
while (i < 7)
{
    cout << i - 1 << i
         << -i + 1 << endl;
    i = i + 1;
}
```

3. What does this program fragment display for an input of 11?

```
cin >> n;
ev = 0;
sum = 0;
while (ev < n)
{
    cout << ev;
    sum = sum + ev;
    ev = ev + 2;
}
cout << ev << "*** " << sum << endl;
```

4. How many times is the loop body below repeated? What is displayed during each repetition of the loop body?

```
x = 3;
count = 0;
while (count < 3)
{
    x = x * x;
    cout << x << endl;
    count = count + 1;
}
```

5. Answer the previous exercise if the last statement in the loop is

```
count = count + 2;
```

Programming

1. Write a `while` loop that displays each integer from 1 to 5 together with its square and cube. Display all three values for each integer on a separate line.

**2.** Write a program fragment that produces the output below. Hint: If n is the number in the first column, the number in the second column is 2 to the power n.

```
0    1
1    2
2    4
3    8
4   16
5   32
6   64
```

## 5.2 Accumulating a Sum or Product in a Loop

Loops often accumulate a sum or a product by repeating an addition or multiplication operation, as will be demonstrated in Examples 5.1 and 5.2.

### EXAMPLE 5.1

The program in Listing 5.2 has a `while` loop similar to the loop in Listing 5.1. Besides displaying each employee's weekly pay, it computes and displays the company's total payroll. Prior to loop execution, the statements

```
totalPay = 0.0;
countEmp = 0;
```

initialize both `totalPay` and `countEmp` to zero, where `countEmp` is the counter variable. Here `totalPay` is an accumulator variable, and it accumulates the total payroll value. Initializing `totalPay` is critical; if you omit this step, your final total will be off by whatever value happens to be stored in `totalPay` when the program begins execution.

In the loop body, the assignment statement

```
totalPay = totalPay + pay;           // add next pay
```

adds the current value of `pay` to the sum being accumulated in `totalPay`. Consequently, the value of `totalPay` increases with each loop repetition. Table 5.1 traces the effect of repeating this statement for the three values of pay shown in the sample run.

---

**Listing 5.2** Program to compute company payroll

---

```
// File: computePay.cpp
// Computes the payroll for a company

#include <iostream>
using namespace std;
```

(continued)

**Listing 5.2** Program to compute company payroll (continued)

```cpp
int main()
{
    int numberEmp;          // input - number of employees
    int countEmp;           // counter - current employee number
    float hours;            // input - hours worked
    float rate;             // input - hourly rate
    float pay;              // output - weekly pay
    float totalPay;         // output - company payroll

    // Get number of employees from user.
    cout << "Enter number of employees: ";
    cin >> numberEmp;

    // Process payroll for all employees.
    totalPay = 0.0;
    countEmp = 0;
    while (countEmp < numberEmp)
    {

        cout << "Hours: ";
        cin >> hours;
        cout << "Rate : $";
        cin >> rate;
        pay = hours * rate;
        cout << "Pay is $" << pay << endl << endl;
        totalPay = totalPay + pay;          // add next pay
        countEmp = countEmp + 1;
    }
    cout << "Total payroll is $" << totalPay << endl;
    cout << "All employees processed." << endl;

    return 0;
}
```

```
Enter number of employees: 3
Hours: 50
Rate : $5.25
Pay is $262.5
Hours: 6
Rate : $5
Pay is $30
Hours: 15
```

(continued)

**Listing 5.2**  Program to compute company payroll (continued)

```
Rate : $7
Pay is $105
Total payroll is $397.5

All employees processed.
```

**Table 5.1**  Trace of Three Repetitions of the Loop in Listing 5.2

| Statement | Hours | Rate | Pay | totalPay | countEmp | Effect |
|---|---|---|---|---|---|---|
|  | ? | ? | ? | 0.0 | 0 |  |
| countEmp < numberEmp |  |  |  |  |  | true |
| cin >> hours; | 50.0 |  |  |  |  | get hours |
| cin >> rate; |  | 5.25 |  |  |  | get rate |
| pay = hours * rate; |  |  | 262.5 |  |  | compute pay |
| totalPay = totalPay + pay; |  |  |  | 262.5 |  | add to totalPay |
| countEmp = countEmp + 1; |  |  |  |  | 1 | increment countEmp |
| countEmp < numberEmp |  |  |  |  |  | true |
| cin >> hours; | 6.0 |  |  |  |  | get hours |
| cin >> rate; |  | 5.0 |  |  |  | get rate |
| pay = hours * rate; |  |  | 30.0 |  |  | compute pay |
| totalPay = totalPay + pay; |  |  |  | 292.5 |  | add to totalPay |
| countEmp = countEmp + 1; |  |  |  |  | 2 | increment countEmp |
| countEmp < numberEmp |  |  |  |  |  | true |
| cin >> hours; | 15.0 |  |  |  |  | get hours |
| cin >> rate; |  | 7.0 |  |  |  | get rate |
| pay = hours * rate; |  |  | 105.0 |  |  | compute pay |
| totalPay = totalPay + pay; |  |  |  | 397.5 |  | add pay to totalPay |
| countEmp = countEmp + 1; |  |  |  |  | 3 | increment countEmp |

## Program Style   Writing General Loops

Because the loop in Listing 5.1 uses the loop repetition condition countEmp < 7, it processes exactly seven employees. The loop in Listing 5.2 is more general. It uses the loop repetition condition countEmp < numberEmp so it can process any number of employees. The number of employees to be processed must be read into variable numberEmp before the while statement executes. The loop repetition condition compares the number of employees processed so far (countEmp) to the total number of employees (numberEmp).

## Multiplying a List of Numbers

In a similar way, we can use a loop to accumulate a product, as shown in the next example.

### EXAMPLE 5.2

The next loop multiplies data items as long as the product remains less than 10,000. It displays the product calculated so far before asking for the next data value. The product so far is updated on each iteration by executing the statement

```
product = product * item; // Update product
```

Loop exit occurs when the value of `product` is greater than or equal to 10,000. Consequently, the loop body does not display the last value assigned to `product`.

```
// Multiply data while product remains less than 10000
product = 1;
while (product < 10000)
{
    cout << product << endl;   // display product so far
    cout << "Enter data item: ";
    cin >> item;
    product = product * item; // Update product
}
```

**conditional loop**
A loop that repeats the processing of data while a specified condition is true.

This is an example of a **conditional loop**—a loop that repeats the processing of data while a specified condition is true as indicated by its pseudocode below.

**Conditional Loop**

1. Initialize the *loop control variable.*
2. `while` a condition involving the loop control variable is true
    3. Continue processing.
    4. Update the loop control variable.

For the product computation loop, the loop control variable is `product`, which is initialized to 1. The loop repetition condition is that `product` is less than 10,000, and the steps of the loop body make up the processing mentioned in pseudocode Step 3. We discuss conditional loops in Section 5.4.

## Compound Assignment Operators

We've seen several assignment statements of the form

*variable* = *variable op expression*;

where *op* is a C++ arithmetic operator. These include increments and decrements of loop counters

```
countEmp = countEmp + 1;
time = time - 1;
```

as well as statements accumulating a sum or computing a product in a loop, such as

```
totalPay = totalPay + pay;
product = product * item;
```

C++ provides special assignment operators that enable a more concise notation for statements of this type. For the operations +, -, *, /, and %, C++ defines the compound *op=* assignment operators +=, -=, *=, /=, and %=. A statement of the form

*variable op* = *expression*;

is an alternative way of writing the statement

*variable* = *variable op (expression)*;

Table 5.2 shows some examples using compound assignment operators.

**Table 5.2**   Compound Assignment Operators

| Statement with Simple Assignment Operator | Equivalent Statement with Compound Assignment Operator |
|---|---|
| `countEmp = countEmp + 1;` | `countEmp += 1;` |
| `time = time - 1;` | `time -= 1;` |
| `totalTime = totalTime + time;` | `totalTime += time;` |
| `product = product * item;` | `product *= item;` |
| `n = n * (x + 1);` | `n *= (x + 1);` |

## EXERCISES FOR SECTION 5.2

**Self-Check**

1. What output values are displayed by the `while` loop below for a data value of 5? Of 6? Of 7? In general, what does this loop display?

```
cout << "Enter an integer: ";
cin >> x;
product = 1;
count = 0;
while (count < 5)
{
    cout << product << endl;
    product *= x;
    count += 1;
}
```

2. Answer Self-Check Exercise 1 if the order of the first two statements in the loop body is reversed.

3. The following segment needs some revision. Insert braces where needed, indent properly, and correct the errors. The corrected segment should read five integers and display their sum.

```
count = 0;
while (count <= 5)
cout << "Enter data item: ";
cin >> item;
item += sum;
count += 1;
cout << count << " data items were added;" << endl;
cout << "their sum is " << sum << endl;
```

4. Write equivalents for the following statements using compound assignment operators.

```
r = r % 10;
z = z + x + 1;
q = q - r * m;
m = m - (n + p);
```

Programming

1. Write a loop that produces the output below (hint: each number in the right column is the sum of all values in the left column up to that point):

```
i     sum
0     0
1     1
2     3
3     6
4     10
5     15
6     21
```

2. Write a program that computes `1 + 2 + 3 + ... + (n - 1) + n` using a loop, where n is a data value. Follow the loop with an `if` statement that compares this value to `(n * (n + 1)) / 2` and displays a message that indicates whether the values are the same or different. What message do you think will be displayed?

## 5.3 The **for** Statement

C++ provides the `for` statement as another form for implementing loops, especially for counting loops. The loops we've seen so far are typical of most repetition structures in that they have three loop control components:

- *initialization* of the loop control variable,
- *testing* the loop repetition condition, and
- *updating* the loop control variable.

An important feature of the `for` statement in C++ is that it supplies a designated place for each of these three components. A `for` statement implementation of the loop from Listing 5.2 is shown in Listing 5.3.

**Listing 5.3**   Using a `for` statement in a counting loop

```cpp
// Process payroll for all employees.
totalPay = 0.0;
for (countEmp = 0;              // initialization
     countEmp < numberEmp;  // test
     countEmp += 1)            // update
{

   cout << "Hours: ";
   cin >> hours;
   cout << "Rate : $";
   cin >> rate;
   pay = hours * rate;
   cout << "Pay is $" << pay << endl << endl;
   totalPay += pay;        // accumulate total pay
}
cout << "Total payroll is $" << totalPay << endl;
cout << "All employees processed." << endl;
```

The effect of this `for` statement is exactly equivalent to the execution of the comparable `while` loop in the earlier program (Listing 5.2). Because the `for` statement's heading

```
for (countEmp = 0;          // initialization
     countEmp < numberEmp;  // test
     countEmp += 1)         // update
```

combines the three loop control steps of initialization, testing, and update in one place, separate steps to initialize and update `countEmp` must not appear elsewhere. The `for` statement can be used to count up or down by any interval.

---

**`for` Statement**

**Form:**   `for` (*initialization expression;*
               *loop repetition condition;*
               *update expression*)
               *statement;*

**Example:**   `// Display N asterisks.`
               `for  (countStar = 0;`
                     `countStar < N;`
                     `countStar += 1)`
                     `cout << '*';`

**Interpretation:** First, the initialization expression is executed. Then, the *loop repetition condition* is tested. If it's true, the *statement* is executed, and the *update expression* is evaluated. Then the *loop repetition condition* is retested. The *statement* is repeated as long as the *loop repetition condition* is true. When this condition is tested and found to be false, the `for` loop is exited, and the next program statement after the `for` statement is executed.

**Caution:** Although C++ permits the use of fractional values for counting loop control variables of type `float`, we strongly discourage this practice. Counting loops with type `float` control variables may not execute the same number of times on different computers.

---

## Program Style   Formatting the **`for`** Statement

For clarity, we often place each expression of the `for` heading on a separate line. If all three expressions are very short, we may place them together on one line. Here is an example:

```
// Display nonnegative numbers < max
for (i = 0; i < max; i += 1)
    cout << i << endl;
```

The body of the `for` loop is indented. If the loop body is a compound statement or if we're using a style in which we bracket all loop bodies, we place the opening brace on a separate line after the `for` heading and terminate the statement by placing the closing brace on a separate line. The braces should align with the "f" of `for`.

## Increment and Decrement Operators

The counting loops that we've discussed so far have all included assignment statements of the form

```
counter = counter + 1;
```

or

```
counter += 1;
```

We can also implement this assignment as

```
counter++;
```

or

```
++counter;
```

using the C++ increment operator. The increment operator ++ takes a single variable as its operand. The **side effect** of applying the ++ operator is that the value of its operand is incremented by one. Frequently, ++ is used just for this side effect, as in the following loop in which the variable `counter` is to run from 0 up to (but not including) `limit`:

**side effect**
A change in the value of a variable as a result of carrying out an operation.

```
for (counter = 0; counter < limit; counter++)
    . . .
```

The *value* of the expression in which the ++ operator is used depends on the position of the operator. When the ++ is placed immediately in front of its operand (*prefix increment*), the value of the expression is the variable's value *after* incrementing. When the ++ comes immediately after the operand (*postfix increment*), the expression's value is the value of the variable *before* it's incremented. For example, the second statement below

```
m = 3;
n = m++;
```

assigns 3 to n and then increments m (new value of m is 4). Conversely, the second statement below

```
m = 3;
n = ++m;
```

increments m before the assignment to n (m and n are both 4).

You should avoid using the increment and decrement (--) operators in complex expressions in which the variables to which they are applied appear more than once. C++ compilers are expected to exploit the commutativity and associativity of various operators in order to produce efficient code. For example, the next code fragment may assign y the value 13 (2 * 5 + 3) in one implementation and the value 18 (3 * 5 + 3) in another.

```
x = 5;
i = 2;
y = i * x + ++i;
```

A programmer must not depend on side effects that will vary from one compiler to another.

## EXAMPLE 5.3

Function `factorial` (Listing 5.4) computes the factorial of an integer represented by the formal parameter n. The loop body executes for *decreasing values* of i from n through 2, and each value of i is incorporated in the accumulating product (n × (n−1) × ... × 3 × 2). Loop exit occurs when i is 1.

## Program Style    Localized Declarations of Variables

The example that follows illustrates the use of a localized variable declaration—the loop control variable i. Because `for` loop control variables often

**Listing 5.4**    Function to compute factorial

```
// Computes factorial (n!)
// Pre: n is greater than or equal to zero
int factorial(int n)
{
    int product;      // accumulator for product computation
    product = 1;
    // Computes the product n x (n-1) x (n-2) x  . . .   x2
    for (int i = n; i > 1; i—)
      product = product * i;
    // Returns function result
    return product;
}
```

have meaning only inside the loop, we can declare these variables at the point of first reference—in the `for` loop header. A loop control variable declared this way can be referenced only inside the loop body.

## EXAMPLE 5.4

The `for` statement shown next displays the characters in `firstName`, one character per line. It illustrates the use of the string functions `length` and `at`. If `firstName` is `Jill`, the loop displays the letters `J`, `i`, `l`, `l` on separate lines. The loop repeats exactly `firstName.length()` times.

```
string firstName;
cout << "Enter your first name: ";
cin >> firstName;
for (int posChar = 0; posChar < firstName.length();
     posChar++)
   cout << firstName.at(posChar) << endl;
```

## Increments and Decrements Other than One

We've seen `for` statement counting loops that count up by one and down by one. Now we'll use a loop that counts down by five to display a Celsius-to-Fahrenheit conversion table.

## EXAMPLE 5.5

The table displayed by the program in Listing 5.5 shows temperature conversions from 10 degrees Celsius to 25 degrees Celsius because of the values of the constants `CBEGIN` (10) and `CLIMIT` (-5). The loop update step `celsius -= CSTEP` decreases the value of the counter `celsius` by five after each repetition. Loop exit occurs when `celsius` becomes less than `CLIMIT`, so loop exit occurs when the value of celsius is 210. The last value of `celsius` displayed in the program output is 25.

**Listing 5.5**  Converting Celsius to Fahrenheit

```
// File: temperatureTable.cpp
// Conversion of celsius to fahrenheit temperature

#include <iostream>
#include <iomanip>
using namespace std;
```

(continued)

**Listing 5.5**    Converting Celsius to Fahrenheit (continued)

```cpp
int main()
{
    const int CBEGIN = 10;
    const int CLIMIT = -5;
    const int CSTEP = 5;
    float fahrenheit;

    // Display the table heading.
    cout << "Celsius" << "      Fahrenheit" << endl;

    // Display the table.
    for (int celsius = CBEGIN;
             celsius >= CLIMIT;
             celsius -= CSTEP)
    {
      fahrenheit = 1.8 * celsius + 32.0;
      cout << setw(5) << celsius
           << setw(15) << fahrenheit << endl;
    }

    return 0;
}
```

```
Celsius    Fahrenheit
   10         50.00
    5         41.00
    0         32.00
   -5         23.00
```

## Displaying a Table of Values

The program in Listing 5.5 displays a table of output values. The output state before the loop displays a string that forms the table heading. Within the loop body, the output statement

```cpp
cout << setw(5) << celsius
     << setw(15) << fahrenheit << endl;
```

**manipulators**
Member functions of
class iomanip that
control the format of
input/output list items.

displays a pair of output values each time it executes. The items in color above are **manipulators**—member functions of the class iomanip. Manipulators can precede one or more output list items and they control the format or appearance of these items when they are displayed. The manipulator setw(5) causes the next output value (value of celsius) to be displayed using five character positions on the screen. If a number has less than five characters, blanks appear before the number. If a number requires more than five characters to be displayed correctly, the extra characters will be displayed. The manipulators in the above output statement align the output values for `celsius` and `fahrenheit` in columns under the appropriate heading. We describe manipulators in more detail in Section 8.5.

## EXERCISES FOR SECTION 5.3

Self-Check

1. Trace the execution of the loop that follows for `n = 10`. Show values of `odd` and `sum` after the update of the loop counter for each iteration.

```
sum = 0;
for (odd = 1;
     odd < n;
     odd += 2)
{
   sum = sum + odd;
   cout << odd << ", " << sum << endl;
}

cout << "Sum of positive odd numbers less "
     << "than " << n << " is " << sum << endl;
```

2. Rewrite the loop in Exercise 1 using a `while` statement.

3. Given the constant definitions of Listing 5.5 (repeated here)
```
const int CBEGIN = 10;
const int CLIMIT = -5;
const int CSTEP = 5;
```

indicate what values of `celsius` would appear in the conversion table displayed if the `for` loop header of Listing 5.5 were rewritten as shown:

   a. `for (celsius = CLIMIT;`
      `celsius >= CBEGIN;`
      `celsius += CSTEP)`

   b. `for (celsius = CLIMIT;`
      `celsius <= CBEGIN;`
      `celsius += CSTEP)`

   c. `for (celsius = CLIMIT;`
      `celsius <= CSTEP;`
      `celsius += CBEGIN)`

    **d.** `for (celsius = CSTEP;`
             `celsius >= CBEGIN;`
             `celsius += CLIMIT)`

3. What is the least number of times that the body of a `while` loop can be executed? The body of a `for` loop?

4. Assume i is 3 and j is a. What is the value assigned to variables m, n, and p and what is the value of i and j after each statement below executes?
```
n = ++i * -j;
m = i + j-;
p = i + j;
```

5. Rewrite the code shown in Exercise 4 so the effect is equivalent but no increment/decrement operator appears in an expression with another arithmetic operator. (Hint: the first statement should be ++i; .)

6. What errors do you see in the following fragment? Correct the code so it displays all multiples of 5 from 0 through 100.
```
for mult5 = 0;
mult5 < 100;
mult5 += 5;
cout << mult5 << endl;
```

7. **a.**  Trace the following program fragment:
```
j = 10;
for  (int i = 5; i > 0 ; i-)
{
   cout <<  i << ", " << j;
   j -= 2;
}
```

    **b.**  Rewrite the previous program fragment so that it produces the same output but displays i in the first five columns and j in the next five columns.

## Programming

1. Write a loop that displays a table of angle measures along with their sine and cosine values. Assume that the initial and final angle measures (in degrees) are available in `initDegree` and `finalDegree` (type `int` variables), and that the change in angle measure between table entries is given by `stepDegree` (also a type `int` variable). Remember that the cmath library's `sin` and `cos` functions take arguments that are in radians. Write this loop using a `for` statement and a `while` statement.

2. Write a program to display a centimeter-to-inches conversion table. The smallest and largest number of centimeters in the table are input values. Your table should give conversions in 10-centimeter intervals. One inch equals 2.54 cm.

# 5.4 Conditional Loops

In many programming situations, you won't be able to determine the exact number of loop repetitions before loop execution begins. The number of repetitions may depend on some aspect of the data that is not known in advance but that usually can be stated by a condition. Like the counting loops we considered earlier, a conditional loop typically has three parts that control repetition: (1) initialization, (2) testing of a loop repetition condition, and (3) an update. The general form for a conditional loop is the following:

**Conditional Loop**
Initialize the loop control variable.
while a condition involving the loop control variable is true
    Continue processing.
    Update the loop control variable.

For example, if we're getting the number of employees of a company, we want to continue reading data until a positive number or zero is entered. Another way of saying this is "We want to continue reading numbers as long as all previous data for number of employees were negative." Clearly, the loop repetition condition is

*number of employees < 0*

Because it makes no sense to test this condition unless number of employees has a meaning, getting this value must be the initialization step. We still need to identify the update action—the statement that, if left out, would cause the loop to repeat infinitely. Getting a new number of employees within the loop body is just such a step. Since we've found these three essential loop parts, we can write this validating input loop in pseudocode:

Prompt for number of employees.
Read number of employees.
while number of employees < 0
    Display a warning and another prompt.
    Read number of employees.

This loop can be implemented easily using the C++ while statement:

```
cout << "Enter number of employees: ";
cin >> numEmp;                    // initialization
while (numEmp < 0)                // test
{
    cout << "Negative number invalid; try again: ";
    cin >> numEmp;                // update
}
```

At first, it may seem odd that the initialization and update steps are identical. In fact, this is very often the case for loops performing input operations in situations where the number of input values is not known in advance.

## A Loop with a Decreasing Loop Control Variable

We study another conditional loop in the next case study. In this example, the loop repetition condition involves testing whether the value of the loop control variable has dropped below a critical point. The value of the loop control variable decreases during each iteration.

*case study*   ## Monitoring Oil Supply

### PROBLEM

We want to monitor the amount of oil remaining in a storage tank at the end of each day. The initial supply of oil in the tank and the amount taken out each day are data items. Our program should display the amount left in the tank at the end of each day and it should also display a warning when the amount left is less than or equal to 10 percent of the tank's capacity. At this point, no more oil can be removed until the tank is refilled.

### ANALYSIS

Clearly, the problem inputs are the initial oil supply and the amount taken out each day. The outputs are the oil remaining at the end of each day and a warning message when the oil left in the tank is less than or equal to 10 percent of its capacity.

DATA REQUIREMENTS
**Problem Constant**

```
CAPACITY = 10000        // tank capacity
MINPCT = 0.10           // minimum percent
```

**Problem Inputs**

```
float supply            // initial oil supply
```
*Each day's oil use*

**Problem Output**

```
float oilLevel          // final oil amount
```
*Each day's oil supply*
*A warning message when the oil*
*supply is less than minimum*

**Program Variable**

```
float minOil            // minimum oil supply
```

FORMULAS
*Minimum oil supply is 10 percent of tank's capacity*

## DESIGN

We list the major steps next.

INITIAL ALGORITHM
1. Get the initial oil supply.
2. Compute the minimum oil supply.
3. Compute and display the amount of oil left each day.
4. Display the oil left and a warning message if necessary.

We'll implement Step 3 using function `monitorOil`. The function's analysis and design follows.

## ANALYSIS FOR MONITOROIL

Function `monitorOil` must display a table showing the amount of oil left at the end of each day. To accomplish this, the function must read each day's usage and deduct that amount from the oil remaining. The function needs to receive the initial oil supply and the minimum oil supply as inputs (arguments) from the main function.

FUNCTION INTERFACE FOR **monitorOil**
**Input Parameters**
```
float supply          // initial oil supply
float minOil          // minimum oil supply
```

**Output**
Returns the final oil amount

**Local Data**
```
float usage           // input from user - Each day's oil use
float oilLeft         // output to user - Each day's oil supply
```

## DESIGN OF MONITOROIL

The body of `monitorOil` is a loop that displays the oil usage table. We can't use a counting loop because we don't know in advance how many days it will take to bring the supply to a critical level. We do know the initial supply of oil, and we know that we want to continue to compute and display the amount of oil remaining (`oilLeft`) as long as the amount of oil remaining does not fall below the minimum. So the loop control variable must be `oilLeft`. We need to initialize `oilLeft` to the initial supply and to repeat the loop as long as `oilLeft > minOil` is true. The update step should deduct the daily usage (a data value) from `oilLeft`.

INITIAL ALGORITHM FOR **monitorOil**

1. Initialize `oilLeft` to `supply`.

2. `while (oilLeft > minOil)`

    **2.1.** Read in the daily usage.

    **2.2.** Deduct the daily usage from `oilLeft`.

    **2.3.** Display the value of `oilLeft`.

### IMPLEMENTATION

Listing 5.6 shows the program. Notice that function `monitorOil` performs three critical steps that involve the loop control variable `oilLeft`.

- *Initialize* `oilLeft` to the initial supply before loop execution begins.
- *Test* `oilLeft` before each execution of the loop body.
- *Update* `oilLeft` (by subtracting the daily usage) during each iteration.

### TESTING

To test the program, try running it with a few samples of input data. One sample should bring the oil level remaining to exactly 10 percent of the capacity. For example, if the capacity is 10,000 gallons, enter a final daily usage amount that brings the oil supply to 1,000 gallons and see what happens. Also, verify that the program output is correct when the initial oil supply is below 10 percent of the capacity, as discussed next.

## Zero Iteration Loops

The body of a `while` loop is not executed if the loop repetition test fails (evaluates to false) when it's first reached. You should always verify that a program still generates the correct results for zero iteration loops. If the value read into `supply` is less than 10 percent of the tank's capacity, the loop body in Listing 5.6 would not execute and the main function would display only the line below.

```
The oil left in the tank is less than 1000 gallons.
```

## Program Style    Performing Loop Processing in a Function Subprogram

In Listing 5.6, function `monitorOil` contains a `while` loop that performs the major program task—monitoring the oil remaining in a tank. This program structure is fairly common and quite effective. Placing all loop processing in a function subprogram simplifies the main function.

**Listing 5.6**   Program to monitor oil supply

```cpp
// File: oilSupply.cpp
// Displays daily usage and amount left in oil tank.
#include <iostream>
using namespace std;

float monitorOil(float, float);

int main()
{
   const float CAPACITY = 10000;      // tank capacity
   const float MINPCT = 10.0;         // minimum percent

   float supply;              // input - initial oil supply
   float oilLeft;             // output - oil left in tank
   float minOil;              // minimum oil supply

   // Get the initial oil supply.
   cout << "Enter initial oil supply: ";
   cin >> supply;

   // Compute the minimum oil supply.
   minOil = CAPACITY * (MINPCT / 100.0);

   // Compute and display the amount of oil left each day.
   oilLeft = monitorOil(supply, minOil);

   // Display a warning message if supply is less than minimum
   cout << endl << oilLeft << " gallons left in tank." << endl;
   if (oilLeft < minOil)
      cout << "Warning - amount of oil left is below minimum!"
           << endl;

   return 0;
}

// Computes and displays the amount of oil left each day.
// Pre: initial supply and minimum amount are calculated.
// Returns the amount of oil left at end of last day.

float monitorOil(float supply, float minOil)
{
   // Local data . . .
   float usage;               // input from user - Each day's oil use
```

(continued)

**Listing 5.6** Program to monitor oil supply (continued)

```cpp
    float oilLeft;           // Amount left each day

    oilLeft = supply;
    while (oilLeft > minOil)
    {
        cout << "Enter amount used today: ";
        cin >> usage;
        oilLeft -= usage;
        cout << "After removal of " << usage << " gallons, ";
        cout << "number of gallons left is " << oilLeft
             << endl << endl;
    }

    return oilLeft;
}
```

```
Enter initial oil supply: 7000
Enter amount used today: 1000
After removal of 1000 gallons, number of gallons left is 6000

Enter amount used today: 4000
After removal of 4000 gallons, number of gallons left is 2000

Enter amount used today: 1500
After removal of 1500 gallons, number of gallons left is 500

500 gallons left in tank
Warning - amount of oil left is below minimum!
```

## More General Conditional Loops

Often the loop repetition condition in a conditional loop contains the logical operator && (and). For example, if we know that the oil tank is always refilled after 14 days, we might want to use the loop heading

```cpp
while ((oilLeft > minOil) && (numDays < 14))
```

in function monitorOil. In this case, loop repetition continues only if both relations are true, so loop exit will occur if either one becomes false.

The loop repetition condition uses oilLeft and numDays as loop control variables, so each variable should be initialized before loop entry and update in the loop body. We should initialize numDays to 0 and increment it by one in the loop body.

# EXERCISES FOR SECTION 5.4

## Self-Check

1. Provide an example of data that would cause function `monitorOil` to return without executing the body of the loop.

2. **a.** Correct the syntax and logic of the code that follows so that it displays all multiples of 3 from 0 through 60, inclusive:

```
sum = 0;
while (sum < 60) ;
   sum += 3;
   cout << sum << endl;
```

   **b.** Rewrite the above fragment using a `for` loop. Is this a counting loop? Explain your answer.

3. What output is displayed if this list of data is used for the program in Listing 5.6?

```
5000
4000.5
550.25
```

4. How would you modify the program in Listing 5.6 so that it also determines the number of days (`numDays`) before the oil supply drops below the minimum? Which is the loop control variable, `oilLeft` or `numDays` or both?

5. Trace the execution of the following loop for data values of 5, 4, 10, –5. Are all the data values read in?

```
cin >> n;
while (n > 0 && pow(2, n)   < 1000)
{
    cout << n << ", " << " << pow(2, n) << endl;
    cin >> n;
}
```

## Programming

1. There are 900 people in a town whose population increases by 10 percent (a data item) each year. Write a loop that displays the annual population and determines how many years (`countYears`) it will take for the population to pass 20,000. Verify that your program works if the population doubles each year (an increase of 100%).

2. Rewrite the payroll program (Listing 5.2), moving the loop processing into a function subprogram. Return the total payroll amount as the function result.

**3.** Rewrite function `monitorOil` to allow the tank to have oil added to it as well as removed.

## 5.5   Loop Design and Loop Patterns

In this section, we look more carefully at loop design issues and illustrate some common loop patterns you're likely to encounter in programming. First we summarize the thought processes that went into the design of the loop in Listing 5.6. The comment

```
// Compute and display the amount of oil left each day.
```

that precedes the call to function `monitorOil` in the main function is a good summary of the purpose of the loop. The columns labeled "Answers" and "Implications ..." in Table 5.3 represent one problem solver's approach to the loop design.

**Table 5.3**   Problem-Solving Questions for Loop Design

| Question | Answer | Implications for the Algorithm |
|---|---|---|
| What are the inputs? | Initial supply of oil (`supply`) Amounts removed (`usage`) | Input variables needed: `supply` `usage` Value of `supply` must be input once, but amounts used are entered many times. |
| What are the outputs? | Current amount of oil | Values of `oilLeft` are displayed. |
| Is there any repetition? | Yes. Program repeatedly<br>1. gets amount used<br>2. subtracts the amount used from the amount left<br>3. checks to see whether the amount left has fallen below the minimum. | Program variable `oilLeft` is needed. |
| Do I know in advance how many times steps will be repeated? | No | Loop will not be controlled by a counter. |
| How do I know how long to keep repeating the steps? | As long as current supply not less than or equal to minimum | The loop repetition condition is `oilLeft > minOil` |

## Sentinel-Controlled Loops

Many programs with loops read one or more data items each time the loop body is repeated. Often we don't know how many data items the loop should process when it begins execution. Therefore, we must find some way to signal the program to stop reading and processing data.

One way to do this is to instruct the user to enter a unique data value, called a **sentinel value**, after the last data item. The loop repetition condition tests each data item and causes loop exit when the sentinel value is read. Choose the sentinel value carefully; it must be a value that could not normally occur as data.

**sentinel value**
A data item entered after the last actual data item, used to cause loop exit.

A loop that processes data until the sentinel value is entered has the following form:

> **Sentinel-Controlled Loop**
> 1. Read the first data item.
> 2. `while` the sentinel value has not been read
> 3. Process the data item.
> 4. Read the next data item.

Note that this loop, like other loops we've studied, has an *initialization* (Step 1), a *loop repetition condition* (Step 2), and an *update* (Step 4). Step 1 gets the first data item; Step 4 gets all the other data items and then tries to obtain one more item. This attempted extra input permits entry (but not processing) of the sentinel value. For program readability, we usually name the sentinel by defining a constant.

## EXAMPLE 5.6

A program that calculates the sum of a collection of exam scores is a candidate for using a sentinel value. If the class is large and attendance varies, the instructor may not know the exact number of students who took the exam being graded. The program should work regardless of class size. The following statements (a and b) must be true for a sentinel-controlled loop that accumulates the sum of a collection of exam scores where each data item is read into the variable **score**. The sentinel value must not be included in the sum.

a. **sum** is the total of all scores read so far.
b. **score** contains the sentinel value just after loop exit.

From statement (a) we know that we must add each score to **sum** in the loop body, and that **sum** must initially be zero in order for its final value to be correct. From statement (b) we know that loop exit must occur after the sentinel value is read into **score**.

A solution is to read the first score as the initial value of **score** before the loop is reached and then to perform the following steps in the loop body:

- Add score to sum.
- Read the next score.

The algorithm outline for this solution is shown next.

---

**Sentinel-Controlled Loop for Processing Exam Scores**
1. Initialize sum to zero.
2. Read first score.
3. while score is not the sentinel
     4. Add score to sum.
     5. Read next score.

---

Beginning programmers sometimes try to cut down on the number of Read operations by reversing the order of Steps 4 and 5 above and deleting Step 2. We show this incorrect sentinel loop pattern next.

Incorrect Sentinel Loop for Processing Exam Scores
1. Initialize sum to zero.
2. while score is not the sentinel
     3. Read score.
     4. Add score to sum.

There are two problems associated with this strategy. Because there's no initializing input statement, the initial test of score is meaningless. Also, consider the last two iterations of the loop. On the next-to-last iteration, the last data value is copied into score and added to the accumulating sum; on the last iteration, the attempt to get another score obtains the sentinel value. However, this fact will not cause the loop to exit until the loop repetition condition is tested again. Before this happens, the sentinel is added to sum. For these reasons, it's important to set up sentinel-controlled loops using the recommended structure: one input to get the loop going (the *initialization* input), and a second to keep it going (the *updating* input).

The program in Listing 5.7 uses a while loop to implement the correct sentinel-controlled loop shown earlier. It calls function displayGrade (see again Listing 4.3) to display the grade for each score. Besides summing the scores, the program also computes and displays the average, as discussed in the next section.

**Listing 5.7** A sentinel-controlled loop

```cpp
// File: sumScores.cpp
// Accumulates the sum of exam scores.

#include <iostream>
using namespace std;

void displayGrade(int);              // See Listing 4.3

int main()
{
   const int SENTINEL = -1;          // sentinel value
   int score;                        // input - each exam score
   int sum;                          // output - sum of scores
   int count;                        // output - count of scores
   int average;                      // output - average score

   // Process all exam scores until sentinel is read
   count = 0;
   sum = 0;
   cout << "Enter scores one at a time as requested." << endl;
   cout << "When done, enter " << SENTINEL << " to stop." << endl;
   cout << "Enter the first score: ";
   cin >> score;
   while (score != SENTINEL)
   {
     sum += score;
     count++;
     displayGrade(score);
     cout << endl<< "Enter the next score: ";
     cin >> score;
   }

   cout << endl << endl;
   cout << "Number of scores processed is " << count << endl;
   cout << "Sum of exam scores is " << sum << endl;

   // Compute and display average score.
   if (count > 0)
   {
       average = sum / count;
       cout << "Average score is " << average;
   }
```

(continued)

**Listing 5.7**   A sentinel-controlled loop (continued)

```
    return 0;
}

// Insert function displayGrade here. (See Listing 4.3).
```

```
Enter scores one at a time as requested.
When done, enter -1 to stop.
Enter the first score: 85
Grade is B
Enter the next score : 33
Grade is F
Enter the next score : 77
Grade is C
Enter the next score : -1
Number of scores processed is 3
Sum of exam scores is 195
Average score is 65
```

Let's check what happens when there are no data items to process. In this case, the sentinel value would be entered after the first prompt. Loop exit would occur right after the first and only test of the loop repetition condition, so the loop body would not execute. The variables sum and count would remain zero. Also, the average would not be calculated or displayed.

## Calculating an Average

The program in Listing 5.7 calculates the average exam score as well as the sum. This happens because an extra variable, count, has been added to keep track of the number of scores processed. We initialize count to 0 before entering the loop and use the statement

```
    count++;
```

in the loop body to increment count after each exam score is processed. Notice that count has no role in loop control—the loop repetition condition tests the loop control variable score, not count.

After loop exit, the value of sum is the sum of scores and the value of count is the number of scores processed, so we can divide sum by count to get the average. Notice that this division takes place only when count is nonzero.

## Flag-Controlled Loops

Type `bool` variables are often used as *flags* to control the execution of a loop. The value of the flag is initialized (usually to false) prior to loop entry and is redefined (usually to true) when a particular event occurs inside the loop. A **flag-controlled loop** executes as long as the anticipated event has not yet occurred.

> **flag-controlled loop**
> A loop whose repetition condition is a type `bool` variable that is initialized to one value (either false or true) and reset to the other value when a specific event occurs.

> **Flag-Controlled Loop**
> 1. Set the flag to false.
> 2. `while` the flag is false
>       3. Perform some action.
>       4. Reset the flag to true if the anticipated event occurred.

## EXAMPLE 5.7

Function `getDigit` (Listing 5.8) has no arguments and returns a type `char` value. It scans the data characters entered at the keyboard and returns the first digit character in the data. For example, if the user has typed in the data line `Abc$34%`, the character returned would be 3. The statement

```
ch = getDigit();
```

stores the character returned by `getDigit` in `ch` (type `char`).

Function `getDigit` uses the local variable `digitRead` as a flag to indicate whether a digit character has been read. Because no characters are read before the loop executes, it initializes `digitRead` to false. The `while` loop continues to execute as long as `digitRead` is false because this means that the event "digit character read" has not yet occurred. Therefore, the loop repetition condition is (`!digitRead`), because this condition is true when `digitRead` is false. Inside the loop body, the type `bool` assignment statement

```
digitRead = (('0' <= nextChar) && (nextChar <= '9'));
```

assigns a value of true to `digitRead` if the character just read into `nextChar` is a digit character (within the range `'0'` through `'9'`, inclusive); otherwise, `digitRead` remains false. If `digitRead` becomes true, loop exit occurs and the last character read into `nextChar` is returned as the function result.

Function `getDigit` is a bit different from other functions you've seen. Instead of returning a value that has been computed, it returns a value that was read as a data item. This is perfectly reasonable, and we'll see more examples of problem data items being returned as function outputs in the next section and in Chapter 6.

**Listing 5.8** Function getDigit

```
// Returns the first digit character read
// Pre: The user has entered a line of data
char getDigit()
{
    char nextChar;       // user input - next data character
    bool digitRead;      // status flag - set true
                         // when digit character is read

    digitRead = false;   // no digit character read yet
    while (!digitRead)
    {
        cin >> nextChar;
        digitRead = (('0' <= nextChar) && (nextChar <= '9'));
    }

    return nextChar;     // return first digit character
}
```

## EXERCISES FOR SECTION 5.5

### Self-Check

1. In Listing 5.7, how would program execution change if we made the assignment statement (sum += score;) the last statement in the loop body?

2. You can use a for statement to implement a sentinel-controlled loop. The initialization and update steps would be input operations. Show the loop in Listing 5.4 as a for statement. Make sure you do not use count for loop control.

3. **a.** What would happen if the type bool assignment statement

    ```
    digitRead = (('0' <= nextChar) && (nextChar <= '9'));
    ```

    was accidentally omitted from the loop in Listing 5.8?

    **b.** What is the value of each relational expression in the preceding assignment statement if the value of nextChar is '2'? If the value of nextChar is 'a'?

    **c.** Replace the assignment statement with an if statement that assigns a value of true or false to digitRead.

4. What value of `count` would the program in Listing 5.7 display when the user enters the sentinel value as the first data item? What would happen when the program attempted to compute the average?

Programming

1. Modify the counter-controlled loop in Listing 5.2 so that it's a sentinel-controlled loop. Use a negative value of `hours` as the sentinel.

2. Write a program segment that allows the user to enter values and displays the number of positive and negative values entered. Use 0 as the sentinel value.

3. Write a `while` loop that displays all powers of an integer, n, less than a specified value, `MAXPOWER`. On each line of a table, show the power (0, 1, 2, … ) and the value of the integer n raised to that power.

4. Write a loop that reads in a collection of words and builds a sentence out of all the words by appending each new word to the string being formed. For example, if the three words This, is, one are entered, your sentence would be "This", then "This is", and finally "This is one". Exit your loop when a sentinel word is entered.

5. Write a flag-controlled loop that continues to read pairs of integers until it reads a pair with the property that the first integer in the pair is the same as the second. If the integers are stored in variables m and n, your loop should display each value of m, n, m−n, and n−m.

# 5.6 The `do-while` Statement

The `do-while` statement is used to specify a conditional loop that executes at least once. In the `do-while` statement, the loop repetition test is specified at the bottom of the loop, so the test cannot be made until at least one execution of the loop body has been completed.

We can use a do-while statement to implement a **data-validation loop**—a loop that continues to prompt and read data until a valid data item is entered. Because the user must enter at least one data item before validation can occur, the `do-while` is a convenient loop structure.

**data-validation loop**
A loop that continues to execute until it reads a valid data item.

> **Data-Validation Loop**
> do
>     Prompt for and read a data item
> while data item is not valid.

As an example, we can use the following `do-while` loop to ensure that the value read into `numEmp` (number of employees) is valid (greater than or equal to zero). The loop continues to prompt for and read data until the user enters a number that is not negative. Loop exit occurs when the condition `numEmp < 0` is false.

```
do
{
    cout << "Enter number of employees: ";
    cin >> numEmp;
} while (numEmp < 0);
```

---

**do-while Statement**

**Form:**    do
        *statement*;
        while (*expression*);

**Example:**    do
        {
           cout << "Enter a digit character: ";
           cin >> ch;
        } while ((ch < '0') || (ch > '9'));

**Interpretation:** After each execution of the *statement*, the *expression* is evaluated. If the *expression* is true, the (loop body) is repeated. If the *expression* is false, loop exit occurs and the next program statement is executed.

---

## EXAMPLE 5.8

Function `getIntRange` in Listing 5.9 contains a data-validation loop that continues to read numbers until the user enters a number within a specified range. The function parameters, `min` and `max`, specify the bounds of the range and are included in the range. The loop repetition condition

```
((nextInt < min) || (nextInt > max))
```

is true if `nextInt` is either less than the lower limit or greater than the upper limit. Otherwise, `nextInt` must be in the desired range.

---

**Listing 5.9**   Function `getIntRange`

```
// Returns the first integer in the range min through max
// Pre: min <= max
int getIntRange(int min, int max)   // range boundaries
{
    int nextInt;       // next number read
```

(continued)

**Listing 5.9**  Function getIntRange (continued)

```
    // Enter data until a number between min and max is read.
    do
    {
        cout << "Enter a number between " << min
             << " and " << max << ": ";
        cin >> nextInt;
    } while ((nextInt < min) || (nextInt > max));
    return nextInt;
}
```

## EXAMPLE 5.9

A **do-while** statement is often used to control a menu-driven program that displays a list of choices from which the program user selects a program operation. For example, the menu displayed for a text editing program (see Example 4.20) might look like this:

```
List of edit operations:
D - Delete a substring.
F - Find a string.
I - Insert a string.
R - Replace a substring.
Q - Quit
Enter D, F, I, R, or Q as your selection:
```

The main control routine for such a program would implement the pseudocode that follows.

> do
>     Display the menu.
>     Read the user's choice.
>     Perform the user's choice.
>     Display the edited string.
> while the choice is not Quit.

Listing 5.10 shows the **main** function. For each iteration, function **displayMenu** displays the menu and reads and performs the user's choice. Function **edit** (Listing 4.6) is called with actual arguments **textString** and **choice**. Function **edit** carries out the action specified by the **choice** value (a character in the list **D, F, I, R,** or **Q**). For any other value of **choice**, **edit** does nothing but return control to the loop. Notice that the loop continues to execute for all values of **choice** except **Q** (value of **SENTINEL**). Therefore, if the user enters an invalid value (one not in the menu), function **edit** should not change **textString** and the user gets another chance to enter a correct value.

**Listing 5.10**   main function for text editor program

```cpp
// file textEditor.cpp
// main function to test menu
#include <iostream>
#include <string>
using namespace std;

// Insert function subprogram prototypes here.

int main()
{
   const char SENTINEL = 'Q';
   char choice;         // input - edit operation
   string textString;   // input/output - string to edit

   cout << "Enter string to edit: ";
   getline(cin, textString);

   do
   {
      displayMenu();         // display the menu & prompt
      cin >> choice;
      textString = edit(textString, choice); // edit
                                             // string
      cout << "New string is " << textString << endl;
   } while (choice != SENTINEL);

   return 0;
}

// Insert function subprograms here.
```

## EXAMPLE 5.10

The program in Listing 5.11 uses a **do-while** loop to find the largest value in a sequence of data items. The variable **itemValue** is used to hold each data item, and the variable **largestSoFar** is used to save the largest data value encountered. Within the loop, the **if** statement

```cpp
if (itemValue > largestSoFar)
   largestSoFar = itemValue;    // save new largest number
```

redefines the value of **largestSoFar** if the current data item is larger than all previous data values.

The variable `minValue`, which represents the smallest integer value, serves two purposes in the program shown in Listing 5.11. By initializing `largestSoFar` to `minValue` before loop entry, we ensure that the condition (`itemValue > largestSoFar`) will be true during the first loop repetition. Thus the first data item will be saved as the largest value so far. We're also using `minValue` as a sentinel because it's unlikely to be entered as a data item for a program that is finding the largest number in a sequence. We include the library `limits`, which defines `INT_MIN` in the program shown in Listing 5.11. Because `INT_MIN` is system dependent, your system may display a different value of `INT_MIN`.

**Listing 5.11**    Finding the largest value

```
// File: largest.cpp
// Finds the largest number in a sequence of integer values

#include <iostream>
#include <limits>            // needed for INT_MIN
using namespace std;

int main()
{
   int itemValue;          // input - each data value
   int largestSoFar;       // output - largest value so far
   int minValue;           // the smallest integer

   // Initialize largestSoFar to the smallest integer.
   minValue = INT_MIN;
   largestSoFar = minValue;

   // Save the largest number encountered so far.
   cout << "Finding the largest value in a sequence: " << endl;
   do
   {
      cout << "Enter an integer or " << minValue << " to stop: ";
      cin >> itemValue;
      if (itemValue > largestSoFar)
         largestSoFar = itemValue;   // save new largest number
   } while (itemValue != minValue);

   cout << "The largest value entered was " << largestSoFar
        << endl;

   return 0;
}
```

(continued)

**Listing 5.11** Finding the largest value (continued)

```
Finding the largest value in a sequence:
Enter an integer or -2147483648 to stop: -999
Enter an integer or -2147483648 to stop: 500
Enter an integer or -2147483648 to stop: 100
Enter an integer or -2147483648 to stop: -2147483648
The largest value entered was 500
```

## EXERCISES FOR SECTION 5.6

### Self-Check

1. What output is produced by the following do-while loop (m is type int)?

```
m = 10;
do
{
    cout << m << endl;
    m = m - 2;
} while (m > 0);
```

2. Redo Exercise 1 for an initial value of m = 11.

3. Rewrite the loop repetition condition in Listing 5.10 so that loop exit occurs after the user enters either q or Q or 10 edit operations have been performed.

### Programming

1. Modify function getIntRange so that it uses a flag-controlled loop instead of a do-while.

2. Modify the loop in the largest score program so that it uses a while loop.

3. **a.** Write a while loop that prompts a user for a score between 0 and 100 inclusive and continues to repeat the prompt until a valid entry is provided.

   **b.** Write a do-while loop that prompts a user for a score between 0 and 100 inclusive and continues to read data until a valid entry is provided.

   **c.** Do you prefer version (a) or (b) of these loops? Justify your answer.

# 5.7   Review of **while**, **for**, and **do-while** Loops

C++ provides three loop control statements: `while`, `for`, and `do-while`. The `while` loop executes as long as its loop repetition condition is true; the `do-while` loop executes in a similar manner except that the statements in the loop body are always performed at least once. Normally, we use a `for` loop to implement counting loops. In a `for` loop, we can specify the three loop control steps—initialization, testing, and update—together in the loop heading. Table 5.4 describes when to use each of these three loop forms.

Although we tend to rely on the `while` statement to write most conditional loops, experienced C++ programmers often use the `for` statement instead. Because the format of a `for` statement heading is

```
for (initialization; loop-repetition test; update)
```

all the `while` loops in this chapter can be written using `for` statements. To do this, you simply move the loop control steps to the locations indicated above. For example, we could write the sentinel-controlled loop for Listing 5.7 using the `for` statement heading

```
for (cin >> score; score != SENTINEL; cin >> score)
```

This clearly shows that the initialization and update steps for a sentinel-controlled loop are the same.

It's relatively easy to rewrite a `do-while` loop as a `while` loop (or a `for` loop) by inserting an initialization step that makes the loop-repetition condition true the first time it's tested. However, not all `while` loops can be conveniently expressed as `do-while` loops; a `do-while` loop will always execute at least once, but a `while` loop body may be skipped entirely. For

**Table 5.4**   Three Loop Forms

| | |
|---|---|
| `while` | Most commonly used when repetition is not counter controlled; condition test precedes each loop repetition; loop body may not be executed at all |
| `for` | Used to implement a counting loop; also convenient for other loops with simple initialization and update steps; condition test precedes the execution of the loop body |
| `do-while` | Convenient when at least one repetition of the loop body is required |

this reason, a `while` loop is preferred over a `do-while` loop unless it's clear that at least one loop iteration must always be performed.

As an illustration of the three loop forms, a simple counting loop is written in Listing 5.12. (The dotted lines represent the loop body.) The `for` loop is the best to use in this situation. The `do-while` loop must be nested in an `if` statement to prevent it from being executed when `startValue` is greater than `stopValue`. For this reason, the `do-while` version of a counting loop is least desirable.

In Listing 5.12, the expression

```
count++;
```

is used in all three loops to update the loop control variable `count`. `count` will be equal to `stopValue` after the loops are executed; `count` will remain equal to `startValue` if these loops are skipped.

**Listing 5.12**   Comparison of three loop forms

```
while loop
count = startValue;
while (count < stopValue)
{

   .. .  .  .
   count++;
}  // end while
```

```
for loop
for (count = startValue; count < stopValue; count++)
{

   .. .  .  .
} // end for
```

```
do-while loop
count = startValue;
if (startValue < stopValue)
   do
   {

      .. .  .  .
      count++;
   } while (count < stopValue);
```

Self-Check
1. What does the `while` statement below display? Rewrite it as a `for` statement and as a `do-while` statement.

```
num = 5;
while (num <= 50)
{
    cout << num << endl;
    num += 5;
}
```

2. What does the `for` statement below display? Rewrite it as a `while` statement and as a `do-while` statement.

```
for (n = 3; n > 0; n--)
    cout << n << " cubed is " << pow (n, 3) << endl;
```

3. When would you make use of a `do-while` loop rather than a `while` loop in a program?

Programming
1. Write a program fragment that ignores any negative integer values read as data and finds the sum of only the positive numbers. Write two versions: one using `do-while` and one using `while`. Loop exit should occur after a sequence of three negative values is read.

2. Write a program fragment that could be used as the main control loop in a menu-driven program for updating an account balance (`D` = deposit, `W` = withdrawal, `Q` = quit). Assume that functions `process-Withdrawal` and `processDeposit` already exist and are called with the actual argument `balance`. Prompt the user for a transaction code (D, W, or Q) and call the appropriate function.

# 5.8 Nested Loops

We've used nested `if` statements in earlier programs and now show that it's also possible to nest loops. Nested loops consist of an outer loop with one or more inner loops. Each time the outer loop is repeated, the inner loops are reentered, their loop control components are reevaluated, and all required iterations are performed.

## EXAMPLE 5.11

Listing 5.13 shows a sample run of a program with two nested **for** loops. The outer loop is repeated four times (**for** i equals 0, 1, 2, 3). Each time the outer loop is repeated, the statement

```
cout << "Outer" << setw(7) << i << endl;
```

displays the string **"Outer"** and the value of i (the outer loop control variable). Next, the inner loop is entered, and its loop control variable, j, is reset to 0. The inner loop repeats exactly i times. Each time the inner loop body is executed, the statement

```
cout << "  Inner" << setw(10) << j << endl;
```

displays the string **"  Inner"** and the value of j.

The outer loop control variable i determines the number of repetitions of the inner loop, which is perfectly valid. However, it's best not to use the same variable as the loop control variable of both an outer and inner **for** loop in the same nest.

## EXAMPLE 5.12

The program in Listing 5.14 displays the multiplication table. The first **for** loop displays the table heading. The nested loops display the table body. The outer loop control variable

```
for (int rowVal = 0; rowVal < 10; rowVal++)
```

sets the value for each row of the table. The inner loop control variable

```
for (int colVal = 0; colVal < 11; colVal++)
```

cycles through each of the column values (0 through 10). Inside the inner loop, the statement

```
cout << setw(3) << rowVal * colVal;
```

displays each item in the table body as the product of a row value times a column value. The output statement

```
cout << endl;
```

follows the inner loop and terminates the row of values displayed by that loop.

**Listing 5.13**  Nested for loop program

```cpp
// File: nestedLoops.cpp
// Illustrates a pair of nested for loops

#include <iostream>
#include <iomanip>
using namespace std;

int main()
{
    // Display heading
    cout << setw(12) << "i" << setw(6) << "j" << endl;
    for (int i = 0; i < 4; i++)
    {
        cout << "Outer" << setw(7) << i << endl;
        for (int j = 0; j < i; j++)
            cout << "  Inner" << setw(10) << j << endl;
    }  // end outer loop

    return 0;
}
```

```
                    i       j
    Outer           0
    Outer           1
        Inner               0
    Outer           2
        Inner               0
        Inner               1
    Outer           3
        Inner               0
        Inner               1
        Inner               2
```

## EXERCISES FOR SECTION 5.8

### Self-Check

1. In Listing 5.14, how many times does the line

   ```cpp
   cout << setw(3) << rowVal * colVal;
   ```

   execute? How many times does the line that follows it execute? How would you change the program to display the addition table?

**Listing 5.14**  Displaying the multiplication table

```cpp
// File: multiplication.cpp
// Displays the multiplication table

#include <iostream>
#include <iomanip>
using namespace std;

int main()
{

    // Display table heading
    cout << "     ";
    for (int colHead = 0; colHead < 11; colHead++)
        cout << setw(3) << colHead;
    cout << endl;
    cout << "   ----------------" << endl;

    // Display table, row-by-row
    for (int rowVal = 0; rowVal < 10; rowVal++)
    {
        cout << setw(3) << rowVal << ' ';

        // Display all columns of current row
        for (int colVal = 0; colVal < 11; colVal++)
            cout << setw(3) << rowVal * colVal;
        cout << endl;
    }

    return 0;
}
```

```
  |  0  1  2  3  4  5  6  7  8  9 10
  ---------------------------------
0 |  0  0  0  0  0  0  0  0  0  0  0
1 |  0  1  2  3  4  5  6  7  8  9 10
2 |  0  2  4  6  8 10 12 14 16 18 20
3 |  0  3  6  9 12 15 18 21 24 27 30
4 |  0  4  8 12 16 20 24 28 32 36 40
5 |  0  5 10 15 20 25 30 35 40 45 50
6 |  0  6 12 18 24 30 36 42 48 54 60
7 |  0  7 14 21 28 35 42 49 56 63 70
8 |  0  8 16 24 32 40 48 56 64 72 80
9 |  0  9 18 27 36 45 54 63 72 81 90
```

**2.** What do the following program segments display, assuming m is three and n is five? Trace each loop's execution, showing the values of the loop control variables when each display statement executes.

**a.**
```
for (int i = 0; i < n; i++)
{
    for (int j = 0; j < i; j++)
        cout << "*";
    cout << endl;
}   // end for i
```

**b.**
```
for (int i = m; i > 0; i--)
{
    for (int j = n; j > 0; j--)
        cout << "*";
    cout << endl;
} // end for i
```

**3.** Show the output displayed by the following nested loops:

```
for (int i = 0; i < 2; i++)
{
    cout << "Outer" << setw(5) << i << endl;
    for (int j = 0; j < 3; j++)
        cout << " Inner" << setw(3) << i <<
                << setw(3) << j << endl;
    for (int k = i; k >= 0; k-)
        cout << " Inner" << setw(3) << i
                << setw(3) << k << endl;
} // end for i
```

Programming

**1.** Write nested loops that display the output below.

```
0
0 1
0 1 2
0 1 2 3
0 1 2 3 4
```

**2.** Write nested loops that display the output below.

```
0 1 2 3 4
1 2 3 4
2 3 4
3 4
4
```

**3.** Write a program that displays the pattern below.

## 5.9    Debugging and Testing Programs

Section 2.8 described several categories of errors: syntax, link, run-time, and logic errors. Sometimes the cause of a run-time error or the source of a logic error is apparent and the error can be fixed easily. Often, however, the error is not obvious and you may spend considerable time and energy locating it.

The first step in locating a hidden error is to examine the program output to determine which part of the program is generating incorrect results. Then you can focus on the statements in that section of the program to determine which are at fault. We describe two ways to do this.

### Using a Debugger

Modern Integrated Development Environments (IDEs) include features to help you debug a program while it's executing. In this section, we describe these features in a general way. Specific details for Microsoft Visual C++ and Borland C++ Builder are provided in Appendixes F and G.

You can use a debugger to observe changes in variables as the program executes. Debuggers enable you to single-step through a program, or to execute it statement-by-statement. Before starting execution, you indicate to the IDE that you want to debug or trace the program's execution. You place the names of variables you wish to trace in a **watch window**. As each program statement executes, the value of each variable in the watch window is updated. The program pauses and you can inspect the changes. When you're ready, you instruct the IDE to execute the next statement. With single-step execution, you can validate that loop control variables and other important variables (e.g., accumulators) are incremented as expected during each iteration of a loop. You can also check that input variables contain the correct data after each input operation.

**watch window**
A window listing the variables that are traced during debugging.

Usually you want to trace each statement in a program. However, when you reach a library function call, you should select the "step over" option, which executes the function as a single unit instead of tracing through the individual statements in the C++ library code for that function. For the same reason, you should also select the "step over" option when you reach an input or output statement.

You may not want to single-step through all the statements in your program. You can place the cursor at a specific line and then select `"Run to cursor"`. When the program pauses, you then check the variables in the watch window to see if their values are correct.

You can also divide your program into segments by setting *breakpoints,* a feature that is like a fence between two segments of a program. You should set a breakpoint at the end of each major algorithm step. Then instruct the debugger to execute all statements from the last breakpoint up to the next breakpoint. When the program stops at a breakpoint, you can examine the variables in the watch window to determine whether the program segment has executed correctly. If it has, you'll want to execute through to the next breakpoint. If it hasn't, you'll want to single-step through that segment.

## Debugging without a Debugger

If you cannot use a debugger, insert extra **diagnostic output statements** to display intermediate results at critical points in your program. For example, you should display the values of variables affected by each major algorithm step before and after the step executes. By comparing these results, you may be able to determine which segment of your program contains bugs. For example, if the loop in Listing 5.7 is not computing the correct sum, you might want to insert an extra diagnostic statement, as shown in the second line of the loop below.

**diagnostic output statement**
An output statement that displays intermediate results during debugging.

```
cin >> score;
while (score != SENTINEL)
{
    sum += score;
    cout << "***** score is " << score << " and sum is "
        << sum << endl;
    cout << "Enter the next score : ";
    cin >> score;
}
```

The diagnostic output statement displays the current value of `score` and each sum that is accumulated. This statement displays a string of asterisks at the beginning of an output line. This makes it easier to identify diagnostic output in the debugging runs and to locate the diagnostic `cout` statements in the source program.

Be careful when inserting extra diagnostic output statements. Sometimes you must add braces if a single statement inside an `if` or `while` statement becomes a compound statement when you add a diagnostic output statement.

Once you think you have located an error, you'll want to take out the extra diagnostic statements. You can turn the diagnostic statements into comments by prefixing them with the double slash (`//`). If errors appear again in later testing, you can remove the slashes to get more debugging information.

## Off-by-One Errors

A fairly common logic error in programs with loops is a loop that executes one more time or one less time than required. If a sentinel-controlled loop performs an extra repetition, it may erroneously process the sentinel value along with the regular data.

If a loop performs a counting operation, make sure that the initial and final values of the loop control variable are correct and that the loop repetition condition is right. For example, the loop body below executes n + 1 times instead of n times. If you want the loop body to execute n times, change the loop repetition condition to `count < n`.

```
for (int count = 0; count <= n; count++)
    sum += count;
```

**loop boundaries**
Initial and final values of a loop control variable.

Often you can determine whether a loop is correct by checking the **loop boundaries**—that is, the initial and final values of the loop control variable. For a counting loop, carefully evaluate the initialization step, substitute this value everywhere the counter variable appears in the loop body, and verify that it makes sense as a beginning value. Then choose a value for the counter that still causes the loop repetition condition to be true but that will make this condition false after one more evaluation of the update expression. Check the validity of this boundary value wherever the counter variable appears. As an example, in the `for` loop,

```
k = 1;
sum = 0;
for (int i = -n; i < n - k; i++)
    sum += (i * i);
```

check that the first value of the counter variable `i` is supposed to be `-n` and that the last value is supposed to be n - 2. Next, check that the assignment statement

```
sum += (i * i);
```

is correct at these boundaries. When `i` is `-n`, `sum` gets the value of `n2`. When `i` is `n - 2`, the value of `(n - 2)2` is added to the previous sum. As a final check, pick some small value of `n` (for example, 2) and trace the loop execution to see that it computes `sum` correctly for this case.

## Testing

After you've corrected all errors and the program appears to execute as expected, you should test the program thoroughly to make sure that it works. If the program contains a decision statement, check all paths through this statement. Make enough test runs to verify that the program works properly for representative samples of all possible data combinations. We discuss testing again in Section 6.5.

### EXERCISES FOR SECTION 5.9

**Self-Check**
1. In the subsection entitled "Off-by-One Errors," add debugging statements to the first `for` loop to show the value of the loop control variable at the start of each repetition. Also, add debugging statements to show the value of `sum` at the end of each loop repetition.

## 5.10 Common Programming Errors

Beginners sometimes confuse `if` and `while` statements because both statements contain a parenthesized condition. Always use an `if` statement to implement a decision step and a `while` or `for` statement to implement a loop.

The syntax of the `for` statement header is repeated.

```
for (initialization expression; loop repetition condition;
        update expression)
```

Remember to end the initialization expression and the loop repetition condition with semicolons. Do not put a semicolon before or after the closing parenthesis of the `for` statement header. A semicolon after this parenthesis would have the effect of ending the `for` statement without making execution of the loop body dependent on its condition.

■ *Omitting braces* A common mistake in using `while` and `for` statements is to forget that the structure assumes that the loop body is a single statement. Remember to use braces around a loop body consisting of multiple statements. Some C++ programmers always use braces around a loop body, even if it contains just one statement. Keep in mind that your compiler ignores indentation, so a loop defined as shown (with braces around the loop body left out)

```
while (x > xbig)
    x -= 2;
    xbig++;
```

really executes as

```
while (x > xbig)
    x -= 2; // only this statement is repeated
xbig++;
```

■ *Omitting a closing brace* The C++ compiler can easily detect that there is something wrong with code in which a closing brace has been omitted for a compound statement. However, the error message noting the symbol's absence may be far from the spot where the brace belongs, and other error messages often appear as a side effect of the omission. When compound statements are nested, the compiler will associate the first closing brace encountered with the innermost structure. Even if it is the terminator for this inner structure that is left out, the compiler may complain about the outer structure. In the example that follows, there's no closing brace at the end of the body of the inner `while` statement. But the compiler will associate the closing brace in the last line with the inner loop, and then assume that the code that follows (not shown) is part of the outer loop. The message about the missing brace will not appear until much later in the program source code.

```
sum = 0;
for (int i = 0; i < 9; i++)
{
    for (int j = 0; j < i, j++)
    {
        sum += j;
        cout << j << endl;
    cout << i << endl;
} // end for i
```

■ *Infinite loop* Be sure to verify that a loop's repetition condition will eventually become false (0); otherwise, an infinite loop may result. Be especially careful if you use tests for inequality to control the repetition of a loop. The following loop is intended to process all transactions for a bank account while the balance is positive:

```
cin >> balance;
while (balance != 0.0)
{
    cout << "Next check amount: ";
    cin >> check;
    balance -= check;
}
```

If the bank balance goes from a positive to a negative amount without being exactly 0.0, the loop will not terminate (an infinite loop). This loop is safer:

```
cin >> balance;
while (balance > 0.0)
{
    cout << "Next check amount: ";
    cin >> check;
    balance -= check;
}
```

- *Misuse of = for ==* One common cause of a nonterminating loop is the use of a loop repetition condition in which an equality test is mistyped as an assignment operation. Consider the following loop that expects the user to type the letter Y to continue and anything else to quit:

```
do
{
    . . .
    cout << "Continue execution - Y(Yes)/N(No): ";
    cin >> choice;
} while (choice = 'Y');       // should be: choice == 'Y'
```

This loop will compile but will cause a warning message such as "Possible incorrect assignment". If you run the program, the assignment statement will execute after each loop repetition. Its value (a positive integer) will be considered true, so the loop will not exit regardless of the letter typed in.

- *Bad sentinel value* If you use a sentinel-controlled loop, remember to provide a prompt that tells the program's user what value to enter as the sentinel. Make sure that the sentinel value cannot be confused with a normal data item and is not processed in the loop body.

- *Using do-while instead of while* A do-while always executes at least once. Use a do-while only when there's no possibility of zero loop iterations. If you find yourself adding an if statement to patch your code with a result like this

```
if (condition₁)
    do
    {
      . . .
    } while (condition₁);
```

replace the segment with a while or for statement. Both statements automatically test the loop repetition condition before executing the loop body.

- *Incorrect use of compound assignment* Do not use increment, decrement, or compound assignment operators in complex expressions. At best, such usage leads to expressions that are difficult to read, and at worst, to expressions that produce varying results in different implementations of C++.

- *Incorrect use of increment and decrement operators* Be sure that the operand of an increment or decrement operator is a variable and that this variable is referenced after executing the increment or decrement operation. Without a subsequent reference, the operator's side effect of changing the value of the variable is pointless. Do not use a variable twice in an expression in which it is incremented/decremented. Applying the increment/decrement operators to constants or expressions is illegal.

## Chapter Review

1. A loop is used to repeat steps in a program. Two kinds of loops occur frequently in programming: counting loops and sentinel-controlled loops. For a counting loop, the number of iterations required can be determined before the loop is entered. For a sentinel-controlled loop, repetition continues until a special data value is read. The pseudocode for each loop form follows.

**Counter-Controlled Loop**
Set *loop control variable* to an initial value of 0.
while *loop control variable* < *final value*
　　. . .
　　Increase *loop control variable* by 1.

**Sentinel-Controlled Loop**
Read the first data item.
while the sentinel value has not been encountered

Process the data item.
Read the next data item.

2. Pseudocode forms were introduced for two other kinds of loops:

**General Conditional Loop**
Initialize the loop control variable.
while a condition involving the loop control variable is still true
    Continue processing.
    Update the loop control variable.

**Data-Validation Loop**
do
    Prompt for and read a data item
while data item is not valid.

3. C++ provides three statements for implementing loops: while, for, and do-while. Use for to implement counting loops and do-while to implement loops that must execute at least once, such as data validation loops for interactive programs. Use while or for to code other conditional loops, using whichever implementation is clearer.

4. In designing a loop, the focus should be on both loop control and loop processing. For loop processing, make sure that the loop body contains steps that perform the operation that must be repeated. For loop control, you must provide steps that initialize, test, and update the loop control variable. Make sure that the initialization step leads to correct program results when the loop body is not executed (zero-iteration loop).

## Summary of New C++ Constructs

| Construct | Effect |
| --- | --- |
| **while Statement**<br>```sum = 0;```<br>```while (sum <= maxSum)```<br>```{```<br>```   cout << "Next integer: ";```<br>```   cin >> nextInt;```<br>```   sum += nextInt;```<br>```}``` | A collection of input data items is read and their sum is accumulated in sum. The process stops when the accumulated sum exceeds maxSum. |
| **Counting for Statement**<br>```for (int currentMonth = 0;```<br>```     currentMonth < 12;```<br>```     currentMonth++)```<br>```{```<br>```     cin >> monthSales;```<br>```     yearSales += monthSales;```<br>```}``` | The loop body is repeated 12 times. For each month, the value of monthSales is read and added to yearSales. |

## Summary of New C++ Constructs (continued)

| Construct | Effect |
|---|---|
| **Counting for Loop with a Negative Step**<br><pre>for (volts = 20;<br>     volts >= -20;<br>     volts -= 10)<br>{<br>    current = volts / resistance;<br>    cout << setw(5) << volts<br>         << setw(10) << current<br>         << endl;<br>}</pre> | For values of volts equal to 20, 10, 0, –10, –20, the loop computes value of current and displays volts and current. |
| **Sentinel-Controlled while Loop**<br><pre>product = 1;<br>cout << "Enter -999 to quit: ";<br>cout << "Enter first number: "<br>cin >> dat;<br>while (dat != -999)<br>{<br>   product *= dat;<br>   cout << "Next number: ";<br>   cin >> dat;<br>}</pre> | Computes the product of a list of numbers. The product is complete when the user enters the sentinel value (–999). |
| **Data Validation do–while Loop**<br><pre>do<br>{<br>   cout << "Positive number < 10: ";<br>   cin >> num;<br>} while (num < 1 && num >= 10);</pre> | Repeatedly displays prompt and stores a number in num until user enters a number that is in range 1 through 9. |
| **Flag-Controlled while Loop**<br><pre>divisible = false;<br>while (!divisible)<br>{<br>   cout << "Enter an integer: ";<br>   cin >> n;<br>   divisible = ((n % 2 == 0) ||<br>               (n % 3 == 0));<br>}</pre> | Continues to read in numbers until a number that is divisible by 2 or by 3 is read. |
| **Increment / Decrement**<br><pre>z = ++j * k--;</pre> | Stores in z the product of the incremented value of j and the current value of k. Then k is decremented. |
| **Compound Assignment**<br><pre>ans *= (a - b);</pre> | Assigns to ans the value of ans * (a - b). |

## Quick-Check Exercises

1. A loop that continues to process input data until a special value is entered is called a _____ loop.

2. It's an error if a `for` loop body never executes. (True/False)

3. The sentinel value is always the last value added to a sum being accumulated in a sentinel-controlled loop. (True/False)

4. Which loop form (`for, do-while, while`)

   **a.** executes at least one time?

   **b.** should be used to implement a sentinel loop?

   **c.** should be used to implement a counting loop?

   **d.** should be used to implement a menu-controlled loop?

5. What does the following segment display?

```
product = 1;
counter = 2;
while (counter < 5)
    product *= counter;
    counter++;
cout << product;
```

6. What does the segment of Exercise 5 display if the two statements that are indented are in braces?

7. For the program segment below:

```
for (int i = 0; i < 9; i++)
{
    for (int j = 0; j <= i; j++)
        cout << setw(4) << (i * j);
    cout << endl;
}
```

   **a.** How many times does the first `cout` statement execute?

   **b.** How many times does the second `cout` statement execute?

   **c.** What is the last value displayed?

8. If the value of m is 5 and n is 3, what is the value of the following expression?

   `m++ * --n`

9. What are the values of m and n after the expression in Exercise 8 executes?

10. What does the following code segment display? Try each of these inputs: 345, 82, 6. Then describe the action of the code.

```
cout << "Enter a positive integer: ";
cin >> num;
do
{
    cout << num % 10;
    num /= 10;
} while (num > 0);
cout << endl;
```

## Answers to Quick-Check Exercises

1. sentinel-controlled loop

2. False

3. False; the sentinel should not be processed.

4. a. do-while   b. while   c. for

5. Nothing; the loop executes "forever" because only one statement is repeated.

6. The value of $1 \times 2 \times 3 \times 4 \times 5$ (or 24).

7. a. $1 + 2 + 3 + \ldots + 9 + 10$ (or 45)   b. 9   c. 64

8. 10 (product of 5 times 2)

9. m is 6 (incremented after the multiplication), n is 2(decremented before the multiplication)

10. ```
    Enter a positive integer: 345
    543
    Enter a positive integer: 82
    28
    Enter a positive integer: 6
    6
    ```

   The code displays the digits of an integer in reverse order.

## Review Questions

1. How does a sentinel value differ from a program flag as a means of loop control?

2. For a sentinel value to be used properly when reading in data, how many input statements should there be and where should the input statements appear?

3. Write a program to read a collection of employee data (hours and rate) entered at the terminal and to calculate and display the gross pay for each employee. Your program should stop when the user enters a sentinel value of -0 for hours.
    ```

**4.** Hand trace the program below given the following data:

```
4 2 8 4  1 4 2 1  9 3 3 1 -22 10 8 2  3 3 4 5
// File: Slope.cpp
// Calculates the slope of a line

#include <iostream>
using namespace std;

int main()
{
   const float SENTINEL = 0.0;
   float slope;
   float y2, y1, x2, x1;

   cout << "Enter 4 numbers: " << endl;
   cout << "The program terminates if the last two";
   cout << " numbers are the same." << endl;
   cout << "Numbers entered will be in the order: "
        << "y2, y1, x2, x1." << endl << endl;
   cout << "Enter four numbers: ";
   cin >> y2 >> y1 >> x2 >> x1;

   while ((x2 - x1) != SENTINEL)
   {
      slope = (y2 - y1) / (x2 - x1);
      cout << "Slope is " << slope << endl;
      cout << "Enter 4 more numbers: ";
      cin >> y2 >> y1 >> x2 >> x1;
   }

   return 0;
}
```

**5.** Rewrite the `while` loop appearing in Exercise 4 as a

**a.** do-while loop.

**b.** flag-controlled loop.

**6.** Consider the following program segment:

```
count = 0;
for (i = 0; i < n; i++)
{
   cin >> x;
   if (x % i == 0)
      count++;
}
```

    **a.** After loop exit, what does the value of count represent.

    **b.** Write a while loop equivalent to the for loop.

    **c.** Write a do-while loop equivalent to the for loop.

**7.** Write a do-while loop that repeatedly prompts for and reads data until a value in the range 0 through 15 inclusive is entered.

**8.** Write a program that will find the product of a collection of data values. Your program should ignore any negative data and should terminate when a zero value is read.

## Programming Projects

**1.** Write a program that reads a collection of positive and negative numbers and multiplies only the positive integers. Loop exit should occur when three consecutive negative values are read.

**2.** The greatest common divisor (gcd) of two integers is the largest integer that divides both numbers. Write a program that inputs two numbers and implements the following approach to finding their gcd. We'll use the numbers 252 and 735. First, we find the remainder of the larger number divided by the other.

$$
\begin{array}{r}
2 \\
252\,\overline{\smash{\big)}\,735} \\
\underline{504} \\
231
\end{array}
$$

Now we calculate the remainder of the old divisor divided by the remainder found.

$$
\begin{array}{r}
1 \\
231\,\overline{\smash{\big)}\,252} \\
\underline{231} \\
21
\end{array}
$$

We repeat this process until the remainder is zero.

$$
\begin{array}{r}
11 \\
21\,\overline{\smash{\big)}\,231} \\
\underline{21} \\
21 \\
\underline{21} \\
0
\end{array}
$$

The last divisor (21) is the gcd.

3. Write a program to find the largest, smallest, and average values in a collection of n numbers where the value of n will be the first data item read.

4. **a.** Write a program to read in a collection of exam scores ranging in value from 0 to 100. Your program should display the category of each score. It should also count and display the number of outstanding scores (90 to 100), the number of satisfactory scores (60 to 89), and the number of unsatisfactory scores (0 to 59).

   **b.** Modify your program so that it also displays the average score at the end of the run.

   **c.** Modify your program to ensure that each score is valid (in the range 0 to 100).

5. Write a program to process weekly employee time cards for all employees of an organization. Each employee will have three data items: the employee's name, the hourly wage rate, and the number of hours worked during a given week. Employees are to be paid time-and-a-half for all hours worked over 40. A tax amount of 3.625 percent of gross salary will be deducted. The program output should show each employee's name, gross pay, and net pay, and should also display the total net and gross amounts and their averages. Use zzzzzz as a sentinel value for name.

6. Write a menu-driven savings account transaction program that will process the following sets of data:

Group 1

```
I   1234    1054.07
W           25.00
D           243.35
W           254.55
Z
```

Group 2

```
I   5723    2008.24
W           15.55
Z
```

Group 3

```
I   2814    128.24
W           52.48
D           13.42
W           84.60
Z
```

Group 4

```
I   7234    7.77
Z
```

Group 5

```
I   9367    15.27
W           16.12
D           10.00
Z
```

Group 6

```
I   1134    12900.00
D           9270.00
Z
```

The first record in each group contains the code (I) along with the account number and its initial balance. All subsequent transaction records show the amount of each withdrawal (W) and deposit (D) made for that account, followed by a sentinel value (Z). Display the account number and its balance after processing each record in the group. If a balance becomes negative, display an appropriate message and take whatever corrective steps you deem proper. If there are no transactions for an account, display a message stating this. A transaction code (Q) should be used to allow the user to quit program execution.

7. Suppose you own a soft drink distributorship that sells Coca-Cola (ID number 1), Pepsi (ID number 2), Canada Dry (ID number 3), and Hires (ID number 4) by the case. Write a program to do the following:

   a. Read in the case inventory for each brand at the start of the week.

   b. Process all weekly sales and purchase records for each brand.

   c. Display the final inventory.

   Each transaction will consist of two data items. The first will be the brand identification number (an integer). The second will be the amount purchased (a positive integer) or the amount sold (a negative integer). You can assume that you always have sufficient foresight to prevent depletion of your inventory for any brand.

8. Revise the previous project to make it a menu-driven program. The menu operations supported by the revised program should be as follows:

   (E)nter inventory

   (P)urchase soda

   (S)ell soda

   (D)isplay inventory

   (Q)uit program

   Negative quantities should no longer be used to represent goods sold.

9. Write a simple arithmetic expression translator that reads in expressions such as 25.5 + 34.2 and displays their value. Each expression has two numbers separated by an arithmetic operator. (*Hint:* Use a switch statement with the operator symbol (type char) as a selector to determine which arithmetic operation to perform on the two numbers. For a sentinel, enter an expression with zero for both operands.)

**10.** Complete the text editor program (Listings 4.6 and 5.10). You need to write only function `displayMenu` and the function subprograms called by function `edit`.

**11.** Bunyan Lumber Company needs to create a table of the engineering properties of its lumber. The dimensions of the wood are given as the base and the height in inches. Engineers need to know the following information about lumber:

$$\text{cross-sectional area: } base \times height$$

$$\text{moment of inertia: } \frac{base \times height^3}{12}$$

$$\text{section modulus: } \frac{base \times height^2}{6}$$

The owner makes lumber with base sizes of 2, 4, 6, 8, and 10 inches. The height sizes are 2, 4, 6, 8, 10, and 12 inches. Produce a table with appropriate headings to show these values and the computed engineering properties. The first part of the table's outline follows.

```
Lumber       Cross-Sectional     Moment of     Section
Size         Area    Inertia     Modulus
2 x 2
2 x 4
2 x 6
2 x 8
2 x 10
2 x 12
4 x 2
4 x 4
.
.
.
```

**12.** Write a program that reads in a collection of strings and displays each string read with the vowels removed. For example, if the data strings are:

```
hat
dog
kitten
*** (sentinel)
```

the output would be:

```
ht
dg
kttn
```

Write and call a function `removeVowel` with prototype

```
string removeVowel(string);
```

that returns its argument string with the vowels removed.

13. Write a loop that reads a collection of words and builds a sentence out of all the words by appending each new word to the string being formed. For example, if the three words "This", "is", and "one." are entered, your sentence would be "This", then "This is", and finally "This is one." Exit your loop when a word that ends with a period is entered or the sentence being formed is longer than 20 words or contains more than 100 letters. Do not append a word if it was previously entered.

14. A prime number is a number that is divisible only by itself and 1. Write a program that asks a user for an integer value and then displays all prime numbers less than or equal to that number. For example, if the user enters 17, the program should display:

```
Prime numbers less than or equal to 17:
2
3
5
7
11
13
17
```

# Mike Weisert

*Mike Weisert is currently the tools manager at Integrated Systems, where he is responsible for creating a productive development environment for embedded systems programmers. Before moving to Integrated Systems, Weisert helped develop successful C and C++ products at Borland International. One such example is Turbo C, for which Weisert developed the user interface. Turbo C offered C programmers an integrated development environment (providing an editor and compiler options) for the first time.*

**What is your educational background?**
Science, math, and art were my passions in college, though my degree was in business. My computer education began with a Sinclair ZX-80 computer that my dad gave me in high school. These early personal computers were more work to use than the benefit they returned to the user.

I was fascinated with the interaction between computers and people. So, my degree in business administration led me to study how computers could increase productivity for people in business environments.

**How did you become interested in computer science?**
I found the puzzles of computer science more entertaining than any other discipline. I was pleasantly surprised when I found that the skills I learned were in high demand and that people would pay me to do what I liked to do.

**What was your first job in the computer industry? What did it entail?**
I started in a C programming position on a project that was canceled two months after I started on it. Welcome to business and the Silicon Valley. My software career began in earnest as a technical support engineer at Borland International in 1985 because of my experience with Modula-2 [a programming language developed by Niklaus Wirth and released in 1980]. After three months of answering questions about hard sector floppies, configuration files, and Pascal programming, I turned in my resignation to take an Ada programming position. However, I was convinced to stay at Borland as a Modula-2 programmer.

I proceeded to develop software in Modula-2. Following techniques I learned in school, such as stepwise refinement and structured programming, I developed a graphics package for single-board computers and helped develop a CPM-based development tool. Later, I had the luck to build development tools for BASIC and C. The first product to ship out of this effort was Turbo C 1.0. Integration and automation of the development tool were forever altered. The user interfaces for Turbo Basic, Turbo C, and Turbo Pascal became known as IDEs, or Integrated Development Environments.

**What is a typical day like for you?**

My day starts with about an hour of e-mail regarding previous product releases or general business stuff. This is followed by individual discussion with engineers to solve problems, maybe a team or status meeting. Then I use the software we are developing to find rough spots and better ways to integrate and automate features.

**Do you have any advice for students learning C++?**

Focus on the concept rather than the syntax. Languages come and go and improve with time. The underlying concepts of programming are always the same and are better expressed with newer languages.

**How do you see C++ evolving over the next few years?**

C++ will serve a special purpose. It will be used for applications that have no user interface, such as server software. C++ is portable until you add the user interface. So, it's better to write server code in C++ and client code in a highly portable language like Java.

**What kind of project are you currently working on?**

Development tools (IDEs) for embedded software engineers. We use several server components that provide the information needed by the user interface to accomplish the tasks of building and debugging embedded programs that run on a variety of chip architectures. All of our non-UI components are coded in C++, while the user interface components are written in Java.

**What do you enjoy most about working on a software development team?**

The ability to build something bigger than one person alone can create, and organizing an effort to build a shared vision. I've heard it said that managing programmers is like herding cats, so when I manage to have a team deliver a finished product, I feel accomplished.

**What is some general advice you have about programming?**

C++ is one instance of an object-oriented programming language. It has strengths and weaknesses like anything else. As a manager of many high-powered programmers, I had the opportunity to see really good programmers abuse the language with undesirable results and I've seen novice programmers apply object-oriented techniques (independent of language) to C++ projects with excellent results. The point is that you must consider the overall results of what you are trying to do when selecting a language. Code almost always has a future. One question to ask yourself is who might have to read and modify the code you are writing. A programming language is a tool, and you have to pick the best tool for the job you are doing.

# Modular Programming

## Chapter Objectives

- To learn how to return function results through a function's arguments
- To understand the differences between call-by-value and call-by-reference
- To understand the distinction between input, inout, and output parameters and when to use each kind
- To learn how to modularize a program system and pass information between system modules (functions)
- To understand how to document the flow of information using structure charts
- To learn testing and debugging techniques appropriate for a program system with several modules

A CAREFULLY DESIGNED PROGRAM that has been constructed using functions has many of the properties of a stereo system. Each stereo component is an independent device that performs a specific operation. Electronic audio signals move back and forth over wires linking the stereo components. Plugs on the back of the stereo receiver are marked as inputs or outputs. Wires attached to the input plugs carry electronic signals into the receiver, where they are processed. These signals may come from the cassette deck, tuner, or CD player. The receiver sends new electronic signals through the output plugs to the speakers or back to the cassette deck for recording. You can connect the components and listen to your favorite music without knowing what electronic parts each component contains or how it works.

In Chapter 3 you learned how to write the separate components—the functions—of a program. The functions correspond to the individual steps in a problem solution. You also learned how to provide inputs to a function and how to return a single output. In this chapter you complete your study of functions, learning how to connect the functions to create a program system—an arrangement of separate modules that pass information from one to the other.

# 6.1    Value and Reference Parameters

At this point we know how to write functions that return up to one result. In this section, we'll learn how to write functions that use output parameters to return more than one result.

## EXAMPLE 6.1

Function `computeSumAve` at the bottom of Listing 6.1 has four parameters: two for input (`num1` and `num2`) and two for output (`sum` and `average`). The symbol `&` (ampersand) in the function header indicates that the parameters `sum` and `average` are output parameters. The function computes the sum and average of its inputs but doesn't display them. Instead, these values are assigned to formal parameters `sum` and `average` and returned as function results to the `main` function that displays them.

The function call

```
computeSumAve(x, y, sum, mean);
```

sets up the argument correspondence below.

| Actual Argument | Corresponds to formal parameter |
|:---:|:---:|
| x | num1 (input) |
| y | num2 (input) |
| sum | sum (output) |
| mean | average (output) |

The values of `x` and `y` are passed into the function when it's first called. These values are associated with formal input parameters `num1` and `num2`. The statement

```
sum = num1 + num2;
```

stores the sum of the function inputs in the calling function variable `sum` (the third actual argument). The statement

```
average = sum / 2.0;
```

divides the value stored in the calling function variable `sum` by `2.0` and stores the quotient in the calling function variable `mean` (the fourth actual argument).

**Listing 6.1** Function to compute sum and average

```cpp
// File: computeSumAve.cpp
// Tests function computeSumAve.

#include <iostream>
using namespace std;

// Function prototype
void computeSumAve(float, float, float&, float&);

int main()
{
    float x,           // input - first number
          y,           // input - second number
          sum,         // output - their sum
          mean;        // output - their average

    cout << "Enter 2 numbers: ";
    cin >> x >> y;

    // Compute sum and average of x and y
    computeSumAve(x, y, sum, mean);

    // Display results
    cout << "Sum is " << sum << endl;
    cout << "Average is " << mean << endl;

    return 0;
}

// Computes the sum and average of num1 and num2.
// Pre: num1 and num2 are assigned values.
// Post: The sum and average of num1 and num2 are
//       computed and returned as function outputs.
void computeSumAve
    (float num1,          // IN -   values used in
     float num2,          //        computation
     float& sum,          // OUT - sum of num1 and num2
     float& average)      // OUT - average of num1 and
num2
{
    sum = num1 + num2;
    average = sum / 2.0;
}   // end computeSumAve
```

```
Enter 2 numbers: 8 10
Sum is 18
Average is 9
```

Figure 6.1 shows the main function data area and function compute-SumAve's data area after the function call but before the execution of computeSumAve begins; Figure 6.2 shows these data areas just after computeSumAve finishes execution. The execution of computeSumAve sets the values of calling function variables sum and mean to 18.0 and 9.0, respectively. We explain how this happens next.

## Call-by-Value and Call-by-Reference Parameters

In C++, you insert the symbol & immediately following the type of a formal parameter to declare an output parameter. Therefore, in function compute-SumAve in Listing 6.1, the formal parameters sum and average are output parameters, and num1 and num2 are input parameters.

The compiler uses the information in the parameter declaration list to set up the correct *argument-passing mechanism* for each function parameter. For parameters used only as input, C++ uses **call-by-value** because the *value* of the argument is copied to the called function's data area and there's no further connection between the formal parameter and its corresponding actual argument. In Figures 6.1 and 6.2, the dashed arrows pointing to num1 and num2 indicate this situation. The top dashed arrow shows that the

**call-by-value**
An argument-passing mechanism in which the value of an actual argument is stored in the called function's data area.

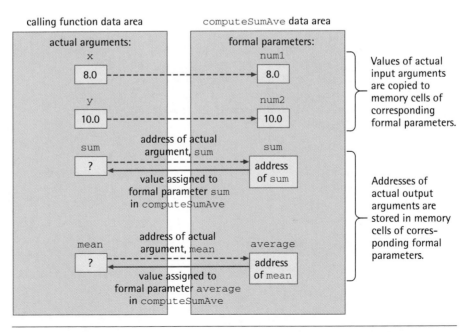

**Figure 6.1**   Data areas after call to computeSumAve (before execution)

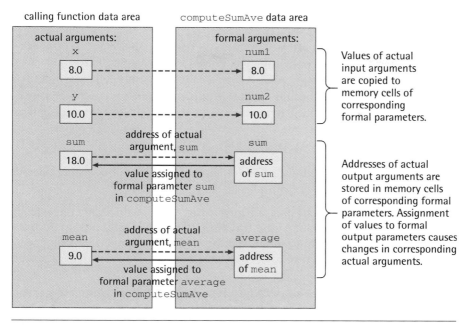

calling function data area          `computeSumAve` data area

Figure 6.2   Data areas after execution of `computeSumAve`

value of the actual argument `x` is passed to the formal parameter `num1` in function `computeSumAve`.

For output parameters, C++ uses **call-by-reference**. For *reference parameters,* the compiler stores in the called function's data area the memory *address* of the actual variable that corresponds to each reference parameter. Through this address, the called function can access the actual argument in the calling function, which enables the called function to modify the actual argument value or to use it in a computation. In Figure 6.2, a dashed arrow and a solid arrow connect a reference parameter in `computeSumAve` with its corresponding actual argument in the calling function. The dashed arrow in color shows that the address of variable `mean` in the calling function is passed to formal parameter `average` in `computeSumAve`; the solid arrow in color shows that the value assigned to formal parameter `average` in `computeSumAve` is actually stored in variable `mean` in the calling function.

Remember to place the `&` (for reference parameters) in the formal parameter list only, not in the actual argument list. Also, you must insert `&`s in the function prototype to indicate that the third and fourth formal parameters are reference parameters:

```
void computeSumAve(float, float, float&, float&);
```

call-by-reference
An argument-passing mechanism in which the address of an actual argument is stored in the called function's data area.

## `void` Functions Can Return Results

Beginning programmers are sometimes confused by the fact that compute-SumAve is declared as a `void` function but still returns results to the calling function. By declaring computeSumAve as `void`, we're only telling C++ that it doesn't return a value through execution of a `return` statement. But computeSumAve is still permitted to return results through its output parameters.

## When to Use a Reference or a Value Parameter

How do you decide whether to use a reference parameter or a value parameter? Here are some rules of thumb:

- If information is to be passed into a function and doesn't have to be returned or passed out of the function, then the formal parameter representing that information should be a value parameter (for example, num1 and num2 in Figure 6.1). A parameter used in this way is called an **input parameter**.

- If information is to be returned to the calling function through a parameter, then the formal parameter representing that information must be a reference parameter (sum and average in Figure 6.1). A parameter used in this way is called an **output parameter**.

- If information is to be passed into a function, perhaps modified, and a new value returned, then the formal parameter representing that information must be a reference parameter. A parameter used in this way is called an **input/output parameter** (or **inout parameter**).

**input parameter**
A parameter used to receive a data value from the calling function.

**output parameter**
A parameter used to return a result to the calling function.

**input/output (inout) parameter**
A parameter that receives a data value from the calling function and returns a value to it.

Although we make a distinction between output parameters and input/output parameters, C++ does not. Both must be specified as reference parameters (using the ampersand), so that the address of the corresponding actual argument is stored in the called function data area when the function is called. For an input/output parameter (as well as for an input parameter), we assume there are some meaningful data in the actual argument before the function executes; for an output parameter, we make no such assumption.

## Program Style    Writing Formal Parameter Lists

In Listing 6.1, the formal parameter list

```
(float num1,      // IN - values used
 float num2,      //      in computation
 float& sum,      // OUT - sum of num1 and num2
 float& average)  // OUT - average of num1 and num2
```

is written on four lines to improve program readability. The value parameters are on the first two lines with comments that document their use as input parameters. The reference parameters are on the next two lines followed by comments that document their use as function outputs.

Generally, we follow this practice in writing formal parameter lists. We list input parameters first, input/output parameters next, and output parameters last.

## Comparison of Value and Reference Parameters

Table 6.1 summarizes what we've learned so far about value and reference parameters.

## Protection Afforded by Value Parameters

Reference parameters are more versatile than value parameters because their values can be used in a computation as well as changed by the function's execution. Why not make all parameters, even input parameters, reference parameters? The reason is that value parameters offer some protection for data integrity. Because copies of value parameters are stored locally in the called function data area, C++ protects the actual argument's value and prevents it from being erroneously changed by the function's execution. For example, if we insert the statement

```
num1 = -5.0;
```

at the end of function `computeSumAve`, the value of formal parameter `num1` will be changed to `-5.0`, but the value stored in x (the corresponding actual argument) will still be `8.0`.

**Table 6.1**   Comparison of Value and Reference Parameters

| Value Parameters | Reference Parameters |
| --- | --- |
| • Value of corresponding actual argument is stored in the called function. | • Address of corresponding actual argument is stored in the called function. |
| • The function execution cannot change the actual argument value. | • The function execution can change the actual argument value. |
| • Actual argument can be an expression, variable, or constant. | • Actual argument must be a variable. |
| • Formal parameter type must be specified in the formal parameter list. | • Formal parameter type must be followed by & in the formal parameter list. |
| • Parameters are used to store the data passed to a function (input parameters). | • Parameters are used to return outputs from a function (output parameters) or to change the value of a function argument (input / output parameters). |

If you forget to declare a formal output parameter as a reference parameter (using the ampersand), then its value (not its address) will be passed to the function when it's called. The argument value is stored locally, and any change to its value will not be returned to the calling function. This is a very common error in parameter usage.

## Argument/Parameter List Correspondence Revisited

We first discussed argument/parameter list correspondence in Section 3.5. We used the acronym **not** to indicate that an argument list used in a function call must agree with the called function's parameter list in **n**umber, **o**rder, and **t**ype. We repeat these three rules below and add one more.

### Argument/Parameter List Correspondence

- **N**umber: The number of actual arguments used in a call to a function must be the same as the number of formal parameters listed in the function prototype.
- **O**rder: The order of arguments in the lists determines correspondence. The first actual argument corresponds to the first formal parameter, the second actual argument corresponds to the second formal parameter, and so on.
- **T**ype: Each actual argument must be of a data type that can be assigned to the corresponding formal parameter with no unexpected loss of information.
- For reference parameters, an actual argument must be a variable. For value parameters, an actual argument may be a variable, a constant, or an expression.

The last rule states that you can use expressions (or variables or constants) as actual arguments corresponding to value parameters but not to reference parameters. For example, the function call

```
computeSumAve(x + y, 10, mySum, myAve);
```

calls `computeSumAve` to compute the `sum` (returned in `mySum`) and the `average` (returned in `myAve`) of the expression `x + y` and the integer `10`.

Only variables can correspond to reference parameters, so `mySum` and `myAve` must be declared as type `float` variables in the calling function. This restriction is imposed because an actual argument corresponding to a formal reference parameter may be modified when the called function executes; it makes no sense to allow a function to change the value of either a constant or an expression.

## EXAMPLE 6.2

Listing 6.2 shows the outline of a **main** function and a lower-level function called **test**.

The prototype for function **test** shows that **test** has two type **int** value parameters (**a** and **b**), two type **float** reference parameters (**c** and **d**), and one type **char** reference parameter (**e**). You could use any of the following function calls in the **main** function:

```
test(m + 3, 10, x, y, next);
test(m, -63, y, x, next);
test(35, m * 10, y, x, next);
```

In each call above, the first two arguments are type **int** variables, constants, or expressions; the next two arguments are type **float** variables; the last parameter is a type **char** variable (**next**). Table 6.2 shows the correspondence specified by the first argument list.

**Listing 6.2**   Functions main and test

```
// Functions used  . . .
void test(int, int, float&, float&, char&);

int main()
{ . . .
   float x, y;
   int m;
   char next;
   . . .
}

void test(int a, int b,                 // IN
          float& c, float& d, char& e)  // OUT
{
   . . .
}  // end test
```

**Table 6.2**   Argument/Parameter Correspondence for test(m + 3, 10, x, y, next)

| Actual Argument | Formal Parameter | Description |
|---|---|---|
| m + 3 | a | int, value |
| 10 | b | int, value |
| x | c | float, reference |
| y | d | float, reference |
| next | e | char, reference |

Table 6.3 Invalid Function Calls

| Function Call | Error |
|---|---|
| `test(30, 10, m, 19, next);` | The constant 19 cannot correspond to reference parameter d. Note that the integer m would be converted to floating point by the compiler. |
| `test(m, 19, x, y);` | Not enough actual arguments. |
| `test(m, 10, 35, y, 'E');` | Constants 35 and `'E'` cannot correspond to reference parameters. |
| `test(m, 3.3, x, y, next);` | This is legal; however, the type of 3.3 is not an integer so the fractional part will be lost. |
| `test(30, 10, x, x + y, next);` | Expression x + y cannot correspond to a reference parameter. |
| `test(30, 10, c, d, e);` | c, d, and e are not declared in the main function. |

All the function calls in Table 6.3 contain errors. The last function call points out an error often made in using functions. The last three actual argument names (c, d, e) are the same as their corresponding formal parameters. However, they are not declared as variables in the main function, so they cannot be used as actual arguments.

When writing relatively long argument lists such as those in this example, be careful not to transpose two actual arguments. If you transpose arguments, you may get a syntax error. If no syntax rule is violated, the function execution will probably generate incorrect results.

## EXERCISES FOR SECTION 6.1

### Self-Check

1. The function definitions below are from Example 6.2.

```
int main()
{
    float x, y;
    int m;
    char next;
    . . .
}

void test(int a, int b,                    // IN
          float& c, float& d, char& e)     // OUT
{
    . . .
}   // end test
```

For each argument list below, provide a table similar to Table 6.2 if the argument list is correct. Otherwise, indicate the reason(s) the argument list would not be correct.

```
test(m, -63, y, x, next);
test(35, m * 10, y, x, next);
test(m, m, x, m, 'a');
```

2. Correct the syntax errors in the prototype parameter lists below.

```
(int&, int&; float)
(value int, char x, y)
(float x + y, int account&)
```

3. Assume that you've been given the following declarations:

```
// Functions used ...
void massage (float&, float&, int);

    // Local data ...
    const int MAX = 32767;

    float x, y, z;
    int m, n;
```

Determine which of the following function calls are invalid and indicate why. If any standard conversions are required, indicate which one(s) and specify the result of the conversion.

a.  `massage(x, y, z);`

b.  `massage(x, y, 8);`

c.  `massage(y, x, n);`

d.  `massage(m, y, n);`

e.  `massage(25.0, 15, x);`

f.  `massage(x, y, m+n);`

g.  `massage(a, b, x);`

h.  `massage(y, z, m);`

i.  `massage(y+z, y-z, m);`

j.  `massage(z, y, x);`

k.  `massage(x, y, m, 10);`

l.  `massage(z, y, MAX);`

Programming

1.  Write a function that accepts a real number as input and returns its whole and fractional parts as outputs. For example, if the input is –5.32, the function outputs should be the integer –5 and the real value –0.32.

2.  Write a function that accepts an input argument consisting of two words with a space between them and returns each word through its two output parameters. All three parameters should be type `string`. If the input argument has only one word, the second output parameter should store the string `" "`.

3.  Write a function that accepts a real number as input and returns the largest integer that is smaller than the real number and the smallest integer that is larger than the real number. Hint: Use `cmath` functions `floor` and `ceil`.

# 6.2 Functions with Output and Input Parameters

In previous examples, we passed information to a function through its input parameters and returned a result from a function through its output parameters. In this section, we study three functions that have only output or inout (input/output) parameters.

## EXAMPLE 6.3

Function `getFrac` in Listing 6.3 reads a common fraction typed in by a user and returns the numerator and denominator through two type `int` output parameters. For example, if the user types in 4 / 7, the function returns 4 through `numerator` and 7 through `denominator`. The `main` function calls `getFrac` to read a fraction and then displays the fraction read.

This example illustrates a curious phenomenon. Notice that function `getFrac`'s outputs (`numerator` and `denominator`) are actually data items that are entered at the keyboard. Although this seems strange at first, it's a fairly common occurrence in programming. It illustrates that data elements in a program system can have different purposes in different modules. For example, `numerator` and `denominator` are output parameters of function `getFrac` and return their values to `main` program variables `num` and `denom`. In the `main` function, the values of `num` and `denom` are considered problem inputs because they are entered by the program user.

**Listing 6.3**   Testing function `getFrac`

```cpp
// File: testGetFrac
// Test function getFrac

#include <iostream>
using namespace std;

void getFrac(int&, int&);

int main()
{
   int num,           // input - fraction numerator
       denom;          // input - fraction denominator

   cout << "Enter a common fraction "
        << "as 2 integers separated by a slash: ";

   getFrac(num, denom);

   cout << "Fraction is " << num
        << " / " << denom << endl;

   return 0;
}

// Reads a fraction.
// Pre: none
// Post: Returns fraction numerator through numerator
//        Returns fraction denominator through denominator
void getFrac(int& numerator,          // OUT
             int& denominator)        // OUT
{
   char slash;        // temporary storage for slash
   cin >> numerator >> slash >> denominator;
}
```

```
Enter a fraction as 2 integers separated by a slash: 3 / 4
Fraction is 3 / 4
```

Similarly, if we wrote a function to display the fraction, we'd have to pass the fraction's numerator and denominator values to the display function through its input parameters. The display function would then display its inputs on the screen. In this case, the numerator and denominator are problem outputs, but they are inputs to the display function.

## EXAMPLE 6.4

In this example, we illustrate multiple calls to a function. Function `readFracProblem` in Listing 6.4 reads a problem involving two common fractions. A sample problem would be 2/4 + 5/6 . The function outputs would be the numerator and denominators of both fractions and the operation as a character ('+' for the sample). Function `read-FracProblem` calls `getFrac` twice. Programming Project 10 at the end of this chapter describes a program that uses `readFracProblem`.

Notice that the data for a fraction numerator (or denominator) has different names in each function. We use the name `numerator` in function `getFrac`, and we use the names `num1` and `num2` in function `getFracProblem`. The parameter `numerator` in `getFrac` corresponds to parameter `num1` in the first call and parameter `num2` in the second. If we use the statement

```
readFracProblem(n1, d1, n2, d2, op);
```

to call `readFracProblem`, argument `n1` will receive the value returned through `num1` and argument `n2` will receive the value returned through `num2`. Table 6.4 summarizes the argument/parameter list correspondence.

**Listing 6.4**   Function `readFracProblem`

```
// Reads a fraction problem
// Pre: none
// Post: Returns first fraction through num1, denom1
//       Returns second fraction through num2, denom2
//       Returns operation through op
void readFracProblem(
    int& num1, int& denom1,              // OUT - 1st fraction
    int& num2, int& denom2,              // OUT - 2nd fraction
    char& op)                            // OUT - operator
{
    getFrac(num1, denom1);
    cin >> op;
    getFrac(num2, denom2);
}
```

**Table 6.4**   Argument/Parameter Correspondence for `readFracProblem(n1, d1, n2, d2, op);`

| Actual Argument | `readFracProblem` Parameter | `getFrac` Parameter |
|---|---|---|
| n1 | num1 | numerator  (in first call) |
| d1 | denom1 | denominator (in first call) |
| n2 | num2 | numerator (in second call) |
| d2 | denom2 | denominator (in second call) |

## EXAMPLE 6.5

In this example, we illustrate multiple calls to a function with inout parameters. The `main` function in Listing 6.5 reads three data values into `num1`, `num2`, and `num3` and rearranges the data so that they are in increasing sequence, with the smallest value in `num1`. The three calls to function `order` perform an operation known as **sorting**.

Each time that function `order` executes, the smaller of its two argument values is stored in its first actual argument and the larger is stored in its second actual argument. Therefore, the first function call

```
order(num1, num2);          // order the data in num1 & num2
```

stores the smaller of `num1` and `num2` in `num1` and the larger in `num2`. In the sample run shown, `num1` is `7.5` and `num2` is `9.6`, so these values are not changed by the function execution. However, the function call

```
order(num1, num3);          // order the data in num1 & num3
```

switches the values of `num1` (initial value is `7.5`) and `num3` (initial value is `5.5`). Table 6.5 traces the `main` function execution.

The body of function `order` is based on the `if` statement from Example 4.13. The function heading

```
void order(float& x, float& y)   // INOUT - numbers to sort
```

identifies `x` and `y` as inout (input/output) parameters because the function uses the current actual argument values as inputs and may return new values.

During the execution of the second function call

```
order(num1, num3);          // order the data in num1 & num3
```

the formal parameter `x` contains the address of the actual argument `num1`, and the formal parameter `y` contains the address of actual argument `num3`. In testing the condition

```
(x > y)
```

the variable corresponding to `x` (`num1`) has value `7.5` and the variable corresponding to `y` (`num3`) has value `5.5` so the condition is true. Executing the first assignment statement in the true task

```
temp = x;
```

causes `7.5` to be copied into the local variable `temp`. Figure 6.3 shows a snapshot of the values in memory immediately after execution of this assignment statement.

Execution of the next assignment statement

```
x = y;
```

**sorting**
Rearranging data values so they are in an ordered sequence.

replaces the `7.5` in the variable corresponding to `x` (`num1`) with the value (`5.5`) of the variable corresponding to `y` (`num3`). The final assignment statement

```
y = temp;
```

copies the contents of the temporary variable (`7.5`) into the variable corresponding to `y` (`num3`). This completes the swap of values.

**Listing 6.5**   Function to order three numbers

```cpp
// File: sort3Numbers.cpp
// reads three numbers and sorts them in ascending order

#include <iostream>
using namespace std;

// Functions used . . .
// Sorts a pair of numbers
void order(float&, float&);   // INOUT - numbers to sort

int main()
{

    float num1, num2, num3;    // user input - numbers to sort

    // Read 3 numbers.
    cout << "Enter 3 numbers to sort: "
    cin >> num1 >> num2 >> num3;

    // Sort them.
    order(num1, num2);              // order data in num1 & num2
    order(num1, num3);              // order data in num1 & num3
    order(num2, num3);              // order data in num2 & num3

    // Display results.
    cout << "The three numbers in order are:" << endl;
    cout << num1 << " " << num2 << " " << num3 << endl;

    return 0;
}

// Sorts a pair of numbers represented by x and y
// Pre: x and y are assigned values.
// Post: x is the smaller of the pair and y is the larger.
void order(float& x, float& y)        // INOUT - numbers to sort
{
```

(continued)

**Listing 6.5** Function to order three numbers (continued)

```
        // Local data  . . .
        float temp;                 // storage for number in x

        // Compare x and y, exchange values if not in order.
        if (x > y)
        {                           // exchange the values in x and y
            temp = x;               // store old x in temp
            x = y;                  // store old y in x
            y = temp;               // store old x in y
        }
    } // end order
```

```
Enter 3 numbers to sort: 7.5 9.6 5.5
The three numbers in order are:
5.5 7.5 9.6
```

**Table 6.5** Trace of Program to Sort Three Numbers

| Statement | num1 | num2 | num3 | Effect |
|---|---|---|---|---|
| cin >> num1 >> num2 >> num3; | 7.5 | 9.6 | 5.5 | Enters data |
| order(num1, num2); | | | | No change |
| order(num1, num3); | 5.5 | | 7.5 | Switches num1 and num3 |
| order(num2, num3); | | 7.5 | 9.6 | Switches num2 and num3 |
| cout << num1 << num2 << num3 << endl; | | | | Displays 5.5, 7.5, 9.6 |

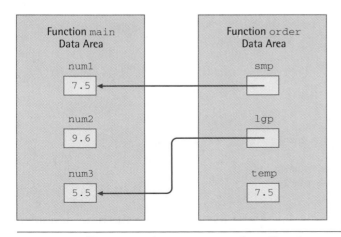

**Figure 6.3** Data areas after temp = x; for call order(num1, num3);

## EXERCISES FOR SECTION 6.2

Self-Check

1. Examine the functions below and answer the questions after function `sumDiff`.

```cpp
#include <iostream>
using namespace std;

void sumDiff(int, int);

int main()
{
    int w, x, y, z;

    x = 5;   y = 3;   z = 7;   w  = 9;
    cout << "    x    y    z    w " << endl;
    cout << "  " << x << "   " << y << "   " << z
         << "   " << w << endl;

    sumDiff(x, y, z, w);
    cout << "  " << x << "   " << y << "   " << z
         << "   " << w << endl;

    sumDiff(y, x, w, z);
    cout << "  " << x << "   " << y << "   " << z
         << "   " << w << endl;

    sumDiff(y, x, y, x);
    cout << "  " << x << "   " << y << "   " << z
         << "   " << w << endl;

    sumDiff(z, w, y, x);
    cout << "   " << x << "   " << y << "   " << z
         << "   " << w << endl;

    return 0;
}

void sumDiff(
    int num1, int num2,         // IN:
    int& num3, int& num4)       // INOUT:
{
    num3 = num1 + num2;
    num4 = num1 - num2;
}   // end sumDiff
```

**a.** Show the output displayed by function show in the form of a table of values for w, x, y, and z.

**b.** Briefly describe what function `sumDiff` computes. Include a description of how the input and input/output parameters to `sumDiff` are used.

**c.** Write the preconditions and postconditions for function `sumDiff`.

**2. a.** Refer to Listing 6.5 and trace the execution of the three function calls

```
order(num3, num2);
order(num3, num1);
order(num2, num1);
```

for the data sets:  15   20   4 and 4   15   20.

**b.** What is the effect of this sequence of calls?

Programming
**1.** Write the function `sumDiff` in Self-Check Exercise 1 as two separate functions `sum` and `diff` that take two input arguments. Function `sum` performs the addition, and function `diff` performs the subtraction. Rewrite the `main` function to use `sum` and `diff` to compute the same results as before.

**2.** Write function `doFrac` that returns a string representing a common fraction given its numerator and denominator as input arguments and also returns the decimal value of the function. If the input arguments are 1 and 4, the string should be `"1/4"` and the decimal value should be `0.25`. Make sure you don't use integer division to calculate the decimal value (1 / 4 is 0 using integer division).

## 6.3  Stepwise Design with Functions

Using argument lists to pass information to and from functions improves problem-solving skills. If the solution to a subproblem cannot be written easily using just a few C++ statements, code it as a function. The case study demonstrates stepwise design of programs using functions.

*case study*   **General Sum and Average Problem**

### PROBLEM

You have been asked to accumulate a sum and to average a list of data values using functions. Because these tasks surface in many problems, design a general set of functions you can reuse in other programs.

## ANALYSIS

Let's look again at the loop in Figure 5.2, which computed a company's total payroll. We can use a similar loop here to sum a collection of data values. To compute an average, divide a sum by the total number of items, being careful not to perform this division if the number of items is zero.

### DATA REQUIREMENTS
#### Problem Input

| | |
|---|---|
| int numItems | *// number of data items* |
| the data items | |

#### Problem Output

| | |
|---|---|
| float sum | *// accumulated sum of data items* |
| float average | *// average of all data items* |

### FORMULA
Average = Sum of data / number of data items

## DESIGN

### INITIAL ALGORITHM
1. Read the number of items.

2. Read the data items and compute the sum of the data (computeSum).

3. Compute the average of the data (computeAve).

4. Print the sum and the average (printSumAve).

The structure chart in Figure 6.4 documents the data flow between the main problem and its subproblems. We'll implement each step as a separate function; the label under a step denotes the name of the function implementing that step.

Figure 6.4 clarifies the data flow between the main function and each subordinate function. All variables whose values are set by a function are *function outputs* (indicated by an arrow pointing out of the function). All variables whose values are used in a computation but are not changed by a function are *function inputs* (indicated by an arrow pointing into the function). The role of each variable depends on its usage in a function and changes from step to step in the structure chart.

Because the step "Read the number of data items" defines the value of numItems, this variable is an output of this step. Function computeSum needs the value of numItems to know how many data items to read and sum; consequently, numItems is an input to function computeSum. The variable sum is an output of function computeSum but is an input to functions

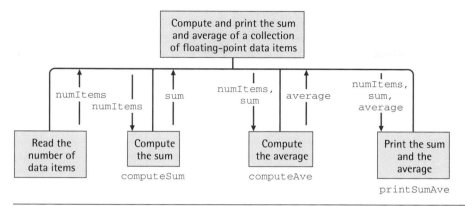

**Figure 6.4** Structure chart for general `sum` and `average` problem

`computeAve` and `printSumAve`. The variable `average` is an output of function `computeAve` but is an input to function `printSumAve`.

## IMPLEMENTATION

Using the data flow information in the structure chart, you can write the main function even before refining the algorithm. Follow the approach described in Section 3.1 to write function `main`. Begin by converting the data requirements shown earlier into local declarations for function `main`. Declare all the variables that appear in the structure chart in the main function, because they store data passed to a function or results returned from a function. Omit the declaration for a variable that stores the individual data items, since it doesn't appear in the structure chart. However, remember to declare this variable later in the function that uses it (`computeSum`). Next, move the initial algorithm into the main function body, writing each algorithm step as a comment.

To complete the main function (see Listing 6.6), code each algorithm step *in-line* (as part of the main program code) or as a function call. Code the data entry step in-line because it consists of a simple prompt and data entry operation.

The data flow information in Figure 6.4 tells you the actual arguments to use in each function call. It also tells you the name of the main program variable that will hold the function result. For example, use the assignment statement

```
sum = computeSum(numItems);
```

to call `computeSum` and set the value of `sum`. In this call, `numItems` is passed as an input argument to function `computeSum` and the function result

**Listing 6.6**    Main function for general sum and average problem

```cpp
// File: computeSumAve.cpp
// Computes and prints the sum and average of a collection of data.

#include <iostream>
using namespace std;

// Functions used  . . .
// Computes sum of data
float computeSum
    (int);                  // IN - number of data items

// Computes average of data
float computeAve
    (int,                   // IN - number of data items
     float);                // IN - sum of data items

// Prints number of items, sum, and average
void printSumAve
    (int,                   // IN - number of data items
     float,                 // IN - sum of the data
     float);                // IN - average of the data

int main()
{
    int numItems;           // input - number of items to be added
    float sum;              // output - accumulated sum of data
    float average;          // output - average of data being processed

    // Read the number of items to process.
    cout << "Enter the number of items to process: ";
    cin >> numItems;

    // Compute the sum of the data.
    sum = computeSum(numItems);

    // Compute the average of the data.
    average = computeAve(numItems, sum);

    // Print the sum and the average.
    printSumAve(numItems, sum, average);

    return 0;
}

// Insert definitions for functions computeSum, computeAve,
// and printSumAve here.
```

(determined by the `return` statement) is assigned to `sum`. Similarly, use the statement

```
average = computeAve(numItems, sum);
```

to call `computeAve`. Finally, use the statement

```
printSumAve(numItems, sum, average);
```

to call `printSumAve`, which has three input parameters and returns no result.

## ANALYSIS FOR `computeSum`

In specifying the data requirements for `computeSum`, begin with the function interface information. This function is given the number of items to be processed as an input parameter (`numItems`). It's responsible for reading and computing the sum of this number of values. This sum is then returned using the `return` statement.

> FUNCTION INTERFACE FOR `computeSum`
> **Input Parameters**
>
> `int numItems`     *// number of items to process*
>
> **Output Parameters**
>
> (none)
>
> **Function Return Value**
>
> the sum (`float`) of the data items processed

Besides a variable to store the sum, `computeSum` needs two more local variables: one for storing each data item (`item`) and one for loop control (`count`).

> **Local Data**
>
> `float item`     *// Contains each data item as it is read in*
> `float sum`      *// Used to accumulate the sum of data read in*
> `int count`      *// The number of data items processed so far*

## DESIGN OF `computeSum`

The loop control steps must ensure that the correct number of data items are read and summed. Since you know the number of items to sum beforehand (`numItems`), use a counting loop. Use these steps to write the algorithm for `computeSum`; Listing 6.7 shows the code for `computeSum`.

> INITIAL ALGORITHM FOR `computeSum`
> 1. Initialize `sum` to zero.
>
> 2. For each value of `count` from 0, as long as `count < numItems`

**Listing 6.7** Function computeSum

```
// Computes sum of data.
// Pre: numItems is assigned a value.
// Post: numItems data items read; their sum is stored in sum.
// Returns: Sum of all data items read if numItems >= 1;
//          otherwise, 0.

float computeSum
    (int numItems)      // IN: number of data items
{
    // Local data  . . .
    float item;         // input: contains current data item
    float sum;          // output: used to accumulate sum of data
                        //         read in

    // Read each data item and accumulate it in sum.
    sum = 0.0;
    for (int count = 0; count < numItems; count++)
    {
        cout << "Enter a number to be added: ";
        cin >> item;
        sum += item;
    }  // end for

    return sum;
}  // end computeSum
```

**2.1.** Read in a data item.

**2.2.** Add the data item to sum.

**3.** Return sum.

### ANALYSIS FOR computeAve AND printSumAve

Both computeAve and printSumAve are relatively straightforward. We list their interface information and algorithms next. Neither function requires any local data, but both algorithms include a test of numItems. If numItems isn't positive, it makes no sense to compute or display the average of the data items.

FUNCTION INTERFACE FOR computeAve
**Input Parameters**

| | |
|---|---|
| int numItems | // the number of data items to be processed |
| float sum | // the sum of all data processed |

**Output Parameters**

(none)

**Function Return Value**

the average of all the data (`float`)

## DESIGN OF `computeAve`

INITIAL ALGORITHM

1. If the number of items is less than 1

    **1.1.** display "invalid number of items" message.

    **1.2.** return a value of 0.

2. Return the value of the sum divided by `numItems`.

FUNCTION INTERFACE FOR `printSumAve`

**Input Parameters**

```
int numItems      // the number of data items to be processed
float sum         // the sum of all data processed
float average     // the average of all the data
```

**Output Parameters**

(none)

## DESIGN OF `printSumAve`

INITIAL ALGORITHM

1. If the number of items is positive

    **1.1.** Display the number of items and the sum and average of the data.

    Else

    **1.2.** Display "invalid number of items" message.

## IMPLEMENTATION OF `computeAve` AND `printSumAve`

The implementation of the `computeAve` and `printSumAve` functions is shown in Listings 6.8 and 6.9.

## TESTING

The program that solves the general `sum` and `average` problem consists of four separate functions. In testing the complete program, you should make sure that `sum` and `average` are displayed correctly when `numItems` is positive and that a meaningful diagnostic is displayed when `numItems` is zero or negative. Listing 6.10 shows a sample run of the complete program system.

**Listing 6.8**    Function `computeAve`

```
// Computes average of data
// Pre:  numItems and sum are defined; numItems must be
//       greater than 0.
// Post: If numItems is positive, the average is computed
//       as sum / numItems;
// Returns: The average if numItems is positive;
// otherwise, 0.

float computeAve
    (int numItems,      // IN: number of data items
     float sum)         // IN: sum of data
{
    // Compute the average of the data.
    if (numItems < 1)  // test for invalid input
    {
        cout << "Invalid value for numItems = " << numItems
            << endl;
        cout << "Average not computed." << endl;
        return 0.0; // return for invalid input
    }  // end if

    return sum / numItems;
}  // end computeAve
```

**Listing 6.9**    Function `printSumAve`

```
// Prints number of items, sum, and average of data
// Pre: numItems, sum, and average are defined.
// Post: Displays numItems, sum and average if numItems > 0.

void printSumAve
    (int numItems,              // IN: number of data items
     float sum,                 // IN: sum of the data
     float average)             // IN: average of the data
{
    // Display results if numItems is valid.
    if (numItems > 0)
    {
        cout << "The number of items is " << numItems << endl;
        cout << "The sum of the data is " << sum << endl;
        cout << "The average of the data is " << average << endl;
```

(continued)

**Listing 6.9** Function `printSumAve` (continued)

```
    }
    else
    {
        cout << "Invalid number of items = " << numItems << endl;
        cout << "Sum and average are not defined." << endl;
        cout << "No printing done. Execution terminated." << endl;
    } // end if
} // end printSumAve
```

**Listing 6.10** Sample run of general `sum` and `average` problem

```
Enter the number of items to process: 3
Enter a number to be added: 5
Enter a number to be added: 6
Enter a number to be added: 17
The number of items is 3
The sum of the data is 28.00
The average of the data is 9.3333
```

## Multiple Declarations of Identifiers in a Program

The identifiers `sum` and `numItems` are declared as variables in the `main` function and as formal parameters in the three subordinate functions. From the discussion of scope of names (see Section 3.6), you know that each of these declarations has its own scope, and the scope for each formal parameter is the function that declares it. The argument lists associate the main function variable `sum` with each of the other identifiers named `sum`. The value of variable `sum` (in function `main`) is initially defined when function `computeSum` finishes execution because variable `sum` is assigned the function result. This value is passed into function `computeAve` because variable `sum` corresponds to `computeAve`'s input parameter `sum`, and so on.

To avoid the possible confusion of seeing the identifier `sum` in multiple functions, we could have introduced different names in each function (e.g., `total`, `mySum`). But the program is easier to read if the name `sum` is used throughout to refer to the sum of the data values. Make sure that you remember to link these separate uses of identifier `sum` through argument list correspondence.

## Program Style     Use of Functions for Relatively Simple Algorithm Steps

All but the first step of the general sum and average problem are performed by separate functions. Even though it was relatively easy to implement the step for computing the average, we used a function (computeAve) rather than writing the code inline in the main function. We want to encourage the use of separate functions even for relatively easy-to-implement algorithm steps. This helps you keep the details of these steps separate and hidden and makes the program system easier to debug, test, and even modify at some future date. Also, you may be able to reuse this function later. From this point on, your main functions should consist primarily of a sequence of function calls.

## Program Style     Cohesive Functions

Function computeSum only computes the sum. It doesn't read in the number of data items (Step 1 of the main function), nor does it display the sum of the data (role of function printSumAve).

Functions that perform a single operation are called *functionally cohesive*. It's good programming style to write such single-purpose, highly cohesive functions, as this helps to keep each function relatively compact and easy to read, write, and debug. You can determine whether a function is highly cohesive from the comment describing what the function does. If the comment consists of a short sentence or phrase with no connectives such as "and" or "or," then the function should be highly cohesive. If more than one or two connectives or separate sentences are needed to describe the purpose of a function, this may be a hint that the function is doing too many things and should be further decomposed into subfunctions.

## EXERCISES FOR SECTION 6.3

### Self-Check

1. Function computeAve returns a single value using a return statement. Rewrite this function to return this result through an output parameter. Why is this not as good a solution as the one used in the case study?

2. Draw the before and after data areas for the main function and revised computeAve (see Self-Check Exercise 1) assuming computeAve is called with sum equal to 100.0 and numItems equal to 10.

3. Draw the main function and printSumAve data areas given the data value assumptions in Self-Check Exercise 2.

4. Consider the three functions `computeSum`, `computeAve`, and `printSumAve` as though the code to validate the value of the parameter `numItems` had been omitted. For each of these functions, describe what would happen now that the function would be allowed to proceed with its work even if `numItems` were zero or negative.

5. Design an algorithm for `readNumItems` that uses a loop to ensure that the user enters a positive value. The loop should continue reading numbers until the user enters a positive number.

Programming
1. Implement the solution to Self-Check Exercise 5.

# 6.4 Using Objects with Functions

C++ provides two ways that you can use functions to modify objects.

1. You can use dot notation to apply a member function to an object (also called "sending the object a message"). The member function may modify one or more data attributes of the object to which it is applied.

2. You can pass an object as an argument to a function.

We illustrate both approaches in the next example.

## EXAMPLE 6.6

Listing 6.11 shows function `moneyToNumberString`, which has a single inout argument of type `string`. This function removes a dollar sign and any commas that appear in its argument string. For example, if the argument string passed to the function is `"-$5,405,123.65"`, the argument string will be changed to `"-5405123.65"` by the function execution.

The `if` statement checks for the presence of a `$`. If the argument string begins with a `$`, the true task removes it. The `else` clause removes only the `$` from a string that begins with the substring `"-$"`. Next, the `while` loop removes all commas from the argument string, starting with the leftmost one. If a comma is found, the loop repetition condition is true, so the comma is removed and the next one is searched for. The loop repetition condition fails when there are no commas left in the argument string. We will say more about objects as arguments in Chapter 10.

**Listing 6.11** Testing function `moneyToNumberString`

```cpp
// File: moneyToNumberTest.cpp
// Tests function moneyToNumberString
#include <string>
#include <iostream>
using namespace std;

// Function prototype
void moneyToNumberString(string&);

int main()
{
   string mString;                 // input - a "money" string

   cout << "Enter a dollar amount with $ and commas: ";
   cin >> mString;

   moneyToNumberString(mString);

   cout << "The dollar amount as a number is " << mString
        << endl;

   return 0;
}

// Removes the $ and commas from a money string.
// Pre: moneyString is defined and may contain commas and
//      begin with $ or -$.
// Post: $ and all commas are removed from moneyString.
void moneyToNumberString
   (string& moneyString) // INOUT - string with possible $ and commas
{
   // Local data . . .
   int posComma;        // position of next comma

   // Remove $ from moneyString
   if (moneyString.at(0) == '$')           // Starts with $ ?
      moneyString.erase(0, 1);             // Remove $
   else if (moneyString.find("-$") == 0)   // Starts with -$ ?
      moneyString.erase(1, 1);             // Remove $

   // Remove all commas
   posComma = moneyString.find(",");                // Find first ,
```

(continued)

**Listing 6.11**   Testing function `moneyToNumberString` (continued)

```
    while (posComma >= 0 &&
           posComma < moneyString.length())    // Is posComma valid ?
    {
        moneyString.erase(posComma, 1);         // Remove ,
        posComma = moneyString.find(",");       // Find next ,
    }
}  // end moneyToNumberString
```

```
Enter a dollar amount with $ and commas: -$5,405,123.65
The dollar amount as a number is -5405123.65
```

## EXERCISES FOR SECTION 6.4

### Self-Check

1. Trace the execution of function `moneyToNumberString` for the data value shown in Listing 6.11. Show all values assigned to `posComma`.

### Programming

1. Write a function `compress` that removes all blanks from its string argument. If the argument is `"  this  Is      One"` it should be changed to `"thisIsOne"`.

2. Write a function `doRemove` that removes the first occurrence of a substring (an input argument) from a second argument string (input/output).

## 6.5   Debugging and Testing a Program System

As the number of statements in a program system grows, the possibility of error also increases. If we keep each function to a manageable size, the likelihood of error increases much more slowly. It's also easier to read and test each function.

Just as you can simplify the overall programming process by writing a large program as a set of independent functions, you can simplify testing and debugging if you test in stages as the program evolves. Two kinds of testing are used: top-down testing and bottom-up testing. You should use a combination of these methods to test a program and its functions.

### Top-Down Testing and Stubs

Though a single programmer or a programming team may be developing a program system, not all functions will be ready at the same time. It's still possible to test the overall flow of control between the main program and its level-1 functions and to test and debug the level-1 functions that are complete. Testing the flow of control between a `main` function and its subordinate functions is called **top-down testing**.

**top-down testing**
The process of testing flow of control between a `main` function and its subordinate functions.

Because the `main` function calls all level-1 functions, we need for all functions that are not yet coded a substitute called a **stub**—a function heading followed by a minimal body, which should display a message identifying the function being executed and should assign simple values to any outputs. Listing 6.12 shows a stub for function `computeSum` that could be used in a test of the `main` function in Listing 6.6. The stub arbitrarily returns a value of `100.0`, which is reasonable data for the remaining functions to process. Examining the program output tells us whether the `main` function calls its level-1 functions in the required sequence and whether data flows correctly between the `main` function and its level-1 functions.

**stub**
A function with a heading and a minimal body used in testing flow of control.

## Bottom–Up Testing and Drivers

**unit test**
A test of an individual function.

When a function is completed, it can be substituted for its stub in the program. However, we often perform a preliminary **unit test** of a new function before substitution because it's easier to locate and correct errors when dealing with a single function rather than with a complete program system. We can perform such a unit test by writing a short driver function to call it.

It isn't a good idea to spend a lot of time creating an elegant driver function, because it will be discarded as soon as the new function is tested. A driver function should contain only the declarations and executable statements necessary to test a single function. A driver should begin by reading or assigning values to all input arguments and to input/output arguments.

**Listing 6.12**  Stub for function `computeSum`

```
// Computes sum of data - stub
// Pre: numItems is assigned a value.
// Post: numItems data items read; their sum is stored in sum.
// Returns: Sum of all data items read if numItems >= 1;
//    otherwise 0.0.
float computeSum
   (int numItems)      // IN - number of data items

{
    cout << "Function computeSum entered" << endl;
    return 100.0;
}  // end computeSum stub
```

Next comes the call to the function being tested. After calling the function, the driver should display the function results. Listing 6.13 shows a driver for the completed function `computeSum`. Since we have no need to save the function result, we inserted the function call directly in the output statement.

Once you're confident that a function works properly, you can substitute it for its stub in the program system. The process of separately testing individual functions before inserting them in a program system is called **bottom-up testing**. Tests of the entire system are called **system integration tests**.

By following a combination of top-down and bottom-up testing, a programming team can be fairly confident that the complete function system will be relatively free of errors when it's finally put together. Consequently, the final debugging sessions should proceed quickly and smoothly.

**bottom-up testing**
The process of separately testing individual functions of a program system.

**system integration tests**
Testing a system after replacing all its stubs with functions that have been pretested.

## Debugging Tips for Program Systems

The following suggestions will prove helpful when debugging a program system.

1. Carefully document each function parameter and local variable using comments as you write the code. Also describe the function's purpose using comments.

2. Create a trace of execution by displaying the function name as you enter it.

3. Trace or display the values of all input and input/output parameters upon entry to a function. Check that these values make sense.

**Listing 6.13**  A driver to test `computeSum`

```cpp
int main()
{

    int n;
    // Keep calling computeSum and displaying the result.
    do
    {
        cout << "Enter number of items or 0 to quit: ";
        cin >> n;
        cout << "The sum is " << computeSum(n) << endl;
    } while (n != 0);

    return 0;
}  // end driver
```

4. Trace or display the values of all function outputs after returning from a function. Verify that these values are correct by hand computation. Make sure you declare all input/output and output parameters as reference parameters (using the & symbol).

5. Make sure that the function stub assigns a value to each output parameter.

You should plan for debugging as you write each function rather than adding debugging statements later. Include any output statements that you might need to help determine that the function is working. When you're satisfied that the function works as desired, you can remove these debugging statements. In Section 5.9, it was suggested that you turn them into comments.

Another way to "turn debugging off and on" is to introduce a type bool flag called DEBUG. First, make each debugging statement a dependent statement that executes only if DEBUG is true.

```
if (DEBUG)
    cout << "***** score is " << score << " and sum is "
         << sum << endl;
```

To "turn on debugging," insert the statement

```
const bool DEBUG = true;
```

before your main function, making it visible in all your functions. Setting the debugging flag to true causes the debugging statements to execute. To "turn off debugging," set the constant DEBUG to false instead of true.

## Identifier Scope and Watch Window Variables

You can use a debugger to trace values passed into a function's input arguments and to trace the values returned by a function. The values displayed in the Watch window are determined by the normal scope rules for identifiers. Consequently, a function's local variables and formal parameters will be considered undefined until that function begins execution. Upon exit from the function, its local variables and formal parameters will again become undefined.

## Black–Box Versus White–Box Testing

**black-box (or specification-based) testing** A testing process that assumes the tester has no knowledge of the code; the tester must compare a function or the system's performance with its specification.

There are two basic ways to test a completed function or system: (1) black-box testing and (2) white-box testing. In **black-box** (or **specification-based**) **testing**, we assume that the program tester has no information about the code inside the function or system. The tester's job is to verify that the function or system meets its specifications. For each function, the tester must ensure that its postconditions are satisfied whenever its preconditions are met. Because the tester cannot look inside the function or system, the tester must prepare sufficient sets of test data to verify that the system output is correct for all valid input values. The tester should also find out whether the function or system will crash for invalid data. The tester should especially check the *boundaries* of the system, or particular values where the system performance changes. For example, a boundary for a payroll program would be the value of hours worked that triggers overtime pay. Black-box testing is most often done by a special testing team or by program users.

In **white-box** (or **glass-box**) **testing**, the tester has full knowledge of the code for the function or system and must ensure that each section of code has been thoroughly tested. For a selection statement (if or switch), this means checking all possible paths through the selection statement. The tester must determine that the correct path is chosen for all possible values of the selection variable, taking special care at the boundary values where the path changes.

**white box (or glass box) testing**
A testing process that assumes the tester knows how the system is coded and requires checking all possible execution paths.

For a repetition statement, the tester must make sure that the loop always performs the correct number of iterations and that the number of iterations isn't off by one. Also, the tester should verify that the computations inside the loop are correct at the boundaries—that is, for the initial and final values of the loop control variable. Finally, the tester should make sure that the function or system still meets its specification when a loop executes zero times and that under no circumstances can the loop execute forever.

## EXERCISES FOR SECTION 6.5

### Self–Check
1. Show the output you'd expect to see for the sum and average program (Listing 6.6) using the stub in Listing 6.12 when numItems is 10.

2. Write a driver program to test function computeAve.

3. Explain the difference between black-box and white-box testing, between bottom-up and top-down testing, between unit tests and system integration tests.

4. Explain the difference between stubs and drivers. Which would be more useful in bottom-up testing? Which would be more useful in top-down testing?

### Programming
1. Write a driver function to test function computeAve.

# 6.6    Recursive Functions (Optional)

C++ allows a function to call itself. A function that calls itself is a *recursive function*. Sometimes it's simpler to implement a repeated operation using recursion instead of iteration. A recursive function calls itself repeatedly, but with different argument values for each call.

**stopping case**
An alternative task in a recursive function that leads to no further recursive calls.

Just as we did for a loop, we need to identify a situation (called a **stopping case**) that stops the recursion; otherwise, the function will call itself forever. Usually a recursive function has the following form:

> **Template for a Recursive Function**
> 1.   If the stopping case is reached
> >    1.1. Return a value for the stopping case
> >    Else
> >    1.2. Return a value computed by calling the function again with different arguments.

The `if` statement tests whether the stopping case has been reached. When it is reached, the recursion stops and the function returns a value to the caller. If the stopping case isn't reached, the function calls itself again with different arguments. The arguments in successive calls should bring us closer and closer to reaching the stopping case.

In this section we describe a recursive function that returns an integer value representing the factorial of its argument. The *factorial of n* is the product of all positive integers less than or equal to $n$ and is written in mathematics as $n!$. For example, 4! is the product $4 \times 3 \times 2 \times 1$ or 24. We provide a recursive definition for $n!$ next.

$$n! = 1 \qquad\qquad \text{for } n = 0 \text{ or } 1$$
$$n! = n \times (n{-}1)! \qquad \text{for } n > 1$$

We can translate this definition into pseudocode using the template shown earlier:

> 1.   If $n$ is 0 or 1
> >    1.1. Return 1
> >    Else
> >    1.2. Return $n \times (n{-}1)!$

Listing 6.14 shows function `factorial` rewritten as a recursive function. The stopping case is reached when $n$ is less than or equal to 1. When $n$ is greater than 1, the statement

```
return n * factorial(n-1);
```

executes, which is the C++ form of the second formula. The expression part of this statement contains a valid function call, `factorial(n-1)`, which calls function `factorial` with an argument that is 1 less than the current argument. This function call is a *recursive call.* If the argument in the initial call to `factorial` is 3, the following chain of recursive calls occurs:

```
factorial(3)  →  3 * factorial(2)  →  3 * (2 * factorial(1))
```

In the last call above, n is equal to 1, so the statement

```
return 1;
```

executes, stopping the chain of recursive calls.

When it finishes the last function call, C++ must return a value from each recursive call, starting with the last one. This process is called **unwinding the recursion**. The last call was `factorial(1)` and it returns a value of 1. To find the value returned by each call for n greater than 1, multiply n by the value returned from `factorial(n-1)`. Therefore, the value returned from `factorial(2)` is 2 * the value returned from `factorial(1)` or 2; the value returned from `factorial(3)` is 3 * the value returned from `factorial(2)` or 6 (see Figure 6.5).

**unwinding the recursion**
The process of returning a value from each recursive call.

For comparison purposes, Listing 6.15 shows an iterative factorial function that uses a loop to accumulate partial products in local variable `productSoFar`. The `for` statement repeats the multiplication step when n is greater than 1. If n is 0 or 1, the `for` loop body doesn't execute, so `productSoFar` retains its initial value of 1. After loop exit, the last value of `productSoFar` is returned as the function result.

**Listing 6.14**   Recursive function factorial

```
// Pre: n is >= 0
// Returns: The product 1 * 2 * 3 *   . . .   * n for n >
1;
//          otherwise 1.

int factorial(int n)
{
   if (n <= 1)
      return 1;
   else
      return n * factorial(n-1);
}
```

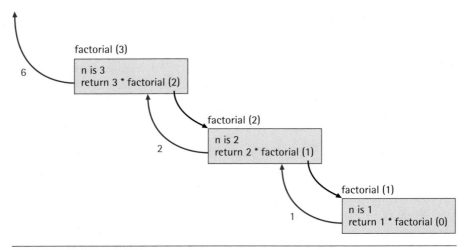

**Figure 6.5**    Unwinding the recursion

**Listing 6.15**    Iterative factorial function

```
// Pre: n is >= 0
// Returns: The product 1 * 2 * 3 *   . . .   * n for n > 1;
//          otherwise 1.
int factorial(int n)
{
   int productSoFar;              // output: accumulated product

   // Initialize accumulated product
   productSoFar = 1;

   // Perform the repeated multiplication for i > 1.
   for (int i = n; i > 1; i--)
      productSoFar = productSoFar * i;

      return productSoFar;
}
```

## EXERCISES FOR SECTION 6.6

### Self-Check

1. Show the chain of recursive calls to function `mystery` when `m` is 5 and `n` is 3. What do you think `mystery` does?

```
int mystery(int m, int n)
{
    if (n == 1) then
        return m;
    else
        return m * mystery(m, n-1);
}
```

2. Complete the recursive definition of function `gcd` which computes the greatest common divisor of two integers (`gcd(20, 15)` is 5).

```
//  precondition:  m is greater than or equal to n
int gcd(int m, int n)
{
    if (n > m)
        return gcd(#, );     //exchange arguments
    else if (m % n == 0)
        return __;           //the result is known
    else
        return gcd( ,  ); //find gcd of n and
                            //remainder of m / n
}
```

### Programming

1. Write a recursive function that, given an input value of `n`, computes:

```
n + n-1 +  ...  + 2 + 1.
```

2. Write a function `c(n, r)` that returns the number of different ways $r$ items can be selected from a group of $n$ items. The mathematical formula for `c(n, r)` follows. Test `c(n, r)` using both the recursive and the nonrecursive versions of function `factorial`.

$$c(n, r) = \frac{n!}{r!(n - r)!}$$

## 6.7    Common Programming Errors

Many opportunities for error arise when you use functions with parameter lists, so be extremely careful. Proper use of parameters is difficult for beginning programmers to master, but it's an essential skill. One obvious pitfall is not ensuring that the actual argument list has the same number of items as the formal parameter list. Each actual input argument must be of a type that can be assigned to its corresponding formal parameter. An actual output argument or inout argument should be the same data type as the corresponding formal parameter. Let's now look at two specific errors that can occur with reference parameters.

- *Parameter inconsistencies with call-by-reference parameters:* In Chapter 3, we indicated that argument/parameter inconsistencies involving character, integer, and floating-point data usually don't cause even a warning message from the compiler. However, such inconsistencies will cause a warning message if they occur when using reference parameters.

  For example, if `initiate` has the prototype

  ```
  void initiate(char &);
  ```

  and `sum` is type `float`, the call

  ```
  initiate(sum);
  ```

  will result in a compiler warning such as

  ```
  "Temporary used for parameter 1 in call to 'initiate
   (char &)'"
  ```

  Even though this is only a warning, it does indicate a possible error. Check the function call carefully to ensure that you're passing the correct argument.

- *Forgetting to use an & with call-by-reference parameters:* Make sure you remember to use an & in the function prototype and function header (but not the call) before each output or inout parameter. Forgetting the & doesn't cause an error message; however, C++ will treat the formal parameter as call-by-value instead of call-by-reference. Therefore, any change made to the parameter by the called function will not be returned to the calling function.

# Chapter Review

1. Functions provide a mechanism for separating and hiding the details for each component of a program system. The use of functions makes it possible to carry this separation through from the problem analysis and program design stages to the implementation of a program in C++.

2. Parameters enable a programmer to pass data to functions and to return multiple results from functions. The parameter list provides a highly visible communication path between a function and its calling program. Using parameters enables a function to process different data each time it executes, thereby making it easier to reuse the function in other programs.

3. Parameters may be used for input to a function, for output or sending back results, and for both input and output. An input parameter is used only for passing data into a function. The actual argument corresponding to an input parameter may be an expression or a constant. The parameter's declared type should be the same as the type of the argument.

4. C++ uses call-by-value for input parameters and call-by-reference for output and inout (input/output) parameters. For call-by-value, the actual argument's value is passed to the function when it's called; for call-by-reference, the actual argument's address is passed to the function when it's called. C++ uses the symbol & after the parameter type to indicate a reference parameter in a function prototype and in a function definition but not in a function call.

5. Output and inout parameters must be able to access variables in the calling function's data area, so the actual argument corresponding to an output or inout parameter must be a variable. The parameter's declared type should be the same as the type of the data.

## Summary of New C++ Constructs

| Construct | Effect |
|---|---|
| **Function Prototype**<br>`void doIt (float, char, float&, char&);` | Prototype for a function having two input and two output parameters. |
| **Function Definition**<br><pre>void doIt<br>  (float x,        // IN<br>   char op,        // IN<br>   float& y,       // OUT<br>   char& sign)     // OUT<br>{<br>    switch(op)<br>    {<br>      case '+':<br>         y = x + x;<br>         break;<br>      case '*':<br>         y = x * x;<br>         break;<br>    }<br>    if (x >= 0.0)<br>       sign = '+';<br>    else<br>       sign = '-';<br>}    // end doIt</pre> | x and op are input parameters that contain valid values passed in from the calling function. The memory cells corresponding to the output parameters y and sign are undefined upon entrance to function doIt, but they contain valid values that are passed back to the calling function upon exit. |
| **Function Call Statement**<br>`doIt(-5.0, '*', p, mySign);` | Calls function doIt. -5.0 is passed into x and '*' is passed into op. 25.0 is returned to p, and '-' is returned to mySign. |

### Quick-Check Exercises

1. Actual arguments appear in a function _____; formal parameters appear in a function _____ and function _____. Formal parameters are optional in a function _____.

2. Constants and expressions may be used as actual arguments corresponding to formal parameters that are _____ parameters.

3. In a function header, _____ parameters used for function output are designated by using the symbol _____ placed _____ the parameter type.

4. A _____ must be used as an actual argument corresponding to a call-by-reference formal parameter. You can use an _____ as an actual argument corresponding to a call-by-value parameter.

5. For _____ parameters, the argument's address is stored in the called function data area for the corresponding formal parameter. For _____ parameters, the argument's value is stored in the called function data area for the corresponding formal parameter.

6. If a function returns all its results (type `double`) through its formal parameters, what would the type of the function be?

7. Is a driver or a stub used to allow an upper-level function to be tested before all lower-level functions are complete?

8. Does a testing team use white-box or black-box testing?

9. What output lines are displayed by the program below?

```
void silly(int);

int main()
{
    int x, y;
    // Do something silly.
    x = 8;   y = 5;
    silly(x);
    cout << x << ", " << y << endl;
    silly(y);    // values here
    cout << x << ", " << y << endl;

    return 0;


}


void silly(int x)

{
    int y;

    y = x;
    x *= 2;
    cout << x << ", " << y << endl;
} // end silly
```

10. Answer Quick-Check Exercise 9 if `silly`'s parameter is a reference parameter.

11. In what ways can a function return values to its caller?

## Answers to Quick-Check Exercises

1. call; definition, prototype; prototype

2. value (or call-by-value)

3. reference (or call-by-reference), &, after

4. variable, expression

5. call-by-reference; call-by-value

6. void

7. stub

8. black-box testing

9. ```
   16,  8
    8,  5
   10,  5
    8,  5
   ```

10. ```
    16,  8
    16,  5
    10,  5
    16, 10
    ```

11. A function can return values by using a `return` statement or by assigning the values to be returned to reference parameters.

## Review Questions

1. Write the prototype for a function named `pass` that has two integer parameters. The first parameter should be a value parameter and the second a reference parameter.

2. Write a function called `letterGrade` with a type `int` input parameter called `score`. The function should return through an output parameter (grade) the appropriate letter grade using a straight scale (90 to 100 is an A; 80 to 89 is a B; 70 to 79 is a C; 60 to 69 is a D; and 0 to 59 is an F). Return through a second output parameter a plus symbol if the student just missed the next higher grade by one or two points (for example, if a student got an 88 or 89, the second output parameter should be '+'). If the student just made the grade (for example, got a grade of 80 or 81), return a '−' for the second output parameter. The second output parameter should be blank if the student did not just miss or just make the grade.

3. Would you write a function that computes a single numeric value as a non-void function that returns a result through a return statement or as a `void` function with one output parameter? Explain your choice.

4. Explain the allocation of memory cells when a function is called. What is stored in the called function's data area for an input parameter? What is stored for an output parameter? What is stored for an inout parameter?

5. Write a driver program to test the function that you wrote for Review Question 2.

6. What are the two kinds of reference parameters? Explain the differences between them.

7. Sketch the data areas of functions main and silly as they appear immediately before the return from the first call to silly in Quick-Check Exercise 9 as modified in 10.

8. Present arguments against these statements:
   a. It's foolish to use function subprograms because a program written with functions has many more lines than the same program written without functions.
   b. The use of function subprograms leads to more errors because of mistakes in using argument lists.

## Programming Projects

1. Write a function that computes and prints the fractional powers of its first argument as shown below for a first argument of 2 (1/2, 1/4, 1/8, and so on). The function should also print the decimal value of each fraction as shown below. The range of powers printed should be determined by the function's second and third input arguments (1 and 3 for the example below). Write a driver program to test the function.

| Power | Fraction | Decimal Value |
|-------|----------|---------------|
| 1     | 1/2      | 0.5           |
| 2     | 1/4      | 0.25          |
| 3     | 1/8      | 0.125         |

2. The assessor in your town has estimated the market value of all of the properties in the town and would like you to write a program that determines the tax owed on each property and the total tax to be collected. The tax rate is 150 mils per dollar of assessed value (a mil is 0.1 of a penny). The assessed value of each property is 28 percent of its estimated market value. (This assessed value is the value to be used in computing the taxes owed for each property.)

Design and implement a program for the town assessor. First develop the structure chart indicating the functions you'll need and the relationships among them. Carefully develop the data tables for these functions, and be sure to add the input and output parameter information to the structure chart. Test your program on the following market values:

| $150,000 | $248,000 | $245,500 | $197,000 | $137,600 | $247,100 |
|----------|----------|----------|----------|----------|----------|
| $365,000 | $353,350 | $228,000 | $158,000 | $152,250 |          |
| $156,500 | $243,700 |          |          |          |          |

Your program should continue to read and process market values until a market value of 999999 is read. A meaningful, readable table of output values should be produced by your program. The table should consist of four columns of information: the name of the owner of each property, the market value of each property, the assessed value, and the taxes owed. At the end of the table, the total taxes and the count of the number of properties processed should be printed. Don't forget to print column headers for your column output. Also, be sure to include some other information at the top of the assessor's report, such as the assessor's name, the name of your township, and the date of the report. You should provide separate functions at least for the following subproblems (and maybe more):

- Display instructions to the user of your program.
- Display the informational heading (name, date, etc.) at the top of the report.
- Process all market values (and print table).
- Display final totals.

3. The trustees of a small college are considering voting a pay raise for their 12 faculty members. They want to grant a 2.5-percent pay raise; however, before doing so, they want to know how much this will cost. Write a program that will print the pay raise for each faculty member and the total amount of the raises. Also, print the total faculty payroll before and after the raise. Test your function for the salaries:

| $52,500 | $64,029.50 | $56,000 | $53,250 |
|---------|-----------|---------|---------|
| $65,500 | $42,800 | $45,000.50 | $68,900 |
| $53,780 | $77,300 | $84,120.25 | $64,100 |

**4.** Redo Programming Project 3 assuming that faculty members earning less than $50,000 receive a 3-percent raise, those earning more than $70,000 receive a 3.5-percent raise, and all others receive a 2.5-percent raise. For each faculty member, print the raise percentage as well as the amount.

**5.** Patients required to take many kinds of medication often have difficulty in remembering when to take their medicine. Given the following set of medications, write a function that prints an hourly table indicating what medication to take at any given hour. Use a counter variable `clock` to go through a 24-hour day. Print the table based on the following prescriptions:

| Medication | Frequency |
|---|---|
| Iron pill | 0800, 1200, 1800 |
| Antibiotic | Every 4 hours starting at 0400 |
| Aspirin | 0800, 2100 |
| Decongestant | 1100, 2000 |

**6.** A monthly magazine wants a program that will print out renewal notices to its subscribers and cancellation notices when appropriate. Using functions when needed, write a program that first reads in the current month number (1 through 12) and year (00 through 99). For each subscription processed, read in four data items: the account number, the month and year the subscription started, and the number of years paid for the subscription.

Read in each set of subscription information and print a renewal notice if the current month is either the month prior to expiration or the month of expiration. A cancellation notice should be printed if the current month comes after the expiration month. Sample input might be:

10, 2003       for a current month of October 2003

1364, 4, 2003, 3    for account 1364 whose 3-year subscription began in April 2003

**7.** The square root of a number $N$ can be approximated by repeated calculation using the formula

$$NG = 0.5 \, (LG + N/LG)$$

where $NG$ stands for *next guess* and $LG$ stands for *last guess*. Write a function that implements this computation. The first parameter will be a positive real number, the second will be an initial guess of the square root of that number, and the third will be the computed result.

The initial guess will be the starting value of *LG*. The function will compute a value for *NG* using the formula above. To control the computation, we can use a `while` loop. Each time through the loop, the difference between *NG* and *LG* is checked to see whether these two guesses are almost identical. If so, the function returns *NG* as the square root; otherwise, the next guess (*NG*) becomes the last guess (*LG*) and the process is repeated (i.e., another value is computed for *NG*, the difference is checked, and so forth).

For this problem, the loop should be repeated until the magnitude of the difference between *LG* and *NG* is less than 0.005. Use an initial guess of 1.0 and test the function for the numbers 4.0, 120.5, 88.0, 36.01, and 10,000.0.

8. Develop a collection of functions to solve simple conduction problems using various forms of the formula

$$H = \frac{kA(T_2 - T_1)}{X}$$

where *H* is the rate of heat transfer in watts, *k* is the coefficient of thermal conductivity for the particular substance, *A* is the cross-sectional area in m$^2$ (square meters), $T^2$ and $T^1$ are the Kelvin temperatures on the two sides of the conductor, and *X* is the thickness of the conductor in meters.

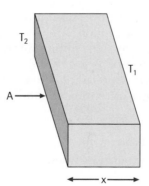

Define a function for each variable in the formula. For example, function `calcH` would compute the rate of heat transfer, `calcK` would figure the coefficient of thermal conductivity, `calcA` would find the cross-sectional area, and so on.

Develop a driver function that interacts with the user in the following way:

Respond to the prompts with the data known. For the
unknown quantity, enter -999

Rate of heat transfer (watts) : 755.0
Coefficient of thermal conductivity (W/m-K) : 0.8
Cross-sectional area of conductor (m^2) : 0.12
Temperature on one side (K) : 298
Temperature on other side (K) : -999
Thickness of conductor (m) : 0.003

$$H = \frac{kA\ (T2 - T1)}{X}$$

Temperature on the other side is 274 K.
```
H = 755.0 W                    T2 = 298 K
k = 0.800 W/m-K                T1 = 274 K
A = 0.120 m^2                  X = 0.0003 m
```

9. Write a program to model a simple calculator. Each data line should
consist of the next operation to be performed from the list below and
the right operand. Assume the left operand is the accumulator value
(initial value of 0). You need a function scan_data with two output
parameters that returns the operator and right operand scanned from
a data line. You need a function do_next_op that performs the
required operation. do_next_op has two input parameters (the operator and operand) and one input/output parameter (the accumulator).
The valid operators are:

+   add
−   subtract
*   multiply
/   divide
^   power (raise left operand to power of right operand)
q   quit

Your calculator should display the accumulator value after each operation. A sample run follows.

```
+ 5.0
result so far is 5.0
^ 2
result so far is 25.0
/ 2.0
result so far is 12.5
q 0
final result is 12.5
```

10. Write a function that reads a problem involving two common fractions such as 2/4 + 5/6. After reading the common fractions problem, call a function to perform the indicated operation (call `addFrac` for +, call `multiplyFrac` for *, and so on). Pass the numerator and denominator of both fractions to the function that performs the operation; the function should return the numerator and denominator of the result through its output parameters. Then display the result as a common fraction. (Hint: Use functions `readFracProblem` and `getFrac`; see Listings 6.3 and 6.4.)

11. Write a function to calculate the day number for a given day represented by three type `int` values (the function input). The day number should be between 1 and 365 (366 if the year is a leap year). Also, write a function that returns true if its first date (first three `int` arguments) comes after its second date (last three `int` arguments). Then write a recursive function that determines the number of days between two dates, each represented by three integers. Use the following algorithm:

    If the first date comes after the second date

       Reverse the dates and calculate the days between them

    Else if the year of both dates is the same

       The result is the day number of the second date minus

       the day number of the first date

    Else

       The result is the day number of the second date +

       the number of days between the first date and the last

       day of the previous year

    The recursive function requires the second date to follow the first. If it doesn't, the task under the first condition should return the result of calling the function with the arguments reversed, so the second date will follow the first in this next call.

    If the dates are in the correct order and the year is the same (tested by the second condition), the result is just the difference in the day numbers for each date. Otherwise, the last task calculates the result by adding the day number of the second date to the number of days between the first date and the end of the year just before the year of the second date. For example, if the second date is January 5, 2003, the result is 5 + the number of days between the first date and December 31, 2002. The next call to the function will calculate the latter value either by executing the second task (if 2002 is the year of the first date) or by adding 365 (the number of days in 2002) to the difference between the first date and December 31, 2001, and so on.

# Robert Sebesta

*Dr. Sebesta received his Ph.D. in Computer Science from Penn State University, and he currently teaches Perl programming, among other subjects, at the University of Colorado at Colorado Springs. His research is in the areas of compiler design and programming language design, and he has been teaching computer science for over s8 years. He is a member of ACM and the Computer Society of IEEE. He is the author of many programming books, including* Concepts of Programming Languages *and* Programming the World Wide Web.

**What is your educational background, and how did you decide to study computer science?**
I have a B.S. in Applied Mathematics (University of Colorado at Boulder), an M.S. in Computer Science (Penn State), and a Ph.D. in Computer Science (Penn State). I decided to study computer science for two reasons: (1) I minored in computer science as an undergraduate and enjoyed programming, and (2) most of the jobs available for someone with a B.S. in applied math were in software development. I thought that if I was going to be a software developer, I needed more education in computer science.

**What was your first job in the computer industry?**
I worked half time in a government research lab during my last two years of undergraduate school. I was a programmer for a small group of scientists who were doing research on wave propagation.

**Which person in the field has inspired you most?**
One early inspiration for me was the researcher for whom I worked as an undergraduate. He was very interested in computer applications in his research. I learned much about scientific computing and in the process discovered that I really enjoyed doing that kind of work.

**Do you have any advice about programming in C++?**
Because of its widespread use in industry, all undergraduate students in computer science must learn it. However, by most reasonable measures, C++ is a large, complex language that includes more insecurities than some other languages, such as Java and C#. Because of its complexity, C++ programs are more difficult to maintain than programs written in some other languages.

**What advice do you have for students entering the computer science field?**
First, computer science is not an easy discipline, so plan on spending large amounts of time studying and working on programming projects. Although the job market is less than great right now, there are still companies and agencies that are hiring programmers. Furthermore, I believe that the market for pro-

grammers will improve over the next few years.

**What is the most challenging part of your job?**

Because only a small percentage of people can easily become great programmers, the challenge for educators is to find ways to teach as many of the others as we can.

**What kind of projects are you currently working on?**

I spend a great deal of my evenings and weekends writing textbooks for college-level computer science courses. One area of research in which I'm working is the general problem of software security Specifically, I'm interested in finding new ways to determine whether software has been damaged, intentionally or by accident.

**How has C++ evolved in the last few years?**

Although new class libraries are always being created, the language itself has not changed much in the last few years. The changes that would be required to make the language less complex and more reliable are substantial and unlikely to happen.

**What is your vision for the future of the C++ programming language?**

I think C++ will remain a very popular language in industry, in part because there is a great deal of legacy software that is written in C++. However, the popularity of C++ has been eroded by the widespread use of Java. Furthermore, I think C# will replace C++ in many applications over the next few years.

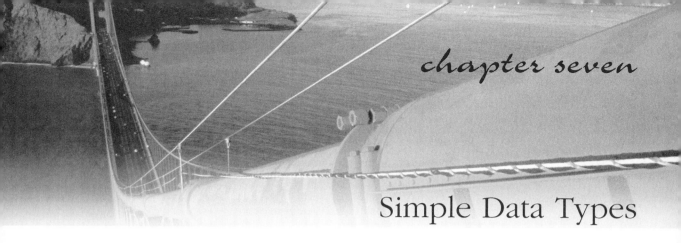

# Simple Data Types

Chapter Objectives

- To learn how to define constants using the #define compiler directive
- To understand the differences between fixed-point and floating-point representations of numbers
- To learn about additional data types for representing very large integers and real numbers, and the range of numbers that can be represented by these different data types
- To learn how to manipulate character data using functions in library cctype
- To understand the encoding of character data using the ASCII character set
- To learn how to write and use bool functions in programming
- To understand how to use enumeration types and enumerators to define a data type and its associated values

SO FAR WE'VE used four *predefined data types* of C++: int, float, char, and bool. In this chapter, we look more closely at these data types and introduce some variants of them. We examine the forms in which these types of values are stored in memory, and we introduce some new operators that can be applied to these types. We also introduce the *enumeration type*. A characteristic shared by all of these data types is that only a single value can be stored in a variable of the type. Such types are often referred to as *simple* or *scalar data types*.

# 7.1 Constants Revisited

## The #define Compiler Directive

We begin by reexamining the concept of constants in C++. Constant definitions have the form

```
const type identifier = constant;
```

where *constant* is a value of the same type as the identifier.

C++ provides another way to define important constants. The #define line is a compiler directive that can be used to associate an identifier with a particular sequence of characters called the *replacement-text*. The general form of the #define line is as follows:

```
#define identifier  replacement-text
```

Once this line appears in a program, any occurrence of *identifier* (not enclosed in quotes and not part of another name) will be replaced by the associated *replacement-text* during compilation. The *identifier* has the same form as any C++ identifier. The *replacement-text* can be any sequence of characters. It's not a character string, so it's not enclosed in quotes.

---

### EXAMPLE 7.1

We can use either the constant declaration

```
const float PI = 3.14159;
```

or the #define line

```
#define PI 3.14159
```

to associate the constant PI with the value 3.14159. In the first form, C++ allocates a memory cell named PI and stores 3.14159 in that cell. In the second form, the compiler replaces all textual references to the identifier PI by the constant 3.14159 during the compilation process, just as a word processor would perform the substitution. Using this form, PI is simply an identifier; it's not treated as a variable and has no storage associated with it.

---

The #define line is often used to name constants in the C language. Because C++ permits const declarations, we rarely use the #define line.

Self-Check

1. Which of the constants declared below are valid and which are invalid?
   Explain your answers briefly.

```
const int MAXINT = 32767;
const int MININT = -MAXINT;
const char FIRST_FEMALE = "Eve";
const int MAX_SIZE = 50;
const int MIN_SIZE = MAX_SIZE - 10;
const int ID = 4FD6;
const int KOFFMAN_AGE = 57;
const int FRIEDMAN_AGE = z56;
const float PRICE = $3,335.50;
const float PRICE = 3335.50;
const float PRICE = "3335.50";
```

2. Why would you declare an identifier as a constant rather than as a
   variable?

3. Explain the difference between the #define line and the constant
   declaration.

# 7.2   Internal Representations of Numeric Data Types

In this section, we look at the numeric data types and discuss the differences in their representations.

## Fixed-Point and Floating-Point Data Types

The data types int and float are used to represent numeric information.
We use integer variables as loop counters to represent data, such as exam
scores, that do not have fractional parts. In most other instances, we use
type float numeric data.

   You may be wondering why it's necessary to have two numeric types.
Can the data type float be used for all numbers? The answer is yes, but on
many computers, operations involving integers are faster than those
involving type float numbers and less storage space may be needed to
store integers. Also, operations with integers are always precise, but there
may be some loss of accuracy when dealing with type float numbers.

   These differences result from the way type float numbers and integers
are represented internally in a computer's memory. All data are represented

in memory as strings of *binary digits*, or *bits* (0s and 1s). But the binary string stored for the integer 13 isn't the same as the binary string stored for the type `float` number 13.0. The actual internal representation depends on the computer, but the general forms are consistent in all computers. For example, the integer 13 would be represented as 1101 preceded by a sequence of 0 digits.

The internal representation of floating-point data is analogous to scientific notation. Recall that in scientific notation $3.57 \times 10^3$ refers to the same number as 3570. Similarly, $3.57 \times 10^{-4}$ refers to 0.000357.

The storage area for a floating-point number is segmented into a *characteristic* and a *mantissa*. Usually, the mantissa is a binary fraction between 0.5 and 1.0 for positive numbers (and between $-0.5$ and $-1.0$ for negative numbers). The characteristic is normally a power of 2. The mantissa and characteristic are chosen to satisfy the formula

$$float\text{-}number = mantissa \times 2^{characteristic}$$

Because the size of a memory cell is finite, not all floating-point numbers (in the mathematical sense) can be represented precisely in the range of type `float` numbers provided on your computer system. We'll talk more about this later.

Besides the capability of storing fractions, the range of numbers that may be represented in type `float` form is considerably larger than for the integer form. For example, positive type `float` numbers on microcomputers might range between $10^{37}$ (a very small fraction) and $10^{37}$ (a rather large number), whereas positive type `int` values might range from 1 to +32767 ($2^{15}$). The actual ranges depend on the particular C++ compiler and the computer being used. Specifically, they depend on the number of bits that the compiler uses to store these different data types.

## Integer Types

C++ provides three sizes of integers: `short int` (or `short`), `int`, and `long int` (or `long`). The actual lengths corresponding to the sizes are implementation-defined. C++ does, however, place some restrictions on the lengths of *short integers* (minimum of 16 bits) and *long integers* (minimum of 32 bits). It also requires that the following must be true:

- Short integers may be no longer than type `int` values.
- Type `int` values may be no longer than long integers.

The use of short integers can save space in programs with large volumes of integer data. However, as we've noted, the largest positive integer that may be stored in a short integer on most computers is $2^{15} \times 1$, or 32767. (Remember, one bit is used for the sign of the integer, leaving 15 bits to store the magnitude of the integer. See the Self-Check Exercises at the end of this section for more details.) This may not always be sufficient for storing and manipulating your data.

## Floating–Point Types

C++ provides three sizes of floating-point types: `float`, `double`, and `long double`. As with integers, these are implementation-defined, but with the following restrictions: `double` isn't less precise than `float`, and `long double` isn't less precise than `double`. Some C++ compilers provide a `double` type with approximately twice the precision of `float` and a `long double` type with twice the precision of `double`.

## Types of Numeric Literals

The data type of a numeric literal is determined in the following way. If the literal has a decimal point, then it's considered to be of type `float`. For example, `-67.345` and `2.998E+5` (read as $2.998 \times 10^5$ or 299800.0) are floating-point literals. A literal written with a decimal scale factor is also considered to be a floating-point literal whether or not it has a decimal point. For example, the value `5E2` is considered type `float` (with a value of 500.0) because it has a scale factor.

## Value Ranges for Integer and Floating–Point Types

C++ provides names for the ranges of integer and floating-point types. Some of these names, their interpretations, and the values they represent are shown in Table 7.1. These definitions are included along with many others in the standard C++ libraries named `climits` and `cfloat`. The values shown in this table are acceptable minimum (or maximum) values for these constant identifiers; the actual values are computer dependent.

## Numerical Inaccuracies

The representation of floating-point data can cause numerical inaccuracies to occur in floating-point computations. Just as certain numbers cannot be represented exactly in the decimal number system (e.g., the fraction 1/3 is 0.333333 . . .), some numbers cannot be represented exactly in floating-point form. The **representational error** will depend on the number of bits used in the mantissa: the more bits, the smaller the error.

**representational error** An error that occurs when a finite number of bits is used to represent a real number.

**Table 7.1**   Special C++ Constants

| From `climits` | | |
|---|---|---|
| Name | Value | Interpretation |
| `CHAR_BIT` | 8 | Number of bits in a character type item |
| `INT_MAX` | +32767 | Maximum value of `int` (16 bits) |
| `INT_MIN` | −32768 | Minimum value of `int` (16 bits) |
| `LONG_MAX` | +2147483647L | Maximum value of long integer (32 bits) |
| `LONG_MIN` | −2147483648L | Minimum value of long integer (32 bits) |
| `SHRT_MAX` | +32767 | Maximum value of short integer (16 bits) |
| `SHRT_MIN` | −32768 | Minimum value of short integer (16 bits) |
| From `cfloat` | | |
| Name | Value | Interpretation |
| `FLT_DIG` | 6 | Number of decimal digits of precision (32-bit float type) |
| `FLT_MAX` | 1E+37 | Maximum floating-point number |
| `FLT_MIN` | 1E−37 | Minimum floating-point number |
| `FLT_EPSILON` | 1E−5 | Minimum positive number $x$ such that $1.0 + x$ does not equal 1.0 |
| `DBL_DIG` | 10 | Decimal digits of precision for `double` |
| `DBL_EPSILON` | 1E−9 | Minimum positive number $x$ such that $1.0 + x$ does not equal 1.0 |
| `LDBL_DIG` | 10 | Decimal digits of precision for `long double` |

The number 0.1 is an example of a number that has a representational error. The effect of a small error can become magnified through repeated computations. As a result, the loop shown next may fail to terminate on some computers because the effect of adding 0.1 to itself ten times isn't exactly 1.0.

```
for (float trial = 0.0;
        trial != 1.0;
        trial += 0.1) {
    ...
}
```

If the loop repetition test is changed to `trial < 1.0`, the loop might execute 10 times on one computer and 11 times on another. This is yet another reason why it's best to use integer variables whenever possible in loop repetition tests.

**cancellation error**
An error due to applying an arithmetic operator to two operands of very different magnitudes; the effect of the smaller number is lost.

Other problems can occur when manipulating very large or very small real numbers. If you add a large number to a small number, the larger number may "cancel out" the smaller number—resulting in a **cancellation error**.

If $x$ is much larger than $y$, then $x + y$ may have the same value as $x$ (e.g., 1000.0 + 0.0001234 is equal to 1000.0 on some computers).

If two very small numbers are multiplied and the result is too small to be represented accurately, it will be represented as zero. This phenomenon is called **arithmetic underflow**. Similarly, if two very large numbers are multiplied, the result may be too large to be represented. This phenomenon, called **arithmetic overflow**, is handled in different ways by C++ compilers. Arithmetic overflow can occur when processing very large integer values as well.

**arithmetic underflow** An error in which a very small computational result is represented as zero.
**arithmetic overflow** An error due to an attempt to represent a computational result that is too large.

## Mixing Types: Promotions

In Chapter 2 (Section 2.6), we first introduced the notion of mixed-type expressions and assignments with type `int` and `float` data. In Chapters 3 and 6, we discussed the correspondence of formal and actual arguments. We recommended that you match the type of an actual argument in a function call with its corresponding formal parameter type.

C++ allows many uses of mixed types: in expressions, in assignment, and in argument passing. When data values of mixed type are used in expressions, the compiler examines the operands involved with each operation and *converts* (or *promotes*) mixed operands to make them the same. For example, short integers and characters would be promoted to type `int`, type `int` to type `float`, and type `float` to `double`. The result of the operation is the same type as the operands after promotion.

For example, in the expression

```
3 + x / 2
```

where x is type `float`, the constant 2 is promoted to `float` before the division is performed. Because the result of the division is type `float`, the constant 3 would be promoted to `float` before the addition is performed.

All such conversions are intended to be *value-preserving*. For the most part, an integral conversion (`char` to `int`, `short int` to `int`) won't alter the value of the data. This is also true when integers are converted to floating point, except that some loss of accuracy can occur because not all type `float` values can be precisely represented in the computer.

## Type Conversions

Conversions similar to those just described for expressions are performed whenever mixed assignments are specified. Again the conversions are intended to preserve value. However, value preservation sometimes isn't possible when the type conversion is in the "other direction." In these cases, actual changes in value are likely to occur. For example, the assignment of a type `float` value to an integer variable will result in the *truncation* (chopping off) of the fractional part of the floating-point value (the assignment of the value 13.78 to the integer variable m stores the integer 13 in m). A few other examples are shown next.

```
i = 3.89;     // Truncates floating-point value 3.89.
              //    Stores 3 in i (type int).
ch = 64.97;   // Truncates floating-point value 64.97.
              // Stores character with ASCII value 64
              //       ('@') in ch (type char).
printInt(27.7); // Argument 27.7 is converted to 27.
                // Function printInt has the prototype
                // void printInt(int);
```

## Type Casting

Besides relying on automatic conversion, you can specify an explicit type conversion operation using a **cast**. For example, if sum and n are type `int` and average is type `float`, we can use the statement

```
average = float(sum) / float(n);
```

to perform an accurate computation of the average value that retains the fractional part of the result. The casting operator `float` in the expression `float(sum)` converts the value of sum to a type `float` number before the division, so the division result is type `float`. Without casting, a type `int` result would be calculated. The actual values stored in sum and n are still type `int` and aren't changed by the casting operation.

Although we cast both operands in the expression above, we need to cast only one. The other would be converted automatically because of the way C++ evaluates mixed-type expressions.

Notice that the expression

```
average = float(sum / n);
```

wouldn't achieve the desired goal of retaining the fractional part of the average value. The cast takes place after the integer division, so a real number with a fractional part of zero would be assigned to variable **average**.

## EXAMPLE 7.2

Sometimes we want to compute the value of a positive number rounded to **two** decimal places. The statement

```
x = float(int(x * 100.0 + 0.5)) / 100.0;
```

uses the casting operators int and **float** to accomplish this. For example, if **x** is 7.0562, the argument for the cast operator int would be 706.12 (705.62 + 0.5). The result of this cast operation would be the integer 706. The cast operator **float** converts 706 to a floating-point number. The result of dividing by 100.0 is assigned to variable **x** (value is 7.06).

## EXERCISES FOR SECTION 7.2

Self–Check

1. What is the largest positive integer that may be stored (with sign) in a type int variable of size 2 bytes (16 bits)?

2. How does a cancellation error differ from a representational error?

3. In Example 7.2, what is the value of the assignment statement

```
x = float(int(x * 100 + 0.5)) / 100.0;
```

for x = 6.875? For x = − 6.875?

Write an if statement that rounds to two decimal places for negative numbers as well as positive numbers.

4. Write the algorithm for a decision step that rounds any real number to $n$ decimal places.

Programming

1. Write a C++ program to display the largest long integer and largest type double value that can be used on your computer system.

2. Write a function that has two formal input parameters, a real number x and an integer n. The function result should be x rounded to n decimal places. Use the if statement in Self-Check Exercise 4.

## 7.3 Character Data and Functions

C++ provides a character data type for storing and manipulating individual characters such as those that compose a person's name, address, and other personal data. We use the type specifier char to declare character variables. A type char literal consists of a single printable character (a letter, digit, punctuation mark, or the like) enclosed in single quotes. We can also use escape sequences (see Section 2.3) to represent character literals. We can associate a character value with a constant identifier or assign it to a character variable. We can compare character values using the equality and relational operators.

```
const char STAR = '*';
const char ENDLINE = '\n';
char nextLetter;
nextLetter = 'C';
if (nextLetter >= 'A')
```

To understand the result of an order comparison (using a relational operator), you must know something about the way your computer represents characters internally. Each character has its own unique numeric code; the binary form of this code is stored in a memory cell to represent a character value. C++ compares these binary numbers using the relational operators in the normal way.

The number of bits used to store a character value must be sufficient to store any member of the character set being used by your C++ language system. The ASCII (American Standard Code for Information Interchange) character set is most often used in C++ systems (see Appendix A). In ASCII, one byte (8 bits) is used to represent characters. Only the rightmost 7 bits are used, so the numeric codes for all character values are in the range 0 to 127 (the value of $2^7 - 1$).

If you examine the ASCII code shown in Appendix A, you'll see that consecutive codes (decimal code values 48 through 57) represent the digit characters '0' through '9' respectively. The order relationship shown below holds for the digit characters:

'0'<'1'<'2'<'3'<'4'<'5'<'6'<'7'<'8'<'9'.

For the uppercase letters 'A', 'B', ... 'Z', the following order relationship holds:

'A'<'B'<'C'<   ...   <'X'<'Y'<'Z'.

In the ASCII code, these characters are also represented using consecutive decimal values (decimal code values 65 through 90).

A similar situation is true for lowercase letters. Once again, the expected order relationship holds in the ASCII code:

```
'a'<'b'<'c'<  ...  <'x'<'y'<'z'.
```

The lowercase letters have the consecutive decimal code values 97 through 122 in ASCII.

In ASCII, the printable characters have codes from 32 (the code for a blank or space) to 126 (the code for the symbol ~). The other codes represent nonprintable control characters (represented in a C++ program using escape sequences). Sending a control character to an output device causes the device to perform a special operation, such as returning the cursor to column one, advancing the cursor to the next line, or sounding a beep.

Because characters are represented by integer codes, C++ permits conversion of type char to type int and vice versa. For example, you could use the following to find out the code for a question mark:

```
cout << "Code for ? is " << int('?') << endl;
```

The next example uses the casting operator char to convert an integer to a character.

## EXAMPLE 7.3

A *collating sequence* for characters is the ordering of characters according to their numeric codes. The program in Listing 7.1 displays part of the C++ collating sequence for the ASCII character set. It lists the characters with numeric codes 32 through 126, inclusive. The first character displayed is a blank (numeric code 32); the last one is the tilde (numeric code 126).

## Some Useful Character Functions

Table 7.2 lists several useful character functions found in the C++ standard library cctype. The first two functions, tolower and toupper, change the case of a letter. They take a type char argument and return a type char result. If the argument for tolower is an uppercase letter, tolower returns its lowercase equivalent (that is, 'c' for an argument of 'C'). If the argument for tolower isn't an uppercase letter, tolower returns its argument unchanged. The remaining functions are used to test a character argument

**Listing 7.1**    ASCII collating sequence illustration

```cpp
// File: collate.cpp
// Displays part of the character collating sequence

#include <iostream>
using namespace std;

int main()
{
   const MIN = 32;    // smallest numeric code
   const MAX = 126;   // largest numeric code
   char nextChar;     // output - character form of next code

   // Display sequence of characters.
   for (int nextCode =  MIN; nextCode <= MAX; nextCode++) {
      nextChar = char(nextCode);
      cout << nextChar;
      if (nextChar == 'Z')
         cout << endl;
   }

   return 0;
}
```

```
!"#$%&'()*+,-./0123456789;:<=>?@ABCDEFGHIJKLMNOPQRSTUVWXYZ
[/]^_'abcdefghijklmnopqrstuvwxyz{ }~
```

to see if it's a particular kind of character (for example, is it a letter?). All the test functions take a type `char` argument, and all return a type `bool` result (either `true` or `false`).

## EXAMPLE 7.4

Sometimes we want to convert a digit character to an equivalent number. For example, the digit character `'7'` should convert to the number 7. Function `digitToNumber` (Listing 7.2) performs this conversion. If its input argument isn't a digit character, function `digitToNumber` returns −1.

We use the `bool` function `isdigit` to determine whether parameter `ch` contains a digit character (a character in the set `{'0', '1', '2', ... '9'}`).

**Table 7.2** Some Character Functions from the Standard Library `cctype`

| Function Prototype | Purpose |
|---|---|
| `char tolower(char)` | If c is uppercase, this function returns the corresponding lowercase letter; otherwise, returns c. |
| `char toupper(char)` | If c is lowercase, this function returns the corresponding uppercase letter; otherwise, it returns c. |
| `bool isalnum(char)` | Returns `true` if either `isalpha(c)` or `isdigit(c)` is nonzero; otherwise, returns `false`. |
| `bool isalpha(char)` | Returns `true` if either `isupper(c)` or `islower(c)` is `true`; otherwise, returns `false`. |
| `bool iscntrl(char)` | Returns `true` if c is a control character; otherwise, returns `false`. |
| `bool isdigit(char)` | Returns `true` if c is a digit character (`'0'`, `'1'`, `'2'`, . . . , `'9'`); otherwise, returns `false`. |
| `bool isgraph(char)` | Returns true if c is a printable character (other than a space); otherwise, returns `false`.* |
| `bool islower(char)` | Returns `true` if c is a lowercase letter; otherwise, returns `false`. |
| `bool isprint(char)` | Returns `true` if c is a printable character (including the space); otherwise, returns `false`. |
| `bool ispunct(char)` | Returns `true` if c is a printable character other than a space, letter, or digit; otherwise, returns `false`. |
| `bool isspace(char)` | Returns `true` if c is a space, newline, formfeed, carriage return, tab, or vertical tab; otherwise, returns `false`. |
| `bool isupper(char)` | Returns `true` if c is an uppercase letter; otherwise, returns false. |

*A printable character is any character in the ASCII table between the space (ASCII value 32) and the tilde (~, ASCII value 126).

**Listing 7.2** Function `digitToNumber`

```
// Returns the number corresponding to its argument
//   if its argument is a digit character; otherwise
//   returns -1.
int digitToNumber(char ch)
{
   if (isdigit(ch))
      return (int(ch) - int('0'));
   else
      return -1;
}
```

We read the `if` statement in Listing 7.2 as follows:

If ch is a digit character, execute the statement
```
    return (int(ch) - int('0'));
```
else execute the statement
```
    return false;
```

The expression

```
int(ch) - int('0')
```

yields the difference between the code for the character stored in ch and the code for '0'. This difference is the number we're seeking. For example, if ch is '7', its code is 55 and the code for '0' is 48.

Follow a similar process if you want to determine the relative position of a letter in the alphabet. For example, if letChar is a type char variable storing an uppercase letter, the expression

```
int(letChar) - int('A')
```

returns the position in the alphabet of letChar relative to A (at position 0).

## EXERCISES FOR SECTION 7.3

Self-Check

1. Evaluate the following C++ expressions using the ASCII character set.

   a.  `int('d') - int('a')`

   b.  `char((int('M') - int('A')) + int('a'))`

   c.  `int('7') - int('0')`

   d.  `char(int('5') + 1)`

2. What is the purpose of the type cast operators int and char used in the previous exercise?

3. Briefly explain the result of each of the following function references. (First indicate the type of the result and then its actual value.)

   a.  `isdigit('a');`

   b.  `isdigit('7');`

   c.  `isdigit(9);`

   d.  `toupper('#');`

   e.  `tolower('A');`

   f.  `tolower('p');`

   g.  `digitToNumber('0');`

4. In Listing 7.2, what is the effect of the `if` statement?

5. What values are returned by `digitToNumber` for the three data characters: x, $, 3?

**Programming**

1. Write your own version of function `toupper` (call it `myToupper`). Hint: See Self-Check Exercise 1b.

2. Write your own version of function `islower` (call it `myIslower`).

3. Write a C++ function called `getDigitValue` that reads data characters until it reads a digit character. Your function should return the numeric value of the first digit character read. Your function should use functions `isdigit` and `digitToNumber` (from Listing 7.2).

# 7.4 Type **bool** Data and Logical Expressions

Type `bool` data was introduced in Chapter 2, and we've used type `bool` expressions as conditions in `if` statements and for loop control. There are only two type `bool` literals—`true` and `false`. We now describe some additional features of logical expressions.

## Complementing Logical Expressions

We use the logical operator `!` (not) to form the complement or opposite of a condition. If a logical expression is true, then its complement is false and vice versa.

The ability to complement a condition is useful when you write `if` and `while` statements in C++. For example, certain expressions involving the use of the `!` operator are more difficult to read and think about than an equivalent *complement expression* written without the `!` operator. We can complement a simple condition just by changing the relational operator as shown below.

| Operator | Operator in Complement |
|:---:|:---:|
| < | >= |
| <= | > |
| > | <= |
| >= | < |
| == | != |
| != | == |

If a simple logical expression such as `!(x <= y)` is used in a condition, its equivalent condition may be obtained by removing the `!` operator and complementing the relational operator. This process would yield the simpler but equivalent condition `x > y`.

DeMorgan's theorem explains how to complement a compound logical expression:

1. Write the complement of each simple logical expression.

2. Change each `&&` (and) to `||` (or) and each `||` to `&&`, respectively.

---

**DeMorgan's Theorem**

`!( expression₁ && expression₂ )`    `!(expression₁ || expression₂)`

is the same as    is the same as

`!expression₁ || !expression₂`    `!expression₁ && !expression₂`

---

Another way to complement a logical expression is to precede the entire expression with the not (`!`) operator. Table 7.3 shows the complements of more complicated logical expressions as determined by applying DeMorgan's theorem. We see that `flag` and `swap` are type `bool` variables; `next` is type `char`; and x, y, m, and n are type `int`. In the complement of the expression on the first line, the relational operators are complemented (e.g., `>=` is changed to `<`) and the operator `&&` (and) is changed to `||` (or). The last two lines show two complements of the same expression. In the last line, the expression is complemented by simply inserting the logical operator `!` (not) in front of the entire condition. Any logical expression can be complemented in this way.

**Table 7.3**   Complements of Logical Expressions

| Expression | Complement |
| --- | --- |
| `x >= 1 && x <= 5` | `x < 1 || x > 5` |
| `!flag || x <= y` | `flag && x > y` |
| `flag && !swap` | `!flag || swap` |
| `(n % m == 0) && flag` | `(n % m != 0) || !flag` |
| `next == 'A' || next == 'a'` | `next != 'A' && next != 'a'` |
| `next == 'A' || next == 'a'` | `!(next == 'A' || next == 'a')` |

## Type **bool** Functions

Most of the functions listed in Table 7.2 are examples of type bool functions—they return either true or false values. We use these functions to determine the status of type char variables. You can write similar functions, give them meaningful names, and use them to write clear and concise conditions with calls to these functions.

## EXAMPLE 7.5

We can use bool functions to simplify loop repetition conditions. For example, a bill-paying program should continue to pay monthly bills as long as the account balance is positive and there are more bills to pay. The main processing loop might have the heading

```
while (balance > 0.0 && moreBills())
```

Loop exit occurs if the balance becomes zero or negative or if the user indicates there are no more bills to pay.

Function moreBills should ask the user if there are more bills. Listing 7.3 shows one possible implementation. The function returns true if the user enters Y or y after the prompt Any more bills (Y/N):.

Inside the loop, we use the toupper function to set the character in answer to uppercase. This step simplifies the loop repetition condition (see Self-Check Exercise 4). The do-while loop executes until answer is either Y or N. The loop repetition condition is equivalent to

```
!(answer == 'Y' || answer == 'N')
```

After loop exit, the statement

```
return (answer == 'Y');
```

evaluates the condition in parentheses (type bool) and returns its value (true or false). This is simpler than using an if statement to return either true or false (see Programming Exercise 3).

## Input and Output of Type **bool** Data

When you display type bool data, the value false displays as the integer 0 and true displays as the integer 1. Similarly, you must enter 0 (false) and 1 (true) to represent type bool data. These restrictions aren't likely to affect you, since you usually won't want to read bool data and will only display bool data during debugging. If you want to read or display false and

**Listing 7.3** Function `moreBills`

```cpp
// Returns true if the user has more bills to pay
bool moreBills()
{
    char answer;            // Stores user's answer

    do {
        cout << "Any more bills (Y/N): ";
        cin >> answer;
        answer = toupper(answer); // to uppercase
    } while (answer != 'Y' && answer != 'N');

    return (answer == 'Y');
}
```

`true` as type `bool` data (instead of 0 or 1), insert the following lines of C++ code before the input or output statements.

```cpp
cin.setf(ios::boolalpha);   // to read true/false
cout.setf(ios::boolalpha); // to display true/false
```

## EXERCISES FOR SECTION 7.4

Self-Check

1. Write the complements of the conditions below. Assume the variables are all of type `int` except for `flag` (type `bool`). Use DeMorgan's theorem.

   a. `x <= y && x == 25`

   b. `x > y && x != 15 || z <= 7`

   c. `x != 15 || z == 7 && x <= y`

   d. `flag || !(x != 15)`

   e. `!flag && x > 8`

2. What does the following function do:

   ```cpp
   bool inRange(int item, int min, int max)
   {
       return (item >= min && item <= max)
   }
   ```

   What values can the function return?

3. The loop below uses function `readInt` from Exercise 2. Describe what the loop does and the value that n will have after loop exit. Also, explain the comment at the end of the loop and write the condition in a simpler way using the complement operator.

```
int n;
do {
    cout << "Enter a number in the range 1 to 10: ";
    cin >> n;
} while (inRange(n, 1, 10) == false); // == false is
                                      // not necessary
```

4. Trace the execution of function `moreBills` for the data characters q, y.

Programming

1. Write a type `bool` function that has two integer input parameters m and n and returns `true` if the value of m is a divisor of n and `false` otherwise.

2. Write a loop that continues prompting and reading exam scores until the user enters a score that is in range (0 through 100). Use function `inRange` from Self-Check Exercise 2.

3. Rewrite function `moreBills` using an `if` statement to return the result. Which approach do you think is more efficient?

## 7.5 Enumeration Types

Good solutions to many programming problems require new data types. For example, in a budget program you might distinguish among the following categories of expenses: entertainment, rent, utilities, food, clothing, automobile, insurance, and miscellaneous. C++ allows you to associate a numeric code with each category by creating an **enumeration type** that has its own list of meaningful values.

For example, the enumerated type `expense` has eight possible values:

> **enumeration type**
> A user-defined data type with a list of values for that type.

```
enum expense {entertainment, rent, utilities, food,
              clothing, automobile, insurance,
              miscellaneous};
```

Defining type `expense` as shown causes the identifier `entertainment` to be associated with the integer 0, `rent` to be associated with the integer 1, and so on. We can use our new type name `expense` in variable declarations just as we would use a standard type such as `int` or `double`. Here is a declaration of variable `expenseKind`:

```
expense expenseKind;
```

We can manipulate variable `expenseKind` and its eight possible values (called **enumerators**) just as we would any other integers. The `if` statement that follows tests the value of `expenseKind` and displays an appropriate message.

**enumerator**
An identifier defined in an enumeration type.

```
if (expenseKind == entertainment)
    cout << "Postpone until after your payday.";
else if (expenseKind == rent)
    cout << "Pay before the first of the month!";
...
else if (expenseKind == miscellaneous)
    cout << "Do you really need that?";
```

The `if` statement with enumerators is more readable than an equivalent `if` statement with integer values. This is the primary motivation for using enumeration types. For example, without enumerators, we would write the first condition as `(expenseKind == 0)`, which has no special meaning.

## EXAMPLE 7.6

The enumeration type **day** declared below has the values **sunday**, **monday**, and so on.

```
enum day {sunday, monday, tuesday, wednesday,
              thursday, friday, saturday}; // days of the week
```

The enumerator **sunday** has the value 0; **monday** has the value 1, and so on.
We can alter this default association by explicitly specifying a different association for some or all of the identifiers in an enumeration type, as shown in the next two examples.

## EXAMPLE 7.7

The 12 enumerators for enumeration type **month** are associated with the constant integer values 1, 2, 3, ..., 12. Because the value 1 is specified for enumerator **jan**, enumerator **feb** has the value 2, enumerator **mar** has the value 3, and so on.

```
enum month {jan = 1, feb, mar, apr, may, jun, jul, aug,
              sep, oct, nov, dec};
```

---

**Enumeration Type Declaration**

**Form:**     *enum enumeration-type {enumerator-list};*

**Example:**  enum `classId` {freshman, sophomore,
                              junior, senior};

**Interpretation:** A new integral data type (an *enumeration-type*) is declared. The enumerators associated with this type are specified in the *enumerator-list*. The enumerators in the list may be identifiers. The enumerator values start at 0 and increase by one.

If an *enumerator* is defined using the form

> *identifier = constant-expression*

the enumerator is given the value of the *constant-expression*. The values of subsequent enumerators increase by increments of one until another enumerator is defined using this form. The values associated with enumerators in a particular enumeration type do not have to be unique. However, an enumerator, like any other identifier, cannot appear in more than one enumeration type declaration within its scope of definition.

---

## Characters as Enumerator Values

Because characters also have integer values, you can use character constants to specify the value of an enumerator. In this case, the value of the enumerator is determined by the character's numeric code.

## EXAMPLE 7.8

We can define an enumeration type to associate names with some of the common special characters.

```
enum specialChars
   {backspace = '\b', bell = '\a', newline = '\n',
    return = '\r',    tab = '\t',  vtab = '\v'};
```

The value of the enumerator **backspace** is the ASCII code for the control character '\b'. We can use the enumerator **backspace** to represent the backspace character in our C++ code.

## Comparisons Involving Enumeration Types

The order relationship among the enumerators of an enumeration type is fixed when the enumeration type is declared. For example, for types `day` and `expense`, the following order relationships are all true:

```
sunday < monday
wednesday != tuesday
wednesday == wednesday
wednesday >= tuesday
entertainment < rent
other >= automobile
utilities != food
```

## Distinctions among Integral Types

When using enumeration types, it's important to remember that each declaration of an integral type is different from all the others (and therefore also different from the `int` type). These different types cannot be mixed in an expression. The expressions

```
entertainment + wednesday
```

and the order relation

```
entertainment < wednesday
```

would cause a syntax error because the values shown are associated with two different enumeration types.

## Reading and Writing Enumeration Type Values

Enumeration types are defined by the programmer, so their values aren't known in advance, and the C++ input/output systems cannot read or write these values. But you can write your own functions for this purpose. The next example illustrates one approach to displaying the value of an enumeration variable in a readable form.

Notice that the switch statement shown in Listing 7.4 has enumerators as case labels. Make sure you do not attempt to use a character string (such as `"green"`) as a case label. Enumerators are allowed as case labels; character strings aren't.

## EXAMPLE 7.9

Function `writeColor` in Listing 7.4 displays a character string that represents a value of type `color`.

```
enum color {red, green, blue, yellow};
```

If the value of **eyeColor** (type `color`) is defined, the statement

```
writeColor(eyeColor);
```

displays the value of **eyeColor** as a string.

**Listing 7.4**   Function to display a value of type `color`

```
// Displays the value of thisColor
// Pre : thisColor is assigned a value.
// Post: The value of thisColor is displayed as a string
void writeColor
  (color thisColor)     // IN: color to display as a string
{
  // Display color value as a string.
  switch (thisColor)
  {
    case red:
      cout << "red ";
      break;
    case green:
      cout << "green ";
      break;
    case blue:
      cout << "blue ";
      break;
    case yellow:
      cout << "yellow ";
      break;
    default:
      cout << "*** ERROR: Invalid color value."
           << endl;
  }
}
```

## EXAMPLE 7.10

Function `readColor` in Listing 7.5 "reads" an enumerator value. It does this by reading a character representing a color (R, G, B, Y) and then returning the enumerator corresponding to that color (red for R, and so on). If `eyeColor` is type `color`, you could use the statements

```
cout << "Reading eye color";
eyeColor = readColor();
```

to assign to `eyeColor` a color value based on a data character.

**Listing 7.5**    Function to read a value of type `color`

```
// Reads a color value
// Returns the color value corresponding to a data character.
color readColor()
{
    // Local data  . . .
    char colorChar;           // storage for data character

    // Continue reading until data character is valid.
    do
    {
        cout << "Enter first letter of color (R,G,B, or Y): ";
        cin >> colorChar;
        colorChar = toupper(colorChar);   // to uppercase

        // Return color value if valid character read.
        switch(colorChar)
        {
            case 'R' : return red;
            case 'G' : return green;
            case 'B' : return blue;
            case 'Y' : return yellow;
            default  : cout << "Try again!" << endl;
        } // end switch
    } while (true);
}
```

The `switch` statement returns the enumerator corresponding to the first valid color character read. Instead of using a break statement, we return immediately to the calling function. The loop executes forever (its repetition condition is `true`), so executing one of the `return` statements is the only way to exit the loop.

## Program Style   Using Returns in a Switch Statement

Usually we end each case in a `switch` statement with a `break` statement, and we end a function with a single `return` statement. In some situations, replacing every `break` with a `return` statement can lead to more readable code. If you want to return after executing every case in a `switch` statement, consider using `return` statements instead of a `break`.

## Placement of Enumeration Type Declarations

When you use enumeration types, you'll normally need to provide functions similar to `readColor` and `writeColor`. Because these functions (and possibly other functions) need to reference the enumeration type `color` and its enumerators, you must declare the enumeration type before the function prototypes. This gives the enumeration type global scope and enables all functions to reference it and its enumerators. Listing 7.6 shows a small driver program that declares and uses enumeration type `color`.

## Enumeration Types as Cast Operators

You can use enumeration types as cast operators. For the enumeration type `month` from Listing 7.7

```
enum month {jan = 1, feb, mar, apr, may, jun, jul, aug,
            sep, oct, nov, dec};
```

the cast operation `month(3)` returns the enumerator (`mar`) in the list above corresponding to 3. Function `readMonth` (Listing 7.7) uses this feature to return the type `month` enumerator corresponding to an integer read as data. First, it calls function `getIntRange` (Listing 5.9) to read an integer in the range 1 through 12. Next it casts this value to type `month` and returns the result.

**Listing 7.6**    Using enumeration type color

```cpp
// File: color.cpp
// Tests the enumeration type color.

#include <iostream>
using namespace std;

enum color {red, green, blue, yellow};

// Function prototypes
void writeColor(color);
color readColor();

int main()
{
   color eyeColor, hairColor;

   cout << "Reading eye color" << endl;
   eyeColor = readColor();
   cout << endl << "Reading hair color" << endl;
   hairColor = readColor();

   cout << endl << "Eye color is ";
   writeColor(eyeColor);
   cout << ", hair color is ";
   writeColor(hairColor);
   cout << endl;

   return 0;
}
// Insert functions readColor and writeColor here.
```

```
Reading eye color
Enter first letter of color (R,G,B, or Y): e
Try again!
Enter first letter of color (R,G,B, or Y): b
Reading hair color
Enter first letter of color (R,G,B, or Y): Y
Eye color is blue, hair color is yellow
```

**Listing 7.7**   Function to read a value of type month

```
// Reads a month value as an integer
// Returns the corresponding month value
month readMonth()
{
    // Local data  . . .
    int monthValue;            // storage for integer data

    // Read a valid integer.
    cout << "Reading month"
    monthValue = getIntRange(1, 12);

    return (month(monthValue));
}
```

## EXERCISES FOR SECTION 7.5

**Self–Check**

1. What are the integer values associated with the type `color` enumerators? With the type `day` enumerators? With the type `specialChars` enumerators?

2. Evaluate each of the following, assuming before each operation that `today` (type `day`) is `wednesday`.

   **a.** `int(monday)`
   **b.** `int(today)`

   **c.** `today < tuesday`
   **d.** `day(int(today) + 1)`

   **e.** `wednesday + monday`
   **f.** `int(today) + 1`

   **g.** `today >= thursday`
   **h.** `wednesday + thursday`

3. Indicate whether each sequence of type declarations below is valid or invalid. Explain what is wrong with each invalid sequence.

   **a.** `enum logical {true, false};`

   **b.** `enum letters {A, B, C};`
       `enum twoLetters {A, B};`

c. ```
enum day {sun, mon, tue, wed, thu, fri, sat};
enum weekDay {mon, tue, wed, thu, fri};
enum weekEnd {sat, sun};
```

d. ```
enum trafficLight {red, yellow, green};
int green;
```

4. Trace the execution of function `readMonth` in Listing 7.7 for data values of 15 and 7. What value is returned by the function?

Programming

1. Write a `switch` statement with a selector expression of type `day` that displays a message indicating the corresponding day of the week followed by the message `" is a weekday"` or `" is a weekend day"`. For example, if the selector expression has a value 0, the message `"Sunday is a weekend day"` should be displayed.

2. Write function `writeMonth` for enumeration type `month`.

# 7.6   Common Programming Errors

Be careful when writing complicated expressions, especially those involving the use of parentheses. Watch out for the following errors.

- *Omitting pairs of parentheses:* This error will often go undetected by the compiler because the resulting expression may be syntactically valid even though it's logically incorrect. For example, the statement

```
m = y2 - y1 / x2 - x1;
```

might be intended to compute the slope of a line through two points, (x1, y1) and (x2 , y2), in the xy-plane. Yet because of the missing parentheses, the expression will actually compute m as

```
y2 - (y1 / x2) - x1
```

- *Unbalanced parentheses:* Omitting a single left or right parenthesis is also quite common in programming. This error will be detected by the compiler, causing a message such as `"parse error before )"`.

  To help prevent such errors in the use of parentheses, review the C++ operator precedence rules summarized in Appendix D. Also, you can break a complicated expression into subexpressions that are separately assigned to temporary variables, and then manipulate these temporary variables. For example, instead of the single assignment statement

```
z = sqrt(x + y) / (1 + sqrt(x + y));
```

write the three assignment statements

```
temp1 = sqrt(x + y);
temp2 = 1 + temp1;
z = temp1 / temp2;
```

which have the same effect. Using three assignment statements is also more efficient because the square root operation is performed only once; it's performed twice in the single assignment statement above.

■ *Mixing operators and operands of different types:* It's easy to make mistakes when writing expressions using mixed data types. To make matters worse, most errors of this nature aren't detected by the compiler. The expressions '3' + '4' and grossPay != '3' (grossPay of type float) are syntactically correct but will yield an unexpected and undesirable result at execution time.

   The best advice we can give for avoiding these problems is to not mix data types in the first place. Instead, use casting operators to specify explicitly all desired conversions.

■ *Operator precedence errors:* Because of the operator precedence hierarchy in C++, very little use of parentheses is normally required when writing expressions involving relational and equality operators. The one major exception lies in the use of the not operator, !, which has a higher precedence than most of the other operators used so far. For example, if x is true and y is false, then !x && y is false, but !(x && y) is true.

   We list the precedence of operators in Appendix D. Notice that the unary operators have a higher precedence than the others (except for parentheses) and that they associate right to left, instead of left to right. Logical expressions such as

```
-5.0 <= x && x <= 5.0
```

may be written correctly without parentheses. You may find such expressions easier to read when parentheses are used:

```
(-5.0 <= x) && (x <= 5.0)
```

■ *Using enumeration types:* When declaring enumeration types, remember that the enumerators must be identifiers. Strings, characters, and numbers aren't allowed. Make sure that the same enumerator does not appear in more than one enumeration-type declaration in a given declaration scope. Remember that there are no standard functions available to read or write the values of an enumeration type.

   C++ treats enumeration and char data as integral data types (having integer values) and it's therefore possible to perform the standard arithmetic and relational operations on values of these data types. You must be careful, however; neither the compiler nor the run-time system will attempt to verify that the results of the arithmetic operations fall within the range of meaningful values for these types. Remember, each enumeration type you define is considered to be a different integral type, so you shouldn't mix enumerators from different types in the same expression.

You can't assign a type `int` value to an enumeration type without first applying the appropriate type casting operator. Use the statement

```
today = day(i);    // correct assignment
```

to assign the value of integer `i` to `today` (type `day`), not the statement

```
today = i;         // incorrect assignment
```

## Chapter Review

1. Type `int` and `double` data have different internal representations. Type `int` values are represented as binary numbers with the leftmost bit containing the sign of the number. Type `double` data are represented by a binary exponent and mantissa.

2. Additional integer types are `short` and `long`. Type `short` typically represents a smaller range of integers than type `int`; type `long` represents a larger range.

3. Additional floating-point types are `double`, which typically represents a larger range than type `float`, and `long double`, which may represent an even larger range.

4. Arithmetic with floating-point data may not be precise, because not all real numbers can be represented exactly. Other types of numerical errors include cancellation error and arithmetic overflow and underflow.

5. Type `char` data are represented by storing a binary code value for each symbol. ASCII is a commonly used character code.

6. The character function library `cctype` contains several useful character functions for converting the case of a letter (`tolower` and `toupper`) and for testing the kind of data stored in a type `char` variable (`isdigit`, `isletter`, and so on).

7. DeMorgan's theorem describes how to complement a logical expression involving logical operators. For example, the expression `!((x < y) || (y > z))` is equivalent to `(x >= y) && (y <= z)`.

8. Data types in C++ can be declared using the reserved word `enum`. Defining an enumeration type requires listing the identifiers that are the values (enumerators) of the type. Each value is represented by an integer. Using enumeration types makes programs more readable because you can choose enumerators that are meaningful for a particular application.

9. A variable or expression can be cast to another type by writing the new type's name before the value to convert and enclosing the value in parentheses. Such a cast is a very high-precedence operation.

## Summary of New C++ Constructs

| Construct | Effect |
| --- | --- |
| **Integer Variants** | |
| `const long INT_BIG = 123456789L;` | A long integer constant |
| `const short INT_SMALL = 32;` | A short integer constant |
| **Floating-Point Variants** | Provides additional accuracy over `float` |
| `double x;` | |
| **Enumeration Types** | |
| `enum coins {penny=1, nickel=5,` | A data type for representing United States coins and their values |
| `dime=10, quarter=25, halfDollar=50};` | |

## Quick-Check Exercises

1. **a.** Evaluate the logical expression

   ```
   flag && ((m % n) == 0)
   ```

   when `flag` is `true`, m is 16, and n is 5.
   **b.** Is the outer pair of parentheses required?
   **c.** What about the inner pair?
   **d.** Write the complement of this expression in two ways.

2. Assuming m and k are integers (k = 13),
   **a.** What value is assigned to m by the statement

   ```
   m = 2.5 + k / 2;
   ```

   **b.** If m is type `float`, what is the value assigned to m?
   **c.** Rewrite the assignment statement in part (a) so that the addition and division become type `float` operations and the fractional part of the result is truncated before the assignment to m.
   **d.** If k is type `int`, is the division in `float(k / 2)` integer division or real division? Explain.

3.  What is the value of each of the following?
    **a.** `char(int('a'))`          **b.** `char(int('a') + 3)`
    **c.** `char(int('z') - 20)`     **d.** `char(int('z') - 32)`
    **e.** `int('z') - 32`           **f.** `ch - '0'` (where `ch` is any digit character)

4.  If `ch` contains the character `'a'`, what is the value of the expression

    `isdigit(ch) || iscntrl(ch)`

    What kind of an expression is this?

5.  Can an enumerator of the enumeration type `day` be assigned to a variable of another enumeration type? In other words, is the assignment

    `today = entertainment`

    valid if `today` is a variable of type `day` and `entertainment` is an enumerator of type `expense`?

6.  Assume that two variables aren't of the same integral type (`int`, `long int`, `char`, enumeration, and so on).
    **a.** Can they be mixed in the same arithmetic expression?
    **b.** Can one be assigned to the other?

7.  Under what circumstance can a type `int` variable or value be assigned to a variable of an enumeration type?

8.  What is wrong with the following enumeration type declarations?

    ```
    enum prime {2, 3, 5, 7, 11, 13};
    enum vowels {'a', 'e', 'i', 'o', 'u'};
    ```

9.  Write a function with the prototype

    ```
    bool isUpperCase(char);
    ```

    that returns `true` if its argument is an uppercase letter. Write a `while` loop that uses this function in a repetition condition. The loop should ignore any characters entered by the user that aren't uppercase letters. After loop exit, the input variable should store the first uppercase letter that is entered.

## Answers to Quick-Check Exercises

1.  **a.** `false`
    **b.** The outer pair isn't required.
    **c.** The inner pair isn't required.
    **d.** `!(flag && (m % n == 0))` or `!flag || (m % n != 0)`

**2. a.** `m = 2.5 + 13 / 2;` 8 is assigned to m (the integral part of `8.5`).

   **b.** `8.5` is assigned to m.

   **c.** `m = int(2.5 + float(k) / 2.0);` 9 is assigned to m (the integral part of `2.5 + 6.5`).

   **d.** In `float(k  / 2)` the division of k by 2 is type `int`. It's performed first and then the result is cast to type `float`.

**3. a.** `'a'`  **b.** `'d'`  **c.** `'f'`  **d.** `'R'`  **e.** 82
   **f.** The result is the integer form of the character—e.g., 7 if ch is `'7'`.

**4.** `false || false` is `false`; this is a logical expression involving calls to two type `bool` functions.

**5.** no

**6. a.** Yes, but carefully. Remember that these data are each considered to be different C++ types and are subject to the C++ conversion/promotion rules in Section 7.2.
   **b.** The same applies to assignment except that integer type values may not be assigned to variables of enumeration types.

**7.** This can happen only if the enumeration variable's type cast is applied to the type `int` variable or value before the assignment (e.g., `today = day(i);`).

**8.** Type `int` and `char` values aren't allowed as enumerators in enumeration types.

## Review Questions

1. Explain why it's useful to have a data type `int` for integers instead of using data type `float` for all numbers.

2. List and explain three computational errors that may occur in type `float` expressions.

3. **a.** Write an enumeration type declaration for `fiscal` as the months from `July` through `June`.
   **b.** Write an enumeration type declaration for `winter` as `December` through `February`.
   **c.** Can you declare both enumerated types in the same function? Explain your answer.

4. Write a function for writing the value of a variable of type `season` as a string:

   ```
   enum season {winter, spring, summer, fall};
   ```

5. Write a `bool` function `isWeekend` that returns `true` if the value of `today` (of type `day`; see Listing 7.6) is a weekend day. Otherwise the function should return `false`.

6. Write a `switch` statement that tests to see if the type `day` variable `today` is a working day (`Monday` through `Friday`). Display the message "Workday" or "Weekend". Also, write an `if` statement that does this. Remember you can compare enumerators of the same type using the relational operators.

7. Write an `if` statement that will write out `true` or `false` according to the following conditions: either `flag` is `true` or `color` is `red`, or both `money` is `plenty` and `time` is up.

8. Write a function that returns `true` if a worker's hours (the function input) are greater than 40. Otherwise, the function should return `false`.

9. What are the rules followed by C++ when type `float` variables are mixed with type `double` variables?

10. Write a C++ function that receives an integer argument between 0 and 9, inclusive, and returns an equivalent character value (e.g., `'0'` for 0, `'1'` for 1).

## Programming Projects

1. An integer $n$ is divisible by 9 if the sum of its digits is divisible by 9. Develop a program to determine whether or not the following numbers are divisible by 9:

   $n$ = 154368
   $n$ = 621594
   $n$ = 123456

2. Redo the previous programming project by reading each digit of the number to be tested into the type `char` variable `digit`. Form the sum of the numeric values of the digits. (Hint: The numeric value of `digit` is `int (digit) - int ('0')`.)

3. If a human heart beats on an average of once per second (60 beats per minute), how many times does the heart beat in a lifetime of 78 years? (Use 365.25 for the number of days in a year.) Rerun your program for a heart rate of 75 beats per minute. Implement the program first using beats per minute and years as integers and total beats and all constants as type `double`. Then try changing all type `double` data to type `float` and see what happens. Can you explain the difference (if any) in the execution output of the two versions?

4. A number is said to be *perfect* if the sum of its divisors (except for itself) is equal to itself. For example, 6 is a perfect number because the sum of its divisors (1 + 2 + 3) is 6. The number 8 is said to be *deficient* because the sum of its divisors (1 + 2 + 4) is only 7. The number 12 is

said to be *abundant* because the sum of its divisors $(1 + 2 + 3 + 4 + 6)$ is 16. Write a program that lists the factors of the numbers between 1 and 100 and classifies each number as perfect, deficient, or abundant.

5. Write a program for printing a bar graph summarizing the rainfall in Bedrock for one year. Include the average monthly rainfall and the maximum monthly rainfall during the year as part of the program output.

   Prompt the user for the amount of rainfall for a particular month and instruct the computer to send an appropriate output line to the printer. Assume that no one month will have more than 14 inches of rainfall. Your graph should resemble the following:

```
January      |* * * * * * * * * * * * * * * * *
             |
February     |* * * * * * * * * * * *
             |
March        |
             |
December     |* * * * * * * * * * * * * * * * * * * * * * * * * * * * * * * * * *
             |-----1-----2-----3-----4-----5-----6-----7-----8-----9...
                            Inches of Rainfall
```

Write functions corresponding to the prototypes shown below as part of your solution.

```
// Write the month value as a string
void writeMonth
   (int);        // IN - month to be written as a string

// Get rainfall for month; update totals
// User is prompted for inches of rainfall during a month.
// Max inches and total inches are updated to contain
//    the maximum and total inches of rainfall input so far.
void getMonthlyTotal
   (int,         // IN - current month
    float&,      // OUT - inches of rain for month
    float&,      // INOUT - max inches of rain
    float&);     // INOUT - total inches of rain

// Draw bar of length given by inches
// Draw a bar whose length is computed from inches with
//    label determined by the value of month.
void drawBar
   (int,         // IN: the month to be written as a string
    float);      // IN: the inches of rain for the month

// Draw scale and label at bottom of graph
void drawScaleLine();
```

6. The interest paid on a savings account is compounded daily. This means that if you start with *startbal* dollars in the bank, at the end of the first day you'll have a balance of

```
startbal * (1 + rate/365)
```

dollars, where *rate* is the annual interest rate (0.10 if the annual rate is 10 percent). At the end of the second day, you'll have

```
startbal * (1 + rate/365) * (1 + rate/365)
```

dollars, and at the end of *n* days you'll have

```
startbal * (1 + rate/365)n
```

dollars. Write a program that processes a set of data records, each of which contains values for `rate`, `startbal`, and n and computes the final account balance.

7. Experiments that are either too expensive or too dangerous to perform are often simulated on a computer when the computer is able to provide a good representation of the experiment. Find out how to call the random-number generator (usually a function returning a floating-point value in the range 0 to 1) for your C++ system. (Look up the functions `rand` and `srand` in the library `cstdlib`.) Write a program that uses the random-number generator to simulate the dropping of glass rods that break into three pieces. The purpose of the experiment is to estimate the probability that the lengths of the three pieces are such that they might form the sides of a triangle.

   For the purposes of this experiment, you may assume that the glass rod always breaks into three pieces. If you use the line segment 0 to 1 (on the real number line) as a mathematical model of the glass rod, a random-number generator (function) can be used to generate two numbers between 0 and 1 representing the coordinates of the breaks. The triangle inequality (the sum of the lengths of two sides of a triangle are always greater than the length of the third side) may be used to test the length of each piece against the lengths of the other two pieces.

   To estimate the probability that the pieces of the rod form a triangle, you'll need to repeat the experiment many times and count the number of times a triangle can be formed from the pieces. The probability estimate is the number of successes divided by the total number of rods dropped. Your program should prompt the user for the number of rods to drop and allow the experiment to be repeated. Use a sentinel value of 21 to halt execution of the program.

8. Julian day numbers are used to provide a number for a day of the year so that calculations can be performed relatively easily to determine the

difference between two dates. For example, if you wanted to determine the number of days between the day you were born and today, this would be a very tedious calculation. You would need to determine how many days followed the day you were born in that year, how many days were in each year between the year you were born and the current year, and how many days were in the current year up to today. This is complicated by the fact that leap years have 366 days (see Programming Project 11 in Chapter 6). The Julian day number for a day is the number of days that have elapsed between that day and a base date of January 1, 4713 B.C.E. Code the following algorithm for computing the Julian day number as a type long function where day is an integer from 1 to 31, month goes from 1 to 12, and year goes from − 4713 (4713 B.C.E.) to whatever.

```
long julianDayNumber(int month, int day, int year)
{
    jyear = year;
    jmonth = month;
    if (year < 0)
        increment jyear by 1;    // no year 0
    if (month > 2)
        increment jmonth by 1;
    else
        increment jmonth by 13 and decrement jyear by 1

    long julian = floor(362.25 * jyear) +
                  floor(30.6001 * jmonth) +
                  day + 1720995.0;
    if  the argument date is not before October 15, 1582
          int jCorrection = 0.01 * jyear;
          julian = julian + 2 - jCorrection +
                  0.25 * jCorrection;
    return julian;
}
```

Write and test a function to calculate the Julian day number for a given day. (The date October 9, 1995 is Julian day 2,450,000; the date October 15, 1582 is Julian day number 2,299,161.) Use this function to determine how many days you've been alive.

# Thomas Drake

*Thomas Drake is a member of the Senior Executive Service (SES) in the United States government and also a Technical Director for Software Engineering Implementation, where he leads a software engineering leadership center focused on improving the maturity of software design, development, and delivery. In addition, he is responsible for creating and sponsoring team-based software development environments that create cost-effective, functionally fit, high quality, and customer-driven products and services, while taking advantage of best practices from both inside and outside the government.*

**What is your educational background?**
I received a B.A. degree in government from the University of Maryland. I also received an M.A. degree in 1988 from the University of Arizona, majoring in national security policy and international relations. I hold an Applied Science degree from the Community College of the Air Force, and an Advanced Certificate from the Information Management/Decision Sciences and Policy Sciences doctorate degree program at the University of Maryland, Baltimore County.

**How did you get interested in computer science?**
My U.S. Air Force military experience, where I was introduced to very advanced computer and data processing technology, piqued my interest in computer science and software-based information technology systems.

**What is a typical day like for you?**
I lead several enterprise-wide software engineering teams. We are increasingly focused on web-based applications and messaging, advanced object-oriented programming, software reuse services, and independent verification and validation. You can also find me sponsoring groups and projects that support engineering management and developer-level best practices, including the instantiation of agile methods within projects and process improvement for organizations.

**Which person in the computer science field has inspired you?**
If there were one person to name, it would be Alan Kay. He is one of the inventors of the Smalltalk programming language and one of the fathers of the idea of object-oriented programming. He is also largely credited for originating the concepts behind the laptop computer, and is one of the leading architects of the modern windowing graphical user interface. If you ever get a chance to hear him speak, go listen!

**Do you have any advice for students learning C++?**
Use assertions! Assertions provide for the checking of your arguments and making sure that your functional assumptions are true. Peer and code reviews are also one of the best ways of uncovering design and logic flaws. Comment your code. You never know how

long your program will hang around. And have someone else test your code. Spend the bulk of your time in analysis and design, not programming.

**How has C++ evolved over the last few years?**
Well, it was very possible for software developers to "roll" C++ code that had terrible performance and maintenance issues. Now there is much more emphasis on design and execution—a good thing!

**What is your vision for the future of the C++ programming language?**
I see patterns becoming more and more important for C++. Also, we are moving to an era where we will generate code from the design logic rather than hand-code after the fact—already happening with code-generation technology.

**What is software entropy? What can be done about it?**
Software entropy is really the tendency of code to become rapidly complex after just a few changes. This usually means that the software has an inherent tendency to break down based on the number and degree of dependent relationships. The key is reducing complexity by increasing the functionality for any given amount of code and keeping it as simple as possible. I subscribe to the "weak-link" theory for software development—the code is only as strong as its weakest functionality. It is the "change state" of the code that really determines its functional robustness.

**What kind of stumbling blocks do C++ programmers tend to run into when it comes to program quality?**
Many programmers still don't consider the critical software process activities that are the foundation for high-quality software engineering. Quality must be built in, and not after code is developed. We are talking about designing and developing error "free-er" coding the first time.

Comments are another area. If your program isn't worth commenting, it probably is not worth running. After all, comments make it more understandable for you, but most importantly, for any developer coming after you.

Invariants! An invariant is a set of assertions about an instance or a class that must be true for all "stable" times. Bertrand Meyer, the designer of the Eiffel programming language and author on object-oriented methods, has defined this as the period before a method is invoked in the object or class and immediately after the method is invoked. By documenting the "invariants" you provide information on how the class can be used.

# Streams and Files

Chapter Objectives

- To learn how to use external files for program input and output
- To learn how to read program data from input streams (type `ifstream`) and write program results to output streams (type `ofstream`)
- To become familiar with functions for manipulating streams in the C++ library `fstream`
- To learn when and how to use functions `get`, `getline`, and `ignore` to read character and string data
- To learn how to use manipulators in the C++ library `iomanip` to format output

THIS CHAPTER DISCUSSES streams and files in C++. It describes the input and output facilities provided by the C++ libraries that support stream input and output. The chapter will also present more about the standard input/output streams, `cin` and `cout`, how to use disk files for input/output, and how to format data items that are written to output streams.

## 8.1 The Standard Input/Output Streams

**stream**
A sequence of characters used for program input or output.

A **stream** is a sequence of characters used for program input or output. So far, we've used the *standard input stream* (named `cin`) and the *standard output stream* (named `cout`). Including the `iostream` header file enables a program to access these streams. When we first introduced streams in Chapter 2, we mentioned that `cin` and `cout` are objects of type `istream` and `ostream` respectively. The user-defined types `istream` and `ostream` are defined by classes in the `iostream` library, and `cin` and `cout` are declared as objects of these types. Normally, `cin` is connected to your keyboard, so when a program reads characters from `cin`, it reads characters typed at the keyboard. Similarly, `cout` is connected to your display, so writing characters to the standard output stream object `cout` displays these characters on your screen.

During input, the stream operators must convert sequences of characters into their appropriate internal representations before storing them in memory. For example, if the character sequence starting with `123.45` (digit character 1, digit character 2, and so on) is being read into a type `float` variable, the stream extraction operator `>>` must convert this sequence to the floating point form of the real number 123.45 for storage. If the same character sequence (`123.45`) is being read into a type `int` variable, only the first three characters will be extracted and converted into a fixed point number (binary equivalent of 123) for storage. The characters (`.45`) remain in the stream. Finally, if this sequence is being read into a type `char` variable, only the first character (`'1'`) is extracted and stored.

During output, the reverse process takes place. When writing a floating point number to an output stream, the insertion operator `<<` must first convert its internal representation to a sequence of characters and then write this character sequence to the output stream. A similar process takes place for the other data types in C++ (see Figure 8.1).

Any character, whether printable or not, may be read from or written to a stream. Thus nonprintable characters such as `'\a'` and `'\n'` may also be read from or written to streams. As their name suggests, these characters are not displayed. Rather, on many computers, they cause special actions to occur, such as sounding a beep (`'\a'`) or moving the cursor to the beginning of the next line (`'\n'`).

## EXAMPLE 8.1

**newline character**
A character that partitions a stream into a sequence of lines.

The **newline character** (`'\n'`) partitions a stream into a sequence of lines. We call this a *logical partition*, because it reflects the way we often think and talk about a stream. Don't forget, however, that a stream is physically just a sequence of characters with the newline character interspersed. For example, the following represents a stream of two lines of data consisting of letters, blank characters, `'.'` (a period), and `'!'` (an exclamation point). The symbols `<nwln>` represent the newline character.

```
This is a stream!<nwln>It is displayed as two lines.<nwln>
```

The `<nwln>` character separates one line of data in the stream from the next. The letter I following the first `<nwln>` is the first character of the second line. If we were to display this stream, each `<nwln>` character would cause a *line feed* and a *carriage return*, ensuring that everything that follows it would appear at the beginning of a new line. The displayed stream would appear as follows:

```
This is a stream!
It is displayed as two lines.
```

A stream has no fixed size. As we write (insert) information to a stream, we're simply adding characters to the end of the stream (increasing its size). The C++ stream output library functions keep track of the size of the stream. As we read (extract) information from a stream, the C++ stream input library functions keep track of the last character read using an *input stream buffer pointer*. Each new attempt to get information from an input stream begins at the current position of this pointer.

When reading data from a stream using the extraction operator >>, any leading *white space* (blanks, tabs, and newline characters) is skipped until

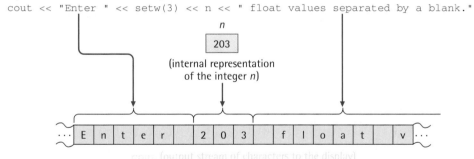

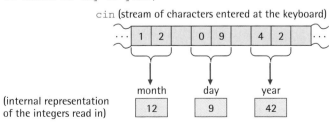

**Figure 8.1**  Conversion of data during stream input/output

the first non-white-space character is found. This is the case whether you're reading data into a type `char`, `int`, `float`, or `bool` variable or into a type `string` object. After the data characters are extracted, the input stream buffer pointer is advanced to the next character to be read.

## EXAMPLE 8.2

For the input stream

```
     CIS 642   ...
```
the line
```
cin >> ch;          // ch is a type char variable
```

causes the five blanks (indicated by the symbol [blank]) at the start of the stream to be skipped. The character **c** is then extracted from the stream and stored in the variable **ch** (type **char**). The stream buffer pointer then is positioned at the character **I**.

When reading a numeric value, all characters that are part of the numeric value (a sign, digits, etc.) are processed until a character that's not legally part of a number in C++ is read. At this point, the number processed is returned to the program. If no digits are read before an illegal numeric character is encountered, the value returned is not defined.

## EXAMPLE 8.3

If **myAge** and **n** are type **int**, for the input stream

```
347an old man
```

the line

```
cin >> myAge;      // myAge is a type int variable
```

reads the characters 347 and stops when the character a is encountered. The integer value 347 would be stored in myAge. The stream buffer pointer then points to the character a. If the next input statement is

```
cin >> n;          // n is a type int variable
```

reading would stop as soon as the **a** is encountered, and the result stored in **n** would be undefined.

## EXAMPLE 8.4

Consider the input stream consisting of exam score *records* (three initials and a score) for each of four students, where each record is entered as a single line, with the return key pressed after each score is typed:

```
flf 78<nwln>ebk 89<nwln>jas 95<nwln>pac 66<nwln>
```

Assuming that the variable `score` is type `int`, and `firstInit`, `midInit`, and `lastInit` are type `char`, the C++ instructions

```
for (int i = 0; i < numStudents; i++)
{
   cin >> firstInit >> midInit >> lastInit >> score;
   // Process the information just read.
    ...
}
```

may be used to read in this information. If `numStudents` is 4, this loop would extract (read) four data elements (three characters and an integer) at a time from the stream just shown until all four student records have been processed. In each `for` loop iteration, the next student's initials would be extracted and stored in the character variables, `firstInit`, `midInit`, and `lastInit`, and the integer that follows them would be read and stored in `score`.

The newline character in the stream has no special impact on the processing of the data just shown. Leading white space, including blanks and the newline character, is always skipped when reading a data element using `cin`. After the score for the first student has been read, the input stream buffer pointer is positioned at the `<nwln>` character that stopped the processing:

```
flf 78<nwln>ebk 89<nwln>jas 95<nwln>pac 66<nwln>
        ↑
```

When reading data for the second student, the white space (`<nwln>`) that precedes this student's first initial is skipped. If we replace each newline with a blank, the processing would be the same. In fact, if there were no white-space characters anywhere in the line, the processing of the line would not change (Listing 8.1). In this case, the letter **e** would terminate the reading of the first score, and **e** would then be read as the first initial of the second student.

Listing 8.1    An input stream without white space

```
flf78ebk89jas95pac66
```

## Reading One Character at a Time

In many situations, we want to treat white space the same way as any other character. The following examples illustrate how this might be done using the stream input and output functions `get` and `put`, which are part of the C++ `iostream` library. Function `get` is used to read one character at a time; function `put` is used to display one character at a time.

---

### EXAMPLE 8.5

The program in Listing 8.2 counts and displays the number of characters in each line of a stream entered at the keyboard. It also counts and displays the number of lines in the stream. The outer loop repeats as long as the condition `!cin.eof()` is true. Function `eof` (end-of-file) detects the end of a stream of characters. This function returns a value of **false** as long as there are more characters to be read in a stream. When the end of the stream is reached, it returns the value **true**. Consequently the outer loop repeats until the end of the stream is reached. You indicate the end of a stream by typing a special control character which is system dependent. On PCs, you enter this character by pressing and holding the CONTROL key and then pressing Z (CTRL-Z). On UNIX computers, the character CTRL-D is used.

The inner loop condition `(next != nwln)` is true as long as the newline character has not been read. Therefore, this inner loop processes all of the characters in the current data line, including the blanks. The **put** function displays each character in the line after it is read. When the newline character is read by the inner call to `get`, the inner **while** loop expression evaluates to false, and loop exit occurs. At this point, the newline is displayed (marking the end of the current line of output), the line count is incremented, and the number of characters in the line is displayed. This sequence of steps repeats as long as the outer loop condition is true.

---

Notice that the `eof` function does not return a value of true until after the `get` function reads the end-of-file character `<eof>` that marks the end of a stream. We use dot notation to indicate which stream (`cin` or `cout`) is involved in each stream operation (for example, `cin.eof()`).

We summarize the new functions together with other stream input/output functions in Table 8.1. The `open`, `fail`, and `close` functions are used only with external file streams, described in the next section.

**Listing 8.2**   Processing individual characters in a stream

```cpp
// File: countChars.cpp
// Counts number of characters in a line and lines in a stream

#include <iostream>
#include <string>
using namespace std;

#define ENDFILE "CTRL-Z"

int main()
{
   const char NWLN = '\n';   // newline character
   char next;            // next character in current line
   int charCount;        // number of characters in current line
   int lineCount;        // keeps track of number of lines in file

   lineCount = 0;
   cout << "Enter a line or press " << ENDFILE << ": ";
   cin.get(next);              // get first char of new line
   while (!cin.eof())
   {
      charCount = 0;    // initialize character count for new line
      while (next != NWLN)
      {
         cout.put(next);
         charCount++;         // Increment character count.
         cin.get(next);       // Get next character.
      } // end inner while

      cout.put(NWLN);   // Mark end of current display line.
      lineCount++;
      cout << "Number of characters in line " << lineCount
           << " is " << charCount << endl;
      cout << "Enter a line or press " << ENDFILE << ": ";
      cin.get(next);                    // Get next character.
   } // end outer while

   cout << endl << endl << "Number of lines processed is "
        << lineCount << endl;

   return 0;
}
```

(continued)

**Listing 8.2**    Processing individual characters in a stream (continued)

```
Enter a line or press CTRL-Z: This is one.
This is one.
Number of characters is 12
Enter a line or press CTRL-Z: Hello!
Hello!
Number of characters is 6
Enter a line or press CTRL-Z: CTRL-Z
Number of lines processed is 2
```

**Table 8.1**    The File Manipulation Member Functions

| Member Function | Purpose |
| --- | --- |
| *fs*.open(*fname*); | Opens stream *fs* for input or output. Connects the stream *fs* to the external file designated by *fname*. |
| *fs*.get(*ch*); | Extracts the next character from stream *fs* and places it in the character variable *ch*. |
| *fs*.put(*ch*); | Inserts (writes or displays) character *ch* into stream *fs*. |
| *fs*.close(); | Disconnects stream *fs* from its associated external file. |
| *fs*.eof(); | Tests for the end-of-file condition on stream *fs*. Returns true when the end-of-file is reached. This is detected when a program attempts to read the <eof> character marking the end of a file. |
| *fs*.fail(); | Returns true if an operation on stream *fs* such as open failed to execute properly. |

## Program Style   Using a Stream in a Condition

As an alternative to using the eof function to test for the end of a stream, C++ programmers can test the status of the stream by using the stream name directly in a condition. For example, to test whether an input operation on stream cin was successful, you can evaluate the condition (cin) just after the input operation. If the input operation in question was cin.get(next), you can use the condition (cin.get(next)). Because an input operation on stream cin returns a reference to stream cin, the status of stream cin is tested. The condition value is true if the input operation was successful; the condition value is false if the input operation was unsuccessful (for example, because the <eof> character was read).

Using this technique, we can write the outer loop control for Listing 8.2 as shown next.

```
cout << "Enter a line or press " << ENDFILE << ": ";
while (cin.get(next))     // get first char of new line
```

```
    {
        // insert loop body including inner while loop.
        . . .
        cout << "Enter a line or press " << ENDFILE << ": ";
    } // end outer while
```

This loop repeats until the user enters the `<eof>` character instead of a data line. Notice that the input operation (`cin.get(next)`) appears only in the loop repetition condition. In Listing 8.2, we called function `get` twice: just before entering the loop and at the end of the loop body.

## EXERCISES FOR SECTION 8.1

**Self-Check**

1. Explain what would happen in Listing 8.2 if the function calls `cin.get(next)` were replaced by `cin >> next;`.

2. Let x be type `float`, n type `int`, and c type `char`. Indicate the contents of each variable after each read operation is performed on the input stream below.

       1374 37 15.125 pqr*<nwln>233 $ <nwln>

   Assume the input stream buffer is reset to the first character before each file read operation.

   **a.**  `cin >> n >> x; cin >> c >> n;`

   **b.**  `cin >> n; cin.get(c);`

   **c.**  `cin >> x >> n >> c; cin.get(c); cin >> n;`

   **d.**  `cin >> c >> n >> x; cin >> c;`

   **e.**  `cin >> c >> c >> c >> x >> n;`

3. Write one input statement that reads the input stream for Self-Check Exercise 2 and stores `15.125` in x, `233` in n, and $ in c.

4. What would happen to the displayed output for Listing 8.2 if the line `cout.put(NWLN);` were omitted from the program?

5. Describe the behavior of the program in Listing 8.2 if the statement containing the innermost `cin.get` were omitted.

6. Describe the behavior of the program in Listing 8.2 if the input stream being processed were empty (contained no data at all).

Programming

1. Write a function that simulates what the extraction operator does when it reads an integer value. Your function should skip leading whitespace and read each digit character until it reaches a nondigit character. Your function should return the numeric value of the digit characters read. For example, if it reads the digit characters 3, 4, 5, your function should return the number 345. (Hint: Accumulate the numeric value by adding the numeric value of the current digit character (int(dig) – int('0')) to ten times the numeric value for the previous digit characters. If the previous sum is 34 and 5 is the next digit character, the next sum is 340 + 5 or 345.)

# 8.2    External Files

## Interactive versus Batch Processing

So far this chapter focused on interactive input. Interactive programs read their input data from the cin stream associated with the keyboard, and they display their output to the cout stream associated with a display. This mode of operation is fine for small programs. However, as you begin to write larger programs, you'll see that there are many advantages to using external data files. External files are stored on a secondary storage device, normally a disk, and are semipermanent. They will remain on the disk until you delete or overwrite them.

You can create an external data file using a text editor in the same way that you create a program file. Once the data file is entered in computer memory, you can carefully check and edit each line and then save the final data file as a disk file. When you enter data interactively, you don't always have the opportunity to examine and edit the data. Also, the data are processed as they are entered—they are not saved permanently.

**batch processing**
Reading data from an external file instead of through interaction with the user.
**echo-print**
The immediate display of a value read as data.

After the data file is saved on disk, you can instruct your program to read from the data file rather than from the keyboard. This mode of execution is called **batch processing**. Because the program data are supplied before execution begins, prompting messages are not required for batch programs. Instead, batch programs should contain display statements that print back, or **echo-print**, those data values read by the program. This provides a record of the values read and processed in a particular program run, which can be useful, especially for debugging and testing.

In addition to giving you the opportunity to check for errors in your data, using data files provides another advantage. A data file can be read many times. Therefore, during debugging you can rerun the program many times without needing to type in the test data each time.

You can also instruct your program to write its output to a disk file rather than display it on the screen. When output is written to the screen, it disappears when it scrolls off the screen and cannot be retrieved. However, if program output is written to a disk file, you have a permanent copy of it. You can get a **hard copy** of the file—a permanent copy on paper—by sending it to your printer, or you can read it using an editor or word processor.

**hard copy**
A permanent copy of program output on paper.

Finally, you can use the output generated by one program as a data file for another program. For example, a payroll program may compute employee salaries and write each employee's name and salary to an output file. You could then run a second program (for example, a program that prints employee checks) that uses the output from the payroll program as its input data file.

## Directory Names for External Files

To access a file in a program, you must know the file's directory name. The directory name consists of the path to the file followed by the file name. For example, on a PC you'd use the directory name C:\MyFiles\Payroll.txt for a file named Payroll.txt stored in directory MyFiles on disk drive C. The details of providing directory names are system-dependent. If your program and external files are in the same disk directory, you can usually refer to the external file using just its file name.

File names must follow whatever conventions apply on a particular computer system. For example, UNIX computers don't permit blanks in file names. We use the *extension* .txt to designate data files.

## Attaching Streams to External Files

We mentioned earlier that the input and output stream objects cin and cout are attached to the keyboard and display, respectively, by the C++ language system. However, to read from or write to an external data file, we must first attach or connect a stream object to that file.

In C++, we use the open statement (see Table 8.1) to connect a stream object to an external file. We show how to do this next.

## EXAMPLE 8.6

For security reasons, it is a good idea to have a backup or duplicate copy of a file in case the original is lost. The program in Listing 8.3 creates a copy of a file by writing each character in the input file (file `inData.txt`) to the output file (file `outData.txt`).

Before we can read or write an external file in a program, we must first declare a stream object for each stream/file to be processed by our program. In Listing 8.3, the declarations

```
ifstream ins;
ofstream outs;
```

involve two new data types: `ifstream` (input file stream) and `ofstream` (output file stream). Both are defined in the C++ library `fstream`. Once the stream objects have been declared, we can open the files:

```
ins.open(inFile);
outs.open(outFile);
```

This function communicates with the operating system and attaches a stream (`ins`, for example) to the external file specified as the argument (`ins` is connected to `inFile`). We show the connections established by the `open` statements in Listing 8.3.

The use of the `#define` compiler directive enables us to associate the name of a stream used by the program (for example, `inFile`) with the actual directory name of an external file (such as `inData.txt`). This association enables us to easily reuse this program with different input and output files. All we would need to change are the two `#define` lines in the program, and the program would be ready to run with different files.

The `if` statement after the call to the `open` function tests whether the `open` operation was successful. If the last operation on stream object `ins` failed, function `fail` returns true. If the last operation succeeded, function `fail` returns false. You should always test whether an `open` operation is successful and terminate execution of the program if the value returned by `fail` is true. A return with the value `EXIT_FAILURE` (defined in library `cstdlib`) may be used to report unsuccessful termination to the operating system.

---

**Listing 8.3**   Copying a file

---

```
// File: copyFile.cpp
// Copies file InData.txt to file OutData.txt

#include <cstdlib>     // for the definition of EXIT_FAILURE
#include <fstream>     // for external file streams
using namespace std;

// Associate stream objects with external file names
```

(continued)

**Listing 8.3**  Copying a file (continued)

```cpp
#define inFile "InData.txt"        // directory name for inFile
#define outFile "OutData.txt"      // directory name for outFile

// Functions used  . . .
// Copies one line of text
int copyLine(ifstream&, ofstream&);

int main()
{
   int lineCount;     // output: number of lines processed
   ifstream ins;      // ins is an input stream
   ofstream outs;     // outs is an output stream

   // Open input and output file, exit on any error.
   ins.open(inFile);  // connects ins to file inFile
   if (ins.fail())
   {
      cerr << "*** ERROR: Cannot open " << inFile
           << " for input." << endl;
      return EXIT_FAILURE;   // failure return
   }

   outs.open(outFile);  // connect outs to file outFile
   if (outs.fail())
   {
      cerr << "*** ERROR: Cannot open " << outFile
           << " for output." << endl;
      return EXIT_FAILURE;  // failure return
   }

   // Copy each character from inData to outData.
   lineCount = 0;
   while (!ins.eof())
   {
      if (copyLine(ins, outs) != 0)
         lineCount++;
   }

   // Display a message on the screen.
   cout << "Input file copied to output file." << endl;
   cout << lineCount << " lines copied." << endl;

   ins.close();       // close input file stream
   outs.close();      // close output file stream
```

(continued)

Listing 8.3    Copying a file (continued)

```
      return 0;              // successful return
}


// Copy one line of text from one file to another
// Pre:    ins is opened for input and outs for output.
// Post:   Next line of ins is written to outs.
//         The last character processed from ins is <nwln>;
//         the last character written to outs is <nwln>.
// Returns: The number of characters copied.
int copyLine
    (ifstream& ins,          // IN: ins stream
     ofstream& outs)         // OUT: outs stream
{
   // Local data  . . .
   const char NWLN = '\n';            // newline character

   char nextCh;                       // inout: character buffer
   int charCount = 0;                 // number of characters copied

   // Copy all data characters from stream ins to
   //    stream outs.
   ins.get(nextCh);
   while ((nextCh != NWLN) && !ins.eof())
   {
      outs.put(nextCh);
      charCount++;
      ins.get(nextCh);
   }  // end while

   // If last character read was NWLN write it to outs.
   if (!ins.eof())
   {
      outs.put(NWLN);
      charCount++;
   }

   return charCount;
}  // end copyLine
```

```
Input file copied to output file.
37 lines copied.
```

Besides the standard iostreams `cin` and `cout`, there's another standard stream, `cerr`, the *standard error stream*, which is usually connected to your display. The `if` statement just discussed writes an error message to stream `cerr` when an error occurs in attempting to open the input file.

The program in Listing 8.3 uses the `get`, `put`, and `eof` functions with external files. It also uses the function `close` to disconnect each external file before the program terminates. This is a good programming practice.

## Function `copyLine`

In the main function in Listing 8.3, the loop that does the actual copying follows the `open` instructions. This loop calls function `copyLine` to copy one line of information at a time from the input file to the output file. Function `copyLine` returns the count of characters in the line just read. The `main` function loop counts the number of lines copied. Loop repetition continues as long as the end of the input file has not been reached. After loop exit, the number of lines copied is displayed on the screen and both files are closed.

Function `copyLine` copies one line of the input file to the output file. The `while` loop header in `copyLine`

```
while ((nextCh != NWLN) && !ins.eof())
```

controls a loop that copies one character at a time as long as neither a newline character nor the end of the input file has been encountered. When either of these events occurs, loop exit occurs. If the newline character caused loop exit (`!ins.eof()` is true), a newline character is written to the output file before `copyLine` returns to the main function.

Reading from or writing to a file stream modifies the file position pointer associated with the stream. For this reason, we must pass all file stream arguments by reference.

## More on the Newline Character

Let's review how function `copyLine` processes newline characters. Consider the input file shown next:

```
This is a text file!<nwln>It has two lines.<nwln><eof>
```

When the first `<nwln>` is read during the execution of the `while` loop, the input and output files (and their respective stream buffer pointers) would appear as follows:

*Input file*
```
This is a text file!<nwln>It has two lines.<nwln><eof>
                                 ↑
```

*Output file*
```
This is a text file!
                    ↑
```

If the lines

```
// If last character read was NWLN write it to outData.
if (!ins.eof())
{
    outs.put(NWLN);
    charCount++;
}
```

were omitted from `copyLine`, the `<nwln>` character just read from the input file would not be written to the output file. As this continued throughout the program, the output file `OutData.txt` would contain all the characters in `InData.txt`, except for the line separators:

```
This is a text file!It has two lines.
```

The call to function `put` following the `while` loop in function `copyLine` ensures that a newline character is written to the output file at the end of each complete line. Once the `<nwln>` has been copied to the output file, control is returned to the calling program. When `copyLine` is called the next time, the input and output files would appear as shown below:

*Input file*
```
This is a text file!<nwln>It has two lines.<nwln><eof>
                          ↑
```

*Output file*
```
This is a text file!<nwln>
                          ↑
```

The first call to function `get` (just prior to the `while` loop in `copyLine`) causes the next character (the `I` in `It`) to be read. This loop continues copying characters from input to output until the second newline is encountered. This newline then is copied to the output file, and control is returned to the calling function. What happens upon the next call to `copyLine` is left as an exercise at the end of this section (see Self-Check Exercise 1).

In Microsoft Visual C++, the newline character is actually a pair of characters representing the carriage return and line feed. Since we define NWLN as the line feed character '/n' and the line feed is the second character of the pair, this should not affect the examples in this chapter.

## Using `getline` with a File Stream

Instead of writing our own function `copyLine`, we can use function `getline` to read each line of the file stream into a string object. We can replace the main function loop in Listing 8.3 with the one below.

```
string line;              // Next data line
lineCount = 0;
getline(ins, line);
while (line.length() != 0)
{
   lineCount++;
   outs << line << endl;
   getline(ins, line);
}
```

In this loop, each function call

```
getline(ins, line);
```

reads the next data line into string object `line`. If the number of characters read is nonzero, we increment `lineCount`, write the current line to stream `outs`, and repeat the process.

## Program Style    Reading a File Name

In Listing 8.3, we use the #define compiler directive to specify the actual directory name of an external file:

```
#define inFile "InData.txt"
```

This instructs the compiler to replace `inFile` in the `open` statement with the string `"InData.txt"`:

```
ins.open("InData.txt");
```

Sometimes program users need to enter interactively the name of a data file. You can enable this to happen by removing the compiler directive above and replacing the `open` statement with the statements:

```
    string fileName

    cout << "Enter the input file name: ";
    cin >> fileName;
    ins.open(fileName.c_str());
```

The file name that's typed in after the prompt will be read into string `file-Name` and associated with stream `ins`. The function call `fileName.c_str()` converts the string in `fileName` to a C-style string, which has a different format than a C++ string. The `open` statement has a C-style string (see Section 9.9) as its argument.

## EXERCISES FOR SECTION 8.2

### Self-Check

1. The next character to extract in the stream below is the letter e:

   ```
   This is a text file!<nwln>It has two lines.<nwln><eof>
                                    ↑
   ```

   Examine the file copy program shown in Listing 8.3 and provide a complete, step-by-step description of the completion of the processing of this line.

2. What is the purpose of the `close` function, the `open` function, and the `eof` function?

3. What are some of the advantages to having external (permanent) storage files in which to store program input and output?

### Programming

1. Rewrite the program shown in Listing 8.2 (counting the number of characters in a line and lines in a stream) to read from an external file named `MyData.txt` (rather than from the keyboard). Also, display the total number of characters in the file including the newline characters.

2. Rewrite the copy program shown in Listing 8.3 as a reusable function component with two arguments—specifically, the input and output file streams. The function should return an integer indicating the number of lines copied (0, if the input file is empty).

3. List the changes needed in Listing 8.3 to enable the user to type in the file name.

# 8.3  Using External Files for Communication between Programs

The following case study shows how one program can communicate with another using an intermediate disk file. If one program writes its output to a disk file rather than to the screen, a second program may use this output file as its own data file.

*case study*   **Preparing a Payroll File**

### PROBLEM STATEMENT

You've been asked to write two programs for processing the company payroll. The first program reads a data file consisting of employee salary data. The data for each employee is stored in a single data record containing the employee's first and last names, hours worked, and hourly rate, as shown next for a file consisting of three data records:

```
Jim Baxter       35.5    7.25<nwln>
Adrian Cybriwsky   40.0   6.50<nwln>
Ayisha Mertens     20.0   8.00<nwln><eof>
```

The first program reads the input for each employee and computes the employee's gross salary as the product of the hours worked and the hourly pay rate. Next, it writes the employee's name and gross salary to an output file and accumulates the gross salary amount in the total company payroll. After processing all employees, it displays the total payroll. Processing the sample input file above would create the sample output file:

```
Jim Baxter $257.38<nwln>
Adrian Cybriwsky $260.00<nwln>
Ayisha Mertens $160.00<nwln><eof>
```

The second program reads the file above as its data file and prints payroll checks based on its contents. For example, the first check issued should be a check for $257.38 made out to Jim Baxter.

### PROBLEM ANALYSIS

We'll write the first program now and leave the second one as Programming Project 1 at the end of this chapter. As already explained, our program reads each employee record, computes the gross salary, and writes the employee's name and salary to the output file. Finally, the gross salary is added to the payroll total.

DATA REQUIREMENTS
**Streams Used**

```
ifstream eds        // employee data information
ofstream pds        // payroll data information
```

**Problem Input (from stream eds)**

for each employee:
```
string firstName
string lastName
float hoursWorked
float hourlyRate
```

**Problem Output (to stream pds)**

for each employee:
```
string firstName
string lastName
float salary
```

**Problem Output (to stream cout)**

```
float totalPayroll       // total company payroll
```

## PROGRAM DESIGN

Function `main` prepares the streams and associated files for input and output. It then calls function `processEmp` to process the data for the company employees and determine the total company payroll amount. After the return from `processEmp`, the function `main` displays the final payroll total. We show the algorithm for function `main` next.

ALGORITHM FOR FUNCTION **main**
1. Prepare streams and associated files for processing.

2. Process all employees and compute payroll total.

3. Display the payroll total.

## ANALYSIS AND DESIGN FOR `processEmp`

Function `processEmp` reads each employee's data record from the input file and writes a corresponding output record to the output file. The function interface and algorithm follow.

INTERFACE FOR **processEmp**

**Input Arguments**

```
ifstream eds        // input stream - employee data stream
ofstream pds        // output stream - payroll data stream
```

**Output Arguments**

(none)

*Function Return Value*

```
float totalPayroll       // total company payroll
```

ALGORITHM FOR **processEmp**

1. Initialize payroll total to 0.0.

2. While there are more employees

   **2.1.** Read employee's first and last names and salary data from eds.

   **2.2.** Compute employee's salary.

   **2.3.** Write employee's first and last names and salary to pds; add it to payroll total.

## IMPLEMENTATION

We show the C++ code for function main in Listing 8.4. Only the three streams cout, eds (employee data stream), and pds (payroll data stream) and the total payroll variable need to be visible in this function. The individual employee data (first and last name, hours worked, hourly rate, and salary) will be used exclusively in processEmp and therefore are not declared until needed. Function main has no need to know this information.

Listing 8.5 shows function processEmp. We declare variables first-Name, hours, rate, and salary as local variables in processEmp because they are referenced only in processEmp. Notice that the lines

```
eds >> firstName >> lastName >> hours >> rate;
```

and

```
pds << firstName << " " << lastName
    << " " << salary << endl;
```

are written in exactly the same form that we've been using since Chapter 2 for doing stream I/O with streams cin and cout. We simply changed the names of the streams to eds and pds.

**Listing 8.4** Creating a payroll file (function `main`)

```cpp
// File: payrollFile.cpp
// Creates a company employee payroll file
//     computes total company payroll amount

#include <fstream>    // required for file streams
#include <cstdlib>    // for definition of EXIT_FAILURE
using namespace std;

// Associate streams with external file names
#define inFile "EmpFile.txt"   // employee file
#define outFile "Salary.txt"   // payroll file

// Functions used  . . .
// PROCESS ALL EMPLOYEES AND COMPUTE TOTAL
float processEmp(ifstream&, ofstream&);

int main()
{
   ifstream eds;        // input: employee data stream
   ofstream pds;        // output: payroll data stream
   float totalPayroll;  // output: total payroll

   // Prepare files.
   eds.open(inFile);
   if (eds.fail ())
   {
      cerr << "*** ERROR: Cannot open " << inFile
           << " for input." << endl;
      return EXIT_FAILURE;  // failure return
   }

   pds.open(outFile);
   if (pds.fail())
   {
      cerr << "***ERROR: Cannot open " << outFile
           << " for output." << endl;
      eds.close();
      return EXIT_FAILURE;  // failure return
   }

   // Process all employees and compute total payroll.
   totalPayroll = processEmp(eds, pds);
```

(continued)

**Listing 8.4** Creating a payroll file (function `main`) (continued)

```
        // Display result.
        cout << "Total payroll is $" << totalPayroll << endl;

        // Close files.
        eds.close();
        pds.close();

        return 0;
    }
    // Insert processEmp here.


    Total payroll is $677.38
```

## TESTING

For the sample data file shown in the problem statement, function `processEmp` would create the output file also shown in the problem statement. After the return from `processEmp`, the main function would display the line

```
    Total payroll is $677.38
```

Before you run this program, type in the data file using an editor and save it in the same directory as your program. Make sure you press the RETURN key after typing the last line.

**Listing 8.5** Implementation of `processEmp`

```
// File: payroll.cpp
// Process all employees and compute total payroll amount
// Pre:  eds and pds are prepared for input/output.
// Post: Employee names and salaries are written from eds to pds
//       and the sum of their salaries is returned.
// Returns: Total company payroll
float processEmp
    (ifstream& eds,     // IN: employee file stream
     ofstream& pds)     // IN: payroll file stream
{
    string firstName;   // input: employee first name
    string lastName;    // input: employee last name
    float hours;        // input: hours worked
```

(continued)

Listing 8.5   Implementation of `processEmp` (continued)

```
    float rate;          // input: hourly rate
    float salary;        // output: gross salary
    float payroll;       // return value - total company payroll

    payroll = 0.0;
    // Read first employee's data record.
    eds >> firstName >> lastName >> hours >> rate;
    while (!eds.eof())
    {
       salary = hours * rate;
       pds << firstName << " " << lastName
           << " " << salary << endl;
       payroll += salary;
       // Read next employee's data record.
       eds >> firstName >> lastName >> hours >> rate;
    }  // end while

    return payroll;
}  // end processEmp
```

## EXERCISES FOR SECTION 8.3

### Self-Check

1. In the payroll program:

   **a.** What would be the effect, if any, of leading blanks in an employee record (see Listing 8.5)?

   **b.** What would be the effect of blank lines (empty data records)?

2. Write a statement that reads the information in the record below from stream `eds` into string variables `first` and `last` and float variables `hours` and `rate`.

   ```
   Karina Haavik     30.0     7.75<nwln>
   ```

3. Show how you could use the `getline` function and the extraction operator to read the employee's data when that data is written on two lines.

   ```
   Karina Haavik<nwln>
   30.0     7.75<nwln>
   ```

Programming

1. Write a program that reads from file `Salary.txt` produced by the payroll program and displays the total salary for all employees and their average salary.

2. Modify function `processEmp` to count the number of records processed and to return this value as well as the total payroll. Return both values through output parameters.

# 8.4   More on Reading String Data

Each employee in the employee data file has a first name and a last name. If we want to allow more flexibility (for example, a middle initial or middle name), we can use the `getline` function first introduced in Section 3.7 to read the entire name and store it in a string object. To do this correctly, we need to separate the employee name from the rest of the data in the employee record. We show a modified data file next that uses the pound character '#' to mark the end of each employee name:

```
Jim Andrew Baxter#      35.5    7.25<nwln>
Adrian Cybriwsky#       40.0    6.50<nwln>
Ayisha W. Mertens#      20.0    8.00<nwln><eof>
```

We can identify the pound character as a string delimiter symbol by passing it as the third argument in a call to function `getline`. The statement

```
getline(eds, name, '#');   // # is string delimiter
```

extracts from input stream `eds` a sequence of characters ending with # and stores all characters except the # in string object `name`.

## Using **ignore** to Advance Past the Newline Character

Often we use the `getline` function to extract a sequence of characters up to and including a newline character. However, remember that `getline` does not skip leading white space, so if a newline character is encountered at the beginning of the characters to be extracted, `getline` will stop immediately and won't perform the expected task.

This can happen when both the extraction operator and the `getline` function are used to extract data from the same input stream. To illustrate, let's consider putting each employee's data on two lines instead of using # as a delimiter character after the name:

```
Jim Andrew Baxter<nwln>
35.5    7.25<nwln>
Adrian Cybriwsky<nwln>
40.0    6.50<nwln>
Ayisha W. Mertens<nwln>
20.0    8.00<nwln><eof>
```

We can use the next `while` loop to read and process all records of this file. For each employee, it reads the contents of the first line into string object `name` and the contents of the second line into variables `hours` and `rate`. Loop exit occurs when the end of the data file is reached.

```
payroll = 0.0;

// Get name of first employee.
getline(eds, name);
while (!eds.eof())
{
    // Get current employee salary data.
    eds >> hours >> rate;
    salary = hours * rate;
    pds << name << " " << salary << endl;
    payroll += salary;

    // Get name of next employee.
    getline(eds, name);
}   // end while
```

Given our six-line data sample, the first call to `getline` reads the first employee's name. Executing the first input statement in the loop

```
eds >> hours >> rate;
```

advances the input stream buffer pointer for stream `eds` to the `<nwln>` character at the end of the second line:

```
35.5    7.25<nwln>
            ↑
```

**null string**
An empty string containing zero characters.

If we leave the input stream buffer pointer here, the next call to `getline` (to extract the second employee's name) would process just the `<nwln>` without reading any characters into string object `name`. The **null string**—an empty string containing zero characters—would be stored in `name`.

At this point, the next character in the stream would be the first letter of an employee's name (the `A` in `Adrian`). The next input statement to execute

Table 8.2   Functions `getline` and `ignore`

| | |
|---|---|
| `getline(istream& ins, string& str)` | Reads all characters from input stream `ins` up to the first newline into string `str`. The newline character is extracted but not stored. |
| `getline(istream& ins, string& str, char delimiter)` | Reads all characters from input stream `ins` up to the first occurrence of `delimitor` into string `str`. The character is extracted but not stored. |
| `ins.ignore(int n, char delimiter)` | Extract (but do not store) up to n characters from stream `ins` through the first occurrence of the `deliminator` character. If the `delimitor` is one of the first n characters, it will be extracted but not stored. |

```
eds >> hours >> rate;
```

attempts to read a number into `hours` and into `rate`. Because the next character to read is the letter A, each read operation terminates immediately. The value of `hours` and `rate` are undefined, so an output record with an empty name and meaningless payroll data will be written to the output file.

One way to skip the newline character and avoid this problem is to use the `fstream` function `ignore` just before the call to `getline` in the `while` loop:

```
// Get name of next employee.
eds.ignore(100, '\n');   // skip through first '\n'
getline(eds, name);
```

This call to the `ignore` function skips up to 100 characters in the specified stream (`eds`) until the character argument `'\n'` is encountered. The character argument is also extracted and ignored. The `ignore` acts like an input operation except it does not store the characters extracted from the stream. Table 8.2 summarizes the functions `getline` and `ignore`.

## EXERCISES FOR SECTION 8.4

### Self-Check

1. Change `processEmp` (Listing 8.5) to write the name and salary for a given employee on separate lines. Explain the changes that have to be made.

2. Explain the differences between using the input operator `>>` and function `getline` to read string data.

3. Explain the effect of the statement

```
eds.ignore(80, '*');
```

4. If we use `getline(eds, name, '#')` in `processEmp` (Listing 8.5) to read an employee's name:

   a. What would be the effect, if any, of trailing blanks and the `<nwln>` character at the end of an employee data record in the input stream?

   b. What would be the effect, if any, of leading blanks in an employee record in the input stream?

Programming

1. Write a function `skipNewline` that reads one character at a time in the designated stream up to and including the next newline (if any), and then leaves the stream pointer at the first character in the stream after the newline. Function `skipNewline` should require only one argument—the stream for which the skip operation is to be carried out.

2. Write a function `compress` that removes all white space (blanks and newline characters) from a file. Function `compress` should have two arguments, the input file and the output file.

## 8.5   Input/Output Manipulators

Section 5.3 described the input/output manipulator `setw`, which controls the width of an output field. Earlier, we introduced an additional manipulator, `endl`, which is used to insert the newline character into an output stream. In this section, we complete the discussion of I/O manipulators by introducing three other manipulators: `setprecision`, `fixed`, and `showpoint`. The manipulators are defined in libraries `iostream` and `iomanip`.

### EXAMPLE 8.7

The next output statement uses three manipulators to control the appearance of **x** (type `float`).

```
cout << "The value of x is "
     << fixed
     << showpoint
     << setprecision(4) << x << endl;
```

The manipulator **fixed** causes real numbers to be displayed in decimal rather than scientific notation. The manipulator **showpoint** ensures that the decimal point will always appear (even for whole numbers) and that trailing zeros will be shown. The manipulator `setprecision(4)` sets the precision to four decimal places. These manipulators remain in effect (until changed) for future output statements.

Next we show how the earlier output statement would display some sample values of x. Notice that all the numbers have a decimal point followed by four digits.

```
The value of x is 3.4500
The value of x is 67.1234
The value of x is -1.0000
The value of x is 567890.5123
```

Table 8.3 shows some of the manipulators. To use `setw` and `setprecision`, you need to include library `iomanip`. To use the others, you need to include library `iostream`. The last pair of manipulators, `skipws` and `noskipws`, affects input operations only.

The manipulator `left` changes justification from right-justification (the default) to left-justification. Often, it is preferable to display strings left-justified in a field. After displaying the string, the manipulator `right` should be used to reset justification to the default.

**Table 8.3**   Input/Output Manipulators

| | |
|---|---|
| `setw(int n)` | Sets the width of the next output value only to the argument. After output, the width returns to the default of 0. |
| `setprecision(int n)` | Sets the precision to the argument. The default is 6. |
| `boolalpha` | Enables `false` and `true` to be extracted from an input stream or inserted into an output stream as values of type `bool` variables. The default is to use 0 for false and 1 for true. |
| `noboolalpha` | Resets `bool` input/output to the default values (0 and 1). |
| `fixed` | Causes all floating-point numbers to be displayed in decimal notation. |
| `scientific` | Causes all floating-point numbers to be displayed in scientific notation. |
| `showpoint` | Causes a decimal point to always be displayed. |
| `noshowpoint` | A decimal point may not be displayed for whole numbers. |
| `left` | Left-adjust output in field. |
| `right` | Right-adjust output in field (the default). |
| `skipws` | Skip white space on input (the default). |
| `noskipws` | Don't skip white space on input. |

## EXERCISES FOR SECTION 8.5

Self-Check

1. Show the effect of executing the output statement

   ```
   cout << fixed << showpoint << setprecision(2)
        << setw(10) << 15.9853
        << setw(10) << 13.45 << endl;
   ```

2. How would the output for Self-Check Exercise 1 change if manipulator `scientific` were used instead of `fixed`?

3. Show the effect of executing the output statement

   ```
   cout << setw(10) << left << "Jane"
        << setw(10) << right << "Doe" << endl;
   ```

   How many blanks would appear between the two strings?

4. Answer Self-Check Exercise 3 with the words `left` and `right` transposed.

Programming

1. Write a program fragment that displays the table below. Left-align each column heading with the columns of numbers that follow. Leave 10 spaces between the column headings.

   ```
   n          n x n
   1          1
   2          4
   3          9
   .  .  .
   12         144
   ```

# 8.6   Common Programming Errors

When you first start using external files, there are many opportunities for error. The operating system must be able to connect an external file to its associated input stream. Your program must be able to correctly determine when all the data in a file have been read. We discuss some common errors next.

- *Connecting streams and external files:* To use an external file in your program, you first must declare a stream object and establish a connection between the file name as it is known to the operating system and the name of the stream object in your program. In C++, you establish this connection with function open. Once you establish this connection, use the stream name in all references to the file in your program. Normally, you won't receive a compiler or an execution-time diagnostic if a call to the open function fails to open a file successfully. For this reason, use function fail to verify that function open did its job. If the operating system was unable to find the file you were trying to connect to stream ins, the function call ins.fail() will return true.

- *Using input and output streams incorrectly:* Always be careful to prefix each call to a file processing function with the correct stream name. For example, using an output stream name with a file input operation such as get will cause a compiler error message such as "Get is not a member of ofstream". This message indicates that you've incorrectly tried to use the get function with an output file stream.

- *Reading past the end of a file:* An execution time error such as "attempt to read beyond end of file" will occur if a read operation is performed after all data in a file have been processed. The most likely cause for such an error is a loop that executes once too often.

- *Matching data in an input stream to input data stores:* Make sure that the order and type of the data stores (objects and variables) listed after the extraction >> operators are consistent with the order and type of the data in the specified stream. Usually you won't get a run-time error because of data inconsistencies. Instead, incorrect and sometimes undefined information will be stored. When debugging and testing a program, start by echo-printing the values stored in input variables to verify that your test data was read correctly. Remember that any character (not just white space) that's not a valid numeric character will terminate the reading of a numeric input value. The numeric value of the characters read to that point will be stored. If no characters were read, the value stored is undefined.

- *White space and input:* For all input involving the extraction operator, leading white space is ignored—even when reading a single character or character string. If your program requires that white space be treated as any other character, use function get to read a single character at a time. Trailing white space also terminates the extraction of characters for strings and for numeric data. You can read a string that contains white space by using the member function getline. However, you must use some character (often the newline) to mark the end of the string to be extracted.

- *Proper handling of the newline character during input:* When reading character or string data mixed with numeric data, you must make sure that you handle the newline character properly. Often, you must use the ignore function to skip over a newline character at the end of a number before reading a string that ends with a newline.

■ *Input/output settings:* Most format settings will remain set in a particular state until changed. However, the field width setting always reverts back to your system default value (usually 0) if it is not set again prior to the input or output of the next data element. When this occurs, data elements may be inserted into an output stream with no separating blanks and will be hard to read.

## Chapter Review

1. Function `get` is used to extract characters from an input stream and function `put` to insert characters into an output stream. Unlike the extraction operator >>, the `get` function does not skip white space.

2. The operating system keeps a directory of all external files associated with your computer. These files are known to the system by an external file name.

3. The C++ `iostream` library function `open` establishes a connection between the external file name and the name of the stream to be processed by your program.

4. Input streams should be declared as type `ifstream` objects and output streams as type `ofstream` objects.

5. The `eof` function can be used to test for the end of a stream and the `close` function to disconnect an external file from its associated stream.

6. The newline character breaks a stream into a sequence of lines. Be especially careful reading string data when the string delimiter is the newline character. In this case, leading newline characters won't be skipped but will terminate data entry. Use the `ignore` function to skip over a leading newline character. You can also pass a third argument to the `endline` function if you want to use a different character as a string delimiter.

7. The input/output manipulators in Table 8.3 are used to control the format or appearance of displayed output.

## Summary of New C++ Constructs

| Construct | Effect |
| --- | --- |
| **Stream Declarations**<br>`ifstream ins;`<br>`ofstream outs;` | Declares `ins` and `outs` as stream variables. |
| **open, fail, and close operations on Data File Streams**<br>`ins.open(inData);` | Establishes the connection between the external file named `inData` and the stream `ins`. |
| `if (ins.fail())`<br>`{`<br>`    cerr << "Oops! " << endl;`<br>`    return EXIT_FAILURE;`<br>`}` | Displays an error message and returns immediately if the open operation failed. |
| `ins.close();` | Closes or disconnects stream `ins`. |
| **Input/Output with get, put, getline, and ignore**<br>`ins.get(ch);`<br>`ins >> i;` | Gets the next character from the stream `ins`.<br>The next integer is read from file `ins` as a string of characters, then converted to a binary number and stored in `i`. |
| `outs.put(ch);`<br>`outs << i;` | Puts the character in `ch` to the stream `outs`, followed by a sequence of characters representing the value of `i`. |
| `ins.ignore(80, '\n');` | Extracts and skips up to 80 characters in input stream `ins` up to and including the first occurrence of the delimiter `'\n'`. |
| `getline(ins, name);` | Extracts the characters in input stream `ins` through the next newline and stores all characters except the newline in `name`. |
| `getline(ins, name, '#');` | Extracts the characters in input stream `ins` through the next character # and stores all characters except the # in `name`. |
| **End-of-File Function**<br>`ins.get(ch);`<br>`while (!ins.eof())`<br>`{`<br>`    outs.put(ch);`<br>`    ins.get(ch);`<br>`}` | Data characters are read from stream `ins` and written to stream `outs` until the end of the stream is reached. |

## Quick-Check Exercises

1. The statement

   _____._____(_____);

   associates external file `data.txt` with stream `ins`.

2. Write a condition that's true when the operation described above for stream `ins` does not succeed.

3. The _____ character separates a stream into lines.

4. When would you use `getline` to read a string from a stream rather than the extraction operator `>>` ?

5. What function often needs to be called after `getline` and why?

6. Correct the C++ program segment shown below. Explain the changes you make.

   ```
   while (!ins.eof())
   {
       ins.get(ch);
       outs.put(ch);
   }
   ```

7. What does the symbol `endl` represent? What do we call this symbol in C++? Where is it defined?

8. Write a call to function `getline` that extracts up to 60 characters from stream `ins` or all characters through the first `*` character.

9. Write an output statement that displays the value of x right-justified in a field of width `10`, in decimal notation with four decimal places of precision.

10. If `x` has the value `34.567`, show how `x` would be displayed by the statement:

    ```
    outs << fixed << setprecision(2) << x << "*"
         << scientific << x << endl;
    ```

11. What error could occur if you forget to close an output file?

## Answers to Quick-Check Exercises

1. `ins.open("data.txt");`

2. `(ins.fail())`

3. newline or `'\n'`

4. You'd use `getline` when the string may contain an embedded blank.

5. If the next item to be read is a string, you need to call function `ignore` to advance past the newline character.

6. 
```
ins.get( ...);
while (!ins.eof())
{
    outs.put( ...);
    ins.get( ...);
}
```

The original version will attempt to insert a character into the stream `outs` even after the end of file has been encountered (and there are no more characters to be processed). There will be two copies of the last character read.

7. `endl` represents the newline character; it is a manipulator defined in library `iostream`.

8. `getline(ins, 60, '*');`

9. 
```
cout << setw(10) << fixed << showpoint
        << right << setprecision(4) << x << endl;
```

10. `34.57*3.46e+01`

11. The information in the output buffer may not be appended to the end of the output file, so the output file may be incomplete.

## Review Questions

1. List three advantages to using files for input and output as opposed to the standard input and output you've used so far in this course.

2. Explain how `get` and `cin` differ in reading data items from a stream.

3. **a.** Explain why there are usually three distinct names associated with a file.

   **b.** What conventions are followed for choosing each name?

   **c.** What does the name appearing in a program represent?

   **d.** Which name appears in the stream variable declaration?

   **e.** Which name is known to the operating system?

4. Let `x` and `y` be type `float`, `m` and `n` type `int`, `ch1` and `ch2` type `char`, and `str` type `string`. Show the final contents of each variable affected by the input operations below. Indicate any errors that might occur when the statements in each part execute. Assume that the input stream pointer is reset to the first input character before each part executes.

   ```
   345.27  wxyz <nwln>
   50   40<nwln>
   ```

    **a.** `ins >> x >> y >> ch1 >> ch2 >> str;`
       `ins >> x >> m >> n;`

    **b.** `ins >> m >> n >> x >> ch1 >> ch2 >> str;`

    **c.** `ins >> x >> y >> str;`
       `ins >> m >> ch1 >> n >> ch2 >> str;`

    **d.** `ins >> m >> n >> x >> str;`

5. Write a loop that reads up to ten integer values from a data file and displays them on the screen. If there are not ten integers in the file, the message `"That's all, folks"` should be displayed after the last number.

6. Write a function that copies several data lines typed at the keyboard to an external file. The copy process should be terminated when the user enters an empty line (indicated by two consecutive newlines).

7. Explain how the following manipulators format output data.

    **a.** The manipulator `right` when inserting a string of length 6 in a field of size 20

    **b.** The manipulator `noshowpoint` when inserting a floating-point value such as `65.0` into an output stream

    **c.** The manipulator `setprecision(5)` when inserting a floating-point value such as `25.635248` into an output stream

    **d.** The manipulator `setw` when inserting an integer value such as `250` into a field of width 8 in an output stream

    **e.** The manipulator `scientific` when inserting a floating-point value such as `25000143.6352` into an output stream

## Programming Projects

1. Write a program system that prints payroll checks using the file produced by the payroll program described in Section 8.3. The format of the checks should be similar to the one shown in Figure 8.2.

2. Each year the state legislature rates the productivity of the faculty of each of the state-supported colleges and universities. The rating is based on reports submitted by the faculty members indicating the average number of hours worked per week during the school year. Each faculty member is rated, and the university receives an overall rating. The faculty productivity ratings are computed as follows:

    **a.** Highly productive means over 55 hours per week reported.

    **b.** Satisfactory means reported hours per week are between 35 and 55.

```
Temple University                    Check No. 12372
Philadelphia, PA                     Date: 03-17-03


Pay to the
Order of:   William Cosby        $    20000.00


                                     Jane Smith
```

**Figure 8.2**   Format of check for Programming Project 1

c. Overpaid means reported hours per week are less than 35.

Read the following data from a data file:

| Name | Hours |
|------|-------|
| Herm | 63 |
| Flo | 37 |
| Jake | 20 |
| Maureen | 55 |
| Saul | 72 |
| Tony | 40 |
| Al | 12 |

Your program should include functions corresponding to the function prototypes shown below as part of your solution.

```
// Displays table heading
void printHeader();

   // Displays productivity ranking given hours worked
void displayProductivity
  (float); // IN: hours worked per week

// Reads and displays one faculty name from a data stream file
void processName
  (ifstream&);  // IN: stream of names and hours worked

// Reads data lines from file facHours and displays body
//    of table. returns number of faculty and sum of hours
//    worked.
// Uses: processName and displayProductivity.
void processData
  (ifstream&,    // IN: stream containing names and hours
   int&,         // INOUT: count of number of faculty
   float&);      // INOUT: sum of hours worked by faculty
```

3. Write a program system that reads several lines of information from a data file and prints each word of the file on a separate line of an output file followed by the number of letters in that word. Also print a count of words in the file on the screen when done. Assume that words are separated by one or more blanks. Reuse as many functions introduced in the text or in the C++ library as possible.

4. Compute the monthly payment and the total payment for a bank loan, given the following:

   **a.** Amount of loan

   **b.** Duration of loan in months

   **c.** Interest rate for loan

   Your program should read in one loan at a time, perform the required computation, and print the values of the monthly payment and the total payment.

   Test your program with at least the following data (and more if you want).

   | Loan | Months | Rate |
   | --- | --- | --- |
   | 16000 | 300 | 6.50 |
   | 24000 | 360 | 5.25 |
   | 30000 | 300 | 5.0 |
   | 42000 | 360 | 5.0 |
   | 22000 | 300 | 4.5 |
   | 100000 | 360 | 4.25 |

   Hints:

   **a.** The formula for computing a monthly payment is

   $$monthlyPay = \frac{ratem \times expm^{months} \times loan}{expm^{months} - 1.0},$$

   where

   ```
   ratem = rate / 1200.0,
   expm = (1.0 + ratem).
   ```

   **b.** The formula for computing the total payment is

   ```
   total = monthlyPay * months.
   ```

   Use type `double` data for all calculations.

**5.** Use your solution to Programming Project 4 as the basis for writing a program that will write a data file containing a table of the following form:

Loan Amount: $1000

| Interest rate | Duration (years) | Monthly payment | Total payment |
|---|---|---|---|

The output file produced by your program should contain payment information on a $1000 loan for interest rates from 4 percent to 7 percent with increments of 0.25 percent. The loan durations should be 20, 25, and 30 years.

**6.** Whatsamata U. offers a service to its faculty in computing grades at the end of each semester. A program will process three weighted test scores and will calculate a student's average and letter grade (A is 90 to 100, a B is 80 to 89, etc.). It will read the student data from a file and write each student's ID, test score, average, and grade to an output file.

Write a program system to provide this valuable service. The data will consist of the three test weights followed by three test scores and a student ID number (four digits) for each student. Calculate the weighted average for each student and the corresponding grade. This information should be printed along with the initial three test scores. The weighted average for each student is equal to

$$\texttt{weight1} \times \texttt{score1} + \texttt{weight2} \times \texttt{score2} + \texttt{weight3} \times \texttt{score3}$$

For summary statistics, print the "highest weighted average," "lowest weighted average," "average of the weighted averages," and "total number of students processed." Sample data:

```
0.35   0.25   0.40          (test weights)
100    76     88    1014    (test scores and ID)
```

**7.** Write a program to read in a string of characters that represent a Roman numeral and then convert it to Arabic form (an integer). The character values for Roman numerals are as follows:

M  1000
D   500
C   100
L   50

X   10

V   5

I   1

Test your program with the following data: LXXXVII (87), CCXIX (219), MCCCLIV (1354), MMDCLXXIII (2673), MCDLXXVI (1476).

8. Because text files can grow very large, some computer systems supply a handy utility program that displays the head and tail of a file where the head is the first four lines and the tail is the last four lines. Write a program that asks the user to type in a file name and then displays the head of the file, a line of dots (three or four dots will do), and the tail of the file. If the file is eight lines long or less, just display the entire file.

9. Write a program to manage a dictionary. Your dictionary should be stored on a text file named `diction.txt` and consist of an alphabetized list of words, one per line. When a user enters a word, scan the dictionary looking for the word. If the word is in the dictionary, say so. If not, display the dictionary word immediately preceding and the word immediately following so the user can see words that are close in spelling. Then ask whether the user wants to add this new word to the dictionary. If the answer is yes, do so and go back to request the next word.

   To insert a word into a file in alphabetical order, simply copy the file to a new, temporary file named `diction.tmp` and move words one at a time from this temporary file back to the original file, inserting the new word when you reach its correct position alphabetically.

10. Write a program that reads two input files whose lines are ordered by a key data field. Your program should merge these two files, writing an output file that contains all lines from both files ordered by the same key field. As an example, if two input files contain student names and grades for a particular class ordered by name, merge the information as shown below.

| File 1 | File 2 | Output file |
|---|---|---|
| Adams  C | Barnes  A | Adams  C |
| Jones  D | Johnson  C | Barnes  A |
| King  B | | Johnson  C |
| | | Jones  D |
| | | King  B |

You must read one line of a file at a time and either write it or the last line read from the other data file to the output file. A common merge algorithm is the following:

```
Read a line from each data file
While the end of both files has not been reached
    If the line from file 1 is smaller than the line from file 2
        Write the line from file 1 to the output file and read a new
        line from file 1.
    Else
        Write the line from file 2 to the output file and read a new
        line from file 2.

Write the remaining lines (if any) from file 1 to the output file.
Write the remaining lines (if any) from file 2 to the output file.
```

# Anita Borg

*Dr. Anita Borg was a computer science pioneer who made it her goal to revolutionize both the world of technology and women's role in it. She was the founding director of the Institute for Women and Technology, an organization whose mission is to increase the impact of women on all aspects of technology and to increase the positive impact of technology on the lives of the world's women. She also created Systers, one of the oldest global electronic networks of women in computer science, and co-founded the Grace Hopper Celebration of Women in Computing, a prestigious conference for women in the computer science field. In 1999, President Clinton appointed her to the Commission of the Advancement of Women and Minorities in Science, Engineering, and Technology (CAWMSET), and in 2002 she received the Heinz Award for Technology, the Economy and Employment.*

*Anita Borg died in April 2003, as this book was being prepared for publication. We were honored to have this inspirational computer scientist contribute an interview to this book's previous edition in 1999, and that interview is included here.*

**Why did you decide to study computer science, and how did you become interested in the field?**

I started as a math major in college, and I later taught myself COBOL from program instruction manuals. Then I went back to school and majored in computer science, and just got completely hooked. I loved the problem solving and the challenge. I loved figuring out how to make these contraptions do what I wanted them to do.

**What was your first job in the industry and what did it entail?**

My very first job, in 1969, was writing some simple programs for an insurance company. Once I was out of graduate school, I worked for a startup, where I was the lead designer of a fault-tolerant version of the UNIX operating system.

**What kind of projects are you doing for the Institute for Women and Technology?**

One project is a partnership with MIT, Purdue, Texas A&M, and Santa Clara University, where interdisciplinary groups of students and faculty develop technology projects based on ideas that come out of workshops with nontechnical women in the local community, brainstorming about ways in which technology could have a positive impact on their families and communities. One of the ideas is a family scheduler that helps coordinate all members of the family.

**What is a typical day like for you?**

Running an organization is a very busy thing. I spend my time between writing and communicating with people, either on the phone or via e-mail. I probably give two talks a week. This fall I've been traveling. I give speeches, hold meetings, and find out what women in other countries are doing. For instance, the Third World Organization for Women in Science brought 300 female scientists and engineers from 60 developing countries together to discuss science and technology for sustainable human development. I gave the keynote speech on information technology.

### What do you do as a member of CAWMSET?

We've conducted hearings and collected information and next we will put together a report that will be recommendations to the nation, both to the president and Congress, to the states and to industry about how to improve representation of women and minorities in science.

### What advice do you have for students entering the computer science field?

I think that it is very, very important to get involved in projects that are connected to real needs and to experience what that's like. So, if there's some way to work on something that is not just an abstract problem, where there are real customers and real users, where you can see the reality of this stuff, it's just incredibly valuable.

I envision a transformation from a technology-driven world in which we wind up with solutions in search of problems to one in which we really look at the problems that are out there and let those drive the technology. This definitely is not happening. The technology culture is one in which we train students to talk to and listen to other brilliant technologists. We train them to believe that by talking to other brilliant technologists, they will come up with ideas for projects and research to work on. Most students don't understand that ordinary people have tremendously brilliant ideas for things that they could work on that would then really push the boundaries of technology.

### Besides technical skills, what kind of skills do you think are most important to have for students wanting to go into computer science?

Technical skills are clearly core. However, I think that students should strive for a very broad background, educationally. I think students should study some art, some political science, some sociology, and really try to get as broad a background as they can as undergraduates, because all of that helps them to think. Building an ability to think well in a variety of different disciplines, on a variety of different topics, is really important.

Students should also have a lot of understanding of cultural differences internationally. They should make an effort to get international experience if possible. We are building tools that are at the cutting edge of connecting the entire world; we can't build this stuff in a vacuum.

*chapter nine*

# Data Structures: Arrays and Structs

**Chapter Objectives**

- To learn how to declare and use arrays for storing collections of values of the same type
- To understand how to use a subscript to reference the individual values in an array
- To learn how to process the elements of an array in sequential order using loops
- To learn a method for searching an array
- To learn a method for sorting an array
- To become familiar with Big-O notation for estimating an algorithm's efficiency
- To learn how to declare and use structs to store collections of values of different types
- To understand how to use dot notation to reference the individual values in a struct
- To learn how to use character arrays and C-style strings

SIMPLE DATA TYPES, whether built in (`int`, `float`, `bool`, `char`) or user defined (e.g., enumeration type `day`), use a single variable to store a value. To solve many programming problems, it's more efficient to group data items together in main memory than to allocate a different variable to hold each item. For example, it's easier to write a program that processes exam scores for a class of 100 students if you can store all the scores in one area of memory and can access them as a group. C++ allows a programmer to group such related data items together into a single composite structured variable. Without such a structured variable, we'd have to allocate 100 different variables to hold each individual score. In this chapter, we look at two structured data types: the array and the struct.

# 9.1    The Array Data Type

array
A collection of data items stored under the same name.

array element
Each individual element in an array.

An **array** is a collection of data items associated with a particular name—for example, all the exam scores for a class of students could be associated with the name scores. We can reference each individual item—called an **array element**—in the array. We designate individual elements by using the array name and the element's position, starting with 0 for the first array element. The first element in the array named scores is referred to as scores[0], the second element as scores[1], and the tenth element as scores[9]. In general, the *k*th element in the array is referred to as scores[k-1].

C++ stores an array in consecutive storage locations in main memory, one item per memory cell. We can perform some operations, such as passing the array as an argument to a function, on the whole array. We can also access individual array elements and process them like other simple variables.

## Array Declaration

Arrays in C++ are specified using *array declarations* that specify the type, name, and size of the array:

```
float x[8];
```

C++ associates eight memory cells with the name x. Each element of array x may contain a single floating-point value. Therefore, a total of eight floating-point values may be stored and referenced using the array name x.

### EXAMPLE 9.1

Assume **x** is the array shown in Figure 9.1. Table 9.1 shows some statements that manipulate the elements of this array. Figure 9.2 shows the array after the statements in Table 9.1 execute. Note that only x[2] and x[3] are changed.

| x[0] | x[1] | x[2] | x[3] | x[4] | x[5] | x[6] | x[7] |
|------|------|------|------|------|------|------|------|
| 16.0 | 12.0 | 6.0 | 8.0 | 2.5 | 12.0 | 14.0 | -54.5 |
| First | Second | Third | | ... | | | Eighth |

**Figure 9.1**   Array **x**

**Table 9.1**   Statements that Manipulate Elements of Array **x** in Figure 9.1

| Statement | Explanation |
|-----------|-------------|
| `cout << x[0];` | Displays the value of `x[0]`, or 16.0. |
| `x[3] = 25.0;` | Stores the value 25.0 in `x[3]`. |
| `sum = x[0] + x[1];` | Stores the sum of `x[0]` and `x[1]`, or 28.0, in the variable `sum`. |
| `sum += x[2];` | Adds `x[2]` to `sum`. The new `sum` is 34.0. |
| `x[3] += 1.0;` | Adds 1.0 to `x[3]`. The new `x[3]` is 26.0. |
| `x[2] = x[0] + x[1];` | Stores the sum of `x[0]` and `x[1]` in `x[2]`. The new `x[2]` is 28.0. |

| x[0] | x[1] | x[2] | x[3] | x[4] | x[5] | x[6] | x[7] |
|------|------|------|------|------|------|------|------|
| 16.0 | 12.0 | 28.0 | 26.0 | 2.5 | 12.0 | 14.0 | -54.5 |
| First | Second | Third | | ... | | | Eighth |

**Figure 9.2**   Array **x** after execution of statements in Table 9.1

## EXAMPLE 9.2

The declarations for the plant operations program shown below allocate storage for four arrays, `onVacation`, `vacationDays`, `dayOff`, and `plantHours`.

```
const int NUM_EMP = 10;      // number of employees
bool onVacation[NUM_EMP];
int vacationDays[NUM_EMP];
enum day {sunday, monday, tuesday, wednesday, thursday,
          friday, saturday};
day dayOff[NUM_EMP];
float plantHours[7];
```

The arrays `onVacation` and `vacationDays` (Figure 9.3) have 10 elements, each with subscripts 0 through 9 (value of `NUM_EMP` − 1). Each element of array `onVacation` can store a type `bool` value. The contents of this array indicate which employees are on vacation (`onVacation[i]` is `true` if employee `i` is on vacation). If employees 0, 2, 4, 6, and 8 are on vacation, the array will have the values shown in Figure 9.3. Array `vacationDays` shows the number of vacation days each employee has remaining.

| | onVacation | | vacationDays | | dayOff |
|---|---|---|---|---|---|
| [0] | true | [0] | 10 | [0] | monday |
| [1] | false | [1] | 12 | [1] | wednesday |
| [2] | true | [2] | 3 | [2] | tuesday |
| [3] | false | [3] | 8 | [3] | friday |
| [4] | true | [4] | 15 | [4] | friday |
| [5] | false | [5] | 5 | [5] | monday |
| [6] | true | [6] | 6 | [6] | thursday |
| [7] | false | [7] | 9 | [7] | wednesday |
| [8] | true | [8] | 10 | [8] | tuesday |
| [9] | false | [9] | 15 | [9] | thursday |

**Figure 9.3**    Arrays `onVacation`, `vacationDays`, and `dayOff`

**parallel arrays**
Two or more arrays with the same number of elements used to store related information about a collection of objects.

The array `dayOff` (Figure 9.3) also has 10 elements. Each element stores an enumerator from the enumeration type `day`, and the value of `dayOff[i]` indicates the weekday employee `i` has off. Because the data stored in `onVacation[i]`, `vacationDays[i]`, and `dayOff[i]` relate to the `i`th employee, the three arrays are called **parallel arrays**.

The array `plantHours` (Figure 9.4) has seven elements with subscripts 0 through 6. We can use the subscripts 0 through 6 or the enumeration type `day` to reference these elements. The array element `plantHours[sunday]` (or `plantHours[0]`) indicates how many hours the plant was operating

| | |
|---|---|
| plantHours[sunday] | 0.0 |
| plantHours[monday] | 8.0 |
| plantHours[tuesday] | 16.0 |
| plantHours[wednesday] | 24.0 |
| plantHours[thursday] | 8.0 |
| plantHours[friday] | 16.0 |
| plantHours[saturday] | 0.0 |

**Figure 9.4**    Array `plantHours`

during Sunday of the past week. The array shown in Figure 9.4 indicates that the plant was closed on the weekend, operating single shifts on Monday and Thursday, double shifts on Tuesday and Friday, and a triple shift on Wednesday.

## Array Initialization

The next example shows how to specify the initial contents of an array as part of its declaration.

### EXAMPLE 9.3

The statements below declare and initialize three arrays (see Figure 9.5). The list of initial values for each array is enclosed in braces and follows the assignment operator =. The first array element (subscript 0) stores the first value in each list, the second array element (subscript 1) stores the second value, and so on.

```
const int SIZE = 7;
int scores[SIZE] = {100, 73, 88, 84, 40, 97};
char grades[] = {'A', 'C', 'B', 'B', 'F', 'A'};
char myName[SIZE] = {'F', 'R', 'A', 'N', 'K'};
```

The length of the list of initial values can't exceed the size of the array. If the list contains fewer elements than the array size allows, then the value of any element not initialized is system dependent (indicated by ? in Figure 9.5). If the size of the array is not specified, indicated by an empty pair of brackets [ ], the compiler sets the array size to match the number of elements in the initial value list.

Array scores (size 7)

| 100 | 73 | 88 | 84 | 40 | 97 | ? |
|-----|----|----|----|----|----|---|
| [0] | [1] | [2] | [3] | [4] | [5] | [6] |

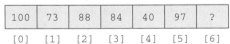

Array grades (size 6)

| 'A' | 'C' | 'B' | 'B' | 'F' | 'A' |
|-----|-----|-----|-----|-----|-----|
| [0] | [1] | [2] | [3] | [4] | [5] |

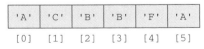

Array myName (size 7)

| 'F' | 'R' | 'A' | 'N' | 'K' | ? | ? |
|-----|-----|-----|-----|-----|---|---|

**Figure 9.5** Initialization of three arrays

## EXAMPLE 9.4

The array declaration

```
string kidNames[] = {"Richard", "Debbie", "Robin",
                     "Shelley", "Dara"};
```

allocates storage for an array of five strings called **kidNames**, storing the string literals shown in the initialization list in this array. The statement

```
cout << kidNames[0] << '/' << kidNames[4] << endl;
```

displays the output line

```
Richard/Dara
```

---

### Array Declaration

**Form:**     *element-type array-name*[ *size* ]**;**
              *element-type array-name*[ *size* ] = { *initialization-list* }**;**

**Example:**  `char myName[5];`
              `float salaries[NUM_EMP];`
              `char vowels[] = {'A', 'E', 'I', 'O', 'U'};`

**Interpretation:** The identifier *array-name* describes a collection of array elements, each of which may be used to store data values of type *element-type*. The *size*, enclosed in brackets, [ ], specifies the number of elements contained in the array. The *size* value must be a constant expression consisting of constant values and constant identifiers. This value must be an integer and must be greater than or equal to 1. There is one array element for each value between 0 and the value *size* –1.

In the initialized array declaration, the *size* in brackets is optional. In this case, the number of values in the *initialization-list* determines the array size. The *initialization-list* consists of constant expressions of type *element-type* separated by commas. Element 0 of the array being initialized is set to the first constant, element 1 to the second, and so on.

---

## Array Subscripts

**array subscript**
A value or expression enclosed in brackets after the array name, specifying which element to access.

**subscripted variable**
A variable followed by a subscript in brackets, designating a particular array element.

To process the data stored in an array, we must be able to access its individual elements. We use the array name (a variable) and the **array subscript** to do this. The array subscript is enclosed in brackets after the array name and selects a particular array element for processing. For example, if x is the array with eight elements shown earlier in Figure 9.2 and repeated below, then the **subscripted variable** x[0] (read as "x sub 0") references the first element of the array x, x[1] the second element, and x[7] the eighth element. The number enclosed in brackets is the array subscript.

| x[0] | x[1] | x[2] | x[3] | x[4] | x[5] | x[6] | x[7] |
|------|------|------|------|------|------|------|------|
| 16.0 | 12.0 | 28.0 | 26.0 | 2.5 | 12.0 | 14.0 | -54.5 |
| First element | Second element | Third element | | . . . | | | Eighth element |

Understanding the difference between an array subscript value and an array element value is key. The subscripted variable x[i] references a particular element of array x. If i has the value 0, the subscript value is 0, and x[0] is referenced. The value of x[i] in this case is 16.0. If i has the value 2, the subscript value is 2, and the value of x[i] is 28.0.

A subscript can be an expression of any integral type (int, long, short, char, or an enumeration type). However, to create a valid reference, the value of this subscript must be between 0 and one less than the array size. If i has the value 8, the subscript value is 8, and we can't predict the value of x[i] because the subscript value is out of the allowable range.

## EXAMPLE 9.5

Table 9.2 shows some simple statements involving the array x shown above and in Figure 9.2. In these statements, i is assumed to be type int with value 5. Make sure you understand each statement. The two attempts to display element x[10], which is not in the array, may result in a run-time error, but they're more likely to display incorrect results.

The last cout line in Table 9.2 uses int(x[4]) as a subscript expression. Because this evaluates to 2, the value of x[2] (*not* x[4]) is displayed. If the value of int(x[4]) were outside the range 0 through 7, its use as a subscript expression would reference a memory cell outside the array.

Two different subscripts are used in each of the three assignment statements at the bottom of the table. The first assignment statement copies the value of x[6] to x[5] (subscripts i+1 and i); the second assignment statement copies the value of x[5] to x[4] (subscripts i-1 and i). The last assignment statement causes a syntax error because there is an expression to the left of the assignment operator.

---

**Array Subscript**

**Form:**      *name*[ *subscript* ]

**Example:**   x[ 3*i-2 ]

**Interpretation:** The *subscript* must be an integral expression. Each time a subscripted variable is encountered in a program, the *subscript* is evaluated and its value determines which element of array *name* is referenced. The *subscript* value should be between the range 0 and one less than the array size (inclusive). If the *subscript* value is outside this range, a memory cell outside the array will be referenced.

**Table 9.2**    Some Simple Statements Referencing Array x in Figure 9.2

| Statement | Effect |
|---|---|
| `cout << 3 << ' ' << x[3];` | Displays 3 and 26.0 (value of x[3]). |
| `cout << i << ' ' << x[i];` | Displays 5 and 12.0 (value of x[5]). |
| `cout << x[i] + 1;` | Displays 13.0 (value of 12.0 + 1). |
| `cout << x[i] + i;` | Displays 17.0 (value of 12.0 + 5). |
| `cout << x[i+1];` | Displays 14.0 (value of x[6]). |
| `cout << x[i+i];` | Value in x[10] is undefined. |
| `cout << x[2*i];` | Value in x[10] is undefined. |
| `cout << x[2*i-3];` | Displays −54.5 (value of x[7]). |
| `cout << x[(int(x[4])];` | Displays 28.0 (value of x[2]). |
| `x[i] = x[i+1];` | Assigns 14.0 (value of x[6]) to x[5]. |
| `x[i-1] = x[i];` | Assigns 14.0 (new value of x[5]) to x[4]. |
| `x[i] - 1 = x[i-1];` | Illegal assignment statement. Left side of an assignment operator must be a variable. |

## EXERCISES FOR SECTION 9.1

### Self-Check

1. What is the difference between the expressions x3 and x[3]?

2. For the following declarations, how many memory cells are reserved for data and what type of data can be stored there?

   **a.** `float prices[15];`

   **b.** `char grades[20];`

   **c.** `bool flags[10];`

   **d.** `int coins[5];`

3. Write array declarations for each of the following:

   **a.** Array names with element type string, size 100

   **b.** Array checks with element type float, size 20

   **c.** Array madeBonus with element type bool, size 7

4. Which of the following array declarations are legal? Defend your answer and describe the result of each legal declaration. For question (e), use enumeration type day as defined in Example 9.2.

   **a.** `float payroll[friday];`

   **b.** `int workers[3] = {6, 8, 8, 0};`

c. `char vowels[] = {'a', 'e', 'i', 'o', 'u'};`

d. `int freq[12] = {0, 0, 3, 7, 10, 16, 28, 31};`

e. `day firstDay[] = {monday, friday, wednesday, saturday,`
`                    friday};`

Programming

1. Provide array type declarations for representing the following:

   a. A group of rooms (living room, dining room, kitchen, etc.) that have a given area

   b. A group of rooms as in part (a), but the array elements should indicate whether the room is carpeted

   c. Elementary school grade levels (0 through 6, where 0 means kindergarten) with a given number of students per grade

   d. A selection of colors (strings) representing the eye color of five people

   e. Answer (d) above assuming each array element stores an enumerator from the enumeration type below.

   ```
   typedef color = {blue, green, hazel, brown, black};
   ```

# 9.2   Sequential Access to Array Elements

Many programs process all the elements of an array in sequential order, starting with the first element (subscript 0). To enter data into an array, print its contents, or perform other sequential processing tasks, use a for loop whose loop-control variable (i) is also the array subscript (x[i]). Increasing the value of the loop-control variable by 1 causes the next array element to be processed.

## EXAMPLE 9.6

The array `cube` declared below stores the cubes of the first 10 integers (for example, `cube[1]` is 1, `cube[9]` is 729).

```
int cube[10];      // array of cubes
```

The `for` statement

```
for (int i = 0; i < 10; i++)
    cube[i] = i * i * i;
```

initializes this array as shown in Figure 9.6.

| [0] | [1] | [2] | [3] | [4] | [5] | [6] | [7] | [8] | [9] |
|---|---|---|---|---|---|---|---|---|---|
| 0 | 1 | 8 | 27 | 64 | 125 | 216 | 343 | 512 | 729 |

**Figure 9.6** Array cube

## EXAMPLE 9.7

In Listing 9.1, the statements

```
const int MAX_ITEMS = 8;
float x[MAX_ITEMS];                    // array of data
```

allocate storage for an array **x** with subscripts 0 through 7. The program uses three **for** loops to process the array. The loop-control variable **i**, with **i** in the range (0 <= i <= 7), is also the array subscript in each loop. The first **for** loop,

```
for (int i = 0; i < MAX_ITEMS; i++)
   cin >> x[i];
```

reads one data value into each array element (the first item is stored in **x[0]**, the second item in **x[1]**, and so on). The **cin** line executes for each value of **i** from 0 to 7; each repetition causes a new data value to be read and stored in **x[i]**. The subscript **i** determines the array element to receive the next data value. The data shown in the first line of the sample execution of Listing 9.1 cause the array to be initialized as shown in Figure 9.1.

**Listing 9.1**   Displaying a table of differences

```
// File: showDiff.cpp
// Computes the average value of an array of data and displays
//    the difference between each value and the average
#include <iostream>
#include <iomanip>
using namespace std;

int main()
{
   const int MAX_ITEMS = 8;
   float x[MAX_ITEMS];              // array of data
   float average;                   // average value of data
   float sum;                       // sum of the data

   // Enter the data.
   cout << "Enter " << MAX_ITEMS << " numbers: ";
   for (int i = 0; i < MAX_ITEMS; i++)
      cin >> x[i];
```

(continued)

**Listing 9.1**   Displaying a table of differences (continued)

```
// Compute the average value.
sum = 0.0;                            // initialize sum
for (int i = 0; i < MAX_ITEMS; i++)
    sum += x[i];                      // add next element to sum
average = sum / MAX_ITEMS;            // get average value

cout << "The average value is " << average << endl << endl;

// Display the difference between each item and the average.
cout << "Table of differences between x[i] and the average."
     << endl;
cout << setw(4) << "next" << setw(8) << "x[next]"
     << setw(14) << "difference" << endl;
for (int i = 0; i < MAX_ITEMS; i++)
    cout << setw(4) << i << setw(8) << x[i]
         << setw(14) << (x[i] - average) << endl;

    return 0;
}
```

```
Enter 8 numbers: 16   12   6   8   2.5   12   14   -54.5
The average value is 2

Table of differences between x[i] and the average.
    i      x[i]      difference
    0        16          14
    1        12          10
    2         6           4
    3         8           6
    4       2.5         0.5
    5        12          10
    6        14          12
    7      -54.5       -56.5
```

The second **for** loop accumulates the sum of all eight elements of array **x** in the variable **sum**. Each time the **for** loop body repeats, the statement

```
sum += x[i];                    // add next element to sum
```

adds the next element of array **x** to **sum**. Table 9.3 traces the first three loop iterations. The last **for** loop displays a table showing each array element, **x[i]**, and the difference between that element and the average value, **x[i] - average**.

**Table 9.3** Trace of Second for Loop in Listing 9.1 (three iterations)

| Statement Part | i | x[i] | sum | Effect |
|---|---|---|---|---|
| sum = 0.0; | | | 0.0 | Sets sum to zero |
| for (i = 0; i < MAX_ITEMS; i++) | 0 | 16.0 | | Sets i to zero |
| sum += x[i]; | | | 16.0 | Add x[0] to sum |
| increment and test i | 1 | 12.0 | | 1 < 8 is true |
| sum += x[i]; | | | 28.0 | Add x[1] to sum |
| increment and test i | 2 | 6.0 | | 2 < 8 is true |
| sum += x[i]; | | | 34.0 | Add x[2] to sum |

## Strings and Arrays of Characters

A string object uses an array whose elements are type char to store a character string. That's why the position of the first character of a string object is 0, not 1. If name is type string, we can use either name[i] or name.at(i) to access the ith character in string name.

## EXAMPLE 9.8

The program in Listing 9.2 forms a *cryptogram*, or coded message, by replacing each letter in a message (a data string) with its code symbol. For example, in the simple next-letter-substitution code, we want to replace all as with b, all bs with c, and so on. In Listing 9.2, the string constant **ALPHABET** contains all 26 lowercase letters and the string **CODE** contains the corresponding code symbols that appear under each letter.

The **for** loop heading

```
for (int i = 0; i < message.length(); i++)
```

processes each character in string **message** from the first to the last (subscript message.length() – 1). The statement

```
message[i] = CODE.at(pos);
```

replaces the letter in **message[i]** with its corresponding code symbol. This statement executes only if the value of **pos** is between 0 and 25, or when function **find** is able to locate the lowercase form of **message[i]** in string **ALPHABET**. See Table 3.3 to review the string functions.

**Listing 9.2**   Cryptogram generator

```cpp
// File: cryptogram.cpp
// Displays a cryptogram.

#include <string>
#include <iostream>
#include <cctype>
using namespace std;

int main()
{
   const string ALPHABET = "abcdefghijklmnopqrstuvwxyz";
   const string CODE =     "bcdefghijklmnopqrstuvwxyza";
   string message;          // message to encode
   char ch;                 // next message character
   int pos;                 // its position

   cout << "Enter a string to encode: ";
   getline(cin, message);

   // Encode message.
   for (int i = 0; i < message.length(); i++)
   {
      ch = tolower(message.at(i));   // ch to lowercase
      pos = ALPHABET.find(ch);       // find position of ch
      if ((pos >= 0) && (pos < 26))
         message[i] = CODE.at(pos);
   }

   cout << "The cryptogram is       : " << message << endl;

   return 0;
}
```

```
Enter a string to encode: This is a string.
The cryptogram is       : uijt jt b tusjoh.
```

# EXERCISES FOR SECTION 9.2

Self-Check

1. **a.** If an array has 10 elements, what is displayed by the fragment below?

```
for (int i = 9; i >= 0; i--)
    cout << i << " " << x[i] * x[i] << ",";
cout << endl;
```

**b.** What is displayed by the fragment below?

```
i = 0;
while (i < 10)
{
    cout << x[i] << " ";
    i += 2;
}
cout << endl;
```

2. The sequence of statements below changes the initial contents of array x displayed by the program in Listing 9.1. Describe what each statement does to the array and show the final contents of array x after all statements execute.

```
i = 3;
x[i] = x[i] + 10.0;
x[i-1] = x[2*i-1];
x[i+1] = x[2*i] + x[2*i+1];
for (int i = 4; i < 7; i++)
    x[i] = x[i+1];
for (int i = 2; i >= 0; i--)
    x[i+1] = x[i];
```

3. Trace the execution of the for loop in Listing 9.1 when the string read into message is "4 Aces.".

Programming

1. Write program statements that will do the following to array x, shown in Listing 9.1:

   **a.** Display all elements with even subscripts on one line.

   **b.** Calculate the sum of the elements with even subscripts only.

2. Write a loop that displays the characters in string message in reverse order.

3. Write a program to store in string reverse the characters in string message in reverse order and to display "Is  a  palindrome" if message and reverse contain the same string.

# 9.3 Array Arguments

The C++ operators (for example, <, ==, >, +, -) can be used to manipulate only one array element at a time. Consequently, an array name in an expression will generally be followed by its subscript. The next example shows the use of array elements as function arguments.

## Array Elements as Arguments

### EXAMPLE 9.9

You can use function **exchange** (see Listing 9.3) to switch the contents of its two floating-point arguments. The formal parameters **a1** and **a2** are used for both input and output and are therefore passed by reference.

This function may be used to exchange the contents of any two floating-point variables. The statement

```
exchange(x, y);
```

switches the original contents of the floating-point variables **x** and **y**.

This function may also be used to exchange the contents of any pair of elements of a floating-point array. For example, the function call

```
exchange(s[3], s[5]);
```

switches the contents of array elements **s[3]** and **s[5]** (see Figure 9.7). C++ treats the call to **exchange** in the same way as the earlier call involving **x** and **y**. In both cases, the contents of two floating-point memory locations (**s[3]** and **s[5]**) are exchanged.

**Listing 9.3**  Function to exchange the contents of two floating-point memory locations

```
void exchange
  (float& a1, float& a2)     // INOUT
{
    // Local data  . . .
    float temp;
    temp = a1;
    a1 = a2;
    a2 = temp;
}
```

| s[0] | s[1] | s[2] | s[3] | s[4] | s[5] | s[6] | s[7] |
|------|------|------|------|------|------|------|------|
| 16.0 | 12.0 | 28.0 | 26.0 | 2.5 | 12.0 | 14.0 | -54.5 |

| s[0] | s[1] | s[2] | s[3] | s[4] | s[5] | s[6] | s[7] |
|------|------|------|------|------|------|------|------|
| 16.0 | 12.0 | 28.0 | 12.0 | 2.5 | 26.0 | 14.0 | -54.5 |

**Figure 9.7** Array s before (top) and after (bottom) exchange of s[3] and s[5];

Besides passing individual array elements to functions, we can write functions that have arrays as arguments. Such functions can manipulate some, or all, of the elements corresponding to an actual array argument.

## Passing an Array Argument

We can pass an entire array to a function by writing its name with no subscript in the argument list of a function call. What is actually stored in the function's corresponding formal parameter is the address of the initial array element. In the function body, we can use subscripts with the formal parameter to reference the array's elements. However, the function manipulates the actual array, not its own personal copy, so an assignment to one of the array elements by a statement in the function changes the contents of the actual array.

The next two examples illustrate the use of arrays as function arguments. We assume the calling function declares three floating-point arrays, x, y, and z, each of size 5:

```
const int MAX_SIZE = 5;        // size of arrays
float x[MAX_SIZE];
float y[MAX_SIZE],
float z[MAX_SIZE];
```

## EXAMPLE 9.10

Function **sameArray** in Listing 9.4 determines whether two arrays, represented by formal array parameters **a** and **b**, are identical. We consider two arrays to be identical if the first element of one is the same as the first element of the other, the second element of one is the same as the second element of the other, and so on.

We can determine that the arrays are not identical by finding a single pair of unequal elements. Before each iteration, the second part of the **while** loop condition

```
while ((i < size-1) && (a[i] == b[i]))
```

**Listing 9.4**   Function `sameArray`

```
// File: sameArray.cpp
// Compares two float arrays for equality by comparing
//    corresponding elements

// Pre:  a[i] and b[i] (0 <= i <= size-1) are assigned
//       values.
// Post: Returns true if a[i] == b[i] for all i in range
//       0 through size - 1; otherwise, returns false.

bool sameArray
  (float a[],                 // IN: float arrays to be compared
   float b[],
   const int size)           // IN: size of the arrays
{
   // Local data  . . .
   int i;                 // loop control variable and array subscript
   i = 0;
   while ((i < size-1) && (a[i] == b[i]))
      i++;

   return (a[i] == b[i]);     // define result
}
```

compares the `i`th elements of the actual arrays corresponding to formal array parameters **a** and **b**. Loop exit occurs when a pair of unequal elements is found or just before the last pair is tested.

After loop exit, the statement

```
return (a[i] == b[i]);             // define result
```

defines the function result (true or false). If loop exit occurs because the pair of elements with subscript `i` is not equal, the function result is false. If loop exit occurs because the last pair of elements is reached (i equal to size-1), the function result will be true if these elements are equal and false if they're not.

As an example of how you might use function **sameArray**, the **if** statement

```
if (sameArray(x, y, MAX_SIZE))
   cout << "The arrays x and y are identical. " << endl;
else
   cout << "The arrays x and y are different. " << endl;
```

displays a message indicating whether the actual argument arrays **x** and **y** are identical.

Notice that we write the actual array **x** without brackets in the function call. Also, we declare formal array parameter **a** as `float a[]` in the parameter list for function **sameArray**. We discuss the reasons for this after the next example.

## EXAMPLE 9.11

The assignment statement

```
z = x + y;      // invalid array operation
```

is invalid because the operator + can't be used with array arguments. However, we can use function **addArray** (see Listing 9.5) to add together, element by element, the contents of any two floating-point arrays of the same size. The function stores the sum of each pair of elements with subscript $i$ in element $i$ of a third floating-point array. The function call

```
addArray(MAX_SIZE, x, y, z);
```

causes the addition of corresponding elements in arrays **x** and **y** with the result stored in the corresponding element of array **z**.

Figure 9.8 shows the argument correspondence for arrays established by the function call

```
addArray(MAX_SIZE, x, y, z);
```

Because C++ always passes arrays by reference, arrays **a**, **b**, and **c** in the function **addArray** data area are represented by the addresses of the actual arrays **x**, **y**, and **z** used in the call. Thus the values of the elements of **x** and **y** used in the addition are taken directly from the arrays **x** and **y** in the calling function, and the function results are stored directly in array **z** in the calling function. After execution of the function, **z[0]** will contain the sum of **x[0]** and **y[0]**, or 3.8; **z[1]** will contain 6.7; and so on. Arrays **x** and **y** will be unchanged. In fact, the use of the reserved word **const** in front of the formal parameters **a** and **b** ensures that the contents of the corresponding actual arguments (**x** and **y**) can't be changed by the function. We use **const** in the declaration of formal parameter **size** for the same reason.

Notice that the formal parameter list in Listing 9.5 doesn't indicate how many elements are in the array parameters. Because C++ doesn't allocate space in memory for a copy of the actual array, the compiler doesn't need to know the size of an array parameter. In fact, since we don't provide the size, we have the flexibility to pass to function **addArray** three arrays of any size. In each call to **addArray**, the first argument tells the function how many elements to process. In the function prototype, we use **float[ ]** to represent each formal array parameter:

```
void addArray(int, const float[], const float[], float[]);
```

**Listing 9.5** Function `addArray`

```
// File: addArray.cpp
// Stores the sum of a[i] and b[i] in c[i]

// Sums pairs of array elements with subscripts ranging from 0
//     to size-1
// Pre:  a[i] and b[i] are defined (0 <= i <= size-1)
// Post: c[i] = a[i] + b[i] (0 <= i <= size-1)

void addArray
   (int size,                 // IN: the size of the arrays
    const float a[],          // IN: the first array
    const float b[],          // IN: the second array
    float c[])                // OUT: result array
{
    // Add corresponding elements of a and b and store in c.
    for (int i = 0; i < size; i++)
       c[i] = a[i] + b[i];
}
```

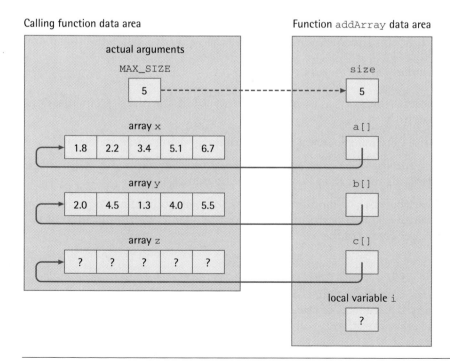

**Figure 9.8** Argument correspondence for `addArray(MAX_SIZE, x, y, z);`

We summarize important points about arrays as function arguments next.

---

### Arrays as Function Arguments

- In C++, arrays are passed by reference. Therefore, a formal array parameter in a function (c in Listing 9.5) represents the address of the first element of the actual array argument (z in Figure 9.8). All references to the formal array parameter are therefore references to the corresponding actual array argument in the calling function.
- In a function definition or a function prototype, we use empty brackets [ ] to inform the compiler that a formal parameter represents an array. We don't need to specify the size of this array because the compiler doesn't allocate storage for a copy of the actual array in the called function data area.
- The reserved word `const` indicates a formal array parameter that can't be changed by a function. If a function attempts to modify the contents of such an array, the compiler will generate an error message.
- In the function call, write the name of an actual argument array without using brackets after the array name.

---

## EXERCISES FOR SECTION 9.3

### Self–Check

1. In function `sameArray`, what will be the value of i when the statement

   ```
   return (a[i] == b[i]);
   ```

   executes if array a is equal to array b? If the third elements don't match?

2. Write the `return` statement for `sameArray` using an `if` statement.

3. Rewrite the `exchange` and `sameArray` functions to work with integer operands rather than floating-point operands.

4. Describe how to modify function `addArray` to obtain a new function, `multArray`, that performs an element-by-element multiplication of two integer arrays of the same size.

### Programming

1. Write a function that assigns a value of `true` to element i of the output array if element i of one input array has the same value as element i of the other input array; otherwise, assign a value of `false`.

2. Write a function `scalarMultArray` that multiplies an entire floating-point array x (consisting of $n$ elements) by a single floating-point scalar c. Array x should be used for input/output.

# 9.4 Reading Part of an Array

Often a programmer doesn't know in advance exactly how many elements will be stored in an array. As an example, let's say you're writing a program to process exam scores. There may be 150 students in one section, 200 in the next, and so on. Because you must declare the array size before program execution begins, you must allocate enough storage space so that the program can process the largest expected array without error.

When you read the array data into memory, you should begin filling the array starting with the first element (at subscript 0) and be sure to keep track of how many data items are actually stored in the array. The part of the array that contains data is called the **filled subarray**. The *length* of the filled subarray is the number of data items that are actually stored in the array.

**filled subarray**
The portion of a partially filled array that contains data.

## EXAMPLE 9.12

Function `readScores` in Listing 9.6 reads and stores in its array argument `scores` up to `MAX_SIZE` exam scores, where `MAX_SIZE` is an input argument that represents the size of the actual array corresponding to `scores`. The output argument `sectionSize` represents the length of the filled subarray and is initialized to zero. Within the loop, the statements

```
scores[sectionSize] = tempScore;   // save score just read
sectionSize++;
```

store the score just read (value of `tempScore`) in the next array element and increment `sectionSize`. After loop exit, the value of `sectionSize` is the length of the filled subarray **array**. The `if` statement displays a warning message when the array is filled (when `sectionSize` equals `MAX_SIZE`).

**Listing 9.6**   Function `readScores`

```cpp
// File: readScores.cpp
// Reads an array of exam scores for a lecture section
//    of up to MAX_SIZE students.

// Pre:  None
// Post: The data values are stored in array scores.
//       The number of values read is stored in sectionSize.
//       (0 <= sectionSize < MAX_SIZE).
```

(continued)

**Listing 9.6** Function `readScores` (continued)

```
void readScores
   (int scores[],        // OUT: array to contain all scores read
    const int MAX_SIZE,  // IN: max size of array scores
    int& sectionSize)    // OUT: number of elements read
{
    // Local data  . . .
    const int SENTINEL = -1;    // sentinel value
    int tempScore;              // temporary storage for each score

    // Read each array element until done.
    cout << "Enter next score after the prompt or enter "
         << SENTINEL << " to stop." << endl;
    sectionSize = 0;            // initial class size

    cout << "Score: ";
    cin >> tempScore;
    while ((tempScore != SENTINEL) && (sectionSize < MAX_SIZE))
    {
        scores[sectionSize] = tempScore;  // save score just read
        sectionSize++;
        cout << "Score: ";
        cin >> tempScore;
    } // end while

    // Sentinel was read or array is filled.
    if (tempScore != SENTINEL)
    {
        cout << "Array is filled!" << endl;
        cout << tempScore << " not stored" << endl;
    }
}
```

Often when processing array data, we prefer to read the data from a file rather than type it in each time. Function `readScoresFile` (Listing 9.7) performs this operation assuming `ifstream` parameter `ins` is associated with a data file. We based this function on `readScores`. The major difference is the addition of parameter `ins` and the use of the `eof` function to detect the end of the data file instead of using a sentinel value. Also, we removed the prompts. If you prefer to use a sentinel value, the only change to function `readScores` in Listing 9.6 would be to add parameter `ins`, replace `cin` by `ins`, and delete all prompts.

**Listing 9.7**   Function `readScoresFile`

```cpp
// File: readScoresFile.cpp
// Reads an array of exam scores for a lecture section
//    of up to MAX_SIZE students from a file.

// Pre:  None
// Post: The data values are read from a file and stored
//        in array scores.
//        The number of values read is stored in sectionSize.
//        (0 <= sectionSize < MAX_SIZE).
void readScoresFile
  (ifstream& ins,        // IN:  input stream of scores
   int scores[],         // OUT: array to contain all scores read
   const int MAX_SIZE,   // IN: max size of array scores
   int& sectionSize)     // OUT: number of elements read
{
   // Local data  . . .
   int tempScore;               // temporary storage for each score

   // Read each array element until done.
   sectionSize = 0;             // initial class size
   ins >> tempScore;
   while (!ins.eof() && (sectionSize < MAX_SIZE))
   {
      scores[sectionSize] = tempScore;  // save score just read
      sectionSize++;
      ins >> tempScore;
   }  // end while

   // End of file reached or array is filled.
   if (!ins.eof())
   {
      cout << "Array is filled!" << endl;
      cout << tempScore << " not stored" << endl;
   }
}
```

## EXERCISES FOR SECTION 9.4

Self-Check

1. Describe the changes necessary to use function `readScores` for reading floating-point data.

2. In function readScores, what prevents the user from entering more than MAX_SIZE scores?

3. Explain how you would modify function readScoresFile if the number of scores to read was included in the data file. Where should this number be placed?

Programming

1. Rewrite readScoresFile so that it stops reading when either a sentinel value is read, the end of the file is reached, or the array is filled.

# 9.5  Searching and Sorting Arrays

This section discusses two common problems in processing arrays: searching an array to determine the location of a particular value and sorting an array to rearrange the elements in an ordered fashion. As an example of an array search, we might want to search the array scores to determine which student, if any, got a particular score. An example of an array sort would be rearranging the array elements so that they're in increasing order by score. This would be helpful if we wanted to display the list in order by score or if we needed to locate several different scores in the array.

## Finding the Smallest Value in an Array

We begin by solving a different kind of search problem: finding the smallest value in a subarray.

1. Assume that the first element is the smallest so far and save its subscript as "the subscript of the smallest element found so far."
2. For each array element after the first one
   2.1. If the current element < the smallest so far
      2.1.1. Save the subscript of the current element as "the subscript of the smallest element found so far."

Function findIndexOfMin in Listing 9.8 implements this algorithm for any subarray of floating-point elements. During each iteration of the loop, minIndex is the subscript of the smallest element so far and x[minIndex] is its value. The function returns the last value assigned to minIndex, which is the subscript of the smallest value in the subarray. Arguments startIndex and endIndex define the boundaries of the subarray, x[startIndex] through x[endIndex], whose smallest value is being found. Passing these subscripts as arguments results in a more general function. To find the minimum element in the entire array, pass 0 to startIndex and the array size − 1 to endIndex.

**Listing 9.8**   Function `findIndexOfMin`

```
// File: arrayOperations.cpp
// Finds the subscript of the smallest value in a subarray.

// Returns the subscript of the smallest value in the subarray
// consisting of elements x[startindex] through x[endindex]
// Returns -1 if the subarray bounds are invalid.
// Pre:  The subarray is defined and 0 <= startIndex <= endIndex.
// Post: x[minIndex] is the smallest value in the array.

int findIndexOfMin
    (const float x[],       // IN: array of elements
     int startIndex,        // IN: subscript of first element
     int endIndex)          // IN: subscript of last element
{
    // Local data  . . .
    int minIndex;           // index of the smallest element found
    int i;                  // index of the current element

    // Validate subarray bounds
    if ((startIndex < 0) || (startIndex > endIndex))
    {
        cerr << "Error in subarray bounds" << endl;
        return -1;                          // return error indicator
    }

    // Assume the first element of subarray is smallest and check
    //    the rest.
    // minIndex will contain subscript of smallest examined so far.
    minIndex = startIndex;
    for (i = startIndex + 1; i <= endIndex; i++)
        if (x[i] < x[minIndex])
            minIndex = i;

    // Assertion: All elements are examined and minIndex is
    //    the index of the smallest element.
    return minIndex;                        // return result
} // end findIndexOfMin
```

Note that function `findIndexOfMin` returns the subscript (or index) of
the smallest value, not the smallest value itself. Assuming `smallSub` is type
`int`, and `yLength` is the number of array elements containing data, the following statements display the smallest value in array `y`.

```
smallSub = findIndexOfMin(y, 0, yLength - 1);
if (smallSub != -1)
   cout << "Value of smallest element in array y is "
        << y[smallSub] << endl;
else
   cerr << "Error - invalid array range" << endl;
```

## Program Style    Assertions as Comments

assertion
A comment that makes
a statement about the
program that must be
true.

Normally we use a comment to document the purpose of the statements that follow it. In Listing 9.8, we introduced a different kind of comment called an **assertion**—a statement about the program that must be true at this point in the program. Instead of summarizing the intent of the statements that follow it, an assertion helps clarify the rationale for those statements. Programmers sometimes use assertions to help them prove that a program is correct. We'll use them to describe the expected status or state of the program.

## Array Search

We can search an array for a particular element by comparing each array element, starting with the first (subscript 0), to the target, the value we're seeking. If a match occurs, we have found the target in the array and can return its subscript as a search result. If we test all array elements without finding a match, we return –1 to indicate that the target was not found. We choose –1 because no array element has a negative subscript.

INTERFACE FOR A SEARCH FUNCTION

**Input Arguments**

| | |
|---|---|
| `int items[]` | *// array to search* |
| `int size` | *// number of items to be examined* |
| `int target` | *// item to find* |

**Output Arguments**

(none)

**Returns**

Subscript of the first element of the array containing the target (return –1 if no element contains the target)

We use the linear search algorithm below and implemented in Listing 9.9 to search the input array for the target value.

**1.** For each array element
   **1.1.** If the current element contains the target
   **1.2.** Return the subscript of the current element.
**2.** Return –1.

**Listing 9.9** The function `linSearch`

```cpp
// File: arrayOperations.cpp
// Searches an integer array for a given element (the target)

// Array elements ranging from 0 to size -1 are searched for
//    an element equal to target.
// Pre:  The target and array are defined.
// Post: Returns the subscript of target if found;
//       otherwise, returns -1.

int linSearch
  (const int items[],       // IN: the array being searched
   int target,              // IN: the target being sought
   int size)                // IN: the size of the array
{
    for (int next = 0; next < size; next++)
       if (items[next] == target)
           return next;            // found, return subscript

    // Assertion: All elements were tested without success.
    return -1;
} // end linSearch
```

## Sorting an Array in Ascending Order

Many programs execute more efficiently if the data they process are sorted before processing begins. For example, a check-processing program executes more quickly if all checks are in order by checking account number. Other programs produce more readable output if the information is sorted before it's displayed. For example, your university might want your instructor's grade report sorted by student ID number. In this section, we describe one simple sorting algorithm.

## EXAMPLE 9.13

The *selection sort* is a fairly intuitive sorting algorithm. To perform a selection sort of an array of $n$ elements (subscripts 0 through $n - 1$), we locate the smallest element in the array and then switch the smallest element with the element at subscript 0, thereby placing the smallest element at location 0. We then locate the smallest element remaining in the subarray with subscripts 1 through $n - 1$ and switch it with the element at subscript 1, thereby placing the second smallest element at location 1. We continue this process until all elements have been placed in their correct locations.

DATA REQUIREMENTS FOR A SORT FUNCTION

### Input Arguments

`float items[]`   *// array to sort*
`int n`           *// number of items to sort*

### Output Arguments

`int items[]`     *// original array sorted in ascending order*

### Local Variables

`int i`           *// subscript of first element in each subarray*
`int minSub`      *// subscript of each smallest item located by*
                  `findIndexOfMin`

ALGORITHM

1. Starting with the first item in the array (subscript 0) and ending with the next-to-last item:

   1.1. Set `i` equal to the subscript of the first item in the subarray to be processed in the next steps.

   1.2. Find the subscript ($_{minSub}$) of the smallest item in the subarray with subscripts ranging from i through $_{n-1}$;

   1.3. Exchange the smallest item found in step 1.2 with item i (exchange $_{items[minSub]}$ with $_{items[i]}$).

Figure 9.9 traces the operation of the selection sort algorithm on an array with four elements. The first array shown is the original array. Then we show each step as the next smallest element is moved to its correct position. The shaded portion of each array represents the subarray that is sorted. We stop when the next to last element is placed in its correct position, so `n-1` exchanges will be required to sort an array with `n` elements.

We can use function `findIndexOfMin` (see again Listing 9.8) to perform step 1.2. Function `selSort` in Listing 9.10 implements the selection sort algorithm. Local variable `minSub` holds the index of the smallest value found so far in the current subarray. At the end of each pass, we call function `exchange` (see again Listing 9.3) to exchange the elements with subscripts `minSub` and `i`. After execution of function `selSort`, the array element values will be in increasing order.

---

The selection sort illustrates the importance of component reuse in problem solving and program engineering. We always strive to break down a complicated problem into simpler subproblems so that we can solve many of these subproblems using existing and tested components. Occasionally, we may need to make some minor modification to these components to adapt them to the current problem. But this is preferable to designing, implementing, and testing a new function from scratch.

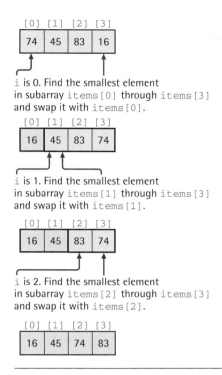

i is 0. Find the smallest element
in subarray `items[0]` through `items[3]`
and swap it with `items[0]`.

i is 1. Find the smallest element
in subarray `items[1]` through `items[3]`
and swap it with `items[1]`.

i is 2. Find the smallest element
in subarray `items[2]` through `items[3]`
and swap it with `items[2]`.

**Figure 9.9**  Trace of selection sort

**Listing 9.10**  Function `selSort`

```
// File: arrayOperations.cpp

// Sorts an array (ascending order) using selection sort algorithm
//    Uses exchange and findIndexOfMin
// Sorts the data in array items (items[0] through items[n-1]).
// Pre:  items is defined and n <= declared size of actual argument
//       array.
// Post: The values in items[0] through items[n-1] are in
//       increasing order.
void selSort(float items[], int n)
{
    // Local data  . . .
    int minSub;  // subscript of each smallest item located by
                 // findIndexOfMin

    for (int i = 0; i < n-1; i++)
    {
```

(continued)

**Listing 9.10**   Function `selSort` (continued)

```
    // Find index of smallest element in unsorted section of
    //     items.
    minSub = findIndexOfMin(items, i, n-1);

    // Exchange items at position minSub and i
    exchange(items[minSub], items[i]);
  }
}
```

## EXERCISES FOR SECTION 9.5

Self-Check

1. For the linear search function in Listing 9.9, what happens if

   **a.** the last element of the array matches the target?

   **b.** several elements of the array match the target? The subscript of which one will be returned?

2. Trace the execution of the selection sort on the following list:

   55   34   56   76   5   10

   Show the array after each exchange occurs. How many comparisons are required? How many exchanges?

3. How could you modify the selection sort algorithm to arrange the data items in the array in descending order (smallest first)?

4. Modify the `exchange` function (Listing 9.3) to work for integer data.

5. In selection sort, there is no need to exchange the value in element i with the smallest value found if the smallest value is the same as the one at position i. How would you modify the algorithm to avoid this unnecessary exchange? How would this change affect the number of comparisons? How would it affect the number of exchanges?

Programming

1. Write a function to count the number of items in an integer array having a value greater than 0.

2. Another method of performing the selection sort is to place the largest value in position n-1, the next largest in n-2, and so on. Write this version.

3. Write function `linSearchLast` that finds the last occurrence of a target value in an array.

4. Rewrite function `selectSort` by writing step 1.2 of the algorithm (Find index of smallest item ... ) as a loop with loop control variable `j` instead of calling function `findIndexOfMin`.

# 9.6 Analyzing Algorithms: Big-O Notation

Often we want to estimate the efficiency of an algorithm. In this section, we provide a brief introduction to the topic of algorithm analysis, focusing on the searching and sorting algorithms just introduced.

There are many algorithms for searching and sorting arrays. Because arrays can be very large, these operations can become time-consuming, so we need to know the relative efficiency of various algorithms for performing the same task. Because it's difficult to get a precise measure of the efficiency of an algorithm or program, we normally try to approximate the effect on an algorithm of a change in the number of items, $n$, that the algorithm processes. This way, we can see how an algorithm's execution time increases with $n$, so we can compare two algorithms by examining their growth rates.

Usually, growth rates are described in terms of the largest contributing factor as the value of $n$ gets large (for example, as it grows to 1,000 or more). If we determine that the expression

$$2n^2 + n - 5$$

expresses the relationship between the processing time of an algorithm and $n$, we say that the algorithm is an $O(n^2)$ algorithm, where O is an abbreviation for "the order of magnitude." This notation is known as big-O notation. The reason that this is an $O(n^2)$ algorithm rather than an $O(2n^2)$ algorithm or an $O(2n^2 + n - 5)$ algorithm is that the dominant factor in the relationship is the $n^2$ term. For large values of $n$, the largest exponent term has by far the greatest impact on our measurements. For this reason, we tend to ignore the "smaller" terms and constants.

## Analysis of a Search Algorithm

To search an array of $n$ elements using the linear search function, we have to examine all $n$ elements if the target is not present in the array. If the target is in the array, then we have to search only until we find it. However, the target could be anywhere in the array—it's equally as likely to be at the beginning of the array as at the end. So, on average, we have to examine

$n/2$ array elements to locate a target value in an array. This means that linear search is an $O(n)$ process; that is, the growth rate is linear with respect to the number of items being searched.

## Analysis of a Sort Algorithm

To determine the efficiency of a sorting algorithm, we normally focus on the number of array element comparisons and exchanges that it requires. Performing a selection sort on an array of $n$ elements requires $n - 1$ comparisons during the first pass, $n - 2$ during the second pass, and so on. Therefore, the total number of comparisons is represented by the series

$$1 + 2 + 3 + \ldots + (n - 2) + (n - 1)$$

The value of this series is

$$\frac{n \times (n - 1)}{2} = n^2/2 - n/2$$

At the end of each pass through the unsorted subarray, we exchange the smallest value with the array element at position $i$. Therefore, the number of exchanges is $n$ and the growth rate for exchanges is $O(n)$.

Because the dominant term in the expression for the number of comparisons shown earlier is $n^2/2$, the selection sort is considered an $O(n^2)$ process and the growth rate is said to be quadratic (proportional to the square of the number of elements). What difference does it make whether an algorithm is an $O(n)$ or $O(n^2)$ process? Table 9.4 shows the evaluation of $n$ and $n^2$ for different values of $n$. A doubling of $n$ causes $n^2$ to increase by a factor of 4. Because $n^2$ increases much more rapidly than $n$, the performance of an $O(n)$ algorithm is not as adversely affected by an increase in array size as is an $O(n^2)$ algorithm. For large values of $n$ (say, 100 or more), the difference in the performances of an $O(n)$ and an $O(n^2)$ algorithm is significant (see the last three lines of Table 9.4).

Other factors besides the number of comparisons and exchanges affect an algorithm's performance. For example, one algorithm may take more time preparing for each exchange or comparison than another. Also, one algorithm might exchange subscripts, whereas another might exchange the array elements themselves. The second process can be more time consuming. Another measure of efficiency is the amount of memory required by an algorithm. Further discussion of these issues is beyond the scope of this book.

**Table 9.4**   Table of Values of $n$ and $n^2$

| $n$ | $n^2$ |
|-----|-------|
| 2 | 4 |
| 4 | 16 |
| 8 | 64 |
| 16 | 256 |
| 32 | 1024 |
| 64 | 4096 |
| 128 | 16384 |
| 256 | 65536 |
| 512 | 262144 |

## EXERCISES FOR SECTION 9.6

Self-Check

1. Determine how many times the cout line is executed in each of the following fragments. Indicate whether the algorithm is O($n$) or O($n^2$).

   **a.** `for (i = 0; i < n; i++)`
      `for (j = 0; j < n; j++)`
         `cout << i << ' ' << j;`

   **b.** `for (i = 0; i < n; i++)`
      `for (j = 1; j <= 2; j++)`
         `cout << i << ' ' << j;`

   **c.** `for (i = 0; i < n; i++)`
      `for (j = n; j > 0; j--)`
         `cout << i << ' ' << j;`

2. What does it mean for a term to dominate an equation? To get a feel for the answer, calculate the value of $n$, $n^2 + n - 5$, $n^2 - n + 5$, and $2n^2$ for values of $n = 1, 10, 100, 1000,$ and $10000$. You may want to write a small program to do this. Notice that each value of $n$ is 10 times the previous value.

Programming

1. Write a program to compute and print the values of y1 and y2 (below) for *n*, from 10 to 1000 inclusive, in increments of 25. Does the result surprise you?

$$y1 = 100n + 10$$
$$y2 = 5n^2 + 2$$

# 9.7    The Struct Data Type

Arrays are useful data structures for storing a collection of data elements of the same type. But many programming problems require us to store collections of related data that have different types, such as the **struct**, a data structure that can be used to store related data items with different types. For example, we can use a struct to store a variety of information about a person, such as name, marital status, age, and date of birth. The individual component of a struct is called a **member**. In this section, we show how to declare and process structs.

**struct**
A data structure that can be used to store a collection of related data items with different types.
**member**
An individual component of a struct.

## Declaring a Struct Type and Struct Variables

### EXAMPLE 9.14

The manager of a software firm has asked you to keep organized, accessible information about her staff. As part of her plan, she would like certain information about each employee. An example might look like this:

ID: 1234
Name: Noel Goddard
Gender: Female
Number of dependents: 0
Hourly rate: 12.00
Total wages: 480.00

This information can be stored in a struct with six data elements. The struct type declaration describes the format of each struct including the name and type of each data element, or *struct member*. To store the preceding information, you can use the struct type **employee** shown next with two integer fields, a **string** field, a character field (for gender), and two **float** fields:

```
struct employee
{
    int id;
    string name;
    char gender;
    int numDepend;
    float rate;
    float totWages;
};
```

The above sequence of C++ statements (ending with a semicolon) defines a new struct data type named **employee** consisting of six members. There is no memory associated with this type. However, once it has been defined, you can declare *structure variables* of this type. The declaration

```
employee organist, janitor;
```

allocates storage space for two variables, **organist** and **janitor**, in the form defined by the structured type **employee**. Thus the memory allocated for these variables consists of storage space for six distinct values. The variable **organist** shown in Figure 9.10 stores the values presented earlier in the example.

As with other identifiers in C++ programs, use member names that describe the information to be stored and select a data type that's appropriate for that kind of information. For example, struct type **employee** uses a string field for storage of an employee's name.

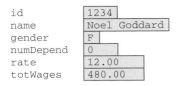

| | |
|---|---|
| id | 1234 |
| name | Noel Goddard |
| gender | F |
| numDepend | 0 |
| rate | 12.00 |
| totWages | 480.00 |

**Figure 9.10**   The struct variable **organist**

> **struct Type Declaration**
>
> **Form:**    struct *struct-type*
>              {
>                *type₁ id-list₁*;
>                *type₂ id-list₂*;
>                       .
>                       .
>                       .
>                *typeₙ id-listₙ*;
>              };
>
> **Example:**    struct complex
>                {
>                     float realPart, imaginaryPart;
>                };
>
> **Interpretation:** The identifier *struct-type* is the name of the struct being declared. Each *id-listᵢ* is a list of one or more member names of the same type separated by commas, and each *id-listᵢ* is separated from the next *id-list* of a possibly different type by a semicolon. The data type of each member in *id-listᵢ* is specified by *typeᵢ*.
>
> You must declare a struct type before you can declare any variables of that type. We recommend that you declare a struct type before the function prototypes in a program system. This placement makes the struct type global, which means that all functions in the program system can use it. Make sure you follow the closing brace with a semicolon.

## Accessing Members of a Struct

**member access operator**
The period placed between a struct variable name and a member name for that struct type.

We can access a struct member using the **member access operator**, a period placed between a struct variable name and a member name for that struct type. If s is a struct variable and m is a member of that struct, then s.m accesses member m of the **struct s**.

### EXAMPLE 9.15

The statements below store data in the struct variable **organist**. Refer back to Figure 9.10 to view the contents of **organist** after these statements execute.

```
organist.id = 1234;
organist.name = "Noel Goddard";
organist.gender = 'F';
organist.numDepend = 0;
organist.rate = 12.00;
organist.totWages = 480.0;
```

Once data are stored in a struct, they can be manipulated in the same way as other data in memory. For example, the assignment statement

```
organist.totWages += (organist.rate * 40.0);
```

computes the organist's new total wages by adding this week's wages to her previous total wages. The computed result is saved in the struct member `organist.totWages`.

The statements

```
cout << "The organist is ";
switch (organist.gender)
{
   case 'F': case 'f':
      cout << "Ms. ";
      break;
   case 'M': case 'm':
      cout << "Mr. ";
      break;
   default:
      cout << organist.gender
           << " is bad character for gender!" << endl;

}
cout << organist.name << endl;
```

display the organist's name after an appropriate title (**"Ms."** or **"Mr."**); the output line follows:

```
The organist is Ms. Noel Goddard
```

## EXERCISES FOR SECTION 9.7

### Self-Check

1. Describe what happens when the following assignment is executed:
   ```
   organist.rate *= 2;
   ```

2. Explain what is wrong with the statement below, which is supposed to set an employee's gender.
   ```
   employee.gender = 'M';
   ```

### Programming

1. A catalog listing for a textbook consists of the author's name as well as the title, edition, publisher, and year of publication. Declare a struct `catalogEntry` and a variable `cPlusBook` and write assignment statements that store the relevant data for a C++ textbook in `cPlusBook`.

2. A company represents each part in an inventory by its part number, a descriptive name, the quantity on hand, and the price. Define a struct `part`.

# 9.8    Structs as Operands and Arguments

Programmers often need to write functions that process entire structs. In this section we discuss passing structs as function arguments and other operations on entire structs.

## Struct Copy or Assignment

We can copy all of the members of one struct variable to another struct variable of the same type. If `organist` and `janitor` are both struct variables of type `employee`, the statement

```
organist = janitor;   // Copy janitor to organist
```

copies each member of `janitor` into the corresponding member of `organist`.

## Passing a Struct as an Argument

A struct can be passed as an argument to a function, provided the actual argument is the same type as its corresponding formal parameter. The use of structs as arguments can shorten argument lists considerably, because one argument (a struct variable) can be passed instead of several related arguments.

### EXAMPLE 9.16

You have been asked to organize a grading program, which keeps track of a student's name, three exam scores, the average exam score, and letter grade based on the average. Previously you would have stored these data in separate variables, but now you can group them together as a struct.

```
struct examStats
{
    string stuName;
    int scores[3];
    float average;
    char grade;
};
```

```
int main ()
{
    examStats aStudent;
```

Struct variable **aStudent** (type **examStats**) contains all the data regarding the student's exam performance. Notice that member **scores** is an array of integers. We use the notation **aStudent.scores[0]** to access the first element of this array. Figure 9.11 shows a sketch of variable **aStudent**.

Function **printStats** (Listing 9.11) displays the value stored in each member of its struct argument (type **examStats**). For the sample data shown, the statement

```
printStats(aStudent);
```

would display the following output:

```
Exam scores for Judy: 55 90 87
Average score: 77.3333
Letter grade : C
```

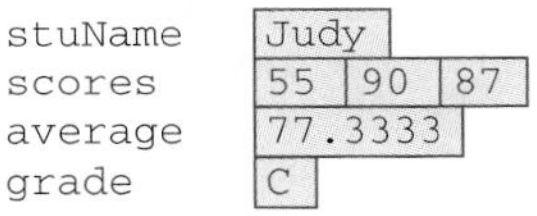

**Figure 9.11**  Variable **aStudent**

**Listing 9.11**  Function **printStats**

```
// File: printStats.cpp
// Prints the exam statistics

// Pre:  The members of the struct variable stuExams are
//       assigned values.
// Post: Each member of stuExams is displayed.

void printStats
   (examStats stuExams)        // IN:
                               // the struct to be displayed
{
    cout << "Exam scores for " << stuExams.stuName << ": "
    cout << stuExams.scores[0] << ' ' << stuExams.scores[1]
         << ' ' << stuExams.scores[2] << endl;
    cout << "Average score: " << stuExams.average << endl;
    cout << "Letter grade : " << stuExams.grade << endl;
}
```

In `printStats`, the struct argument was declared as a value argument, so storage is allocated for a copy of its actual argument in the function data area. You can pass a struct as a reference argument, as illustrated in the next section.

## Reading a Struct

Function `readEmployee` in Listing 9.12 reads data into the first five members of a struct variable of type `employee` represented by the reference parameter `oneEmployee`. The address of the actual struct argument is stored in the function data area, so `oneEmployee.id` references member `id` of the actual struct argument. The function call

```
readEmployee(organist);
```

causes the data read to be stored in struct variable `organist`.

---

**Listing 9.12**    Function `readEmployee`

```cpp
// File: readEmp.cpp
// Reads one employee record into oneEmployee

#include <string>
#include <iostream>

// Pre:  None
// Post: Data are read into struct oneEmployee

void readEmployee
   (employee& oneEmployee)      // OUT: The destination for the data read
{
   cout << "Enter a name terminated with the symbol # : ";
   getline(cin, oneEmployee.name, '#');
   cout << "Enter an id number: ";
   cin >> oneEmployee.id;
   cout << "Enter gender (F or M): ";
   cin >> oneEmployee.gender;
   cout << "Enter number of dependents: ";
   cin >> oneEmployee.numDepend;
   cout << "Enter hourly rate: ";
   cin >> oneEmployee.rate;
}
```

## Efficiency of Reference Arguments

For efficiency reasons, programmers sometimes prefer not to pass structs as value arguments because C++ must make a local copy of a struct passed as a value argument in the called function's data area. But they can still get the protection afforded by value arguments by using the word `const` in a formal parameter declaration. For example, the function header

```
void printStats
    (const examStats& stuExams) // IN:
                                // the struct to be displayed
```

declares `stuExams` as a reference argument that can't be changed by the execution of function `printStats`. Instead of making a local copy of the actual struct argument during a call to `printStats`, C++ passes the actual argument's address to function `printStats`. This enables `printStats` to access the data stored in its actual argument, but C++ doesn't allow `printStats` to modify the data in its actual argument.

## EXERCISES FOR SECTION 9.8

**Self-Check**

1. For variables `aStudent` and `bStudent` (type `examStats` in Example 9.16), describe the meaning of each of the valid references below. Which are invalid?

   **a.** `aStudent.stuName`       **e.** `aStudent.scores[2]`

   **b.** `aStudent.stuName[0]`     **f.** `examStats.scores[0]`

   **c.** `examStats.stuName`       **g.** `aStudent = bStudent;`

   **d.** `aStudent.scores[3]`      **h.** `aStudent.scores[0] =`
                                        `bStudent.grade;`

2. Write statements that calculate the average score for `aStudent` and assign a letter grade based on a straight scale (90–100 an A, 80–89 a B, and so on).

3. You can return a struct as a function result. This means it would be possible to write a function `readEmp` with prototype

   ```
   employee readEmp();
   ```

   to read in an employee's data. Write a statement to call `readEmp` to read in an organist's data.

Programming

1. Write function `readEmp` described in Self-Check Exercise 3.

2. Write a function that reads in the data for a struct of type `date`:

```
struct date
{
    string month;
    int day;
    int year;
};
```

The function should return the values read through a single argument of type `date`.

3. Consider the struct `employee` given in Example 9.14. Write a function `printEmployee` to print all the members of a structure variable of type `employee` and show how you would call it.

# 9.9    Strings as Arrays of Characters (Optional)

Before C++ had a string class as part of its standard library, a string in C++ (or C) was stored in an array of characters. These strings are often called *C-Style strings*. For historical reasons, we show how to process strings stored as arrays of characters in this section.

## Declaring and Initializing an Array of Characters

The declaration

```
char name[] = "Jackson";
```

or

```
char name[8] = "Jackson";
```

allocates storage for an array of eight characters and stores each character of the string literal `"Jackson"` in an element of that array (see Figure 9.12). Recall that you don't need to declare the size of an array when you provide initial values for its elements. The last character stored is `'\0'`, the **null character**, that C++ uses to denote the end of a string in a character array. C++ actually stores each string literal that occurs in a program as an array of characters terminated by the null character.

```
[0]   [1]   [2]   [3]   [4]   [5]   [6]   [7]
'J'   'a'   'c'   'k'   's'   'o'   'n'  '\0'
```

**Figure 9.12**  Array name

## Reading and Writing Character Arrays

You can display the string stored in name as an entity by using the extraction operator

```
cout << name << endl;
```

Or you can use the following loop to display each individual character in the array.

```
// Display each character up to '\0'
int i = 0;
while (name[i] != '\0') {
   cout << name[i];
   i++;
}
```

In either case, all characters up to, but not including, the null character are displayed.

The declaration

```
char flower[10];
```

allocates storage for a string of at most nine characters because the last character stored should always be the null character. You can read a string into array flower by using the insertion operator

```
cin >> flower;
```

Or you can read each individual character from a data line using a sentinel-controlled loop as shown in the following fragment. The loop reads each individual character and stores it in the next array element, starting with the one at position 0. Loop repetition stops when either the newline character is read or nine data characters are stored in the array. The statement following the loop is critical; however, it's easy to forget. Its purpose is to store the null character after the last data character stored in the array. The test `j < 9` ensures that at most 9 data characters will be stored and there will be space in the array for the null character.

```
int j = 0;
char ch;

cin.get(ch);              // read first character
while (ch != '\n' && j < 9) {
   flower[j] = ch;        // store data character
                          // in next array element
   j++;
   cin.get(ch);           // read next character
}
flower[j] = '\0';         // terminate string with
                          // null character
```

You can't assign a string literal to a character array that has already been declared. We discuss how to store a string literal in an array next.

## Some Useful Functions for Character Arrays

The standard library `cstring` has several useful functions for manipulating strings stored in character arrays (called *C-style strings*). You can use function `strlen` to return the length of a C-style string. The null character is not counted, so the function call

```
strlen(name)
```

returns 7 for the array shown in Figure 9.12.

You can't assign a string to a character array after storage has been allocated to the array. However, you can use the string copy function, `strcpy`, to change the contents of a character array. The statement

```
strcpy(flower, "Rose");
```

stores the five characters `'R'`, `'o'`, `'s'`, `'e'`, `'\0'` in the character array `flower` (size 10). Take care not to overflow the storage area allocated to a character array. The assignment statement

```
strcpy(flower, "Chrysanthemum");   // string is too long
```

will overwrite data in memory cells that follow the ones allocated to array `flower`. This could lead to execution errors because C++ doesn't prevent string overflow from happening.

In Section 8.3, we mentioned that the standard string library has a method `c_str` that converts a C++ string to an array of characters (C-style string). We used that function to enable the user to provide the external file name (needed for function `open`) as a data item. The argument of `open` must be a C-style string. If `fileName` stores a standard C++ string and `aStream` is a stream, the statement below associates stream `aStream` with the file whose name is stored in `fileName`.

```
aStream.open(fileName.c_str());
```

Another useful string function, `atoi`, is found in the standard library `cstdlib`. You can use `atoi` to convert a numeric string consisting of only digit characters to a type `int` value. If the `string` variable `yearStr` stores a numeric string (for example, `"2003"`), the fragment below stores the corresponding integer value (`2003`) in `year` (type `int`). The argument of `atoi` is the C-style string corresponding to `yearStr`.

```
year = atoi(yearStr.c_str());
```

## EXERCISES FOR SECTION 9.9

### Self-Check

1. Correct the errors in each of the statements below.

```
char dayName[] = "Sunday";
cout << "length is " << dayName.length();
char monthName[5];
monthName = "February";
string fName = "data.txt";
aStream.open(fName);
string year = "2004";
year++;
char initial[3];
initial[0] = 'E';   initial[1] = 'B';      initial[2] = 'K';
```

### Programming

1. Write a function `readCharArray` that reads the data to be stored in its character array argument from a data line. The second function argument should be the declared size of the array. The function should store the null character in the array. If too many characters are provided, ignore any extra characters at the end of the line.

2. Write a function `concat` that returns through its third character array argument, the concatenation of its first two arguments. The fourth

argument should be the declared size of the output array. If the declared size is too small to store the entire result, store only the characters that will fit without causing overflow.

# 9.10   Common Programming Errors

Most errors in using arrays are due to subscript range errors. Be especially careful when writing loops that process arrays. Make sure that the subscript values at the loop boundaries are within range.

- *(Arrays) Out-of-range subscript references:* Array subscript references that are out-of-range (less than zero, or greater than or equal to the array size) won't be detected by the compiler or the run-time system. Instead, they will cause access to memory locations outside the range of the array, causing unpredictable program behavior.

  Such errors are very difficult to identify; they may not become readily apparent until a statement in your program executes that appears unrelated to the point where the problem occurred. It's the programmer's responsibility to prevent these errors from happening.

- *(Arrays) Unsubscripted array references:* Arrays may be used as function arguments. However, unsubscripted array references in expressions are invalid and will generate an error message. For example, if x is an integer array and y is an integer, the expression

  ```
  y = y + x;
  ```

  will generate an error message.

- *(Arrays) Subscripted references to nonarray variables:* Subscripted references to nonarray variables, such as the reference b[10] in

  ```
  a = a + b[10];
  ```

  where a and b are both simple variables, causes an error message to be generated indicating an "Invalid operation."

- *(Arrays) Mixing types in passing arrays to functions:* When array arguments are passed to functions, differences between actual argument and formal parameter types will produce error messages. For example, passing an integer array actual argument when a character array is expected will cause the compiler to generate a message such as

  ```
  "Type mismatch in parameter y in call to findMatch."
  ```

- *(Structs) References to a struct member with no prefix:* Always use the member access operator (a period) when referencing a member of a variable of some structured type. If you don't use the period, the compiler assumes that you're referencing a variable that isn't part of a structured variable.

- *(Structs) Reference to a struct member with incorrect prefix:* If v is a structured variable with a member named comp and x is a structured variable with no member of that name, then the reference x.comp will generate an "Undefined symbol 'comp'" message. If you use a struct type name (for example, coord) instead of a struct variable name before the dot, then a message such as "Improper use of typedef 'coord'" might be generated. This tells you that the a user-defined type name (coord, in this case) has been used illegally.

- *(Structs) Missing semicolon following a struct declaration:* If the semicolon required at the end of a struct declaration is missing, a variety of error messages might be generated, depending on what follows the declaration. Frequently, another declaration will follow the faulty one. If so, the second declaration is considered part of the struct, and the compiler will generate a diagnostic such as "Too many types in declaration."

## Chapter Review

1. A data structure is a grouping of related data items in memory.

2. An array is a data structure used to store a collection of data items of the same type.

3. To reference an array element, a subscript is placed in brackets immediately after the array name.

4. The initial element of array x is referenced as x[0]. If x has *n* elements, the final element is referenced as x[n-1].

5. A for loop whose counter variable runs from 0 to one less than an array's size enables us to reference all the elements of an array in sequence by using the loop counter as the array subscript.

6. For an array declared as a local variable, space is allocated in the function data area for all the array elements.

7. For an array declared as a function parameter, space is allocated in the function data area for only the address of the initial element of the actual array argument.

8. A struct is a data structure used for storing a collection of related data items of different types.

9. The individual members of a struct are accessed by placing the name of the member after the name of the struct, separating the two by the member access operator (a period).

10. The time required to perform a linear search of an array is proportional to the size of the array, so the growth rate for linear search is $O(n)$.

11. The time required to perform a selection sort on an array is proportional to the size of the array squared, so the growth rate for linear search is $O(n^2)$.

## Summary of New C++ Constructs

| Construct | Effect |
|---|---|
| **Array Declaration** | |
| `int cube[10];`<br>`int count[10];` | cube and count are arrays with 10 type int elements. |
| **Array References** | |
| `for (i = 0; i < 10; i++)`<br>`   cube[i] = i * i * i;` | Saves i cubed in the ith element of array cube. |
| `if (cube[5] > 100)`<br>`   cout << cube[0] << cube[1];` | Compares cube[5] to 100.<br>Displays the first two cubes if cube[s] is larger. |
| **struct Declaration** | |
| `struct part`<br>`{`<br>`  int id;`<br>`  int quantity;`<br>`  float price;`<br>`};`<br>`part nuts, bolts;` | A struct part is declared with data fields that can store two ints and a float value. nuts and bolts are struct variables of type part. |
| **struct References** | |
| `totalCost = nuts.quantity *`<br>`          nuts.price` | Multiplies two members of nuts. |
| `cout << bolts.id;` | Displays the id field of bolts. |
| `bolts = nuts;` | Copies struct nuts to bolts. |

### Quick-Check Exercises

1. What structured data types were discussed in this chapter? What is a structured data type?

2. Which fundamental types can't be array subscript types? Array element types?

3. Can values of different types be stored in the same array?

4. When an array is initialized, you don't need to declare the size of the array. (True/False)

5. An array is always passed by reference. (True/False)

6. When can the assignment operator be used with array elements? With entire arrays? Answer the same questions for the equality operator.

7. The elements of an array can be accessed in _____ order; however, use a _____ statement to access the elements of an array in sequential order.

8. What is the primary difference between an array and a struct? Which would you use to store the catalog description of a course? Which would you use to store the names of the students in the course?

9. When can you use the assignment operator with struct operands? When can you use the equality operator?

10. For a`Student` declared as follows, provide a statement that displays the name of a student in the form *last name, first name.*

```
struct student
{
    string first;
    string last;
    int age;
    int score;
    char grade;
}; // end student

student aStudent;
```

11. How many members are there in struct `student`?

12. Write a function that displays a variable of type `student`.

13. Explain the reason you might use `const student& stu` in a parameter list instead of `student stu`.

## Answers to Quick-Check Exercises

1. Arrays and structs. A structured data type is a named grouping of related values.

2. Floating-point types can't be used for array subscript types; all types can be element types.

3. no

4. true

5. true

6. Both the assignment and equality operators may be used with array elements. Neither the assignment operator nor the equality operator may be used with entire arrays.

7. random, `for` or `while`

8. The values stored in an array must all be the same type; the values stored in a struct don't have to be the same type. You would use a struct for the catalog item and use an array for the list of names.

9. The assignment operator may be used between structs of the same type. The equality operator may not be used to compare structs.

10. `cout << aStudent.last << ", " << aStudent.first << endl;`

11. five

12.
```
void writeStudent
    (student oneStu)      // IN: The data to display
{
    cout << "Student is " << oneStu.first << " "
        << oneStu.last << endl;
    cout << "Age is " << oneStu.age << endl;
    cout << "Score is " << oneStu.score << endl;
    cout << "Grade is " << oneStu.grade << endl;
}
```

13. The formal parameter `const student stu&` is a reference parameter whereas `student stu` is a value parameter. In the former, the data for the actual argument struct is referenced by the function but the data can't be changed. The latter creates a local copy of the actual argument, which requires extra storage and time. This extra time can be a factor for structs that store a lot of data.

## Review Questions

1. Identify the error in the following code segment. When will the error be detected?

```
int main()
{
    int x[8];
    for (int i = 0; i <= 8; i++)
```

```
        x[i] = i;
    return 0;
}
```

2. Declare an array of floating-point elements called week that can be referenced by using any day of the week as a subscript. Assume sunday is the first subscript.

3. Does C++ give you a compile-time error or a run-time error if you have a subscript out of the valid range?

4. Write a C++ program segment to print out the index of the smallest and the largest character in an array letters of 20 characters.

5. The arguments for a function are two arrays of type float and an integer that represents the length of the arrays. The function copies the first array in the argument list to the other array using a loop structure. Write the function.

6. How many exchanges are required to sort the following list of integers, using the selection sort? How many comparisons are required?

   20 30 40 25 60 80 15

7. Declare a struct called subscriber that contains the member's name, streetAddress, monthlyBill (how much the subscriber owes), and which paper the subscriber receives (morning, evening, or both).

8. Write a C++ program to read and then display the contents of the variable competition declared as follows:

```
struct olympicTrial
{
    string event;
    string entrant;
    string country;
    int place;
};

olympicTrial trackMeet;
```

9. Identify and correct the errors in the following program:

```
int main()
{
    struct summerHelp
    {
        string name;
        int empID;
```

```
            string startDate;
            float payRate
            int hoursWorked;
        }

    summerHelp operator;

    summerHelp.name = "James Borden";
    summerHelp.startDate = "June 1, 2004";
    summerHelp.hoursWorked = 29.3;
    cout << operator << endl;
    return 0;
    }
```

10. Declare the proper data structure to store the following student data:

    studentName, GPA, major, and address (consisting of streetAddress, city, state, zipCode). Use whatever data types are most appropriate for each member.

## Programming Projects

1. Write a program to read *n* data items into two arrays, x and y, of size 20. Store the products of corresponding pairs of elements of x and y in a third array, z, also of size 20. Print a three-column table that displays the arrays x, y, and z. Then compute and print the square root of the sum of the items in z. Make up your own data, with *n* less than 20.

2. Write a program for the following problem. You're given a file that contains a collection of IDs and scores (type int) for an exam in your computer course. You're to compute the average of these scores and assign grades to each student according to the following rule:

    If a student's score is within 10 points (above or below) of the average, assign a grade of satisfactory. If a student's score is more than 10 points above average, assign a grade of outstanding. If a student's score is more than 10 points below average, assign a grade of unsatisfactory.

    The output from your program should consist of a labeled three-column list that shows each ID, score, and corresponding grade. As part of the solution, your program should include functions that correspond to the function prototypes that follow.

```
// reads exam scores into array scores
void readStuData
   (ifstream &rss,        // IN: data file
    int scores[],          // OUT: the scores
```

```
   int id[],           // OUT: the IDs
   int &count,         // OUT: Number of students read
   bool &tooMany);     // OUT: A flag to indicate that more
                       // than MAX_SIZE scores items are in
                       // input file.


// computes average of count student scores
float mean(int scores[], int count);


// Displays a table showing each student's ID, score and grade
// on a separate line
// Uses: printGrade
void printTable(int score[], int ID[], int count);


// Prints student grade after comparing oneScore to average
void printGrade(int oneScore, float average);
```

3. Redo Programming Project 2 using a struct to store each student's data and an array of structs to store the whole class. The struct should have a data member for id, score, and grade.

4. The bubble sort is another technique for sorting an array. A bubble sort compares adjacent array elements and exchanges their values if they're out of order. In this way, the smaller values "bubble" to the top of the array (toward element 0), while the larger values sink to the bottom of the array. After the first pass of a bubble sort, the last array element is in the correct position; after the second pass, the last two elements are correct, and so on. Thus, after each pass, the unsorted portion of the array contains one less element. Write and test a function that implements this sorting method.

5. The results of a survey of the households in your township are available for public scrutiny. Each record contains data for one household, including a four-digit integer identification number, the annual income for the household, and the number of household members. Write a program to read the survey results into three arrays and perform the following analyses.

   **a.** Count the number of households included in the survey and print a three-column table displaying the data. (Assume that no more than 25 households were surveyed.)

   **b.** Calculate the average household income, and list the identification number and income of each household that exceeds the average.

   **c.** Determine the percentage of households that have incomes below the poverty level. Compute the poverty level income using the formula

$$p = \$7000.00 + \$850.00 \times (m - 2)$$

where $m$ is the number of members of each household. This formula shows that the poverty level depends on the number of family members, $m$, and that the poverty-level income increases as $m$ gets larger. Test your program on the following data.

| Identification Number | Annual Income | Household Members |
| --- | --- | --- |
| 1041 | 12,180 | 4 |
| 1062 | 13,240 | 3 |
| 1327 | 19,800 | 2 |
| 1483 | 35,000 | 7 |
| 1900 | 17,000 | 2 |
| 2112 | 28,500 | 6 |
| 2345 | 15,623 | 2 |
| 3210 | 3,200 | 6 |
| 3600 | 6,500 | 5 |
| 3601 | 11,970 | 2 |
| 4724 | 8,900 | 3 |
| 6217 | 10,000 | 2 |
| 9280 | 6,200 | 1 |

6. Assume that your computer has the very limited capability of being able to read and write only single-integer digits and to add two integers consisting of one decimal digit each. Write a program that can read two integers up to 20 digits each, add these integers together, and display the result. Test your program using pairs of numbers of varying lengths. (Hint: Store the two numbers in two `int` arrays of size 20, one digit per array element. If the number is less than 20 digits in length, enter enough leading zeros (to the left of the number) to make the number 20 digits long.) You'll need a loop to add the digits in corresponding array elements. Don't forget to handle the carry digit if there is one!

7. A number expressed in scientific notation is represented by its mantissa (a fraction) and its exponent. Write a function that reads a character string that represents a number in C++ scientific notation and stores the number in a struct with two members. Write a function that prints the contents of this struct as a real value. Also write functions that compute the sum, product, difference, and quotient of two numbers in scientific notation stored in two struct arguments. (Hint: The string `-0.1234E20` represents a number in scientific notation. The fraction `-0.1234` is the mantissa, and the number `20` is the exponent.)

**8.** A prime number is any number that's divisible only by one and itself. Write a program to compute all the prime numbers less than 1000. One way to generate prime numbers is to create an array of `bool` values that are true for all prime numbers, but are false otherwise. Initially set all the array entries to true. Then, for every number from 2 to 1000, set the array locations indexed by multiples of the number (but not the number itself) to false. When done, output all numbers whose array location is true. These will be the prime numbers.

**9.** Write a program that generates the Morse code for a sentence that ends in a period and contains no other characters except letters and blanks. After reading the Morse code into an array of strings, your program should read each word of the sentence and display its Morse equivalent on a separate line. The Morse code is as follows:

A .-  B -...  C -.-.  D -..  E .  F ..-.  G --.  H ....  I ..  J .---  K -.-  L .-..  M--
N -.  O ---  P .--.  Q --.-  R .-.  S ...  T -  U ..-  V ...-  W .--  X -..-  Y -.--
Z --..

Your program should include functions corresponding to the prototypes shown next.

```
// Stores Morse codes read from codeFile in array code.
void readCode(ifstream& codeFile, string codeArray[]);

// Writes Morse equivalent for a letter.
void writeCode (string codeArray[], char letter);
```

**10.** Write an interactive program that plays the game of Hangman. Read the word to be guessed into `word`. The player must guess the letters belonging to `word`. The program should terminate when either all letters have been guessed correctly (player wins) or a specified number of incorrect guesses have been made (computer wins). (Hint: Use `solution` to keep track of the solution so far. Initialize `solution` to a string of symbols `'*'`. Each time a letter in `word` is guessed, replace the corresponding `'*'` in `solution` with that letter.)

**11.** Write a function that will merge the contents of two sorted (ascending order) arrays of type `double` values, storing the result in an array output parameter (still in ascending order). The function shouldn't assume that both its input parameter arrays are the same length but can assume that one array doesn't contain two copies of the same value. The result array should also contain no duplicate values.

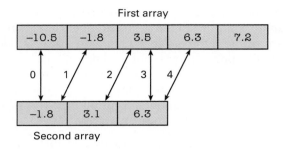

Hint: When one of the input arrays has been exhausted, don't forget to copy the remaining data in the other array into the result array. Test your function with cases in which (1) the first array is exhausted first, (2) the second array is exhausted first, and (3) the two arrays are exhausted at the same time (i.e., they end with the same value). Remember that the arrays input to this function *must already be sorted.*

12. The *binary search* algorithm that follows may be used to search an array when the elements are sorted. This algorithm is analogous to the following approach for finding a name in a telephone book.

   **a.** Open the book in the middle, and look at the middle name on the page.

   **b.** If the middle name isn't the one you're looking for, decide whether it comes before or after the name you want.

   Take the appropriate half of the section of the book you were looking in and repeat these steps until you land on the name.

   ALGORITHM FOR BINARY SEARCH

   1. Let `bottom` be the subscript of the initial array element.

   2. Let `top` be the subscript of the last array element.

   3. Let `found` be false.

   4. Repeat as long as `bottom` isn't greater than `top` and the target has not been found.

       5. Let `middle` be the subscript of the element halfway between `bottom` and `top`.

       6. If the element at middle is the target

**7.** Set `found` to `true` and `index` to `middle`.

> Else if the element at `middle` is larger than the target

**8.** Let `top` be `middle` - `1`.

> Else

**9.** Let `bottom` be `middle` + `1`.

Write and test a function `binarySearch` that implements this algorithm for an array of integers. When there is a large number of array elements, which function do you think is faster: `binarySearch` or the linear search function of Listing 9.9?

**13.** The insertion sort algorithm is a more efficient means of sorting an array. This algorithm is analogous to the procedure that card players follow when picking up cards and inserting them in their hand to form a run in a particular suit. A player makes room for a new card by shifting over the ones that follow it and then inserting it where it belongs in the hand. In sorting an array, all values are available when you begin, but you can assume that the array is not sorted and start by inserting the value currently in the second array element by comparing it to the first element. This gives you a sorted subarray consisting of the first two elements. Next, you insert the value currently in the third array element where it belongs compared to the first two, which gives you a sorted subarray of three elements, and so on. You're finished after you insert the value in the last element. Follow the algorithm below to insert the next value in an array.

ALGORITHM FOR INSERTING THE NEXT VALUE

**1.** Save the value to be inserted in `newValue`.

**2.** Using a loop, compare `newValue` to the elements already inserted in the array starting with the last one inserted. If an element is larger than `newValue`, shift it to the next array element. Exit the loop when a value that is not larger than `newValue` is reached.

**3.** Insert `newValue` at the initial position of the last element that was shifted.

# User-Defined Classes

### Chapter Objectives

- To learn how to define your own classes
- To understand why it's useful to have separate header files and implementation files for classes
- To understand the differences between the public and private section of a class and what to declare in each section
- To understand the reason for constructors in a class and how to write them
- To learn how to use the scope resolution operator in an implementation file
- To learn how to use objects as method arguments
- To understand the client/server relationship as it pertains to user programs and classes

IN THIS CHAPTER, we expand our capability to practice data abstraction and object-oriented programming by further study of the C++ class. The C++ class provides a mechanism to encapsulate, or build a protective wall around, its data and function members. A class contains a public and a private section, and only the information in the public section of the class is accessible from the outside—everything else is hidden. The class construct enables us to build truly self-contained program components that may be designed, implemented, and tested separately and then integrated into a larger program system.

We show how to use classes to define our own user-defined data types as encapsulations of data and operations. Then, we show how to declare and manipulate objects that are instances of the new class type. We implement a variety of classes, including a class for a counter, common fraction, circle, simple string, and bank account.

# 10.1   Class Definition and Use

From the start, we've been using a number of data abstractions in our programming. The types int, float, double, and char are examples of data abstractions that are *built into* the C++ language. We've also studied string and stream types that are provided through C++ class libraries. Section 7.5 presented a definition of simple data types called *enumeration types*. All of these abstract data types consist of data items and a collection of operations that can be performed on those items.

As an example, the type float abstraction might consist of four bytes (32 bits) of memory. The leftmost bit indicates the sign of the number, and the remaining bits are divided into two parts, the *characteristic* and the *mantissa*. The operations defined on variables of type float include addition, multiplication, subtraction, and division. These operations manipulate the sign, characteristic, and mantissa of their operands to produce type float results. We don't need to know the details of either the storage of type float values or their manipulation. We simply declare variables of this type and use the operations defined on them.

With this in mind, we now turn our attention to the definition of *user-defined data types*. We'll illustrate how to define our own data types as extensions to the C++ language, tailoring them as necessary to the particular problem to be solved, while at the same time making them general enough that they can be reused in other problems. The C++ class construct gives us this capability.

Although beyond the scope of this book, the C++ class also enables experienced C++ programmers to derive new classes from existing classes through a process called **inheritance**. Using inheritance, a programmer creates new classes from an existing class by adding additional data or new functions, or by redefining functions. Inheritance enhances reusability because it allows a programmer to modify existing classes easily to fit new situations, rather than having to start from scratch (see Appendix E).

**inheritance**
The process of deriving new classes with additional data or new functions from existing classes.

## The counter Class

We've seen many examples of the use of counter variables in programs. It might be useful to develop our own counter data type. A variable of this type would need to keep track of the current `count` value. The data type should provide common operations involving counters. These include the ability to increment (by one) and decrement (by one) the counter value, to set the counter to a specific value, and to retrieve the counter value. The combination of data (the counter value) and operations (`increment`, `decrement`, `setCount`, `getCount`) constitute an **abstract data type**. In C++, we use classes to define and implement abstract data types. The specification for the `counter` class abstract data type follows. Notice that we've added an additional attribute for an item of type `counter`—the maximum value that it can attain (the minimum value is zero). We also include operators to set and retrieve the maximum value.

> **abstract data type**
> A data type combined with the operations that can be performed on an object of that type.

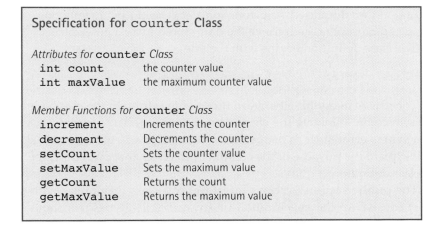

```
Specification for counter Class

Attributes for counter Class
    int count        the counter value
    int maxValue     the maximum counter value

Member Functions for counter Class
    increment        Increments the counter
    decrement        Decrements the counter
    setCount         Sets the counter value
    setMaxValue      Sets the maximum value
    getCount         Returns the count
    getMaxValue      Returns the maximum value
```

Figure 10.1 shows a diagram for the `counter` class. The diagram indicates that the `counter` data and operations are encapsulated in the class. A user of this class can access the data only by calling the operators shown in the diagram. This protects the data from being manipulated incorrectly.

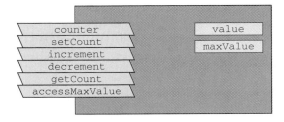

**Figure 10.1**   Class diagram for `counter` class

## Class Definition for the **counter** Class

Listing 10.1 shows an example of a class definition for a simple abstraction that we call a counter. The class contains two single integer variables count and maxValue, declared at the bottom of Listing 10.1. The variable count represents the current counter value; the variable maxValue represents the maximum counter value where 0 is always the minimum counter value. The value of maxValue is set when we allocate storage for a counter object (more on this later). The variables count and maxValue represent the counter **state**—the current status of an object as indicated by the values of its internal variables. Just like any variable you used as a counter in an earlier program, a counter object can be set to an initial value in its range (use function setCount) and its value can be increased (use function increment) or decreased (use function decrement) by 1. Functions get-Count and getMaxValue retrieve the data stored in a counter object.

**state**
The current status of an object as indicated by the values of its internal variables.

The class definition begins with the line

```
class counter
```

and consists of everything between the opening through the closing braces. The semicolon following the closing brace is required; if you omit it, you'll get a syntax error such as Declaration terminated incorrectly. Later, we'll explain the purpose of the compiler directives that precede and follow the class definition.

**public section (or class interface)**
The specification of variables, data types, constants, and functions that are accessible to other program components.

The **public section** (or **class interface**) of a class (beginning with pub-lic:) consists of the specification of any variables, types, constants, and function prototypes that are accessible to another program component. The information in the class interface is all that a programmer needs to know in order to use the class successfully. This is also all the compiler needs to know to compile a program that uses the class. Identifiers that are declared in the public section of a class (for example, setCount, increment, and decrement in Listing 10.1) may be accessed inside or outside of the class. The public section for class counter declares eight functions (through their prototypes). We define these functions in Section 10.2.

**private section**
The specification of variables, data types, constants, and functions that are accessible only to the class member functions.

The **private section** of a class (beginning with private:) consists of the specification of any variables, constants, data types, and function prototypes to be hidden from other program components. Identifiers declared in the private section, such as the variable count, can be accessed only within the class itself.

**class header file**
A file with extension .h that contains a class definition.

The **class header file** (shown in Listing 10.1) is a file with extension .h that contains the class definition, including the public and private sections, down to and including the semicolon following the right brace. In Section 10.2, we discuss the .cpp file, which contains the class implementation.

**Listing 10.1** Definition of class counter

```
// File: counter.h
// Counter class definition

#ifndef COUNTER_H          // used to avoid multiple definitions
#define COUNTER_H          //    not part of the class

class counter
{
   public:
      // Member Functions
      // Constructors
      counter();
      counter(int);

      // Increment counter
      void increment();

      // Decrement counter
      void decrement();

      // Set counter value
      void setCount(int);

      // Set maximum counter value.
      void setMaxValue(int);

      // Return current counter value
      int getCount() const;

      // Return maximum counter value
      int getMaxValue() const;

   private:
      // Data members (attributes)
      int count;
      int maxValue;

}; // Note — a class definition MUST end with a semicolon
#endif // COUNTER_H
```

Although you don't need to store classes in separate files, we recommend you do so. This practice lets you keep each file fairly small and makes it easier to locate and reuse classes as the need arises. Also, the header file gives a concise, clear description for anyone who wants to use the class, and hides unnecessary detail that is found in the implementation file.

The functions declared (through their prototypes in Listing 10.1) in the class definition are referred to as the **member functions** of the class. The variables, constants, and data types are referred to as the **data members** or **storage attributes** of the class.

**member functions**
Functions declared in a class definition.
**data members (or storage attributes)**
Variables, constants, and data types specified in a class definition.

Normally, we place the data members in the private section of the class because the user doesn't need to know either their names or internal representations. This allows us to control access to the data members and ensure that they are always manipulated in a safe and predicable way and only by the member functions that are provided in the class. The member functions provide the interface between the user and the data, so they are normally found in the public section of the class.

## Compiler Directives in File `counter.h`

The purpose of the first two lines in the `counter.h` file

```
#ifndef COUNTER_H        // used to avoid multiple
                         //    definitions -
#define COUNTER_H        //    not part of class
```

is to prevent multiple definitions of the identifiers defined in class `counter` during compilation of a program system in which more than one file includes the `counter` class. These lines precede the class definition and cause the compiler to skip all lines through the last line in the file

```
#endif // COUNTER_H
```

Each time, except for the first time, the compiler encounters the directive

```
#include "counter.h"
```

The line beginning with `#ifndef` (if not defined) tests whether identifier `COUNTER_H` has been defined yet. If it hasn't, the second line defines `COUNTER_H` giving it the value `NULL`. Then the compiler processes the rest of the lines in file `counter.h`. When your compiler attempts to include this file at a later time, the first line it processes

```
#ifndef  COUNTER_H            // used  to  avoid  multiple
                             //    definitions -
```

will determine that `COUNTER_H` is defined, so all lines through `#endif` will be skipped, thereby preventing multiple definitions of the identifiers in the class. There is nothing magical about the name COUNTER_H; we formed it by adding _H to the end of the class name.

## Using the **counter** Class

To help us understand the counter class, let us look at an example program that uses it (see Listing 10.2). This program declares two counters, c1 and c2. It performs several operations on each counter and displays the final counter value.

The first two lines of code in the main function

```
counter c1;
counter c2(10);
```

declare two objects of type counter. These declarations resemble those we've used previously. The first counter object, c1, can have a maximum value of INT_MAX, which is the largest integer value on your C++ system (defined in library file climits). The second counter object, c2, can have a maximum value of 10. Both c1 and c2 have an initial value of 0.

**Listing 10.2**   Test program and sample output for user of counter class

```
// File: counterTest.cpp
// Test the counter class

#include "counter.h"
#include <iostream>
using namespace std;

int main()
{
    counter c1;          // variable of type counter - maximum value
                         //    INT_MAX
    counter c2(10);      // variable of type counter - maximum value
                         //    10

    // Test setCount, increment, decrement, and getCount
    //    functions.
    c1.setCount(50);              // SetValue of c1 to 50
    c1.decrement();
    c1.decrement();
    c1.increment();
    cout << "Final value of c1 is " << c1.getCount() << endl;
```

(continued)

Listing 10.2   Test program and sample output for user of `counter` class (continued)

```
    c2.increment();
    c2.increment();
    c2.decrement();
    cout << "Final value of c2 is " << c2.getCount() << endl;

    return 0;
}
```

```
Final value of c1 is 49
Final value of c2 is 1
```

The legal operations on the objects `c1` and `c2` are defined by the member functions declared in the public section of the `counter` class. These are the only operations allowed on the `counter` variables.

The statement

```
    c1.setCount(50);            // SetValue of c1 to 50
```

sets the value of counter `c1` to 50. Because `c1` is an object, we use dot notation to apply the member function `setCount` to it. Next, we decrement `c1` twice and increment it once. The function call `c1.getCount` (in the first line beginning with `cout`) retrieves its final value (49), which is then displayed. The `counter` object `c2` has an initial value of 0. We increment `c2` twice and decrement it once. The last program line retrieves and displays the final value of `c2`, which is 1.

## Compiler Directives in File **CounterTest.cpp**

File `CounterTest.cpp` begins with the line

```
    #include "counter.h"
```

because file `counter.h` provides the class definition for the `counter` class. It also contains the line

```
    #include <iostream>
```

because it accesses operator `<<` and stream `cout`, both defined in class `iostream`.

## EXERCISES FOR SECTION 10.1

Self-Check

1. Explain why the prefixes `c1` and `c2` are required in references to the functions `setCount`, `increment`, `decrement`, and `getCount` as shown in Listing 10.2.

2. What does the line

   ```
   #infdef COUNTER_H
   ```

   do? What about the line

   ```
   #define COUNTER_H
   ```

3. Correct the errors in the statements below.

   **a.** `counter c1 = 20;`    `// initial value of c1 is 20`

   **b.** `c1.setCount("15");`

   **c.** `decrement(c1);`    `// decrement c1`

   **d.** `decrement(c1, 2);`    `// decrement c1 by 2`

4. Explain the effect of the following fragment. What is the final value of `c1` and `c2`?

   ```
   counter c1;
   counter c2(5);
   while (c2.getCount() > c1.getCount())
       c1.increment();
   ```

Programming

1. A `for` loop header that uses a `counter` variable has the form

   ```
   for (int i = 0; i < n; i++)
   ```

   Declare a `counter` variable `i` and rewrite the `for` loop header using the operators for the `counter` class.

2. Write a program that uses a type `counter` variable to display the lines:

   ```
                10
                 9
                ...
                 0
           BLAST-OFF!
   ```

## 10.2    Class Implementation

**implementation file**
A file with extension
`.cpp` that provides
C++ code for the mem-
ber functions of a class.

**scope resolution
operator**
The operator `::` that
precedes the definition
of a class member func-
tion and is itself pre-
ceded by the name of
the class whose member
function is being
defined.

The **implementation file** for the `counter` class (file `counter.cpp` in Listing 10.3) contains the C++ code for the class member functions. By putting these definitions in a separate file, we hide them from the class users, which don't need to know these details. We use the **scope resolution operator** `::` as a prefix to the function name in each function header. This operator tells the compiler that the function being defined is declared (through its prototype) in the class definition whose name precedes the operator. The scope resolution operator also applies to all identifiers in the function definition through the closing brace. These identifiers are data members also declared in the class definition.

**Listing 10.3**    Implementation file for `counter` class

```cpp
// File: counter.cpp
// Counter class implementation
#include "counter.h"
#include <iostream>
#include <climits>            // For INT_MAX
using namespace std;

// Default constructor
counter::counter()
{
   count = 0;
   maxValue = INT_MAX;    // Set maxValue to default maximum
}

// Constructor with argument
counter::counter(int mVal)    // IN: maximum integer value
{
   count = 0;
   maxValue = mVal;       // Set maxValue to mVal
}

// Increment counter
void counter::increment()
{
   if (count < maxValue)
      count++;
   else
```

(continued)

**Listing 10.3   Implementation file for counter class (continued)**

```cpp
      cerr << "Counter overflow. Increment ignored." << endl;
}

// Decrement counter
void counter::decrement()
{
   if (count > 0)
      count--;
   else
      cerr << "Counter underflow. Decrement ignored." << endl;
}

// Set counter value
void counter::setCount(int val)
{
   if (val >= 0  &&  val <= maxValue)
      count = val;
   else
      cerr << "New value is out of range. Value not changed."
           << endl;
}

// Set maximum counter value
void counter::setMaxValue(int val)
{
   if (val >= 0  &&  val <= INT_MAX)
      maxValue = val;
   else
      cerr << "New maxValue is out of range — not changed."
           << endl;
}

// Get current counter value
int counter::getCount() const
{
   return count;
}

// Get maximum counter value
int counter::getMaxValue() const
{
   return maxValue;
}
```

## Constructors

**constructor**
A member function that
executes when an object
of a class is declared
and that sets the initial
state of the new object.

The implementation file begins with two constructors, special member functions with the same name as the class. A **constructor** automatically executes each time an object of type counter is declared. Its purpose is to set the initial state of the new object by initializing its data members. The constructor without an argument is the *default constructor* and is the one that normally executes.

In the default constructor, the statements

```
count = 0;
maxValue = INT_MAX;     // Set maxValue to default maximum
```

set the initial state of the new counter object to the following: count is 0, maxValue is INT_MAX. Notice that the identifier count requires no prefix of the form object.. C++ assumes that count and maxValue are the data members of the object being declared.

The second constructor executes whenever the object declaration has an argument list. It sets the initial state to the following: count is 0, maxValue is the value of the constructor argument. In Listing 10.2, the declaration statement

```
counter c2(10);
```

causes the second constructor to execute, setting count to 0 and maxValue to 10.

A constructor can't specify a return type or explicitly return a value. For this reason, do not precede the constructor name with either void or a data type when writing its prototype or definition.

## Accessor and Modifier Functions

**modifier**
A member function that
modifies the value of a
data member.

**accessor**
A member function that
retrieves the value of a
data member.

You should be able to read and understand the remaining member functions. Functions setCount, increment, and decrement *modify* the counter value and are called **modifiers**. Functions getCount and getMaxValue *retrieve* the counter data and are called **accessors**. Most of the member functions that you write for a class will fall into one of these two categories.

Manipulating the object's data using class modifiers controls how the data will be manipulated. You can't, for example, increment the counter value beyond the value of maxValue, nor can you decrement it so that it becomes negative.

The accessor function headings end with the word const, which indicates to C++ that the function execution doesn't change the state of the object it's applied to. You should do this whenever you define a member function that doesn't change an object's state. Examples of such functions would be member functions that retrieve, display, or test an object's data.

A class member function can access directly all the data members of the class. Therefore, you shouldn't use member functions `setCount` or `get-Count` to process data member `count` when defining the class member functions. However, you must use these functions outside the class.

## Compiler Directives in File **counter.cpp**

Notice that both files `counterTest.cpp` and `counter.cpp` contain the line

```
#include "counter.h"
```

You must place this directive in both files, so that C++ can access the class definition when compiling these files. Again, the line beginning with `#ifn-def` in file `counter.h` prevents multiple definitions of the identifiers defined in the header file. File `counter.cpp` also accesses identifier `INT_MAX` (from the standard library file `climits`), so it must include that file. Similarly, file `counter.cpp` accesses operator `<<` and `cerr`, so it must include library file `iostream`.

## EXERCISES FOR SECTION 10.2

### Self-Check

1. Explain the purpose of the operator `::` in the `counter` class shown in Listing 10.3. Why is this operator needed?

2. Explain why no prefix is required in references to the attribute `count` in functions `setCount`, `increment`, `decrement`, and `getCount`, as shown in Listing 10.3.

3. Explain why function `counter` has two constructors. How does C++ know which one to execute?

### Programming

1. Write two type `bool` member functions called `atMax` and `atMin` that return a value of true when the value of a `counter` object has reached its maximum value or its minimum value (zero), respectively.

2. Write a `bool` member function called `lessThan` that has a single `int` argument and returns true if the counter object is `lessThan` the value of its argument.

# 10.3   Summary of Rules for Use of Classes and Objects

## Objects as Class Instances

The declaration

```
counter c1;
```

creates a new object c1 that is called an *instance* of the class counter. The declaration causes the default constructor to initialize the data members of object c1 to zero. As we pointed out earlier, this declaration is conceptually the same as declarations involving standard data types, such as

```
int count;
```

All of these declarations associate a name with a region of computer memory. We'll continue to refer to names associated with the fundamental types and with enumeration, array, and struct types as variables. We'll refer to names associated with types defined using the class construct as *objects*. Thus c1 is an object (of type counter) in the test program for the counter class; count and maxValue, variables (of type int), are data members or attributes of the class.

The member functions of the class should include at least one constructor that has the same name as the class. A constructor automatically executes each time a counter object is created, and the constructor initializes one or more of the object's data members. The default constructor takes no argument and executes when the object declaration doesn't end with an argument list. A constructor doesn't have a result type and can't return a value.

## Public versus Private Access

Any program component may apply member functions, setCount, increment, decrement, getCount, and getMaxValue, as operations on object c1. In the counter class, the member functions are all publicly accessible. This is not always the case. Classes may have member functions that are private and, therefore, aren't directly accessible outside the class.

Similarly, not all class attributes must appear in the private section of a class. However, you should have a very good reason for placing an attribute in the public section and, therefore, not protecting it from outside access.

A program that uses a class is called a **client** of the class, and the class itself is referred to as the **server**. The client program may declare and manipulate objects of the data type defined by the server class. It may do so without knowing the details of the internal representation of the server's data or the implementation of its operators. Thus the details of the server are hidden from the client. As we proceed through the rest of this book, we'll illustrate the benefits of this information-hiding capability and its impact on the software development process.

client
A program component that uses another predefined class.

server
A program component, usually a class, that provides operators to another program component that enable it to manipulate the server's data.

## Syntax for Class and Member Function Definitions

A summary of the syntax rules for defining a class and its operations is shown in the following two displays.

---

**Class Definition**

**Form:**
```
class className
{
public:
```
- List of class attributes (variables, types, constants, and so on) that may be accessed by name from outside the class
- List of prototypes for each member function that may be accessed by name from outside the class

. . .
```
private:
```
- List of class attributes (variables, types, constants, and so on) that are intended to be hidden for reference from outside the class
- List of prototypes for each member function intended to be hidden from outside of the class

. . .
```
};  // Don't forget the semicolon
```

**Example:**
```
class checkingAccount
{
public:
// Member functions . . .

// Make deposit into checking account
void makeDeposit
(int);    // IN: number of account to
          //     receive deposit

// Set service charge for account
```

---

```
          void setServiceCharge
            (int,                   // IN: account number
             float);                // IN: service charge

          private:
          // Data members . . .
          char initFirst, initMiddle, initLast;
                             // initials
          int accountNum;        // account number
          float balance;         // account balance
          float serviceCharge; // service charge
          };  // Don't forget the semicolon
```

**Interpretation:** The functions, variables, types, and constants that are declared in the class definition are accessible to all class member functions (see next display). However, only those declared as **public** may be accessed by name from outside the class.

---

## Class Member Function Definition

**Form:**      type className :: fname
             ( formal parameter list )
             {
               . . .
               function body
               . . .
             }

**Example:**
```
// Constructor
checkingAccount::checkingAccount()
{
    accountNum = 0;
    balance = 0.0;
}

// Make deposit into checking account
void checkingAccount::makeDeposit
    (int acNum)      // IN: number of account
                     //      to receive deposit
{
    // Local data . . .
    float amount;

    // Make deposit.
    if (accountNum == acNum)
    {
        balance += amount; }
```

```
        else
        cout << "Wrong account number specified."
            << endl;
}
```

**Interpretation:** The function **makeDeposit** is a member of the class **checkingAccount**. It's like any other C++ function except that it has access to all class data and function members. To ensure that C++ knows that the functions are associated with a class, the function names must be preceded by the name of the class followed by the scope resolution operator **: :**.

**Reminder:** Note carefully that all data members (variables, constants, and so on) of a class are directly accessible to the class member functions.

## Comparing Structs and Classes

Both the struct and the class define a data type that is a composite of related data elements that may be of different types. Both may also contain function prototype declarations (although we haven't done this with structs) and both provide the capability to specify three levels of access control to the functions and data: `public`, `protected` (not discussed in this text), and `private`. In fact, the main difference between structs and classes is that with structs, the default access is `public`; with classes, the default access is `private`. We'll use structs in this book only when no functions are involved in the structure definition and when all data are to be publicly accessible; otherwise, we'll use classes.

## Project Files and Separate Compilation

In many C++ systems, you'll need to create a project to facilitate compiling and linking the separate `.cpp` files for your client program (the one that contains the main function) and its classes. The details of doing this are system dependent (see Appendixes F and G). However, your project must contain all the `.cpp` files (but not the `.h` files) for the classes and client program in your program system. As a first step, you should attempt to compile the client program. If you're successful, select the command `Build` to compile the other `.cpp` files and to link the object files together. When this step completes successfully, you can run the executable file created by the `Build` operation. On most systems, selecting the `Run` command will cause all these steps to be carried out in sequence.

There is a distinct advantage to creating projects: if you later modify your client program but haven't changed your class files, only the client program will need to be recompiled. Similarly, if you use the class with another client program, the new client will be compiled but not the class implementation file. The C++ system will link the new object file created by compiling the client program to the existing object files for its classes. If you later modify a class implementation file but not its header file, you can still run all its client programs without recompiling them. However, the C++ system will need to link a client's object file to the new object file for the class before execution.

If you're having difficulty setting up projects but still want to test and debug your classes, you can do this by including the class implementation file at the end of the header file (`.h`) for each class (using `#include "file-Name.cpp"`). Since this is so simple, you might wonder why we bother with projects in the first place. The disadvantage to including the class implementation file is that the C++ system will always recompile it even if you modify only the client program. With projects and separate compilation, only the files that have been changed will be recompiled.

## Combining Arrays, Structs, and Classes

We'll illustrate a class that has an array as one of its data members in Section 10.7. You can combine arrays, structs, and classes in many different ways in C++. For example, the declaration

```
counter counts[10];
```

allocates storage for an array of 10 counter objects named `counts[0]` through `counts[9]`. The default constructor sets the `count` attribute of each `counter` object to 0 and the `maxValue` attribute to `INT_MAX`. We'll provide many examples of combinations of different kinds of data structures in Chapter 11.

## Function Overloading and Polymorphism

**function overloading**
Providing different formal parameter lists for a particular function.

**polymorphism**
The ability of a function to change its operation based on the object it's applied to or its argument list makeup.

There are two constructors in the `counter` class. When translating a `counter` object declaration, the C++ compiler determines which constructor function to use based on the presence or absence of an actual argument. Having multiple functions with the same name is called **function overloading**. The ability of a function to perform different operations based on the context of its call (the object it's applied to and its argument list makeup) is called **polymorphism**.

Another example of polymorphism would be the use of the same function name in different classes. For example, several classes might declare a function named `display` that displays the class attributes. For a particular call of function `display`, C++ determines which `display` function to use by the data type of the object it's applied to. This capability frees the programmer from having to ensure that each function name is unique and that the name doesn't appear in another class.

## EXERCISES FOR SECTION 10.3

### Self-Check

1. For the array of counters declared in this section, write a statement to set the value of `counts[2]` to 5. Write a statement that displays the value stored in `counts[4]`.

### Programming

1. Write a `for` loop that decrements the values of all the counters in the array of counters.

2. Write a constructor for class `checkingAccount` that initializes the data members to the values specified by its two arguments. Show a sample call.

3. Write member functions `setBalance`, `getBalance`, `getAccountNum` and `setAccountNum` for the `checkingAccount` class.

## 10.4  Classes as Operands and Arguments

In Chapter 9, we discussed rules for using arrays and structs as function arguments and as operands of assignment, equality, relational, and arithmetic operators. We saw that, with the exception of assignment of structs, using familiar operators with these data structures wasn't permitted.

You can use the assignment operator with two objects of the same class type; however, you can't use the other familiar operators with classes unless you explicitly define them as operators for the class—a process called **operator overloading**. We'll explain how to do this in Section 11.7.

Normally, you don't need to pass objects as member function arguments because you use dot notation to specify the object to which the function is being applied. If you need to specify an operation that involves two objects, you can apply the member function to one and pass the other one as an argument. The rules for using objects as formal arguments follow.

**operator overloading**
The ability to use an operator with objects from more than one class.

## Rules for Using Objects as Formal Parameters

- If `c` is a class type, use `c& ob1` to declare `ob1` as a formal reference parameter.
- If `c` is a class type, use `const c& ob1` to specify that formal parameter `ob1` can't be changed by the function's execution.

The second rule is for efficiency but is not a requirement of C++. You can declare an object as a value argument in a function header, but that requires storing a local copy of the object argument each time the function is called. We illustrate the second rule next.

## EXAMPLE 10.1

Listing 10.4 shows a function called **compareCounter** written as a member function for the class **counter**. The function compares two counter objects and returns –1, 0, or 1 depending on whether the **count** attribute of the counter object it's applied to is less than (–1), equal to (0), or greater than (1), the count attribute of its counter argument. If c1 and c2 are counters, you can use the statement below to call **compareCounter**.

```
c1.compareCounter(c2);
```

If the **count** attribute for **c1** is 3 and the count attribute for **c2** is 5, this function call returns –1.

Each condition compares the **count** attribute of the object to which the function is applied (denoted only by **count**) to the **count** attribute of the function argument (denoted by **aCounter.count**). The function result is based on this comparison.

Some programmers dislike the lack of symmetry in the definition and use of function **compareCounter** and would prefer to use a function call such as

```
compareCounter(c1, c2);
```

in which both objects being compared (not just one) are passed as arguments to function **compareCounter**. We'll see how to do this in Section 11.7.

Objects can also be returned as function results. We illustrate this in the next section.

## EXERCISES FOR SECTION 10.4

### Self-Check

1. What value is returned by the function call `c1.compareCounter(c2)` when `c1.count` is 7 and `c2.count` is 5? Answer the same question for `c2.compareCounter(c1)`.

Listing 10.4   Function compareCounter

```
int counter::compareCounter(const counter& aCounter) const
{
   int result;

   if (count < aCounter.count)
      result = -1;
   else if (count == aCounter.count)
      result = 0;
   else
      result = 1;

   return result;
}
```

Programming

1. Rewrite function compareCounter to base its result on both attributes of a counter object: count and maxValue.

2. Write a function lessThan that returns a value of true when the counter object it's applied to has a smaller value than its counter argument.

## 10.5   A Fraction Class

We can use classes to define useful data types that aren't part of the C++ language or its standard library. As an example, we might want to work with common fractions in performing some mathematical computations. In this section, we design a fraction class that would provide this capability.

### Design of fraction Class

The fraction class should have data members to represent the numerator and denominator (both integers) of a fraction object. It should be able to read and display a fraction and also include operators for performing the common mathematical operations on fractions, add, subtract, multiply, and divide. We summarize these design decisions next.

Notice that we provide three constructors for the fraction class. The first is the default. The second constructor allows us to create a fraction object that represents a whole number (the numerator); the new fraction's denominator will be 1. The third constructor allows us to specify both the numerator and denominator of a new `fraction` object.

Notice that each member function that performs an arithmetic operation is type `fraction`. These functions return a `fraction` object that represents the result of the operation. Listing 10.5 shows the class definition.

---

### Specification for **fraction** Class

*Attributes for* **fraction** *Class*

| | |
|---|---|
| `int num` | Numerator of the fraction |
| `int denom` | Denominator of the fraction |

*Member Functions for* **fraction** *Class*

| | |
|---|---|
| `fraction` | A constructor |
| `setNum` | Sets the numerator |
| `setDenom` | Sets the denominator |
| `multiply` | Multiplies fractions |
| `divide` | Divides fractions |
| `add` | Adds fractions |
| `subtract` | Subtracts fractions |
| `readFrac` | Reads a fraction |
| `displayFrac` | Displays a fraction |
| `getNum` | Returns the numerator |
| `getDenom` | Returns the denominator |

---

**Listing 10.5**   Class definition for `fraction`

```
// File: fraction.h
// Fraction class definition

#ifndef FRACTION_H
#define FRACTION_H

class fraction
{
    public:
        // Member functions
        // Constructors
        fraction();
        fraction(int);
        fraction(int, int);

        // Set numerator and denominator
```

(continued)

**Listing 10.5** Class definition for `fraction` (continued)

```
            void setNum(int);
            void setDenom(int);

            // Multiply fractions
            fraction multiply(fraction f1);

            // Divide fractions
            fraction divide(fraction f1);

            // Add Fractions
            fraction add(fraction f1);

            // Subtract Fractions
            fraction subtract(fraction f1);

            // Read a fraction
            void readFrac();

            // Display a fraction
            void displayFrac() const;

            // Accessors
            int getNum() const;
            int getDenom() const;

        private:
            // Data members (attributes)
            int num;
            int denom;
    };
    #endif // FRACTION_H
```

## Using Class **fraction**

Listing 10.6 shows a driver program (with sample output) that tests the arithmetic functions of class `fraction`. First, it calls `readFrac` to read two fractions (`f1` and `f2`). It then uses the statement

```
    f3 = f1.multiply(f2);
```

to calculate `f1` × `f2` and assign the result to fraction `f3`. Next, it calls method `displayFrac` several times to display the fraction operands and the result of each arithmetic operation.

**Listing 10.6** A driver function to test class `fraction`

```cpp
// File: fractionTest.cpp
// Tests the fraction class.

#include <iostream>
#include "fraction.h"
using namespace std;

int main()
{
   fraction f1, f2;      // input - fraction operands
   fraction f3;          // output - result of operation

   // Read two fractions
   cout << "Enter 1st fraction:" << endl;
   f1.readFrac();
   cout << "Enter 2nd fraction:" << endl;
   f2.readFrac();

   // Display results of fraction arithmetic
   f3 = f1.multiply(f2);
   f1.displayFrac();   cout << " * ";
   f2.displayFrac();   cout << " = ";
   f3.displayFrac();   cout << endl;

   f3 = f1.divide(f2);
   f1.displayFrac();   cout << " / ";
   f2.displayFrac();   cout << " = ";
   f3.displayFrac();   cout << endl;

   f3 = f1.add(f2);
   f1.displayFrac();   cout << " + ";
   f2.displayFrac();   cout << " = ";
   f3.displayFrac();   cout << endl;

   f3 = f1.subtract(f2);
   f1.displayFrac();   cout << " - ";
   f2.displayFrac();   cout << " = ";
   f3.displayFrac();   cout << endl;

   return 0;
}
```

(continued)

Listing 10.6   A driver function to test class `fraction`  (continued)

```
Enter 1st fraction:
Enter numerator / denominator: 3 / 4
Enter 2nd fraction:
Enter numerator / denominator: 5 / 6
3/4 * 5/6 = 15/24
3/4 / 3/6 = 18/20
3/4 + 5/6 = 38/24
3/4 - 5/6 = -2/2
```

The main function displays the result of each arithmetic operation in a very readable format such as

```
3/4 * 5/6 = 15/24
```

The two operands, `f1` and `f2`, and the result appear on the same line because the newline character is not displayed until after `f3` is displayed. You may notice that the fraction results aren't in simplified form. We leave this for a later exercise (see Programming Exercise 3 in Section 12.3).

## Implementation File for Class **fraction**

Listing 10.7 shows the implementation file for class `fraction`. The file begins with three constructors followed by four arithmetic operations. In function `multiply`, the statement

```
fraction temp(num * f.num, denom * f.denom);
```

declares a new fraction named `temp` using the constructor that takes two arguments. It defines the numerator of `temp` as the product of the two operand numerators (`num * f.num`); it defines the denominator of `temp` as the product of the two operand denominators (`denom * f.denom`). The statement

```
return temp;
```

returns fraction `temp` as the function result. The other arithmetic operations are defined in a similar manner.

Function `readFrac` displays a prompt that tells the user to enter a fraction as a numerator and denominator value separated by /. The data entry loop repeats until the variable slash (type `char`) contains `'/'`.

Listing 10.7   Implementation file for class `fraction`

```cpp
// File: fraction.cpp
// Fraction class implementation

#include "fraction.h"
#include <iostream>
using namespace std;

// Member functions
// Constructors
fraction::fraction()
{
   num = 0;
   denom = 1;
}

fraction::fraction(int n)
{
   num = n;        // Fraction for a whole number
   denom = 1;
}

fraction::fraction(int n, int d)
{
   num = n;
   denom = d;
}

// Set numerator and denominator
void fraction::setNum(int n)
{
   num = n;
}

void fraction::setDenom(int d)
{
   denom = d;
}

// Multiply fractions
fraction fraction::multiply(fraction f)
{
   fraction temp(num * f.num, denom * f.denom);
```

(continued)

Listing 10.7   Implementation file for class `fraction`  (continued)

```cpp
      return temp;
}

// Divide fractions
fraction fraction::divide(fraction f)
{
    fraction temp(num * f.denom, denom * f.num);
    return temp;
}

// Add fractions
fraction fraction::add(fraction f)
{
    fraction temp(num * f.denom + f.num * denom,
                  denom * f.denom);
    return temp;
}

// Subtract Fractions
fraction fraction::subtract(fraction f)
{
    fraction temp(num * f.denom - f.num * denom,
                  denom * f.denom);
    return temp;
}

// Read a fraction
void fraction::readFrac()
{
    char slash;        // storage for "/"

    do
    {
        cout << "Enter numerator / denominator: ";
        cin >> num >> slash >> denom;
    }
    while (slash != '/');
}

// Display a fraction
void fraction::displayFrac() const
{
```

(continued)

Listing 10.7    Implementation file for class `fraction` (continued)

```
        cout << num << '/' << denom;
    }

    // Accessors
    int fraction::getNum() const
    {
        return num;
    }

    int fraction::getDenom() const
    {
        return denom;
    }
```

You may be wondering whether it's possible in C++ to use the arithmetic operators *, /, +, and − with fraction operands. The answer is yes, and we'll discuss how to overload operators so that they can be used with operands that are fraction objects in Section 11.7.

## EXERCISES FOR SECTION 10.5

### Self–Check

1. Draw a class diagram for the `fraction` class.

2. Discuss how you might return a simplified fraction as the result of a fraction operation. Assume you have a member function named `simplify` that simplifies a fraction. For example, if `f1` is 9/12, `f1.simplify()` would change `f1` to 3/4.

3. Discuss how you might implement function `subtract` using function `add` and a function `negate` that negates a fraction. For example, if `f1` is 3/4, `f1.negate()` is −3/4. (Hint: If `f1` and `f2` are fractions, `f1 - f2` is equal to `f1 + (-f2)`.)

4. Why do you think the constructor with zero arguments initializes data member `denom` to 1 instead of 0?

### Programming

1. Write function `negate` described in Self-Check Exercise 3.

2. Write a member function `toDecimal` that returns the decimal value of a fraction. Be careful not to return 0 when the decimal value is less than 1.

3. Write a type `bool` member function (`isInfinite`) that tests whether a fraction is infinite. An infinite fraction has a denominator of 0.

4. Write four additional member functions that perform arithmetic operations on a fraction and an integer. For example, `f1.add(6)` should add fraction `f1` to the integer 6. (Hint: In the new function `add`, with a type `int` argument, declare a new fraction and pass it to the existing member function `add`, with a type fraction argument, to perform the addition.)

# 10.6 A Circle Class

In a graphics program, we need to represent simple graphical objects such as circles, squares, rectangles, and triangles. We want to be able to position these objects anywhere on the screen and draw them in various sizes and colors. Besides drawing the objects themselves, we want to display the object's characteristics, including its center coordinates, area, and perimeter. In this section, we design a class that can be used to represent circle objects.

## Design of `circle` Class

Our `circle` class should have data members to represent the *x*- and *y*-coordinates of a circle object's center as well as its radius, color, area, and perimeter. Normally, a user of this class would set values for all of a circle object's attributes except its area and perimeter. These attributes can be computed (using member functions) after its radius is set by the class user.

Since our purpose is to represent objects for display on a screen, we'll use type `int` attributes for the circle's center coordinates and radius. We'll declare an enumeration type `color` with eight values for the circle color. We summarize these design decisions next, and Listing 10.8 shows the class definition.

---

**Specification for `circle` Class**

*Public Data Type for `circle` Class*
| | |
|---|---|
| `color` | An enumeration type with 8 color values |

*Attributes for `circle` Class*
| | |
|---|---|
| `int x` | *x*-coordinate |
| `int y` | *y*-coordinate |
| `float radius` | Radius |
| `color cColor` | Color |

---

| | |
|---|---|
| `float area` | Area |
| `float perimeter` | Perimeter |

*Member Functions for* `circle` *Class*

| | |
|---|---|
| `circle` | A constructor |
| `setCoord` | Sets the *x*- and *y*-coordinates |
| `setRadius` | Sets the circle radius |
| `setColor` | Sets the circle color |
| `computeArea` | Computes the area of the circle: *area = $\pi \times radius^2$* |
| `computePerimeter` | Computes the perimeter of the circle: *perimeter = 2.0 $\times \pi \times radius$* |
| `displayCircle` | Displays circle attributes |
| `getX` | Returns *x*-coordinate value |
| `getY` | Returns *y*-coordinate value |
| `getColor` | Returns circle color |
| `getArea` | Returns circle area |
| `getPerimeter` | Returns circle perimeter |

**Listing 10.8**   Class definition for `circle`

```
// File circle.h
// Circle class definition

#ifndef CIRCLE_H
#define CIRCLE_H

class circle
{
   public:
      // enumeration type
      enum color {black, blue, green, cyan, red,
                  magenta, brown, lightgray, nocolor};

      // Member Functions
      // constructor
      circle();

      // Set center coordinates
      void setCoord(int, int);

      // Set radius
      void setRadius(float);

      // Set color
```

(continued)

**Listing 10.8**   Class definition for `circle`  (continued)

```
        void setColor(color);

        // Compute the area
        void computeArea();

        // Compute the perimeter
        void computePerimeter();

        // Display attributes
        void displayCircle() const;

        // accessor functions
        int getX() const;
        int getY() const;
        float getRadius() const;
        color getColor() const;
        float getArea() const;
        float getPerimeter() const;

    private:
        // Data members (attributes)
        int x;
        int y;
        float radius;
        color cColor;
        float area;
        float perimeter;
};
#endif // CIRCLE_H
```

We declare the enumeration type `color` in the public section of the class, so that a user of the class can access its values. The ninth color value, `nocolor`, indicates that a color value hasn't yet been assigned. Rather than define the enumeration type here, another approach is to define a separate class `color` and to include this class (using `#include "color.h"`) in class `circle`. This modification is left as Programming Project 1 at the end of the chapter.

Notice that we declare member functions `computeArea` and `compute-Perimeter` as `void` functions. You might be tempted to declare them as type `float` because they each compute a floating-point value. However, that value is stored in a class attribute and is not returned as a function result. You can call accessor functions `getArea` and `getPerimeter` (both type `float`) to retrieve the attribute values.

## Using Class `circle`

Listing 10.9 shows a small driver function (with program output) that tests the operation of several member functions of class `circle`. First, it creates `circle` object `myCircle` and sets the value of four attributes. Next, it computes the values for attributes `area` and `perimeter`. Finally, it displays the circle's attributes. Notice that in the call to function `setColor` (in the middle of Listing 10.9), we must use the scope resolution operator `circle::` to inform the compiler that `magenta` is defined in class `circle`.

**Listing 10.9**    A driver function to test class `circle`

```cpp
// File circleTest.cpp
// Tests the Circle class

#include "circle.h"
#include <iostream>
using namespace std;

int main()
{
    circle myCircle;

    // Set circle attributes.
    myCircle.setCoord(150, 100);
    myCircle.setRadius(10);
    myCircle.setColor(circle::magenta);

    // Compute area and perimeter
    myCircle.computeArea();
    myCircle.computePerimeter();

    // Display the circle attributes.
    cout << "The circle attributes follow:" << endl;
    myCircle.displayCircle();

    return 0;
}
```

```
The circle attributes follow:
x-coordinate is 150
y-coordinate is 100
radius is 10
color is 5
area is 314.159
perimeter is 62.8318
```

## Implementation File for Class `circle`

Listing 10.10 shows the implementation file for class `circle`. The file begins by declaring the constant `pi`, which is used by member functions `computeArea` and `computePerimeter`. When a `circle` object is declared, the constructor initializes the numerical attributes to zero and the object's color to `nocolor`. Notice that `displayCircle` casts the value of `cColor` to type `int` before displaying it.

Listing 10.10   Implementation file for class `circle`

```cpp
// File circle.cpp
// Circle class implementation

#include "circle.h"
#include <iostream>
using namespace std;

const float pi = 3.14159;

// Member Functions . . .
// constructor
circle::circle()
{
    x = 0;
    y = 0;
    radius = 0;
    cColor = nocolor;
    area = 0.0;
    perimeter = 0.0;
}

// Set center position
void circle::setCoord(int xArg, int yArg)
{
    x = xArg;
    y = yArg;
}

// Set radius
void circle::setRadius(float r)
{
    radius = r;
    computeArea();
```

(continued)

**Listing 10.10**   Implementation file for class `circle`  (continued)

```cpp
        computePerimeter();
}

// Set color
void circle::setColor(color c)
{
    cColor = c;
}

// Compute the area
void circle::computeArea()
{
    area = pi * radius * radius;
}

// Compute the perimeter
void circle::computePerimeter()
{
    perimeter = 2 * pi * radius;
}

// Display attributes
void circle::displayCircle() const
{
    cout << "x-coordinate is " << x << endl;
    cout << "y-coordinate is " << y << endl;
    cout << "radius is " << radius << endl;
    cout << "color is " << int(cColor) << endl;
    cout << "area is " << area << endl;
    cout << "perimeter is " << perimeter << endl;
}

// accessor functions
circle::color circle::getColor() const
{
    return cColor;
}

//     Insert definitions for rest of accessor functions
//          . . .
```

Notice that member function `setRadius` calls member functions computeArea and `computePerimeter` to redefine the area and perimeter attributes as soon as the radius value is stored. The reason for this is to prevent a circle object from containing inconsistent data. It's incorrect for a circle with a nonzero radius to have a value of zero for its area and perimeter.

In the definition of accessor function `getColor`, we must precede the result type `color` with the scope resolution operator `circle::`. We do this to inform the compiler that `color` is declared inside class `circle`. We didn't need to do this for the identifier `color` (the formal parameter type) in member function `setColor` because the scope resolution operator `circle::` precedes the parameter declaration. We leave the other accessor functions as Programming Exercise 1 at the end of this section.

## EXERCISES FOR SECTION 10.6

### Self-Check

1. Draw a class diagram for the class `circle`.

2. Why is it not necessary to pass `radius` as an argument to functions `computeArea` and `computePerimeter`?

3. Explain how you would have to modify the class `circle` to form a class `rectangle`.

4. What would be the effect of removing the calls to function `getArea` and `getPerimeter` in the main function in Listing 10.9?

### Programming

1. Write the accessor functions.

2. Write a private member function `writeColor` to display a color value as a string instead of as an integer (see Figure 7.4). Modify displayCircle to use this function.

3. Write two additional constructors for the `circle` class. The first should enable you to specify the coordinates of the circle. The second should enable you to specify all its attributes except the area and perimeter. The second constructor should call `computeArea` and `computePerimeter` to keep these values consistent with the circle radius.

# 10.7    A Simple String Class

If C++ didn't provide a `string` class in its system library, we'd need to write our own. In this section we discuss a simple string class that has an array of characters as one of its data members.

### Design of Class `simpleString`

We don't have the programming expertise to build a string class that has all the capability of library `string`, but we'd like to be able to at least read a sequence of characters from a stream into a simple string object and display the sequence that we stored. Our class should have a data member for storing the characters in a string and a data member that is a count of the number of characters stored. It should also have a constant data member that specifies the maximum number of characters that may be in a string.

We'll provide a minimal set of member functions for our class: a function to read in a string (`readString`), a function to display a string (`writeString`), and a function to retrieve a character at a particular position (`at`). In addition, we provide accessor functions to retrieve the string length, string capacity, and string contents. We summarize these decisions next.

---

**Specification for Class `simpleString`**

*Attributes for* **`simpleString`** *Class*
| | |
|---|---|
| `capacity` | Constant 255 |
| `contents` | string data |
| `length` | string length |

*Member Functions for Class* **`simpleString`**
| | |
|---|---|
| `simpleString` | Constructor |
| `readString` | Reads the string data |
| `writeString` | Writes the string data |
| `at` | Retrieves a character at a specified position |
| `getLength` | Returns the string length |
| `getCapacity` | Returns the string capacity |

---

### Definition of Class `simpleString`

Listing 10.11 shows the definition for class `simpleString`. The class definition shows that attribute `capacity` is an enumerator with value 255. This is how we define constant class attributes because C++ doesn't permit us to initialize a class attribute (using `const int capacity = 255;`) except inside a class constructor. The `string` data is stored in data member contents, which is an array of characters whose size is `capacity`.

**Listing 10.11**   Class definition for `simpleString`

```
// File simpleString.h
// Simple string class definition

#ifndef SIMPLESTRING_H
#define SIMPLESTRING_H

class simpleString
{
   public:
      // Member Functions
      // constructor
      simpleString();

      // Read a simple string
      void readString();

      // Display a simple string
      void writeString() const;

      // Retrieve the character at a specified position
      //   Returns the character \0 if position is out of bounds
      char at(int) const;

      // Return the string length
      int getLength() const;

      // Return the string capacity
      int getCapacity() const;

      // Return the string capacity
      void getContents(char []) const;

   private:
      // Data members (attributes)
      enum {capacity = 255};      // Capacity of a string
      char contents[capacity];    // string data
      int length;                 // string length
};
#endif //SIMPLESTRING_H
```

Figure 10.2 shows how the character string `Philly  cheesesteak` would be stored in object `food` (type `simpleString`). Table 10.1 lists some calls to member functions applied to object `food` and their effect.

## Testing Member Functions of Class `simpleString`

Listing 10.12 shows a small driver function that tests the operation of the member functions of class `simpleString`. First, it reads a character string typed at the keyboard (terminated by pressing RETURN) and displays the string on the next line. It then displays each character on a separate line by executing the `for` statement

```
for (int pos = 0; pos < aString.getLength(); pos++)
    cout << aString.at(pos) << endl;
```

The loop body executes once for each character in the data string, retrieving and displaying that character. The loop repetition test compares the current character position (starting at 0) to the string length.

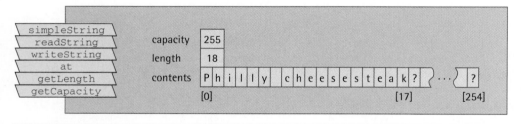

**Figure 10.2**  Class diagram for `simpleString` object `food`

**Table 10.1**  Sample Calls to Member Functions of Class `simpleString`

| Call | Effect |
| --- | --- |
| `food.getLength()` | Returns 18 |
| `food.at(0)` | Returns P |
| `food.at(17)` | Returns k |
| `food.at(18)` | Returns `'\0'`, the null character |
| `food.getCapacity()` | Returns 255 |
| `food.writeString()` | Displays `Philly  cheesesteak` |

## Implementation File for Class `simpleString`

Listing 10.13 shows the implementation file for class `simpleString`. When a `simpleString` object is declared, the constructor initializes the object to an empty string by setting its data member `length` to 0.

Member function `readString` (compare with `readScores` in Listing 9.6) uses a `while` loop to read each data character from the keyboard and store it in the next element of data member `contents`. Loop repetition terminates when the newline character `'\n'` is read or the array is filled (`length` equals `capacity`). Notice that the newline character is not stored in `contents` or counted in the string length.

Member function `writeString` displays each character in data member `contents`, starting with the character at position 0 (the first character)

**Listing 10.12**   Testing class `simpleString`
___

```cpp
// File: simpleStringTest.cpp
// Tests the simple string class

#include "simpleString.h"
#include <iostream>
using namespace std;

int main()
{
   simpleString aString;   // input - data string

   // Read in a string.
   cout << "Enter a string and press RETURN: ";
   aString.readString();

   // Display the string just read.
   cout << "The string read was: ";
   aString.writeString();
   cout << endl;

   // Display each character on a separate line.
   cout << "The characters in the string follow:" << endl;
   for (int pos = 0; pos < aString.getLength(); pos++)
      cout << aString.at(pos) << endl;

   return 0;
}
```

                                                        (continued)

Listing 10.12  Testing class `simpleString`  (continued)

```
Enter a string and press RETURN: Philly cheesesteak
The string read was: Philly cheesesteak
The characters in the string follow:
P
h
i
l
l
y

c
h
e
e
s
e
s
t
e
a
k
```

Listing 10.13  Implementation file for class `simpleString`

```cpp
// File simpleString.cpp
// Simple string class implementation

#include "simpleString.h"
#include <iostream>
using namespace std;

// Member Functions . . .
// constructor
simpleString::simpleString()
{
    length = 0;     // empty string
}

// Read a simple string
void simpleString::readString()
{
    // Local data . . .
```

(continued)

**Listing 10.13** Implementation file for class `simpleString` (continued)

```
    char next;                  // input - next data character
    int pos = 0;                // subscript for array contents

    cin.get(next);              // Get first character from cin
    while ((next != '\n') && (pos < capacity))
    {
        // Insert next character in array contents
        contents[pos] = next;
        pos++;
        cin.get(next);          // Get next character from cin
    }

    length = pos;               // Define length attribute
}
// Write a simple string
void simpleString::writeString() const
{
    for (int pos = 0; pos < length; pos++)
        cout << contents[pos];
}

// Retrieve the character at a specified position
//    Returns the character \0 if position is out of bounds
char simpleString::at(int pos) const  // IN: position of
                                      // character to get
{
    // Local data
    const char NULL_CHARACTER = '\0';

    if ((pos < 0)    (pos >= length))
    {
        cerr << "Character at position " << pos
             << " not defined." << endl;
        return NULL_CHARACTER;
    }
    else
        return contents[pos];
}

// Return the string length
int simpleString::getLength() const
{
```

(continued)

**Listing 10.13**    Implementation file for class `simpleString` (continued)

```
    return length;
}

// Return the string capacity
int simpleString::getCapacity() const
{
    return capacity;
}

// Return the string contents
void simpleString::getContents(char str[]) const
{
    for (int i = 0; i < length; i++)
        str[i] = contents[i];
}
```

and ending with the character at position `length` - 1 (the last character). If `length` is zero (the case for an empty string), the `for` loop body doesn't execute because pos < 0 is false. Therefore, no characters are displayed for an empty string.

Member function `at` begins by testing whether the value of its argument pos is in bounds for the string stored in array `contents`. If it is, the character selected by its argument is returned; otherwise, an error message is printed and a special character called the *null character* (`'\0'`) is returned.

## EXERCISES FOR SECTION 10.7

### Self-Check

1. Does `readString` store leading blanks in a `simpleString` object? If your answer is yes, how could you change it to skip leading blanks?

2. What happens if the user presses the RETURN or ENTER key before typing any characters when reading in string data?

3. Compare the `for` loop in the driver function for `simpleString` with the one in member function `writeString`. Explain why the loop repetition condition in the driver function uses member function `getLength` but the loop in member function `writeString` doesn't.

4. Write statements for a client program that store the contents of a `simpleString` object in a character array and then display that array.

## Programming

1. Modify the constructor to store the null character (`'\0'`) in every character position of a new object of type `simpleString`.

2. Write a member function `concat` that concatenates two `simpleString` objects. (Hint: Pass one `simpleString` object as an argument and append it to the end of the `simpleString` object to which `concat` is applied. Don't forget to modify the length field of the `simpleString` object whose contents is changed.)

3. Write a new constructor and a method `setContents`. Each has a character array argument and stores the contents of this array in a `simpleString` object. Assume the character `'\0'` (null character) follows the last actual character in an argument array. When testing these functions, verify whether you can pass a literal string as an argument. If you write them properly you should be able to do this, because C++ stores literal strings in character arrays that are terminated by the null character.

# 10.8    A Savings Account Class

In this section, we consider how to develop a class for representing a savings account. The case illustrates the use of a private member function to validate the account identification.

*case study*    Using the Savings Account Class

### PROBLEM STATEMENT

You've been asked to define a savings account class that will allow you to represent a savings account and perform all necessary operations on a savings account object.

### ANALYSIS

Your experience in maintaining your own bank account should help you determine what attributes and member functions to include. Associated with each account is the account holder's name, an account identification number, the account balance, and the annual interest rate. The operations performed on a savings account include opening the account, making a deposit, making a withdrawal, checking the balance, adding interest, getting the balance, and closing the account. The specifications for our savings account class follow.

## Specification for Savings Account Class

*Attributes for Savings Account Class*

| | |
|---|---|
| `string name` | The account holder's name |
| `int id` | Account identification |
| `float interestRate` | The annual interest rate (%) |
| `float balance` | The account balance |

*Member Functions for Savings Account Class*

| | |
|---|---|
| `savings` | A constructor |
| `openAccount` | Opens an account |
| `changeName` | Changes the account name |
| `addInterest` | Adds quarterly interest |
| `deposit` | Processes a deposit |
| `withdraw` | Processes a withdrawal |
| `closeAccount` | Closes the account |
| `getBalance` | Gets the account balance |

*Private Member Function for Savings Account Class*

| | |
|---|---|
| `validId` | Validates the account identification before performing an operation |

The class will include a private member function `validId` that will be called by other member functions to validate the user identification before performing a critical operation such as processing a withdrawal or deposit, changing the account name, or closing the account.

### DESIGN

The class definition (Listing 10.14) provides all the information that a user of the class needs to know.

### IMPLEMENTATION

The member functions are implemented next. Listing 10.15 shows the `.cpp` file for the savings account class.

Functions `addInterest`, `deposit`, and `withdraw` all assign a new value to attribute `balance`. Function `addInterest` divides the annual interest rate (a percentage) by 400.0 to convert it to a decimal fraction. Then it adds the interest amount for the quarter to the current balance.

Functions `deposit` and `withdraw` call `validId` to verify that the transaction ID (`ident`) and the account ID match before updating the `balance` attribute. Function `withdraw` also rejects a withdrawal that would lead to a negative balance. Functions `closeAccount` and `changeName` also check for an ID match before performing their operations. This extra check guards against invalid occurrences of these critical operations.

## TESTING

To test this class, you should create a driver function that allocates a type savings object and then performs several of the operations provided in the class. You should try calling member functions with valid and invalid account identification. Listing 10.16 shows a program with sample output that accomplishes this task.

**Listing 10.14**    Definition for class `savings`

```
// File savings.h
// Savings account class definition

#include <string>              // access string class
using namespace std;

#ifndef SAVINGS_H
#define SAVINGS_H

class savings
{
    public:
        // Member Functions . . .
        // constructor
        savings();

        // Open a new account
        void openAccount();

        // Change account name
        void changeName(int, string);

        // Add quarterly interest
        void addInterest();

        // Process a deposit
        void deposit(int, float);
```

(continued)

---

**Listing 10.14**    Definition for class `savings` (continued)

---

```cpp
        // Process a withdrawal
        void withdraw(int, float);

        // Close an account
        void closeAccount(int);

        // Get account balance
        float getBalance() const;

    private:
        // Data members (attributes)
        int id;
        string name;
        float balance;
        float interestRate;

        // Member functions . . .
        // Validate user identification
        bool validId(int) const;
};
#endif // SAVINGS_H
```

---

**Listing 10.15**    File `savings.cpp`

---

```cpp
// File savings.cpp
// Savings account implementation file

#include "savings.h"
#include <string>
#include <iostream>
using namespace std;

// Member Functions . . .
// constructor
savings::savings()
{
    name = "";
    id = 0;
    balance = 0.0;
    interestRate = 0.0;
}
```

(continued)

**Listing 10.15**   File `savings.cpp`  (continued)

```cpp
// Open a new account
void savings::openAccount()
{
   cout << "Account name: ";
   getline(cin, name, '\n');
   cout << "Account ID: ";
   cin >> id;
   cout << "Initial balance: $";
   cin >> balance;
   cout << "Annual interest rate percentage: %";
   cin >> interestRate;
}

// Validate user id
bool savings::validId(int ident) const
{
   if (id == ident)
      return true;
   else
   {
      cerr << "Error - ID's do not match! ";
      return false;
   }
}

// Change account name
void savings::changeName(int ident, string na)
{
   if (validId(ident))
   {
      name = na;
      cout << "Changing account name to " << na << endl;
   }
   else
      cerr << "Reject name change request." << endl;
}

// Add quarterly interest
void savings::addInterest()
{
   // Local data
   float quarterRateFrac;            // quarterly rate as
                                     //    a decimal fraction
```

(continued)

**Listing 10.15** File `savings.cpp` (continued)

```cpp
      quarterRateFrac = interestRate / 400.0;
      balance += balance * quarterRateFrac;
   }

   // Process a deposit
   void savings::deposit(int ident, float amount)
   {
      if (validId(ident))
      {
         balance += amount;
         cout << "Depositing " << amount << endl;
      }
      else
         cerr << "Reject deposit of " << amount << endl;
   }

   // Process a withdrawal
   void savings::withdraw(int ident, float amount)
   {
      if ((validId (ident)) && (amount <= balance))
      {
         balance -= amount;
         cout << "Withdrawing " << amount << endl;
      }
      else
         cerr << "Reject withdrawal of " << amount << endl;
   }

   // Close an account
   void savings::closeAccount(int ident)
   {
      if (validId(ident))
      {
         cout << "Final balance for account number " << id
              << " is " << balance << endl;
         cout << "Account has been closed" << endl;
         balance = 0.0;
         id = 0;
         name = "";
      }
      else
```

(continued)

**Listing 10.15**   File `savings.cpp`  (continued)

```cpp
        cerr << "Account not closed" << endl;
}

// Get account balance
float savings::getBalance() const
{
    return balance;
}
```

**Listing 10.16**   A driver function to test class `savings`

```cpp
// File savingsTest.cpp
// Tests the savings class

#include <iostream>
#include "savings.h"
using namespace std;

int main()
{
    savings myAccount;

    // Open a savings account.
    myAccount.openAccount();
    cout << endl;

    // Make valid and invalid deposit.
    myAccount.deposit(1234, 500.00);
    myAccount.deposit(1111, 300.00);

    // Get and display balance.
    cout << endl << "Current balance is "
         << myAccount.getBalance() << endl;

    // Make valid and invalid withdrawal.
    myAccount.withdraw(1234, 750.00);
    myAccount.withdraw(1234, 15000.00);

    // Add interest.
    myAccount.addInterest();

    // Close the account.
```

(continued)

**Listing 10.16** A driver function to test class `savings` (continued)

```
        myAccount.closeAccount(1234);

        return 0;
}
```

```
Account name: William Gates
Account ID: 1234
Initial balance: $1000.00
Annual interest rate percentage: %5
Depositing $500.00
Error - IDs do not match! Reject deposit of $300.00
Current balance is $1,500.00
Withdrawing $750.00
Reject withdrawal of $15,000.00
Final balance for account number 1234 is $759.38
Account has been closed
```

## EXERCISES FOR SECTION 10.8

### Self-Check

1. Assume you've written a client program that creates two different bank account objects. Explain why it won't be possible to place a deposit intended for one of these accounts in the other.

2. Trace the following code fragment assuming the account is opened with an ID of 1234 and an initial balance of $500.

```
savings a1;
int ident = 1234;
a1.openAccount();
a1.deposit(ident, 500);
a1.withdraw(ident, 200);
a1.getBalance(ident);
a1.closeAccount(ident);
```

### Programming

1. Write a code fragment for a client program that reads transaction data and then calls `withdraw` or `deposit` to update the balance based on whether the transaction type is `W` (for withdrawal) or `D` (for deposit). Assume the account ID is stored in variable `myId`.

## 10.9 Common Programming Errors

This section describes a number of the different error messages you may see when errors occur in your C++ programs. All the examples involve the counter class described in Sections 10.1 through 10.3.

- *Function argument and return value errors:* Return value or argument mismatches involving class member functions may cause the compiler not to recognize the function as a member of the class. For example, if the prototype for function getCount (defined in the counter class) specifies a return value of int but the function definition specifies a return value of float, the message

```
"'counter::getCount()' is not a member function
of 'counter'"
```

will appear when the compiler attempts to compile the function definition. Even though the name of the function is the same, the return value inconsistency causes the compiler to treat the defined function as different from the prototype.

- *Failure to define a function as a member of a class:* This error can be caused in several ways:

  1. Failure to prefix the function definition by the name of its class and the scope resolution operator (::)

  2. Failure to spell the function name correctly

  3. Omission of the function definition from the class

  In any case, the result is the same—a compiler error message indicating that the function you called

```
"is not a member"
```

of the indicated class. Thus, if c1 is an object of type counter and the C++ statement

```
c1.print();
```

appears in a client program, the message

```
"'print' is not a member of 'counter'"
```

will be displayed.

- *Prefixing a class member function call:* Any reference to a class member function must be prefixed by the name of an object to be manipulated.

For example, for function `increment` defined in class `counter`, the function call

```
cObj.increment();
```

is legal only if `cObj` is declared as an object of type `counter`. If `cObj` has a different type, the message

```
"Structure required on left side of ."
```

appears; if the identifier is not defined at all, an

```
"undefined symbol"
```

error will occur.

- *Referencing a private attribute of a class:* Identifiers declared as private attributes or functions in a class can't be referenced from outside the class. Any such reference attempt will produce an

```
"undefined symbol"
```

error. Even if the correct prefix for such a reference is used—for example, `c1.counter::count`—an error message will appear:

```
"'counter::count' is not accessible".
```

This message means that the identifier `count` declared in the class `counter` can't be accessed from outside the class.

- *Failure to include a required header file:* Numerous messages will be generated by this programming error. Because the header file most likely contains the definitions for a number of the identifiers used in your program, perhaps the most common of these errors will be the

```
"undefined symbol"
```

- *Missing semicolon following a class definition:* Failure to place a semicolon at the end of a class definition (after the right brace) will cause many errors when the definition is included in and compiled with another file. The semicolon is required to terminate the class definition and separate it from the rest of the statements in this file. Error messages that might appear as a result of this syntax error include

```
"Declaration right brace won't stop declaration",
"Declaration occurs outside of class"
```

and

```
"className may not be defined",
```

where `className` is the name of the class in which the missing semi-colon was detected.

## Chapter Review

1. Programmers can use C++ classes to implement useful data types that aren't provided as part of C++ or its standard library.

2. Classes also encapsulate private data and protect it from inadvertent access and misuse by other programs. Only public data and function members defined in a class may be accessed from outside a class.

3. The class data members are normally declared in the private section of the class definition and the class member functions are normally declared in the public section.

4. The class definition declares the class data members and declares its member function prototypes. The class implementation provides definitions (C++ code) for the member functions. We recommend you place the class definition and the class implementation in separate source files (`.h` and `.cpp` files, respectively). The information in the `.h` file (header file) is all that a potential client of the class needs to know about the class in order to use it.

5. You can include the implementation file for a class with its client program in a project. The client program contains the main function. If you do this, you can take advantage of separate compilation capability offered by your C++ system. Your C++ system won't need to recompile the class unless you rewrite one of its member functions. If you change the class implementation file but not its header file, your C++ system won't need to recompile a client of the class.

6. C++ supports function overloading, which means we can use the same function name in different classes (and even the same class). C++ determines which version of the function to call based on the object it's applied to and the function's actual arguments.

7. We showed how to define and use five data abstractions using classes: `counter`, `fraction`, `circle`, `simpleString`, and `savings` (a savings account class).

## Summary of New C++ Constructs

| Construct | Effect |
|---|---|
| **Class Definition**<br>```cpp\nclass twoNums\n{\n    public:\n        twoNums();\n        twoNums(int, int);\n        int addTwo();\n        int subtractTwo();\n\n    private:\n        int n1;\n        int n2;\n};\n``` | Defines a class twoNums with public data members n1 and n2 and member functions addTwo and subtractTwo. |
| **Member Function Declaration**<br>```cpp\ntwoNums::twoNums()\n{\n    n1 = 0;\n    n2 = 0;\n}\n``` | A constructor for class twoNums that initializes its data members to zero. |
| ```cpp\nint twoNums::addTwo()\n{\n    return (n1 + n2);\n}\n``` | A member function for class twoNums that returns the sum of its data members. |

### Quick-Check Exercises

1. Why is an object prefix name required before the function name when referencing a member function of a class?

2. How does the C++ compiler know which + operation (int, float, double, etc.) to use when it evaluates an operator-operand-operator triple?

3. A class is an encapsulation of _____ and _____ in a single data structure.

4. A _____ declaration is needed to declare an object of a class type. It causes a _____ to execute.

5. The declared items in the _____ part of a class may not be directly accessed outside the class. Those in the _____ part are accessible outside the class.

6. Write a type declaration for an array of 12 objects of type counter; write an expression to increment the sixth element of your array.

7. Arrays and structs may not be used in the declarations of class attributes. True or false?

8. Why would you declare a private member function?

9. Where do you use member functions to access a class attribute? Where can you access the attribute directly?

10. Explain the difference between an object and a class.

11. What is an advantage of putting data members in the private section of a class instead of the public section?

12. What is an overloaded function? Which functions in a class are normally overloaded? How does the compiler know which one to call when translating a statement with an overloaded function call?

### Answers to Quick-Check Exercises

1. The prefix is required to specify the object to which the member function is applied.

2. The correct operation is chosen solely on the basis of the type of operands used in the triple.

3. data members (attributes), member functions

4. type, constructor

5. private, public

6. `counter myCounts[12];`

   `myCounts[5].increment();`

7. false; they may be used

8. To provide a function that may be used inside of the class by other member functions but not outside of the class

9. Use member functions in a client program. Access the attributes directly in the declaration of a member function of that class.

10. An object is an instance or specific occurrence of a class. A class describes the data members and function members of a collection of objects.

11. If data members are in the private section, they can only be accessed through the class member functions. This enables the class implementor to determine how the data members are processed and to ensure that they are processed in a safe and dependable way.

12. An overloaded function has multiple definitions in a class. Normally constructors are overloaded. The signature of a method (argument list) determines which function to call.

## Review Questions

1. Explain why information hiding, separation of concerns, and language extension and reuse through classes is important to the software designer.

2. Write a C++ class definition for an abstract data type describing a bookstore inventory. Each book has the following attributes:

   - Book title (character string)
   - Book author (character string)
   - Book price (floating-point number having two decimal places)
   - Count of books on hand (integer)

   The member functions are as follows:

   - A constructor that is used to initialize all eight elements of the array (to any values you want)
   - A function that displays in a readable tabular form the contents of the entire book collection
   - A modify function that, once called, prompts the user first for a book number (1 through 8) and then for a code (T, A, P, or C) indicating which attribute (title, author, price, or count) of the indicated book is to be changed; finally, the function should provide a prompt for the new value of the attribute.

   Reasonable tests for valid input should be performed in the modify function. Write the declaration for an object named inventory of the type described by this class.

3. Redo the previous question assuming the following:

   - Your attributes are simply the title, author, price, and count of one book.
   - Your constructor is replaced by an explicit initialization function that initializes the contents of the book objects in your inventory.
   - Your display function displays the information for a single book in your inventory.
   - Your modify function no longer needs the number of the book to be changed (why not?) and begins by prompting for the attribute to be changed.

   (Hint: You'll need to declare an array of objects, size 8, of your book type.) Write a call to your modify function to change an attribute of one book.

4. Which of the following statements is incorrect?

   **a.** All class attributes must appear in the private part of a class.

   **b.** All class member functions must appear in the public part of a class.

   **c.** The attributes of a class are allocated memory each time a member function of the class is called; this memory is deallocated when the called function returns control to its caller.

   **d.** Classes may be used in C++ to model problem data elements.

**5.** Write a client program for the `fraction` class that reads two fractions, asks the user whether to add, subtract, multiply, or divide the two fractions, and then performs the requested operation and displays the result. If the result is different when the two fractions are inverted, show both results (for example, subtraction and division).

**6.** Write a class `rectangle` that has all the data members and member functions as class `circle` (Section 10.6) except that data member `radius` should be replaced by data members `width` and `length`. Write files `rectangle.h` and `rectangle.cpp`.

# Programming Projects

**1.** Write a C++ class for an abstract data type `color` with a public enumeration type `colorType`, that has the color values shown in Listing 10.8. Your abstract data type should have an attribute for storing a single value of type `colorType` and member functions for reading (`readColor`) and writing (`writeColor`) a color value as well as setting and accessing it. The function `readColor` should read a color as a string and store the corresponding color value in the `value` attribute of a type `color` object. The function `writeColor` should display as a string the value stored in the `value` attribute of a type `color` object (see Figure 7.5). Modify class `circle` and the driver function in Listing 10.9 to include and use this class. You'll need to remove the declaration for `color` in class `circle`. Test your modified driver function with the new `color` and `circle` classes.

**2.** Define a class `myInt` that has as its single attribute an integer variable and that contains member functions for determining the following information for an object of type `myInt`:

   **a.** Is it a multiple of 7, 11, or 13?

   **b.** Is the sum of the digits odd or even?

   **c.** What is the square root value?

   **d.** Is it a prime number?

   **e.** Is it a perfect number? (Reminder: The sum of the factors of a perfect number is equal to the number itself—for example, $1 + 2 + 4 + 7$

+ 14 = 28, so 28 is a perfect number.) Write a client program that tests your methods, using the input values 104, 3773, 13, 121, 77, and 3075.

3. Each month, a bank customer deposits $50 into a savings account. Assume that the interest rate is fixed (doesn't change) and is a problem input. The interest is calculated on a quarterly basis. For example, if the account earns 6.5 percent interest annually, it earns one-fourth of 6.5 percent every three months. Write a program to compute the total investment, the total amount in the account, and the interest accrued for each of the 120 months of a ten-year period. Assume that the rate is applied to all funds in the account at the end of a quarter, regardless of when the deposits were made.

Print all values accurate to two decimal places. The table printed by your program when the annual interest rate is 6.5 percent should begin as follows:

| Month | Investment | New amount | Interest | Total savings |
|-------|-----------|-----------|----------|--------------|
| 1 | 50.00 | 50.00 | 0.00 | 50.00 |
| 2 | 100.00 | 100.00 | 0.00 | 100.00 |
| 3 | 150.00 | 150.00 | 2.44 | 152.44 |
| 4 | 200.00 | 202.44 | 0.00 | 202.44 |
| 5 | 250.00 | 252.44 | 0.00 | 252.44 |
| 6 | 300.00 | 302.44 | 4.91 | 307.35 |
| 7 | 350.00 | 357.35 | 0.00 | 357.35 |

Design a class to model the customer bank account, including the attributes for each account and at least five methods needed to initialize, update, and display the information in each account.

4. Redo the previous programming project, adding columns to allow comparison of interest compounded monthly (one-twelfth of the annual rate every month) with interest compounded continuously. The formula for continuously compounded interest is

*Amount = Principle $\times$ $e^{rate \times time}$*

where *rate* is the annual interest rate and *time* is expressed in years.

5. An employee time card is represented as one long string of characters. Write a program that processes a collection of these strings stored in a data file and writes the results to an output file.

a. Compute gross pay using the formula

*Gross = Regular hours $\times$ Rate + Overtime hours $\times$ 1.5 $\times$ Rate*

**b.** Compute net pay by subtracting the following deductions:

$Federal\ tax = 0.14 \times (Gross - 13 \times Dependents)$

$Social\ security = 0.052 \times Gross$

$City\ tax = 4\% \times Gross$ if employee works in the city

$Union\ dues = 6.75\% \times Gross$ for union member

The data string for each employee has the following form:

| Positions | Data |
|---|---|
| 1-10 | Employee last name |
| 11-20 | Employee first name |
| 21 | Contains C for city office or S for suburban office |
| 22 | Contains U (union) or N (nonunion) |
| 23-26 | Employee identification number |
| 27 | Blank |
| 28-29 | Number of regular hours (a whole number) |
| 30 | Blank |
| 31-36 | Hourly rate (dollars and cents) |
| 37 | Blank |
| 38-39 | Number of dependents |
| 40 | Blank |
| 41-42 | Number of overtime hours (a whole number) |

Declare the attributes of the class and define and implement five class methods.

**6.** Write a menu-driven program that contains the following options:

Creating a data file to be processed by the payroll program described in the previous programming project. (The user should be prompted to enter several time "cards" from the keyboard.)

- Adding new time cards to the end of an existing file.
- Deleting time cards from an existing file based on their ordinal position within the file (e.g., deleting the seventh time card).
- Quitting the program.

To add or delete lines from a text file requires copying the original data file to a *scratch*, or temporary, file and then back to the original file. During the copy process, time cards to be deleted are simply not copied to the scratch file. New time cards are added to the end of the file after all the time cards from the original file have been copied to the scratch file. Use classes as you see fit to model the additional abstract data types.

7. Your university runs many hundreds of courses each semester and needs to keep track of key information on each one. Among the data needed for each course would be the following:

- University course identification number
- Department course ID and section number (for multiple sections of the same course)
- Number of credits for the course
- Days and times the course meets
- Room in which the course meets (building ID and room number)
- Maximum course enrollment
- Campus on which the course is held
- Name of the course instructor
- Number of students currently enrolled and the student ID of each such student
- Course status: open (for additional enrollment), closed, or canceled

You must be able to change the value of each of these ten data items and, upon request, display all of this information. Initially, the values of the first seven items are known—the last three aren't. Design and implement an abstract data type that can be used to model this university course entity.

8. Write a C++ class definition for an abstract data type money that allows you to do basic arithmetic operations (addition, subtraction, multiplication, and division) on floating-point numbers having exactly two digits to the right of the decimal point. You need not write the implementations for the operations but be sure to include the prototypes for all member functions that would be needed in this class, including any that might be private to the class.

9. Write a C++ class definition for an abstract data type date that models a day of the year. A date object should store three int values. The value of month should be between 1 and 12, day between 1 and 31, and year between 1900 and 2010.

- The constructor with 0 arguments should set the date to January 1, 1900.
- The constructor with three int arguments should set the date based on the values of these arguments.
- The constructor with a string and two int arguments should use the string to set the value of month (1 for "January", and so on).
- Member function displayMonth displays the month as a string.

- Member function `displayDate` displays the entire date using `displayMonth` to display the month.

- Member function `compareDates` returns −1 if the `date` object it's applied to comes before its argument date, 0 if the two dates are the same, and 1 if the `date` object it's applied to comes after its argument date.

- Member function `validMonth` returns true if the value stored in a data object is valid.

- Member function `dayNumber` returns the day number in the year (between 1 and 366) for a particular date object.

- Member function `increment` advances a date object to the next day.

- The last three functions should access an array that stores the number of days in a month. Make sure you account for the fact that February (month 2) has 29 days in a leap year.

10. Write a collection of geometric shape classes similar to class `circle` in Section 10.6. Provide a class for rectangles, right triangles, cylinders, and prisms (rectangular solids). Write a client program that asks the user to enter a shape name and then asks the user for the necessary data for an object of that class. The program should create the object and display all its attributes.

# Timothy Budd

*Timothy Budd is an associate professor of computer science at Oregon State University, where his research areas are object-oriented programming, LEDA (a programming language he developed), and implementation techniques. In addition to his teaching and research, Dr. Budd has also written nine books, including* An Introduction to Object-Oriented Programming, Data Structures in C++ Using the STL, Understanding Object-Oriented Programming with Java, *and most recently,* C++ for Java Programmers. *He received his B.A. from Western Washington State College, and his M.S. and Ph.D. from Yale University.*

### Why did you decide to study computer science?

I took a computer science course in high school but really thought I would be a math major in college. In my third year of college, I was taking courses in functional analysis and abstract algebra, studying topics such as Hilbert spaces and Banach spaces, and I couldn't see any real practical use for these topics. At the same time I had been taking a few computer courses, and they seemed eminently practical. So I decided to move into computer science rather than mathematics. I've never regretted that decision.

### What was your introduction to computers like?

Although my high school had a course in computer programming, it didn't have a computer. This was in the days when you programmed using punch cards, and every day the teacher would travel over to the local college, bringing back the output (paper listings) from the previous day's work. We would pore over the listings, punch up corrections to our programs, and at the end of the day the teacher would take the punch cards back to the college. I got to know some of the students and staff at the college just so I could drop by in the evenings and pick up my output, make a few changes, and resubmit my programs. This allowed me to get twice as much access to the computer as I was getting before. I guess I was pretty good at programming, and before long most of the staff people would recognize me. At the time I was working part-time at a local pizza parlor, mixing the dough and flipping pizzas in the air. One evening I came in to the computer center just covered with flour and tomato sauce. A student who was two years older than I saw me and asked what in the world I had been doing. When I explained, he said that with my talent I could be making just as much money at a desk job, instead of flipping pizzas. True to his word, he put in a recommendation for me, and when I started college in the fall I had a job as a student consultant at the computer center, helping other students (and, sometimes, faculty) learn how to use the machine.

### What kind of computers did the college have?

There were two computers on campus at that time. For serious numerical work, we had an IBM 7090, a machine with core memory that was held in a tank of oil to keep it cool. We always joked about having to change the oil on the computer, but I don't think anybody ever did. The other computer was also an IBM, a 360 model 40. It had 256K worth of memory, but during the day it was always divided into two partitions, so that you could only use half of that.

### What is a typical day like for you?

The thing I like most about being a college professor is that there is no typical day. The most obvious task that a professor does is to lecture. But for every hour of lecture I spend between one and three hours in preparation. There is time spent developing programming assignments. At a research university such as OSU, a considerable amount of time is spent talking to graduate students and supervising their research, and conducting your own research. Finally, and most importantly, there is time spent writing.

### Do you have any advice for students entering the computer science field?

By far the most important skill a computer scientist should possess is the ability to write. Second is the ability to speak in public and work with others. Only third are all the technical skills that we normally teach in computer science courses. During the academic year, most of my writing is for courses and research papers, and during the summer I like to write books.

### What's the story behind Phyl, the platypus that appears on several of your book covers?

A platypus was a casual illustration I tossed out in the first chapter of *An Introduction to Object-Oriented Programming*, an example of the two ideas of inheritance and overriding, since a platypus is a mammal but does almost everything different from other mammals. When it came time to design the cover, the artist asked me for ideas. I gave them several, one of which was the platypus. For some reason the artist liked that one. Some people wonder if Phyl isn't some sort of caricature of the author, but personally I don't see the resemblance. There are other funny stories about Phyl that you can read on my web page (www.cs.orst.edu/~budd).

*chapter eleven*

# Data Abstraction and Object-Oriented Design

### Chapter Objectives

- To learn how to declare and use multidimensional arrays for storing tables of data
- To learn how to use arrays with elements that are structs and classes
- To understand the use of template classes in C++ and how to define template classes
- To learn how to use a particular template class, the indexed list
- To become familiar with object-oriented design techniques
- To learn how to use the vector template class

THE FOCUS IN this chapter is on modeling data with combinations of arrays, structs, and classes. We begin by studying the multidimensional array, which is an array whose elements are arrays. Next, we discuss arrays whose elements are structs and classes.

In the previous chapter, we saw that a class is an improvement over a struct because it encapsulates data (class attributes) and operators (member functions). In this chapter, we study a data abstraction, the indexed list, which is an improvement over the array data structure. Like an array, you can use an indexed list object to provide storage for a collection of elements of the same data type, including array types, struct types, or classes. However, unlike an array, you can't accidentally access storage space outside of an indexed list. We also include member functions for reading, displaying, searching, and sorting an indexed list object. We study a case that uses an indexed list object for storing a personal telephone directory.

The chapter concludes with a discussion of the **vector** class. A vector, like an indexed list, is a better indexed collection than is an array. The vector is one of the classes that is part of the C++ Standard Template Library (STL).

# 11.1 Multidimensional Arrays

The array data structure allows a programmer to organize information in arrangements that are more complex than the linear or one-dimensional arrays discussed so far. We can declare and use arrays with several dimensions of different sizes.

---

**Multidimensional Array Declaration**

**Syntax:**     *element-type aname*[ *size*$_1$ ] [ *size*$_2$ ] ... [ *size*$_n$ ] ;

**Example:**     `float table[NROWS][NCOLS];`

**Interpretation:** The array declaration allocates storage space for an array *aname* consisting of *size*$_1$ × *size*$_2$ × ... × *size*$_n$ memory cells. Each memory cell can store one data item whose data type is specified by *element-type*. The individual array elements are referenced by the subscripted variables *aname*`[0][0]` ... `[0]` through *aname*[ *size*$_1$–1 ] [ *size*$_2$–1 ] ... [ *size*$_n$–1 ]. An integer constant expression is used to specify each *size*$_i$.

---

## Declaring Two–Dimensional Arrays

**two-dimensional array**
An array used to store information that is normally represented as a two-dimensional table.

**Two-dimensional arrays**, the most common multidimensional arrays, store information that we normally represent in table form. Let's first look at some examples of two-dimensional arrays—game boards, seating plans, and matrixes.

### EXAMPLE 11.1

The array declaration

```
char ticTacToe[3][3];
```

allocates storage for a two-dimensional array (ticTacToe) with three rows and three columns. This array has nine elements, each of which must be referenced by specifying a

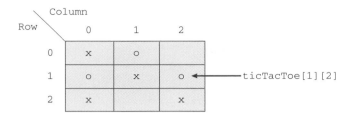

**Figure 11.1** A tic-tac-toe board stored as array ticTacToe

row subscript (0, 1, or 2) and a column subscript (0, 1, or 2). Each array element contains a character value. For the array shown in Figure 11.1, the character O is stored in the subscripted variable

```
ticTacToe[1][2]
```

## EXAMPLE 11.2

Your instructor wants to store the seating plan (Figure 11.2) for a classroom on a computer. The declarations

```
const int NUM_ROWS = 11;
const int SEATS_IN_ROW = 9;
string seatPlan[NUM_ROWS][SEATS_IN_ROW];
```

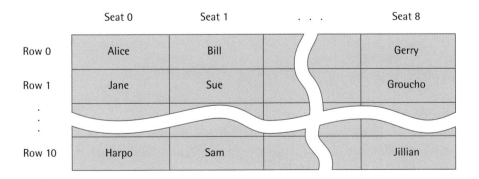

**Figure 11.2** A classroom seating plan

allocate storage for a two-dimensional array of strings called seatPlan. Array seatPlan could be used to store the first names of the students seated in a classroom with 11 rows and 9 seats in each row. The statement

```
seatPlan[0][8] = "Gerry";
```

stores the string "Gerry" in the last seat of the first row.

## Initializing Two–Dimensional Arrays

### EXAMPLE 11.3

The statements

```
const int NUM_ROWS = 2;
const int NUM_COLS = 3;
float matrix[NUM_ROWS][NUM_COLS] = {{5.0, 4.5, 3.0},
                                    {-16.0, -5.9, 0.0}};
```

allocate storage for the array matrix with two rows and three columns. In the initialization list enclosed in braces, each inner pair of braces contains the initial values for a row of the array matrix, starting with row 0, as shown below.

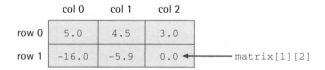

## Nested Loops for Processing Two–Dimensional Arrays

You must use nested loops to access the elements of a two-dimensional array in row order or column order. If you want to access the array elements in row order (the normal situation), use the row subscript as the loop control variable for the outer loop and the column subscript as the loop control variable for the inner loop.

## EXAMPLE 11.4

The nested for statements that follow display the seating plan array from Figure 11.2 in tabular form. The top row of the table lists the names of the students sitting in the last row of the classroom; the bottom row of the table lists the names of the students sitting in the first row of the classroom (closest to the teacher).

```
for (int row = NUM_ROWS - 1; row >= 0; row--)
{
    for (int seat = 0; seat < SEATS_IN_ROW; seat++)
        cout << setw(10) << seatPlan[row][seat];
    cout << endl;
}
```

## Two-Dimensional Arrays as Function Arguments

You can pass two-dimensional arrays as function arguments. In the function call, simply list the actual array name, just as you would for one-dimensional arrays. In the formal argument list, you must list the column dimension, but the row dimension is optional. For example, you could use the function prototype

```
float sumMatrix
    (float table[][NUM_COLS],     // IN: array to be summed
     int rows)                    // IN: number of rows
                                  //          (rows > 0)
```

for function sumMatrix (see Listing 11.1), which calculates the sum of all the elements in an array of floating-point values with NUM_COLS (a constant) columns. The second function argument represents the number of rows to be included in the sum. You can use the statement

```
total = sumMatrix(matrix, NUM_COLS);
```

to assign to total the sum of the element values in the array matrix from Example 11.3.

You may be wondering why you only need to specify the column dimension (NUM_COLS) in the declaration of the formal array parameter table. Because the array elements are stored in row order, starting with row 0, C++ must know the number of elements in each row (value of NUM_COLS) in order to access a particular array element. For example, if NUM_COLS is 3, the first

**Listing 11.1**    Function sumMatrix

```
// File: sumMatrix.cpp
// Calculates the sum of the elements in the first rows
//    of an array of floating point values
//    with NUM_COLS (a constant) columns.
// Pre:  The type int constant NUM_COLS is defined (NUM_COLS > 0)
//       and the array element values are defined and rows > 0.
// Post: sum is the sum of all array element values.
// Returns:  Sum of all values stored in the array.
float sumMatrix
   (float table[][NUM_COLS],      // IN: array to be summed
    int rows)                     // IN: number of rows in array
                                  //        (rows > 0)


{
    float sum = 0.0;      // sum of all element values
                          //   - initially 0.0
    // Add each array element value to sum.
    for (int r = 0; r < rows; r++)
        for (int c = 0; c < NUM_COLS; c++)
            sum += table[r][c];

    return sum;
}
```

row is stored in array positions 0, 1, and 2, the second row is stored in array positions 3, 4, and 5, and so on. C++ uses the formula

```
NUM_COLS * r + c
```

to compute the array position for array element `table[r][c]`. For example, array element `table[1][0]`, the first element in the second row, is stored at array position 3 * 1 + 0 (array position 3).

## Arrays with Several Dimensions

C++ doesn't limit the number of dimensions an array may have, although arrays with more than three dimensions are rare. The array `sales` declared here

```
const int PEOPLE = 10;
const int YEARS = 5;
float sales[PEOPLE][YEARS][12];
```

is a three-dimensional array with 600 (value of $10 \times 5 \times 12$) elements that may be used to store the monthly sales figures for the last five years for the 10 sales representatives in a company. Thus `sales[0][2][11]` represents the dollar amount of sales for the first salesperson (person subscript is 0) during December (month subscript is 11) of the third year (year subscript is 2). As you can see, three-dimensional and higher arrays consume memory space very quickly.

## EXAMPLE 11.5

The following fragment finds and displays the total dollar amount of sales for each of the 10 sales representatives.

```
// Find and display the total dollar amount of sales by
//    person
for (int person = 0; person < PEOPLE; person++)
{
    totalSales = 0.0;
    // Find the total sales for the current person.
    for (int year = 0; year < YEARS; year++)
        for (int month = 0; month < 12; month++)
            totalSales += sales[person][year][month];

    cout << "Total sales amount for salesperson "
         << person << " is " << totalSales << endl;
}
```

Because we're displaying the total sales amount for each person, we use the salesperson subscript (person) as the loop control variable in the outermost loop. We set the value of totalSales to zero before executing the inner pair of nested loops. This pair accumulates the total sales amount for the current salesperson. The statement beginning with cout displays the accumulated total for each individual.

## EXERCISES FOR SECTION 11.1

### Self-Check

1. Assuming the following declarations

```
const int MAX_ROW = 9;
const int MAX_COL = 5;
float matrix[MAX_ROW][MAX_COL];
```

answer these questions:

**a.** How many elements are in array `matrix`?

**b.** Write a statement to display the element in row 3, column 4.

**c.** How would you reference the element in the last column of the last row?

**d.** How would you reference the element in the exact middle of the array?

2. Write the declarations for a multidimensional array used to store the number of students enrolled in each section of the introductory programming course. Four different professors teach the course and each one teaches three sections. Answer this question if the course is taught at three campuses and there are five sections at each campus.

3. Explain why it isn't necessary to specify the first dimension (number of salespeople) when you declare a formal parameter that is an array with the same form as the one in Example 11.5. Describe the storage order for elements of this array in memory. Give a formula that will compute the position of array element `sales[i][j][k]`.

Programming

1. For the array `matrix` declared in Self-Check Exercise 1, do the following:

   **a.** Write a loop that computes the sum of the elements in row 4.

   **b.** Write a loop that computes the sum of the elements in column 3.

   **c.** Write nested loops that compute the sum of all the array elements.

   **d.** Write nested loops that display the array elements in the following order: display column 3 as the first output line, column 2 as the second output line, column 1 as the third output line, and column 0 as the fourth output line.

2. For the array `sales` in Example 11.5, do the following:

   **a.** Write a program fragment that displays the total sales amount in a table whose rows are years and whose columns are months.

   **b.** Write a program fragment that displays the total sales amount for each year and the total for all years.

# 11.2  Array of Structs

Earlier we showed that you can declare a struct with an array component. You can also declare an array of structs.

## EXAMPLE 11.6

The declaration

```
employee company[10];
```

allocates storage for an array with 10 elements of struct type employee (see Figure 11.3). We use the subscripted variable company[0] to access the first element (a struct) of this array. We use the notation company[9].name to access the name component (a string) of the last employee.

## EXAMPLE 11.7

Array company provides storage for 10 elements of type employee, and function readEmployee (see again Listing 9.12) reads data into a single type employee variable. Function readCompany (Listing 11.2) reads data into all 10 elements of array company. The statement

```
readEmployee(company[i]);
```

reads employee data into the array element with subscript i. Because i goes from 0 through 9, all 10 elements receive data.

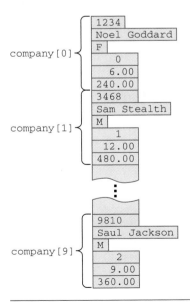

**Figure 11.3**  **Sketch of array company**

**Listing 11.2**   Function `readCompany`

```cpp
// File: readCompany.cpp
// Reads 10 employee records into array company

// Pre:  None
// Post: Data are read into array company
void readCompany
   (employee company[])     // OUT: array being read
{
   // Read 10 employees.
   for (int i = 0; i < 10; i++)
   {
      cout << "Enter data for employee " << i+1 << ":" << endl;
      readEmployee(company[i]);
   }
}
```

## EXAMPLE 11.8

C++ provides a great deal of flexibility in the use of arrays and structs. The struct type gradeBook declared next has three components. The last component is an array of 100 structs of type examStats (see again Example 9.16) containing exam data for each student. Figure 11.4 shows a sketch of variable mySection (type gradeBook).

```cpp
struct gradeBook
{
   string sectionId;
   int numStudents;     // Count of students in section
   examStats students[100];  // Storage for 100 students
};

gradeBook mySection;
```

You use `mySection.sectionId` to access the section ID number, and use `mySection.numStudents` to access the count of students. You use `mySection.students[0]` to access the data for the first student (struct type `examStats`). You use `mySection.students[0].stuName` to access the first student's name and `mySection.students[0].scores[0]` to access her first exam score. You use `mySection.students[numStudents-1]` to access the data for the last student in the section.

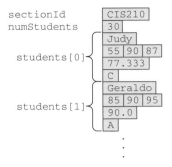

**Figure 11.4**  Sketch of variable mySection

---

## EXERCISES FOR SECTION 11.2

### Self-Check

1. For array `company`, describe the meaning of each of the valid references below. Which are invalid?

   **a.** `company[1].gender`    **e.** `company[1].employee`

   **b.** `id.company[0]`    **f.** `company[1].employee.gender`

   **c.** `company[9]`    **g.** `company[9].name`

   **d.** `company[10]`    **h.** `company[2].company[1]`

2. For variable `mySection` (Figure 11.4), write the correct way to reference each data item described below.

   **a.** First student's name    **e.** First student's score on the first exam

   **b.** Section ID    **f.** Number of students in the section

   **c.** All data for the last student    **g.** Last student's average

   **d.** First student's letter grade    **h.** Last student's score on the last exam

3. For variable `company` (Figure 11.3), show how you'd reference each of the data items below.

   **a.** Noel Goddard    **c.** Sam Stealth

   **b.** 3468    **d.** 1234

### Programming

1. Write a function that displays the data in variable `mySection`. Use function `printStats` (Listing 9.11) to display each student's data.

**2.** Write a function that decreases each employee's total wages in array `company` (Figure 11.3) by a specified percentage (a function argument) for a tax deduction. Assume that data field `totWages` contains the employee's salary amount.

# 11.3    Template Classes

As we begin to define more complicated data abstractions, we'd like them to be as general as possible. For example, let's say we declare an abstract data type that performs several operations on a collection of integers (such as ordering the values, summing the values, finding the median, and so on). It would be very convenient to use the same abstract data type to manipulate a collection of real numbers.

The C++ template feature lets us do this. If you write

```
template <class T>
```

before a class definition, you enable the class to be used with any data type (represented by `T`). This makes the class definition much more versatile.

## Definition of a Template Class

As an example, Listing 11.3 provides a header file and definition for a template class `dummy` that provides storage for a data member, `item`, of type `T`. The type `bool` data member `defined` indicates whether a data item is stored in `item` (yes, if `defined` is true). Parameter `T` is a placeholder for an actual data type. You can substitute for type T any of the C++ predefined data types (`int`, `char`, and so on) or any other user-defined or system-defined data type.

Parameter `T` appears in the formal parameter list for member function `setItem`:

```
void setItem(const T&);     // IN: the value to be stored
```

Because `T` may be any previously defined data type, including a struct or class type, we use `const  T&` for formal parameters that can't be modified.

The data type corresponding to `T` is determined when we declare an instance of class `dummy`. For example, the declaration

```
dummy<int> dayNum;
```

**Listing 11.3**   Header file for template class dummy

```cpp
// File: dummy.h
// Header file for template class dummy
#ifndef DUMMY_H
#define DUMMY_H

template <class T>
class dummy
{
   public:
     // constructor
     dummy();

     // Stores a value of type T
     void setItem(const T&);   // IN: value to store

     // Retrieves a value of type T
     T getItem() const;

   private:
     T item;             // Storage for a value of type T
     bool defined;       // Indicates whether item is defined
};
#endif   // DUMMY_H
```

creates an object dayNum with storage for a type int attribute (item). It also causes automatic generation of the function prototypes:

```cpp
void setItem(const int&);   // IN: the value to be stored
int getItem() const;
```

In case you're wondering, we have no real purpose for introducing template class dummy other than to provide a simple example for illustrating the definition and use of template classes.

---

**Template Classes**

Form:        template <class T>
             class *class-name*
             {

```
        public:
        ■ List of class variables, types, constants, etc. (if any) that may be
          accessed by name from outside the class
        ■ Prototype for each function that may be accessed by name from
          outside the class
        • • •
        private:
        ■ List of class variables, types, constants, etc., that are intended to be
          hidden from reference from outside the class

        ■ Prototype for each function (if any) to be hidden from outside the
          class
        • • •
        };
```

**Interpretation:** Class *class-name* is a template class with parameter *T*. *T* is a placeholder for a built-in, system-defined, or user-defined data type.

---

## Object Declarations Using Template Classes

**Form:**     *class-name<type> an-object;*

**Example:**   `indexList<int> intList;`

**Interpretation:** *Type* may be any defined data type. *class-name* is the name of a template class. The object *an-object* is created when the arguments specified between the symbols <> replace their corresponding parameters in the template class. C++ creates instances of all member function prototypes by substituting *type* for the class member *T*.

---

## EXAMPLE 11.9

Listing 11.4 shows a main function that uses template class dummy. The declarations

```
dummy<int> numDepend;        // object numDepend
dummy<string> spouseName;    // object spouseName
```

allocate storage for two objects, numDepend and spouseName, that are instances of template class dummy. We store a type int value in object numDepend and a type string value in object spouseName. Then we retrieve and display the two values stored.

**Listing 11.4** Driver function for template class dummy

```cpp
// File: dummyTest.cpp
// Tests function dummy

#include "dummy.h"
#include <iostream>
#include <string>
using namespace std;

int main()
{
    dummy<int> numDepend;        // object numDepend
    dummy<string> spouseName;    // object spouseName
    int num;
    string name;

    // Store data in objects numDepend and spouseName
    numDepend.setItem(2);
    spouseName.setItem("Caryn");

    // Retrieve and display values stored
    num = numDepend.getItem();
    name = spouseName.getItem();
    cout << num << endl;
    cout << name << endl;

    return 0;
}
```

```
2
Caryn
```

## Implementation of a Template Class

We can implement a template class in two ways. The first method involves inserting the member function definitions directly in the class definition. In Listing 11.5, we rewrite the definition for template class dummy by replacing each function prototype with a complete function definition.

The advantage of this approach is its simplicity. Because the function definitions appear inside the class definition, we don't need to precede each

**Listing 11.5** Template class `dummy` with `member functions inserted`

```
// File: dummyFun.h
// Definition file for template class dummy with functions

#include <iostream>
using namespace std;

#ifndef DUMMY_FUN_H
#define DUMMY_FUN_H

template <class T>
class dummy                    // with function definitions
{
   public:
       // constructor
       dummy()
       {
          defined = false;     // No value stored yet
       }

       // Stores a value of type t
       void setItem(const T& aVal)  // IN: the value to store
       {
          item = aVal;
          defined = true;
       }

       // Retrieves a value of type t
       T getItem() const
       {
          if (defined)
             return item;
          else
             cerr << "Error - no value stored!" << endl;
       }

   private:
       T item;              // Storage for a value of type T
       bool defined;        // Indicates whether item is defined
};

#endif  // DUMMY_FUN_H
```

function name with a scope resolution operator. However, a disadvantage is that we no longer have a clear separation between the class interface and the class implementation. We'd prefer to place the class definition in an interface file (dummy.h) that contains only the information needed by a class user and to hide the implementation details in a separate implementation file (dummy.cpp). Listing 11.6 shows such an implementation file, which includes the original class definition from Listing 11.3 (file dummy.h).

**Listing 11.6** Implementation file for template class dummy

```cpp
// File: dummy.cpp
// Implementation file for template class dummy

#include "dummy.h"
#include <iostream>
using namespace std;

// constructor
template <class T>
dummy<T>::dummy()
{
    defined = false;      // No value stored yet
}

// Stores a value of type t
template <class T>
void dummy<T>::setItem(const T& aVal)  // IN: value to store
{
    item = aVal;
    defined = true;
}

// Retrieves a value of type t
template <class T>
T dummy<T>::getItem() const
{
    if (defined)
        return item;
    else
        cerr << "Error - no value stored!" << endl;
}
```

In Listing 11.6, we place the template prefix line

```
template <class T>
```

before each function header, and we precede each function name with

```
dummy<T>::
```

to tell the compiler that the function being defined is a member of template class `dummy` with parameter `T`. We use the same function bodies that were used in Listing 11.5.

## Compiler Instructions to Support Separate Compilation

Most C++ compilers require special instructions from the programmer when attempting separate compilation of template class header and implementation files. If you're having difficulty compiling a template class, we recommend that you follow one of two approaches. The first would be to include the source code for the implementation file (using `#include`). You can place this line at the end of the header file for the template class, right before the `#endif` directive. The second approach would be to replace each function prototype in the class definition with the corresponding function definition (for example, see Listing 11.5).

## EXERCISES FOR SECTION 11.3

Self-Check

1. Write a driver function that allocates storage for three objects of type `dummy<float>`. Your function should read two numbers, store them in two of the objects, and then retrieve these values and store their sum in the third object. Finally, retrieve and display the sum.

2. What function prototypes are generated by the object declarations in Listing 11.4?

Programming

1. Write member functions `read` and `display` for template class `dummy`. Assume `stream` operators `<<` and `>>` are defined for all data types that will be used as class parameters.

# 11.4    The Indexed List Abstract Data Type

In this section we describe a very versatile data structure called the *indexed list*. We'll implement an indexed list as a template class, so that the elements of an indexed list object can be any data type, including a struct or a class.

## Need for an Indexed List Class

Although the C++ array has proved to be a useful data structure for storing a collection of elements of the same type, it has some deficiencies:

- You can access (or overwrite) data outside of an array if you use a subscript that is too small (< 0) or a subscript that is larger than the maximum allowed for the array.

- If an array has some empty or unfilled storage locations, your program must keep track of how many elements actually contain data, increasing or decreasing the count of filled elements when an array element is inserted or deleted. When processing the array, you must be careful to access only the filled portion of the array.

- You need to write your own functions to perform operations such as finding the smallest and largest values in the array as well as searching, sorting, and reading and displaying an array. You may need different versions of these functions for different array element types.

To remedy these deficiencies, C++ provides some special classes called container classes in its standard library. To see how container classes are implemented, we'll design our own abstract data type, the indexed list class, as an alternative to the array structure. Besides being safer to use than an array, our indexed list class will be more versatile because it can include as methods most of the common array operations that we listed above and coded in Chapter 9.

## Analysis and Design of an Indexed List Class

An indexed list is a collection of data items of the same type. We access the elements of an indexed list through an index, an integral expression with a value between 0 and `size - 1`, where `size` is the actual number of elements stored in the indexed list. The indexed list grows in size when we insert or append new elements and decreases in size when we delete them. We can replace an item at a given index with a new one, we can search for the index of a particular item, and we can sort the list. The complete specification follows.

SPECIFICATION FOR INDEXED LIST CLASS

### Attributes for Indexed List Class

| | |
|---|---|
| `elements[]` | Array of data items |
| `int size` | Count of items |

### Member Functions for Indexed List Class

| | |
|---|---|
| `indexList` | Constructor |
| `append` | Appends a new item to the indexed list (i.e., inserts at the end) |
| `insert` | Inserts an item at a specified index after moving the elements starting at that index to make room |
| `replace` | Replaces an item at a specified index |
| `retrieve` | Retrieves the value stored at a specified index |
| `remove` | Deletes the value stored at a specified index |
| `findMin list` | Locates the smallest value in a portion of an indexed |
| `findMax list` | Locates the largest value in a portion of an indexed |
| `search` | Searches for a target value in an indexed list |
| `sort` | Sorts an indexed list |
| `read` | Reads data into an indexed list from an input file or the keyboard, starting at element 0 |
| `display` | Displays the items in the indexed list |
| `getSize` | Gets the size of the indexed list |

Listing 11.7 shows the template class `indexList`. In the template prefix line

```
template <class T, int maxSize>
```

parameter `T` is a placeholder for the data type of each element stored in an indexed list and `maxSize` (type `int`) represents the maximum size of an indexed list object.

Listing 11.7   Class `indexList` header file

```
// File: indexList.h
// Definition of indexed list template class

#ifndef INDEXLIST_H
#define INDEXLIST_H

#include <iostream>
using namespace std;
```

(continued)

**Listing 11.7** Class `indexList` header file (continued)

```
template <class T, int maxSize>
class indexList
{
  public:
    // Constructor
    indexList();

    // Add an item to the end of an indexed list
    bool append(const T&);   // IN: item appended

    // Replace an element at a specified index
    bool replace(int,         // IN: index
                 const T&);   // IN: item inserted

    // Insert an element at a specified index
    bool insert(int,          // IN: index
                const T&);    // IN: item inserted

    // Retrieve an element at a specified index
    bool retrieve(int,        // IN:  index
                  T&) const;  // OUT: value retrieved

    // Delete an element at a specified index
    bool remove(int);         // IN: index

    // Find index of smallest value in a sublist
    int findMin(int,          // IN:  start index
                int) const;   // OUT: end index

    // Find index of largest value in a sublist
    int findMax(int,          // IN:  start index
                int) const;   // OUT: end index

    // Find index of a target item
    //    Returns -1 if target item not found
    int search(const T&) const;  // IN: target item

    // Sort an indexed list
    void selSort();

    // Read data from an input stream into the list
    void read(istream &);
```

(continued)

**Listing 11.7** Class `indexList` header file (continued)

```
        // Display the list contents
        void display() const;

        // Get the current size
        int getSize() const;

    private:
        T elements[maxSize];   // Storage for elements
        int size;              // Count of elements in list
    };


#endif  // INDEXLIST_H
```

The data member `elements` is an array of type `T` values. Because the size of the array, `maxSize`, is passed as the second template parameter, we can allocate storage for indexed lists with different storage capacities and different element types in the same program. The declaration

```
indexList<int, 50> myList;  // myList is an indexed list of
                            //      integers
```

creates an indexed list object, `myList`, that can hold up to 50 integer values. The data member `size` (0 <= size <= maxSize) is a count of elements in the indexed list.

The public part in Listing 11.7 declares all the member functions described earlier. We use type `T` to represent the element type and type `int` to represent an index. Because `T` may be a class type, we use `const T&` for formal arguments that can't be modified. For example, in the prototype for function `replace`,

```
bool replace(int,        // IN: index
             const T&);  // IN: item inserted
```

the first argument represents the index (type `int`) where the second argument (type `T`) will be placed.

Functions `append`, `insert`, `replace`, `remove`, and `retrieve` return a type `bool` result to indicate success or failure of the operation. For `replace`, `remove`, and `retrieve`, the operation succeeds if the index passed to the function is valid. For `insert` and `append`, the operation succeeds if there is room to store the new element.

Function `read` has a single parameter of type `istream&`. This gives it the flexibility of reading from a data file or from the keyboard. If we pass the standard stream `cin` as an argument to `read`, it will read its data from the keyboard; if we pass a file stream argument to `read`, it will read its data from a file stream.

The arguments for functions `findMin` and `findMax` define the starting and ending points of a sublist:

```
int findMin(int,        // IN:  start index
            int) const; // OUT: end index
```

Function `findMin` returns the index of the smallest value in the sublist and `findMax` returns the index of the largest value. Both functions return −1 if the sublist boundaries are invalid.

## Using the **indexList** Class

You can think of an object of class `indexList` as a user-friendly array. You don't need to keep track of the number of elements currently filled with data, because this will be done automatically. You also don't need to be concerned about accessing storage locations outside the array, because the class member functions won't allow it.

Finally, you don't need to know anything about arrays or subscripts in order to use an indexed list. The member functions perform all array accesses. If you want to retrieve a particular item, you simply pass its index and the variable that will store the item to member function `retrieve`; the function does the rest. For example, to retrieve the element in location 2 of indexed list `myList` and store it in `me`, you write

```
myList.retrieve(2, me);
```

## EXAMPLE 11.10

Function main in Listing 11.8 performs a number of operations using the indexed list class. The declarations

```
indexList<int, 10>    myIntData;    // list of ints
indexList<string, 5> myStringData; // list of strings
```

allocate storage for an indexed list of 10 type int values (myIntData) and an indexed list of five type string values (myStringData), showing that main can process two different kinds of indexed lists at the same time. Function main next stores data items in both lists and sorts them. It then retrieves and displays the first value in each list after sorting. Finally, it displays the number of elements in each list and the sorted lists.

---

**Listing 11.8**    Testing class `indexList`

---

```cpp
// File: indexListTest.cpp
// Testing the indexed list template class

#include "indexList.h"
#include <iostream>
#include <string>
using namespace std;

int main()
{
   indexList<int, 10>   myIntData;     // list of ints
   indexList<string, 5> myStringData;  // list of strings
   string aString;
   int anInt;
   bool aBool;

   // Store the integer data.
   myIntData.append(5);
   myIntData.append(0);
   myIntData.append(-5);
   myIntData.append(-10);

   // Store the string data.
   cout << "Read a list of strings:" << endl;
   myStringData.read(cin);   // read from keyboard

   // Sort the indexed lists.
   myIntData.selSort();
   myStringData.selSort();

   // Retrieve and display the first value in each list.
   aBool = myIntData.retrieve(0, anInt);
   if (aBool)
      cout << "First integer value after sorting is "
           << anInt << endl;
```

(continued)

**Listing 11.8**   Testing class `indexList` (continued)

```
aBool = myStringData.retrieve(0, aString);
if (aBool)
   cout << "First string value after sorting is "
        << aString << endl << endl;

// Display each list size and contents
cout << "The indexed list of integers contains "
     << myIntData.getSize() << " values." << endl;
cout << "Its contents follows:" << endl;
myIntData.display();

cout << endl << "The indexed list of strings contains "
<< myStringData.getSize() << " values." << endl;

cout << "Its contents follows:" << endl;
myStringData.display();

return 0;
}
```

```
Read a list of strings:
Enter number of list items to read: 3
Enter next item - Robin
Enter next item - Beth
Enter next item - Koffman
First integer value after sorting is 210
First string value after sorting is Beth
The indexed list of integers contains 4 values.
Its contents follows:
-10
-5
0
5
The indexed list of strings contains 3 values.
Its contents follows:
Beth
Koffman
Robin
```

Self–Check

1. Trace the following fragment showing the list contents after each statement.

```
indexList<float, 5> smallList;
smallList.append(3.5);
smallList.append(5.7);
smallList.remove(0);
cout << smallList.retrieve(0) << endl;;
smallList.replace(0, 15.5);
smallList.append(5.5);
cout << smallList.search(5.5) << endl;
smallList.sort();
smallList.display();
```

2. C++ allows you to use subscripts with an array that are outside the valid subscript range for the array. Explain how you might prevent out-of-range subscripts in the indexed list class.

Programming

1. Write a client program that allocates three indexed lists, each containing up to 10 type `float` values. Read (using member function `read`) data into all 10 elements of two of the lists and sort them. Then write a function that stores the sum of corresponding elements of these two lists in the third list. Finally display all three lists, one after the other.

## 11.5 Implementing the Indexed List Class

Listing 11.9 shows several member functions for the indexed list class. Every function begins with the template prefix line

```
template <class T, int maxSize>
```

In every function header, we use the parameterized class name and scope resolution operator

```
indexList<T, maxSize>::
```

to tell the compiler that the function being defined is a member of the template class `indexList` with parameters `T` and `maxSize`. Type `T`, `maxSize`, and any members of the class may be referenced directly within each function body.

**Listing 11.9** Some member functions for class `indexList`

```cpp
// File: indexList.cpp
// Indexed list class implementation

#include "indexList.h"
#include <iostream>
using namespace std;

template <class T, int maxSize>
indexList<T, maxSize>::indexList()   // constructor
{
    size = 0;    // list is empty
}

// Add an item to the end of an indexed list
// Pre:  item is defined
// Post: if size < maxSize, item is appended to list
// Returns: true if item was appended; otherwise, false
template <class T, int maxSize>
bool indexList<T, maxSize>::append(const T& item)
{
    bool result;
    // Add item to the end of the list if list is not full.
    if (size < maxSize)
    {
      elements[size] = item;
      size++;
      result = true;
    }
    else
    {
      cerr << "Array is filled - can't append!" << endl;
      result = false;
    }

    return result;
}

// Replace an item at a specified index.
// Pre:  item and index are defined
// Post: item is placed at position index if valid
// Returns: true if item was inserted; otherwise, false
template <class T, int maxSize>
bool indexList<T, maxSize>::replace
```

(continued)

**Listing 11.9** Some member functions for class indexList (continued)

```
   (int index, const T& item)
{
    bool result;
    // Overwrite a list element if index is valid.
    if (index >= 0  &&  index < size)
    {
      elements[index] = item;
      result = true;
    }
    else
    {
      cerr << "Index " << index << " not in filled part"
           << " - can't insert!" << endl;
      result = false;
    }

    return result;
}

// Retrieve an item at a specified index
// Pre:  item and index are defined
// Post: if index is valid, elements[index] is returned
// Returns: true if item was returned; otherwise, false
template <class T, int maxSize>
bool indexList<T, maxSize>::retrieve(int index, T& item) const
{
    bool result;
    // Return a list element through item if index is valid.
    if (index >= 0  &&  index < size)
    {
      item = elements[index];
      result = true;
    }
else
    {
      cerr << "Index " << index << " not in filled part"
           << " - can't retrieve!" << endl;
      result = false;
    }

    return result;
}
```

(continued)

**Listing 11.9** `Some member functions for class indexList` (continued)

```
// Delete an element at a specified index
// Pre:  index is defined
// Post: if index is valid, elements[index] is deleted
//        and size is decremented.
// Returns: true if item was deleted; otherwise, false
template <class T, int maxSize>
bool indexList<T, maxSize>::remove(int index)
{
    int i;
    bool result;
    // Delete element at index i by moving elements up
    if (index >= 0  &&  index < size)
    {
      // Move each element up 1 position
      for (i = index + 1; i < size; i++)
          elements[i-1] = elements[i];
      size--;                 //   decrement size
      result = true;
    }
    else
    {
      cerr << "Index " << index << " not in filled part"
          << " - can't delete!" << endl;
      result = false;
    }

    return result;
}


// Read data from an input stream into the list
// Pre:  none
// Post: All data items are stored in array elements
//        and size is the count of items
template <class T, int maxSize>
void indexList<T, maxSize>::read(istream& ins)
{   int numItems;        // input - number of items to read
    T nextItem;          // input - next data item

    cout << "Enter number of list items to read: ";
    ins >> numItems;
    ins.ignore(80, '\n');   // skip newline

    // If numItems is valid, read each list element,
```

(continued)

**Listing 11.9**   Some member functions for class indexList (continued)

```
      // starting with first element.
      size = 0;                      // The list is empty.
      if (numItems >= 0  &&  numItems <= maxSize)
         while (size < numItems)
         {
            cout << "Enter next item - ";
            ins >> nextItem;
            elements[size] = nextItem;
            size++;
         }
      else
         cerr << "Number of items " << numItems
              << " is invalid" << " - no data entry!" << endl;
}


// Display the list contents
// Pre:  none
// Post: Displays each item stored in the list
template <class T, int maxSize>
void indexList<T, maxSize>::display() const
{
   // Display each list element.
   for (int i = 0; i < size; i++)
      cout << elements[i] << endl;
}


// Find index of a target item
// Pre:  none
// Post: Returns the index of target if found;
//       otherwise, return -1.
template <class T, int maxSize>
int indexList<T, maxSize>::search
   (const T& target) const
{
   for (int i = 0; i < maxSize; i++)
      if (elements[i] == target)
          return i;         // target found at position I

   // target not found
   return -1;
}

// Sort the indexed list
```

(continued)

**Listing 11.9**  `Some member functions for class indexList` (continued)

```
template <class T, int maxSize>
void indexList<T, maxSize>::selSort()
{
    // Selection sort stub - do nothing
}

// Get the current size
template <class T, int maxSize>
int indexList<T, maxSize>::getSize() const
{
    return size;
}
```

Function `read` begins by setting data member `size` to zero. Next it reads and validates the number of elements to be inserted. If valid, it reads one data item at a time from its stream argument, storing the data item at index `size`, and then incrementing `size`. To read the indexed list data from an external file, a client program must first open the file and connect it to a type `ifstream` object.

Function `append` checks whether the list is full. If it isn't full, `append` inserts a new element at the list position with subscript `size` and then increments `size`, thereby placing the new element at the end of the list. Function `replace` overwrites the element at the list position specified by its first argument with the type `T` item passed as its second argument. Function `retrieve` accesses the list element at the position specified by its first argument and returns that list element to its second argument.

Function `remove` deletes the element at the list position specified by its argument (`index`). It accomplishes this by moving all elements in the array up one position (closer to subscript 0), starting with the element at position `index + 1`. The first move operation overwrites the item to be deleted with the one that follows it. After all elements are moved, we decrement the size of the indexed list.

Functions `findMin`, `findMax`, and `selSort` are similar to functions shown in Chapters 9 and 10, so we leave them as an exercise (see Programming Exercise 3). We also leave function `insert` as a programming exercise (see Programming Exercise 4). Function `display` uses the insertion operator `<<` to display each item stored in the list, and function `read` uses the extraction operator `>>`. Functions `findMin`, `findMax`, and `selSort` work only if the operators `==`, `<`, and `>` are defined for class `T`. We discuss these requirements further in Section 11.7.

## EXERCISES FOR SECTION 11.5

### Self-Check

1. What does the following member function return?

```
template <class T, int maxSize>
int indexList<T, maxSize>::mystery() const
{
    int count;
    count = 0;
    for (int i = 0; i < size-2; i++)
        if (elements[i+1] > elements[i])
            count++;
    return count;
}
```

2. Why is the following search function body incorrect?

```
template <class T, int maxSize>
int indexList<T, maxSize>::search
    (const T& target) const
{
    for (int i = 0; i < size-2; i++)
        if (elements[i] == target)
            return i;
        else
            return -1;
}
```

### Programming

1. Write a member function that returns true if its indexed list object is all filled up.

2. Write member functions findMin, findMax, and selSort.

3. Write member function insert. You need to verify that the index is valid and there is room in the list before doing the insertion. Shift all elements starting at position index down one position before inserting the new element. (Hint: Start by moving the element at position size – 1. See function remove, which shifts elements up one position.)

4. Write a constructor for the indexed list class with a third argument that is an initial value to be stored in all elements of the indexed list.

5. Write a constructor for the indexed list class that loads an indexed list with the values stored in its array argument. Copy each element of the array into the corresponding element of the indexed list.

# 11.6    Illustrating Object-Oriented Design

In this section, we solve a programming problem using *object-oriented design (OOD)*. Although a complete discussion of this topic is beyond the scope of this book, we can summarize an approach to object-oriented design:

## Object-Oriented Design Methodology

1. Identify the objects and define the services to be provided by each object.

2. Identify the interactions among objects in terms of services required and services provided.

3. Determine the specification for each object.

4. Implement each object.

Unlike traditional software design, there is no sharp division between the analysis phase and the design phase. In fact, in object-oriented design, programmers often follow the prototyping design practice of designing a little, implementing a little, and testing a little, rather than attempting to build a complete piece of software all at once.

## *case study*    A Telephone Directory Program

### PROBLEM

We've been asked to design a program to store and retrieve a growing collection of names and telephone numbers in a telephone directory. We create an initial directory by reading a list of names and numbers of people called frequently. The directory program should also be able to insert new names and numbers, change numbers, retrieve selected numbers, and delete names and numbers.

### ANALYSIS AND DESIGN

In OOD, we focus on the data objects and the services (operators) that they provide. There are really two distinct data objects to consider: the directory as a whole and each individual entry. We focus on a directory entry first.

Each directory entry should contain a person's name and telephone number, and it should have a unique name that distinguishes it from the other entries. The specification for a directory entry follows.

SPECIFICATION FOR A DIRECTORY ENTRY

### Attributes for a Directory Entry

`string name`     *// person's name*
`string number`   *// person's number*

### Member Functions for a Directory Entry

`entry`        *// a constructor*
`setEntry`     *// stores a name and number in the entry*
`getName`      *// retrieves the name attribute*
`getNumber`    *// retrieves the number attribute*

### Operators for a Directory Entry

`==`   *// equality operator*
`<`    *// less than*
`>`    *// greater than*
`<<`   *// insertion operator*
`>>`   *// extraction operator*

As shown above, we'll use two string objects for storing a directory entry's attributes. In our specification for a directory, we include a list of operators that are familiar symbols. We plan to overload some of the C++ equality, relational, and input/output operators, so that a client program can use them to compare two type `entry` objects or to perform input/output operations on a type `entry` object. We'll show how to do this in Section 11.7. Listing 11.10 summarizes the design decisions so far in the header file for class `entry`.

We list the second argument in the prototype for member function `setEntry` as `nr = ""`. This means that the default value for `nr` is the empty string if a second argument isn't explicitly passed. This allows us to call function `setEntry` with either one or two arguments. There can be no default for the first argument.

Next we turn our attention to the services provided by a directory object. We should be able to read in an initial directory and add a new entry, delete an entry, and update an entry when a phone number changes. We also should be able to locate a particular name in the directory and retrieve that person's number. After we update the directory through multiple insertions and deletions, we should be able to sort the entries so they're in alphabetical order by name. Finally, we should be able to display the directory entries. This list of operations may sound familiar to you. It should because these are precisely the operations that can be performed on an indexed list. Therefore we'll use an indexed list object for storing our directory.

**Listing 11.10**   Header file for a directory entry

```cpp
// File: entry.h
// Definition for a directory entry class

#include <iostream>
#include <string>
using namespace std;

#ifndef ENTRY_H
#define ENTRY_H

class entry
{
  public:
    // Member functions
    // constructor
    entry();

    // Store data in an entry
    void setEntry(const string&, const string& nr = "");

    // accessor functions
    string getName() const;
    string getNumber() const;

    // operators - explained in Section 11.7
    bool operator == (const entry&);
    bool operator <  (const entry&);
    bool operator >  (const entry&);

    // friends - explained in Section 11.7
    friend ostream& operator << (ostream&, const entry&);
    friend istream& operator >> (istream&, entry&);

  private:
    string name;      // Person's name
    string number;    // and phone number
};

#endif  // ENTRY_H
```

## Using a Telephone Directory

We can now write a client program that maintains our telephone directory. We'll write a menu-driven program that enables the user to select the operations to be performed in any order. We start by reading the directory before entering the menu-driven loop.

DATA REQUIREMENTS

**Problem Input**

```
telDirec        // telephone directory
char choice     // each operation selected
```

**Problem Output**

```
telDirec        // updated telephone directory
```

ALGORITHM

1. Read the initial directory.

2. do

    **2.1.** Display the menu.

    **2.2.** Read the user's selection.

    **2.3.** Perform the operation selected.

```
while the user is not done
```

The main function consists of a do-while loop that calls function select to perform each operation (Step 2.3). The telephone directory and user's selection are passed as arguments to function select.

## ANALYSIS AND DESIGN FOR SELECT (STEP 2.3)

Function select is a decision structure (a switch statement) in which each case performs a different operation on the indexed list. For each case, we must read any required data and call the appropriate member functions from class entry or class indexList. We show the design for function select next.

DATA REQUIREMENTS FOR **select**

**Input Argument**

```
char choice        // operation selected
```

**Input/Output Argument**

```
telDirec           // telephone directory
```

**Local Variables**

```
entry anEntry       // input—data for an entry
string aName        // input—a name to be found
int index           // index for a particular name
```

ALGORITHM FOR SELECT

Choose one of the cases listed below:

■ `Case 'Av:`        // *Add*

> Read the entry to add.
> Append it to the directory.

■ `Case 'C':`        // *Change an entry*

> Read the modified entry.
> Search for its name in the directory.
> `if` the name is found
>> Replace current entry at the index position with new entry.
> `else`
>> Append the entry to the directory if user approves.

■ `Case 'D':`        // *Delete an entry*

> Read the name of entry to delete.
> Search for the name in the directory.
> `if` the name is found
>> delete the entry.

■ `Case 'G':`        // *Get a number*

> Read the name of the entry to retrieve.
> Search for the name in the directory.
> `if` the name is found
>> Retrieve the entry.
>> Retrieve and display the entry's number attribute.

■ `Case 'S':`        // *Sort*

> Call the sort function.

■ `Case 'P':`        // *Print*

> Call the display function.

■ `Case 'Q':`        // *Do nothing*

By using classes `indexList` and `entry`, we can accomplish this substantial programming task with minimal effort. The resulting client program (Listing 11.11) is very concise and readable.

**Listing 11.11** Menu-driven program for telephone directory

```cpp
// FILE: telDirecMenu.cpp
// Menu driven telephone directory update program

#include "indexList.h"
#include "entry.h"
#include <cctype>            // For toupper
#include <iostream>
#include <string>
using namespace std;

typedef indexList<entry, 100> telIndexList;

// Function prototype
// Performs user selection
void select(telIndexList&, char);
int main()
{
    telIndexList telDirec;              // telephone directory
    char choice;                        // menu choice

    // Read the initial directory.
    cout << "Enter the initial directory entries -" << endl;
    telDirec.read();

    // Keep reading and performing operations until user enters Q
    do
    {
        // Display the menu.
        cout << "Enter your choice -" << endl;
        cout << "A(Add), C(Change), D(Delete)," << endl
             << "G(Get), S(Sort),   P(Print), Q(Quit): ";
        cin >> choice;
        cin.ignore(80, '\n');       // skip newline

        // Perform the operation selected.
        select(telDirec, choice);
    }
    while (toupper(choice) != 'Q');

    return 0;
}
```

(continued)

**Listing 11.11** Menu-driven program for telephone directory (continued)

```cpp
// Performs user selection
void select(telIndexList& telDirec,   // INOUT : directory
            char choice)              // IN: selection
{
   // Local data
   entry anEntry;      // one entry
   string aName;       // input - entry name
   int index;          // index of name in directory
   char answer;        // input - indicates whether to add
                       //         entry for missing name

   switch (toupper(choice))
   {
      case 'A':   // Add an entry
         cout << "Enter entry to add - ";
         cin >> anEntry;
         telDirec.append(anEntry);
         break;

      case 'C':   // Change an entry
         cout << "Enter entry to change - ";
         cin >> anEntry;
         index = telDirec.search(anEntry);
         if (index >= 0)
            telDirec.replace(index, anEntry);
         else
         {
            cout << "Name not in directory. "
                 << "Do you wish to add it (Y or N): ";
            cin >> answer;
            if (toupper(answer) == 'Y')
               telDirec.append(anEntry);
         }
         break;

      case 'D':   // Delete an entry
         cout << "Enter name of entry to delete: ";
         getline(cin, aName, '\n');
         anEntry.setEntry(aName);
         index = telDirec.search(anEntry);
         if (index >= 0)
```

*(continued)*

**Listing 11.11** Menu-driven program for telephone directory (continued)

```
                 telDirec.remove(index);
           else
              cout << "Entry not found - no deletion" << endl;
           break;

        case 'G':    // Get a number
           cout << "Enter name of entry to get: ";
           getline(cin, aName, '\n');
           anEntry.setEntry(aName);
           index = telDirec.search(anEntry);
           if (index >= 0)
           {
              telDirec.retrieve(index, anEntry);
              cout << "The number you requested is "
                   << anEntry.getNumber() << endl;
           }
           else
              cout << "Not in directory." << endl;
           break;

        case 's':    // Sort directory
           telDirec.selSort();
           break;

        case 'P':    // Print directory
           telDirec.display();
           break;

        case 'Q':    // Quit directory
           cout << "Exiting program" << endl;
           break;

        default:
           cout << "Choice is invalid - try again" << endl;
           //cin.ignore(80, '\n');
     }
  }  // end select
```

Before the main function, the line

```
    typedef indexList<entry, 100> telIndexList;
```

associates the identifier `telIndexList` with a particular data type, an indexed list of up to 100 type `entry` objects. This enables us to use the line

```
telIndexList telDirec;          // telephone directory
```

in function `main` to create an object of this type named `telDirec`.

Listing 11.12 shows a sample run of our program. We discuss the implementation of class `entry` in the next section.

**Listing 11.12**   Sample run of telephone directory program

```
Enter the initial directory entries -
Enter number of list items to read: 1
Enter next item - Enter name: Maria Sanchez
Enter number: 215-555-1234
Enter your choice -
A(Add), C(Change), D(Delete),
G(Get), S(Sort),   P(Print), Q(Quit): A
Enter entry to add - Enter name: Tom Brown
Enter number: 301-555-5643
Enter your choice -
A(Add), C(Change), D(Delete),
G(Get), S(Sort),   P(Print), Q(Quit): C
Enter entry to change - Enter name: Maria Sanchez
Enter number: 215-555-9876
Enter your choice -
A(Add), C(Change), D(Delete),
G(Get), S(Sort),   P(Print), Q(Quit): G
Enter name of entry to get: Maria Sanchez
The number you requested is 215-555-9876
Enter your choice -
A(Add), C(Change), D(Delete),
G(Get), S(Sort),   P(Print), Q(Quit): D
Enter name of entry to delete: Maria Sanchez
Enter your choice -
A(Add), C(Change), D(Delete),
G(Get), S(Sort),   P(Print), Q(Quit): P
Name   is Tom Brown
Number is 301-555-5643
Enter your choice -
A(Add), C(Change), D(Delete),
G(Get), S(Sort),   P(Print), Q(Quit): Q
Exiting program
```

Self-Check

1. Explain how the C++ compiler knows whether a function in Listing 11.11 is a member function of class `entry` or class `indexList`.

2. List all changes that would be needed if function `select` were a member function of class `indexList`.

Programming

1. Modify the telephone directory client program to read the initial directory from an external file.

2. Modify the telephone directory client program to insert a new element at a specified index.

3. Add a case to function `select` that determines whether there is more than one entry for a particular name. (Hint: You'll have to sort the indexed list first and see whether the name in the entry following the one selected by `search` matches the name in the entry selected by `search`.)

## 11.7 Operator Overloading and Friends

From our discussion of the telephone directory program, we know that the data members of a directory entry consist of two `string` components: `name` and `number`. We need to provide member functions `setEntry`, `getName`, and `getNumber` and operators ==, <, >, >> and << for class `entry`. In this section we learn how to overload operators so that they can process operands of different types.

### Operator Overloading

Let's first look at how we might overload the < operator so that it can compare two objects of type `entry` using a relation of the form `e1 < e2`. We need to place the prototype

```
bool operator < (const entry&);
```

in the definition file for class `entry`. This prototype identifies < as an *operator* that can be applied to a type `entry` object (`e1` in `e1 < e2`). The parameter list in parentheses indicates that the right operand of < must also be type `entry` (object `e2` in `e1 < e2`). The word `bool` before `operator` indicates that the result of applying the operator is type `bool`.

Listing 11.13 shows the code for operator < that would appear in the implementation file for class entry. It resembles a member function definition except that we write `operator` < instead of a function name before the formal parameter list. The `return` statement returns true if the name attribute of the left operand is lexically less than the name attribute of the right operand (represented by dE in Listing 11.13).

## EXAMPLE 11.11

If a, b, and c are type entry objects, the expression

```
a < b && b < c
```

compares the name attribute of objects a and b and then compares the name attribute of objects b and c. The expression value is true if the name attribute for a is lexically less than the name attribute for b, which is lexically less than the name attribute for c.

## Friends

Let's consider another way to implement the "less than" operation for class entry. Instead of implementing operator <, let's write a member function lessThan that has two arguments of type entry. For example, lessThan(a, b) would be true if the name field of object a was lexically less than the name field of object b. We can do this in C++ by introducing the concept of a friend function.

In the definition for class entry, we could use the following prototype for function lessThan:

```
friend bool lessThan(const entry& e1, const entry& e2);
```

This identifies lessThan as a friend of class entry. The parameter list indicates that function lessThan takes two type entry arguments. A **friend** of a class is a member function or operator that has two or more operands from the class being defined or an operand from another class. Listing 11.14 shows the definition of function lessThan written as a friend.

**friend**
A member function or operator that has two or more operands (arguments) from the class being defined or at least one operand from another class.

**Listing 11.13**   Class entry operator <

```
// Returns true if the name attribute of its left operand is
// lexically less than the name attribute of its right operand.
bool entry::operator < (const entry& dE)
{
    return (name < dE.name);
}
```

**Listing 11.14**    Function `lessThan` as a friend

```
// Returns true if the name attribute of its first argument
// is less than the name attribute of its second argument
bool lessThan(const entry& entry1,
              const entry& entry2)
{
    return (entry1.name < entry2.name);
}
```

Notice that `entry::` doesn't appear before the function name `lessThan`. This is because function `lessThan` isn't a member function of class `entry` but rather a friend of the class.

A friend has all the access privileges of a member function; it may directly access the private data members of its object arguments or operands, and it may also call any private member functions. However, a friend function can't be a `const` function.

Next let's consider how we might overload an operator that takes two operands from different classes. For example, we might want to use the operators >> and << with a type `entry` operand:

```
ins >> anEntry;
outs << anEntry;
```

In both examples above, the left-hand operand is a stream and the right-hand operand is type `entry`.

To accomplish this, we declare << and >> as friends of class `entry` by inserting the following prototypes in the class definition.

```
friend ostream& operator << (ostream&, const entry&);
friend istream& operator >> (istream&, entry&);
```

Each definition indicates that the designated operator is a friend of class `entry`. The parameter list in parentheses indicates that the left operand is a stream and the right operand is type `entry`. Each operator modifies its stream operand, as indicated by the result type following the word `friend`. We show the implementation of these functions later in this section.

## EXAMPLE 11.12

If entry1 and entry2 are two type entry objects, the statement

```
cout << entry1;
```

displays entry1 and in the process modifies stream cout. The statement

```
cout << entry2 << endl;
```

first displays entry2, modifying cout. The new cout becomes the left operand for the second insertion operator (<< endl), which places a newline character in stream cout.

---

**Friend Function (Operator) Declaration**

**Form:**    friend *result-type function-name* ( *argument-list* ) ;

        friend *result-type* operator *op-symbol* ( *argument-list* ) ;

**Example:**  friend bool equals (const entry&,
                        const entry&);

friend bool operator == (const entry&,
                        const entry&);

**Interpretation:** The friend function indicated by *function-name* or the friend operator indicated by *op-symbol* returns a value of type *result-type*. The argument list should contain one or more arguments of the class type in which the friend is defined. The friend can access all private data members and function members of the class. Instead of using dot notation to apply a friend function to an object, we pass the object through its argument list and place a friend operator between its left and right operands.

---

## Implementing the Directory Entry Class

Listing 11.15 shows the implementation file (`entry.cpp`) for class `entry`.

**Listing 11.15**  `File entry.cpp`

```
// File: entry.cpp
// Implementation file for class entry

#include "entry.h"
#include <iostream>
#include <string>
using namespace std;
```

*(continued)*

**Listing 11.15** File `entry.cpp` (continued)

```cpp
// constructor
entry::entry()
{
    name = "";
    number = "";
}

// Store data in an entry
void entry::setEntry(const string& na,      // IN: name
                     const string& nr)      // IN: number
{
    name = na;
    number = nr;
}

// Get name
string entry::getName() const
{
    return name;
}

// Get number
string entry::getNumber() const
{
    return number;
}

// Operators
bool entry::operator == (const entry& dE) // IN: right-operand
{
    return (name == dE.name);
}

bool entry::operator < (const entry& dE) // IN: right-operand
{
    return (name < dE.name);
}

bool entry::operator > (const entry& dE) // IN: right-operand
{
    return (name > dE.name);
}
```

(continued)

**Listing 11.15** File entry.cpp (continued)

```cpp
// friends
ostream& operator << (ostream& outs,     // INOUT: stream
                      const entry& dE) // IN: entry displayed
{
   outs << "Name    is " << dE.name << endl;
   outs << "Number is " << dE.number << endl;
   return outs;
}

istream& operator >> (istream& ins, // INOUT: stream
                      entry& dE)    // OUT: entry read
{
   cout << "Enter name: ";
   getline(ins, dE.name, '\n');
   cout << "Enter number: ";
   ins >> dE.number;
   return ins;
}
```

The equality and relational operators base their result only on the name
attribute of a directory entry, which is what we desire. The definition of
operator == enables us to determine if an entry currently in our list has the
same name as a target entry. Assuming target and elements[i] are the
same data type, the condition

```cpp
(elements[i] == target)
```

in function search of class indexList is true (a match) if target and elements[i] have the same name attribute. Similarly, the definition of operator
< enables us to sort the directory entries by name. The condition

```cpp
(elements[i] < elements[minIndex])
```

in function findMin of class indexList is true if the name in elements[i]
is lexically less than the name in elements[minIndex].

## EXERCISES FOR SECTION 11.7

### Self-Check

1. In the definition of friend operator >>, we use the operators << and >>. How can we do this? Explain which insertion or extraction operator C++ associates with each occurrence of these operators in the function body.

2. Explain why we used `getline` in friend operator >> instead of the string extraction operator to read a person's name.

3. Write the declaration for operator * as it would appear in the header file for the fraction class (Listing 10.5).

### Programming

1. Write definitions for operators <=, >=, and != for class `entry`.

2. Write the C++ code for operators *, /, +, and – for the fraction class (see Listing 10.7).

## 11.8 The vector Class

**container**
a special class that is part of the standard template library that stores a collection of objects

**vector**
an indexed container whose size automatically increases as elements are inserted and automatically decreases as elements are removed.

The C++ Standard Template Library (STL) provides a number of container classes where a **container** stores a collection of objects. One container class, the **vector**, is an indexed collection of elements just like an array. However, the vector class has many of the properties of the indexed list class. We can use a vector to provide storage for the phone directory instead of an indexed list. Vectors have the following properties:

■ The size of a vector can increase or decrease as needed.

■ A vector has knowledge of its size (the number of elements it stores).

■ Elements can be added to the end of a vector or deleted from the end of a vector.

■ Elements can be inserted in the middle of a vector.

■ Proper use of the vector at and size functions can prevent the occurrence of subscript range errors.

To use a vector, we need the compiler directive

```
#include <vector>
```

We declare a vector just as we declare any object of a template class. The syntax is

```
vector<element-type> vector-name(size);
```

The *element-type* appears in angle brackets after the class name and the vector *size* appears in parentheses after the *vector-name*. For example:

```
vector<int> intVec(10);    // a vector of 10 int elements
                           //    with value 0
vector<float> hours(5, 0.5);  // a vector of 5 float
                              // elements with value 0.5
```

As shown in the declaration above, you can specify the initial value of all vector elements using a second argument for the constructor. The default initial value is 0 for integers or real numbers.

You can also declare a vector without indicating its size. In this case, the vector will initially be empty (size is 0), and its size will increase as you add new elements. If you remove elements, its size will decrease. Because we don't know how many elements will be in our phone directory, we can use the declaration

```
vector<entry> telDirec;
```

to create an initially empty vector that can store elements of type `entry`.

You can access vector elements using subscript notation the same way you access array elements. For example, the loop below finds the sum of the 10 elements of vector `intVec`.

```
sum = 0;
for (int i = 0; i < intVec.size(); i++)
{
     sum += intVec[i];
}
```

The function call `telDirec.size()` returns the current size of this vector.

A better approach is to use function `at` to access each element of vector `intVec` in the loop above:

```
sum += intVec.at(i);    // a better way to access vector
                        //    elements
```

Use the `at` operator instead of a subscript because `at` checks that the index is within the range 0 to `size()-1` while the subscript operator makes no checks. You should use function `at` to access, but not change, the elements of a vector.

Each program in the book that processes an array would work exactly the same if you use a vector object with the same name, element type, and size instead of using an array. In Listing 9.1, for example, if you replace

```
float x[MAX_ITEMS];
```

with

```
vector<float> x(MAX_ITEMS);
```

the rest of the program would remain unchanged.

## Vector Functions

Table 11.1 shows some of the functions of the `vector` class. Data type $T$ represents the data type of the elements stored in the vector.

You can access the first element in a vector using member function `front` and the last element in a vector using function `back`:

```
cout << "first element is " << myValues.front()
        << ", last element is " << myValues.back() << endl;
```

You can use function `push_back` to append an element to the end of a vector. You can remove the last element from a vector using function `pop_back`. The size of the vector automatically adjusts after each insertion or deletion. The statements below replace the last element of vector `myValues` (a vector of real numbers) with `999.9`, and then display that value.

```
myValues.pop_back();
myValues.push_back(999.9);
```

**Table 11.1**  Some Member Functions for the `vector` Class

| | |
|---|---|
| `int size() const` | Returns the size of a vector. |
| `T at(int) const` | Returns the element at the position indicated by its argument. The argument must be between 0 and size()-1. |
| `T front()` | Returns the first element in a vector (at position 0). |
| `T back()` | Returns the last element in a vector (at position size()–1). |
| `void push_back(const T&)` | Appends an element to the end of a vector, increasing its size by 1. |
| `void pop_back(int)` | Removes the last element of a vector, decreasing its size by 1. |
| `void resize(int)` | Increases the vector size to the size specified by its argument. |

```
cout << "New last element is "
    << myValues.at(myValues.size()-1) << endl;
```

In the line above, the argument of member function `at` is the subscript (9) of the last element in the vector.

You can use member function `resize` to expand a vector. The statement below changes the size of vector `myValues` to 20.

```
myValues.resize(20);
```

## Accessing a Vector through an Iterator

C++ provides additional operations on vectors and other containers that require you to use an **iterator**— a pointer-like type that references elements of a container and which is used to navigate through a container object. The statement

```
vector<float>::iterator index;
```

declares an iterator `index` for any vector of floating point values. For any container class, the member functions `begin()` and `end()` define iterators that point to the first item in the container object and to the item just past the last one, respectively.

The next `for` statement uses the iterator `index` to display all elements of the vector `myValues`.

```
for (index = myValues.begin(); index != myValues.end();
        index++)
    cout << *index << endl;
```

The iterator `index` initially points to the first vector element. The operator `++` advances the iterator to the next vector element. The condition `index != myValues.end()` is true after the iterator has passed the last vector element. The notation `*index` denotes the element of the container pointed to by iterator `index`. Table 11.2 describes vector functions that use the Member function `insert` inserts an element in the vector and increases its size by 1. The statement

```
myValues.insert(myValues.begin() + 1, -777);
```

inserts `-777` just before the second element.

**Table 11.2**   Member Functions for `vector` Class With Iterators

| | |
|---|---|
| `iterator begin()` | Returns an iterator that points to the first element |
| `iterator end()` | Returns an iterator that points to the element following the last element in the vector. |
| `void insert(iterator, T)` | Inserts the second argument in the vector at the element pointed to by the iterator argument. The element at this position prior to the insertion is shifted down, as are all elements that follow it. The vector size is increased by 1. |
| `void erase(iterator)` | Deletes the element pointed to by the iterator argument. The elements that follow the one deleted are moved up. The vector size is decreased by 1. |

## Standard Algorithms

C++ provides a library of algorithms that you can use with certain container classes. These algorithms perform searching and sorting operations, among others. To use them, insert the `algorithm` header in your program file:

```
#include <algorithm>
```

Many of these algorithms require iterators as arguments. For example, the statement

```
sort(myValues.begin(), myValues.end());
```

sorts all elements in the vector `myValues`. The function arguments are iterators that point to the first vector element and one past the last vector element, respectively. These are the boundaries for the sort operation. The operator < must be defined for the elements stored in the container being sorted.

The statement

```
index = find(myValues.begin(), myValues.end(), target);
```

calls function `find` to search for the value of `target` (its third argument) in the vector elements bounded by its two iterator arguments. If `target` is in the vector, the iterator `index` is set to point to the first vector element that matches `target`. If target isn't found, the iterator `index` gets the value of the iterator `myValues.end()`. We can use the `if` statement below to display the search results.

```
if (index != myValues.end())
    cout << *index << " found in the array." << endl;
else
    cout << target << " not found!" << endl;
```

If `target` is found, this statement displays the vector element pointed to by `index` (element `*index`) which is the same as `target`.

## Using **vector** and **algorithm** classes in the Telephone Directory Program

We can use the `vector` and `algorithm` classes to implement the menu-driven program for the telephone directory shown in Listing 11.11. We'll store our directory in a vector of `entry` objects that is initially empty. Next, we discuss how we implement each menu option, shown in the table below. Listing 11.16 shows the program.

| Menu option | Implementation |
|---|---|
| Add | Use function `push_back` to add elements to the end of the directory |
| Change | Use function `find` to return an iterator that points to the entry to be changed. Use function `erase` to delete the existing entry and function `insert` to put the new entry at that position. |
| Delete | Use function `find` to return an iterator that points to the entry to be deleted. Use function `erase` to delete the entry. |
| Get | Use function `find` to return an iterator that points to the desired entry and access that entry. |
| Sort | Use function `sort` to sort the elements in the vector. |
| Print | Use function `display` to cycle through the entries in the vector and display each entry. |

**Listing 11.16**   Menu-driven program for telephone directory using a vector

```
// FILE: teleMenuVector.cpp
// Menu driven telephone directory update program with vector

#include "entry.h"
#include <cctype>          // For toupper
#include <iostream>
#include <string>
#include <algorithm>
```

(continued)

**Listing 11.16** Menu-driven program for telephone directory using a vector (continued)

```cpp
#include <vector>
using namespace std;

// Function prototypes
void select(vector<entry>&, char);
void display(const vector<entry>&);

int main()
{
   vector<entry> telDirec(10);   // telephone directory
   char choice;                  // menu choice

   // Keep reading and performing operations until user enters Q
   do
   {
     // Display the menu.
     cout << "Enter your choice -" << endl;
     cout << "A(Add), C(Change), D(Delete)," << endl
          << "G(Get), S(Sort),   P(Print), Q(Quit): ";

     cin >> choice;

     // Perform the operation selected.
     select(telDirec, choice);
   }
   while (toupper(choice) != 'Q');

   return 0;
}


// Performs user selection
void select(vector<entry>& telDirec,   // INOUT: directory
            char choice)               // IN: selection
{
   // Local data
   entry anEntry;      // one entry
   string aName;       // input - entry name
   vector<entry>::iterator index; // index of name
                                  // in directory
   char answer;        // input - indicates whether to add
                       //         entry for missing name
```

(continued)

**Listing 11.16**   Menu-driven program for telephone directory using a vector (continued)

```
switch (toupper(choice))
{
   case 'A':    // Add an entry
      cout << "Enter entry to add - ";
      cin >> anEntry;
      telDirec.push_back(anEntry);
      break;

   case 'C':    // Change an entry
      cout << "Enter entry to change - ";
      cin >> anEntry;

      index = find(telDirec.begin(), telDirec.end(),
                   anEntry);
      if (index != telDirec.end()) {
         telDirec.erase(index);
         telDirec.insert(index, anEntry);
      }
      else
      {
         cout << "Name not in directory. "
              << "Do you wish to add it (Y or N): ";
         cin >> answer;
         if (toupper(answer) == 'Y')
            telDirec.push_back(anEntry);
      }
      break;

   case 'D':    // Delete an entry
      cout << "Enter name of entry to delete: ";
      cin.ignore(1, '\n');
      getline(cin, aName, '\n');
      anEntry.setEntry(aName);
      index = find(telDirec.begin(), telDirec.end(),
                   anEntry);
      if (index != telDirec.end())
         telDirec.erase(index);
      else
         cout << "Entry not found - no deletion" << endl;
      break;

   case 'G':    // Get a number
```

(continued)

**Listing 11.16    Menu-driven program for telephone directory using a vector (continued)**

```cpp
            cout << "Enter name of entry to get: ";
            cin.ignore(1, '\n');
            getline(cin, aName, '\n');
            anEntry.setEntry(aName);
            index = find(telDirec.begin(), telDirec.end(),
                         anEntry);
            if (index != telDirec.end())
            {
               anEntry = *index;
               cout << "The number you requested is "
                    << anEntry.getNumber() << endl;
            }
            else
               cout << "Not in directory." << endl;
            break;

         case 'S':   // Sort directory
            sort(telDirec.begin(), telDirec.end());
            break;

         case 'P':   // Print directory
            display(telDirec);
            break;

         case 'Q':   // Quit directory
            cout << "Exiting program" << endl;
            break;

         default:
            cout << "Choice is invalid - try again" << endl;
            cin.ignore(80, '\n');
      }
   }  // end select

   // Displays each entry in vector telDirec
   void display(const vector<entry>& telDirec) {
      for (int ix = 0; ix < telDirec.size(); ix++)
         cout << telDirec.at(ix);
   }
```

## EXERCISES FOR SECTION 11.8

### Self-Check

1. Trace the execution of the fragment below. Explain the effect of each statement.

```
vector<char> s(10);
s[0] = 'a';
s[9] = 'z';
s.push_back('$');
for (int i = 0; i < s.size(); i++)
    cout << s.at(i);
char ch1 = s.front();
char ch2 = s.back();
cout << ch1 << "***" << ch2 << endl;
```

2. Trace the execution of the fragment below. Explain the effect of each statement.

```
vector<int> x(10, 5);
vector<int>::iterator ix;
ix = x.begin();
ix++;
*ix = 15;
while (ix != x.end()) {
    cout << *ix;
    ix++;
}
```

### Programming

1. Write a function that loads a vector of ints from an array of ints. The vector should contain the same elements in the same order as the array.

## 11.9   Common Programming Errors

Review the common programming errors sections for Chapters 9 (arrays and structs) and 10 (classes) because many of the same errors can occur when you process combinations of these data structures.

- *Subscript range errors* When you use multidimensional arrays, make sure the subscript for each dimension is always in range. If you use nested `for` loops to process the array elements, check carefully that the loop control variables used as array subscripts are in the correct order. The order of the loop control variables determines the sequence in which the array elements are processed.

- *Improper use of brackets* Be careful not to make the mistake of writing all subscripts inside one pair of brackets (e.g., `sales[1, 2, 3]` is wrong, `sales[1][2][3]` is correct).

- *Misuse of subscript notation or dot notation* For arrays of structs or arrays of classes, use the array name followed by a subscript to access the entire array element. To reference an individual data item stored in an array of structs, you must specify both the array subscript and the name of the struct component using the notation `x[i].comp` where `x[i]` is the `i`th element of array `x` and `comp` is a structure component.

- *Errors in defining template classes* For template classes, you must provide the template class prefix before the header of each member function that is defined in a separate `.cpp` file. Also, the class name with arguments and the scope resolution operator `::` must precede the function name in the function header. If you have difficulty linking the components of a program that uses a template class whose member functions are defined in a separate `.cpp` file, you should determine whether any special compiler directives or `typedef` declarations are required on your system. As an alternative, you can consider placing the function definitions directly in the header file. If you do this, don't forget to remove the template class prefix line and the class name and scope resolution operator from the function header.

- *Errors in using friend functions* For friend functions or operators, begin the function prototype (in the header file) with the word `friend`. In the function definition (in the implementation file), remove the class name and scope resolution operator. Remember that friends can't be `const` functions or operators.

## Summary of New C++ Constructs

| Construct | Effect |
|---|---|
| **Two-Dimensional Array** | |
| `int matrix[10][5];` | `matrix` is a two-dimensional array with 10 rows and 5 columns. |
| `sum = 0;`<br>`for (int i = 0; i < 10; i++)`<br>`   for (int j = 0; j < 5; j++)`<br>`      sum += matrix[i][j];` | Stores the sum of all elements of array `matrix` in `sum`. |
| **Array of Structs** | |
| `struct city`<br>`{`<br>`   string name;`<br>`   string state;`<br>`};` | Declares a struct `type city` with storage for two string components, `name` and `state`. |

## Summary of New C++ Constructs (continued)

| Construct | Effect |
|---|---|
| `city capitals[50];` | Allocates storage for an array `capitals` whose 50 elements are structs of type `city`. |
| `capitals[49].name = "Juno";` | Stores "Juno" in the `name` field of `capitals[49]`. |

**Array of Objects**

| Construct | Effect |
|---|---|
| ```cpp
class point
{
    public:
        point();
        void read();
        void print();
    private:
        int x;
        int y;
};
``` | Each `point` object has two private data members, `x` and `y`. The class has three public member functions: `point`, `read`, and `print`. |
| `point coords[5];` | Allocates storage for an array `coords` whose five elements are objects of type `point`. |
| `coords[0].print();` | Applies `print` to the first object in array `coords`. |

**Template Class**

| Construct | Effect |
|---|---|
| ```cpp
template<class T, int n>
class myList
{
    public:
        myList();
        void read();
        void display();
    private:
        T stuff[n];
};
``` | Template class `myList` has one private data member `stuff` that provides storage for an array of n elements of type `T`. Both `T` and n are parameters. There are three public member functions: `myList` (a constructor), `display`, and `read`. |
| ```cpp
template<class T, int n>
void myList<T, n>::read()
``` | Function header for definition of member function `read` of template class `myList` in a separate implementation file. |
| `myList<point, 3> triangle;` | Object `triangle` is an instance of template class `myList` that provides storage for three objects of type point. |
| `triangle.display();` | Applies member function `display` to object `triangle`. |

**Operator Prototype**

| Construct | Effect |
|---|---|
| `bool operator < (const el&);` | Overloads operator < so it can take two operands of class `el`. |
```

## Summary of New C++ Constructs (continued)

| Construct | Effect |
|---|---|
| **Friend Function Prototype** | |
| `friend bool same`<br>`    (const el&, const el&);` | Declares a friend function same that has two operands of class `el`. |
| `vector declaration`<br>`vector<float> hours;` | Declares a vector hours for storing type float elements. Its size may vary. |
| `iterator declaration`<br>`vector<float>::iterator index;` | Declares an iterator index that may be used with a vector of type float elements. |

# Chapter Review

1. You can model a variety of problem data using combinations of C++ built-in data structures: arrays, structs, and classes.

2. You can model tables and board games with two-dimensional arrays. You can use an array with three dimensions to represent a company's sales volume broken down by salesperson, year, and quarter.

3. Classes can be used to store a collection of data along with operators that process that data. The use of template classes enables us to store and process different kinds of data in the same data structure.

4. We wrote an indexed list template class that acts as a safe array for storage of data of different kinds and sizes. The class includes operators for reading, displaying, searching, sorting, replacing, and deleting its data. We also showed how to model and maintain a telephone directory stored as an indexed list.

5. You can overload C++ operators by providing operator declarations (prototypes) and definitions. An operator definition resembles a function definition, except the word `operator` and the operator symbol, not a function name, precedes the formal parameter list.

6. You can write a function or operator with two formal parameters that are the same class type as a friend of that class. If you want to use the stream operators `<<` and `>>` with a class type, you must define the stream operators as friends of that class.

7. A vector is a useful data structure that is part of the Standard Template Library (STL). A vector is indexed like an array and has many of the features of the non-standard indexed list class implemented in this chapter. Using the member function `at`, you can ensure safe access to

elements of a vector. You can easily add elements to the end of a vector and access elements at the beginning and end of a vector. You can also use iterators to access elements of a vector in sequence.

## Quick–Check Exercises

1. What control structure can be used to sequentially access all the elements in a multidimensional array?

2. List the storage sequence for elements of the two-dimensional array `matrix` with 3 rows and 2 columns.

3. Write a program segment to display the sum of the values in each column of a $5 \times 3$ array `table` with base type `float` elements. How many column sums will be displayed? How many elements are included in each sum?

4. Write a type declaration for a data structure that stores a baseball player's name, salary, position (pitcher, catcher, infielder, outfielder, utility), batting average, fielding percentage, number of hits, runs, runs batted in, and errors.

5. Write the type declaration for a data structure that stores the information in the previous exercise for a team of 25 players.

6. If the elements of the array `team` have the structure described in Quick-Check Exercise 4, write a program segment that displays the first two structure members for the first five players.

7. Write a type declaration for an array of 12 objects of type `counter` (see Figure 10.1). Write an expression to increment the sixth element of your array.

8. Write a declaration that allocates storage for an indexed list of 25 players from Quick-Check Exercise 4.

9. Redo question 8 using an indexed list and a vector.

10. Assuming that the variable `aPlayer` contains a player's data, write a statement to add `aPlayer` to the end of the vector in the previous exercise.

11. Write statements to place `aPlayer` in the first position of the vector but first move the player currently in the first position to the end of the vector.

12. Can you have two vectors of `float` numbers in the same client program? Can you have a vector of integers and a vector of characters in the same client program?

13. Write a program segment that removes from a vector `x` of `int`s the element just before the last element. Use an iterator.

## Answers to Quick–Check Exercises

1. nested for loops

2. `matrix[0][0]`, `matrix[0][1]`, `matrix[1][0]`, `matrix[1][1]`, `matrix[2][0]`, `matrix[2][1]`

3.
```
for (int c = 0; c < 3; c++)
{
    columnSum = 0.0;
    for (int r = 0; r < 5; r++)
        columnSum += table[r][c];
    cout << "Sum for column " << c << " is "
        << columnSum << "." << endl;
} // end for c
```
three column sums; five elements added per column

4. The data elements are of different types:
```
enum position {pitcher, catcher, infielder, outfielder,
                utility};
struct player
{
    string name;
    float salary;
    position place;
    float battingAve, fieldPct;
    int hits, runs, rbis, errors;
}; // end player
```

5. `player team[25];`

6.
```
for (int i = 0; i < 5; i++)
    cout << team[i].name << "    "
        << team[i].salary << endl;
```

7.
```
counter counters[11];
counters[5].increment ();
```

8.
```
indexList<player, 25> team;
    vector<player> team(25);
```

9. `team.push_back(aPlayer);`

10.
```
bPlayer = team.at(0);
team[0] = aPlayer;
team.push_back(bPlayer);
```

| s.top | 2 | | |
|---|---|---|---|
| s.items | & | * | $ |

11. yes; yes

12. ```
vector<int>::iterator ix;
ix = x.end();
ix--;
ix--;
x.erase(ix);
```

## Review Questions

1. Write the declarations for the array `cpuArray` that will hold 20 records of type `cpu`. The structure `cpu` has the following fields: `idNumber` (a string), `make` (a string), `location` (a string), and `ports` (integer).

   *Use the following declarations for questions 2 through 4:*

   ```
   const int NUM_EMPLOYEES = 20;
   struct employee
   {
        int id;
        float rate;
        float hours;
   };   // end employee
   employee allEmployees[NUM_EMPLOYEES];
   ```

2. Write the function `totalGross` that will return the total gross pay given the data stored in the array `allEmployees`.

3. Write a program fragment that displays the ID number of each employee who works between 10.0 and 20.0 hours per week.

4. Write a program fragment that displays the ID number of the employee who works the most hours.

5. Write the declarations for an array of structs that can be used to store all the top 40 hits for one week of the year. Assume that the data stored for each hit is the title, artist, production company, cost, and month of issue (an enumerator).

6. Answer the previous question for a data structure that stores the same data for each of the 52 weeks of a year.

7. Provide the definition for a class whose attributes store the information described in Review Question 5. Declare member functions that perform operations analogous to the ones for class `entry` in Listing 11.10.

8. Provide declarations for indexed lists (not arrays) that store the data described in Review Question 5 using the class from the previous question to store data for each hit.
   ```

9. Explain the advantages of using an indexed list instead of an array to store the data about the top 40 hits.

10. Describe two circumstances when you'd use a friend function instead of a member function.

11. Provide an implementation file with definitions for each member function of the class in Review Question 7. Base the results of a comparison on the title attribute.

12. Show the effect of each of the operations below on `vector<char>` s. Assume that `y` (type `char`) contains the character `'&'`. What are the final values of x and the contents of vector s?

```
s.push_back('+');
x = s.back();

s.push_back('(');
s.push_back(y);
    s.pop_back();
x = s.back();
```

# Programming Projects

1. Write a program that generates the Morse code for a sentence that ends with a period and contains no other characters except letters and blanks. After reading the Morse code into an array of strings, your program should read each word of the sentence and display its Morse code equivalent on a separate line. The Morse code is as follows:

A .-    B -...    C -.-    D -..    E .    F ..-.    G --.    H ....    I ..    J .---

K -.-    L .-..    M --    N -.    O ---    P .--.    Q --.-    R .-.    S ...    T -

U ..-    V ...-    W .--    X -..-    Y -.--    Z --..

Each letter and its Morse code equivalent should be stored in an indexed list of structs, and an appropriate set of functions should be defined for this data abstraction.

2. Develop a C++ class to model the mathematical notion of a matrix. At a minimum, your class should include functions for addition, subtraction, and multiplication of two matrices, plus at least three other matrix operations that you know about. (If you don't know much about matrices, find a mathematics book that can help.) Before performing the required data manipulation, each function you write

should validate its input arguments. In particular, the dimensions of the matrices involved in an operation must be compatible for that operation.

3. The voting district in which you live is partitioned into five precincts. Write a program that reads the election results from each of these precincts and tabulates the total vote in your district for all of the candidates running for election. The program should begin by asking the user to enter the number of candidates, nmbrCandidates, running for office. It should then read the election returns for each precinct for each candidate, compute the total vote for each candidate, and display the input and the results in the form shown in the table on the next page.

For each candidate, the program should also compute and display the percentage of the total vote. If there is one candidate whose percentage is better than 50 percent, display a message declaring that candidate to be the winner of the election. If there is no such candidate, display out a message indicating the names of the top two vote-getters and indicate that a run-off election will be required. The voting data should be stored in an indexed collection of structured elements, each of which contains the name of a candidate, the number of votes in each precinct for that candidate, and the vote total. The relevant information about each candidate should be modeled by a class containing the definitions of the necessary attributes and functions required for one candidate.

Test your program for the data shown below and also when candidate C receives only 108 votes in precinct 4.

| Precinct | Candidate A | Candidate B | Candidate C | Candidate D | Total Vote |
|---|---|---|---|---|---|
| 1 | 192 | 148 | 1206 | 137 | 1483 |
| 2 | 147 | 190 | 1312 | 121 | 1570 |
| 3 | 186 | 112 | 1121 | 138 | 1357 |
| 4 | 114 | 121 | 1408 | 139 | 1582 |
| 5 | 267 | 113 | 1382 | 129 | 1691 |
| Totals | 906 | 184 | 1429 | 164 | 2683 |

4. Modify the previous programming project to make it an interactive, menu-driven program. Menu options should include the following:

■ Initializing the vote table (prompt the user for the number of candidates, their names, and the number of votes in each precinct)

■ Displaying the candidates' names and votes received (raw count and percentage of votes cast)

- Displaying the winner's name (or names of the top two vote-getters in the case of a run-off)

- Exiting the program

5. The HighRisk Software Company has employed us to develop a general sales analysis program that they can market to a number of different companies. The program will be used to enter monthly sales figures for a specified range of years and display these values and some simple statistical measures as requested by the user. The user is to be given a menu from which to choose one of the options shown in the table on the next page.

| Options | Description |
|---|---|
| 0 | *Display help information*—presents more detailed information about the other options available. |
| 1 | *Display sales data*—provides sales data for the entire range of years using two tables, one covering January–June and the other covering July–December. |
| 2 | *Compute annual sales totals*—computes the sum of the monthly sales for each year in the specified range. |
| 3 | *Display annual sales totals*—presents the sum of the monthly sales for each year in the specified range. |
| 4 | *Display largest monthly sales amount*—finds and displays the largest monthly sales amount for a specified year. |
| 5 | *Graph monthly sales data*—provides a histogram for the 12 months of sales for a specified year. |
| 6 | *Exit*—exits from the program. |

The program is to run interactively and should begin by asking the user to enter the range of years involved. Next it should prompt the user for the sales data for each of the specified years. From this point on, the program should display the options menu, allow the user to make a choice, and carry out the user's selection. This process should continue repeatedly until the user enters option 6.

6. Design and implement a C++ class to model a telephone directory for a company. The directory should contain space for up to 100 names, phone numbers, and room numbers. You should have operators to do the following:

- Create an empty directory (all names blank).

- Read in the telephone directory from a file.

- Retrieve the entry corresponding to a given name.

- Display the telephone directory.

■ Add a new entry to the directory.

■ Also design and implement a class with attributes and functions required to model an individual telephone entry.

7. Write a menu-driven program that tests the operators in the previous programming project.

8. Design and implement a C++ class to model a building (floors 1 to 3, wings A and B, and rooms 1 to 5). Each entry in the array will be a `struct` containing a person's name and phone number. Provide operators to do the following:

■ Create an empty building (all names are blank).

■ Read data into the building.

■ Display the entire building.

■ Display a particular floor of the building.

■ Retrieve the entry for a particular room.

■ Store a new entry in a particular room.

To designate a particular room, the program user must enter a floor number, wing letter, and room number as data. Also design and implement a class with attributes and functions required to model a single room in the building.

9. Most supermarkets use computer equipment that allows the checkout clerk to drag an item across a sensor that reads the bar code on the product container. After the computer reads the bar code, the store inventory database is examined, the item's price and product description are located, counts are reduced, and a receipt is printed. Your task is to write a program that simulates this process.

   Your program will read the inventory information from the data file on disk into an array of records. The data in the inventory file is written one item per line, beginning with a two-digit product code, followed by a 30-character product description, its price, and the quantity of that item in stock. Your program will copy the revised version of the inventory to a new data file after all purchases are processed.

   Processing customers' orders involves reading a series of product codes representing each person's purchases from a second data file. A zero product code is used to mark the end of each customer's order. As each product code is read, the inventory list is searched to find a matching product code. Once located, the product price and description are printed on the receipt, and the quantity on hand is reduced by 1. At the bottom of the receipt, print the total for the goods purchased by the customer.

**10.** Write a program that simulates the movement of radioactive particles in a 20 × 20-foot two-dimensional shield around a reactor. Particles enter the shield at some random position in the shield coordinate space. Once a particle enters the shield, it moves 1 foot per second in one of four directions. The direction for the next second of travel is determined by a random number from 1 to 4 (forward, backward, left, right). A change in direction is interpreted as a collision with another particle, which results in a dissipation of energy. Each particle can have only a limited number of collisions before it dies. A particle exits the shield if its position places it outside the shield coordinate space before K collisions occur. Determine the percentage of particles that exit the shield, where K and the number of particles are input as data items. Also, compute the average number of times a particle's path crosses itself during travel time within the shield. (*Hint:* Mark each array position occupied by a particle before it dies or exits the shield.)

**11.** Write a program to monitor the flow of an item (a widget) into and out of a warehouse. The warehouse will have numerous deliveries and shipments for this item during the time covered. A shipment out is billed at a profit of 50 percent over the cost of a widget. Unfortunately, each shipment received may have a different cost associated with it. The accountants for the firm have instituted a last-in, first-out system for filling orders. This means that the newest widgets are the first ones sent out to fill an order. This function of inventory can be represented using a vector. The `push_back` operator will insert a shipment received. The `pop_back` operator will delete a shipment out. Input data should consist of the following:

- `S` or `O`: shipment received or an order to be sent

- `quantity`: quantity received or shipped out

- `cost`: cost per widget (for received shipments only)

- `vendor`: a character string that names the company sent to or received from

For example, the data fragment below indicates that 100 widgets were received from RCA at $10.50 per widget and 50 were shipped to Boeing:

```
S 100 10.50 RCA
O 50 Boeing
```

Output for an order will consist of the quantity and the total price for all the widgets in the order. (Hint: Each widget price is 50 percent higher than its cost. The widgets to fill an order may come from multiple shipments with different costs.)

**12.** Write a program that can be used to compile a simple arithmetic expression without parentheses. For example, the expression

$$A + B * C - D$$

should be compiled as shown in the table below.

| Operation | Operand 1 | Operand 2 | Result |
|:---:|:---:|:---:|:---:|
| * | B | C | Z |
| + | A | Z | Y |
| − | Y | D | X |

The table shows the order in which the operations are performed (*, +, −) and the operands for each operator. The Result column gives the name of an identifier (working backward from Z) chosen to hold each result. Assume that the operands are the letters A through F and the operators are +, −, *, and /.

Your program should read each character and process it as follows. If the character is a blank, ignore it. If it is an operand, push it onto the end of the operand vector. If the character isn't an operator, display an error message and terminate the program. If it is an operator, compare its precedence with that of the operator at the end of the operator vector (* and / have higher precedence than + and −). If the new operator has higher precedence than the one currently at the end (or if the operator vector is empty), it should be pushed onto the operator vector.

If the new operator has the same or lower precedence, the operator at the end of the operator vector must be evaluated next. This is done by removing it from the operator vector along with the last two operands from the end of the operand vector and writing a new line of the output table. The character selected to hold the result should then be pushed onto the end of the operand vector. Next, the new operator should be compared to the new operator at the end of the operator vector. Continue to generate output table lines until the operator at the end of the operator vector has lower precedence than the new operator or until the vector is empty. At this point, add the new operator to the end of the operator vector and examine the next character in the data string. When the end of the string is reached, remove any remaining operator along with its operand pair as just described. Remember to add the result character onto the end of the operand vector after each table line is generated.

# John Lakos

*In 2001, Dr. Lakos joined Bloomberg LP in New York City, where he is the Meta architect and mentor for C++ software development worldwide. Previously, Dr. Lakos was a Managing Director Principal for Bear Stearns, where he directed the design and development of infrastructure libraries for proprietary analytic financial applications and later for Global Information Technologies. For 12 years prior to joining Bear Stearns, Dr. Lakos worked at Mentor Graphics developing large frameworks and advanced ICCAD applications, for which he holds multiple software patents. He received a Ph.D. in Computer Science and anSc. D. in Electrical Engineering (1989) from Columbia University. Dr. Lakos received his undergraduate degrees from MIT in Mathematics and Computer Science. He is the author of the book* Large Scale C++ Software Design.

**What is your educational background, and how did you decide to study computer science?**

I have always been strong in mathematics; I finished all of high school math in the first two months of ninth grade, and then joined the Advanced Placement Calculus class with two other students who were both seniors. It was around that time that Hewlett-Packard had come out with their first scientific pocket calculators: the HP-35, HP-45, and shortly thereafter, the programmable HP-65. It was by programming that calculator in 10th grade that I learned to program "efficiently." I will never forget my high school physics teacher John Roeder (a Ph.D. in nuclear physics from Princeton) exclaiming, "You mean that thing has the wherewithal to record your programs on those tiny magnetic strips?" Between HP, my physics teacher, and my father, Eugene Lakos, a civil engineer from CalTech, I believe I was destined to become a mathematically oriented scientific engineer working with computers.

**Describe your work at Bloomberg.**

My work at Bloomberg is focused on improving quality, time-to-market, and throughput over a longer time horizon. In any commercial software activity, software managers will traditionally trade off quality, delivery date, and cost to achieve an optimal business solution for any given product. My job is to "move the playing field" so managers operate in a space that is inherently better in all three of these dimensions. To achieve this goal, we must develop relevant prefabricated, finely graduated, granular software that is easy to use (reuse), easy to understand, high-performance, portable, and reliable. Developing such integrated solutions takes time; hence, this approach is not a solution that improves productivity immediately. By providing a stable foundation and working with key application developers, a critical mass of what we call "software capital" emerges. The more software capital we have, the easier it is to develop new applications, and with each new application, more software capital is extracted and made available for future use. This recipe for productivity is inherently exponential. The larger the corporation, the more profitable this approach becomes.

## What was your first job in the computer industry?

My first summer job (1978) was as a software engineer working at New York Telephone. There I learned to program in PL-1 by organically growing a single "while" loop into a 5000-line formatter program (BAD IDEA). My second summer job (1979) was at Chase Manhattan Bank working on the "Home Banking on the Apple Computer" project. As a separate exercise, I decided to learn 6502 assembler by writing an assembly level symbolic debugger (in 6502 assembler). Much of what I know about assemblers and debuggers derives from this experience.

## Which person in the field inspired you most?

There are several people in the field of Computer Science that have inspired me. Before doing my Ph.D. research, Bjarne Stroustrup had set the tone for the kind of code that I develop: efficient, consistent, compile-time type-safe, and minimal. As I researched the field for my 1997 Computer Science Ph.D. Dissertation, I was reminded of the remarkable software engineering contributions of David Parnas and Edsger Dijkstra.

## What advice do you have for students entering the computer science field?

Learn as much as you can. I have studied everything about computers from device physics to Turing machines. The more you know, the better you are at making correct practical decisions. Details matter. When I am interviewing people, I am most concerned with their ability to analyze and solve detailed problems. Along with being an abstract thinker, being a hands-on programmer always makes you more valuable.

## What kind of projects are you currently working on?

My "project" for now, and for the foreseeable future, is to create and extend an enterprise-wide component-based meta-framework for developing high-performance middleware, applications frameworks, and application-developer-oriented solutions to recurring business problems that ensures quality and maximizes throughput in the long-term steady state.

## How has C++ evolved in the last few years?

Poorly. Most of what I need day-to-day existed in 1990 in Cfront 3.0. There is essentially no need to change or extend C++ any further. Sure, member templates and partial template specialization have their place, but for all practical purposes, the best thing for C++, in my opinion, is for it to stabilize and stop changing—especially in ways that are incompatible with existing code. Enough is enough.

## What is your vision for the future of the C++ programming language?

C++, in my opinion, has replaced C as the general purpose, high-performance language of choice for at least the next few decades. Other "cool" languages will come and go, but I suspect C++, with its immense embedded knowledge and practical benefit, will be around long after I am not.

# Recursion

## Chapter Objectives

- To understand how recursion is used as a problem solving tool
- To learn how to write recursive functions
- To see how to implement mathematical functions with recursive definitions as C++ functions
- To learn how to use recursion to solve problems involving arrays
- To learn how to write a recursive binary search function
- To understand a recursive solution to the Towers of Hanoi Problem

A RECURSIVE FUNCTION is able to call itself. Each time it is called, the recursive function can operate on different arguments. You can use recursion as an alternative to iteration (looping). In many instances, the use of recursion enables programmers to specify natural, simple solutions to problems that would otherwise be difficult to solve. For this reason, recursion is an important and powerful tool in programming and problem solving—especially in solving problems such as proving theorems, writing compilers, and in searching and sorting algorithms.

## 12.1 The Nature of Recursion

**recursive function**
A function that calls
itself.

In this section we demonstrate recursion using a simple function and we develop rules for writing **recursive functions**, or functions that call themselves. We show how to apply recursive techniques to problem solving next.

### EXAMPLE 12.1

Consider the computer solution to the problem "Raise 6 to the power 3." A computer can multiply but it can't perform the operation "Raise to a power." However, we know that $6^3$ is 6 times $6^2$, so we can split the problem "Raise 6 to the power 3" into two subproblems:

**Subproblems generated from "Raise 6 to the power 3":**

Problem 1.  Raise 6 to the power 2.
Problem 2.  Multiply the result of problem 1 by 6.

Because a computer can multiply, we can solve problem 2 but not problem 1. However, problem 1 is an easier version of the original problem. We can split it into the two problems 1.1 and 1.2 below, leaving us three problems to solve, two of which are multiplication problems.

**Subproblems generated from "Raise 6 to the power 2":**

Problem 1.1        Raise 6 to the power 1.
Problem 1.2        Multiply the result of problem 1.1 by 6.

You can program a computer to recognize that the result of raising any number to the power 1 is that number. Therefore, we can solve problem 1.1 (the answer is 6), and then solve problem 1.2 (the answer is 36), which gives us the solution to problem 1. Multiplying this result by 6 (problem 2) gives us 216, which is the solution to the original problem.

Listing 12.1 shows the implementation of this solution in the form of the recursive function power, which returns the result of raising its first argument, m, to the power indicated by its second argument, n. If n is greater than 1 (the usual situation), the statement

```
return m * power(m, n - 1);       // recursive step
```

executes. To evaluate the return expression, C++ first calls function power with its second argument reduced by 1. The result returned by this call is then multiplied by m. Therefore, we have split the original problem into two simpler problems as desired:

Problem 1.        Raise m to the power n - 1 (power(m, n - 1))
Problem 2.        Multiply the result by m.

**Listing 12.1**   Recursive function power

```
// File: power.cpp
// Recursive power function

// Raises its first argument to the power indicated by its
// second argument.
// Pre:     m and n are defined and n > 0.
// Post:    Returns m raised to the power n.

int power(int m, int n)      // IN: raise m to power n
{
   if (n <= 1)
      return m;                        // stopping case
   else
      return m * power(m, n - 1);  // recursive step
}
```

If the new second argument is greater than 1, there will be additional calls to function power. We call this step the **recursive step** because it contains a call to function power.

The first case in Listing 12.1 causes an immediate return from the function when the condition n <= 1 becomes true. We call this a **stopping case** because it ends the recursion. A condition that's true for a stopping case is called a **terminating condition**.

For now, we'll assume that function power performs as desired. We'll see how to trace the execution of a recursive function in the next section.

**recursive step**
The step in a function or algorithm that contains a recursive call.

**stopping case**
The statement that causes recursion to terminate.

**terminating condition**
A condition that evaluates to true when a stopping case is reached.

## Properties of Recursive Problems and Solutions

Problems that can be solved by recursion have the following characteristics:

- One or more simple cases of the problem (called *stopping cases*) have a straightforward, nonrecursive solution.
- The other cases of the problem can be reduced (using recursion) to one or more problems that are closer to stopping cases.
- Eventually the problem can be reduced to only stopping cases, which are relatively easy to solve.

Follow these steps to solve a recursive problem.

1. Try to express the problem as a simpler version of itself.
2. Determine the stopping cases.
3. Determine the recursive steps.

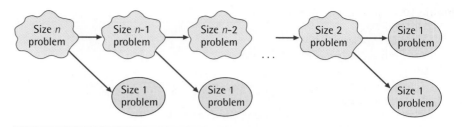

**Figure 12.1**    Splitting a problem into smaller problems

Figure 12.1 illustrates these steps. Assume that for a particular problem of size $n$, we can split the problem into a problem of size 1, which we can solve (a stopping case), and a problem of size $n - 1$. We can split the problem of size $n - 1$ into another problem of size 1 and a problem of size $n - 2$, which we can split further. If we split the problem $n$ times, we'll end up with $n$ problems of size 1, each of which we can solve.

The recursive algorithms that we write will generally consist of an `if` statement with the form:

> `If`  the stopping case is reached
>     Solve the problem.
> `else`
>     Split the problem into simpler cases using recursion.

In some situations, we represent a recursive algorithm as an `if` statement whose dependent statement is the recursive step. The condition tests whether a stopping case has been reached. If not, the recursive step executes; otherwise, an immediate return occurs.

> `If`  the stopping case is NOT reached
>     Split the problem into simpler cases using recursion.

## EXERCISES FOR SECTION 12.1

### Self-Check

1. List all the problems that would be generated to solve the problem "Raise 6 to the power 3." Answer the same question for the problem "Raise 3 to the power 6."

Programming

1. Write a recursive function `multiply` to compute the same result as a *
   b without using the operator *.

2. Write a recursive function `divide` to compute the same result as a / b
   without using the operator / or %.

## 12.2   Tracing Recursive Functions

Hand tracing the execution of an algorithm provides us with valuable
insight as to how that algorithm works. This is particularly true for recursive functions, as shown next.

### Tracing a Recursive Function

In the last section, we wrote the recursive function `power` (see Listing 12.1).
We can trace the execution of the function call `power(6, 3)` by drawing an
**activation frame** corresponding to each function call. An activation frame
shows the argument values for each call and summarizes its execution.

Figure 12.2 shows three activation frames generated to solve the problem of raising 6 to the power 3. The part of each activation frame that executes before the next recursive call is in color; the part that executes after
the return from the next call is in gray.

The value returned from each call appears alongside each black arrow.
The return arrow from each function call points to the operator * because
the multiplication is performed just after the return.

Figure 12.2 also shows that there are three calls to function `power`.
Argument m has the value 6 for all calls; argument n has the values 3, 2, and
finally 1. Because n is 1 in the third call, the value of m (6) is returned as the
result of that call. After the return to the second activation frame, the value

**activation frame**
A logical device showing
argument and local variable values for each
recursive call and its
execution.

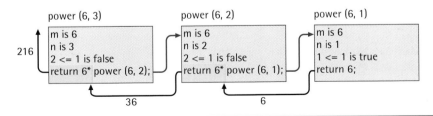

**Figure 12.2**   Trace of function `power`

**Listing 12.2** Recursive function power with tracing

```
// Recursive power function modified to trace its execution
int power(int m, int n)    // IN: raise m to power n
{
    int answer;        // temporary storage for function result

    cout << "Entering power with m = " << m
         << " and n = " << n << endl;
    if (n <= 1)
        answer = m;                     // stopping step
    else
        answer = m * power(m, n - 1);   // recursive step

    cout << "power(" << m << ", " << n << ") returns "
         << answer << endl;

    return answer;                      // return result
}
```

of m is multiplied by this result, and the product (36) is returned as the result of the second call. After the return to the first activation frame, the value of m is multiplied by this result, and the product (216) is returned as the result of the original call to function power.

We can modify a recursive function to provide a trace of its own execution by inserting display statements at the points of entry to and exit from the function. Listing 12.2 shows a version of function power that traces its execution.

In the if statement, we use local variable answer to store the function result rather than returning as soon as it is calculated. The output from the revised function power with actual arguments (8, 3) would appear as follows:

```
Entering power with m = 8 and n = 3
Entering power with m = 8 and n = 2
Entering power with m = 8 and n = 1
power(8, 1) returns 8;
power(8, 2) returns 64;
power(8, 3) returns 512;
```

## Displaying Characters in Reverse Order

Function reverse in Listing 12.3 is an unusual recursive function because it has no argument, and it doesn't return a value. It reads in a sequence of

**Listing 12.3** Function `reverse`

```
// File: reverseTest
// Tests a function which displays keyboard input in reverse

#include <iostream>
using namespace std;

// Function prototype
void reverse();

int main()
{
    reverse();    // Reverse the keyboard input
    cout << endl;
    return 0;
}

// Displays keyboard input in reverse
void reverse()
{
    char next;

    cout << "Next character or * to stop: ";
    cin >> next;

    if (next != '*')
    {
        reverse();            // recursive step
        cout << next;         // Display next after return
    }
}
```

```
Next character or * to stop: c
Next character or * to stop: a
Next character or * to stop: t
Next character or * to stop: *
tac
```

individual characters and displays the sequence in reverse order. If the user enters the data characters a, b, c, d, e, * (the sentinel), they will be displayed in the order e, d, c, b, a.

The body of function `reverse` first reads a data character into `next`. Then it executes the `if` statement. The stopping case is reached when `next` contains the character `'*'`. Otherwise, the recursive step executes

```
reverse();        // recursive step
cout << next;     // Display next after return
```

The character just read is not displayed until later. This is because the output statement follows the recursive function call;that means the output statement doesn't execute until after the recursive call to `reverse` is completed. For example, the third character that's read is not displayed until after the function execution for the second character is done—the third character is displayed after the second character, which is displayed after the first character.

To see why this is so, let's trace the execution of function `reverse` assuming the characters c, a, t, * are entered as data. The trace (Figure 12.3) shows three activation frames for function `reverse`. Each activation frame shows the value of `next` for that frame. Note that the sentinel character * is not displayed.

The statements that execute for each frame are shown in Figure 12.3. Tracing the green arrows and then the black arrows in Figure 12.3 gives us the sequence of events listed in Figure 12.4. To help you understand this list, all the statements for a particular activation frame are indented to the same column.

As shown, there are four calls to function `reverse`. The function returns always occur in the reverse order of the function calls; that is, we return from the last call first, then we return from the next to last call, and so on. After we return from a particular execution of the function, the function displays the character that was read into `next` just prior to that function call. The process of returning from a succession of recursive calls is called **unwinding the recursion**.

**unwinding the recursion**
The process of returning from a succession of recursive calls.

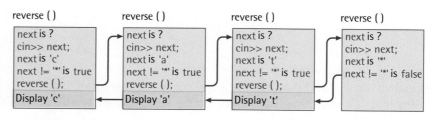

**Figure 12.3**   Trace of function `reverse`

**Figure 12.4**   Sequence of events for trace of `reverse(3)`

Call `reverse`.
    Read the first character (`c`) into `next`.
    `next` is not `'*'`—Call `reverse`.
        Read the second character (`a`) into `next`.
        `next` is not `'*'`—Call `reverse`.
            Read the third character (`t`) into `next`.
            `next` is not `'*'`—Call `reverse`.
                Read the fourth character (`*`) into `next`.
                `next` is `'*'`—Return from fourth call.
            Display the third character (`t`).
            Return from third call.
        Display the second character (`a`).
        Return from second call.
    Display the first character (`c`).
    Return from original call.

## Stack for Function Calls

Java uses a special data structure called a **stack** to keep track of critical data for a recursive function as it changes from call to call. A stack is analogous to a stack of dishes or trays. In a stack of dishes in a buffet line, clean dishes are always placed on top of the stack. When you need a dish, you always remove the last one placed on the stack. This causes the next to last dish placed on the stack to move to the top of the stack.

Whenever a function call occurs (recursive or otherwise), a number of items are placed onto the stack. They include the argument values for that call, a storage location for each local variable during that call, and the instruction to return to after that call is finished. Whenever `next` is referenced in function `reverse`, C++ accesses the top storage location for `next` allocated on the stack. When a function `return` occurs, the storage locations for that call at the top of the stack are removed, and the storage locations for the previous call "move" to the top.

Let's look at the stack right after the first call to `reverse`. To simplify our discussion, we consider only the storage locations for local variable `next` that are allocated on the stack. There is one storage location on the stack and its value is initially undefined.

Stack right after first call to reverse

`?`

**stack**
A data structure in which the last component stored is the first one removed.

The letter c is read into this storage location:

Right after the second call to reverse, another storage location for next is allocated on the stack:

Stack right after second call to reverse

The letter a is read into this storage location:

Right after the third call to reverse, another storage location for next is allocated on the stack:

Stack right after third call to reverse

The letter t is read into this storage location:

Right after the fourth call to reverse, another storage location for next is allocated on the stack:

Stack right after fourth call to reverse

The character * is read into this storage location:

Because `next` is `'*'` (the stopping case), an immediate return occurs. The function `return` causes the value at the top of the stack to be removed, as shown next.

After first return from reverse

Control returns to the output statement, so the value of `next` (t) at the top of the stack is displayed. Another return from function `reverse` occurs, causing the value currently at the top of the stack to be removed.

After second return from reverse

Again, control returns to the output statement, and the value of `next` (a) at the top of the stack is displayed. Another return from function `reverse` occurs, causing the value currently at the top of the stack to be removed.

After third return from reverse

Again, control returns to the output statement, and the value of `next` (c) at the top of the stack is displayed. Another return from function `reverse` occurs, causing the value currently at the top of the stack to be removed. Now, the stack is empty and control returns to the statement in the main function that follows the original call to function reverse.

## Implementation of Argument Stacks in C++

The compiler maintains a single stack for function arguments and return points. Each time a call to a function occurs, all of its arguments and local variables are pushed onto the stack along with the memory address of the calling statement. This memory address gives the computer the return point after execution of the function. Although multiple copies of a function's arguments may be saved on the stack, only one copy of the function body is in memory. Section 11.8 showed you how to declare and manipulate stacks yourself. Because these steps are all done automatically by C++, we can write recursive functions without worrying about the stack. We'll see how to declare and manipulate our own stacks in Section 13.4.

Self-Check

1. Explain why the six output trace statements shown at the beginning of Section 12.2 for function `power` appeared in the order they did. For example, be sure to explain why the three entry displays (`"Entering power   ..."`) appeared before any of the exit displays (`"power   ... returns   ..."`).

2. Assume the characters q, w, e, r, * are entered when function `reverse` is called. Show the contents of the stack immediately after each recursive call and return.

3. Trace the execution of `power(5,   4)` and show the stacks after each recursive call.

4. Given the following function and the call `whatDo(4)`, what would be the output?
   ```
   void whatDo(int i)
   {
       if (i > 1)
       {
           cout << i << endl;
           whatDo(i - 1);
           cout << i << endl;
       }
   }
   ```

Programming

1. Modify function `reverse` so that it also displays the sentinel character.

## 12.3    Recursive Mathematical Functions

Many mathematical functions are defined recursively. An example is the factorial of a number $n$ (represented as $n!$).

- 0! is 1
- $n!$ is n $\times$ $(n-1)!$, for $n > 0$

This is the definition of $n!$ . Thus 4! = 4 $\times$ 3! = 4 $\times$ 3 $\times$ 2!, and so on. It's quite easy to implement this definition as a recursive function in C++.

## EXAMPLE 12.2

Function factorial in Listing 12.4 computes the factorial of its argument n. The recursive step

```
return n * factorial( n - 1 );
```

implements the second line of the definition above. This means that the result of the current call (argument n) is determined by multiplying the result of the next call (argument n – 1) by n.

A trace of a call to factorial,

```
factorial(3)
```

is shown in Figure 12.5. The value returned from the original call, factorial(3), is 6. Be careful when using the factorial function; the value computed increases rapidly and could lead to an integer-overflow error (for example, 10! may come out as 24320 on your computer instead of the correct value, 3628800).

---

Although the recursive implementation of function `factorial` follows naturally from its definition, this function can be implemented easily using iteration. The iterative version is shown in Listing 12.5.

Note that the iterative version contains a loop as its major control structure, whereas the recursive version contains an `if` statement. Also, a local variable, `factorial`, is needed in the iterative version to hold the accumulating product.

**Listing 12.4**   Recursive factorial function

```cpp
// File: factorial.cpp
// Recursive factorial function

// Computes n!// Pre:     n is defined and n >= 0.
// Post:     none
// Returns: n!

int factorial(int n)
{
    if (n <= 0)
        return 1;
    else
        return n * factorial(n-1);
}
```

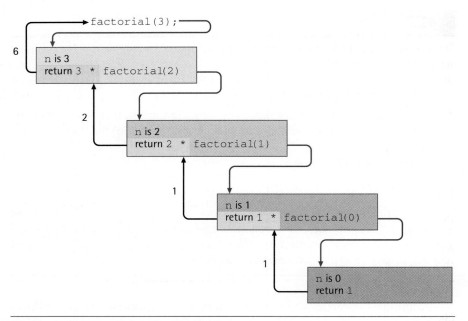

**Figure 12.5** Trace of `factorial(3)`

**Listing 12.5** Iterative factorial function

```cpp
// File: factorialI.cpp
// Iterative factorial function

// Computes n!
// Pre:     n is defined and n >= 0.
// Post:    none
// Returns: n!
int factorialI(int n)
{
   // Local data
   int factorial;    // accumulating product

   factorial = 1;
   for (int i = 2; i <= n; i++)
      factorial *= i;

   return factorial;
}
```

## Example 12.3

The Fibonacci numbers are a sequence of numbers that have many varied uses. They were originally intended to model the growth of a rabbit colony. We won't go into details of the model here, but you can see that the Fibonacci sequence 1, 1, 2, 3, 5, 8, 13, 21, 34, . . . increases rapidly. The fifteenth number in the sequence is 610, and that's a lot of rabbits!

The Fibonacci sequence is defined using the following recurrence relations:

- $fib_1$ is 1
- $fib_2$ is 1
- $fib_n$ is $fib_{n-2} + fib_{n-1}$, for $n > 2$.

Simply stated, $fib_n$ is the sum of the two preceding numbers. Verify for yourself that the above sequence of numbers is correct.

A recursive function that computes the nth Fibonacci number is shown in Listing 12.6. Although easy to write, the Fibonacci function is not very efficient because each recursive step generates two calls to function Fibonacci.

**Listing 12.6**    Recursive Fibonacci number function

```
// File: fibonacci.cpp
// Recursive fibonacci number function

// Computes the nth fibonacci number
// Pre:     n is defined and n > 0.
// Post:    None
// Returns: The nth Fibonacci number.
int fibonacci(int n)
{
   if (n <= 2)
      return 1;
   else
      return fibonacci(n-2) + fibonacci(n-1);
}
```

## EXAMPLE 12.4

Euclid's algorithm for finding the greatest common divisor of two positive integers is defined recursively below. The **greatest common divisor** of two integers is the largest integer that divides them both. For example, the greatest common divisor of 20 and 5 is 5; the greatest common divisor of 20 and 15 is also 5.

greatest common divisor
The largest integer that is a divisor of two integers.

*Algorithm for finding greatest common divisor of m and n (m >= n)*

If n is a divisor of m
    The greatest common divisor is n
else
    Find the greatest common divisor of n and m % n (the remainder of m
    divided by n).

Listing 12.7 shows a driver program and function gcd that implements this algorithm. In gcd, the first condition tests whether m is the smaller number. If m is smaller, function gcd calls itself with the arguments transposed, so that the smaller number is passed to the second argument as it should be. Otherwise, if n divides m, then the result is n (the stopping case). If n doesn't divide m, return the result of calling function gcd with arguments n and m % n (the remainder of m divided by n).

---

**Listing 12.7** Euclid's algorithm for the greatest common divisor

```cpp
// FILE: gcdTest.cpp
// Program and recursive function to find greatest common divisor

#include <iostream>
using namespace std;

// Function prototype
int gcd(int, int);

int main()
{
    int m, n;    // the two input items

    cout << "Enter two positive integers: ";
    cin >> m >> n;
    cout << endl << "Their greatest common divisor is "
         << gcd(m, n) << endl;

    return 0;
}

// Finds the greatest common divisor of two integers
// Pre:     m and n are defined and both are > 0.
// Post:    None
// Returns: The greatest common divisor of m and n.
```

(continued)

**Listing 12.7**  Euclid's algorithm for the greatest common divisor (continued)

```
int gcd(int m, int n)
{
    if (m < n)
        return gcd(n, m);        // transpose arguments
    else if (m % n == 0)
        return n;                // n is GCD
    else
        return gcd(n, m % n);    // recursive step
}
```

```
Enter two positive integers: 24 84
Their greatest common divisor is 12
```

## EXERCISES FOR SECTION 12.3

Self-Check

1. Complete the following recursive function, which calculates the value
   of a number (base) raised to a power (power). The value of power can
   be positive, negative, or zero. There should be two stopping cases.

```
float powerRaiser(int base, int power)
{
    if (base == 0)
        return _____;
    else if (power == 0)
        return _____;
    else if (power < 0)
        return 1.0 / _____;
    else
        return _____;
}
```

2. What does function strange compute?

```
int strange(int n)
{
    if (n == 1)
        return 0;
    else
        return 1 + strange(n / 2);
}
```

3. Explain what would happen if the terminating condition for the Fibonacci number function were (n <= 1).

4. If a program had the call fibonacci(5), how many calls to fibonacci would be generated?

**Programming**

1. Write a recursive function, findSum, that calculates the sum of successive integers starting at 1 and ending at $n$ (i.e., findSum(n) = $(1 + 2 + ... + (n - 1) + n)$.

2. Write an iterative version of the Fibonacci function. Compare this version to the recursive version shown in Listing 12.6. Which is simpler? Which is more efficient?

3. Write an iterative function for the greatest common divisor problem.

4. Write a recursive function to compute the sequence of squares $sq_n$, of a nonnegative integer $n$ using the following relations:

$$\left.\begin{array}{l} sq_0 = 0, \\ d_0 = 1, \end{array}\right\} \text{ for } n = 0$$

$$\left.\begin{array}{l} sq_n = sq_{n-1} + d_{n-1}, \\ d_n = d_{n-1} + 2, \end{array}\right\} \text{ for } n > 0$$

Note that $d_n$ always represents the difference between the $n$th and $n$–1st squares and that for each $n$, $d_n$ increases by a constant amount, 2. The first three values of $sq_n$ are 0, 1, and 4; the first three values of $d_n$ are 1, 3, and 5.

# 12.4   Recursive Functions with Array Arguments

So far our recursive examples have used arguments that are integers. Recursive functions also can process arguments that are data structures or objects. In this section we'll study two recursive functions with array arguments.

A recursive solution to an array processing problem involves splitting the problem up into two or more problems with smaller size arrays. For example, we may be able to solve a problem involving an n-element array if we can split it into a problem involving an n-1 element array and a single array element. Normally an array with one element is a stopping case.

## EXAMPLE 12.5

Function findSum in Listing 12.8 finds the sum of the integers stored in an n-element array. The stopping case is a 1-element array; the sum is just the value stored in the element with subscript 0. The recursive step

```
return x[n-1] + findSum(x, n-1);       // recursive step
```

splits the original problem into one involving an array with n-1 elements and a single-array element. It says that the result is obtained by adding the last integer in the array (x[n-1]) to the sum of the integers in the subarray with n-1 elements.

**Listing 12.8**   Function findSum

```cpp
// File: findSumTest.cpp
// Program and recursive function to sum an array's
elements

#include <iostream>
using namespace std;

// Function prototype
int findSum(int[], int);

int main()
{
   const int SIZE = 10;
   int x[SIZE];             // array of 10 elements
   int sum1;                // result of recursive sum
   int sum2;                // calculated sum

   // Fill array x
   for (int i = 0; i < SIZE; i++)
      x[i] = i + 1;         // Store 1, 2, 3, ... in x

  // Calculate sum two ways
   sum1 = findSum(x, SIZE);
   sum2 = (SIZE * (SIZE + 1)) / 2;

   cout << "Recursive sum is " << sum1 << endl;
   cout << "Calculated sum is " << sum2 << endl;

   return 0;
}
```

(continued)

**Listing 12.8** Function findSum (continued)

```
// Finds the sum of integers in an n-element array
int findSum(int x[], int n)
{
    if (n == 1)
        return x[0];                           // stopping case
    else
        return x[n-1] + findSum(x, n-1);   // recursive step
}
```

```
Recursive sum is 55
Calculated sum is 55
```

The main function fills an array with the integers 1 through 10. It then calls findSum to compute the sum and displays this result along with the sum calculated using a formula. The results are identical (see Self-Check Exercise 4).

## *case study* Binary Search

Earlier we implemented a linear search algorithm for finding a target key in an array (see Listing 9.9), examining the elements in sequence from first to last. Because the algorithm requires an average of $n/2$ comparisons to find a target in an array of $n$ elements and $n$ comparisons to determine that a target is not in the array, linear search is not very efficient for large arrays ($n > 100$).

### PROBLEM

If the elements of the array being searched have been sorted, we can make use of a more efficient search algorithm known as binary search. In binary search, we're able to reduce the problem of searching an $n$-element array to a search involving an $n/2$ element array. Write a function that implements the binary search algorithm.

### ANALYSIS

The *binary-search algorithm* uses the ordering of array elements to eliminate half the array elements with each probe into the array. Consequently, if the array has 1,000 elements, it either locates the target value or eliminates 500 elements with its first probe, 250 elements with its second probe, 125 elements with its third probe, and so on. For this reason, a binary search of an ordered array is an $O(\log_2 n)$ process. This means that you could use the binary-search algorithm to find a name in a large metropolitan telephone directory using 30 or fewer probes (230 is approximately equal to 1,000,000,000).

Because the array is sorted, we only need to compare the target value with the middle element of the subarray we're searching. If their values are the same, we're done. If the middle element value is larger than the target value, we should search the lower half of the subarray next; otherwise, we should search the upper half of the subarray.

The subarray being searched has indices `first` through `last`. The variable `middle` is the index of the middle element in this range. Figure 12.6 shows an example in which the target is 35, `first` is 0, `last` is 8, and `middle` is 4. The upper half of the array (indices `middle` through `last`) is eliminated by the first probe.

The argument `last` needs to be reset to `middle-1` to define the new subarray to be searched, and `middle` should be redefined as shown in Figure 12.7. The target value, 35, would be found on this probe.

FUNCTION INTERFACE

***Input Parameters***

```
table     // array to search
target    // target value
first     // index of first element in subarray
last      // index of last element in subarray
```

***Function Result***

location of target value in array if found or –1

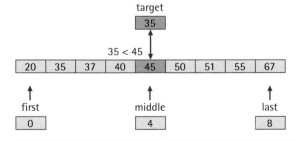

**Figure 12.6**  First probe of binary search

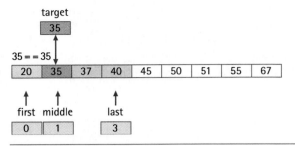

**Figure 12.7** Second probe of binary search

## DESIGN

We can write the binary-search algorithm without too much effort using recursion. There are two stopping cases:

- The array bounds are improper (`first > last`).
- The middle value is the target value.

In the first case, the function returns -1 to indicate that the target is not present in the array. In the second case, `middle` is returned as the index of the target value. The recursive step is to search the appropriate subarray.

    BINARY SEARCH ALGORITHM

1. Compute the subscript of the middle element of the array.
2. `if` the array bounds are improper

   3. `target` not present, return -1

   `else if target` is the middle value

   4. Return subscript of middle value

   `else if target` is less than the middle value

   5. Search subarray with indices `first` through `middle-1`

   `else`

   6. Search subarray with indices `middle+1` through `last`.

For each of the recursive steps (Steps 5 and 6), the bounds of the new subarray must be listed as actual arguments in the recursive call. The actual arguments define the search limits for the next probe into the array.

## IMPLEMENTATION

In the initial call to the recursive function, `first` and `last` should be defined as the first and last elements of the entire array, respectively. For example, you could use the function call

```
binSearch(x, 35, 0, 8)
```

to search an array x with nine elements for the target value 35. The position of the target element in array x will be returned as the function result if 35 is found. Function `binSearch` is shown in Listing 12.9.

The statement

```
int middle = (first + last) / 2;
```

computes the index of the middle element by finding the average of first and last. The value has no meaning when first is greater than last, but it does no harm to compute it.

**Listing 12.9**  Recursive binary search function

```
// Searches for target in elements first through last of array
//    Precondition : The elements of table are sorted &
//                   first and last are defined.
//    Postcondition: If target is in the array, return its
//                   position; otherwise, returns -1.
int binSearch(int table[],  // IN: array being searched
              int target,   // IN: target element
              int first,    // IN: first element to search
              int last)     // IN: last element to search
{
    int middle;

    middle = (first + last) / 2;      // middle of array

    if (first > last)
        return -1;                    // unsuccessful search
    else if (target == table[middle])
        return middle;                // successful search
    else if (target < table[middle])  // search lower half of array
        return binSearch(table, target, first, middle-1);
    else                              // search upper half of array
        return binSearch(table, target, middle+1, last);
}
```

TESTING

Check for targets in the first and last elements of the array. Check for targets that aren't present. Check the algorithm for even- and odd-length arrays. Also check arrays with multiple target values. See what happens when the array size gets very large—say, 1,000.

## EXERCISES FOR SECTION 12.4

Self-Check

1. Trace the execution of `binSearch` for the array shown in Figure 12.6 and a `target` value of 40.

2. What would happen if `binSearch` were called with the precondition of elements in increasing order violated? Would `binSearch` still find the item?

3. What does the following recursive function do?

```
int mystery(int x[], int n)
{
    // Local data   ...
    int temp;

    // Do whatever I do now.
    if (n == 1)
        return x[0];
    else
    {
        temp = mystery(x, n-1);
        if (x[n-1] > temp)
            return x[n-1];
        else
            return temp;
    }   // end outer else
}   //end mystery
```

4. Show that the sum of integers 1 through $n$ for $n$ equals 4 and 5 can be calculated using the formula $(n \times (n + 1)) / 2$. Can you explain why this is so? (Hint: The sum of 1 and $n$ is $n + 1$, the sum of 2 and $n - 1$ is also $n + 1$. So we get the same result if each of these four numbers is replaced by $(n + 1) / 2$.)

Programming

1. Sorting algorithms need to know where in a sorted array a new item should be inserted. Write a recursive function `insertLocation` that returns a location where `target` could be inserted into an array and still maintain correct ordering.

# 12.5    Problem Solving with Recursion

In this section we develop an elegant recursive solution to a problem that would be very difficult to solve without recursion. In our analysis, we'll express the solution to the original problem in terms of simpler versions of itself, leading to a recursive solution.

*case study*    The Towers of Hanoi

### PROBLEM STATEMENT

The Towers of Hanoi problem involves moving a specified number of disks that are all of different sizes from one tower to another. The puzzle has three towers and, in its initial state, all of the disks are on one tower with the largest at the bottom, the next largest on top of it, and so on (see Figure 12.8). Legend has it that the world will come to an end when the problem is solved for 64 disks. We'll ignore that risk and write a program to solve the Towers of Hanoi problem for $n$ disks, where $n$ is the number of disks to be moved from one tower to another.

### ANALYSIS

In the version of the problem shown in Figure 12.8, there are five disks (numbered 1 through 5) and three towers (lettered A, B, C). The goal is to move the five disks from tower A to tower C, subject to the following rules:

- Only one disk may be moved at a time, and this disk must be the top disk on a tower.
- A larger disk can never be placed on top of a smaller disk.

A stopping case of the problem involves moving one disk only (for example, "move disk 1 from tower A to tower C"). Problems that are simpler than the original would be to move four disks subject to the rules

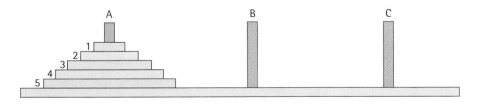

**Figure 12.8**    Towers of Hanoi

above, or to move three disks, and so on. Therefore, we want to split the original five-disk problem into one or more problems involving fewer disks. Let's consider splitting the original problem into the three problems:

1. Move four disks (numbered 1 through 4) from tower A to tower B.
2. Move disk 5 from tower A to tower C.
3. Move the four disks (1 through 4) from tower B to tower C.

In problem 1, we move all disks but the largest to tower B, an auxiliary tower for the original problem. In problem 2, we move the largest disk to the goal tower for the original problem, tower C. Finally, we move the remaining disks from B to the goal tower, where they will be placed on top of the largest disk.

Let's assume that we can simply "follow the directions" indicated in problems 1 and 2 (a stopping case); Figure 12.9 shows the status of the three towers after the completion of the tasks described in these problems. At this point, it should be clear that we can solve the original five-disk problem if we can complete problem 3 (Move four disks from tower B to tower C). In problem 3, tower C is the goal tower and tower A becomes the auxiliary tower.

Unfortunately, we still don't know how to perform problems 1 or 3. Both, however, involve four disks instead of five, so they are easier than the original problem. We should be able to split them into even simpler problems in the same way that we split the original problem. For example, problem 3 involves moving four disks from tower B to tower C. We split this problem into two three-disk problems and a one-disk problem, as follows:

**3.1.** Move three disks from tower B to tower A.

**3.2.** Move disk 4 from tower B to tower C.

**3.3.** Move three disks from tower A to tower C.

Figure 12.10 shows the status of the towers after the tasks described in problems 3.1 and 3.2 have been completed. We now have the two largest

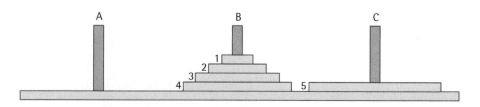

**Figure 12.9**　Towers of Hanoi after steps 1 and 2

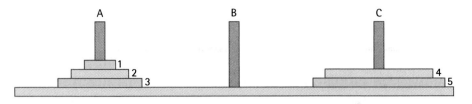

**Figure 12.10** Towers of Hanoi after steps 1, 2, 3.1, and 3.2

disks on tower C. Once we complete problem 3.3, all five disks will be on tower C as required.

By repeatedly splitting each *n*-disk problem into two problems involving *n*–1 disks and a one-disk problem, we'll eventually reach all cases of one disk, which we know how to solve.

The solution to the Towers of Hanoi problem consists of a printed list of individual disk moves. We need a recursive function that can be used to move any number of disks from one tower to another, using the third tower as an auxiliary.

We'll pass the function the number of disks involved (an integer), the tower that is the source of disks (the *from tower*), the tower that is the goal for the disks (the *to tower*), and the tower that can be used as an auxiliary (the *auxiliary tower*). The roles of the towers will, of course, change from one function call to the next. We'll pass a tower name as a character argument (`'A'`, `'B'`, or `'C'`).

FUNCTION INTERFACE

**Input Parameters**

```
int n            // the number of disks to be moved
char fromTower   // the from tower
char toTower     // the to tower
char auxTower    // the auxiliary tower
```

**Function Result**

Displays the list of moves required to move the disks.

DESIGN

**Algorithm**

1. If n is 1

   **1.1.** Move disk 1 from the *from* tower to the *to* tower.

   else

   **1.2.** Move n–1 disks from the *from* tower to the *auxiliary* tower.

　**1.3.** Move disk n from the *from* tower to the *to* tower.

　**1.4.** Move n–1 disks from the *auxiliary* tower to the *to* tower.

If n is 1, a stopping case is reached. If n is greater than 1, the recursive step (following `else`) splits the original problem into three smaller problems, one of which is a stopping case. Each stopping case displays a move instruction. Verify that the recursive step generates the three problems (3.1, 3.2, 3.3) listed earlier when n is 5, the *from* tower is A, and the *to* tower is C.

### IMPLEMENTATION

The implementation of this algorithm is shown as function `tower` in Listing 12.10. Function `tower` has four arguments, `fromTower`, `toTower`, `auxTower`, and n. The main function asks the user for the number of disks (`numDisks`) before calling function `tower` to move them from tower A to tower C. When `numDisks` is 5, the function call

```
tower('A', 'C', 'B', numDisks);   // move disks from A to C
```

solves the original problem of moving five disks from tower A to tower C, using tower B as an auxiliary.

In Listing 12.10, the stopping case (move disk 1) is implemented as an output statement. Each recursive step consists of two recursive calls to `tower` with an output statement sandwiched between them. The first recursive call solves the problem of moving n–1 disks to the *auxiliary* tower. The output statement displays a message to move disk n to the *to* tower. The second recursive call solves the problem of moving the n–1 disks from the *auxiliary* tower to the *to* tower.

**Listing 12.10** Recursive function `tower`

```cpp
// File: tower.cpp
// Recursive tower of hanoi function

#include <iostream>
using namespace std;

// Function prototype
void tower(char, char, char, int);

int main()
{
    int numDisks;      // input - number of disks
    cout << "How many disks: ";
    cin >> numDisks;
```
*(continued)*

**Listing 12.10** Recursive function `tower` (continued)

```
     tower('A', 'C', 'B', numDisks);     // Move disks from A to C
     return 0;
}

// Recursive function to "move" n disks from fromTower
//    to toTower using auxTower
// Pre:   fromTower, toTower, auxTower, and n are defined.
//        and at least n disks are on the fromTower.
// Post: The top n disks are moved to the toTower
//        and each disk is smaller than the one below it.
//        Displays the required moves.
void tower
  (char fromTower,     // IN: fromTower
   char toTower,       // IN: toTower
   char auxTower,      // IN: auxTower
   int  n)             // IN: number of disks
{
   if (n == 1)
      cout << "Move disk 1 from tower " << fromTower
           << " to tower " << toTower << endl;
   else
   {
      tower(fromTower, auxTower, toTower, n-1);
      cout << "Move disk " << n << " from tower " << fromTower
           << " to tower " << toTower << endl;
      tower(auxTower, toTower, fromTower, n-1);
   }
}  // end tower
```

## TESTING

The function call statement

```
    tower('A', 'C', 'B', 3);
```

solves the three-disk problem "Move 3 disks from tower A to tower C." Its execution is traced in Figure 12.11; the output generated is shown in Listing 12.11. Verify for yourself that this list of steps does indeed solve the three-disk problem. Try running this program with up to 10 disks. If the number of disks gets much larger, you may find it takes too long to run the program.

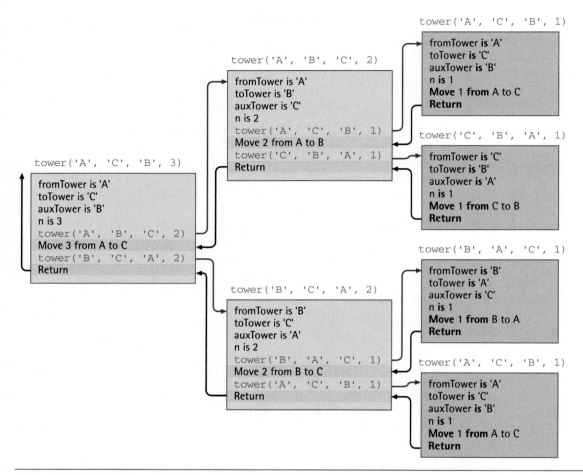

**Figure 12.11**    Trace of tower('A', 'C', 'B', 3);

**Listing 12.11**    Output generated by tower ('A', 'C', 'B', 3);

```
Move disk 1 from tower A to tower C
Move disk 2 from tower A to tower B
Move disk 1 from tower C to tower B
Move disk 3 from tower A to tower C
Move disk 1 from tower B to tower A
Move disk 2 from tower B to tower C
Move disk 1 from tower A to tower C
```

## Comparison of Iteration and Recursive Functions

It's interesting to consider that the function `tower` in Listing 12.10 will solve the Towers of Hanoi problem for any number of disks. The solution to the three-disk problem requires seven calls to function `tower` and is solved by seven disk moves. The five-disk problem requires 31 calls to function `tower` and is solved in 31 moves. In general, the number of moves required to solve the $n$-disk problem is $2^n - 1$. Because each function call requires the allocation and initialization of a local data area in memory, the computer time increases exponentially with the problem size. For this reason, be careful about running this program with a value of $n$ that is larger than 10.

The dramatic increase in processing time for larger towers is a function of this problem, not a function of recursion. However, in general, if there are recursive and iterative solutions to the same problem, the recursive solution will require more time and space because of the extra function calls.

Although recursion was not really needed to solve the simpler problems in this section, it was extremely useful in formulating an algorithm for the Towers of Hanoi problem. For certain problems, recursion leads naturally to solutions that are much easier to read and understand than their iterative counterparts. In these cases, the benefits gained from increased clarity far outweigh the extra cost (in time and memory) of running a recursive program.

### EXERCISES FOR SECTION 12.5

**Self-Check**

1. How many moves are needed to solve the six-disk problem?

2. Write a `main` function that reads in a data value for n (the number of disks) and calls function `tower` to move n disks from A to B.

## 12.6 Common Programming Errors

■ *Stopping condition for recursive functions:* The most common problem with a recursive function involves the specification of the terminating condition. If this condition is not correct, the function may call itself indefinitely or until all available memory is used up. Normally, a `"stack overflow"` run-time error is an indication that a recursive function is not terminating. Make sure that you identify all stopping cases and provide the correct condition for each one. Also be sure that each recursive step leads to a situation that's closer to a stopping case and that repeated recursive calls will eventually lead to stopping cases only.

■ *Missing return statements:* Every path through a function that returns a value should lead to a `return` statement. When multiple returns are used in a function, it's easy to omit one of these returns. The compiler won't detect this omission, but it will return an incorrect value whenever the sequence of statements requiring the return is executed.

■ *Optimizations for recursive functions:* The recopying of large arrays or other large data structures inside a recursive function can quickly consume large amounts of memory. You should do this only when data protection is required.

Checking for errors inside a recursive function is extremely inefficient, so you may want to use a nonrecursive function to validate the correctness of a recursive function's initial arguments. The nonrecursive function would be called to start the recursion. It will validate the arguments, call the recursive function, and return the last result of the recursive function execution.

It's sometimes difficult to observe the result of a recursive function's execution. If each recursive call generates a large number of output lines and there are many recursive calls, the output will scroll down the screen more quickly than it can be read. On most systems, it's possible to stop the scrolling temporarily by pressing a special key or control character sequence. If this can't be done, it's still possible to cause your output to stop temporarily by displaying a prompting message such as

```
cout << "Press the space bar to continue.";
```

followed by a keyboard input operation such as

```
cin >> nextChar;
```

(where `nextChar` is type `char`). Your program will resume execution when you enter a character data item.

■ *Using a debugger with recursive functions:* If you're using a debugger, you can trace into a recursive function. Just before the first statement executes, you can check the values of the function arguments to verify that they are correct. You can also view the system call stack to see the sequence of function calls made by the system.

To view the value returned from each call, add a local variable to temporarily hold the function result as we did in Listing 12.2. Then replace each `return` statement in the `if` statement with a statement that assigns a value to this local variable, and insert a single `return` statement at the end of the function. You can check the value of the variable that holds the result just before this `return` statement executes.

# Chapter Review

1. A recursive function is one that calls itself. You can use recursion to solve problems by splitting them into smaller versions of themselves.

2. Each recursive function has one or more stopping cases and recursive steps. The stopping cases can be solved directly; the recursive steps lead to recursive calls of the function.

3. Recursive functions can be used with arguments that are simple types or structured types. Recursive functions can implement mathematical operations that are defined by recursive definitions.

4. Binary search is a search algorithm that can search a large array in *O(log n)* time.

## Quick-Check Exercises

1. Explain the use of a stack in recursion.

2. Which is generally more efficient, recursion or iteration?

3. Which control statement do you always find in a recursive function?

4. How do you specify a recursive call to a function?

5. Why would a programmer conceptualize a problem solution using recursion and implement it using iteration?

6. In a recursive problem involving n items, why must n be a call-by-value argument?

7. What kind of a programming error could easily cause a "stack over-flow" message?

8. What can you say about a recursive algorithm that has the following form?

   if (condition)
     Perform recursive step.

9. What is the relation between a terminating condition and a stopping case?

10. Returning from a series of recursive calls is called _____ the recursion.

## Answers to Quick-Check Exercises

1. The stack is used to hold all argument and local variable values and the return point for each execution of a recursive function.

2. Iteration is generally more efficient than recursion.

3. The `if` statement is always found in a recursive function.

4. By writing a call to the function in the function itself.

5. When its solution is much easier to conceptualize using recursion but its implementation would be too inefficient.

6. If n were a call-by-reference argument, its address, not its value, would be saved on the stack, so it wouldn't be possible to store a different argument value for each call.

7. Too many recursive calls due to a missing or incorrect terminating condition.

8. Nothing is done when the stopping case is reached.

9. A terminating condition is true when a stopping case is reached.

10. unwinding

## Review Questions

1. Explain the nature of a recursive problem.

2. Discuss the efficiency of recursive functions.

3. Differentiate between stopping cases and a terminating condition.

4. Write a recursive function that returns the accumulating sum of the ASCII values corresponding to each character in a character string. For example, if the string value is `"a boy"`, the first value returned would be the ASCII value of a, then the sum of ASCII values for a and the space character, then the sum of the ASCII values for a, space, b, and so on.

5. Write a recursive function that returns the accumulating sum of ASCII values corresponding to each character in a character string (as in the preceding review question). However, this time exclude any space characters from the sum.

6. Convert the following iterative function to a recursive one. The function calculates an approximate value for e, the base of the natural logarithms, by summing the series

$$1 + 1/1! + 1/2! + \ldots + 1/n!$$

until additional terms do not affect the approximation (at least not as far as the computer is concerned).

```
float elog()
{
    // Local data  ...
    float enl, delta, fact;
    int n;
    enl = 1.0;
    n = 1;
    fact = 1.0;
    delta = 1.0;
    do
    {
        enl += delta;
        n++;
        fact *= n;
        delta = 1.0 / fact;
    }   while (enl != enl + delta);
    return enl;
}   // end elog
```

# Programming Projects

1. The expression for computing $C(n, r)$, the number of combinations of $n$ items taken $r$ at a time is

$$C(n,r) = \frac{r!}{r!(n-r)!}$$

Write and test a function for computing $C(n, r)$ given that $n!$ is the factorial of $n$.

2. A palindrome is a word that's spelled exactly the same when the letters are reversed. Words such as *level, deed,* and *mom* would be examples of palindromes. Write a recursive function that returns a value of 1 (true) if a word, passed as an argument, is a palindrome and that returns 0 (false) otherwise.

3. Write a recursive function that returns the value of the following recursive definition:

$F(X, Y) = X - Y$                        if $X$ or $Y < 0$;

$$F(X, Y) = F(X - 1, Y) + F(X, Y - 1) \ \text{otherwise.}$$

4. Write a recursive function that lists all of the two-letter subsets for a given set of letters. For example:

['A', 'C', 'E', 'G'] → ['A', 'C'], ['A', 'E'], ['A', 'G'], ['C', 'E'], ['C', 'G'], ['E', 'G']

5. The bisection function finds an approximate root for the equation $f(x)$ = 0 on the interval xLeft to xRight, inclusive (assuming that function $f(x)$ is continuous on this interval). The interval endpoints (xLeft and xRight) and the tolerance for the approximation (epsilon) are input by the user.

   One stopping criterion for the bisection function is the identification of an interval [xLeft, xRight] that's less than epsilon in length over which $f(x)$ changes sign (from positive to negative or vice versa). The midpoint [xMid = (xLeft + xRight)/2.0] of the interval will be an approximation to the root of the equation when $f$(xMid) is very close to zero. Of course, if you find a value of xMid such that $f$(xMid) = 0, you have found a very good approximation of the root, and the algorithm should also stop.

   To perform the recursive step, replace either xLeft or xRight with xMid, depending on which one has the same sign as xMid. Write a program that uses the bisection function to determine an approximation to the equation

$$5x^3 - 2x^3 + 3 = 0$$

   over the interval [-1,1] using epsilon = 0.0001.

6. Write a program which, given a list of up to 10 integer numbers and a sum, will find a subset of the numbers whose total is that sum if one exists or indicate that none exists otherwise. For example, for the list: 5, 13, 23, 9, 3, 3 and sum = 28, your program should find: 13, 9, 3, 3.

7. mergeSort is an $O(N \times \log N)$ sorting technique with the following recursive algorithm:

   if the array to sort has more than 1-element
       mergeSort the left-half of the array.
       mergeSort the right-half of the array.
       merge the two sorted subarrays to form the sorted array.

   As an example, to mergeSort the array 10, 20, 15, 6, 5, 40, follow the steps:

   mergeSort the subarray 10, 20, 15 giving 10, 15, 20.

mergeSort the subarray 6, 5, 40 giving 5, 6, 40.
merge the two sorted subarrays giving 5, 6, 10, 15, 20, 40.

Of course, each call to mergeSort above will generate two more recursive calls (one for a one-element array and one for a two-element array). For a one-element array, mergeSort is a stopping case.

8. Write a function that accepts an 8-by-8 array of characters that represents a maze. Each position can contain either an 'x' or a blank. Starting at position [0][0], list any path through the maze to get to location [7][7]. Only horizontal and vertical moves are allowed (no diagonal moves). If no path exists, write a message indicating this. Moves can be made only to positions that contain a blank. If an 'x' is encountered in a path, that path is to be considered blocked and another must be chosen. Use recursion.

# Marshall Cline

*Dr. Cline is the president of MT Systems Company, a technology consulting firm. In 1991 he created the C++ FAQ [Frequently Asked Questions] on the Internet, which demonstrates how to use C++. It was subsequently published as a book, C++ FAQs. Dr. Cline also helped develop the CORBA FAQ on the Internet. In addition, he speaks widely on object-oriented technology. He received his Ph.D. in electrical and computer engineering from Clarkson University.*

**What was your first job in the computer industry? What did it entail?**
I developed software systems to automate some complex, error-prone processes in the testing and repair of a manufacturing plant. I worked a lot of overtime and took my project personally. In a rather short time I developed a software system that automatically "learned" as it gained more experience, and that system was still in use for many years after I left.

**Please give some background on your current position and company.**
I am president of MT Systems Company, a small consulting firm. We help large companies succeed on software development projects.

After years of doing this, I can say with certainty that most problems associated with large software development projects are a result of people issues, not technology issues. The lesson here is to develop good people skills. Simply knowing the technology is not enough. The most important thing you can do for your career is to develop big-picture life skills. Don't be so centered in tech-nology that you forget people. Your success will ultimately hinge on your ability to work with people, not merely your understanding of technology.

**How does this emphasis on communication affect your work?**
One of the most important things I've learned is to listen before you talk, to ask before you answer. When I arrive at a new client's site, I meet the people and spend a lot of time listening and understanding their perspective. The real goal is to develop rapport, since without a good rapport with people, you will fail no matter how good you are with technology. After I develop rapport with the management and with each developer, I gradually dig deeper and deeper into the technology issues. Throughout the process I make it a point to talk with both the management and the developers, the goal being to keep communication lines open.

**Do you have any advice for students learning C++?**
When you are learning C++, make sure you learn how to think in objects. C++ can be used as an object-oriented lan-

guage, but without thinking in terms of objects, you will probably make a lot of mistakes in your C++ programming.

The other key lesson when learning C++ is to learn how to make your code simpler. If you can figure out a shorter, simpler way to do the same thing, it is probably better to do it shorter and simpler. Some programmers get this backward: they seem to think it shows how smart they are if they develop something large and complex, but in reality it is the opposite: the smarter programmer is the one who is able to do the same thing with less complexity. Complexity is your mortal enemy.

**Do you have any advice for students entering the computer science field?**
Don't worry if some of the things you are learning are irrelevant to your ultimate job. The real issue is your ability to learn. Employers generally retrain people anyway, so the main thing they want to see is that you are teachable.

Don't ignore business and communication. These courses may seem "low tech" today, but you will be grateful you took them in ten or twenty years. Related to this point, don't succumb to a bad attitude toward management. Managers understand that technology is ultimately about creating business value—it is a means to an end rather than an end in itself, and great technologists not only accept this, they embrace it and run with it.

Finally, don't become a technology bigot. Every programmer seems to have a favorite programming language, which is fine, but don't get to the point where you argue with others as to which language is "better." The fact is that one language is rarely *better* or *worse* than another, but instead it is merely *more appropriate* or *less appropriate* for a particular problem. In other words, languages are like tools, and you should use the right tool for the job. If you always think your language is better than the others, you won't try to figure out which is the best tool for this particular job, and you might end up choosing wrong.

**What do you think the future of the C++ language is?**
C++ is standardized with the ISO and ANSI standards. There will be relatively minor updates, and when major revisions are brought forth, they will focus mainly on the libraries rather than the language's syntax and semantics. New libraries are being developed to make it easier to build GUIs, and to make it easier to integrate C++ with every conceivable database, device, and programming language. Some of these libraries will become standardized, others will remain proprietary, but it will be valuable for you as a programmer to gain experience in these libraries.

**What is your connection to the C++ FAQ?**
I created the C++ FAQ on the Internet in 1991 or so. Since that time the C++ FAQ has grown into a substantial document that shows how to properly use C++ as an object-oriented language. It shows people "best practices"—how they should use the language.

Interestingly, the C++ FAQ is not written like most FAQs. The questions and answers in the FAQ did not come from the newsgroups proper; instead I sat down and developed an online course in object-oriented programming and C++, using the questions and answers as a device to present that course.

*chapter thirteen*

# Pointers and Dynamic Data Structures

### Chapter Objectives

- To understand dynamic allocation and the new operator
- To learn how to use pointers to access structs
- To learn how to use pointers to build linked data structures
- To understand and use the STL list class
- To learn how to use the STL stack class and how to implement its operators
- To learn how to use the STL queue class and how to implement its operators
- To understand basic concepts of binary trees
- To learn how to use the binary search tree ADT and how to implement its operators

IN THIS CHAPTER we shift our attention from static structures, such as arrays and structs, to dynamic data structures. Unlike static structures, in which the size of the data structure is established during compilation and remains unchanged throughout program execution, dynamic data structures expand and contract as a program executes.

The first dynamic data structure we'll study is the linked list—a collection of elements (called *nodes*) that are structs. Each node has a special field called a *pointer* that connects it to the next node in the list.

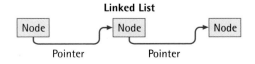

Linked lists are extremely flexible. It's easy to add new information by creating a new node and inserting it between two existing nodes. It's also relatively easy to delete a node.

We'll also examine several other abstract data types (ADTs), including lists, stacks, queues, and trees. We'll learn how to use the C++ Standard Template Library (STL) classes for each of these ADTs and also how to implement them as linked data structures.

## 13.1 Pointers and the new Operator

This section discusses what pointers are and how to use them. The declaration

```
float *p;
```

**pointer or pointer variable**
A memory cell that stores the address of a variable or data object.

identifies p as a **pointer variable** of type "pointer to float." This means that we can store the *memory address* of a type float variable in p. The statement

```
p = new float;
```

calls the C++ operator new, which creates a variable of type float and places the address of this variable in the pointer variable p. Once storage is allocated for the type float value pointed to by p, we can store a value in that memory cell and manipulate it. **Dynamic allocation** is the process of allocating new storage during program execution.

**dynamic allocation**
The process of allocating new storage during program execution.

The actual memory address stored in pointer variable p is a number that has no meaning for us. Consequently, we represent the value of p by drawing an arrow to a memory cell:

The ? in the memory cell pointed to by p indicates that its contents are undefined just after p = new float; is executed. In the next section, we'll see how to write C++ instructions to store information in the memory cell pointed to by p.

C++ allocates storage at different times for the memory cells shown in the preceding diagram. Storage is allocated for pointer variable p during compilation when its variable declaration is reached, and for the cell pointed to by p when the new statement is executed.

---

**Pointer Type Declaration**

**Form:**   *type* *\*variable;*

**Example:** `float *p;`

**Interpretation:** The value of the pointer variable **p** (a pointer) is a memory address. A data element whose address is stored in this variable must be of the specified *type*.

---

**new Operator**

**Form:**   `new` *type;*
       `new` *type[ n ];*

**Example:** `new float;`

**Interpretation:** Storage for a new data element is allocated, and a pointer to this element is returned. The amount of storage allocated is determined by the *type* specified. With the second form shown, **n** elements of the specified *type* are allocated. If sufficient storage isn't available, a C++ exception is raised and the program will terminate.

---

## Accessing Data with Pointers

The asterisk symbol * is called the *indirection operator.* The assignment statement

```
*p = 15.5;
```

stores the float value `15.5` in memory location `*p` (the location pointed to by p), as shown next.

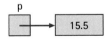

The statements

```
float *p;
p = new float;
*p = 15.5;
cout << "The contents of the memory cell pointed to by p is "
     << *p << endl;
```

produce the result

```
The contents of the memory cell pointed to by p is 15.5
```

## Pointer Operations

A pointer variable can contain only a memory address. If p is the pointer variable declared above, the following statements are invalid; you can't assign a type int or a type float value to a pointer variable:

```
p = 1000;      // invalid assignment
p = 15.5;      // invalid assignment
```

If p and q are pointer variables of the same type, they can be manipulated with the assignment operator and the equality operators (== and !=). For example, the *pointer assignment statement*

```
q = p;
```

copies the address stored in pointer variable p to pointer variable q. As a result, both p and q point to the same memory area.

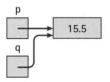

In this instance, the condition p  ==  q is true and p  !=  q is false.

## Pointers to Structs

We can declare pointers to structured data types as well as to simple data types. Often, we declare pointers to structs or to objects. The declarations

```
struct electric
{
    string current;
    int volts;
};
electric *p, *q;
```

identify the variables p and q to be of type "pointer to electric." Type electric is a struct type with two members: current and volts.

Variables p and q are pointer variables that can be used to reference variables of type electric (denoted by *p and *q). The statement

```
p = new electric;
```

allocates storage for a struct of type electric and stores its memory address in pointer p. The data components of the struct pointed to by p are initially undefined.

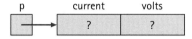

Recall that we use student.name to reference the name field of struct variable student. We can use the member access operator . to reference a member of a struct pointed to by a pointer variable. For example, we use (*p).current to reference the current field of the struct pointed to by p (struct *p). The assignment statements

```
(*p).current = "AC";
(*p).volts = 115;
```

define the fields of the struct pointed to by p as shown in the diagram below.

The form (*p).volts first applies the indirection operator to the variable p of type "pointer to electric," yielding an expression of type electric, and then applies the member access operator to this expression, yielding an expression of type int. If you omit the parentheses, C++ would apply the member access operator first (p.volts), which would be an invalid operation.

Because accessing members of structures through pointers is a common operation, C++ provides a special notation. You can write the statements above as

```
p->current = "AC";
p->volts = 115;
```

> ### Structure Member Access Through a Pointer
>
> **Form:** *p -> m*
>
> **Example:** p->volts
>
> **Interpretation:** If **p** is a pointer to a struct (or class), and if *m* is a member of that struct, then *p->m* accesses the member, *m*, of the struct pointed to by **p**.

The statement

```
cout << p->current << p->volts << endl;
```

displays the data components of the struct pointed to by p. For the struct in the preceding diagram, the statement displays the line

```
AC115
```

The statement

```
q = new electric;
```

stores the address of a new struct of type `electric` in q. The next statements copy the contents of the struct pointed to by p to the struct pointed to by q, and change the `volts` field of the struct pointed to by q.

```
*q = *p;
```

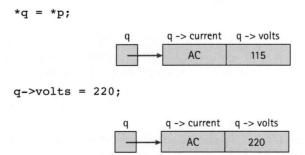

```
q->volts = 220;
```

Finally, the pointer assignment statement

```
q = p;
```

resets pointer q to point to the same struct as pointer p. The old struct pointed to by q still exists in memory but can no longer be accessed. Such a struct is called an *orphan*.

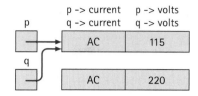

## EXERCISES FOR SECTION 13.1

### Self-Check

1. If p and q are pointers to structs of type `electric`, explain the effect of each valid assignment statement. Which are invalid?

   **a.** p->current = "CA";          **e.** p->current = "HT";

   **b.** p->volts = q->volts;        **f.** p->current = q->volts;

   **c.** *p = *q;                    **g.** p = 54;

   **d.** p = q;                      **h.** *q = p;

2. If a, b, and c are pointers to structures of type `electric`, draw a diagram of pointers and memory cells after the following operations. Indicate any orphaned `data areas`.

   **a.** a = new electric;          **d.** a = b;

   **b.** b = new electric;          **e.** b = c;

   **c.** c = new electric;          **f.** c = a;

### Programming

1. Write a program fragment that creates a collection of seven pointers to the struct type below, allocates memory for each pointer, and places the musical notes do, re, mi, fa, so, la, and ti in the data areas.

```
struct musicNote
{
    note : string;
};
```

## 13.2   Manipulating the Heap

When **new** executes, where in memory is the new struct stored? C++ maintains a storage pool of available memory cells called a **heap**; memory cells from this pool are allocated whenever the new operator executes.

**heap**
A storage pool of memory cells from which new storage is allocated whenever the new operator executes.

### Effect of the **new** Operator on the Heap

If p is a pointer variable of type "pointer to `electric`" (declared in the last section), the statement

```
p = new node;
```

allocates memory space for a struct that stores a string and an `int` variable. The memory cells in this struct are originally undefined (they retain whatever data were last stored in them), and the memory address of the first cell allocated is stored in p. Allocated cells are no longer considered part of the heap. The only way to reference allocated locations is through a pointer variable (for example, p->current or p->volts).

Figure 13.1 shows the pointer variable p and the heap (as a collection of bytes with addresses 1000, 1001, ..., etc.) before and after the execution of p = new node;. The *before* diagram shows pointer variable p as undefined before the execution of p = new node;. The *after* diagram shows p pointing to the first of four memory cells allocated for the new struct (assuming that four memory locations can accommodate a struct of type `electric`). The cells still considered part of the heap are in gray.

For example, if the memory cells with addresses 1000 through 2000 were originally in the heap, after the execution of p = new electric;, the memory cells with addresses 1000 through 1003 are no longer part of the

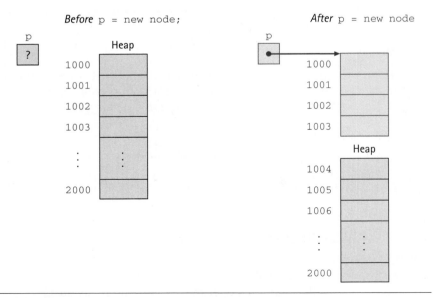

**Figure 13.1**   Heap before and after execution of p = new node;

heap. The address 1000 would be stored in pointer variable p, and that cell would contain the first byte of p->current; memory cell 1002 would contain the first byte of p->volts.

## Returning Cells to the Heap

The operation

```
delete p;
```

returns the memory cells pointed to by p to the heap, restoring the heap to the state shown on the left of Figure 13.1. At this point, the value of pointer variable p becomes undefined and the data formerly associated with *p are no longer accessible. The four cells that are returned to the heap can be reused later when another new operator is executed.

Often, more than one pointer variable points to the same structure. For that reason, be careful when you return the storage occupied by a struct to the heap. If cells are reallocated after they're returned, errors may result if they're later referenced by another pointer that still points to them. Make sure that you have no need for a particular structure before you return the storage occupied by it. Also make sure that only pointer variables that were set with values returned by the new operator are used as an argument to the delete operator.

---

**The delete Operator**

**Form:**      delete *variable*;

**Example:**      delete p;

**Interpretation:** The memory pointed to by **p** (which was set from the invocation of the **new** operator) is returned to the heap. This memory can be reallocated when the **new** operator is next called.

---

## EXERCISES FOR SECTION 13.2

Self-Check

1. In a program that is allocating memory space for temporary data items, what would be the consequences of failing to use delete when the data items are no longer needed?

## 13.3    Linked Lists and the `list` Class

We can arrange groups of dynamically allocated structs into a flexible data structure called a **linked list**. Linked lists are like chains of children's "pop beads," where each bead has a hole at one end and a plug at the other (see Figure 13.2). We can connect the beads in the obvious way to form a chain and easily modify it. We can remove the color bead by disconnecting the two beads at both its ends and reattaching this pair of beads. We can add a new bead by connecting it to the bead at either end of the chain. We can insert a new bead in the middle by breaking the chain (between beads A and B) and connecting one end of the new bead to bead A and the other end to bead B. We show how to perform these operations to rearrange the items in a linked list next.

**linked list**
A group of data objects that are connected.

In this section we use pointers to create linked lists. We can add a pointer member to a struct and then build a linked list by connecting structs with pointer members.

### Declaring Nodes

We can connect two nodes if we include a pointer member in each node. The declarations

```
struct node
{
    string word;
    int count;
    node *link;
};
node *p, *q, *r;
```

allocate storage for three pointer variables. Each pointer variable can point to a struct of type `node` that has three components: `word`, `count`, and `link`. The first two components store a string and an integer value; the

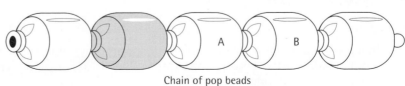

Pop bead                                        Chain of pop beads

**Figure 13.2**    Children's pop beads in a chain

third component, link (type node *—pointer to node), stores an address, as shown in the following diagram:

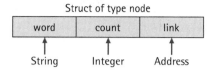

## Connecting Nodes

The statements

```
p = new node;
q = new node;
```

allocate storage for two structs of type node. The assignment statements

```
p->word = "hat";
p->count = 2;
q->word = "top";
q->count = 3;
```

define two fields of each node, as shown in Figure 13.3. The link fields are still undefined. The statement

```
p->link = q;
```

stores the address of the struct pointed to by q in the link field of the struct pointed to by p, thereby connecting these two nodes (see Figure 13.4).

The link field of the first node, p->link, points to the second node in the list and contains the same address as pointer q. We can therefore use

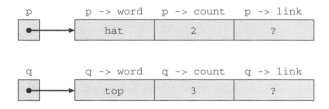

**Figure 13.3**   Nodes pointed to by p and q

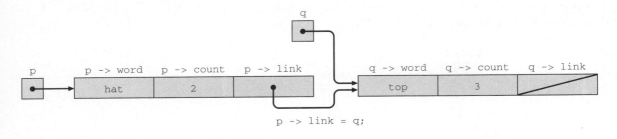

**Figure 13.4**    List with two elements

either member accessor q->word or p->link->word to access the word field (contents is "top") of the second node in the list.

We normally store a special pointer value, NULL, in the pointer field of the last element in a list. We can use either of the following statements to accomplish this result. We usually represent the value NULL by drawing a diagonal line in a pointer field.

        q->link = NULL;                |              p->link->link = NULL;

## Inserting a Node in a List

To insert a new node between the nodes pointed to by p and q, we start with the statements

```
r = new node;
r->word = "the";
r->count = 5;
```

They allocate and initialize a new node, which is pointed to by r. The statements

```
// Connect node pointed to by p to node pointed to by r
p->link = r;
// Connect node pointed to by r to node pointed to by q
r->link = q;
```

assign new values (shown by color arrows) to the link fields of the node pointed to by p and the node pointed to by r. The first statement connects the node pointed to by p to the new node; the second statement connects the new node to the node pointed to by q. Figure 13.5 shows the effect of these statements. The gray arrow shows the old value of p->link. Notice that we no longer need pointer variables q and r to access the list nodes

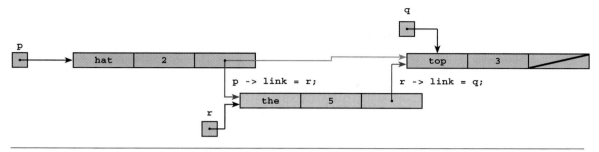

**Figure 13.5**   Inserting a new node in a list

because we can reach each node by following a trail of pointers from pointer variable p. The first node is called the **list head**. Table 13.1 shows some valid references to the list data, starting from the list head.

list head
The first node in a linked list.

## Insertion at the Head of a List

Although we usually insert new data at the end of a data structure, it's easier and more efficient to insert a new item at the head of a list. The following program fragment allocates a new node and inserts it at the head of the list pointed to by p. Pointer oldHead points to the original list head. After the insertion, p points to the new list head, which is linked to the old list head, as shown in Figure 13.6. The new pointer values are shown as color arrows; the gray arrow shows the old value of pointer p:

```
// Save pointer to old list head
oldHead = p;
// Point p to a new node
p = new node;
// Connect new list head to old list head
p->link = oldHead;
```

**Table 13.1**   References to List Nodes in Figure 13.5

| List References | Data Accessed |
| --- | --- |
| p->word | hat |
| p->link | link field of first node |
| p->link->word | the |
| p->link->link | link field of second node |
| p->link->link->count | 3 |

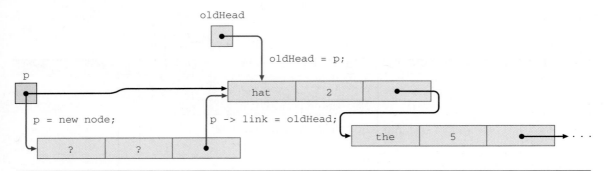

**Figure 13.6** Insertion at the head of a list

## Insertion at the End of a List

Inserting an item at the end of a list is less efficient because we usually do not have a pointer to the last list element, and so we must follow the pointer trail from the list head to the last list node and then perform the insertion. When last is pointing to the last list node (Figure 13.7), the statements

```
// Attach a new node to list end.
last->link = new node;
// Mark new list end.
last->link->link = NULL;
```

insert a node at the end of the list. The first statement allocates a new node that is pointed to by the link field of the last list node (before the insertion), so the new node is now the last node in the list. The second statement sets the link field of the new last node to NULL.

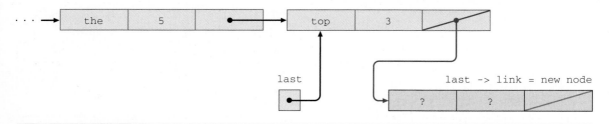

**Figure 13.7** Insertion at the end of a list

## Deleting a Node

To delete a node from a linked list, we simply change the link field of the node that points to it (its *predecessor*). We want the predecessor to point to the node that follows the one being deleted (its *successor*). For example, to delete the node pointed to by r from the three-element list in Figure 13.8, we change the `link` field of the node pointed to by p (the predecessor) to point to the successor of the node pointed to by r. The statement

```
// Disconnect the node pointed to by r.
p->link = r->link;
```

copies the address of the successor node to the `link` field of the predecessor node, thereby deleting the node pointed to by r from the list. The statements

```
// Disconnect the node pointed to by r from its successor.
r->link = NULL;
// Return the node pointed to by r to the heap.
delete r;
```

are then used to disconnect the node pointed to by r from the list and return its storage to the heap.

## Traversing a List

In many list-processing operations, we must process each node in the list in sequence, a procedure called **traversing a list**. We start at the list head and follow the trail of pointers.

**traversing a list**
Processing the nodes in a list in order, from first to last.

One typical operation performed on most data structures is to display the data structure's contents. To display the contents of a list, we must

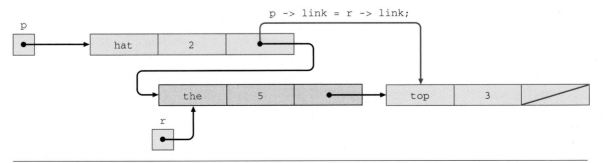

**Figure 13.8**   Deleting a list node

display only the values of the information fields, not the link fields. Function `printList` in Listing 13.1 displays the information fields of each node in the list shown in Figure 13.8 (after the deletion). The function call statement

```
printList(p);
```

displays the output lines

```
hat 2
top 3
```

The `while` condition

```
(head != NULL)
```

is common in loops that process lists. If the list to be displayed is empty, this condition is true initially and the loop body is skipped. If the list isn't empty, the loop body executes and the last statement in the loop,

```
head = head->link;          // Advance to next list node
```

advances the pointer head to the next list element, which is pointed to by the link field of the current list element. After the last data value in the list is printed, this statement assigns the address NULL to head and loop exit occurs.

Because head is a value argument, a local copy of the pointer to the first list element is established when the function is entered. This local pointer is advanced, but the corresponding pointer in the calling function remains unchanged. What would happen to our list if head was a reference argument?

---

**Warning About Reference Arguments for Pointers**
Consider the effect of parameter **head** being a reference argument instead of a value argument. This would allow the function to change the corresponding actual argument, regardless of your intentions. In **printList** and many similar functions, the last value assigned to the pointer argument is **NULL**. If **head** is a reference argument, the corresponding actual argument would be set to **NULL**, thereby disconnecting it from the list it pointed to before the function call.

Passing a pointer as a value argument protects that pointer from being changed by the function. However, you should realize that any changes made to other pointers in the list during the function's execution will remain.

**Listing 13.1**  Function `printList`

```
// File: printList.cpp
// Display the list pointed to by head
// Pre:  head points to a list whose last node has a pointer
//       member of NULL
// Post: The word and count members of each list node
//       are displayed and the last value of head is NULL
void printList
   (listNode *head)     // IN: pointer to list to be printed
{
   while (head != NULL)
   {
      // No prior value of head was NULL.
      cout << head->word << " " << head->count << endl;
      head = head->link;          // Advance to next list node.
   }
}  // end printList
```

## Circular Lists and Two-Way Lists (Optional)

You can traverse a list in only one direction, and you can't move past the last element. To get around these restrictions, programmers sometimes use either circular or two-way lists.

A **circular list** is one in which the last list node points back to the list head. In the circular list below, you can start anywhere in the list and still access all list elements.

**circular list**
A list in which the last list node contains a link to the first list node.

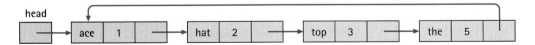

In a **two-way** or **doubly-linked list**, each node has two pointers: one to the node's successor (right) and one to the node's predecessor (left). For the node pointed to by next shown here the statement

**two-way (or doubly-linked) list**
A list in which each node has a link to its predecessor and successor.

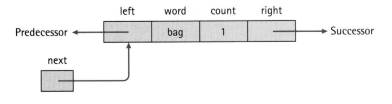

```
next = next->right;
```

moves pointer next to the successor node, and the statement

```
next = next->left;
```

moves pointer next to the predecessor node.

## The `list` Class

The C++ STL provides a `list` container class that is implemented as a two-way list. You can use this class instead of implementing your own linked list template class. You can insert or remove at either end of a `list`, or anywhere in the middle. You access the first and last elements and traverse a `list` in either direction. A `list` isn't indexed, so you can't use subscript notation with a `list` object. However, you can use an iterator (see Section 11.8) to traverse a `list` in either the forward or backward direction. Table 13.2 shows some functions of class `list`. In this table, *T* represents the data type of a `list` element.

Listing 13.2 shows an example that uses the `list` class. We first push three strings onto a list using member function `push_front` and then append three strings to the end of a list using member function `push_back`.

**Table 13.2**   Some Member Functions for the `list` Class

| | |
|---|---|
| `int size() const` | Returns the size of the list. |
| `T front()` | Returns the element at the list head. |
| `T back()` | Returns the last element in a list. |
| `void push_back(const T&)` | Appends an element to the end of a list, increasing its size by 1. |
| `void push_front(const T&)` | Inserts an element at the head of a list, increasing its size by 1. |
| `void pop_back(int)` | Removes the last element of a list, decreasing its size by 1. |
| `void pop_front(int)` | Removes the first element of a list, decreasing its size by 1. |
| `void insert(iterator, const T&)` | Inserts the specified element (2nd argument) at the position of the iterator (1st argument), increasing the list size by 1. |
| `void remove(const T&)` | Removes the specified element from the list, decreasing the list size by 1. |

Next we search for "`Dara`" using function `find` and insert "`Shelly`" in front of her. We display the first and last elements and also traverse and display the list elements using an iterator. Then we modify the list by removing two elements and inserting two elements and display the list after these operations.

We also traverse the two-way list in the backward direction (from last element to first element). The statement

```
list <string>::reverse_iterator rindex;
```

declares a reverse iterator `rindex`. In the `for` loop header

```
for (rindex = l.rbegin(); rindex != l.rend(); rindex++)
```

the initialization step sets `rindex` to point to the last list element; the repetition condition is true as long as `rindex` has not passed the first list element.

**Listing 13.2** Using `list` class

```cpp
#include <list>
#include <string>
#include <iostream>
using namespace std;

int main()
{
    list <string> l;

    // Push three strings onto the front of the list.
    l.push_front("Rich");
    l.push_front("Robin");
    l.push_front("Sam");

    // Append three strings to the end of the list.
    l.push_back("Mark");
    l.push_back("Dara");
    l.push_back("Debbie");

    // Insert Shelly before Dara.
    l.insert(find(l.begin(), l.end(), "Dara"), "Shelly");
```

(continued)

**Listing 13.2** Using `list` class (continued)

```
// Display first and last elements
cout << "List head is " << l.front()
     << ", end of list is " << l.back() << endl;

// Display entire list
list <string>::iterator index;
for (index = l.begin(); index != l.end(); index++)
   cout << *index << " ";
cout << endl;

// Remove Mark and Sam; insert Dustin and Jonathan
// before Rich
l.remove("Mark");
l.remove("Sam");
index = find(l.begin(), l.end(), "Rich");
l.insert(index, "Dustin");
l.insert(index, "Jonathan");

// Display list after changes
for (index = l.begin(); index != l.end(); index++)
   cout << *index << " ";
cout << endl;

// Display list in reverse direction
list <string>::reverse_iterator rindex;
for (rindex = l.rbegin(); rindex != l.rend(); rindex++)
   cout << *rindex << " ";

return 0;
}
```

```
List head is Sam, end of list is Debbie
Sam Robin Rich Mark Shelly Dara Debbie
Robin Dustin Jonathan Rich Shelly Dara Debbie
Debbie Dara Shelly Rich Jonathan Dustin Robin
```

## EXERCISES FOR SECTION 13.3

Self-Check

1. For the three-element list in Figure 13.5, explain the effect of each statement. Assume the list is restored to its initial state before each statement executes.

a. `r->link = p;`

b. `p->link = NULL;`

c. `p->link = r;`

d. `p->link = q->link;`

e. `p = p->link;`

f. `p->word = r->word;`

g. `p->count = p->link->`
   `        link->count;`

h. `p->link->link = NULL;`

j. `while (p != NULL)`
   `{`

i. `q->link = new node;`
   `q->link->word = "zzz";`
   `q->link->count = 0;`
   `q->link->link = NULL;`

   `    (p->count)++;`
   `    p = p->link;`
   `}`

2. How would you delete the node at the head of a list? How would you delete a node if you were given only a pointer to the node to be deleted and a pointer to the list head?

3. Answer Self-Check Exercise 2 using functions from the `list` class.

Programming

1. Write a function that finds the length of a list.

2. Write a fragment to advance pointer last to the last node of a list whose head is pointed to by `p`, then insert a new list node at the end of the list. Make sure you consider the special case of an initially empty list (`p` is NULL).

3. Redo Programming Exercise 2 using functions from the `list` class.

## 13.4    The Stack Abstract Data Type

A **stack** is a data structure in which only the top element can be accessed. To illustrate, the plates stored in the spring-loaded device in a buffet line perform like a stack. A customer always takes the top plate; when a plate is removed, the plate beneath it moves to the top. Also, when a clean plate is returned to the stack, it's always placed on the top of the stack.

The diagram in Figure 13.9 shows a stack s of four characters. The symbol * is the character at the top of the stack and is the only character that we can access. We must remove the symbol * from the stack in order to access

**stack**
a data structure in which only one element can be accessed

**Figure 13.9**    A stack of characters

the letter c. Removing a value from a stack is called **popping the stack**. Storing a data item in a stack is called **pushing** it onto the stack. A stack is called a **Last-In-First-Out (LIFO)** data structure because the last element inserted on a stack is the first one removed.

Compilers push a function's arguments onto a stack when a function is called; the arguments are popped off the stack after returning from the function. Compilers also use stacks for data storage while translating expressions. In general, we use stacks in a program to remember a sequence of data objects or actions in the reverse order from that in which they were encountered.

## The C++ **stack** Class

C++ provides a **stack** class that we can use instead of writing our own template class. To use a **stack**, we need the compiler directive

```
#include <stack>
```

We declare a **stack** just like we declare an object of any template class:

```
stack <type> stack-name;
```

For example:

```
stack <string> nameStack;    // stack of strings
stack <char> s;              // stack of characters
```

Table 13.3 describes the **stack** class member functions **empty**, **push**, **top**, and **pop**. We use function **top** to access the top value (without removal) and then call function **pop** to remove it.

**Table 13.3**   Some Member Functions for the `stack` Class

| | |
|---|---|
| `void push(const T&)` | Pushes its argument onto the stack. |
| `T top() const` | Returns the element at the top of the stack. |
| `void pop()` | Removes the element at the top of the stack. |
| `bool empty() const` | Returns `true` if the stack is empty. |

## EXAMPLE 13.1

In stack **s** shown on the left in Figure 13.10, the first element placed on the stack was
`'2'` and the last element placed on the stack was `'*'`. For this stack, the value of
`s.empty()` is `false`. The statement

```
x = s.top();
```

stores `'*'` in **x** (type `char`) without changing **s**. The statement

```
s.pop();
```

removes `'*'` from **s**. The new stack **s** contains three elements, as shown in the middle
of Figure 13.10.
    The statement

```
s.push('/');
```

pushes `'/'` onto the stack. The new stack **s** contains four elements and is shown on
the right of Figure 13.10.

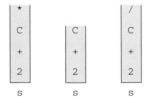

**Figure 13.10**   Stack s (left) after pop (middle) and push (right) operations

## EXAMPLE 13.2

The program in Listing 13.3 calls `fillStack` to read a collection of data strings ending with the sentinel string (`"***"`). Function `fillStack` pushes each string read except the last onto a stack. Then it calls `displayStack` to pop each string from the stack and display it, thereby displaying the strings in reverse order.

---

**Listing 13.3** Using a stack of characters

```cpp
// File: StackTest.cpp
// Use a stack to store strings and display them in reverse order

#include <stack>          // Uses stack template class
#include <string>
#include <iostream>
using namespace std;

typedef stack<string> stringStack;

int fillStack(stringStack& s);
void displayStack(stringStack& s);

int main()
{
   // Local data
   stringStack s;

   // Read data into the stack.
   fillStack(s);

   // Display the stack contents
   displayStack(s);

   return 0;
}


//    Reads data characters and pushes them onto stack s.
//    Pre : s is an empty stack.
//    Post: s contains the strings read in reverse order.
//    Returns the number of strings read not counting the sentinel.

int fillStack(stringStack& s)    // OUT: stack to fill
{
```

(continued)

**Listing 13.3** Using a stack of characters (continued)

```
    // Local data
       string nextStr;              // next string
       int numStrings;              // count of strings read
       const string sentinel = "***";  // sentinel string

    // Read and push strings onto stack until done.
    numStrings = 0;
    cout << "Enter next string or " << sentinel << "> ";
    cin >> nextStr;
    while (nextStr != sentinel)
    {
       s.push(nextStr);   // Push next string on stack S.
       numStrings++;
       cout << "Enter next string or " << sentinel << "> ";
       cin >> nextStr;
    }

    return numStrings;
}  // end fillStack

//    Pops each string from stack s and displays it.
//    Pre : Stack s is defined.
//    Post: Stack s is empty and all strings are displayed.
void displayStack(stringStack& s)  // IN: stack to display
{
    // Local data
    string nextStr;

    // Pop and display strings until stack is empty.
    while (!s.empty())
    {
       nextStr = s.top();
       s.pop();                 // Pop next string off stack.
       cout << nextStr << endl;
    }
}  // end displayStack
```

```
Enter next string or ***> Here
Enter next string or ***> are
Enter next string or ***> strings!
Enter next string or ***> ***
strings!
are
Here
```

The line

```
typedef stack<string> stringStack;
```

associates the data type `stack<string>` with the identifier `stringStack`. Therefore, we can use `stringStack` as the stack type in the formal argument lists for `fillStack` and `displayStack`.

## Implementing a **stack** Template Class

In this section, we consider how we might implement our own `stack` class as a template class. You can visualize a stack as a linked list or as a vector in which all insertions and deletions occur at the same end. Just like a linked list or a vector, a stack will expand and contract as needed as your program executes. A linked list representation of a stack `s` is shown at the top of Figure 13.11. The first element of the list, pointed to by `s.topP`, is at the top of the stack. If a new node is pushed onto the stack, it should be inserted in front of the node that is currently at the head of the list. Stack `s` after insertion of the symbol `'*'` is shown at the bottom of the figure. If we pop the stack shown in Figure 13.11 (bottom), we'll remove the character * that we just inserted.

Each element of a stack can be stored in a node with a data field of type `stackElement`. In the template class `stackList` (see Listing 13.4), we declare a `struct` (type `stackNode`) to hold the data and a pointer to the next node. In class `stackList`, data member `topP` (type `stackNode*`) is a pointer to the top of the stack.

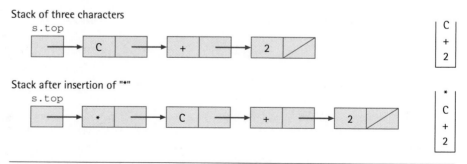

Stack of three characters

Stack after insertion of "*"

**Figure 13.11**  Physical stack **s** (left) and abstract stack (right)

**Listing 13.4**    Header file for template class `stackList`

```cpp
// File: stackList.h
// Definition of a template class stackList using a linked list

#ifndef STACK_LIST_H
#define STACK_LIST_H

template <class stackElement>
class stackList
{
   public:
      // Member functions ...
      // constructor to create an empty stack
      stackList();

      // Push an element onto the stack
      void push
        (const stackElement& x); // IN: item pushed onto stack

      // Pop an element off the stack
      void pop();

      // Access top element of stack without popping
      stackElement top () const;

      // Test to see if stack is empty
      bool empty() const;

   private:
      struct stackNode
      {
         stackElement item;         // storage for the node data
         stackNode* next;           // link to next node
      };

      // Data member
      stackNode* topP;       // pointer to node at top of stack
};
#endif  // STACK_LIST_H
```

## Implementing the Stack Operators

Listing 13.5 shows the implementation file for class `stackList`. The constructor `stackList` sets `topp` to `NULL`, creating an empty stack. Function `push` allocates a new node (pointed to by `topP`), stores its argument `x` in the new node's data member (`topP->item`), and connects the new node to the rest of the stack (pointed to by `oldTop`). Function `top` returns the item at the top of the stack without changing the stack.

Function `pop` first checks to see if the stack is empty. If so, an error message is displayed. Otherwise, the first element is removed. Function `empty` returns true if `topP` is `NULL`.

**Listing 13.5**   Implementation file for template class `stackList`

```
// File: stackList.cpp
// Implementation of template class stackList as a linked list

#include "stackList.h"
#include <cstdlib>                  // for NULL
using namespace std;

// Member functions ...
// constructor to create an empty stack
template <class stackElement>
stackList<stackElement>::stackList()
{
   topP = NULL;
}  // end stackList

// Push an element onto the stack
// Pre:  The element x is defined.
// Post: The item is pushed
//       onto the stack
template <class stackElement>
void stackList<stackElement>::push
  (const stackElement& x)  // IN: Element pushed onto stack
{
   // Local data
   stackNode* oldTop;

   oldTop = topP;              // save old top
   topP = new stackNode;       // allocate new node at top of stack
   topP->next = oldTop;        // link new node to old stack
   topP->item = x;             // store x in new node
```

(continued)

**Listing 13.5**   Implementation file for template class `stackList`  (continued)

```
}   // end push
// Pop an element off the stack
// Pre:  none
// Post: If the stack is not empty, the value at the top
//       of the stack is removed.
//       If the stack is empty, an error message is displayed.
template <class stackElement>
void stackList<stackElement>::pop()
{
   // Local data
   stackNode* oldTop;

   if (topP == NULL)
      cerr << "No element to remove" << endl;
   else
   {
      oldTop = topP;           // save old top of stack
      topP = oldTop->next;     // reset top of stack
      delete oldTop;           // return top node to the heap
   }
}   // end pop


// Access top element of stack without popping
// Pre:  none
// Post: If the stack is not empty, the value at the top is
//       returned. If the stack is
//       empty, an error message is displayed
template <class stackElement>
stackElement stackList<stackElement>::top() const
{
   // Local data
   if (topP == NULL)
   {
      cerr << "stack is empty" << endl;
      return NULL;
   }
   else
      return topP->item;
}   // end top
```

(continued)

**Listing 13.5**    Implementation file for template class `stackList`  (continued)

```
// Test to see if stack is empty
// Pre : none
// Post: Returns true if the stack is empty; otherwise,
//       returns false.
template <class stackElement>
bool stackList<stackElement>::empty() const
{
   return topP == NULL;
}  // end empty
```

## Testing the Stack ADT

We can use the program shown in Listing 13.3, which reads a list of strings and displays them in reverse order. To use the list implementation of a stack instead of the STL `stack` class, we need to change only two lines. Replace the line

```
#include <stack>
```

with

```
#include "stackList.h"
```

Also, replace the line

```
typedef stack<string> stringStack;
```

with

```
typedef stackList<string> stringStack;
```

We can then run the program as before.

## EXERCISES FOR SECTION 13.4

### Self-Check

1. Assume that stack s is defined as in Figure 13.10 (left). Perform the sequence of operations shown below. Show the result of each operation and the new stack if it is changed. Rather than draw the stack each

time, use the notation |2 + c * to represent the stack. (The bar "|" represents the bottom of the stack.)

```
s.push('$');
s.push('-');
s.pop();
nextCh = s.top();
if (s.empty())
    cout << "stack is empty" << endl;
```

2. Declare a stack that can store values of type `entry`.

3. Provide an algorithm for a member function `copyStack` that makes a copy of an existing stack. (Hint: You'll need to pop each node and store its data in a temporary stack.)

4. Discuss the similarities and differences between a stack and a vector. Explain how you might implement a stack using a vector. Give the vector operator that corresponds to each stack operator.

Programming

1. Write a function `displayStack` for class `stackList`.

2. Write a member function `copyStack` for class `stackList` that uses the stack operators to make a copy of an existing stack.

## 13.5 The Queue Abstract Data Type

A **queue** (pronounced "Q") is a list-like structure in which items are inserted at one end and removed from the other. In contrast, stack elements are inserted and removed from the same end (the top of the stack).

In a queue, the element that has been stored the longest is removed first, so a queue is called a **First-In-First-Out (FIFO) structure**. A queue can be used to model a line of customers waiting at a checkout counter or a stream of jobs waiting to be printed by a printer.

Figure 13.12(a) shows a queue of three customers waiting for service at a bank. The name of the customer who has been waiting the longest is McMann (pointed to by `frontP`); the name of the most recent arrival is Carson (pointed to by `rearP`). The customer pointed to by `frontP` will be the first one removed from the queue when a teller becomes available, and pointer `frontP` will be reset to point to Wilson. Any new customers will be inserted after Carson in the queue, and pointer `rearP` will be adjusted accordingly. Figure 13.12(b) shows the queue after removing customer McMann, and Figure 13.12(c) shows the queue after inserting customer Perez at the end of the queue.

**queue**
A data structure in which elements are inserted at one end and removed from the other end.

**First-In-First-Out (FIFO) structure**
A data structure in which the first element stored is the first one removed.

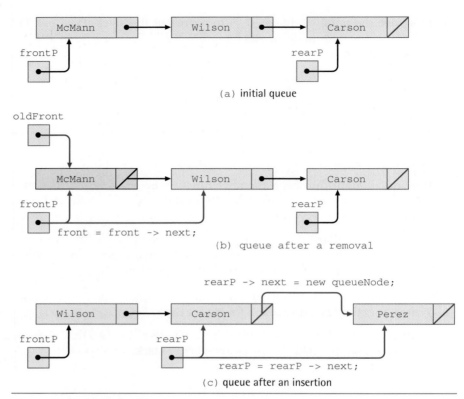

**Figure 13.12** Queue of customers

## The C++ `queue` Class

The STL C++ provides a `queue` class that we can use instead of writing our own template class. To use a queue, we need the compiler directive

```
#include <queue>
```

We declare a queue just like we declare an object of any template class:

```
queue <type> queue-name;
```

For example:

```
queue <string> customers;   // queue of strings
```

Table 13.4 describes the `queue` class member functions `empty`, `push`, `top`, and `pop`. We use function `top` to access the top value (without removal) and then call function `pop` to remove it.

Table 13.4 Some Member Functions for the `queue` Class

| | |
|---|---|
| `void push(const T&)` | Pushes its argument onto the rear of the queue. |
| `T top() const` | Returns the element at the front of the queue. |
| `void pop()` | Removes the element at the front of the queue. |
| `void empty() const` | Returns true if the queue is empty. |
| `int size() const` | Returns the size of the queue. |

## Implementing a Queue ADT

If we implement a queue as a linked list, removing elements from a queue is no different from removing them from a stack—except that the element at the front of the queue is removed first. Because new elements are inserted at the rear of the queue, we need a pointer to the last list element as well as the first. We can represent a queue as an object with two data members, `frontP` and `rearP`. Pointer `frontP` points to the node at the front of the queue, and pointer `rearP` points to the node at the rear of the queue. Because we might also want to know how many elements are in a queue, we'll add a third data member, `numItems`. Each queue node (type `queue-Node`) is a struct with an information part (type `queueElement`) and a link to the next queue node. Listing 13.6 shows the header file for template class `queueList<class queueElement>`.

Listing 13.6    Header file for `queue` template class

```
// File: queueList.h
// Definition of a template class queue using a linked list

#ifndef QUEUE_H
#define QUEUE_H

// Specification of the class queueList<queueElement>
// Elements:      A queue consists of a collection of elements
//                that are all of the same type, queueElement.
// Structure:     The elements of a queue are ordered according
//                to time of arrival. The element that was first
//                inserted into the queue is the only one that
//                may be removed or examined. Elements are
//                removed from the front of the queue and
//                inserted at the rear of the queue.
```

(continued)

**Listing 13.6** Header file for queue template class (continued)

```cpp
template<class queueElement>
class queueList
{
   public:
      // Member functions ...
      // constructor - create an empty queue
      queueList();

      // Insert an element into the queue
      void push
         (const queueElement& x);   // IN: Element to insert

      // Access the element at the front of the queue
      queueElement top() const;

      // Remove the element at the front of the queue
      void pop();

      // Test for empty queue
      bool empty() const;

      // Get queue size
      int size() const;

   private:
      // Data members ...
      struct queueNode
      {
         queueElement item;
         queueNode* next;
      };

      queueNode* frontP;      // the front of the queue
      queueNode* rearP;       // the rear of the queue
      int numItems;           // the number of items currently
                              // in the queue
};
#endif    // QUEUE_H
```

Next we implement the queue member functions. Constructor queueList (Listing 13.7) sets pointer fields frontP and rearP to NULL.

**Listing 13.7**   Implementation file for queue template class

```cpp
// File: queueList.cpp
// Implementation of template class queue using a linked list

#include "queueList.h"
#include <cstdlib>          // for NULL
using namespace std;

// Member functions
// constructor - create an empty queue
template<class queueElement>
queueList<queueElement>::queueList()
{
   numItems = 0;
   frontP = NULL;
   rearP = NULL;
}


// Insert an element into the queue
// Pre : none
// Post: The value x is inserted
//       at the rear of the queue.
template<class queueElement>
void queueList<queueElement>::push
  (const queueElement& x)     // IN: Element to insert
{
   if (numItems == 0)              // Test for empty queue
   {
      rearP = new queueNode;       // Allocate first queue node
      frontP = rearP;              // queue with one element
   }
   else                            // Add to existing queue
   {
      rearP->next = new queueNode; // Connect new last node
      rearP = rearP->next;         // Point rear to last node
   }
   rearP->item = x;                // Store data in last node
   numItems++;
}  // end push
```

(continued)

**Listing 13.7**    Implementation file for queue template class (continued)

```cpp
// Access the element at the front of the queue
// Pre : none
// Post: If the queue is not empty, the value at the front of
//       the queue is retrieved. If the queue is empty, an error
//       is displayed.
  template<class queueElement>
  queueElement queueList<queueElement>::top() const
  {
     if (numItems == 0)
     {
        cerr << "queue is empty" << endl;
        return NULL;
     }
     else
        return frontP->item;
  } // end top


// Remove the element from at the front of the queue
// Pre : none
// Post: If the queue is not empty, the value at the front of
//       the queue is removed. If the queue is empty,
//       an error is displayed.
template<class queueElement>
void queueList<queueElement>::pop()
{
   // Local data
   queueNode* oldFront;

   if (numItems == 0)                // Test for empty queue
   {
      cerr << "empty queue" << endl;     // queue was empty
   }
   else                             // Remove first node
   {
      oldFront = frontP;  // Point oldFront to first node
      frontP = frontP->next;      // Bypass old first node
      oldFront->next = NULL;    // Disconnect old first node
      delete oldFront;             // Return its storage
      numItems--;                  // Decrement queue size
   }
} // end pop
```

(continued)

**Listing 13.7** Implementation file for queue template class (continued)

```cpp
// Test whether queue is empty
template<class queueElement>
bool queueList<queueElement>::empty() const
{
    return (numItems == 0);
}


// Returns queue size
template<class queueElement>
int queueList<queueElement>::size() const
{
    return numItems;
}
```

In operator push, the statements

```cpp
rearP = new queueNode;   // Allocate first queue node
frontP = rearP;          // queue with one element
```

execute when the queue is empty. These statements create a new node and set both `rearP` and `frontP` to reference it. If the queue isn't empty, the statements

```cpp
rearP->next = new queueNode; // Connect new last node
rearP = rearP->next;         // Point rear to last node
```

append a new list node at the end of the queue and then reset `rearP` to point to this new node.

If the queue isn't empty, operator pop uses the statement

```cpp
frontP = frontP->next;      // Bypass old first node
```

to reset `frontP` to point to the successor of the node being removed, as shown in Figure 13.12(b). Next, pop disconnects the old front of the queue (pointed to by `oldFront`) and returns its storage to the heap.

**EXERCISES FOR SECTION 13.5**

**Self-Check**

1. Redraw the queue in Figure 13.12(a) after the insertion of customer Harris and the removal of one customer from the queue. Which customer is removed? How many customers are left? Show pointers `frontP` and `rearP` after each operation.

2. Trace operators `push` and `pop` as the operations in Self-Check Exercise 1 are performed. Show before and after values for all pointers.

3. Write a new `rudeInsert` operator that inserts at the front of the queue rather than the end.

4. A circular queue is a queue in which the node at the rear of the queue points to the node at the front of the queue (see circular lists in Section 13.3). Draw the queue in Figure 13.12 as a circular queue with just one pointer field named `rearP`. Explain how you'd access the queue element at the front of a circular queue.

**Programming**

1. Write operator `size`.

2. Add a new operator `display`, which writes the data stored in a queue.

3. Is it possible to simulate the operation of a queue using two stacks? Write an ADT for the queue object assuming that two stacks are used for storing the queue. What performance penalty do we pay for this implementation?

# 13.6    Binary Trees

**leaf node**
A node with two empty subtrees.

**root node**
The first node in a binary tree.

**left subtree**
The part of a tree connected to the left link of a node.

**right subtree**
The part of a tree connected to the right link of a node.

We can extend the concept of linked data structures to structures containing nodes with more than one pointer component. One such structure is a **binary tree** (or **tree**), whose nodes contain two pointer components. Because one or both pointers can have the value NULL, each node in a binary tree can have 0, 1, or 2 successor nodes.

Figure 13.13 shows two binary trees. For the tree (a), each node stores a three-letter string. The nodes on the bottom of the tree have 0 successors and are called **leaf nodes**. All other nodes have two successors. For tree (b), each node stores an integer. The nodes containing 40 and 45 have a single successor; all other nodes have 0 or 2 successors. A binary tree can be defined recursively: A *binary tree* is either empty (no nodes) or it consists of a node, called the **root**, and two disjoint binary trees called its **left subtree** and **right subtree**, respectively.

In the definition for binary tree, the phrase *disjoint subtrees* means that a node can't be in both a left and a right subtree of the same root node. For the trees shown in Figure 13.13, the nodes containing FOX and 35 are the root nodes for each tree. The node containing DOG is the root of the left subtree of the tree whose root is FOX; the node containing CAT is the root of the left subtree of the tree whose root is DOG; the node containing CAT is a leaf node because both its subtrees are empty trees.

A binary tree resembles a family tree and the relationships among the members of a binary tree are described with the same terminology as a family tree. In Figure 13.13 the node containing HEN is the **parent** of the nodes containing HAT and HOG. Similarly, the nodes containing HAT and HOG are *siblings*, because they're both *children* of the same parent node. The root of a tree is an *ancestor* of all other nodes in the tree, and they in turn are *descendants* of the root node.

For simplicity, we did not show the pointer components in Figure 13.13. Be aware that each node has two pointer components and that the nodes in (b) containing integers 45 and 42 are stored as follows:

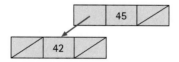

## Binary Search Tree

In the rest of this chapter, we focus our attention on the binary search tree—a particular kind of binary tree structure that stores data in such a way that it can be retrieved very efficiently. Every item stored in a binary search tree

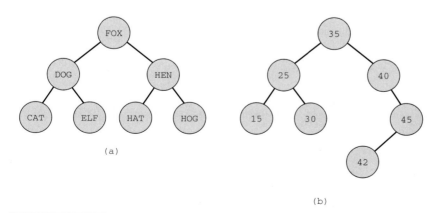

(a)

(b)

**Figure 13.13**   Binary trees

**key**
A unique identifier associated with the data stored in each node of a binary search tree.

**binary search tree**
A binary tree with the property that the item in each node has a larger key than all items in its left subtree and a smaller key than all the items in its right subtree.

has a special data component (called a **key**) whose value is unique to that item. A **binary search tree** is a binary tree that either is empty or has the property that the item in each node has a larger key than each item in its left subtree and a smaller key than each item in its right subtree.

The trees in Figure 13.13 are examples of binary search trees; each node has a single data component that is its key. For tree (a), the string stored in every node is alphabetically larger than all strings in its left subtree and alphabetically smaller than all strings in its right subtree. For tree (b), the number stored in every node is larger than all numbers in its left subtree and smaller than all numbers in its right subtree. Notice that this must be true for every node in a binary search tree, not just the root node. For example, the number 40 must be smaller than both numbers stored in its right subtree (45, 42).

## Searching a Binary Search Tree

Next we explain how to search for an item in a binary search tree. To find a particular item—say, el—we compare el's key to the root item's key. If el's key is smaller, we know that el can only be in the left subtree, so we search it. If el's key is larger, we search the root item's right subtree. We write this recursive algorithm in pseudocode below; the first two cases are stopping cases.

### Algorithm for Searching a Binary Search Tree

> if the tree is empty
> > The target key isn't in the tree.
> else if the target key is in the root item
> > The target key is found in the root item.
> else if the target key is smaller than the root's key
> > Search the left subtree.
> else
> > Search the right subtree.

Figure 13.14 traces the search for 42 in a binary search tree containing integer keys. The pointer root indicates the root node whose key is being compared to 42 at each step. The color lines show the search path. The search proceeds from the top (node 35) down to the node containing 42.

## Building a Binary Search Tree

Before we can retrieve an item from a binary search tree, we must, of course, build the tree. To do this, we must process a collection of data items

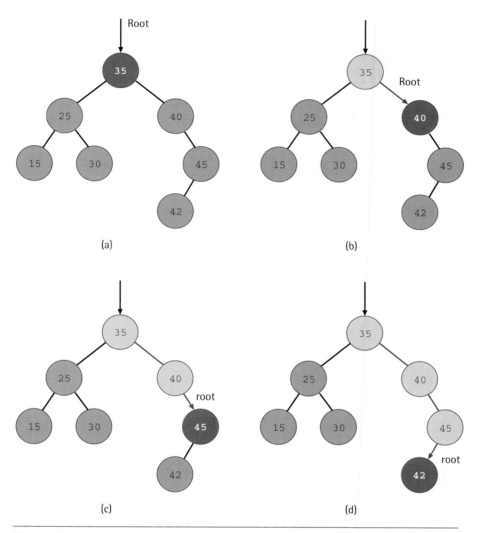

**Figure 13.14**   Searching for key 42

that is in no particular order and insert each one individually, making sure that the expanded tree is a binary search tree. We build a binary search tree from the root node down, so we must store the first data item in the root node. To store each subsequent data item, we must find its parent node in the tree, attach a new node to the parent, and then store that data item in the new node.

When inserting an item, we must search the existing tree to find that item's key or to locate its parent node. If our search is successful, the item's key is already in the tree, so we won't insert the item. (Duplicate keys are not allowed.) If the search is unsuccessful, it will terminate at the parent of the item. If the item's key is smaller than its parent's key, we attach a new node as the parent's left subtree and insert the item in this node. If the item's key is larger than its parent's key, we attach a new node as the parent's right subtree and insert the item in this node. The recursive algorithm below maintains the binary search tree property; the first two cases are stopping cases.

### Algorithm for Insertion in a Binary Search Tree

if the tree is empty
    Insert the new item in the tree's root node.
else if the root's key matches the new item's key
    Skip insertion—duplicate key.
else if the new item's key is smaller than the root's key
    Insert the new item in the tree's left subtree.
else
    Insert the new item in the tree's right subtree.

Figure 13.15 builds a tree from the list of keys: 40, 20, 10, 50, 65, 45, 30. The color lines show the search path followed when inserting each key.

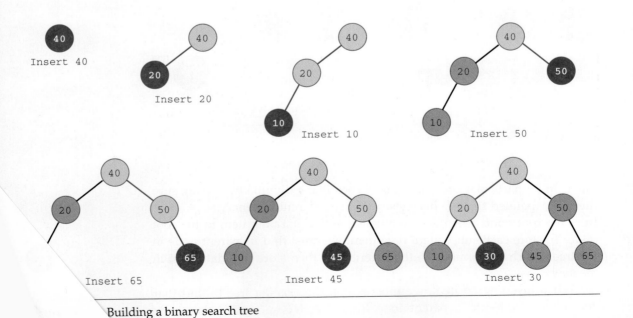

Building a binary search tree

The last node inserted (bottom right diagram) contains the key 30 and is inserted in the right subtree of node 20. Let's trace how this happens using the tree just to the left of the bottom-right tree. Target key 30 is smaller than 40, so we insert 30 in the left subtree of node 40; this tree has 20 in its root. Target key 30 is greater than 20, so we insert 30 in the right subtree of node 20, an empty tree. Because node 20 has no right subtree, we allocate a new node and insert target 30 in it; the new node becomes the root of 20's right subtree.

Be aware that we would get a very different tree if we changed the order in which we inserted the keys. For example, if we inserted the keys in increasing order (10, 20, 30, ... ), each new key would be inserted in the right subtree of the previous key and all left pointers would be NULL. The resulting tree would resemble a linked list. We'll see later (Section 13.8) that the insertion order also affects search efficiency.

## Displaying a Binary Search Tree

To display the contents of a binary search tree so that its items are listed in order by key value, use the recursive algorithm below.

### Algorithm for Displaying a Binary Search Tree

1. if the tree is not empty
   2.. Display left subtree.
   3. Display root item.
   4. Display right subtree.

For each node, the keys in its left subtree are displayed before the key in its root; the keys in its right subtree are displayed after the key in its root. Because the root key value lies between the key values in its left and right subtrees, the algorithm displays the items in order by key value as desired. Because the nodes' data components are displayed in order, this algorithm is also called an *inorder traversal*.

Table 13.5 traces the sequence of calls generated by the display algorithm for the last tree in Figure 13.15. Completing the sequence of calls for the last step shown, "Display right subtree of node 40." is left as an exercise. The trace so far displays the item keys in the sequence 10, 20, 30, 40.

**Table 13.5**     Trace of Tree Display Algorithm

Display left subtree of node 40.

 Display left subtree of node 20.

  Display left subtree of node 10.

   Tree is empty—return from displaying
   left subtree of node 10.

  Display item with key 10.

  Display right subtree of node 10.

   Tree is empty—return from displaying
   right subtree of node 10.

  Return from displaying left subtree of node 20.

 Display item with key 20.

 Display right subtree of node 20.

  Display left subtree of node 30.

   Tree is empty—return from displaying
   left subtree of node 30.

  Display item with key 30.

  Display right subtree of node 30.

   Tree is empty—return from displaying
   right subtree of node 30.

  Return from displaying right subtree of node 20.

 Return from displaying left subtree of node 40.

Display item with key 40.

Display right subtree of node 40.

## EXERCISES FOR SECTION 13.6

### Self-Check

1. Are the following trees binary search trees? Show the list of keys as they would be displayed by an inorder traversal of each tree. If the trees below were binary search trees, what key values would you expect to find in the left subtree of the node containing key 50?

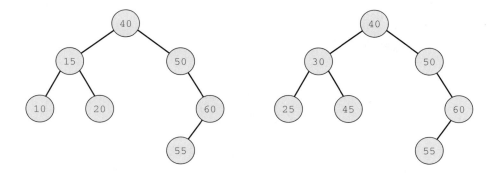

2. Complete the trace started in Table 13.5.

3. Show the binary search trees that would be created from the lists of keys below. Which tree do you think would be the most efficient to search? What can you say about the binary search tree formed in parts (b) and (c)? What can you say about the binary search tree formed in part (d)? How do you think searching it would compare to searching a linked list with the same keys?

   **a.** 25, 45, 15, 10, 60, 55, 12

   **b.** 25, 12, 55, 10, 15, 45, 60

   **c.** 25, 12, 10, 15, 55, 60, 45

   **d.** 10, 12, 15, 25, 45, 55, 60

4. What would be displayed by an inorder traversal of each tree in Self-Check Exercise 3?

## 13.7   Binary Search Tree Abstract Data Type

Next, we design and implement a binary search tree abstract data type.

### Design of Binary Tree Class

The pointer to the tree root is the only attribute of a binary tree. Besides the member functions discussed so far (`search`, `insert`, and `display`), we include a function retrieve to get the tree item whose key matches a target key. We provide the specification for a binary tree class next.

```
Specification for Binary Search Tree

Attributes for Binary Tree Class
    root                // a pointer to the tree root

Member Functions for Binary Tree Class
    binaryTree          // a constructor
    insert              // inserts an item into the tree
    retrieve            // retrieves all the data for a given key
    search              // locates the node for a given key
    display             // displays a binary tree
```

We declare these member functions in the public part of the class definition (see Listing 13.8). The function prototypes show that all of them, except for display, return a type bool result, which indicates whether the function was able to perform its task.

**Listing 13.8**    Template class specification for `tree<treeElement>`

```
// File: binaryTree.h
// Definition of template class binary search tree

#include <cstdlib>        // for NULL
using namespace std;

#ifndef BINARY_TREE_H
#define BINARY_TREE_H

// Specification of the class binTree<treeElement>
// Elements:      A tree consists of a collection of elements
//                that are all of the same type, treeElement.
// Structure:     Each node of a binary search tree has zero, one,
//                or two subtrees connected to it. The key value in
//                each node of a binary search tree is larger than
//                all key values in its left subtree and smaller
//                than all key values in its right subtree.

template<class treeElement>
   binaryTree
```

(continued)

**Listing 13.8**   Template class specification for `tree<treeElement>`  (continued)

```
{
public:
    // Member functions  . . .
    // constructor - create an empty tree
    binaryTree();
    // Insert an element into the tree
    bool insert
        (const treeElement& el );        // IN: Element to insert
    // Retrieve an element from the tree
    bool retrieve
        (const treeElement& el) const;  // OUT: element retrieved
    // Search for an element in the tree
    bool search
        (const treeElement& el) const;  // IN: element being
                                        //      searched for
    // Display a tree
    void display() const;
private:
    // Data type  . . .
    struct treeNode
    {
        treeElement info;       // the node data
        treeNode *left;         // pointer to left-subtree
        treeNode *right;        // pointer to right-subtree
    };
    // Data member
    treeNode* root;             // the root of the tree
    // Private member functions  . . .
    // Searches a subtree for a key
    bool search(treeNode*,                      // root of a subtree
                const treeElement&) const;      // key being
                                                // searched for
    // Inserts an item in a subtree
    bool insert(treeNode*&,             // root of a subtree
                const treeElement&);    // item being inserted
    // Retrieves an item in a subtree
    bool retrieve(treeNode*,            // root of a subtree
                  treeElement&) const;          // item to retrieve
    // Displays a subtree
    void display(treeNode*) const;
};
#endif  // BINARY_TREE_H
```

The private part shows that each binary search tree node (struct `treeNode`) contains a data component, `info`, which is type `treeElement`, and two pointers, `left` and `right`, that connect it to its children. These internal pointers can't be accessed by a user of the binary tree class.

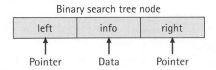

Binary search tree node

A binary tree object contains storage for a single pointer component, `root`, which points to the root node of that tree.

There are three private member functions and three public member functions with the same names—`search`, `insert`, and `retrieve`. Each private member function has a different signature (parameter list) than does the public member function with the same name. We'll explain the reason for the private member functions shortly.

## Implementation of Binary Tree Class

We'll write the member function definitions for the implementation file in stages. As shown in Listing 13.9, the constructor `binaryTree` sets the `root` pointer of its object instance to `NULL`, thereby creating an empty tree.

**Listing 13.9**　Member functions `binaryTree` and `search`

```cpp
// File: binaryTree.cpp
// Implementation of template class binary search tree

#include "binaryTree.h"
#include <iostream>
using namespace std;

    // Member functions  . . .
    // constructor - create an empty tree
    template<class treeElement>
    binaryTree<treeElement>::binaryTree()
    {
        root = NULL;
```

(continued)

**Listing 13.9** Member functions `binaryTree` and `search` (continued)

```cpp
// Searches for the item with same key as el
//  in a binary search tree. (public)
// Pre : el is defined.
// Returns true if el's key is located,
//    otherwise, returns false.
template<class treeElement>
bool binaryTree<treeElement>::search
  (const treeElement& el) const    // IN: Element to search for
{
    return search(root, el); // Start search at tree root.
} // search

// (private) Searches for the item with same key as el in the
// subtree pointed to by aRoot. Called by public search.
// Pre : el and aRoot are defined.
// Returns true if el's key is located,
//    otherwise, returns false.
template<class treeElement>
bool binaryTree<treeElement>::search
  (treeNode *aRoot,                 // IN: Subtree to search
    const treeElement& el) const    // IN: Element to search for
{
  if (aRoot == NULL)
    return false;                   // Tree is empty.
  else if (el == aRoot->info)
    return true;                    // Target is found.
  else if (el <= aRoot->info)
    return search(aRoot->left, el); // Search left.
  else
    return search(aRoot->right, el); // Search right.
} // search
```

Public member function `search` initiates a search for the tree node with the same key as item `el`, the target item, by calling private member function `search`. Normally, only the key component of `el` would be defined. Member function search implements the recursive search algorithm illustrated in Figure 13.14, beginning at the root of the tree to be searched. The operators `==` and `<` compare the keys of item `el` and the root node in the normal way. Both operators must be defined for type `treeElement`.

Member function `retrieve` (see Programming Exercise 1 at the end of this section) returns the tree element with the same key as `el`. Normally, only the key component of `el` would be defined. Its implementation would be similar to that of `search`. When `retrieve` (like `search`) locates item `el`'s key, use the statements

```
el = aRoot->info;     // Return tree element with same key.
success = true;       // Target is found and retrieved.
```

to return the tree data through `el` (a reference argument) and to indicate the result of the retrieval operation.

Public member function `insert` (see Listing 13.10) calls private member function insert to perform the actual insertion, beginning at the root of the tree receiving the insertion message. Member function `insert` implements the recursive insertion algorithm illustrated in Figure 13.15.

**Listing 13.10** Member functions `insert`

```
// Inserts item el into a binary search tree. (public)
// Pre : el is defined.
// Post: Inserts el if el is not in the tree.
//       Returns true if the insertion is performed.
//       If there is a node with the same key value as el,
//       returns false.
template<class treeElement>
bool binaryTree<treeElement>::insert
  (const treeElement& el)  // IN - item to insert
{
    return insert(root, el);
} // insert

// Inserts item el in the tree pointed to by aRoot. (private)
// Called by public insert.
// Pre : aRoot and el are defined.
// Post: If a node with same key as el is found,
//       returns false. If an empty tree is reached,
//       inserts el as a leaf node and returns true.
template<class treeElement>
bool binaryTree<treeElement>::insert
  (treeNode*& aRoot,                // INOUT : Insertion subtree
   const treeElement& el)           // IN    : Element to insert
{
    / Check for empty tree.
     (aRoot == NULL)
        Attach new node
```

(continued)

**Listing 13.10**   Member functions `insert` (continued)

```
      aRoot = new treeNode;               // Connect aRoot to new node.
      aRoot->left = NULL;                 // Make new node a leaf.
      aRoot->right = NULL;
      aRoot->info = el;                   // Place el in new node.
      return true;
   }
   else if (el == aRoot->info)
      return false;                       // duplicate key found.
   else if (el <= aRoot->info)
      return insert(aRoot->left, el);     // insert left.
   else
      return insert(aRoot->right, el);    // insert right.
} // insert
```

In `insert`, if `aRoot` is NULL, the statements

```
aRoot = new treeNode;       // Connect aRoot to new node.
aRoot->left = NULL;         // Make new node a leaf.
aRoot->right = NULL;
aRoot->info = el;   // Insert el in node pointed to by
                    // aRoot.
```

allocate a new tree node that is pointed to by `aRoot` and store `el`'s data in it. The new node is a leaf node because its pointers are NULL. The node that has `aRoot` as its left or right pointer is the parent of the new node. Figure 13.16 illustrates this for the insertion of 30 in a binary search tree. The right pointer of node 20 is NULL before the insertion takes place.

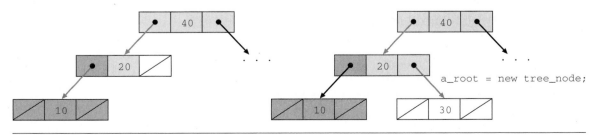

**Figure 13.16**   Inserting a node in a tree

Public member function `display` (Listing 13.11) calls recursive member function `display` (private) to display the tree items in order by key. Private member function `display` assumes that the insertion operator `<<` is defined for type `treeElement` and uses it to display each item.

**Listing 13.11**   Member functions `display`

```
// Displays a binary search tree in key order. (public)
// Pre : none
// Post: Each element of the tree is displayed.
//       Elements are displayed in key order.
template<class treeElement>
void binaryTree<treeElement>::display() const
{
   display(root);
} // display

// (private) Displays the binary search tree pointed to
// by aRoot in key order. Called by display.
// Pre : aRoot is defined.
// Post: displays each node in key order.
template<class treeElement>
void binaryTree<treeElement>::display
   (treeNode *aRoot) const          // IN : Subtree to display
{
   if (aRoot != NULL)
   { // recursive step
     display(aRoot->left);          // display left subtree.
     cout << aRoot->info << endl;    // display root item.
     display(aRoot->right);          // display right subtree.
   }
} // display

// Insert public and private member functions retrieve.
```

## EXERCISES FOR SECTION 13.7

### Self-Check

1. For each reference to function `insert`, how does C++ know which `insert` member function to call?

2. Explain the effect of the program segment below if `myTree` is type `binaryTree` and `treeElement` is type `int`. Draw the tree built by the sequence of insertions. What values would be displayed?

```
binaryTree<int> myTree;
int myData;
bool success;
success = myTree.insert(3000);
success = myTree.insert(2000);
success = myTree.insert(4000);
success = myTree.insert(5000);
success = myTree.insert(2500);
success = myTree.insert(6000);
success = myTree.search(2500);
success = myTree.search(1500);
myData = 6000;
success = myTree.retrieve(myData);
myTree.display();
```

3. Deleting an entry in a binary tree is more difficult than insertion. Given any node in a tree that is to be deleted, what are the three cases for deletion and what must be done in each case? Be sure your approach preserves the binary search tree order.

### Programming

1. Write both member functions `retrieve`.

2. Write a member function that reads a list of data items from a binary file into a binary search tree. Use member function `insert` to place each item where it belongs.

## 13.8   Efficiency of a Binary Search Tree

Searching for a target data value in an array or in a linked list is an $O(N)$ process. This means that the time required to search a list or array increases linearly with the size of the data. Searching a binary search tree can be a much more efficient process. If the left and right subtrees of every node are the exact same size, each move to the left or the right during a search eliminates the nodes of the other subtree from the search process. Since one subtree need not be searched, the number of nodes we do have to search is cut in half in each step. This is a *best-case analysis,* since, in reality, it's unlikely that a binary search tree will have exactly the same number of nodes in the left and right subtrees of each node. Nevertheless, this best-case analysis is useful for showing the power of the binary search tree.

As an example, if $N$ is 1023, it will require searching ten trees ($N = 1023$, 511, 255, 127, 63, 31, 15, 7, 3, 1) to determine that a target is missing. It should require fewer than 10 probes to find a target that is in the tree. The number 1024 is a power of 2 (1024 is 2 raised to the power 10), so searching such a tree is an $O(\log_2 N)$ process ($\log_2 1024$ is 10). (Keep in mind that not all binary search trees will have equal size left and right subtrees!)

Does it matter whether an algorithm is an $O(N)$ process or an $O(\log_2 N)$ process? Table 13.6 evaluates $\log_2 N$ for different values of $N$. A doubling of $N$ causes $\log_2 N$ to increase by only 1. Since $\log_2 N$ increases much more slowly with $N$, the performance of an $O(\log_2 N)$ algorithm isn't as adversely affected by an increase in $N$.

**Table 13.6**    Values of $N$ versus $\log_2 N$

| $N$ | $\log_2 N$ |
| --- | --- |
| 32 | 5 |
| 64 | 6 |
| 128 | 7 |
| 256 | 8 |
| 512 | 9 |
| 1024 | 10 |

## EXERCISES FOR SECTION 13.8

**Self-Check**

1. Given the following binary tree, how many comparisons are needed to find each of the following keys or to determine that the key isn't present? List the keys compared to the target for each search.

    **a.** 50              **b.** 65

    **c.** 55              **d.** 52

    **e.** 10              **f.** 48

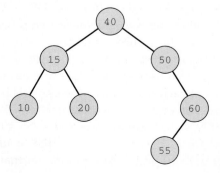

2. Why is it unlikely that a given binary tree will have exactly the same number of elements in the left and right subtrees of every node? For what numbers of nodes is this possible?

3. If the elements of a binary tree are inserted in order, what will the resulting tree look like? What is the big-O notation for searching in this tree?

# 13.9     Common Programming Errors

## Syntax Errors

■ *Misuse of * and ->:* Make sure that you use the dereferencing operator `*` and the member access (with pointer) operator `->` whenever needed. For example, if `p` is a pointer variable pointing to a node defined as a `struct`, then `*p` refers to the whole node and `p->x` refers to the member `x`.

■ *Misuse of* `new` *and* `delete`: The `new` operator allocates storage and returns a pointer. The results should be assigned to a pointer variable having the same type as specified in using the `new` operator. The `delete` operator deallocates storage. It takes a pointer variable as its argument. For example, `p = new node` is correct, but `*p = new node` is not; `delete p` is correct, but `delete *p` is not.

## Run-Time Errors

■ *Missing braces:* There are some typical run-time errors that can occur in writing list traversal code. For example, the `while` loop

```
while (next != NULL)
    cout << next->word;
    next = next->link;
```

will repeatedly display the `word` member of the same node because the pointer assignment statement isn't included in the loop body, so `next` isn't advanced down the list.

■ *NULL pointer reference:* The `while` loop

```
while (next->id != 9999)
    next = next->link;
```

may execute "beyond the last list node" if a node with `id == 9999` isn't found. When `next` becomes `NULL`, you'll get a `NULL pointer reference` run-time error. The statement should be coded as

```
while ((next != NULL) && (next->id != 9999))
   next = next->link;
```

- *Pointers as reference parameters:* If a pointer next is a function parameter that corresponds to a list head pointer, make sure it's a value parameter. Otherwise, the last value assigned to next will be returned as a function result. This may cause you to lose some of the elements originally in the linked list.

- *Heap overflow and underflow:* Problems with heap management can also cause run-time errors. If your program gets stuck in an infinite loop while you're creating a dynamic data structure, it's possible for your program to consume all memory cells on the heap. It's important to check the results of new to make sure it isn't the NULL pointer. If new returns a NULL pointer, all of the cells on the heap have been allocated.

- *Referencing a node on the heap:* Make sure that your program doesn't attempt to reference a list node after the node is returned to the heap. Such an error is difficult to debug because the program may appear to function correctly under some circumstances. Also, returning a node to the heap twice can cause "strange" results on some systems.

## Chapter Review

1. Pointers can be used to reference and connect elements of a dynamic data structure. The new operator allocates additional elements, or nodes, of a dynamic data structure; the delete operator returns memory cells to the storage heap.

2. A linked list is a data structure in which it's easy to insert new elements or delete existing elements. Unlike an array, the existing information in the data structure doesn't have to be moved when performing an insertion or deletion. Instead, we need to redirect the links (pointers) stored in each node of the list.

3. A stack can be implemented as a linked list. A stack is a LIFO (last-in, first-out) structure in which all insertions (push operations) and deletions (pop operations) are done at the list head. Stacks have many varied uses in computer science, including saving argument lists for recursive modules and translation of arithmetic expressions.

4. A queue is a FIFO (first-in, first-out) structure in which insertions are done at one end and deletions (removals) at the other. Queues are used to save lists of items waiting for the same resource (e.g., a printer).

5. A binary tree is a linked data structure in which each node has two pointer fields leading to the node's left and right subtrees. Each node

in the tree belongs to either the left or right subtree of an ancestor node, but it can't be in both subtrees of an ancestor node.

6. A binary search tree is a binary tree in which each node's key is greater than all keys in its left subtree and smaller than all keys in its right subtree. Searching for a key in a binary search tree is an $O(\log_2 N)$ process.

## Quick-Check Exercises

1. Operator _____ allocates storage space for a data object that is referenced through a _____; operator _____ returns the storage space to the _____.

2. When an element is deleted from a linked list represented using pointers, it's automatically returned to the heap. True or false?

3. All pointers to a node that is returned to the heap are automatically reset to NULL so that they can't reference the node returned to the heap. True or false?

4. Why do you need to be wary of passing a list pointer as a reference argument to a function?

5. If a linked list contains three elements with values "Him", "Her", and "It", and h is a pointer to the list head, what is the effect of the following statements? Assume that each node in the list is a struct with data member pronoun and link member next, and that p and q are pointer variables.

```
p = h->next;

p->pronoun = "She";
```

6. Answer Quick-Check Exercise 5 for the following segment:

```
p = h->next;

q = p->next;

p->next = q->next;

delete q;
```

7. Answer Quick-Check Exercise 5 for the following segment:

```
q = h;

h = new node;

h->pronoun = "His";

h->next = q;
```

8. Write a single statement that will place the value NULL in the last node of the three-element list in Quick-Check Exercise 5.

9. Draw the list representation of the following stack:

10. If A, B, and C are inserted in sequence into a stack and a queue, what would be the order of removal for the stack? For the queue?

11. Often computers allow you to type characters ahead of the program's use of them. Should a stack or a queue be used to store these characters?

12. Assume that the left pointer of each node in the tree below is NULL. Is it a binary search tree? What would be displayed by its inorder traversal? Write a sequence for inserting these keys that would create a binary search tree whose NULL pointers were all at the lowest level. Is there more than one such sequence?

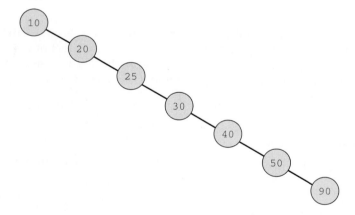

13. If a binary search tree has an inorder traversal of 1, 2, 3, 4, 5, 6, and the root node contains 3 and has 5 as the root of its right subtree, what do we know about the order that numbers were inserted in this tree?

14. What is the relationship between the left child and the right child in a binary search tree? Between the left child and the parent? Between the right child and the parent? Between a parent and all descendants in its left subtree?

## Answers to Quick-Check Exercises

1. new; pointer; `delete`; heap

2. false; `delete` must be called

3. false

4. The value of the actual argument could be advanced down the list as the function executes, changing the value of the pointer that was originally passed to the function, and part of the list will be lost.

5. "`Her`", the pronoun member of the second node, is replaced by "`She`".

6. Detaches the third list element and then deletes it.

7. Inserts a new list value "`His`" at the front of the list.

8. `h->next->next->next = NULL;`

9.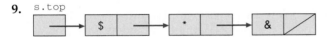

10. for stack: C, B, A; for queue: A, B, C

11. queue

12. yes; 10, 20, 25, 30, 40, 50, 90;

    30, 20, 10, 25, 50, 40, 90; yes

13. 3 was inserted first and 5 was inserted before 4 and 6.

14. left child < parent < right child; parent > all of its descendants

## Review Questions

1. Differentiate between dynamic and nondynamic data structures.

2. Describe a simple linked list. Indicate how the pointers are used to establish a link between nodes. Also indicate any other variables that would be needed to reference the linked list.

3. Give the missing type declarations and show the effect of each of the following statements. What does each do?

```
p = new node;

p->word = "ABC";

p->next = new node;

q = p->next;

q->word = "abc";

q->next = NULL;
```

Assume the following type declarations:

```
struct listNode
{
    string name;
    listNode *next;
};

listNode *theList;
```

4. Write a program segment that places the names Washington, Roosevelt, and Kennedy in successive elements of the list `theList`.

5. Write a program segment to insert the name Eisenhower between Roosevelt and Kennedy in Review Question 4.

6. Write a function to delete all nodes with the data value "`Smith`" from an argument of type `listNode*` as defined in Review Question 4.

7. Write a function `deleteLast` that deletes the last node of `theList` (defined following Review Question 3).

8. Write a function `copyList` that creates a new list that is a copy of another list.

9. Show the effect of each of the operations below on `stack<char> s`. Assume that `y` (type `char`) contains the character `'&'`. What are the final values of `x` and stack `s`? Assume that `s` is initially empty. Show the stack contents after each operation.

```
s.push('+');

x = s.top();

s.pop();

s.push('(');

s.push(y);

x = s.top();

s.pop();
```

10. Write a member function `moveToRear` that moves the element currently at the front of a queue to the rear of the queue. The element that was second in line in the queue will then be at the front of the queue. Use the member functions `push`, `top`, and `pop` from the queue template class.

11. Write a member function `moveToFront` that moves the element currently at the rear of a queue to the front of the queue. Use member functions `push`, `top`, and `pop` from the queue template class.

12. Discuss the differences between a simple linked list and a binary tree. Consider such things as the number of pointer fields per node, search technique, and insertion algorithm.

13. How can you determine if a binary tree node is a leaf?

14. Trace an inorder traversal of the following tree as it would be performed by member function display of class binaryTree.

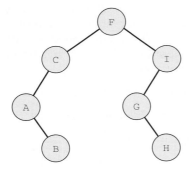

15. What happens when all the elements in a binary search tree are inserted in order? In reverse order? How does this affect the performance of programs that use the tree?

## Programming Projects

1. Write a client program that uses the `queue` class to simulate a typical session for a bank teller. `queueElement` should represent a customer at a bank. Define a class `bankCustomer` that contains the customer's name, transaction type, and amount. Include operators to read and write customers in the class. After every five customers are processed, display the size of the queue and the names of the customers who are waiting. As part of your solution, your program should include functions that correspond to the following function prototypes:

```
// Simulate arrival of a single customer
void arrive
    (queue& waitingLine)              // INOUT
// Simulate departure of a single customer
void depart
```

```
   (queue& waitingLine)              // INOUT
// Display the size and contents of the customer queue
void show
   (const queue& waitingLine);        // IN
```

2. Write a program to monitor the flow of an item into and out of a warehouse. The warehouse will have numerous deliveries and shipments for this item (a widget) during the time covered. A shipment out is billed at a profit of 50 percent over the cost of a widget. Unfortunately, each shipment received may have a different cost associated with it. The accountants for the firm have instituted a last-in, first-out system for filling orders. This means that the newest widgets are the first ones sent out to fill an order. This member function of inventory can be represented using a stack. The push operator will insert a shipment received. The pop operator will delete a shipment out. Input data should consist of the following:

   - S or O: shipment received or an order to be sent

   - amount: the quantity received or shipped out

   - cost: cost per widget (for received shipments only)

   - vendor: a character string that names the company sent to or received from

   For example, the data fragment below indicates that 100 widgets were received from RCA at $10.50 per widget and 50 were shipped to Boeing:

   ```
   S 100 10.50 RCA

   O 50 Boeing
   ```

   Output for an order will consist of the quantity and the total price for all the widgets in the order. (Hint: Each widget price is 50 percent higher than its cost. The widgets to fill an order may come from multiple shipments with different costs.)

3. Write a program that can be used to compile a simple arithmetic expression without parentheses. For example, the expression

   ```
   A + B * C - D
   ```

   should be compiled as shown in the table below.

   | Operation | Operand 1 | Operand 2 | Result |
   | --- | --- | --- | --- |
   | * | B | C | Z |
   | + | A | Z | Y |
   | - | Y | D | X |

The table shows the order in which the operations are performed (*, +, -) and the operands for each operator. The result column gives the name of an identifier (working backward from z) chosen to hold each result. Assume that the operands are the letters A through F and the operators are +, -, *, and /.

Your program should read each character and process it as follows. If the character is a blank, ignore it. If it's an operand, push it onto the operand stack. If the character isn't an operator, display an error message and terminate the program. If it's an operator, compare its precedence with that of the operator on top of the operator stack (* and / have higher precedence than + and -). If the new operator has higher precedence than the one currently on top (or if the operator stack is empty), it should be pushed onto the operator stack. If the new operator has the same or lower precedence, the operator on the top of the operator stack must be evaluated next. You do this by popping the top operator off the operator stack, popping a pair of operands from the operand stack, and writing a new line of the output table. The character selected to hold the result should then be pushed onto the operand stack. Next, the new operator should be compared to the new top of the operator stack. Continue to generate output table lines until the top of the operator stack has lower precedence than does the new operator or until the stack is empty. At this point, push the new operator onto the top of the operator stack and examine the next character in the data string. When the end of the string is reached, pop any remaining operator along with its operand pair as just described. Remember to push the result character onto the operand stack after each table line is generated.

4. A polynomial can be represented as a linked list, where each node contains the coefficient and the exponent of a term of the polynomial. The polynomial

$$4x^3 + 3x^2 - 5$$

would be represented as the linked list shown in Figure 13.17.

Write a class `polynomial` that has operators for creating a polynomial, reading a polynomial, and adding and subtracting a pair of polynomials. (Hint: To add or subtract two polynomials, traverse both lists. If a particular exponent value is present in either one, it should also be present in the result polynomial unless its coefficient is zero.)

**Figure 13.17**

5. Each student in the university takes a different number of courses, so the registrar has decided to use a linked list to store each student's class schedule and an array of structs to represent the whole student body. A portion of this data structure is shown in Figure 13.18.

These data show that the first student (ID 1111) is taking section 1 of CIS120 for three credits and section 2 of HIS1001 for four credits; the second student is not enrolled; and so on. Write a class for this data structure. Provide operators for creating the original array, inserting a student's initial class schedule, adding a course, and dropping a course. Write a menu-driven program that uses the class.

6. The radix sorting algorithm uses an array of queues (numbered 0 through 9) to simulate the operation of a card-sorting machine. The algorithm requires that one pass be made for every digit of the numbers being sorted. For example, a list of three-digit numbers would require three passes through the list. During the first pass, the least significant digit (the ones digit) of each number is examined and the number is added to the rear of the queue whose subscript matches the digit. After the numbers have been processed, the elements of each queue, beginning with q[0], are copied one at a time to the end of an eleventh queue prior to beginning the next pass. Then the process is repeated for the next most significant digit (the tens digit) using the order of the numbers in the eleventh queue. The process is repeated again, using the third most significant digit (the hundreds digit). After the final pass, the eleventh queue will contain the numbers in sorted order. Write a program that implements the radix sort using the queue class.

7. A deque (pronounced "deck") is a double-ended queue—that is, a structure in which elements can be inserted or removed from either end. Write a deque class that is similar to the stack and queue classes.

8. Use a binary search tree to maintain an airline passenger list. Each passenger record should contain the passenger name (record key), class (economy, business, first class), and number of seats. The main program should be menu-driven and allow the user to display the data

**Figure 13.18**

for a particular passenger, and for the entire list, create a list, insert or delete a node, and replace the data for a particular passenger. When deleting a node, simply change the number of assigned seats to zero and leave the passenger's node in the tree.

9. Save each word appearing in a block of text in a binary search tree. Also save the number of occurrences of each word and the line number for each occurrence. Use a stack for the line numbers. After all words have been processed, display each word in alphabetical order. Along with each word, display the number of occurrences and the line number for each occurrence.

10. The fastest binary tree is one that is as close to balanced as possible. However, there is no guarantee that elements will be inserted in the right order. It's possible to build a balanced binary tree if the elements to be inserted are in order in an array. Write a procedure and test program that, given a sorted array of elements, builds a balanced binary tree. Augment the binary tree ADT to count the number of nodes that are searched to find an element and display the number of nodes that are searched to find each item in the tree. (Hint: The root of the tree should be the middle (median) of the array. This project is easier to do if you use recursion.)

11. Write a function that performs an inorder traversal of a binary tree without using recursion. It will be necessary to use a stack. Write a suitable test program for your function.

# ASCII Character Set

The following chart shows the numeric values used to represent each character in the ASCII (American Standard Code for Information Interchange) character set. Only the printable characters are shown. The numeric (ordinal) value for each character is shown in decimal (base 10). For example, in ASCII, the numeric (ordinal) value for 'A' is 65 and the ordinal value for 'z' is 122.

**Table A.1**

| Code | Character | Code | Character | Code | Character | Code | Character |
|------|-----------|------|-----------|------|-----------|------|-----------|
| 0 | *null* | 32 | *space* | 64 | @ | 96 | ` |
| 1 | | 33 | ! | 65 | A | 97 | a |
| 2 | | 34 | " | 66 | B | 98 | b |
| 3 | | 35 | # | 67 | C | 99 | c |
| 4 | | 36 | $ | 68 | D | 100 | d |
| 5 | | 37 | % | 69 | E | 101 | e |
| 6 | | 38 | & | 70 | F | 102 | f |
| 7 | *bell* | 39 | ' | 71 | G | 103 | g |
| 8 | *backspace* | 40 | ( | 72 | H | 104 | h |
| 9 | *tab* | 41 | ) | 73 | I | 105 | i |
| 10 | *line feed* | 42 | * | 74 | J | 106 | j |
| 11 | | 43 | + | 75 | K | 107 | k |
| 12 | *form feed* | 44 | , | 76 | L | 108 | l |
| 13 | *carriage returrn* | 45 | – | 77 | M | 109 | m |
| 14 | | 46 | . | 78 | N | 110 | n |
| 15 | | 47 | / | 79 | O | 111 | o |
| 16 | | 48 | 0 | 80 | P | 112 | p |
| 17 | | 49 | 1 | 81 | Q | 113 | q |
| 18 | | 50 | 2 | 82 | R | 114 | r |
| 19 | | 51 | 3 | 83 | S | 115 | s |
| 20 | | 52 | 4 | 84 | T | 116 | t |
| 21 | | 53 | 5 | 85 | U | 117 | u |
| 22 | | 54 | 6 | 86 | V | 118 | v |
| 23 | | 55 | 7 | 87 | W | 119 | w |
| 24 | | 56 | 8 | 88 | X | 120 | x |
| 25 | | 57 | 9 | 89 | Y | 121 | y |
| 26 | | 58 | : | 90 | Z | 122 | z |
| 27 | *escape* | 59 | ; | 91 | [ | 123 | { |
| 28 | | 60 | < | 92 | \ | 124 | | |
| 29 | | 61 | = | 93 | ] | 125 | } |
| 30 | | 62 | > | 94 | ^ | 126 | ~ |
| 31 | | 63 | ? | 95 | _ | 127 | *delete* |

# Appendix B
# Reserved Words and Special Characters

The following identifiers are reserved for use as C++ language keywords and may not be used except as intended.

| | | | | |
|---|---|---|---|---|
| and | default | inline | pret_cast | typename |
| and_eq | delete | int | return | union |
| asm | do | long | short | unsigned |
| auto | double | mutable | signed | using |
| bitand | dynamic_cast | namespace | sizeof | virtual |
| bitor | else | new | static | void |
| bool | enum | not | static_cast | volatile |
| break | explicit | not_eq | struct | wchar_t |
| case | export | operator | switch | while |
| catch | extern | or | template | xor |
| char | false | or_eq | this | xor_eq |
| class | float | private | throw | |
| compl | for | protected | true | |
| const | friend | public | try | |
| const_cast | goto | register | typedef | |
| continue | if | reinter | typeid | |

## Notes

1. Identifiers containing a double underscore (_ _) are reserved for use by C++ implementations and standard libraries and should be avoided by users.

2. The following characters are used for operators or for punctuation in ASCII representations of C++ programs:

   ```
   !   %   ^   &   *   (   )   -   +   =   {   }   |   ~
   [   ]   \   :   "   ;   '   <   >   ?   ,   .   /
   ```

3. The following character combinations are used as operators in C++ :

   ```
   ->   ++   --   .*   ->*   <<   >>   <=   >=      ==   !=   &&
   ||   *=   /=   %=   +=    -=   <<=  >>=  &=      ^=   |=   ::
   ```

4. The tokens # and ## are used by the C++ preprocessor.

# Appendix C
## Selected C++ Library Facilities[1]

**Appendix C**

| Function Name | Description | Number of Arguments | Type(s) of Arguments | Return Type | Header File | Section Number |
|---|---|---|---|---|---|---|
| abs | Integer absolute value | 1 | int | int | cmath cstdlib | — |
| acos | Arc cosine | 1 | double | double | cmath | 3.2 |
| asin | Arc sine | 1 | double | double | cmath | 3.2 |
| at | Returns character in position i (the argument) in source string object (call using dot notation) | 1 | size_t[2] | char | string | 3.7 |
| atan | Arc tangent | 1 | double | double | cmath | 3.2 |
| atan2 | Arc tangent | 2 | double | double | cmath | 3.2 |
| atoi | Converts character string to an integer | 1 | char*[3] | int | cstdlib | — |
| atol | Converts character string to a long integer | 1 | char* | long int | cstdlib | — |
| atof | Converts character string to a double | 1 | char* | double | cstdlib cmath | — |
| bad | Returns nonzero (true) if designated stream is corrupted and recovery is not likely | 0 | (none) | int | iostream | — |
| ceil | Smallest integer not less than the argument | 1 | double or long double | double or long double | cmath | 3.2 |
| clear | Sets error state of designated stream; argument represents the state to be set | 1 | int | void | iostream | — |
| close | Closes file and disassociates it from stream; flushes buffer | 0 | (none) | returns 0 on error | iostream | 8.1 |
| cos | Cosine | 1 | double | double | cmath | 3.2 |
| cosh | Hyperbolic cosine | 1 | double | double | cmath | — |

(continued)

[1]Libraries that begin with the letter c were originally part of the ANSI standard C library . Some functions listed in this table, particularly those in the fixed length string library cstring, are not discussed in the text.

[2]size_t is an unsigned integer type; it is the type of the result returned by the size_of operator.

[3]Type char* is a pointer to a C-style string.

## Appendix C (continued)

| Function Name | Description | Number of Arguments | Type(s) of Arguments | Return Type | Header File | Section Number |
|---|---|---|---|---|---|---|
| c_str | Returns a C-style string with the same characters as the string it is applied to. C-style strings end with the null character '\0' | 0 | (none) | char* | string | — |
| eof | Returns nonzero (true) if end-of-file has been encountered in designated stream | 0 | (none) | int | iostream | 8.1 |
| erase | Starting at position start (1st argument) in source string remove the next count (2nd argument) characters (call with dot notation). | 2 | size_t size_t | pointer to object modified by remove | string | 3.7 |
| exit | Program termination; same as a return statement in function main (closes files, flushes buffers, etc.); 0 argument usually means successful termination; nonzero indicates an error | 1 | int | void | cstdlib | — |
| exp | Exponential function (calculates e to the x power, where x is the argument) | 1 | double | double | cmath | 3.2 |
| fabs | Double absolute value | 1 | double | double | cmath | 3.2 |
| fail | Returns nonzero (true) if an operation on a stream has failed; recovery still possible and stream still usable once fail condition cleared; also true if bad is true | 0 | (none) | int | iostream | 8.1 |
| find | Returns starting position of string target (the argument) in source string object (call using dot notation). | 1 | string | size_t | string | 3.7 |
| floor | Largest integer not greater than the argument | 1 | double or long double | double or long double | cmath | 3.2 |

(continued)

**Appendix C**    (continued)

| Function Name | Description | Number of Arguments | Type(s) of Arguments | Return Type | Header File | Section Number |
|---|---|---|---|---|---|---|
| get | Single character input (extracts single character from stream and stores it in its argument) | 1 | char | int (zero at eof; else nonzero) | iostream | 8.1 |
| get | String input (reads from designated stream until n–1 characters are extracted or until delimiter is read or eof encountered; null character is placed at end of string; delimiter not extracted but is left in stream); fails only if no characters extracted | 3 | char* int n char delim = '\n' | int (zero at eof; else nonzero) | iostream | — |
| getline | String input (reads from designated stream until n characters extracted or until delimiter is read or end of file encountered; null character is placed at end of string; delimiter removed from stream but is not stored in string) | 3 | char* int n char delim = '\n' | int | iostream | 3.7 |
| ignore | causes the number of characters specified (1st argument) in the input stream object to be ignored. If the delimiter (2nd argument) is encountered first, all characters up to and including the delimiter are ignored. | 2 | size_t | pointer to stream | | 8.4 |
| insert | Inserts new string (2nd argument) at position start (1st argument) in source string (call with dot notation). | 2 | size_t string | pointer to object modified by insert | string | 3.7 |
| isalnum | Checks for alphabetic or base–10 digit character | 1 | char | bool | cctype | 7.3 |
| isalpha | Checks for alphabetic character | 1 | char | bool | cctype | 7.3 |
| iscntrl | Checks for control character (ASCII 0–31 and 127) | 1 | char | bool | cctype | 7.3 |

(continued)

## Appendix C   (continued)

| Function Name | Description | Number of Arguments | Type(s) of Arguments | Return Type | Header File | Section Number |
|---|---|---|---|---|---|---|
| isdigit | Checks for base–10 digit character ('0', '1', '2', ..., '9') | 1 | char | bool | cctype | 7.3 |
| islower | Checks for lowercase letter ('a', ..., 'z') | 1 | char | bool | cctype | 7.3 |
| ispunct | Checks for punctuation character (ispunct is true if iscntrl or isspace are true) | 1 | char | bool | cctype | 7.3 |
| isspace | Checks for white space character (space, tab, carriage return, newline, formfeed, or vertical tab) | 1 | char | bool | cctype | 7.3 |
| isupper | Checks for uppercase letter ('A', ..., 'Z') | 1 | char | bool | cctype | 7.3 |
| length | Returns count of characters in string (call with dot notation) | 0 | (none) | size_t | string | 3.7 |
| log | Natural logarithm (ln) | 1 | double | double | cmath | 3.2 |
| log10 | Base–10 logarithm | 1 | double | double | cmath | 3.2 |
| open | Opens a file given as first argument and associates it with designated stream | varies | char* ... | void | fstream | 8.1 |
| peek | Returns next character in designated stream without extracting it; returns EOF if no character present in stream | 0 | (none) | int | iostream | — |
| pow | Exponentiation; first argument raised to the power of the second | 2 | double | double | cmath | 3.2 |
| precision | Sets the number of significant digits to be used when printing floating-point numbers and returns the previous value | 1 | int n = 6 | int | iomanip | |
| put | Inserts a single character to the designated stream | varies | char | int | iostream | 8.1 |
| random | Pseudo-random number generator; returns an integer between 0 and n–1 | 1 | int n | int | cstdlib | — |

(continued)

## Appendix C   (continued)

| Function Name | Description | Number of Arguments | Type(s) of Arguments | Return Type | Header File | Section Number |
|---|---|---|---|---|---|---|
| replace | Starting at position `start` (1st argument) in source string, replace the next count (2nd argument) characters (call with dot notation). | 3 | `size_t` `size_t` `string` | pointer to object modified by replace | `string` | 3.7 |
| seekg | Moves position of "get" pointer to a file; move is relative either to the beginning, current position, or end of the file | 1 or 2 | `long` `int` | `int` | `iostream` | — |
| setf | Turns on the format flags and returns the previous flags | 1 | `long` `lon(bitflags)` | `long` `lon(bitflags)` | `iomanip` | _ |
| setf | Clears the specified bit field and then turns on the format flags; returns previous flags | 2 | `long` `lon(bitflags)` `long` `lon(bitfield)` | `long` `lon(bitflags)` | `iomanip` | _ |
| setpre- cision | Sets the precision to the argument; the default is 6. | 1 | `int` `lon` | `void` | `iomanip` | 8.5 |
| setwidth | Sets the field width for the next output value to the argument; field width is reset to zero after output. | 1 | `int` | `void` | `iomanip` | 5.3, 8.5 |
| sin | Sine | 1 | `double` | `double` | `cmath` | 3.2 |
| sinh | Hyperbolic sine | 1 | `double` | `double` | `cmath` | — |
| sqrt | Square root | 1 | `double or` `long double` | `double` `long` `double` | `cmath` | 3.2 |
| srand | Random number generator (RNG) seed function; the RNG is reinitialized (to same start point) if the seed is 1; the RNG can be set to a new starting point if any other seed is used | 1 | `unsigned` `int` (the seed) | `void` | `cstdlib` | — |
| strcat | String concatenation (appends a copy of the string pointed to by `from` to the end of the string pointed to by `to`) | 2 | `char*` to `const` `char *from` | `char*` | `cstring` | — |

(continued)

**Appendix C**  (continued)

| Function Name | Description | Number of Arguments | Type(s) of Arguments | Return Type | Header File | Section Number |
|---|---|---|---|---|---|---|
| strchr | Search for first occurrence of character in string (returns pointer to first occurrence if found or the null pointer otherwise); any character may be used as the source character (to be found) | 2 | const char* char | char* | cstring | — |
| strcmp | Lexical string comparison (returns <0, 0, >0 if s1 is less than, equal to, or greater than s2, respectively) | 2 | const char* s1 const char* s2 | int | cstring | — |
| strcpy | String copy (copies the string pointed to by from to the string pointed to by to up to and including the null character) | 2 | char* to const char* from | char* | cstring | — |
| strlen | String length (not counting null character, '\0') | 1 | const char* | size_t[2] | cstring | — |
| strncat | String concatenation of up to lim characters (same as strcat except that a maximum of lim characters are concatenated; the to string is always terminated by '\0') | 3 | char* to const char* from size_t lim | char* | cstring | — |
| strncmp | Lexical string comparison of at most lim characters (same as strcmp except at most lim characters are compared) | 3 | const char* s1 const char* s2 size_t lim | int | cstring | — |
| strncpy | String copy of up to lim characters (see strcpy) padded by '\0' if '\0' is found in from string before lim characters copied | 3 | char* to const char* from size_t lim | char* | cstring | — |
| strpbrk | Searches for first occurrence in s of any character in set; returns pointer to first character in s matched by a character in set | 2 | const char* s const char* set | char* | cstring | — |
| strrchr | Reverse search for first occurrence of character in string (otherwise, same as strchr) | 2 | const char* char | char* | cstring | — |

(continued)

[2]size_t is an unsigned integer type; it is the type of the result returned by the size_of operator.

**Appendix C**   (continued)

| Function Name | Description | Number of Arguments | Type(s) of Arguments | Return Type | Header File | Section Number |
|---|---|---|---|---|---|---|
| strstr | Searches for first occurrence in s1 of the substring s2; returns pointer to start of s2 in s1 or the null pointer if s2 not found in s1 | 2 | const char* s1 const char* s2 | char* | cstring | — |
| system | Calls operating system | 1 | const char* | int | ccstdlib | — |
| tan | Tangent | 1 | double or long double | double long double | cmath | 3.2 |
| tanh | Hyperbolic tangent | 1 | double or long double | double long double | cmath | — |
| time | Returns time measured in seconds since 00:00:00 Greenwich Mean Time, January 1, 1970 | 1 | long int (time_t)  [4] | long int* (time_t*) | ctime | — |
| tolower | Converts uppercase letter to lowercase | 1 | char | char | cctype | 7.3 |
| toupper | Converts lowercase letter to uppercase | 1 | char | char | cctype | 7.3 |
| unsetf | Turns off the format flags and returns the previous flags | 1 | long (bitflags) | long (bitflags) | iomanip | — |
| width | Sets the minimum field width to the given size and returns the previous field width (zero means no minimum); the minimum field width is reset to zero after each insertion or extraction | 1 | int | int | iomanip | — |

[4] time_t is a long int type.

# *Appendix D*
# Operators

Table D.1 shows the precedence of C++ operators discussed in the text. Horizontal lines separate the precedence groups. Operators in the same group have the same precedence. Operators in higher groups have higher precedence than operators in lower groups. All operators are left associative except for unary operators and assignment.

**Table D.1**  Operation Precedence and Associativity

operation
*scope resolution operator: class name* `::` *member*

---

*member selection: object* `.` *member*
*member selection operators: pointer* `->` *member*
*subscripting: array*`[`*expression*`]`
*function call: function*`(`*argument list*`)`
*post increment: variable* `++`
*post decrement: variable* `--`

---

sizeof
*logical not:* `!`
*pre increment* `++`*variable*
*pre decrement:* `--`*variable*
*unary* `+`*; unary* `-`
*address of:* `&` *value*
*dereference:* `*` *expression*
`new`      `delete`      `delete [ ]`
*casts (type conversion)*

---

*member selection: object* `.*` *pointer to member*
*member selection: pointer* `->` *pointer to member*

---

*multiplicative binary operators:* `*`   `/`   `%`

---

*additive binary operators:* `+`   `-`

---

*relational operators:* `<`   `>`   `<=`   `>=`

---

*equality operators:* `==`   `!=`

---

*logical and:* `&&`

---

*logical inclusive or:* `||`

---

*assignment operators:* `=` `+=` `-=` `*=` `/=` `%=`

---

*comma:* `,`

---

In this appendix we introduce *inheritance* and *polymorphism,* which are very powerful features of object-oriented languages such as C++. Inheritance allows us to define new classes by extending and adapting existing classes. The new class *inherits* the characteristics of the *parent class,* and it may extend or adapt these features to meet the specific needs of an application. Several classes may be *derived* in this way from a common parent. Each such class represents a different *specialized adaptation* of the parent class. Whenever an object of a derived class is declared, the data members associated with the parent class can be used in the derived class and member functions of the parent are applicable in the derived class. This is often described by saying that the derived class and the parent are bound by the *is-a* relationship, as in "A circle is a specialization of a shape."

## E.1    Subclassing for Specialization

There are at least a half-dozen forms of inheritance that have been identified. The first form is called *subclassing for specialization.* In this form, we begin with a complete parent class (a working software component) and develop modified or extended child classes (subclasses). The indexed list class first introduced in Section 11.4 provides a good example of the utility of this kind of subclassing. The class template contains several member functions, such as `append`, `insert`, `retrieve`, `remove`, and `getSize`, that could be used in almost any application involving the manipulation of objects of the indexed list data type. The class template also contains several functions that are far less universally used with indexed list objects: `findMin`, `findMax`, `search`, and `sort`.

Subclassing for specialization allows the programmer to begin work by defining a *base* or *parent* class containing the most common attributes (such as the array of elements and the size of the array) and member functions (such as `append`, `insert`, `retrieve`, `remove`, and `getSize`). Once this class has been defined and tested, we *specialize on the class* by adding features (attributes and/or functions) that might be useful in specific applications. A few applications may require the data to be sorted. In other applications it might be useful to be able to compute the sum and average of the data in an indexed list. Applications involving the computation of statistical measures such as the average, standard deviation, range, and median of a collection of numeric values might require sum and average functions combined with functions such as sort, findMin, and findMax.

In each case of specialization, we can use the C++ inheritance feature to *derive* new data types from existing types, adding the required functions, and in some cases, additional attributes (for example, sum and ave). The derivation process requires only that we specify the new attributes and functions, as shown in Listing E.1. The parent class (referred to as indexListBase in Listing E.1) remains as shown in Listing 11.7, but without some of the less commonly used attributes and functions, while the derived class (called indexListSpec) can be specified solely in terms of the added features required for the particular application. We have rewritten the modified specification for class indexListBase; it is the same as class indexList shown in Listing 11.7, but without functions findMin, findMax, search, selSort, read, and display. We also changed the word private (as applied to the class attributes) to protected. We will say more about this change in the display that follows Listing E.1.

**Listing E.1**    Class indexListSpec derived from indexListBase parent class

```
// File:indexListBase.h
// Index list base class

#ifndef INDEX_LIST_BASE_H
#define INDEX_LIST_BASE_H

template <class T, int maxSize>
class indexListBase
{
public:
   // Constructor
   indexListBase();

   // Add an element to the end of an indexed list
   bool append(const T&);        // IN: element appended

   // Insert an element at a specified index.
```

(continued)

**Listing E.1**   Class `indexListSpec` derived from `indexListBase` parent class (continued)

```
   bool insert(int,            // IN: insertion index
            const T&);          // IN: element inserted

   // Retrieve an element at a specified index.
   bool retrieve(int,          // IN: index of element to retrieve
            T&) const;          // OUT: value retrieved

   // Remove (delete) an element at a specified index.
   bool remove(int);           // IN: index of element to be remove

   // Get the current number of data elements in the list.
   int getSize() const;

protected:
   T elements[maxSize];     // Storage for data
   int size:                // Count of number of elements in list
};

#endif   // INDEX_LIST_BASE_H

// File:indexListSpec.h
// Index list class specialized from index list parent
//     Includes sum and average attributes and functions
//     Definition and Implementation

#ifndef INDEX_LIST_SPEC_H
#define INDEX_LIST_SPEC_H

template <class T, int maxSize>
class indexListSpec : public indexListBase
{
public:
   // Public member functions inherited from parent class:
   //     append, insert, retrieve, remove, getSize

   // Constructor
   indexListSpec();

   // Compute sum of all data in the list
   T computeSum();
```

(continued)

**Listing E.1**   Class `indexListSpec` derived from `indexListBase` parent class (continued)

```
// Compute average of all data in the list
T computeAverage();

protected:
// Protected data inherited from parent class:
//    list of data elements and the count of elements in list
T sum;            // sum of the data elements in the list
T ave;            // average of the data elements in the list
};
#endif    // INDEX_LIST_SPEC_H
```

Subclassing for specialization saves considerable programming effort because the features of the parent class do not have to be respecified. Yet we also retain the capability of defining and using classes designed to meet the needs of each application without excess, unused features.

The syntax for defining a derived class is shown in the following display.

---

**Defining a Derived Class**

**Form:**      class *derived* : *access base*
          {  ...  };

**Example:** class circle : public figure
          {  ...  };

**Interpretation:** The class *derived* is derived from the class *base*. The *access* specifier may be **public**, **private**, or **protected**. If it is **public**, then **public** (or **protected**) members of the base class are **public** (or **protected**) in the derived class. If it is **private** or (**protected**), then the **public** and **protected** members of the base class become **private** (or **protected**) members of the derived class. The reserved word **protected** indicates a level of protection between **public** and **private**. Recall that items defined after the reserved word **public** can be accessed by any function and that items defined after the reserved word **private** can be accessed only by member functions of the class in which they are declared. Items defined after the reserved word **protected** are accessible by member functions of both the class in which they are declared and classes derived from this class.

**Note:** Constructors are not inherited. Each declaration of an object of the derived class causes execution of the base class constructor (in this case, for **indexListBase**) before the derived class constructor.

---

## E.2   Subclassing for Specification

In Section 10.6 we constructed a class for the geometric shape of a circle. This class included attributes to represent the $x$ and $y$ coordinates, color, radius, and the area and perimeter of the circle. Then we specified functions for defining the coordinates, radius, and color of a circle, for computing the area and the perimeter of a circle, and for displaying a circle. We also included six accessor functions, one for each of the attributes of a `circle`. The circle class specification is shown in Listing 10.8 and a driver program illustrating how to use this class is given in Listing 10.9.

   We could easily devise classes for other shapes, patterned after the circle class. A similar class for a rectangle might contain the same attributes and functions as for the circle class. We would expect to replace the radius attribute with a pair of attributes representing the height and width of the rectangle. With the corresponding changes in the rectangle class functions (replacing `setRadius` and `getRadius` with similar functions for height and width), we would have the specification for the new class. To obtain a similar class for a square, we would simply substitute the length of the side of the square for the radius of the circle.

   This process of developing a separate class for each figure is workable and leads to the definition of three new data types (`circle`, `rectangle`, and `square`). However, because of the commonality among these three classes, the classes would contain much redundant code. In addition, the manipulation of objects of these new data types requires the use of a different object prefix such as

```
myCircle.computeArea();
myRectangle.computeArea();
mySquare.computeArea();
```

Thus, in any program requiring extensive manipulation of geometric shapes, the required use of separate prefixes for each shape makes the code cumbersome—full of statement sequences that are identical except for the designation of object names. Furthermore, if we wish to add new shapes to the list of those to be manipulated, extensive changes would be required in the user program.

   What we would really like is to find a way to reduce, if not eliminate, the code redundancies in the shapes classes as well as in any program that might use these classes. At the same time, we would like a solution that would enable us to add new shapes to our collection with minimal effort and with as little impact as possible on any program that would use our shapes data types. To realize such a solution, we examine a second form of inheritance, called subclassing for specification.

In *subclassing for specification,* the parent class provides a specification of some attributes as well as a list of the member functions common to all (or most) of the subclasses. However, no description of the behavior of these functions is provided. The purpose of the parent class in subclassing for specification is to describe *what must be done* but not *how the listed tasks are to be carried out.* In this case, the member functions specified in each subclass *override* the member function specifications in the parent class and provide a description of exactly how the task is to be carried out for that particular subclass.

Subclassing for specification is useful in situations where many different subclasses inherit data and function members from a parent and where we would like to have the same function protocol (return and argument types), terminology, and behavior used for the attributes and functions in all of the subclasses. We illustrate subclassing for specification next.

*case study*   Areas and Perimeters of Different Figures

### PROBLEM

We want to be able to process a collection of geometric shapes. We will focus on functions and attributes needed to compute the area and perimeter of these shapes. We also provide functions to display the attribute values of each class and functions that enable the program user to enter in the values of the attributes required to compute the area and perimeter.

### ANALYSIS

Figure E.1 provides a graphical representation of the attributes and operations just described for each of the three classes, `circle`, `square`, and `rectangle`. Recall that the width and height measurements of a rectangle are required to compute its area and perimeter, while the radius and side are required to perform these computations for a circle and a square (respectively).

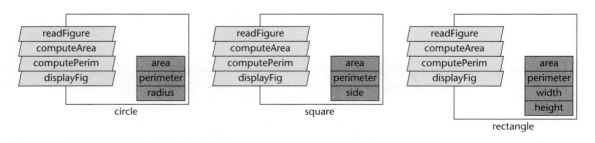

**Figure E.1** The classes `circle`, `square`, and `rectangle`

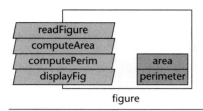

figure

**Figure E.2**    The class `figure`

The subclassing process requires that we be able to abstract the common attributes and functions of these classes into a parent class from which the individual shapes can be derived. From Figure E.1, it is clear that two attributes (area and perimeter) and all four of our functions are common to each class. We can therefore define a class figure that contains the common elements of the three classes as shown in Figure E.2. The member functions in Figure E.2 are shaded. This indicates that while these functions are common to all three figures, the particular implementation details are specific to each kind of figure.

**Listing E.2**    C++ definition of the class `figure`

```
// File: figure.h
// Abstract class figure contains operators and attributes common
//    to all figures.
#ifndef FIGURE_H
#define FIGURE_H

class figure
{
   // Member functions (common to all figures)  ...
   public:
      // Read figure attributes
      virtual void readFigure() = 0;

      // Compute the area
      virtual void computeArea() = 0;

      // Compute the perimeter
      virtual void computePerim() = 0;

      // Compute information about the figure
      virtual void displayFig();
```

(continued)

**Listing E.2**   C++ definition of the class `figure` (continued)

```
    // Attributes common to all figures  ...
    protected:
        float area;                // The area of the figure
        float perimeter;           // The perimeter of the figure
};
#endif       // FIGURE_H
```

Listing E.2 shows the C++ definition of the class `figure`. The reserved word `virtual` that precedes the specifications of the four functions indicates that these *virtual functions* can have different versions for each of the derived classes. When a virtual function is called during execution, the C++ run-time system decides which of the actual (derived class) functions is to be executed.

Function specifications such as

```
    virtual prototype = 0;
```

indicate the declaration of a *pure virtual function*—a virtual function with an undefined body. We use pure virtual functions instead of virtual functions in situations where the steps to be carried out by the function are known only to the derived class, not to the parent. For example, in the shapes problem, we cannot prescribe the computation of the area or perimeter of a figure until we know which figure is involved (the computation of the area of a circle is different from that of a rectangle or a square). The same applies to the function `readFigure`, since it is not possible to know what value(s) need to be read (radius of a circle, length of the side of a square, or the height and width of a rectangle) without knowing which figure is involved. In cases such as these, where there is no other computation to be specified in the function, we leave the body of the function unspecified as shown in Listing E.2. Note that the function `displayFig` is different from the others since the portion of its task

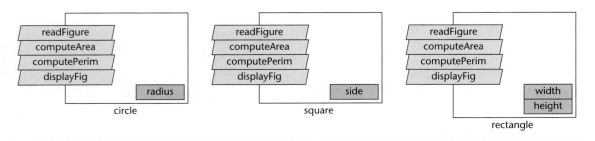

**Figure E.3**   The classes `circle`, `square`, and `rectangle`

**Listing E.3**   The class `circle`

```
// File: circle.h
#ifndef CIRCLE_H
#define CIRCLE_H

#include "figure.h"

// the class circle
class circle : public figure  // a circle is a figure
{
   // Overriding member functions (unique for circles)  ...
   public:
      // Read a circle
      void readFigure();

      // Compute the area of a rectangle
      void computeArea();

      // Compute the perimeter of a rectangle
      void computePerim();

      // Display characteristics unique to rectangles
      void displayFig();

   // Data members (unique to rectangles)  ...
   private:
      float radius;
};
#endif     // CIRCLE_H
```

**Listing E.4**   The class `square`

```
// File: square.h
#ifndef SQUARE_H
#define SQUARE_H

#include "figure.h"

// The class square
class square : public figure      // square is a figure
{

   // Overriding member functions (unique for squares)  ...
   public:
      // Read a square
      void readFigure();
```

(continued)

**Listing E.4** The class **square** (continued)

```cpp
        // Compute area of a square
        void computeArea();

        // Compute perimeter of a square
        void computePerim();

        // Display characteristics unique to squares
        void displayFig();
    // Attributes (unique to squares)  ...
    private:
        float side;                     // length of side of square
};
#endif      // SQUARE_H
```

**Listing E.5** The class rectangle

```cpp
// File: rectangle.h
#ifndef RECTANGLE_H
#define RECTANGLE_H

#include "figure.h"

// the class rectangle
class rectangle : public figure  // a rectangle is a figure
{
    // Overriding member functions (unique for rectangles)  ...
    public:
        // Read a rectangle
        void readFigure();

        // Compute the area of a rectangle
        void computeArea();
        // Compute the perimeter of a rectangle
        void computePerim();

        // Display characteristics unique to rectangles
        void displayFig();

    // Data members (unique to rectangles)  ...
    private:
        float width;                  // width of rectangle
        float height;                 // height of rectangle
};
#endif      // RECTANGLE_H
```

that is common to all derived classes (the display of the area and perimeter of a shape) may be specified in the base class (see Listing E.8).

A class that contains at least one pure virtual function is called an *abstract base class*. Such a class can have no instances; it is used only as the basis for derived classes. An abstract base class, such as the class `figure`, is intended to be used to describe the specification of the attributes and functions common to these derived classes.

Figure E.3 shows unique elements of the classes `circle`, `square`, and `rectangle`. If you overlay each of these on Figure E.2, you will get the full classes as shown in Figure E.1. Listings E.3, E.4, and E.5 show the C++ definitions for each of the classes `circle`, `square`, and `rectangle`, as derived from `figure`.

## DESIGN

Given the parent class `figure` and the derived classes `circle`, `square`, and `rectangle`, we can now design the program for solving the shapes problem. The initial algorithm follows.

**INITIAL ALGORITHM**

1. Determine the type of the figure.

2. Read in the figure characteristics (`readFigure`).

3. Compute the area of the figure (`computeArea`).

4. Compute the perimeter of the figure (`computePerimeter`).

5. Display the complete data for the figure (`displayFig`).

## IMPLEMENTATION

We use the parent class `figure` and the derived classes `circle`, `square`, and `rectangle` as shown in Listings E.2, E.3, E.4, and E.5. These classes contain the member functions required to perform steps 2 through 5.

**CODING THE MAIN FUNCTION**
The `main` function (Listing E.6) declares a variable (`myFig`) of type pointer to `figure`. The function `getFigure` returns a pointer to `figure`. The `main` function `for` loop calls `getFigure`, which carries out Step 1 of the algorithm. Depending upon the input received, the pointer returned by `getFigure` (and stored in `myFig`) will point to a particular kind of figure (`circle`, `square`, or `rectangle`). This object, indicated by `*myFig`, is passed to the function `processFigure` (Listing E.6). The member functions of the class `figure` are called by `processFigure` to perform Steps 2 through 5 of our initial

**Listing E.6**   Figures program main function

```cpp
// File: figuresTest.cpp
// Main program to illustrate the figures class

#include <iostream>
#include <cstddef>
using namespace std;

#include "circle.h"
#include "square.h"
#include "rectangle.h"
#include "figure.h"

// Functions called  ...
// Get the type of figure
figure* getFigure();

// Process one figure
void processFigure
  (figure&);              // INOUT: figure to be processed

int main()
{
   figure* myFig;        // a pointer to a figure

   // Process a selected figure until no more figures selected.
   for (myFig = getFigure(); myFig != 0; myFig = getFigure())
   {
      processFigure(*myFig);
      delete myFig;    // delete this figure
   }

   return 0;
}

// Process one figure
void processFigure
  (figure& fig)              // INOUT: The figure to be processed
{
   fig.readFigure();    // get characteristics of figure
   fig.computeArea();   // compute its area
   fig.computePerim();  // compute its perimeter
   fig.displayFig();    // display characteristics
}
```

algorithm. The `main` function then deletes the object pointed to by `myFig` so that another figure may be defined. The program exits when a zero pointer is returned from `getFigure`. Notice that these functions know only about the class `figure` and not any of the particular figures derived from it; there are simply no references to the derived classes here.

All that remains to be done at this point is to code the function `getFigure`, and the member functions of the classes `figure`, `circle`, `square`, and `rectangle`. The function `getFigure` is shown in Listing E.7. This function prompts for an input character and calls the `new` operator to allocate memory for the particular kind of figure specified. If the letter `x` is input, the

**Listing E.7**   Function `getFigure`

```
// File: figuresTest.cpp (append to Fig. E.9)

// Reads the kind of figure
// Pre: none
// Post: returns a pointer to the type of figure
figure* getFigure()
{
   // local data
   char figChar;   // character indicating figure type

   do
   {
      cout << "Enter the kind of object" << endl;
      cout << "Enter C(Circle), R(Rectangle), or S(Square)"
           << endl;
      cout << "Enter X to exit program" << endl;
      cin >> figChar;
      switch(figChar)
      {
         case 'C': case 'c':
           return new circle;
         case 'R': case 'r':
           return new rectangle;
         case 'S': case 's':
           return new square;
         case 'X': case 'x':
           return 0;
      } // end switch
   } while (true);
}  // end getFigure
```

**Listing E.8**  Implementation of the class `figure`

```cpp
// File: figure.cpp
// Implementation of the base class figure

#include "figure.h"

#include <iostream>
using namespace std;

// Functions readFigure, computeArea, computePerim are pure
// virtual

// Displays the common characteristics of a figure
// Pre:  none
// Post: common characteristics are displayed
void figure::displayFig()
{
   cout << "Area is " << area << endl;
   cout << "Perimeter is " << perimeter << endl;
}  // end displayFig
```

**Listing E.9**  Implementation of the class `circle`

```cpp
// File: circle.cpp
// Implementation of the class circle

#include <iostream>

#include "circle.h"
const float pi = 3.1415927;

// Read data unique to a circle
void circle::readFigure()
{
   cout << "Enter radius > ";
   cin >> radius;
}

// Compute the perimeter (circumference) of a circle
void circle::computePerim()
{
   perimeter = 2.0 * pi * radius;
}
```

(continued)

**Listing E.9**   Implementation of the class `circle` (continued)

```cpp
// Compute the area of a circle
void circle::computeArea()
{
    area = pi * radius * radius;
}


// Display the characteristics of a circle
void circle::displayFig()
{
    // Display the type of figure and its radius.
    cout << "Figure Shape is Circle" << endl;
    cout << "Radius is " << radius << endl;
    // Call the base function to display common
    // characteristics.
    figure::displayFig();
}
```

**Listing E.10**   Implementation of the class `square`

```cpp
// File: square.cpp
// Implementation of the class square

#include <iostream>

#include "square.h"

// Read data unique to a square
void square::readFigure()
{
    cout << "Enter side > ";
    cin >> side;
}

// Compute the perimeter of a square
void square::computePerim()
{
    perimeter = 4.0 * side;
}

// Compute the area of a square
void square::computeArea()
```

(continued)

**Listing E.10**    Implementation of the class `square` (continued)

```cpp
{
   perimeter = 4.0 * side;
}

// Compute the area of a square
void square::computeArea()
{
   area = side * side;
}

// Display the characteristics of a square
void square::displayFig()
{
   // Display the type of figure and its size.
   cout << "Figure shape is Square" << endl;
   cout << "Side is " << side << endl;
   // Call the base function to display common
   // characteristics.
   figure::displayFig();
}
```

**Listing E.11**    Implementation of the class `rectangle`

```cpp
// File: rectangle.cpp
// Implementation of the rectangle class

#include <iostream>
using namespace std;

#include "rectangle.h"

// Read data unique to a rectangle
void rectangle::readFigure()
{
   cout << "Enter width: ";
   cin >> width;
   cout << "Enter height: ";
   cin >> height;
}

// Compute the perimeter of a rectangle
void rectangle::computePerim()
{
```

(continued)

**Listing E.11**  Implementation of the class `rectangle` (continued)

```
    perimeter = 2.0 * (width + height);
}

// Compute the area of a rectangle
void rectangle::computeArea()
{
    area = width * height;
}

// Display the characteristics of a rectangle
void rectangle::displayFig()
{

    // Display the type of figure and its height and width.
    cout << "Figure shape is Rectangle" << endl;
    cout << "Height is " << height << endl;
    cout << "Width is " << width << endl;

    // Call the base function to display common
    // characteristics.
    figure::displayFig();
}
```

function returns a zero pointer to indicate that no figure was specified. If a letter that is not recognized is entered, the function asks for another input.

Listings E.8, E.9, E.10, E.11, and E.12 show the implementations of the classes `figure`, `circle`, `square`, and `rectangle`. With the exception of the function `displayFig`, the functions in the parent class `figure` have little work to do. The function `figure::displayFig` (the function `displayFig` which is a member of the class `figure`) displays the `perimeter` and `area` of a shape, attributes that are common to all of the kinds of figures. The implementation of the other member functions is straightforward. Notice that each class implementation needs to know only about itself and not the other classes. Thus `figure.cpp` needs to include `figure.h`, `circle.cpp` needs to include `circle.h`, and so on, but they do not need to include the definitions for the other classes.

## E.3    Commentary

Without inheritance, we would have to explicitly code the references to each of the member functions of our shapes classes as well as the decisions required to select which functions are to be called (based on the designation of the shape being processed). For example, the simple step of processing one figure, shown in Listing E.6, would be written as shown next (assuming figShape to be of type char):

```
switch (figShape)
{
  case 'c' : case 'C' :
     circle.readFigure();
     circle.computeArea();
     circle.computePerim();
     circle.displayFig();  break;
  case 'r' : case 'R' :
     rectangle.readFigure();
     rectangle.computeArea();
     rectangle.computePerim();
     rectangle.displayFig();  break;
  case 's' : case 'S' :
     square.readFigure();
     square.computeArea();
     square.computePerim();
     square.displayFig();  break;
  default:
     cerr << "Incorrect character for shapes
             designation."
           << "Re-run program." << endl;
}  // end switch
```

Extending this kind of code to include additional figures is not difficult, but it can be a relatively boring, time-consuming, and error-prone exercise.

Compare this with the processFigure function of Listing E.8. This function contains no switch statement. The switch statement is in the function getFigure, and it simply determines which kind of figure is to be created given the user's input. To extend this new version of the figures program for other kinds of figures is very easy. We merely need to define a new class for our new kind of figure and to modify getFigure to recognize an input that designates it. (As an exercise, you might try to extend the figures program to include the figure class rightTriangle. Use the following formulas:

$$area = \frac{1}{2} \, base \times height$$

$$hypotenuse = \sqrt{base^2 + height^2}$$

where *base* and *height* are the two sides that form the right triangle and *hypotenuse* is the side opposite the right angle.)

# E.4  Polymorphism

As illustrated in Listing E.8, a pointer, such as `myFig` or `fig`, to an object of the parent type can point to an object of any of the derived types. Operations such as `computeArea`, which appear in all the derived classes, may be accessed through such a pointer, as in `fig.computeArea()`. The particular `computeArea` function that executes is determined at run-time. This is called *polymorphism* (meaning "many forms").

In this example, we have illustrated one form of polymorphism, known as *overriding through the use of a virtual function.* An overridden function name, such as `computeArea`, is polymorphic in the sense that it can be used to refer to many different functions (five, in our example).

The operator + is also polymorphic; it may be *overloaded.* That is, it can be used to specify integer addition, as in

```
19 + 32
```

or floating-point addition, as in

```
6.1 + 8.8
```

or concatenation, as in

```
firstNameString + " " + lastNameString
```

To the underlying computer, these are three totally distinct operations. To the programmer, + can be viewed as a single operation that allows the use of different types of arguments. The specific underlying computer operation to be performed is determined by the compiler, based upon the operands involved.

The use of inheritance and polymorphism permits us to define a foundation upon which others can build specialized applications. Commercial software vendors provide such foundation classes for a variety of application domains. Two popular domains are in *graphical user interfaces* and in *database management.*

# *Appendix F*
# Using Visual C++

## F.1   Creating a New Project

1. Start Microsoft Visual C++. You will see a screen that looks something like Figure F.1.

2. Select File, New and the screen in Figure F.2 will pop up.

3. Select Win32 Console Application from the list on the left (with tab Projects), type in your project name (HelloWorld) in the text field in the upper right corner, and select OK. You will get the screen in Figure F.3. Select the checkbox "An Empty Project". Press the Finish button and you will get the window in Figure F.4. Press OK and you get the ClassView window on the left of Figure F.5 and the gray screen on the right. Select File, New and you get the window in Figure F.6. Select C++ Source File from the list on the left (with tab Files), type in your file name (HelloWorld), and press OK. You will see the edit window with label HelloWorld.cpp shown in Figure F.7.

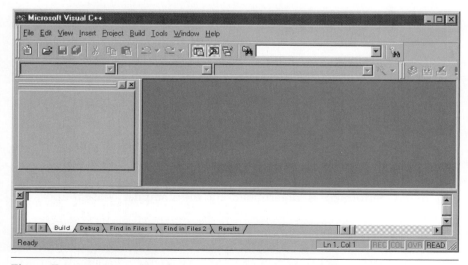

**Figure F.1**

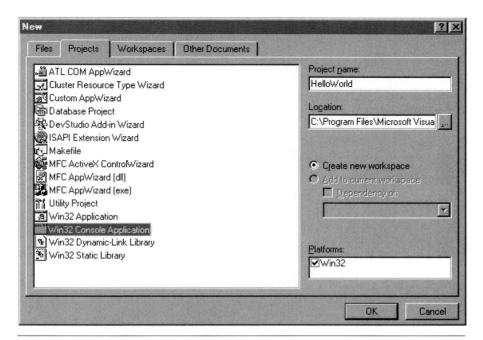

Figure F.2

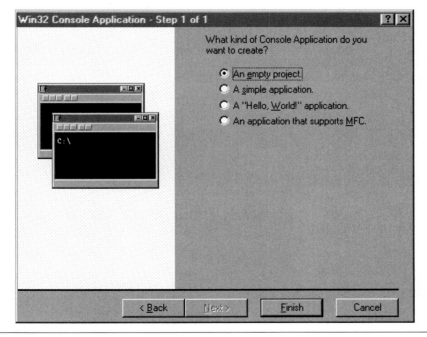

Figure F.3

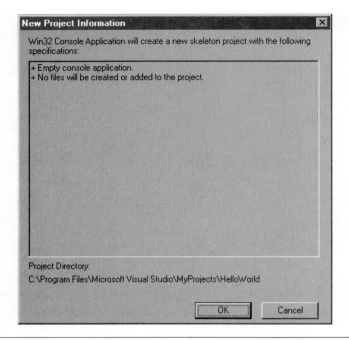

Figure F.4

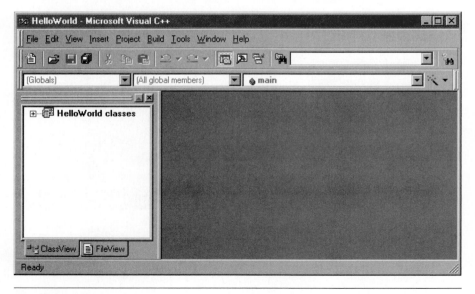

Figure F.5

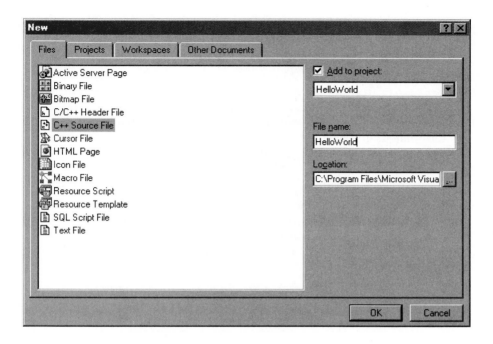

**Figure F.6**

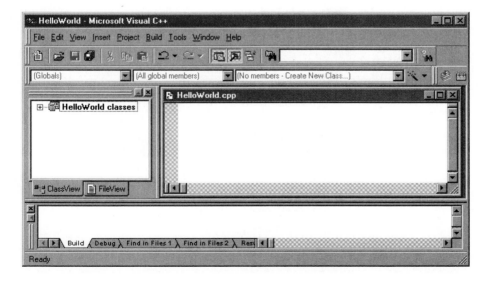

**Figure F.7**

4. Type in your C++ program (Figure F.8). Once you have finished, you can save your program by selecting File, Save or by clicking on the disk icon in the menu bar.

5. To compile and build your program, select Build, Build `Hello-World.exe` from the menu bar. Compiling this program will bring up the error message window shown below the edit window in Figure F.8. The error messages show that the string in the `cout` line is not properly terminated. The newline constant (`endl`) and the semicolon are considered part of the string, so there is no semicolon before the return statement.

6. If you terminate the string properly and select Build, Build `Hello-World.exe` again and then select Build, ! Execute `HelloWorld.cpp` (or just press the icon with the red exclamation point), your program will run and you will see a console window (Figure F.9) with the single output line: `Hello World`. Press any key after you are through examining the program output in the console window.

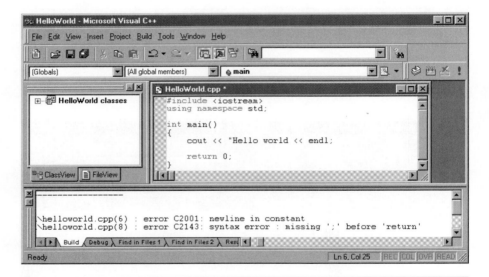

**Figure F.8**

**Figure F.9**

7. To exit from Visual C++, select File, Exit. You may see a dialog window asking you whether you want to save any changes to the program since the last save. Generally you will want to answer Yes.

## F.2   Reopening a Project

To reopen a project at a later date, select File, Open Workspace…and you will see a list of folders. If the one you want is listed, open it and you will see a file with the extension `.dsw` (`HelloWorld.dsw` in Figure F.10). Open that file to open the workspace associated with your project. You will see an edit window containing the original source file.

## F.3   Using the Debugger

Sections 5.9 and 6.5 give general advice about using a debugger that enables you to execute your program incrementally instead of all at once. To use the Visual C++ debugger, select Debug, Start Debug, Step Into. This will cause the debugger to pause before executing the first line of your main function,

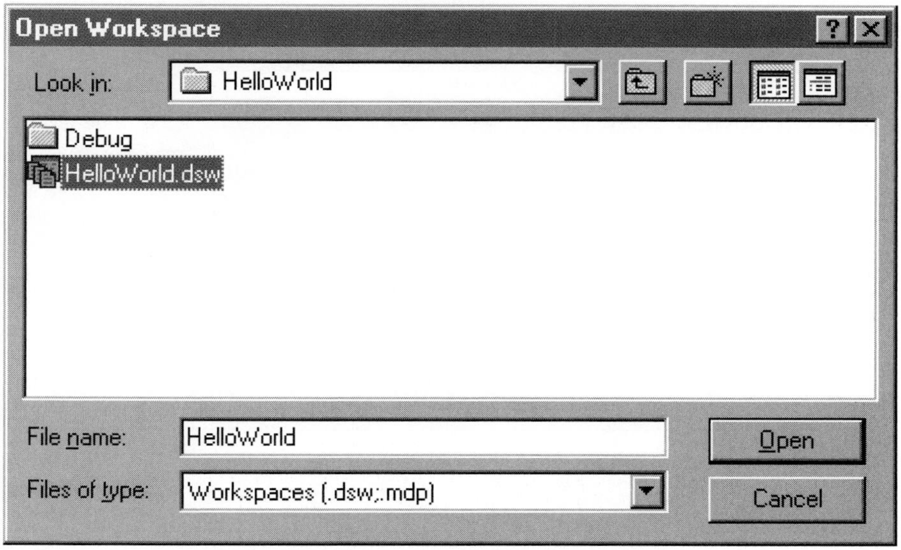

Figure F.10

as indicated by the arrow in the window for file `HelloWorld.cpp` in Figure F.11. The arrow indicates the next statement to execute. At this point you can select any of the four icons appearing in the top row of the menu bar to the right of the arrow. These four icons represent the options Step Into, Step Over, Step Out, and Run to Cursor. You can select Step Over to step over the next statement; i.e., execute it as a unit. This choice executes a function body in a single step. Select Step Into if the next statement is a function call and you want to execute its individual statements one at a time. Unless you are sure you are stepping into your own function, you are better off not selecting Step Into because you may end up tracing a system library function. You can select Step Out to exit from the current function. This is particularly useful if you happen to step into a system function. Alternatively, you can place the cursor at a particular program line and then select Run to Cursor to execute to that line.

The whole purpose of using the debugger is to be able to see the effect of each program statement on your program variables. The name and value of each program variable will appear in the window on the bottom left of your screen (Figure F.12). These values change as you step through your program.

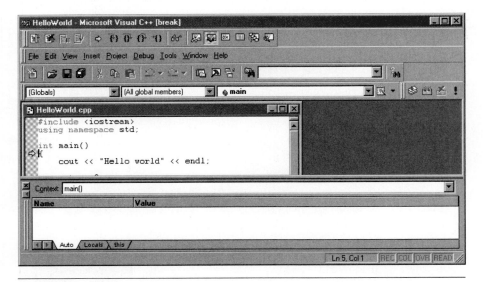

Figure F.11

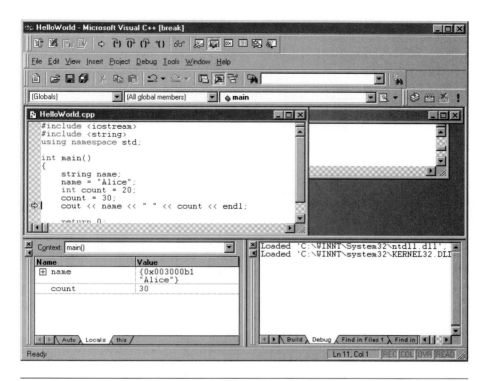

**Figure F.12**

# F.4   Creating Projects with Multiple Files

Visual C++ lets you create projects with multiple files. If you refer back to Figure F.8, you will see a window on the left with a tab called Class View. If you click on the + next to HelloWorld classes, three folders will appear (Source Files, Header Files, and Resource Files). Figure F.13 shows these three folders after the Source File folder has been opened (by clicking on the + next to it). At this point, the only file in the Source Files folder is HelloWorld.cpp. If you want to add one or more .cpp files, choose Select Project, Add Files, and then select a source file to add to your project from the file directory. In a similar manner, you can add header (.h) files to your project. Figure F.14 shows the Source Files and Header Files folders after adding files money.cpp and money.h. You can then Build and Execute the project as before.

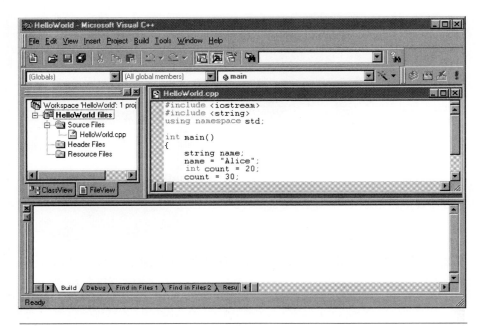

**Figure F.13**

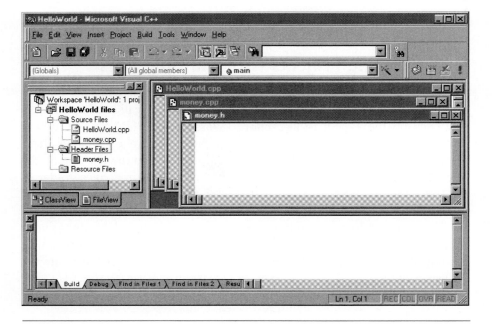

**Figure F.14**

$\mathcal{A}ppendix\ \mathcal{G}$
# Using C++ Builder

## G.1 Creating a New Project

1. Start C++ Builder. You will see a screen that looks something like Figure G.1.
2. Select File, New and the screen in Figure G.2 will pop up.

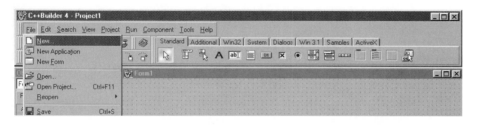

**Figure G.1**

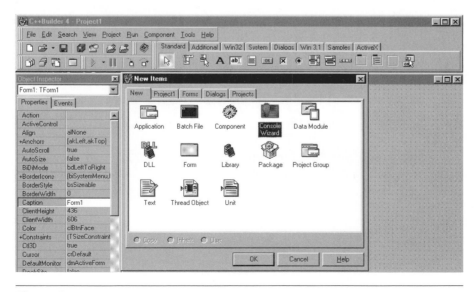

**Figure G.2**

3. Double-click on Console Wizard and you will get the screen in Figure G.3. The checkboxes Console and EXE should be selected. Press the Finish button and you will get an edit window (Figure G.4).

4. You should delete the lines shown in this window before you begin typing in your C++ program (Figure G.4). Once you have finished, you can save your program by selecting File, and Save As. The File name you type in will be used as the project name. For example, if you enter `HelloWorld.bpr`, the project file will be saved as `HelloWorld.bpr` and the edit window will be saved as `HelloWorld.cpp` (your C++ program).

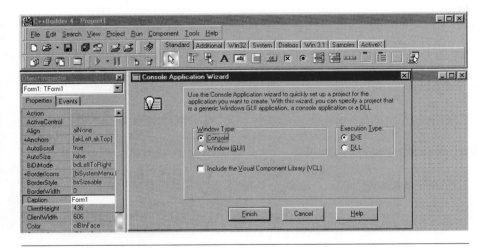

**Figure G.3**

**Figure G.4**

Figure G.5

5. To compile, build, and execute your program, select Run from the top menu bar. Compiling this program will bring up an error message window below the edit window in Figure G.5. This error message window will show that the string in the `cout` line is not properly terminated.

6. If you terminate the string properly and select run again, you will see a console window with the single output line: `Hello World`. You can press <Shift> Print Scrn to print the contents of the console window.

7. To exit from CBuilder, select File, Exit. You may see a dialog window asking you whether you want to save any changes to the program since the last save. Generally you will want to answer Yes.

## G.2   Viewing the Console Window before Exiting Your Program

The console window is interactive and it will show all prompts and data that you type in as your program executes. Unfortunately, when the function `return` statement executes, the console window disappears instantaneously. For this reason, we include the Borland C++ library `conio` (console io) in the program shown in Figure G.5. Just before the function return, we call the `getch` method in this library to keep the Console window displayed so that we can read it and print it. The `getch` function returns the next character typed at the keyboard. As soon as you enter a character, the `return` statement will execute and the console window will disappear.

## G.3    Reopening a Project

To reopen a project at a later date, select File, Reopen and you will see a list of previous projects. If the one you want is listed, highlight it and it will be reopened. Another way to open a project is to select File, Open, which will show you all projects in the Projects subdirectory.

## G.4    Using the Debugger

Sections 5.9 and 6.5 give general advice about using a debugger that enables you to execute your program incrementally instead of all at once. To use the C++ Builder degugger, select Run, Step Over (Figure G.6). This will cause the debugger to pause before executing the first line of your `main` function, as indicated by the arrow and highlight bar in Figure G.7. At this point you can select any of the choices from the Run menu (Figure G.6). You can select Step Over (which executes a function body in a single step) or Trace Into (which allows you to execute individual lines of a function). Unless you are sure you are tracing into your own function, you are better off not selecting Trace Into because you may end up tracing a system library function. You can Trace to the next source line (shown by the dots in Figure G.7). You can place the cursor at a particular program line and then select Run to the cursor to execute to that line.

The whole purpose of using the debugger is to be able to see the effect of each program statement on your program variables. Begin by placing variables you want to trace in the Watch window. To add a variable to the Watch window, double-click on the variable name somewhere in the pro-

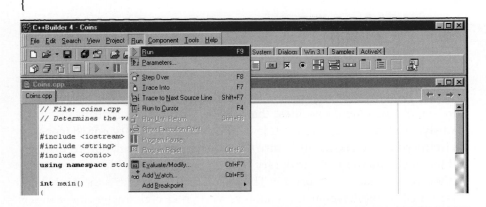

Figure G.6

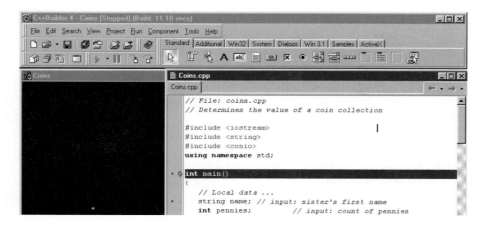

**Figure G.7**

gram. Then select Add Watch from the Run menu. This pops up the dialog box shown in Figure G.8. Press OK to add variable `nickels` to the Watch window (the window to the left of the Edit window). As you step through your program, the values shown for the Watch window variables (`name`, `pennies`, and `nickels`) will be updated (see Figure G.9). The Watch window shows the values read into `name` and `nickels`; the value of `pennies` is about to be read.

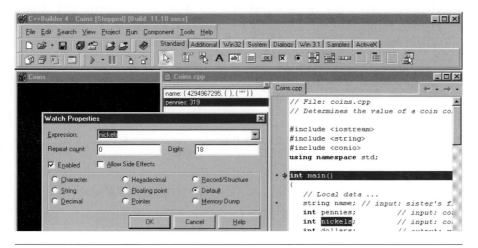

**Figure G.8**

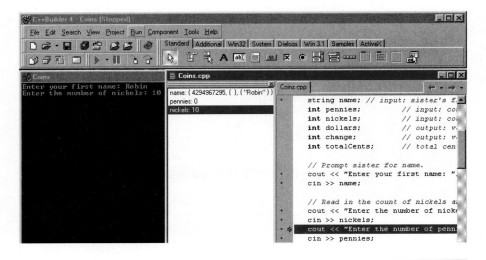

**Figure G.9**

## G.5    Creating Projects with Multiple Files

C++ Builder lets you create projects with multiple files. Figure G.10 shows the Project Manager Window (left) for project `moneyTest` (Select View, Project Manager). Currently there is just one file in the project, `moneyTest.cpp`. To add the file `money.cpp`, select Add to Project from the Project menu or click on the icon with the + symbol under Project in the menu bar. Then select `money.cpp` from the list of files shown. You may need to go to another directory if `money.cpp` is not in the same directory as your main program. Figure G.11 shows the Project Manager Window after `money.cpp` is added.

The Edit window in Figure G.10 shows the main function for the project. Notice that it contains the two lines

```
#pragma hdrstop
#include <condefs>
```

You must insert these compiler directives in the main source file of a C++ Builder multiple file project.

In Figure G.11, the edit window contains two new lines that were inserted by C++ Builder after file `money.cpp` was added to the project:

```
USEUNIT("money.cpp");
//-------------------------------------------------
```

The first line instructs the compiler to use file `money.cpp` in this project.

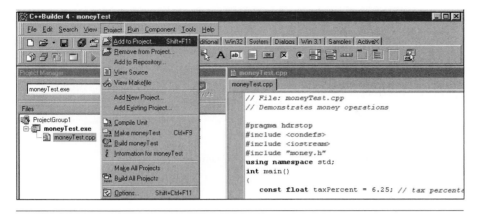

**Figure G.10**

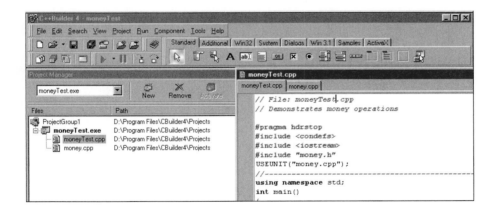

**Figure G.11**

# Answers to Odd Numbered Exercises

## Chapter 1
### Section 1.1

1. microcomputers

   minicomputers

   mainframes and supercomputers

3. The first electronic digital computer was designed in the late 1930s by Dr. John Atanasoff and Clifford Berry. J. Presper Eckert and John Mauchley designed the ENIAC—the earliest, large-scale general-purpose electronic digital computer. The basis for the modern digital computer is credited to Von Neumann, who proposed the stored-program computer.

### Section 1.2

1. cell 1 contains `354`

   cell 998 contains `x`

3. bit, byte, ROM, RAM, floppy disk, zip disk, hard disk

5. The Internet.

7. While it is being typed, a letter may be stored in main memory or RAM. After it is finished, the letter will be stored on a secondary storage device. Usually this will be the computer's hard disk, but it may be stored on a floppy disk or zip disk too. A software package that you purchase is installed on the hard disk. Very large files that are no longer needed would also go on a secondary storage device, but probably not the hard disk.

9. `354 + (-26)` or `328`

### Section 1.3

1. a. Store the difference of `gross` and `net` in `profit`.

   b. Multiply `1.8` times `celsius`, add `32`, and store the sum in `fahren`.

   c. Store `percent` divided by `100.0` in `fraction`.

   d. Store `sum` plus `x` in `sum`.

e. Add the product of `oldPrincipal` times `interest` to `oldPrincipal`. Store the sum in newPrincipal. Another way to say this is: add `interest` to `1.0`. Multiply `oldPrincipal` by this sum. Store the result in `newPrincipal`.

3. Methods are operations that can be performed on an object's data.

5. An abstraction is a computer representation or model of an object or concept. For example, a fraction consists of a numerator and a denominator, both of which are integers. Two fractions can be added, multiplied, etc.

### Section 1.4

1. Syntax errors are found in source files or source programs. The compiler would find any syntax errors. Syntax errors can be corrected by going back to the word processor or to the editor window in an Integrated Development Environment.

3. It is possible that certain programming environments may leave the source program in memory instead of saving it to a disk. A source program could be lost if it is not explicitly saved to disk after every modification, before attempting to run it.

### Section 1.5

1. The five steps/stages of the software development method are:

Problem specification

Problem analysis

Program design

Program implementation

Program testing

3. If an error occurs and you haven't saved your program file on disk, you could lose it if you need to stop running the IDE in order to recover from the error.

### Section 1.6

Algorithm

1. Get the distance in kilometers.

2. Convert the distance to miles.

3. The distance in miles is .621 times the distance in kilometers.

4. Display the distance in miles.

## Section 1.7

1. You might do this in order to preemptively protect against viruses. Hopefully, people that you know will not send you a virus.

# Chapter 2
## Section 2.1

1. The characters kms; are part of the comment and they should not be. Anything after /* and before */ is ignored by the compiler.

```
float miles,      // input:  distance in miles
   kms;           // output: distance in kilometers
```

3. The variable declarations tell the compiler how to allocate storage. Executable statements are translated into machine language. Compiler directives, comments, and using namespace statements are not translated into machine language.

## Section 2.2

1. C++ reserved words can't be used as identifiers.

3. C++ reserved words:      `float, return`
   Valid Identifiers:       `var, so_is_this, cout, xyz123, Bill,`
                            `thisIsLong, under_score, rate,`
                            `include, start`
   Invalid Identifiers:     `x=y*z, Prog#2, hyphen-ate, 123xyz,`
                            `"hello", 'a'`

## Section 2.3

1. Predefined types are built into the language. Class types are defined in class libraries or by the programmer. Predefined types have data stores that are variables; class types have data stores that are objects. A string is a class type.

3. a.  `0.0345`

      `3456000`

      `345678`

   b.  `5.678E3 or 5.678e3`

      `5.6789E2 or 5.6789e2`

      `5.67E-3 or 5.67e-3`

5. The area of a circle would be a `float`. The number of cars passing through an intersection in an hour would be an `int`. A name would be stored in a `string` variable. The first letter of a last name would be stored in a `char`.

7. The first declaration stores the character 'r' in the variable `color` which is of data type `char`. The second declaration stores the literal string "r" in the variable `colors` which is of class type `string`.

## Section 2.4

1. Enter two numbers: *3.0 5.0*    (data entered in italics)

   a = -2

   b = -10

   Note: This assumes a and b are declared as type `double` or `float`.

3. My name is: Doe, Jane

   I live in Ann Arbor, MI and my zip code is 48109

## Section 2.5

1. /* This is a comment?   */

   /* This one */

   /* seems like a comment */

   /* doesn't it */

## Section 2.6

1. 7 15 2 5

3. m = (m / n) * n + (m % n)

   m = 45      n = 5

   45 = (45 / 5) * 5 + (45 % 5)

   45 = 9 * 5 + 0

5. a.  i = a % b;                i is assigned 3

   b.  i = (MAX_I - 990 / a);    i is assigned 3

   c.  i = a % y;                invalid: y must be type int

   d.  i = (990 - MAX_I) / a;    i is assigned $-3$

   e.  i = pi * a;               i is assigned 9

   f.  x = pi * y;               x is assigned $-3.14159$

   g.  x = pi / y;               x is assigned $-3.14159$

   h.  i = (MAX_I - 990) % a     i is assigned 1

i.   `x = a % (a / b);`                 runtime error: cannot divide by 0

j.   `i = a % 0;`                        runtime error: cannot divide by 0

k.   `i = b / 0;`                        runtime error: cannot divide by 0

l.   `i = a % (MAX_I - 990)`            i is assigned 3

m.  `x = a / y;`                        i is assigned $-3.0$

n.   `i = a % (990 - MAX_I);`          system dependent, $-3$ or 3

o.   `x = a / b;`                        x is assigned 0

7. a.   `white = color * 2.5 / purple;`        white is assigned
                                                  1.66667

   b.   `green = color / purple;`               green is assigned
                                                  0.666667

   c.   `orange = color / red;`                 orange is assigned 0

   d.   `blue = (color + straw) / (crayon + 0.3);` blue is assigned
                                                      $-3$

   e.   `lime = red / color + red % color;`     lime is assigned 2

   f.   `purple = straw / red * color;`         purple is assigned 0

## Section 2.7

1.  In interactive programs, the `cout` line just before the `cin` line is used to prompt the user to enter input. In a batch program, there is no need for this prompt because the data items are obtained from a batch data file. In a batch file, after the `cin` line, the `cout` line is used to echo the data. This lets the user know what data values were read.  Input data is provided to an interactive program through the standard input stream (`cin`) or the console; input is provided to a batch program through a batch data file.

# Chapter 3
## Section 3.1

1.  Problem Output

```
float numGallons        //gallons of gas purchased
float milesPerGallon     //amount of gas used up every mile
```

Problem Input

```
float miles              //miles the car can drive
float gasCost            //final gas bill
float costPerGallon      //cost of a gallon of gas
```

Formulas

| number of miles | = number of gallons x miles per gallon |
|---|---|
| cost of gas | = number of gallons x cost per gallon |

Initial Algorithm

1. Get the number of gallons.

2. Get the miles per gallon.

3. Get the cost of a gallon

4. Compute the number of miles.

5. Compute the gas cost.

6. Display the number of miles and gas cost.

Algorithm Refinements

4.1 Assign `numGallons * milesPerGallon` to `miles`

5.1 Assign `numGallons * costPerGallon` to `gasCost`

3. Problem Input

```
float tripDistance        //miles traveled during the trip
float milesPerGallon      //amount of gas used up every mile
float costPerGallon       //cost of a gallon of gas
```

Problem Output

```
float tripCost            //total cost of the trip
```

Formula

number of gallons = distance of trip / miles per gallon

cost of gas          = number of gallons x cost per gallon

Initial Algorithm

1. Get the distance of the trip.

2. Get miles per gallon.

3. Get average cost of a gallon.

4. Compute the total cost of the trip.

5. Display total cost of the trip.

Program variable

```
float numGallons        //number of gallons
```

Algorithm Refinements

4.1 Assign `tripDistance / milesPerGallon` to `numGallons`

4.2 `Assign numGallons * costPerGallon` to `tripCost`

## Section 3.2

1. a. `sqrt(u + v) * w * w`

   b. `log(pow(x,y))`

   c. `sqrt(pow(x-y, 3))`

   d. `fabs((a/c)- (w*z))`

## Section 3.3

1.

3. Program design.

## Section 3.4

1. Prints the 5 by 5 letter O.

   After a line space, prints the 5 by 5 letter H.

   Three lines are skipped.

   Prints the 5 by 5 letter H.

   Prints the 5 by 5 letter I.

   After a line space, prints the 5 by 5 letter M.

3. Neither. The functions execute in the order in which they are called by the main function or by another function that is called by the main function.

## Section 3.5

1. a. `778.0`    b. `18.8495`    c. `12.5664`    d. `7.85397`

3. Function arguments are used to pass information between the separate modules of a program and between the main function and its modules. Arguments make it easier for a function to be reused by other functions or programs. Functions with arguments are building blocks for constructing larger programs.

## Section 3.6

1.

| Name | Visible in scale | Visible in main |
|------|------------------|-----------------|
| scale | yes | yes |
| main | yes | yes |
| num1 | no | yes |
| num2 | no | yes |
| x (float parameter) | yes | no |
| n (int parameter) | yes | no |
| scaleFactor | yes | no |

## Section 3.7

1. line 1:    The variable name is declared as type `string`.

   line 2:    The prompt `name:` is displayed. We type `Jones***John Boy`

   line 3:    The literal that was typed, excluding the newline character, is stored in name.

   line 4:    name is searched until the group `***` is found. The position of the first item in this group is stored in the variable `start`, which is 5.

   line 5: 3    characters of the string are erased, the first is the character at the position indicated by `start`, and the second and third are the characters that come after that. This method call results in the literal `***` being erased and everything after `***` is shifted to the left to fill in the empty space.

   line 6:    A `", "` is inserted into the string at position 5. The characters starting with the second letter `J`, which was previously at position 5, are shifted to the right by one position.

   line 7:    The modified contents in name is displayed: *Jones, John Boy*.

3. `wholeName = lastName + ", " + firstName;`

# Chapter 4
## Section 4.2

1. x = 15.0, y = 10.0

   | | |
   |---|---|
   | x != y | true |
   | x < y | false |
   | x >= (y − x) | true |
   | x == (y+x-y) | true |

   a. Either x must be < 5.1 or x must be >= 5.1 so one of those conditions must be true and the result will be true regardless of the values of x and y.

   b. If q is false, then both p && q and q && r must be false, so the result is false.

3. a. Either x must be < 5.1 or x must be >= 5.1 so one of those conditions must be true and the result will be true regardless of the values of x and y.

   b. If q is false, then both p && q and q && r must be false, so the result is false.

## Section 4.3

1. a. for x = 10 the output is:

      less

      done

      for x = 20 the output is:

      done

   b. O.K.

3. a. "the" is located at position 8 (value of posTarget) and is replaced by "that". testString becomes "Here is that string".

   b. "Here" is located at position 0 (value of posTarget) and replaced by "There". testString becomes "There is the string".

   c. "Where" is not located so the condition involving posTarget is false and the error message is displayed.

### Section 4.4

```
1. if (x > y)
   {
      x = x + 10.0;
      cout << "x bigger than y" << endl;
   }
   else
   {
      y = y + 10.0;
      cout << "x smaller than y" << endl;
   }
   cout << "x is " << x
            << "y is " << y << endl;
```
3. Placing braces around the last two lines in the answer to Question 1 would cause the value of y to be displayed only when x <= y is true.

### Section 4.5

1. Program is more readable and easier to modify.
3. We would have to change only the definition for the constant DUES (new value 25) defined in the main function.

### Section 4.6

1. hours is 41, rate is 5.0. Replace Step 3.1.4 in Table 4.9 with steps 3.1.1, 3.1.2, 3.1.3. gross will be 205.0 and net will be 190.0.

### Section 4.7

1.

| Statement Part | salary | tax | Effect |
|---|---|---|---|
|  | 135000.00 | ? |  |
| if (salary < 0.0) |  |  |  |
| else if (salary < 15000.00) |  |  | 135000.00 < 0.0 is false. |
| else if (salary < 30000.00) |  |  | 135000.00 < 15000.00 is false |
| else if (salary < 50000.00) |  |  | 135000.00 < 30000.00 is false. |
| else if (salary < 80000.00) |  |  | 135000.00 < 50000.00 is false. |
| else if (salary < 150000.00) |  |  | 135000.00 < 80000.00 is false. |
| else if (salary < 150000.00) |  |  | 135000.00 < 150000.00 is true. |
| tax = (salary - 80000.00) |  |  | tax evaluates to 55000.00. |
|    * .25 |  |  | tax evaluates to 13750.00. |
|    + 14250.00 |  | 28000.00 | tax evaluates to 28000.00. |

3. a. There would be a division by zero error without short-circuit evalua-tion (y / x). With short circuit-evaluation, the value would be false. Because (x > 10) && . . . is false, evaluation would stop.

   b. There would be a division by zero error without short-circuit evalua-tion (x / (y − 7)). With short circuit-evaluation, the value would be true. Because (x <= 10) || . . . is true, evaluation would stop.

## Section 4.8

1. ```
   red
   blue
   yellow

   switch (color)
   {
       case 'R': case 'r':
         cout << "red" << endl;
          break;
       case 'B': case 'b':
         cout << "blue" << endl;
          break;
       case 'Y': case 'y':
          cout << "yellow" << endl;
       default:
          cout << "color not determined"
          break;
               << endl;
   }
   ```

3. In Section 4.7, the selection is determined based on a sizable range of values rather than a specific value. With the switch statement, selection is based on a single value or a small, easily listable set of values.

5. Logic error, a wattage of 25 would also be assigned a value of 1000.

## Chapter 5
### Section 5.1

1. a.  The loop will repeat forever (infinite loop), since countEmp remains 0.

   b.  Since countEmp is undefined, the results cannot be predicted.

3. 024681012*** 30
   ```

5. Repetition #1 outputs 9.

   Repetition #2 outputs 81.

## Section 5.2

1.

| Data Value | Data Value | Data Value |
|---|---|---|
| 5 | 6 | 7 |
| Output | Output | Output |
| 1 | 1 | 1 |
| 5 | 6 | 7 |
| 25 | 36 | 49 |
| 125 | 216 | 1296 |
| 625 | 1296 | 2401 |

This loop displays $x^0$ through $x^4$ for every x entered by the user.

3. The segment should read:

```
count = 0;
sum = 0;
while (count < 5)
{
    cout << "Enter data item: ";
    cin >> item;
    sum += item;
    count++;
}
cout << count << " data items were added" << endl;
cout << "their sum is " << sum << endl;
```

## Section 5.3

1. 1, 1

   3, 4

   5, 9

   7, 16

   9, 25

   Sum of positive odd numbers less than 10 is 25

3. a.  Nothing would be displayed because –5 is less than 10.  The loop body will not execute.

   b.  `Celsius`

      `-5`

      `0`

      `5`

      `10`

   c.  `Celsius`

      `-5`

      `5`

   d.  Nothing would be displayed because 5 is less than 10.  The loop body will not execute.

5. `++i;`
   `--j;`
   `n = i * j;`
   `m = i + j;`
   `j--;`
   `p = i + j;`

7.
| i | j | Output |
|---|---|--------|
| 5 | 10 | 5, 10 |
| 4 | 8 | 4, 8 |
| 3 | 6 | 3, 6 |
| 2 | 4 | 2, 4 |
| 1 | 2 | 1, 2 |

## Section 5.4

1. `supply = 990.0`

3. `Enter initial oil supply: 5000`
   `Enter amount used today: 4000.5`
   `After removal of 4000.5 gallons,`
   `number of gallons left is 999.5.`

   `999.5 gallons left in tank.`
   `Warning - amount of oil left is below minimum!`

5.

| n | n >0 && pow(2,n) < 1000 | Output |
|---|---|---|
| 5 | true | 5, 32 |
| 4 | true | 4, 16 |
| 10 | false | |

------------------------------------------------

The while loop exit occurs and —5 is not read in

## Section 5.5

1. The first score would not be included in the sum but the sentinel would be.

3. a.   The loop would repeat forever, since `digitRead` remains false.

   b.   `nextChar = '2'` Both relational expressions are true.

   `nextChar = 'a'` The first relational expression is true but the second is false.

   c.   `if (('0' <= nextChar) && (nextChar <= '9'))`
   `        digitRead = true;`
   `else`
   `        digitRead = false;`

## Section 5.6

1. Output

   10
   8
   6
   4
   2

3. `const int SENTINEL = 'Q';`
   `int count = 0;`
   `do`
   `{`
   `       . . .`
   `     count++;`
   `} while(toupper(choice) != SENTINEL || count < 10);`

**Section 5.7**

1. Output
    a.  5
        10
        15
        20
        25
        30
        35
        40
        45
        50

    b.
```
for (num = 5; num <= 50; num += 5)
{
    cout << num << endl;
}
```
    c.  num = 5;
        do
        {
            cout << num << endl;
            num += 5;
        } while (num <= 50);

3. The `do-while` loop should be used only in situations where it is certain that the loop should execute at least once. It can be used in data entry loops when you know at least one data item will always be entered.

**Section 5.8**

1. 100 times. 10 times.

    The addition table could be printed by modifying the statement within the inner loop to

```
cout << setw(3) << (rowVal + colVal);
```

3. 
```
Outer   0
  Inner   0   0
  Inner   0   1
  Inner   0   2
  Inner   0   0
Outer   1
  Inner   1   0
  Inner   1   1
  Inner   1   2
  Inner   1   1
  Inner   1   0
```

## Section 5.9

1. 
```
sum = 0;
cout << "Enter " << n << " integers and press return:"
    << endl;
for (int count = 0; count <= n; count++)
{
   cout << "count " << count << endl;      // debug
   cin >> item;
   sum += item;
   cout << "sum " << sum << endl;      // debug
} // end for
```
The addition of these debug statements should show that the loop has an "off by 1" error. The prompt is requesting n data items. The loop is expecting n+1 data items. This can be corrected by changing the relational operator from <= to <.

# Chapter 6
## Section 6.1

1. `test(m, -63, y, x, next);`

| Actual Argument | Formal Parameter | Description |
|---|---|---|
| m | a | int, value |
| -63 | b | int, value |
| y | c | float, reference |
| x | d | float, reference |
| next | e | char, reference |

```
test(35, m*10, y, x, next);
```

| Actual Argument | Formal Parameter | Description |
|---|---|---|
| 35 | a | int, value |
| m * 10 | b | int, value |
| y | c | float, reference |
| x | d | float, reference |
| next | e | char, reference |

```
test(m, m, x, m, 'a');
```

Not correct because the fourth parameter should be type `int`. It should also be a variable, not a character literal.

3. Invalid function calls:

   e.   must use variable for call by reference

   g.   a, b not declared in `main`

   i.   must use variable for call by reference

   k.   too many arguments

Calls requiring standard conversion:

   a.   value of `z` is converted to `int`

   d.   float value returned to `m` is converted to `int`. If `m` is used as INOUT, initial value of `m` is converted to `float`.

   j.   value of `x` is converted to `int`

## Section 6.2

1. a.

| x | y | z | w |
|---|---|---|---|
| 5 | 3 | 7 | 9 |
| 5 | 3 | 8 | 2 |
| 5 | 3 | -2 | 8 |
| -2 | 8 | -2 | 8 |
| -10 | 6 | -2 | 8 |

   b.   `sumDiff` computes the sum and difference of its first two arguments and places the answers in its third and fourth parameters. The input parameters cannot be modified, but `sumDiff` changes the value of the output parameters, which are passed by reference.

   c.
```
// Pre:    num1 and num2 are defined.
// Post:   num3 and num4 contain the sum and difference
//         of num1 and num2.
```

### Section 6.3

1.

```
// Pre:          numItems and sum are defined; numItems must be > 0.0
// Post:         If numItems is positive, the average (variable ave) is
//               computed as sum / numItems;  otherwise ave is set to 0.0
// Returns:      The average (variable ave) if numItems is positive;
//               otherwise variable ave is set to 0.0
void computeAve (int numItems,       // IN: number of data items
                 float sum,          // IN: sum of data
                 float & ave)        // OUT: average of data
{
   if (numItems < 1)
   {
      cout << "Invalid value for numItems = " << numItems << endl;
      cout << "Average not computed." << endl;
      ave = 0.0;
   } //endif
   else
      ave = sum / float (numItems);
} // end computeAve
```

The solution is not as good because a function that computes a single value should return that value as its result (by executing a return statement).

3.

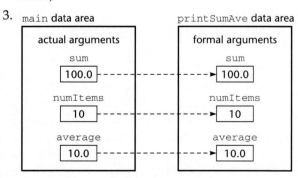

5. 1.   Read the number of items

   2.   while the number of items is <= 0

      3.   Display an error message

      4.   Read the number of items.

## Section 6.4

1.

| Statement | posComma | Effect |
|---|---|---|
| `moneyToNumberString` | | `moneyToNumberString` is passed |
| `(string& "-$5,405,123.65")` | | `"-$5,405,123.65"` by reference |
| `if (moneyString.at(0) == '$')` | | value is false |
| `else if (moneyString.find("-$") == 0)` | | value is true |
| `moneyString.erase(1, 1);` | | removes the `-$` |
| `posComma = moneyString.find(",");` | 2 | `posComma` is assigned 2 |
| `while (posComma >= 0 &&` | | loop while `posComma >= 0` and |
| `posComma < moneyString.length())` | | `<` the length of `moneyString` |
| `moneyString.erase(2, 1);` | | removes the first comma |
| `posComma = moneyString.find(",");` | 5 | `posComma` is assigned 5 |
| `moneyString.erase(5, 1);` | | removes the second comma |
| `posComma = moneyString.find(",");` | >=11 | there are no more commas in `moneyString` |

## Section 6.5

1. ```
Enter the number of items to be processed: 10
Function computeSum entered
The number of items is 10
The sum of the data is 100.00
The average of the data is 10.00
```

3. Black-box testing assumes the tester has no knowledge of the system code. The tester must enter representative data sets and check the correctness of the output for each input sample. White-box testing assumes the tester knows how the system is coded. The tester must provide a data set for each possible execution path. Top-down testing involves testing the flow of control between a main function and its subordinate functions, possibly using stubs for the functions that are not yet completed. Bottom-up testing involves testing each individual function separately as it is completed. Unit testing is the process of thoroughly testing each individual function to be part of a system. System integration testing is the process of putting the system together and testing the entire system after all unit testing has been performed.
```

## Section 6.6

1. mystery(5, 3) -> 5 * mystery(5, 2) -> 5 * (5 * mystery(5, 1)).

   The result would be $5^3$. The function raises its first argument to the power indicated by its second argument.

# Chapter 7
## Section 7.1

1. const int MAXINT = 32767;   valid

   const int MININT = -MAXINT; valid, MININT is -32767

   const char FIRST_FEMALE = "Eve"; invalid char constant

   const int MAX_SIZE = 50.5;   invalid int constant

   const int MIN_SIZE = maxsize - 10; invalid expression

   const int ID = "4FD6"; invalid int constant

   const int KOFFMAN_AGE = 57;   valid

   const int FRIEDMAN_AGE = z56; invalid int constant

   const float PRICE = $3,335.50; invalid float constant

   const float PRICE = 3335.50;      valid

   const float PRICE = "3335.50";    invalid float constant

3. The difference between the #define and the const declaration is that the identifier used in the #define has no storage associated with it. The #define is a compiler directive that tells the compiler to replace one string of characters with another everywhere the first string of characters appears in the source file. Using a const declaration involves placing the constant value in a storage location. The contents of this storage location cannot be changed during program execution.

## Section 7.2

1. $2^{15} - 1$ (32767)

3. For `x = 6.875` the result is `6.88`.
   For `x = -6.875` the result is `−6.87`.

```
if  (x >= 0)
    x = float(int(x * 100 + 0.5)) / 100.0;
else
    x = float(int(x * 100 - 0.5)) / 100.0;
```

## Section 7.3

1. Note it is not really necessary to know the ASCII code. Each of these answers can be determined without using the actual code values.

   a. `int('d') - int('a')`
      `100 - 97 = 3`

   b. `char((int('M') - int('A')) + int('a'))`
      `char((77-65) + 97)`
      `char(109) = 'm'`

   c. `int('7') - int('0')`
      `55 - 48 = 7`

   d. `char(int('5') + 1)`
      `char(53 + 1)`
      `char(54) = '6'`

3.

|     |                        | Type | Value | Explanation |
|-----|------------------------|------|-------|-------------|
| a.  | `isdigit('a');`        | int  | false | `'a'` is not the character representation of a digit. |
| b.  | `isdigit('7');`        | int  | true  | `'7'` is the character representation of a digit. |
| c.  | `isdigit(9);`          | int  | false | 9 is not the character representation of a digit |
| d.  | `toupper('#');`        | char | `'#'` | `'#'` is not a letter. |
| e.  | `tolower('A');`        | char | `'a'` | `'A'` is uppercase; returns corresponding lowercase. |
| f.  | `tolower('p');`        | char | `'p'` | `'p'` is lowercase. |
| g.  | `digitToNumber('0')`   | int  | 0     | Returns the number corresponding to `'0'` |

### Section 7.4

1.    Condition                                Complement

a.    `x <= y && x == 25`                        `x > y || x != 25`

b.    `(x > y && x != 15) || z <= 7`            `(x <= y || x == 15) && z > 7`

c.    `x != 15 || z == 7 && x <= y`             `x == 15 && (z != 7 || x > y)`

d.    `flag || !(x != 15)`                      `!flag && x != 15`

e.    `!flag && x > 8`                          `flag || x <= 8`

3. The loop keeps asking for a number until a number between 1 and 10 inclusive is entered.

When the loop is exits, the value entered that made `inRange()` return true, is retained in n.

The condition at the end of the loop can be written as (`!inRange(n, 1, 10)`)

### Section 7.5

1. The enumerator `red` has value 0, green has value 1, yellow has value 2, and blue has value 3.

The type `day` enumerators have values `0, 1, 2, . . . , 6`. The type `specialChars` enumerators have values `'\b', '\a', '\n', '\r', '\t', '\v'` (8, 7, 10, 13, 9, 11).

3. a. `enum logical {true, false};` invalid: `true` and `false` are values of type `bool`.

b. `enum letters {A, B, C};` valid
   `enum twoletters {A, B};` invalid: an identifier may not be used more than once in any enumeration within the same scope of definition.

c. `enum day {sun, mon, tue, wed, thu, fri, sat};` valid
   `enum weekDay {mon, tue, wed, thu, fri};` invalid: see reason in Part b above

   `enum weekEnd {sat, sun};` invalid: see reason in Part b above

d. `enum trafficLight {red, yellow, green};` valid
   `int green;` invalid: see reason in Part b above

# Chapter 8

## Section 8.1

1. `cin >> next;` skips over white space. Any blank characters in the input would not be counted. The while loop wouldn't terminate on newlines.

3. `cin >> n >> n >> x >> c >> c >> c >> c >> n >> c;`

5. If the innermost `cin.get` were omitted, the program would execute forever as no new data characters would be read.

## Section 8.2

1. The `e` is read in the loop in function `copyLine`. It is written to the output file. The `s` is read next and written to the output file. The `.` is read next and written to the output file. The `<nwln>` is read next, causing loop exit. `<nwln>` is written to the output file. Control passes back to main. `lineCount` is incremented. Since end-of-file is true, the loop in `main` is exited. Statistics are displayed on the screen, files are closed, and execution is terminated.

3. Some advantages of using external (permanent) files for program input and output are as follows:

   a. The input data can be reused without being reentered. This is especially helpful while you are debugging your program.

   b. The input information can be printed and examined as often as needed.

   c. The output information can be used as input data for another program.

## Section 8.3

1. a. Leading blanks are ignored when each employee's first name is read so they cause no problem.

   b. Blank lines in the middle of the data stream would cause no problem because they would be skipped when reading the next employee's first name. A blank line at the end would cause the while loop to execute an extra time.

3. `getline(eds, name, '\n');`

   `eds >> hours >> rate;`

   or if you wanted to read data into `firstName` and `lastName`:

   `getline(eds, firstName, ' ');`

   `getLine(eds, lastName, '\n');`

   `eds >> hours >> rate;`

### Section 8.4

1. To write the name and salary on separate lines use the following statement:

   `pds << name << endl << salary << endl;`

3. This statement extracts and ignores (skips) all characters in the input stream through the next '*' character. If there are more than 80 characters before the next '*' character, it will only skip the first 80 characters.

### Section 8.5

1. `#####15.99#####13.45`   (# represents a space character)

3. `Jane#############Doe`   (# represents a space character)

## Chapter 9

### Section 9.1

1. `x3` is a simple variable. A single value is associated with this single memory location. `x[3]` is a part of a collection of variables, called an array, all having the same data type. An array is a structured variable. `x[3]` refers to the fourth element in this array.

3. a. `string names[100];`

   b. `float checks[20];`

   c. `bool madeBonus[7];`

### Section 9.2

1. a. Each time the body of the loop is executed, the value of `i` is displayed followed by a space and the value in array `x` at index `i`, squared, followed by a comma. This is done 10 times (from 9 down to 0).

b. The loop displays elements with even subscripts (0,2,...,8). There is a single space between values.

3. a. `enum logical {true, false};`  invalid: `true` and `false` are values of type `bool`.

b. `enum letters {A, B, C};`  valid

`enum twoletters {A, B};`  invalid: an identifier may not be used more than once in any enumeration within the same scope of definition.

c. `enum day {sun, mon, tue, wed, thu, fri, sat};`  valid

`enum weekDay {mon, tue, wed, thu, fri};`  invalid: see reason in Part b above

`enum weekEnd {sat, sun};`  invalid: see reason in Part b above

d. `enum trafficLight {red, yellow, green};`  valid

`int green;`  invalid: see reason in Part b above

## Section 9.3

1. `size—1`.

3.
```
   // Pre: a1, a2 are defined.
   // Post: contents of a1 are exchanged with the contents of a2.
   int exchange
       (int& a1,          // item to exchange with a2
        int& a2)          // item to exchange with a1
   {
       int temp;          // stores (saves) contents of a1 prior to moving
                          // contents of a2 into a1

       temp = a1;
       a1 = a2;
       a2 = temp;
   } // end exchange

   // Pre:  a[i] and b[i] (0 <= i <= size-1) are assigned values.
   // Post: Returns true if a[i] == b[i] for all i in range 0 through
   // size-1; otherwise returns false.        int sameArray
       (const int a[],    // IN: char array to be compared to array b
        const int b[],    // IN: char array to be compared to array a
        const int size)   // IN: size of the arrays
   {
       for (int i = 0;
         i < size — 1 && a[i] == b[i];
         i++);

       return a[i] == b[i];

   } // end sameArray
```

### Section 9.4

1. In readScores, the int array scores must be changed to float. Local data SENTINEL and tempScore must be changed from int to float.

3. The number of scores to read could be different from MAX_SIZE (the declared size), so the function should read this number into section-Size from the data file and compare it to MAX_SIZE. If it is larger than MAX_SIZE, reset sectionSize to MAX_SIZE and display a warning that only MAX_SIZE scores can be read – the rest will be ignored. This is all to be done before the while-loop. If sectionSize is smaller or less than MAX_SIZE then execute the while-loop. The value for sectionSize should be the first value in the data file and should be the only value on the first line.

### Section 9.5

1. a. The array subscript of the last item is returned to the calling function.

   b. The array subscript of the first item matching target is returned to the calling function.

3. We could use a function findIndexOfMax to arrange the data items in the array in descending order. We should also change the variable minSub to maxSub to improve readability.

5. Before the call to the function exchange, we could check to see if min-Sub == i. Call exchange only if these two values are not equal.

```
if (i != minSub)
    exchange(items[minSub], items[i]);
```

This if-statement always increases the number of comparisons by 1 for each pass but can decrease the number of exchanges.

### Section 9.6

1. a. Executes $n$ times for each $i$, or $n^2$ times; $O(n^2)$.

   b. Executes 2 times for each $i$, or $2n$ times; $O(n)$.

   c. Executes $n$ times for each $i$, or $n^2$ times; $O(n^2)$.

### Section 9.7

1. The value of the rate component of organist is multiplied by 2.

## Section 9.8

1. a. Accesses the `stuName` component of `aStudent`.

   b. Accesses the first character of the `stuName` component of `aStudent`.

   c. invalid, `examStats` is a type, not a variable.

   d. invalid, `scores[2]` is the last one.

   e. The last score of `aStudent`.

   g. invalid, `examStats` is a type, not a variable.

   g. Copies each member of `bStudent` into `aStudent`.

   h. Assigns the ASCII code for `bStudent.grade` ( type `char`) to `aStudent.score` (type `int`).

3. 
```cpp
void printEmployee (const employee& oneEmployee)
{
    cout << "Name: " << oneEmployee.name << endl;
    cout << "ID: " << oneEmployee.id << endl;
    cout << "Gender: " << oneEmployee.gender << endl;
    cout << "# of Dependents " << oneEmployee.numDepend << endl;
    cout << "Hourly rate:    " << oneEmployee.rate << endl;
}
```

To call this function to display an Employee struct, simply state:

```cpp
printEmployee(oneEmployee);
```

## Section 9.9

1. a. 
```cpp
char dayName[] = "Sunday";
cout << "length is " << strlen(dayName);
```

   b. 
```cpp
char monthName[10];
strcpy(monthName, "February");
```

   c. 
```cpp
string fName = "data.txt";
aStream.open(fName.c_str());
```

   d. 
```cpp
string year = "2004";
int yearN = atoi(year.c_str());  yearN++;
```

   e. 
```cpp
char initial[4];
initial[0] = 'E';  initial[1] = 'B';
initial[2] = 'K';  initial[3] = '\n';
```

# Chapter 10
## Section 10.1

1. These are all member functions of class counter. To call them, we must associate them with a particular object of this class using dot notation.

3. a.  `counter c1(20);`

   b.  `c1.setCount(15);`

   c.  `c1.decrement();`

   d.  `c1.decrement();`

   e.  `decrement();`

## Section 10.2

1. The scope resolution operator `::` is used as a prefix to the function name in each member function header. This operator tells the compiler that the scope of the function name and of the identifiers appearing in the function is the class that precedes the operator `::`.

3. The constructors are used to initialize the data members of a new object of the class type. The argument of the second constructor can be used to set the initial state of the new object. The compiler can determine which overloaded constructor function to use based on the presence or absence of an actual argument.

## Section 10.3

1. `counts[2].setCount(5);`

   `cout << counts[4].getCount();`

## Section 10.4

1. 1, −1

**Section 10.5**

1.

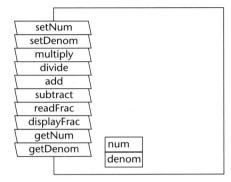

3. Replace the body of function `subtract` with `return`

`f1.add(f2.negate());`. This statement uses method `negate` to negate fraction `f2` and then adds this result to fraction `f1` using function `add`.

**Section 10.6**

1.

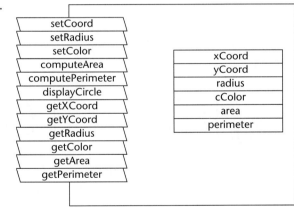

3. To form a rectangle class, substitute the attributes `width` and `length` (type `float`) for the attribute `radius`. Replace member function `setRadius` with `setDimensions`. The function `setDimensions` would have two arguments, representing the width and length of a rectangle. Replace member function `getRadius` with two accessor functions: `getWidth` and `getLength`. Replace `displayCircle` with `displayRectangle`. The bodies of the new member functions would process the new attributes. Functions `computeArea` and `computePerimeter` would do the calculations for a rectangle instead of a circle. The five member functions that set and retrieve the object's coordinates and color would be unchanged.

### Section 10.7

1. It does store the leading blanks. One way to change it would be to use the extraction operator >> to get the first character only instead of function get.

3. Since the driver function is a client program, the details of the class simpleString are to be hidden from the driver function, while the member function writeString has access to the class' data members. So the for loop in the driver function uses the public member function getLength, while the for loop in the member function writeString uses length.

### Section 10.8

1. Each account has a unique id number and the id number must be specified as part of the deposit transaction. Unless the user enters the wrong id number, it would not be possible to place a deposit intended for one account in the other account.

## Chapter 11

### Section 11.1

1. a.  45

   b.  cout << matrix[2][3];

   c.  matrix[8][4]

   d.  matrix[4][2] or

   matrix[MAX_ROW/2][MAX_COL/2]

3. The compiler can compute the offset of any element from the first knowing just the size of the second and third dimensions. The array element order is sales[0][0][0] . . . sales[0][0][11], sales[0][1][0] . . . sales[0][1][11] . . . sales[0][4][0] . . . sales[0][4][11]. Then the same sequence for the first subscript 1, the first subscript 2 . . . the first subscript 9. The last element is sales[9][4][11]. The offset for sales[i][j][k] is computed by the formula

$$\text{offset} = i \times 5 \times 12 + j \times 12 + k$$

For the last element this gives $9 \times 60 + 4 \times 12 + 11$ or 599.

## Section 11.2

1. a. gender attribute of second employee
   b. invalid
   c. the last employee (a struct)
   d. invalid
   e. invalid
   f. invalid
   g. the last employee's name
   h. invalid

3. a. `company[0].name`
   b. `company[1].id`
   c. `company[1].name`
   d. `company[0].id`

## Section 11.3

1. ```
   dummy<float> a, b, c;
   float num1, num2, n1, n2, sum;
   cout << "Enter two numbers: ";
   cin >> num1 >> num2;
   ```
   a. `setItem(num1);`
   b. `setItem(num2);`
   c. ```
      setItem(a.getItem() + b.getItem());
      sum = c.getItem();
      cout << sum << endl;
      ```

## Section 11.4

1. array attribute `smallList.elements` has room for 5 `float` values.

   `smallList.size` is 0.

   contents of `elements` is 3.5, `smallList.size` is 1

   contents of `elements` is 3.5, 5.7, `smallList.size` is 2

   contents of `elements` is 5.7, smallList.size is 1

   display 5.7, `elements` and size are not changed.

   contents of `elements` is 15.5, `smallList.size` is 1

contents of `elements` is 15.5, 5.5, `smallList.size` is 2

display 1, index of 5.5.

contents of `elements` is 5.5, 15.5, `smallList.size` is 2

display array `elements`: 5.5, 15.5, smallList.size is 2.

### Section 11.5

1. It returns the count of array elements that are larger than the array element they follow. For example, if elements contains 3.5, 5.6, 4.6, 7.7, the value returned would be 2 because 5.6 and 7.7 are larger than the array element they follow.

### Section 11.6

1. The compiler determines which class a member function belongs to by the type of object it is applied to.

### Section 11.7

1. In the definition of friend operator >>, all three occurrences of operators << and >> in the body have a stream as the left operand and a string object as the right operand. C++ has defined >> and << for stream and string objects.

```
cout << "Enter name: ";         // << defined in iostream class
getline(ins, dE.name, '\n');   // getline defined in string, iostream class
cout << "Enter number: ";      // << defined in iostream class
ins >> dE.number;              // >> defined in string, iostream class
```

3. `fraction operator * (const fraction&, const fraction&);`

### Section 11.8

1.

| Statment | Effect |
| --- | --- |
| vector<char> s(10); | Creates a character vector of size 10. |
| s[0] = 'a'; | Inserts 'a' at the beginning of vector; s.size() is 1 |
| s[9] = 'z'; | Inserts 'z' at the end of vector; s.size() is 10 |
| Everything in between s[0] and s[9] is NULL. | |
| s.push_back('$'); | Inserts '$' at position 10 of the vector. s.size() is 11. |

```
for(int i = 0; i < s.size();          Will display the line below with 8 spaces
                                      in middle.
        i++) cout << s.at(i);         a z      $


char ch1 = s.front();                 ch1 = 'a'
char ch2 = s.back();                  ch2 = '$'
cout << ch1 << "***"
<< ch2 << endl;                       a***$
```

# Chapter 12
## Section 12.1

1. Raise 6 to the power of 3
   Subproblems generated by 1.
       1.1  Raise 6 to the power of 2.
       1.2  Multiply the result of 1.1 by 6.
   Subproblems generated by 1.1
       1.1.1 Raise 6 to the power of 1.
       1.1.2  Multiply the result of 1.1.1 by 6.
2. Raise 3 to the power of 6
   Subproblems generated by 2.
       2.1 Raise 3 to the power of 5.
       2.2 Multiply the result of 2.1 by 3.
   Subproblems generated by 2.1
       2.1.1 Raise 3 to the power of 4.
       2.1.2 Multiply the result of 2.1.1 by 3
           Subproblems generated by 2.1.1
           2.1.1.1 Raise 3 to the power of 3.
           2.1.1.2 Multiply the result of 2.1.1.1 by 3
               Subproblems generated by 2.1.1.1
               2.1.1.1.1 Raise 3 to the power of 2
               2.1.1.1.2 Multiply the result of 2.1.1.1.1 by 3
                   Subproblems generated by 2.1.1.1.1
                   2.1.1.1.1.1 Raise 3 to the power of 1
                   2.1.1.1.1.2 Multiply the result of 2.1.1.1.1.1 by 3

### Section 12.2

1. Each call to the recursive function displays an entry display before calling the function `power` recursively (until n <= 1). The first exit display is displayed after the stopping case is reached, `power(8, 1)`. The return to the second activation frame is followed by displaying the exit display for `power(8, 2)`. The return to the first activation frame is followed by displaying the exit display for `power(8, 3)`.

3. `power(5, 4)`
   m is 5
   n is 4
   4 <= 1 is false
   answer = m * power(5, 3)
   return answer

   `power(5, 3)`
   m is 5
   n is 3
   3 <= 1 is false
   answer = m * power(5, 2)
   return answer

   `power(5, 2)`
   m is 5
   n is 2
   2 <= 1 is false
   answer = m * power(5, 1)
   return answer

   `power(5, 1)`
   m is 5
   n is 1
   1 <= 1 is true
   answer = m
   return answer

Contents of stacks after each recursive call to `power`:

| power(5, 4) | | power(5, 3) | | power(5, 2) | | power(5, 1) | |
|---|---|---|---|---|---|---|---|
| m | n | m | n | m | n | m | n |
| 5 | 4 | 5 | 3 | 5 | 2 | 5 | 1 |
|   |   | 5 | 4 | 5 | 3 | 5 | 2 |
|   |   |   |   | 5 | 4 | 5 | 3 |
|   |   |   |   |   |   | 5 | 4 |

## Section 12.3

1. 
```
float powerRaiser(int base, int power)
{
    if (base == 0)
          return 0;
    else if (power == 0)
          return 1;
    else if  (power < 0)
          return 1.0 / base;
    else
          return base * powerRaiser(base, power - 1);
}
```

3. If the stopping condition for the Fibonacci number function were just (n == 1), the function would call itself indefinitely. This occurs because not testing for (n == 2) allows n to become less than the stopping value of 1, for example, n − 2 = 0 when n is 2. Since the stopping value of 1 is passed over and can never be reached, 2 is continually subtracted from n, and the function continues indefinitely.

## Section 12.4

1. Parameters `table` and `target` would be the same in each frame, so we have not shown them.

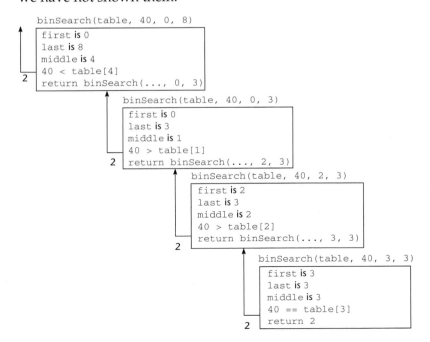

### Section 12.5

1. Sixty-three moves are needed to solve the six-disk problem. The number of moves required to solve the $n$-disk problem is $2^n - 1$.

# Chapter 13
## Section 13.1

1. a. The string "CA" is stored in the current field of the struct pointed to by p.

   b. Copies the volts member of the struct pointed to by q to the volts member of the struct pointed to by p.

   c. The contents of the struct pointed to by q is copied into the struct pointed to by p.

   d. p now contains the same memory address as q; i.e., it points to the same node.

   e. Copies the string "HT" to the current field of the struct pointed to by p.

   f. Invalid; the current field cannot be assigned an integer value.

   g. Invalid; p cannot be assigned an integer.

   h. Invalid.

## Section 13.2

1. The memory is not returned to the heap so it is unavailable for other programs and/or operations that could use it.

## Section 13.3

1. a. Assigns the link field of the struct pointed to by r to point to the same node as p. Node pointed to by q is deleted from this new circular list of 2 nodes.

   b. Assigns NULL to the link field of the struct pointed to by p, thereby denoting that this node is unchanged.

   c. Assigns the link field of the struct pointed to by p to point to the node pointed to by r. The list is unchanged.

   d. Causes the link field of the struct pointed to by p to point to the node pointed to by the link field of the node pointed to by q, NULL. Effectively disconnects the rest of the list from the node pointed to by p.

   e. Assigns p to point to the struct pointed to by p's link field (node pointed to by r). The original first node is deleted from the list.

f.   Copies the `word` field "`the`" from the struct pointed to by `r` to the `word` field of the node that `p` points to.

g.   Assigns the `count` field of the struct pointed to by `p` to the same value as the `count` field of the struct pointed to by `q` (`p`'s count field is assigned the value 3).

h.   Assigns the `link` field of the struct pointed to by `r` to NULL by following the chain of pointers starting from `p`. The node pointed to by `q` is deleted.

i.   Creates a new node and stores its address in the `link` field of the struct pointed to by `q`. Initializes the fields of the newly created node to "`zzz`", 0, and NULL for `word`, `count`, and `link`. Thus, a new node is added to the end of the linked list.

j.   Traverses through the list, incrementing the `count` field of each node by one until all nodes have been processed.

3. Assume the pointer to the node to be removed is a list iterator named `ptr` and the list is referenced by `l`. Use the statement:

```
l.remove(*ptr);
```

**Section 13.4**

```
1. s.push('$');      pushes $,    |$
   s.push('-');      pushes -,    |$-
   s.pop();          pops -,      |$
   nextCh = s.top(); nextCh is $
   if (s.empty())
           cout << "stack is empty" << endl;
```
Stack `s` is not empty. Does not display message.

3. Algorithm for `copyStack`:

1. Allocate storage for a temporary stack.

2. While the existing stack is not empty

   2.1  Retrieve and pop the next item from the existing stack.

   2.2  Push the item onto a temporary stack.

3. While the temporary stack is not empty

   3.1  Retrieve and pop the next item from the temporary stack.

   3.2  Push the item onto the original stack and onto the copy stack.

**Section 13.5**

1.  Original Queue          Queue After Insertion of Harris
    McMann                 McMann
    Wilson                 Wilson
    Carson                 Carson
                           Harris

    After insertion, `front` points to McMann and `rear` points to Harris.

    Original Queue          Queue After Removal of McMann
    McMann                 Wilson
    Wilson                 Carson
    Carson                 Harris

    After removal, `front` points to Wilson and `rear` points to Harris.

    There are three passengers left.

3.

```
// Insert an element at the front of the queue
// Pre : none
// Post: The value x is inserted
//       at the front of the queue.
template<class queueElement>
 void queue<queueElement>::rudeInsert
  (const queueElement& e1)                  // IN — to insert
  {
  // Local data…
  queueNode* oldFront;          // pointer to old front

     if (frontP == NULL)
     { // empty queue
        frontP = new queueNode;
        rearP = frontP;                 // queue w/one element
     }
     else
     {
        oldFront = frontP;            // save old front
        frontP = new queueNode;       // new first element
        frontP->link = oldFront;      // connect up
     }
```

```
        frontP->item = el;                    // insert at front
        numItems++;
    }
```

## Section 13.6

1. The first tree is a binary search tree whereas the second is not.

   Inorder traversal of first tree: 10, 15, 20, 40, 50, 55, 60

   Inorder traversal of second tree: 25, 30, 45, 40, 50, 55, 60

   In the left subtree of the node containing 50, one would expect to find key values that are less than 50 and greater than 40.

3.

a.
```
        25
       /  \
     15    45
    /        \
  10          60
    \        /
    12     55
```

b.
```
        25
       /  \
     12    55
    / \   / \
  10  15 45  60
```

c.
```
        25
       /  \
     12    55
    / \   / \
  10  15 45  60
```

d.
```
   10
     \
      12
        \
         15
           \
```

```
25
  \
   45
     \
      55
        \
         60
```

Trees (b) and (c) are the most efficient to search.

The binary search trees in (b) and (c) are full binary search trees. Every node, except the leaves, has a left and a right subtree. Searching the tree is an O(log N) process.

For the binary search tree in (d), each node has an empty left subtree. Searching (d) is an O(N) process just as in searching a linked list with the same keys.

## Section 13.7

1. The public `insert` function has 1 argument and is called using dot notation. The private `insert` function has 2 arguments.

3. 1. The node has 0 children; the node can be deleted.

   2. The node has 1 child; its parent should connect to this node's child, thereby deleting this node.

   3. The node has 2 children; the item must be replaced by the next larger item that will be found in a leaf of its right subtree. Delete the leaf node (Case 1).

## Section 13.8

1. Excluding the pointer comparisons (testing for NULL):

   a. With a target key of 50, two comparisons are necessary to find the target:

   | *Key* | *Result* | *Subtree Taken* |
   | --- | --- | --- |
   | 40 | 40 < 50 | Right |
   | 50 | 50 == 50 | None |

  b. With a target key of 55, four comparisons are necessary to find the target:

| Key | Result | Subtree Taken |
|-----|--------|---------------|
| 40 | 40 < 55 | Right |
| 50 | 50 < 55 | Right |
| 60 | 60 > 55 | Left |
| 55 | 55 == 55 | None |

  c. With a target key of 10, three comparisons are necessary to find the target:

| Key | Result | Subtree Taken |
|-----|--------|---------------|
| 40 | 40 > 10 | Left |
| 15 | 15 > 10 | Left |
| 10 | 10 == 10 | None |

  d. With a target key of 65, three comparisons are necessary to determine that 65 is not present:

| Key | Result | Subtree Taken |
|-----|--------|---------------|
| 40 | 40 < 65 | Right |
| 50 | 50 < 65 | Right |
| 60 | 60 < 65 | Right, empty |

  e. With a target key of 52, four comparisons are necessary to determine that 52 is not present:

| Key | Result | Subtree Taken |
|-----|--------|---------------|
| 40 | 40 < 52 | Right |
| 50 | 50 < 52 | Right |
| 60 | 60 > 52 | Left |
| 55 | 55 > 52 | Left, empty |

  f. With a target key of 48, two comparisons are necessary to determine that 48 is not present:

| Key | Result | Subtree Taken |
|-----|--------|---------------|
| 40 | 40 < 48 | Right |
| 50 | 50 > 48 | Left, empty |

3. There will be no left subtree for each node, only a right subtree. The big-O notation for searching a tree like this is O(N).

# Index